PRO ORIENTE
BAND XLIV

WIENER PATRISTISCHE TAGUNGEN X

Wiener Patristische Tagungen
Forscher aus dem Osten und Westen Europas an den Quellen des gemeinsamen Glaubens

   I. *Y. de Andia, P. L. Hofrichter* (Hgg.)
      Christus bei den Vätern, Pro Oriente 27 (2004)

  II. *Y. de Andia, P. L. Hofrichter* (Hgg.)
      Der Heilige Geist im Leben der Kirche, Pro Oriente 29 (2005)

 III. *Y. de Andia, P. L. Hofrichter* (Hgg.)
      Gott Vater und Schöpfer, Pro Oriente 31 (2007)

  IV. *Th. Hainthaler, F. Mali, G. Emmenegger* (Hgg.)
      Einheit und Katholizität der Kirche, Pro Oriente 32 (2009)

   V. *Th. Hainthaler, F. Mali, G. Emmenegger* (Hgg.)
      Heiligkeit und Apostolizität der Kirche, Pro Oriente 35 (2010)

  VI. *Th. Hainthaler, F. Mali, G. Emmenegger* und
      M. Lenkaitytė Ostermann (Hgg.)
      Für uns und für unser Heil, Pro Oriente 37 (2014)

 VII. *Th. Hainthaler, F. Mali, G. Emmenegger* und
      M. Lenkaitytė Ostermann (Hgg.)
      Sophia, die Weisheit Gottes, Pro Oriente 40 (2017)

VIII. *Th. Hainthaler, F. Mali, G. Emmenegger* und
      M. Lenkaitytė Ostermann (Hgg.)
      Pronoia, die Vorsehung Gottes, Pro Oriente 42 (2019)

  IX. *Th. Hainthaler, F. Mali, G. Emmenegger* und
      A. Morozov (Hgg.)
      Imago Dei, Pro Oriente 43 (2021)

PRO ORIENTE
BAND XLIV

WIENER PATRISTISCHE TAGUNGEN X

"Inherited sin?" Erbsünde?

Forscher aus dem Osten und Westen Europas
an den Quellen des gemeinsamen Glaubens

Studientagung
Wien, 15. – 19. September 2021
"Inherited sin?"

Herausgegeben von
Theresia Hainthaler, Franz Mali, Gregor Emmenegger und
Alexey Morozov

TYROLIA-VERLAG · INNSBRUCK-WIEN

Gedruckt mit Unterstützung der Fritz Thyssen Stiftung.

Mitglied der Verlagsgruppe „engagement"

Bibliografische Information der Deutschen Nationalbibliothek
Die Deutsche Nationalbibliothek verzeichnet diese Publikation in der Deutschen Nationalbibliografie; detaillierte bibliografische Daten sind im Internet über http://dnb.d-nb.de abrufbar.

2024
© Verlagsanstalt Tyrolia, Innsbruck
Umschlaggestaltung: Wolfgang Bledl
Druck und Bindung: Alcione, Lavis (I)
ISBN 978-7022-4167-4
E-Mail: buchverlag@tyrolia.at
Internet: www.tyrolia-verlag.at

Inhaltsverzeichnis

Archbishop Elpidophoros
    Greeting 11

Bischof Dr. José Rico Pavés
    Grusswort 13

Ysabel de Andia
    Salutation au Cardinal Christoph Schönborn 15

Andrew Louth
    20th anniversary of the Orthodox-Catholic Colloquy 21

Theresia Hainthaler
    Preface 23

Introduction

Theresia Hainthaler
    Introduction to the topic "Inherited sin?" 31

Early Fathers

Zdravko Jovanović
    The Notion of Infancy of Adam and Eve in Theophilus and Irenaeus
    and Its Relevance for Contemporary Theological Anthropology 43

Ysabel de Andia
  Eve *causa mortis* et Marie *causa salutis*.
  Désobéissance d'Adam et d'Eve et obéissance du Christ et de Marie   60

Tomasz Stępień
  The Sin of Embodiment in the Platonic Tradition   73

Jana Plátová
  Sündenlehre bei Clemens von Alexandria   85

Alexey Morozov
  La notion du libre arbitre dans l'héritage littéraire
  de Méthode d'Olympe   98

Mariya Horyacha
  Adam's Inheritance: Macarian Teaching on Indwelling Sin 118

Pablo Argárate
  "Sin was planted in our father Adam and in our mother Eve on the
  day they sinned. It entered and lived in all their children" (*LG* 19, 3)
  Evil and Sin in the Syriac *Liber Graduum* 137

Johannes Arnold
  Zur Frage nach dem Ursprung des Bösen im Menschen
  bei Origenes vor dem Hintergrund
  mittelplatonischer Philosophie 156

Latin Tradition

Alexey Fokin
  Tertullian's doctrine of the "original vice" (*vitium originis*) and its
  contradictory nature 177

Gregor Emmenegger
  Der verdorbene Samen.
  Traduzianismus und dessen naturphilosophische Grundlagen bei
  Tertullian und Augustinus 196

Giuseppe Caruso
    Il peccato di Adamo in Girolamo 220

Franz Mali
    „Die zerrissene Tunica der Unsterblichkeit wurde von Christus wieder zusammengenäht".
    Zur Erlösung von Adams Sünde durch Christus im *Opus imperfectum in Matthaeum*.. 237

Paul Mattei
    Quid habes, o homo, quod non accepisti?
    Remarques sur l'état de l'homme après la chute selon Ambroise 252

Lenka Karfíková
    Hereditary Sin? Augustine and Origen 269

Vittorino Grossi
    Per una rilettura del peccato originale in Agostino d'Ippona
    Modalità attuali della ricerca 286

Vít Hušek
    Inherited Sin in Ambrosiaster and Pelagius 303

Dominique Gonnet
    Césaire d'Arles, le Concile d'Orange II et le péché originel......... 318

Hilary Mooney
    Leaving paradise: Eriugena's theology of 'inherited sin' 334

Greek Tradition

Viacheslav V. Lytvynenko
    The Imagery of Movement in the Descriptions of Sin and Christian Life in the *Vita Antonii* 355

Marta Przyszychowska
    The first sin as a sin of nature according to Gregory of Nyssa 368

Giulio Maspero and Ilaria Vigorelli
Relational Ontology and the Syntactic Dimension of Sin in Gregory
of Nyssa 381

Svetoslav Riboloff
Theodore of Mopsuestia on the Ancestral Sin 404

Michel Stavrou
« Héritiers de la malédiction survenue en Adam »
L'enseignement de Cyrille d'Alexandrie sur le péché des origines ... 416

Georgiana Huian
The Sin of Adam and Eve and the Restoration of the Image of God
through Baptism according to Diadochus of Photike 429

Ioannis Kourempeles
„Die Jungfrau, die die Erlösung vom Fluch gebar":
Die Alte Eva und das neue Paradies in der Dichtung von Romanos
dem Meloden 443

Georgi Kapriev
Das Problem der Erbsünde in der Anthropologie des Maximus Confessor 457

Karolina Kochańczyk-Bonińska
Human Sexuality—One of the Ontic Consequences of Adam's Fall—
Maximus the Confessor's Interpretation 477

Ivan Christov
St Cyril the Philosopher on the Meaning of Theology for Restoring
the Image of God in Man and Overcoming Original Sin 485

Georgios Martzelos
The Concept of inherited sin in the Orthodox Tradition 496

Inhaltsverzeichnis 9

Presse

Pressemitteilung (Wien, Pro Oriente-Informationsdienst, 13.09.21)
    Patristische Tagungen feiern in Wien ihr 20-Jahr-Jubiläum 515

Pressemitteilung (Wien, Pro Oriente-Informationsdienst, 16.09.21)
    Wien: Ökumene braucht Einsatz auf allen Ebenen 517

Pressemitteilung (Wien, Pro Oriente-Informationsdienst, 17.09.21)
    Schönborn: Freundschaften wichtige Voraussetzung für Ökumene .. 519

Пресс-релиз (Вена, Служба коммуникации ОВЦС, 18.09.2021)
    Митрополит Волоколамский Иларион в дистанционном режиме принял участие в конференции патрологов в Вене 522

Press Release (Vienna, DECR, 18.09.2021)
    Metropolitan Hilarion of Volokolamsk takes part remotely in a conference of patristic scholars in Vienna 524

Fotos

    Bilder der Tagung 528

Register

    Biblische Schriften 532
    Frühchristliche und anonyme Schriften 536
    Antike und mittelalterliche Autoren und Personennamen 536
    Moderne Autoren 538
    Abkürzungen 543

Archbishop Elpidophoros, New York (United Staates of America)

Greeting

Dear Prof. Hainthaler

Having received your letter dated August 31, 2021, I would like to communicate with you in order to thank you for informing me of the upcoming 10th Patristic Colloquy, which will be held in Vienna Austria, the days of September 16–18, 2021, and having as its theme, "Inherited sin?"

In response to your gracious invitation, kindly know that my participation in this event will not be possible. Nevertheless, I am most grateful for your thoughtful gesture, and extend to you and all of your fellow colleagues and participants my warmest wishes for fruitful deliberations and a most successful colloquy. Indeed, now more than ever, the role of religion and promotion of dialogue—particularly between the Orthodox and the Roman Catholics—are crucial components in the ongoing healing of a broken world and society that is still recovering from the adverse effects of the COVID-19 pandemic.

Thanking you once again for your kindness, I convey to you my heartfelt prayers and greetings, and remain

Prayerfully yours,

\+ Elpidophoros
Archbishop of America

Bischof Dr. José Rico Pavés, Jerez de la Frontera (Spanien)

Grusswort

Aus Südspanien schließe ich mich an, Gott für den zwanzigsten Jahrestag der Patrologentreffen aus Ost und West zu danken, an denen ich an einigen teilnehmen durfte. Ich gratuliere denen, die in diesen Jahren an ihrer Organisation gearbeitet haben.

Am 31. Juli [2021] habe ich die Diözese Jerez de la Frontera in Besitz genommen, deren Schutzpatron der hl. Dionysius Areopagita ist. Ein schönes Zeichen dafür, dass die Kirche ein gemeinsames Erbe der Heiligkeit besitzt, das wir weiterhin bewahren müssen, um unsere Spaltungen zu überwinden.

Allen ein schönes Jubiläum, möge der Herr Sie segnen.

+ José Rico Pavés
Bischof von Jerez de la Frontera

Ysabel de Andia, Paris (France)

Salutation au Cardinal Christoph Schönborn

Monseigneur,

Nous nous sommes connus lors de nos études de théologie à *l'Institut Catholique de Paris*, à l'époque troublée de mai 68, vous faisiez un doctorat sur *l'icône du Christ* et je découvrais avec vous les Pères de l'Église et l'œcuménisme dans le séminaire du Père Marie-Joseph Le Guillou, dominicain, et du Père Boris Bobrinskoy, orthodoxe. Nous sommes revus en octobre 1999 au second Synode des évêques pour l'Europe, à Rome, où j'ai eu l'honneur d'être invitée, comme expert. Je vous ai demandé si vous acceptiez de réunir une trentaine de patrologues orthodoxes et catholiques européens, autour de vous à Vienne. Vous êtes patrologue et votre thèse sur «L'icône du Christ» a été traduite dans de nombreuses langues européennes.

Quant à Vienne, cette capitale est au centre de l'Europe, à mi-chemin entre Paris et Moscou. Le cadre de cette rencontre ne pouvait être que Pro Oriente qui a justement pour vocation de réunir les Chrétiens d'Orient et d'Occident et le Professeur Hofrichter a volontiers accepté de faire rentrer ce projet dans les Colloques organisés par Pro Oriente, et il me laissa le soin d'organiser le groupe et le programme.

La première réunion eut lieu à Vienne du 7 au 9 juin 2001, il y a vingt ans. J'ai sous les yeux le premier volume publié par *Pro Oriente* :

„Christus bei den Vätern.
Forscher aus dem Osten und Westen Europas an den Quellen des gemeinsamen Glaubens.
Pro Oriente-Studientagung : Christus bei den griechischen und lateinischen Kirchenvätern im ersten Jahrtausend", Wien, 7. – 9. Juni 2001, herausgegeben von Ysabel de Andia und Peter Leander Hofrichter.

Dans l'Introduction aux Actes du Colloque de Vienne à Pro Oriente (juin 2001), j'ai écrit les grandes orientations de ce projet, que je reprends ici.

La première dimension de ce projet est œcuménique

Il s'agissait de se faire rencontrer des Orthodoxes et des Catholiques qui enseignaient la Patristique ou la Théologie dans les Facultés de Lettres ou de Théologie et qui ont en commun l'amour des Pères de l'Église du premier millénaire. La limite du premier millénaire indique la volonté de se situer dans une époque antérieure au grand schisme des Églises grecque et latine, époque où les Églises déployaient la diversité de leurs traditions et trouvaient leur unité dans les Conciles œcuméniques. Comment des Chrétiens du XXe siècle, appartenant à l'une ou l'autre Église, peuvent-ils lire la tradition qui leur est commune et qu'ils interprètent pourtant d'une manière différente? Cette lecture commune était le premier enjeu de ces rencontres et la confrontation des différentes lectures, qui font apparaître les différences, une richesse.

La seconde dimension est universitaire

Les Chrétiens qui sont présents dans cette assemblée ne sont pas des représentants attitrés de leurs Églises, le dialogue ne se fait pas au niveau de la hiérarchie des différentes Églises, comme Pro Oriente est habitué de le faire, mais à celui du travail universitaire qui réunit une communauté de spécialistes de telle ou telle époque ou de tel ou tel auteur, comme lors des Congrès internationaux de Patristique d'Oxford. La méthodologie présupposée est celle enseignée dans les grands centres universitaires. Dans la relation de la foi et de la raison, il y a une part de rationalité touchant la compréhension du texte qui doit permettre une discussion académique.

La troisième dimension est européenne

Ce projet est le fruit du Synode des évêques pour l'Europe et c'est à titre d'européens que les membres de cette assemblée (une trentaine) étaient invités. Une Europe qui ne correspond pas aux frontières de l'Union européenne, mais encore une fois à la postérité des Églises byzantine et latine. Ce sont des Européens chrétiens, orthodoxes et catholiques, qui représentent dix-sept pays européens et témoignent de leur foi à l'intérieur du continent européen actuel en assumant, face au monde contemporain, l'héritage ancien du christianisme. Or l'expérience que ces Chrétiens ont de leur foi et de la culture des pays dans lesquels ils vivent, offre une variété qui dépend notamment des rapports des Églises et de l'État.

La première rencontre comprenait une soirée de débat sur « les racines chrétiennes de l'Europe », telles qu'elles étaient vécues dans les différents pays représentés par les participants. Tout le spectre des situations était représenté, depuis la Grèce majoritairement orthodoxe jusqu'à l'Espagne, majoritairement catholique, en passant par la laïcité française et les pays germaniques ou de la Mitteleuropa. Faut-il approfondir cette réflexion sur « les racines chrétiennes de l'Europe » et comment ? Il est clair toutefois que, pour les Chrétiens, ces « racines » sont les « Pères » de l'Église et l'idée même de « paternité » ou de « racine » nous renvoie aux naissances baptismales de l'Europe.

Jésus-Christ

Comme le Synode des évêques à Rome avait pris comme sujet : « Le Christ, espérance pour l'Europe », c'est autour du Christ qu'a eu lieu la première « réunion ». Si le Christ ne nous « réunit » pas, comment pouvons-nous nous dire encore chrétiens ? Le professeur Peter Hofrichter a ouvert la discussion en faisant le point sur le débat christologique de Pro Oriente : « Der christologische Dialog der Stiftung Pro Oriente und seine europäische Perspektive ». J'avais choisi de traiter la confession de foi ecclésiale de « Jésus, Christ et Seigneur » chez Irénée de Lyon et Basile de Césarée qui ont déployé le caractère trinitaire de ces titres, comme fondement de notre rencontre.

Quelle était la composition des participants ?

J'avais invité mes professeurs et mes amis français et romains :

- Monique Alexandre, professeur de grec et patristique à la Sorbonne,

- Joseph Wolinsky, mon professeur de patristique à l'Institut Catholique de Paris,

- Michel Stavrou théologien de l'Institut Saint Serge à Paris,

- Dominique Gonnet, jésuite, des Sources chrétiennes à Lyon.

- Lenka Karfikova de Prague dont le mari philosophe était venu travailler chez nous, au CNRS (Centre National de la Recherche Scientifique), à Paris.

- Et Franz Mali, professeur à Fribourg en Suisse.

Le Père Vittorino Grossi, augustinien, professeur à l'Augustinianum à Rome, où j'ai fait mon doctorat de théologie. Et José Rico Pavés, actuellement évêque de Jerez en Espagne, que j'avais connu à Rome où il avait fait une thèse sur Denys l'Aréopagite.

Deux personnes qui deviendront célèbres ont participé à cette première rencontre : Hilarion Alfeyev, que j'avais connu à Oxford, où il faisait sa thèse sur Saint Syméon le Nouveau Théologien avec l'évêque Kallistos Ware, et Elpidophoros Lambriniadis, qui était venu à Paris suivre des cours de français. Comme vous le savez, Hilarion Alfeyev est actuellement métropolite de Volokolamsk et directeur du Département des Relations extérieures du Patriarcat russe, à Moscou, et Elpidophoros Lambriniadis est archevêque orthodoxe grec d'Amérique depuis son intronisation le 22 juin 2019 en la cathédrale de la Sainte-Trinité de New York. Un autre ami russe était là, Alexei Muraviev qui travaillait à Munich avec le père Michel van Esbroeck.

Deux participants de cette première rencontre nous ont quitté : le Père Michel van Esbroeck et Serguei Averintsev et je veux rendre hommage à leur mémoire. Le Père Michel van Esbroeck (Malines 1934 – Louvain la Neuve 2003), jésuite, bollandiste et orientaliste, spécialiste des Homéliaires géorgiens, était professeur à l'université de Munich. Il nous divertissait en se mettant au piano et improvisant pour nous.

Mais celui qui m'a fait la plus forte impression c'était Serguei Averintsev (Moscou 1937 – Vienne 2004) qui avait été le professeur, à Moscou, d'Alfeyev et de Muraviev. Il avait fait une thèse sur la poésie byzantine, mais il était spécialiste de la poésie russe de l'Âge d'argent. Après avoir travaillé comme bibliothécaire, pendant toute la période communiste, il devint en 1989, professeur de philologie classique à l'Université Lomonossov, puis, en 1994, professeur d'études slaves à l'Université de Vienne où il mourut en 2004. En 1994, il devint membre de l'académie Pontificale des Sciences Sociales. C'était un grand humaniste qui parlait toutes les langues anciennes, le grec et le latin, bien sûr, mais aussi l'hébreu, et les langues européennes. Il était capable de vous déclamer des vers en toutes les langues.

Faisaient aussi partie de ce premier groupe des orthodoxes :

- Mgr Joseph Pop, métropolite de Roumanie pour l'Europe Occidentale et Méridionale et représentant de l'Église orthodoxe roumaine auprès des Institutions européennes (Limours en France).

les pères

- Vladimir Zelinsky (Brescia),

- Basilius Grolimund (qui a fondé le Skyte de St Spyridon en Allemagne, près de Limburg),
- Andrew Louth (Oxford et Durham),
- l'Archiprêtre Mykola Makar (Milan) qui a participé aux Colloques jusqu'en 2009.

et les professeurs

- Konstantin Sigov (Kiev) qui était venu enseigner aux Hautes Études à Paris,
- István Bugar (Budapest, CEU), qui avait étudié à Louvain,
- Georgi Kapriev (Sofia), qui m'avait été recommandé par Elpidophoros Lambriniadis,
- et Georgios Martzelos (Thessalonique), J'ai déjà cité Michel Stavrou (Paris).

Par la suite, certains organiseront des colloques chez eux : Martzelos à Thessalonique, Ivan Christov, un ami de Kapriev, à Varna en Bulgarie.

Franz Mali (Fribourg en Suisse), qui était venu par Pro Oriente, a assisté à la rencontre. Et puis, «last but not least», Theresia Hainthaler, également de Pro Oriente, que j'avais invitée à cause de ses travaux en Christologie et de ses contacts œcuméniques, était présente à cette première rencontre. Elle m'a remplacée avec le succès que tout le monde reconnaît et a organisé notre rencontre d'aujourd'hui. Qu'elle en soit remerciée.

C'était à Vienne, il y a vingt ans. Vingt ans déjà ! Le temps passe et les choses changent, prenant leur consistance propre : une nouvelle époque, de nouveaux visages…

Merci, Monsieur le Cardinal de votre confiance et de votre espérance qui a permis à ce groupe d'exister

Ysabel de Andia

Andrew Louth, Darlington (United Kingdom)

20th anniversary of the Orthodox-Catholic Colloquy

Your Eminence Christoph Cardinal Schönborn, our convenors, first, Ysabel de Andia, and lately, Theresia Hainthaler, dear sisters and brothers!

Alas, I cannot be with you for our tenth conference, marking the twentieth anniversary of our colloquy, and Theresia has asked me to send some reflections that can be read out during our celebrations. Our first meeting was in Vienna, under the auspices of Pro Oriente, in 2001. From the first, the idea behind our meetings was to take some central theological topic and through papers and discussion to explore it as a group of patristic scholars, who take our faith—Orthodox or Catholic—as seriously as we take our scholarship. Our membership was by invitation; we were not, and did not regard ourselves as, delegates. Our discussion, though searching at times, often continuing outside the formal context of the seminar room, was to be—and proved to be—a discussion that explored the chosen topic for its own sake, from the perspective of Fathers of the Church, Western and Eastern. From the time of our first meetings, there echoed in our ears the appeal by Pope John Paul II, quoting the words of Vyacheslav Ivanov, for the Church once again to breathe with both its lungs.

What have we achieved? Well, first of all, we have, as Orthodox and as Catholics, explored what each of these 'lungs' mean and, to some extent, how each of these lungs operate. Nevertheless, I doubt if any of us would claim, that our research and our discussion has, in any measurable way, advanced the cause of reunion between the Christian East (Greek, Slav, Romanian) and the Latin West. Perhaps more important than the pronouncements of negotiations between our several Churches, we have, over the years, come to know one another, as scholars, as believers, but also as friends. The creation of bonds of friendship between the members of different Churches seems to me as important as any formal agreement about issues that divide us, and what we have achieved on a small scale is but part of a larger movement that has characterized the last century. The last century, which saw the nations of the world tearing one another apart, with regimes based on division and hatred, also saw, especially after the Second World War, growing bonds of friendship through the world of scholarship, perhaps the most noted for patristic scholars, such as we are, the Oxford Patristic Conferences that have taken place every four years in Oxford in 1951—the inspiration of Canon Professor Leslie Cross, who believed that the patient work of scholarship could help Christians to listen to one another, and break down barriers of suspicion and mistrust that have been the result of centuries of division.

To speak personally, for me our Colloquy (even though I have missed a couple of them, this being, I think, the third) seems like a series of jewels stretching over the last twenty years, the brilliant facets of which have been our encounters with one another—encounters in which we have recognized familiar, and increasingly beloved, faces, or occasionally a rare encounter, though precious in the memory (I recall particularly my first encounter with the great Russian scholar, Sergei Sergeevich Averintsev, at our first meeting in Vienna), as well as the time we spent together on our outings together—to the monastery of Heiligenkreuz, where we were informed by the librarian that to be a Cistercian it was necessary to have a 'sexual relationship' with books! Or, more adventurously, when a group of us set out from the Brâncoveanu Monastery at Sâmbăta de Sus in a minibus to explore the Romanian monasteries of Bukovina—with a wildly ambitious itinerary!

I mention all this, because the Church is held together, less by the hierarchy, than by what we might think of as spiritual sinews, that link us all—sinews strengthened by our mutual prayer for one another, sinews that facilitate the movement of the Holy Spirit within the Church, sinews that—yes, also—manifest themselves in bonds of friendship. That is what our colloquies have seemed to me to foster and to nurture; its fruits belong to the future, in God's providence.

Andrew Louth, FBA, DD

Theresia Hainthaler, Frankfurt am Main (Germany)

Preface

The 2021 Patristic Colloquy, which took place in Vienna 20 years after the start of this series in 2001, was held in a historically significant location, namely the Rahner Hall of the Cardinal König House in Vienna. Fifty years ago, in 1971, the so-called Vienna Dialogue with the Oriental Orthodox Churches on Christology, organized by PRO ORIENTE, began at this place, albeit in the former building. In 1994, the first consultation of the Syriac Dialogue, organized by PRO ORIENTE, also was held there, bringing together representatives of presumably all the churches of the Syriac tradition as well as some expert scholars. In 1998, the Cardinal König House was inaugurated in this Rahner Hall, and named after Cardinal König, who also was present, as was Cardinal Schönborn, the Archbishop of Vienna then and now. Even the plenary of the Joint International Commission for theological Dialogue between the Roman Catholic Church and the Orthodox Church in September 2010 took place in this room.

Our colloquies

With the 10th Patristic Colloquy on the subject "Inherited sin?" the Patristic Colloquies came back to Vienna, where they started in 2001. Due to the generosity of PRO ORIENTE, who kindly agreed to organize this conference, we could celebrate the 20 years anniversary. Tirelessly and with great patience General Secretary Bernd Mussinghoff accompanied and carried out all the preparations, aptly supported by Dr. Viola Raheb and the very friendly care of Gudrun Kaiser in the office.

The previous nine Patristic Colloquies took place after 2001 once again in 2003 in Vienna, but then our journey went to several places in Europe, West and East: first in 2005 to Luxembourg mediated by Aglaë Hagg (wife of the Austrian ambassador in Luxembourg with all her connections) and hosted by Archbishop Fernand Franck. We have been invited to Romania in 2007 to Sibiu and to the Brâncoveanu Monastery by Metropolitan Iosif Pop, Romanian Orthodox Metropolitan of Western and Southern Europe, a member of our group from the very beginning. Another member from the very beginning, Georgios Martzelos, was instrumental to bring us to Greece in 2009, to Thessaloniki, a Colloquy hosted by the Orthodox Higher Ecclesial Academy. An invitation in 2012 to Hungary by Atanáz Orosz (member of the group since 2003), Apostolic Exarch (in 2011) and first Hungarian-Catholic Eparch of Miskolc (since 2015), brought us to Esztergom and Budapest where Cardinal Erdő hosted us in his new Conference Centre in Esztergom. Our Bulgarian colleague Ivan Christov made the arrangement that we could go in 2015 to Varna in Bulgaria where Metropolitan Ioan of Varna and Veliko Preslav was our generous host. Our Polish colleague Tomasz Stępień prepared everything—helped also by Karolina Kochańczyk-Bonińska and Marta Przyszychowska—that we could have the Colloquy in 2017 in Warsaw, hosted by Cardinal Nycz who received us in a dinner. Finally, in 2019, we went to L'viv in Ukraine, first prepared by Daria Morozova and Konstantin Sigov with the great help of Roman Zaviyskyy, then Dean of the Theological Faculty of the Ukrainian Catholic University.

At these conferences, we first dealt with topics of Trinitarian theology: Christ and the Fathers, the Holy Spirit in the Church, God the Father and Creator. Then we turned to ecclesiology and held two Colloquies on the marks of the Church, the *notae ecclesiae*, first on unity and catholicity of the Church, then on holiness and apostolicity of the Church. With the topic soteriology in East and West ("For us and for our salvation"), we had a subject, which is already well connected to the theme of "inherited sin". The topics of the following Colloquies, "Sophia. The Wisdom of God" and "Pronoia. The Providence of God" are also in relationship with some aspects of the subject dealt with at the tenth Colloquy in Vienna.

As Ysabel de Andia explained—see p. 16—these meetings can be characterized in a threefold way: on a European scale, in an academic manner and ecumenical with regard to Orthodox and Catholic. All the conferences have been published with the subtitle "Researchers from East and West of Europe at the sources of the common faith" (a list of these conferences can also be found on p. 2 of the respective publications).

These Colloquies, which started on the initiative of Cardinal Schönborn in the framework of PRO ORIENTE, are based on the idea of Ysabel de Andia, who carried out the first three colloquies together with Peter Hofrichter of Salzburg. From 2001 to 2009, the PRO ORIENTE Foundation supported the Colloquies with the help of local sponsors. At the request of Cardinal Schönborn, I took over the academic leadership in 2006. From 2012, we were able to continue the conferences with the help of the Thyssen Foundation, Renovabis and local sponsors, as PRO ORIENTE could no longer host the conferences due to a lack of staff and funding. However, we continued to publish the proceedings in the PRO ORIENTE series "Wiener Patristische Tagungen".

Through the previous conferences, a European network of proven patristic scholars has been formed, which could integrate repeatedly young colleagues. The early church is the unifying basis for Orthodox and Catholic scholars. In times of increasingly difficult relations at the official level, also due to some tensions in Eastern Europe, this cooperation is of particular importance. Though such an initiative is always useful and necessary to support the ecumenical dialogue, this task is even more important in times of difficulties for the international dialogue in order to build and enforce relationships.

The Vienna colloquy 2021

The Colloquy on *Imago Dei* in L'viv, Ukraine, in 2019, marked the beginning of the exploration on the field of theological anthropology. The theme "Inherited sin?" of the Vienna Colloquy in 2021, decided by the participants in 2019, is not an explicitly controversial topic that divides Orthodoxy and the Western churches. There are, however, different theological approaches that need to be addressed with a view to the further official theological dialogue.

In eleven sessions, a total of 36 participants from 17 countries (France, Germany, Italy, Austria, Switzerland, Greece, Great Britain, the Netherlands, Spain, Ireland, the Czech Republic, Poland, Ukraine, Romania, Bulgaria, Serbia and Russia), if countries of origin are included, offered their papers.

Festive Evening

The 20th anniversary of the Colloquies was celebrated with a festive evening on 16 September 2021. The President of PRO ORIENTE, Dr Alfons Kloss, welcomed the guests (in addition to the conference participants and other invited guests) in the evening, moderated by myself. On the podium were Cardinal Schönborn, Archbishop of Vienna, Ysabel de Andia, and Bishop Atanáz Orosz of Miskolc. Further statements of participants from 2001 could be heard via zoom by Metropolitan Hilarion Alfeyev from Moscow, Head of the Department for External Relations of the Moscow Patriarchate, and Rev. Prof. Dr Andrew Louth from the United Kingdom. In addition, the greeting address of H.E. Elpidophoros Lambriniadis, the actual Greek-Orthodox Archbishop of America, was read and a video with a greeting address of Bishop José Rico Pavés of Jerez de la Frontera, Spain—in Spanish and German—was presented.

Cardinal Kurt Koch, president of the Pontifical Council (now: Dicastery) for Promoting Christian Unity, sent his greetings and good wishes from Rome.

The importance of the Patristic Colloquies was emphasized surprisingly clearly in the statements cf. the Press releases (p. 515–517). Cardinal Schönborn described the initiative as a "network of science and friendship", and he added with regard to the official dialogue between the Catholic and Orthodox Churches: "Even if the official dialogue is sometimes laborious, the dialogue at the Patristic Conferences works very well." Metropolitan Hilarion from Moscow underlined that it is very important, that these colloquies should continue. He expressed his hope that sooner or later he will meet us in person. Prof Dr Andrew Louth FBA called the colloquia "a series of jewels stretching over the last twenty years"; they fostered and nourished the spiritual sinews that hold the Church together.

A photo exhibition of the nine previous conferences (2001, 2003, 2005, 2007, 2009, 2013, 2015, 2017 and 2019) with the corresponding programs or communiqués served as a visual reminder of the earlier conferences. We would like to express our sincere thanks to PRO ORIENTE for its efforts in producing prints of old photographs and copies and for organizing the exhibition!

This publication

The section on **early Christian Fathers** comprises the following papers: Zdravko Jovanović dealt with the concept of Adam and Eve being children, found in Theophilus and Irenaeus. Ysabel de Andia showed the juxtaposition of Eve as "causa mortis" and Mary as "causa salutis" in Irenaeus of Lyon. Tomasz Stępień explained the basic ideas of the ancient Platonic tradition, according to which the corporealization of the soul is sin. Jana Plátová unfolded the doctrine of sin in Clement of Alexandria and Alexey Morozov explored the teachings of Methodius of Olympus on free will, based on new editions. Mariya Horyacha focused on the Macarian corpus and its doctrine of indwelling sin as an inheritance from Adam. Pablo Argárate outlined the concept of evil and sin in the Syriac *Liber Graduum*. Johannes Arnold explored the question of the origin of evil in Origen and presented the discussion of this question in research against the background of Middle Platonic philosophy.

The **Latin Tradition** is analyzed in several contributions: Alexey Fokin summarized Tertullian's statements on Adam's sin and its consequences in the various works of Latin scholars, which he saw as an anticipation of Augustine's teaching. On the other hand, Tertullian saw two sources of human sin, on the one hand free will and on the other hand corrupt human nature (in body and soul). Gregor Emmenegger's paper on traducianism in Tertullian and its reception in Augustine shows how Tertullian's traducianism is influenced by ancient medicine. Traducianism offers a plausible explanation of how Adam's sin is transmitted. Giuseppe Caruso OSA presented the understanding of Adam's sin in Jerome. Franz Mali worked out how the *Opus imperfectum in Matthaeum* (the most comprehensive patristic commentary on Matthew) conceptualizes the redemption of Adam's sin through Christ. Paul Mattei dealt with the human condition after the fall of man according to Ambrose. Lenka Karfíková focused on the concept of original sin in Augustine (in contrast to Origen). Vittorino Grossi OSA undertook a relecture of Augustine on original sin. Vít Hušek analyzed original sin in Ambrosiaster and Pelagius. Dominique Gonnet SJ offered a paper on Caesarius of Arles and the Council of Orange, at which the doctrine of original sin was discussed. Hilary Mooney presented John Scotus Eriugena's theology of original sin under the title "Leaving paradise".

The section on the **Greek tradition** opens with reflections on the description of sin and its use of the imagery of movement in Athanasius' life of Antony by Viacheslav Lytvynenko. Marta Przyszychowska dealt with Gregory of Nyssa's understanding of original sin as a sin of nature. Giulio Maspero and Ilaria Vigorelli's work on Gregory of Nyssa was based on a new concept of relational ontology and examined the syntactic dimension of sin (in Gregory of Nyssa). Svet Ribolov dealt with Theodore of Mopsuestia's approach to original sin. Michel Stavrou presented the teaching of Cyril of Alexandria on the sin of the beginning. Georgiana Huian presented how Diadochus of Photike understood the sin of Adam and Eve and how, according to him, the image of God is restored through baptism. Ioannis Kourempeles analyzed the poetry of Romanos Melodos after the old Eve and the new paradise. In his paper on Maximus Confessor, Georgi Kapriev located the problem of original sin in the anthropology of Maximus. Karolina Kochańczyk-Bonińska explored the interpretation of Maximus in relation to human sexuality—one of the ontic consequences of Adam's fall from grace. Ivan Christov dealt with Cyril (the philosopher) on the importance of theology in restoring God's image. Georgios Martzelos gave an overview lecture on the concept of original sin in the Orthodox tradition.

Fr Daniel Buda †

Sadly, we mourn our colleague Fr Daniel Buda (* 7 June 1977) who suffered a cerebrovascular accident in Regensburg February 11 to 12, 2023, at the end of a Conference; finally, he passed away December 26, 2023 in Sibiu, Romania, where he was Dean of the Orthodox Faculty of Theology. He could not finalize his paper of Vienna (on the inherited sin in St John Chrysostom and Augustine). Enthusiastically, he joined our colloquies since 2007. R.i.p. Memory eternal!

Thanks

We express our thanks to the Thyssen foundation and to Renovabis for their financial support of the Conference. PRO ORIENTE was our host and made this Colloquy possible with every help and work as well as financial support. We are deeply grateful for all their efforts! We would also like to thank the Thyssen Foundation for their generous support of the publication.

Sincere thanks go to the staff in Fribourg at the chair of Franz Mali, especially Alexey Morozov, for their great effort and all the care in preparation of the publication. Once again we owe the layout of the print-ready volume to Gregor Emmenegger, who deserves great thanks for all his effort and commitment.

Frankfurt am Main, 29th January 2024   Theresia Hainthaler

Introduction

Theresia Hainthaler, Frankfurt am Main (Germany)

Introduction to the topic "Inherited sin?"

After a basic introduction to our topic, I would like to address a few themes in order to draw attention to the diversity of aspects in our subject, namely, (1.) Contestations—The question mark (in our title), (2.) Old Testament and original sin—a response of Norbert Lohfink, (3.) The heritage (κληρονομία) of Adam. Melito of Sardis' Paschal homily (c. 160–170), and (4.) A debate on original human immortality in Syriac theology.

I. General remarks on "Inherited sin"

The doctrine of original sin, in Latin *peccatum originale*, is biblically based on the story of the fall in Gen 2–3, and in the New Testament on Romans 5: 11–21, often called the *locus classicus* of the doctrine of original sin[1]. However, it must be stated that, as Leo Scheffczyk put it, that "the idea of an 'original sin' ... cannot be sought in the New Testament, especially if one insists on the partial moment of 'inheritance'. However, the generality and universality of sin advocated by the New Testament is a finding that deserves attention."[2]

The "reality and generality of sin [appears] very clearly as the dark foil of redemption", but there are no "statements about a causal link between sins and an original sin", nor does the story of the Fall of Man have any significance in the Synoptics. The reason for the lack of a statement that humanity is sinful from the beginning, for Scheffczyk, is due to the fact that "the formal realization of an original sin endowed with universal effect could only arise where the event of redemption was grasped in all its historical dimensions." [3]

---

[1] L. *Scheffcyzk*, Urstand, Fall und Erbsünde – von der Schrift bis Augustinus = Handbuch der Dogmengeschichte II 3a(1) (Freiburg i.B. 1982), 7, 39.
[2] *Scheffczyk*, Urstand, 36: dass "der Gedanke an eine 'Erbsünde' ... im Neuen Testament nicht gesucht werden [kann], zumal wenn man auf dem Teilmoment des 'Erbes' insistiert. Wohl aber ist die vom Neuen Testament vertretene Allgemeinheit und Universalität der Sünde ein Befund, der Beachtung verdient."
[3] *Scheffczyk*, Urstand, 38: "Die förmliche Erkenntnis einer mit universaler Wirkung ausgestatteten Ursünde konnte erst dort aufkommen, wo das Erlösungsgeschehen in allen seinen geschichtlichen Dimensionen erfaßt war."

This was the case for the Synoptics, but no longer so for Paul, who develops the antiparallel between Adam and Christ and develops "such a detailed answer to the question of the origin of the power of sin that this passage has been understood ever since as the *locus classicus* of the later 'doctrine of original sin'." In this passage, strictly speaking, "the origin of death and not that of sin is the actual topic"[4]. Thus the central passage is Romans 5:12.

For Peter Knauer[5], ἐφ' ᾧ in Rom 5:12 is best related to the preceding θάνατος[6]. Following Hebrews 2:14f, the root of all sins that precedes all offences consists in the predicament of a φόβῳ θανάτου, i.e. in the fact that only a faithless existence is innate, in which one lives under the power of fear for oneself. Therein lies the need for redemption of all people.

In his interpretation of Romans 5:12, Norbert Baumert, too, stated: "Just as we have been reconciled to God through the death of the Son of God as *a* man ..., so also the fact that all men fell into the realm of death is caused by the peculiarity of the act of one man."[7] The sin of the progenitor had the peculiarity of characterizing his entire descendants and therefore dragged them into the state of sin (cf. Rom 5:19). A monograph on Patristic exegesis of Rom 5:12 would be most welcome.

Pier Franco Beatrice pointed out that in ecclesiastical writers the idea that Adam had committed a sexual sin, as is to be found in the encratite Alexandrian tradition (Clement of Alexandria wrote against it!) has found no recording. The idea of a transference of impurity (Origen, Didymus, Ambrose), however, can be found. "For Augustine—as for Origen—the baptism of newborns is proof of the existence of original sin". For Augustin, *superbia* is the root and cause of moral evil; the Pelagians on the other hand, saw Adam's sin only as a bad example and denied that it produced death and original sin[8].

Overviews of the further development of Irenaeus of Lyons, Tertullian, the Cappadocians up to the Pelagian dispute and the unfolding of the powerful doctrine of original sin in Augustine are provided by the corresponding

---

[4] Scheffczyk, Urstand, 39.
[5] P. Knauer, Erbsünde als Todesverfallenheit. Eine Deutung von Röm 5,12 aus dem Vergleich mit Hebr 2,14f., ThGl 58 (1968) 337–349.
[6] Rom 5:12: Διὰ τοῦτο ὥσπερ δι' ἑνὸς ἀνθρώπου ἡ ἁμαρτία εἰς τὸν κόσμον εἰσῆλθεν καὶ διὰ τῆς ἁμαρτίας ὁ θάνατος, καὶ οὕτως εἰς πάντας ἀνθρώπους ὁ θάνατος διῆλθεν, ἐφ' ᾧ πάντες ἥμαρτον.
[7] N. Baumert, Christus – Hochform von 'Gesetz'. Übersetzung und Auslegung des Römerbriefes (Würzburg 2012) 94: "Wie wir durch den Tod des Sohnes Gottes als eines Menschen mit Gott versöhnt worden sind..., so ist auch die Tatsache, dass alle Menschen in den Todesbereich gerieten, durch die Eigenart der Tat eines einzigen Menschen verursacht."
[8] P. F. Beatrice, Sünde V, in: TRE 32 (2001) 392–393.

presentations in lexica and especially the fascicles of the *Handbuch der Dogmengeschichte* by Leo Scheffczyk for the beginnings up to Augustine, and then Manfred Hauke from Augustine to the Greek and Michael Stickelbroeck to the Latin tradition[9].

II. Remarks to some special points

The doctrine of original sin was declared obsolete in the Catholic Church, not least in 1970 by theologians such as Herbert Haag; this indicates the question mark in the title of our conference. As an Old Testament scholar, Norbert Lohfink dealt with this topic and showed his sympathy with a sociological doctrine of original sin, which he combined with the approach of René Girard.

In addition, two topics should be mentioned that were not dealt with at our conference: the Pascha-Homily of Melito of Sardis from the 2nd century, which explicitly speaks of the inheritance of Adam, who left corruption and perdition to his children (§ 49). Furthermore, the debate in Syriac theology as to whether man was created mortal or immortal is illustrated by the views of Jacob of Sarug and Narsai.

1. Contestations—The question mark (in our title)

Urs Baumann's dissertation from 1970 bears the title of our conference in German: *Erbsünde?*, where the subtitle indicates the focus on "its traditional understanding in the crisis of contemporary theology". The Old Testament scholar Herbert Haag wrote in the foreword to this dissertation, that the farewell of the doctrine of original sin will come rather much too late[10]. The doctrine of original sin has therefore been disputed in the Catholic Church for more than 50 years.

---

[9] Besides *Scheffczyk* also *M. Hauke,* Urstand, Fall und Erbsünde. In der nachaugustinischen Ära bis zum Beginn der Scholastik: die griechische Theologie = Handbuch der Dogmengeschichte II 3a (2.Teil) (Freiburg i. B. [u.a.] 2007); *M. Stickelbroeck,* Urstand, Fall und Erbsünde. In der nachaugustinischen Ära bis zum Beginn der Scholastik: die lateinische Theologie = Handbuch der Dogmengeschichte II 3a (3.Teil) (Freiburg i. B. [u.a.] 2007).

[10] *H. Haag,* Geleitwort, in: Urs Baumann, Erbsünde? Ihr traditionelles Verständnis in der Krise heutiger Theologie (Freiburg i.B. 1970) 6: "Nachdem die abendländische Kirche 1500 Jahre einer durch Augustinus irregeleiteten Tradition gehuldigt hat, kommt heute der Abschied von der 'Erbsünde' wahrlich nicht zu früh – eher viel zu spät."

On the other hand, Theodor W. Adorno (1903–1969) spoke in 1966 of a "secularized original sin", in the sense that "whatever the individual or the group undertakes against the totality of which it forms a part is infected by its evil"[11].

Haag assumes right from the start that the church's doctrine of original sin cannot be proven in the texts of the Old and New Testament. However, as Lohfink explains[12], he compares the church's doctrine of original sin according to theological handbooks and catechisms from 1965 and before, in so-called "mythical" form with biblical texts, which he strips of their "mythical" guise. With that method the result is clear: the Bible does not correspond to later church doctrine.

Already the two volumes by Julius Gross[13] of a history of the formation of the doctrine of original sin in 1960 and 1963 (and two other volumes for the later period) present rich material, especially for our patristic time, with the aim to prove that the doctrine of original sin is a mistake. Scheffczyk commented that "with regard to the great work of J. Gross" one can rightly speak of a "war pamphlet"[14], however, Scheffczyk wished to avoid to make history of dogma an apologetic. The question here is probably also what is meant by the doctrine of original sin.

For an orientation on the official teaching of the Catholic Church on original sin reference can be made to the outline of Christoph Schönborn and to the Catechism of the Catholic Church in the first Part on the Profession of Faith[15] in §§ 396–409.

---

[11] *Th. W. Adorno*, Negative Dialektik (Frankfurt 1966) 239: "Was immer der Einzelne oder die Gruppe gegen die Totalität unternimmt, deren Teil sie bildet, wird von deren Bösem angesteckt …Dazu hat die Erbsünde sich säkularisiert."

[12] *N. Lohfink*, Wie sollte man das Alte Testament auf die Erbsünde hin befragen?, in: N. Lohfink, A. Sand, G. Scherer, W. Breuning, Zum Problem der Erbsünde. Theologische und philosophische Versuche (Essen 1981) 9–52, here 10–11.

[13] *J. Gross*, Geschichte des Erbsündendogmas. I Entstehungsgeschichte des Erbsündendogmas von der Bibel bis Augustinus (München, Basel 1960); II Entwicklungsgeschichte des Erbsündendogmas im nachaugustinischen Altertum und in der Vorscholastik (5. – 11. Jahrhundert) (München, Basel 1963); III Entwicklungsgeschichte des Erbsündendogmas im Zeitalter der Scholastik (12. – 15. Jahrhundert) (München, Basel 1971); IV Entwicklungsgeschichte des Erbsündendogmas seit der Reformation (München, Basel 1972).

[14] *Scheffczyk*, Urstand, 5.

[15] I.2.1.1.7. In Brief: 416 By his sin Adam, as the first man, lost the original holiness and justice he had received from God, not only for himself but for all human beings. 417 Adam and Eve transmitted to their descendants human nature wounded by their own first sin and hence deprived of original holiness and justice; this deprivation is called "original sin". 418 As a result of original sin, human nature is weakened in its powers, subject to ignorance, suffering and the domination of death, and inclined to sin (this inclination is called "concupiscence").

In § 404 it is explained how the personal sin committed by Adam and Eve "affected the human nature that they would then transmit in a fallen state (Council of Trent: DS 1511-1512). It is a sin which will be transmitted by propagation to all mankind, that is, by the transmission of a human nature deprived of original holiness and justice. ... that is why original sin is called 'sin' only in an analogical sense: it is a sin 'contracted' and not 'committed'—a state and not an act." Thus, original sin "does not have the character of a personal fault in any of Adam's descendants. It is a deprivation of original holiness and justice, but human nature ... is wounded in the natural powers proper to it, subject to ignorance, suffering and the dominion of death, and inclined to sin—an inclination to evil that is called concupiscence" (§ 405). Though baptism "erases original sin and turns a man back towards God, but the consequences for nature, weakened and inclined to evil, persist in man and summon him to spiritual battle."

Briefly, the Compendium of the Catechism of the Catholic Church § 76 formulates: "Original sin, in which all human beings are born, is the state of deprivation of original holiness and justice. It is a sin 'contracted' by us not 'committed'; it is a state of birth and not a personal act. Because of the original unity of all human beings, it is transmitted to the descendants of Adam 'not by imitation, but by propagation'. This transmission remains a mystery which we cannot fully understand."

2. Old Testament and original sin—a response of Norbert Lohfink

In contrast to Haag, the Old Testament exegete Norbert Lohfink presented some reflections on how to start with an Old Testament doctrine of original sin[16]. In a first section, he reflected on some hermeneutical questions, concluding that Old Israelite thinking of a clan needs to bring a teaching of universal sin in the image of an "original sin" of the father of the whole tribe. This means a threefold type of thinking: typological (a typological figure represents the whole group), etiological thinking (what is today is derived from a founding event in early times), and a genealogical one (the founding event is linked with the person of the fictive father of the whole group).

---

419 "We therefore hold, with the Council of Trent, that original sin is transmitted with human nature, 'by propagation, not by imitation' and that it is ... 'proper to each'". The solemn Professio fidei of Pope Paul VI is quoted here, which he proclaimed on 30 June 1968 on the occasion of the 1900th anniversary of the martyrdom of Saints Peter and Paul, published as Motu Proprio, AAS 60 (1968), no. 8, p. 432-445. Ch. *Schönborn*, Die kirchliche Erbsündenlehre im Umriss, in: idem, A. Görres, R. Spaemann, Zur kirchlichen Erbsündenlehre. Stellungnahmen zu einer brennenden Frage (Einsiedeln - Freiburg 1991) 70-102, esp. 89-102.

[16] *Lohfink*, Wie sollte man das Alte Testament auf die Erbsünde hin befragen?, 9-52.

Approaches of systematic theologians to original sin can be classified as "historical", "evolutionary", sociological and personal—so already Baumann[17]. Lohfink has opted—with good reason—for the sociological path, which he considers the most viable one[18] and including most of the statements of the personal way[19]. Lohfink would choose a sociological way in order to write a doctrine of original sin in the OT, based on the theory of René Girard and Raymund Schwager[20] (Girard's theory: human violence is not overcome by any human society, but they use counter-violence fixed in the society, like sacrifices, or in modern societies the whole juridical system).

On this basis, the classical texts for the OT, Gen 2-4 and Ps 51,7 can be analyzed in order to present an Old Testament "doctrine of original sin", so Lohfink's proposal.

3. The heritage (κληρονομία) of Adam: Melito of Sardis' Paschal homily (c. 160-170)

The homily[21] De pascha (Περὶ πάσχα) is the earliest preserved Easter homily, so Stuart Hall[22], and is ascribed to Melito of Sardis (died before 190), as mostly assumed[23], though not completely secured[24]. A list of Melito's writings in Eu-

---

[17] *Baumann*, Erbsünde?, 181-182; he explains these four models a)-d) on p. 182-190. a) Starting from a historical Adam, a historical original state, and historical fall of Man at the beginning of human history; thus, the Adam figure has universal decision-making power. There is a biological procreative connection with Adam. b) Original state is what man will be in perfection. c) Social character of sin becomes the pivotal point of the doctrine of original sin—social interdependence (ibid.186). d) The historicity of Adam is abandoned. What Scripture says about man, it says about me (ibid. 187).
[18] *Lohfink*, Wie sollte man das Alte Testament auf die Erbsünde hin befragen?, 18-20.
[19] *Lohfink*, Wie sollte man das Alte Testament auf die Erbsünde hin befragen?, 22.
[20] R. *Girard*, La violence et le sacré (Paris 1972); R. *Schwager*, Brauchen wir einen Sündenbock? Gewalt und Erlösung in den biblischen Schriften (München 1978).
[21] Text: Meliton de Sardes. Sur la pâque et fragments. Introd., texte crit., trad. et notes, ed. O. Perler, SC 123 (Paris 1966); German: J. *Blank*, Meliton von Sardes. Vom Passa. Die älteste christliche Osterpredigt. Übersetzt, eingeleitet und kommentiert (Freiburg i.B. 1963) 101-131; English: Melito of Sardis, On Pascha. With the fragments of Melito and other material related to the quartodecimans, translated, introduced and annotated by A. Stewart-Sykes (Crestwood N.Y. 2001) 37-67.
[22] Cf. S. G. *Hall*, art. Melito von Sardes, in: TRE 22 (1992) 424-428, here 425.
[23] Some discussion, however, on the identity of the author of the Easter homily with Melito of Sardis by L. Cohick, Melito of Sardis's Peri Pascha and Its 'Israel', HTR 91 (1998) 351-372, here 354-357.
[24] Cf. *Th. R. Karmann*, Melito von Sardes und das Petrusevangelium, in: Th. J. Kraus, T. Nicklas (hgg.), Das Evangelium nach Petrus. Text, Kontexte, Intertexte = TU 158 (Berlin, New York 2007) 215-235, here 234, n. 112.

sebius HE IV 26,1–4 reveals him as one of the most important Christian theologians of the second half of the second century; the homily is dated usually between 160 and 170[25]. Already in 1949, Alois Grillmeier wrote an analysis on this homily[26], especially with regard to §§ 48–56, dealing with the creation of man and the Fall.

In his homily, Melito parallels Israel's salvation from the bondage of Egypt with Christ's redemption from the Egypt of damnation. In the passage (§§ 48–56), Melito provides a description of the "overall situation of humanity created by Adam", in a manner which can be called a drastic one. This description seems almost modern in mentioning the atrocities we experience in our times (abuse of all kinds—shocking war crimes or experiences of abuse)[27]. In a surprising way—for such an early Christian text—, the idea is found (§ 49): what Adam brought upon himself through his transgression by tasting of the tree, he leaves to his children, the human race, as an inheritance, κληρονομία (twice)[28]. This heritage of Adam is perdition (ἀπώλεια) instead of salvation. Grillmeier commented that it is "unique in early Christian literature" that the whole condition of the human race in the world is called a "kleronomia"[29].

§ 49: "He [scl. Adam] left an inheritance to his children, and as an inheritance he left his children:
not purity but lust, not incorruption but decay, not honor but dishonor, not freedom but bondage, not sovereignty but tyranny, not life but death, not salvation but destruction."[30]

Melito attributes these atrocities to the personified *Hamartia* (§ 50): The people on earth "were grasped by tyrannical sin (ἁμαρτία) and they were led to the land of sensuality, where they were swamped in unsatisfying pleasures: by adultery, by lust, by license, by love of money, by murder, by the shedding

---

[25] *Karmann*, Melito, 217. Karmann shows that Melito's homily is not necessarily literary dependent from Petr-Ev, at least not that clearly "certain" as Perler writes. Cf. Karmann also for bibliography on Meliton.

[26] A. *Grillmeier*, "Das Erbe der Söhne Adams" in der Homilia de Passione Melitos. Ein neues Beispiel griechischer Erbsündelehre aus frühchristlicher Zeit, Schol 20-24 (1949) 481–502; neu bearbeitet in: *idem*, Mit ihm und in ihm (Freiburg i.B. 1975, ²1978), 175–197.

[27] *Grillmeier*, "Das Erbe", 175–176, emphasized already the "power of the formulations" and wrote: "Schon in dem bis jetzt bekannten Schrifttum fällt die Kraft der Formulierungen auf, die sich bei dem besonderen Redestil Melitons sehr einprägsam gestalteten."

[28] Cf. *Grillmeier*, "Das Erbe", 180, 182, n.17; 184.

[29] *Grillmeier*, "Das Erbe", 189: "Daß Meliton den ganzen beschriebenen Zustand der Söhne Adams in der Welt eine Kleronomia nennt, ist in der frühchristlichen Literatur einzigdastehend."

[30] *Melito of Sardis*, De pascha 49: SC 123, p. 86–87; English: Stewart-Sykes, p. 50.

of blood, by the tyranny of evil, by the tyranny of lawlessness"[31]. And Melito elaborates on this with a long series of examples like murder, adultery, abortion (§§ 51–53).

Between sin and death there is a link for Melito (§§ 54–55): Sin works together with death, and he called sin the collaborator of the Death, συνεργὸς τοῦ θανάτος ("collaborateur de la Mort" in SC 123, 91), which "set his sign on every one and those on whom he etched his mark were doomed to death" (§ 54). Here "sin" (hamartia) is understood in a personified manner. Thus the conclusion (§ 55): "all flesh fell under sin, and every body under death, ... and that which was taken from the dust was reduced to dust, and the gift of God was locked away in Hades"[32]. Thus, only the personal sin causes the complete perdition, namely death[33].
Finally in § 56, we read:

> Humanity was doled out by death,
> for a strange disaster and captivity surrounded him;
> he was dragged off a captive under the shadow of death,
> and the father's image (ἡ τοῦ πατρὸς εἰκών) was left desolate.[34]

Thus, we are linked with the topic "Imago Dei" of our last Colloquy in L'viv in 2019.

Melito's homily was also taken up by Scheffczyk, who approvingly reported Grillmeier's essay[35]. It is understandable when Scheffczyk writes that in Melito "the decisive elements of a doctrine of the culpable calamity of all human beings coming from Adam ... receive the strongest emphasis by then"[36]. In addition, the term "inheritance" provides "the clearest relationship to Adam and his disastrous act"[37]. Adam is the "testator" who causes a state of evil— meant as an external condition and disastrous situation. In the background of Melito's approach is Pauline theology of history, even if formal quotations are missing, Rom 5,12–19 is not quoted, while Exodus 12,1–42 more or less literally[38].

---

[31] *Melito of Sardis*, De pascha 50: SC 123, p. 86–89; English: Stewart-Sykes, p. 50.
[32] *Melito of Sardis*, De pascha 54–55: SC 123, p. 90–91; English: Stewart-Sykes, p. 51–52.
[33] This is the conclusion of *Grillmeier*, "Das Erbe", 190–193.
[34] *Melito of Sardis*, De pascha 55–56: SC 123, p. 90–91; English: Stewart-Sykes, p. 52.
[35] *Scheffczyk*, Urstand, 54–57. Cf. *Gross*, Entstehungsgeschichte I, 83–85, who also took up Melito's homily and Grillmeier's essay, criticizing only the talk of original sin in this context; "nach unserm Text zu urteilen, hat Melito zwar an Erbübel geglaubt, von einer Vererbung der Ursünde aber nichts gewußt" (85).
[36] *Scheffczyk*, Urstand, 56.
[37] Ibid.
[38] Cf. *Grillmeier*, "Das Erbe", 193; *Scheffczyk*, Urstand, 57.

4. A debate on original human immortality in Syriac theology

Was Adam created mortal or immortal? The teaching of original human mortality is found with Philo of Alexandria (d. ca 50)[39] who said the earthly Adam was mortal by nature. Theophilus of Antioch dealt with the question whether man was mortal or immortal explicitly in Ad Autolycum II 27, but stating already in II 24: "For man had been made a middle [nature] (μέσος), neither forever mortal, nor immortal at all, but capable of either"[40].

According to Ephrem in his Commentary on Genesis, Adam was created neither mortal nor immortal[41], i.e. Adam was in an intermediate state from the beginning of creation until the fall. He could decide for himself whether he would henceforth exist as a mortal or immortal being[42]. If man had obeyed the commandment (and the will of God), he would have been granted immortality by God. Jacob of Sarug devoted an entire Memro to this question[43]; though it cannot be proven that Jacob "drew directly from Ephrem", "but the similarities are striking"[44]. According to Jacob, man was "modelled" and composed both mortal and immortal; thus he could choose according to his own will[45].

In his Homily IV of Narsai's homilies on Genesis, it is clearly expressed that man was created mortal (in relying on Theodore of Mopsuestia)[46]. Narsai is

---

[39] *Philo of Alex.*, De mundi opificio XLVI. (135) : ed. R. Arnaldez (1961), p. 232-233; "even if man is mortal according to that portion of him which is visible, he may at all events be immortal according to that portion which is invisible; and for this reason, one may properly say that man is on the boundaries of a better and an immortal nature, partaking of each as far as it is necessary for him; and that he was born at the same time, both mortal and the immortal. Mortal as to his body, but immortal as to his intellect (κατὰ τὴν διάνοιαν)." English: https://www.earlyjewishwritings.com/text/philo/book1.html (27.01.2024). Cf. Ph. *Gignoux*, Introduction, PO 34, 493.

[40] *Theophil. Ant.*, Ad Autolycum II 24 et 27: SC 20 (Paris 1948), 158 (Greek), 161 (French); 164-167. Text and transl. R. M. Grant (Oxford 1970), p. 66/67; 68-71.

[41] *Ephrem*, Comm. in Genesim II 17,3: ed. R. M. Tonneau, CSCO 153, Syr 72 (Leuven 1955), p. 26,10-13; CSCO 152, Syr. 71, p. 34,28-31.

[42] Th. *Kremer*, Mundus primus. Die Geschichte der Welt und des Menschen von Adam bis Noach im Genesiskommentar Ephräms des Syrers = CSCO 641, Subs. 128 (Louvain 2012), esp. 269-276, here 269.

[43] *Jacob of Sarug*, Mēmrō de Saint Mār Jacques sur: Adam a-t-il été créé mortel ou immortel [Hom. II]: ed. Kh. Alwan, Jacques de Saroug. Quatre homélies métriques sur la création = CSCO 508, 509, Syr. 214, 215 (Louvain 1989), p. 18-30 (Syr.); 17-32 (French).

[44] *Kremer*, Mundus primus, 274.

[45] *Jacob of Sarug*, Hom. II, 131-146: CSCO 508, p. 23-24 (Syr.); CSCO 509, p. 24.

[46] *Narsai*, Sur la constitution d'Adam et d'Ève et sur la transgression du commandement, ed. Ph. Gignoux, PO 34, 610-637. Cf. vv. 41-58: PO 34, p. 612-613, given the headline "La mortalité originelle du premier homme".

fighting against the opinion that the Creator did not know that we will sin, and that anger changed the will of the Creator:

> Il savait, en nous constituant, qu'il nous faisait mortels;
> Et sa création témoigne qu'il savait qu'elle avait été créée pour des mortels.[47]

Narsai strongly emphasised the pedagogy of God, who wants to educate us more and more[48]. He argues also: if God created man immortal in order to later condemn him to become mortal, then sin would have changed his will; and it would be due to his wrath that man lost his immortality, an idea which would be contrary to his pedagogical plan (Hom. IV, 55–57). Narsai underlines the pedagogical plan of God in the whole history of salvation, a basic theme in East Syriac theology[49], from Cyrus of Edessa to Ishodad of Merv.

Jacob on the other hand, explains that such an assumption would lead to blasphemy[50]. In these words we may touch upon an underlying controversy.

Lucas Van Rompay described the different conceptualization of the history of paradise in Jacob of Sarug and Narsai; they are not independent from one another. Both of them hold that "human discernment was put into work". And Van Rompay concludes that there was a "fruitful encounter and interaction between important ideas and between creative minds"[51] in the School of Edessa—an observation which was already explored by the late Luise Abramowski († 2014) in a chapter in her monograph on Narsai's Christology (written in 2006)[52].

---

[47] *Narsai,* Hom IV, 57–58: PO 34, p. 613.
[48] Cf. *Gignoux,* Introduction, PO 34, 488–495 (F. L'état primitive de l'homme: La doctrine de la mortalité originelle).
[49] Cf. *T. Hainthaler,* in: Jesus der Christus im Glauben der Kirche 2/5: Die Kirche in Persien (Freiburg i.B. 2022) esp. 772–774, 795–796.
[50] *Jacob of Sarug,* Hom. II, 117–124: CSCO 508 and 509, p. 23. Cf. *Kremer,* Mundus primus, 274.
[51] *L. Van Rompay,* Humanity's Sin in Paradise. Ephrem, Jacob of Sarug and Narsai in Conversation, in: G. A. Kiraz (ed.), Jacob of Serugh and His Times. Studies in Sixth-Century Syriac Christianity (Piscataway 2010) 199–217, here 217.
[52] *L. Abramowski,* Die edessenisch-theodorianische Schulung des Kyrillianers Jakob von Sarug, in: Jesus der Christus im Glauben der Kirche 2/5: Die Kirche in Persien, ed. T. Hainthaler (Freiburg i.B. 2022) 200–212.

The discussion on original sin in systematic theology is going on, as is documented by Quaestiones disputatae nr. 316 Die Erbsündenlehre in der modernen Freiheitsdebatte, edited by Christoph Böttigheimer and René Dausner[53], and it might be subject in the theological dialogue between the Roman Catholic Church and the Orthodox Church.

---

[53] *Ch. Böttigheimer, R. Dausner* (eds.), Die Erbsündenlehre in der modernen Freiheitsdebatte = Quaestiones disputatae (Freiburg i.B. 2021).

Early Fathers

Zdravko Jovanović, Belgrade (Serbia)

The Notion of Infancy of Adam and Eve in Theophilus and Irenaeus and Its Relevance for Contemporary Theological Anthropology

Abstract:
The persistent diligence with which both Theophilus' and Irenaeus' extant texts are studied in contemporary scholarship is caused, among other things, by their teaching about the created order as a reality intended for temporal progression and growth. Moreover, their perplexing doctrine of Adam and Eve as νήπιοι relating to the state in which they existed before the Fall and the dynamism of human nature potentially opens up significant possibilities for understanding numerous fundamental topics in theological anthropology. One of the most important subjects recognized by modern scholars is certainly an adequate understanding of the relationship between the adjectives "good" and "perfect" in the context of teaching about the creation of men. In connection with this question, it is important to have a balanced understanding of the relationship between protology and eschatology, which derives directly from the soteriology of Irenaeus and especially from his doctrine of recapitulation. No less important is the significance of human material, bodily existence, and its connection with the temporal dimension of the created world and the flow and the culmination of human history. In the present paper perspectives that potentially arise in the context of the doctrine about the infancy of Adam and Eve for the reevaluation of perpetual theological topics such as the relationship between anthropology and Christology, the ecclesial context of salvation, mysteriology, ethics, and dialogue between theology and science are also discussed.

Given the fact that since its inception, the biological theory of human evolution has had a huge impact on the rethinking of modern anthropological topics, many Christian theologians have tried to find inspiration for a dialogue with science in early Christian thought. On the one hand, the reason for this should be sought in believing that Augustine's traditional understanding of original sin cannot be easily reconciled with the theory of evolution[1], and on the other hand, it was hoped that such an agreement is much more

---
[1] For this and some other reasons Augustine was sometimes accused of "having concocted a doctrine that is found neither in the gospels nor in the Pauline epistles nor in the Greek

likely to happen in the context of the anthropology of Irenaeus of Lyon (c.130–c.200/203) and, to some extent, his predecessor Theophilus of Antioch (c.120–c.183/185). The great attention with which Irenaeus' and Theophilus' texts are read in contemporary theology is also caused by their teaching about creation as a reality created for development and growth, as well as their related teaching about creation which initially existed as "imperfect". For this reason, their theology is seen as a sort of antipode to Augustine's teaching about the Fall, which occurred in the context of the supposedly original perfection of creation[2].

Nevertheless, the teaching of Theophilus and Irenaeus about Adam and Eve, who were not created as perfect from the very beginning, but were like children or infants (νήπιοι) at the time of their "fall", was not generally accepted in early Christian theology. Moreover, this particular aspect of their theological anthropology has not been particularly widely studied even in contemporary theological thought either[3]. This is somewhat surprising, since this theme is present in the only Theophilus' (which probably influenced Irenaeus' theology on this matter) and in both of Irenaeus' preserved texts. Truth be told, neither they themselves provide any extensive interpretation, nor a clear theological definition of the term νήπιος. What remains for the intrigued reader is to look for the meaning of the term by studying a whole range of indicators that exist in the wider contextual environment of this term. The key text in which Theophilus expounds his understanding of the account of the Fall from the Book of Genesis and Adam's mode of existence reads:

---

patristic tradition". H. *Rondet*, Original Sin: The Patristic and Theological Background, transl. C. Finegan (Shannon 1972) 21. According to Rist's interpretation Gilson castigate Augustine for inventing an immoral doctrine that turns a person into a "puppet". *J. Rist*, Augustine on Free Will and Predestination, JThS 20/2 (1969) 420–447, 429, 435. See also: *P. Sanlon*, Original Sin in Patristic Theology, in: H. Madueme, M. Reeves (eds.), Adam, The Fall and Original Sin. Theological, Biblical and Scientific Perspectives (Grand Rapids 2014) 85–107.

[2] *A. M. McCoy*, The Irenaean Approach to Original Sin through Christ's Redemption, in: S. P. Rosenberg et al. (eds.), Finding Ourselves after Darwin. Conversations on the Image of God, Original Sin, and the Problem of Evil (Grand Rapids 2018) 160–172.

[3] Exceptionally valuable are the studies written on this topic by Ysabel de Andia and M. Steenberg. I am indebted very much to their insightful engagement on this delicate topic. See: *M. C. Steenberg*, Children in Paradise. Adam and Eve as 'Infants' in Irenaeus of Lyons, JECS 12/1 (2004) 1–22; *M. C. Steenberg*, Irenaeus on Creation. The Cosmic Christ and the Saga of Redemption (Leiden 2008) 142–145; *Y. de Andia*, Adam-Enfant chez Irénée de Lyon, Le Fruit de l'Esprit. Etudes sur Irénée de Lyon (Paris 2021) 101–113. See also: *J. Lawson*, The Biblical Theology of Saint Irenaeus (London 1948) 207–214; *J. Z. Smith*, The Garments of Shame, in: J. Z. Smith (ed.), Map is Not Territory: Studies in the History of Religions (Leiden 1978) 1–23, especially 18–21.

> The tree of knowledge was good and its fruit was good. For the tree did not contain death, as some suppose; this was the result of disobedience. For there was nothing in the fruit but knowledge, and knowledge is good if one uses it properly. In his actual age, Adam was as old as an *infant* (τῇ δὲ οὔσῃ ἡλικίᾳ ὅδε Ἀδὰμ ἔτη νήπιος ἦν); therefore he was not yet able to acquire knowledge properly. For at the present time when a child is born it cannot eat bread at once, but first it is fed with milk and then, with increasing age, it comes to solid food. So it would have been with Adam. Therefore God was not jealous, as some suppose, in ordering him not to eat of knowledge. Furthermore, he wanted to test him, to see whether he would be obedient to his command. At the same time he wanted the man to remain simple and sincere for a longer time, remaining in *infancy* (ἐπὶ πλείονα χρόνον ἐβούλετο ἁπλοῦν καὶ ἀκέραιον διαμεῖναι τὸν ἄνθρωπον νηπιάζοντα)[4].

When it comes to Irenaeus, he mentions this idea directly five times—twice in his work *Epideixis tou apostolikou kērygmatos* and three times in his work *Adversus Haereses*[5]. The most important and explicit text, according to the interpreters, is in chapter 12 of the *Epideixis*. Irenaeus says the following:

> So, having made the man lord (*dominum*, κύριος) of the earth and everything in it, He (God) made him in secret lord also of the servants in it. They, however, were in their full development, while the lord, that is, the man, was a little one (*nam infans erat*); for he was a child and had need to grow so as to come to his full perfection (*ad perfectionem venire*) [...] But the man was a little one, and his discretion (*consilium*, βουλή) still undeveloped, wherefore also he was easily misled by the deceiver[6].

The term *infant* is simply a translation of the Latin term *infans*, which in turn is a translation of the Greek term νήπιος. Theophilus and Irenaeus opt for this term rather than equivalents such as the terms παιδίον, τέκνον, βρέφος. According to them, Adam and Eve were simply children and they were infantile. This fact is important for understanding another of the key Irenaeus' sections in which this motif appears:

---

[4] *Theophil. Ant.*, Ad Autol. 2.25.1–28: R. M. Grant, Theophilus of Antioch: Ad Autolycum (Oxford 1970), p. 66–67 (text and transl.).
[5] *Iren. Lugd.*, AH 3.22.4: A. Rousseau, L. Doutreleau, SC 211 (Paris 1974), p. 438–444; *Iren. Lugd.*, AH 3.23.5: A. Rousseau, L. Doutreleau, SC 211 (Paris 1974), p. 456–460; *Iren. Lugd.*, AH 4.38.1–2: A. Rousseau, SC 100 (Paris 1965), p. 942–950; *Iren. Lugd.*, Epid. 12: A. Rousseau, SC 406 (Paris 1995), p. 100; *Iren. Lugd.*, Epid. 14: A. Rousseau, SC 406 (Paris 1995), p. 102.
[6] Epid. 12: SC 406, p. 100. English transl. *J. Smith*, St. Irenaeus: Proof of the Apostolic Preaching, ACW 16 (New York 1952), p. 55.

If, however, anyone says, "What then? Could not God have exhibited man as perfect from the beginning (*ab initio Deus perfectum fecisse hominem*; ἀπ' ἀρχῆς ὁ θεὸς τέλειον πεποιηκέναι τόν ἄνθρωπον)?" let him know that, inasmuch as God is indeed always the same and unbegotten as respects Himself, all things are possible to Him. But created things must be inferior to Him who created them, from the very fact of their later origin (*quae autem facta sunt ab eo, secundum quod postea facturæ initium habuerunt, secundum hoc et minora esse oportuit eo qui se fecerit. Nec enim poterant infecta esse, quæ nuper facta sunt*; τὰ δὲ γεγονότα, καθ' ὃ μετέπειτα γενέσεως ἀρχὴν ἰδίαν ἔσχε, κατὰ τοῦτο καὶ ὑστερεῖσθαι ἔδει αὐτὰ τοῦ πεποιηκότος); for it was not possible for things recently created to have been uncreated. But inasmuch as they are not uncreated, for this very reason do they come short of the perfect. Because, as these things are of later date, so are they infantile; so are they unaccustomed to, and unexercised in, perfect discipline (*secundum enim quod sunt posteriora, secundum hoc et infantilia, et secundum quod infantilia, secundum hoc et insueta et inexercitata ad perfectam disciplinam*; καθ' ὃ γὰρ νεώτερα, κατὰ τοῦτο καὶ νήπια, καὶ καθ' ὃ νήπια, κατὰ τοῦτο καὶ ἀσυνήθη καὶ ἀγύμναστα πρὸς τὴν τελείαν ἀγωγήν). For as it certainly is in the power of a mother to give strong food to her infant, [but she does not do so], as the child is not yet able to receive more substantial nourishment; so also it was possible for God Himself to have made man perfect from the first, but man could not receive this [perfection], being as yet an infant (*homo autem impotens percipere illam: infans enim fuit*; ὁ δὲ ἄνθρωπος ἀδύνατος λαβεῖν αὐτό· νήπιος γὰρ ἦν). And for this cause our Lord, in these last times, when He had summed up all things into Himself, came to us, not as He might have come, but as we were capable of beholding Him. He might easily have come to us in His immortal glory, but in that case we could never have endured the greatness of the glory; and therefore it was that He, who was the perfect bread of the Father, offered Himself to us as milk, [because we were] as infants (*Et propter hoc, quasi infantibus, ille qui erat panis perfectus Patris lac nobis semetipsum praestavit*; Καὶ διὰ τοῦτο, ὡς νηπίοις, ὁ ἄρτος ὁ τέλειος τοῦ Πατρὸς γάλα ἡμῖν ἑαυτὸν παρέσχεν). He did this when He appeared as a man, that we, being nourished, as it were, from the breast of His flesh, and having, by such a course of milk nourishment, become accustomed to eat and drink the Word of God, may be able also to contain in ourselves the Bread of immortality, which is the Spirit of the Father[7].

Although any attempt to hermeneutically unpack this notion is somewhat speculative, it seems that in the surviving works of Irenaeus (much more than in Theophilus), there are clear theological statements that shed light on the original intention in postulating this idea. In essence, Irenaeus' understanding of the creation and destiny of man is most closely related to his understanding of human progress, growth, deification and final salvation in Christ.

---

[7] AH 4.38.1: SC 100, p. 942–949. English transl. A. Roberts, J. Donaldson, ANF 1 (Grand Rapids 1953), p. 521.

In other words, Christology and the doctrine of salvation are the basis on which he builds his theological anthropology. Hovever, compared to Irenaeus, Theophilus is significantly less helpful in understanding the full theological capacity of the term νήπιος primarily because of his underdeveloped Christology[8].

Created as Perfect?

As already mentioned, an important reason for the relevance of both Theophilus and Irenaeus in our time is their perception of creation as "imperfect" from the very beginning of its existence. Namely, none of their available texts speaks of the fact that God created man as completely perfect, that is, fully realized. According to Irenaeus, man as a dynamic being who progresses through history could gain perfection only at the end of the historical process, that is, in the eschaton[9]. However, their descriptions of humanity created in a state of "imperfection" and childhood should not be understood as if they indicate that humanity was created sinful. This would mean that they imply that evil is a phenomenon that naturally belongs to creation. Accepting such an attitude would actually mean agreeing with the Gnostics because their view of the creation implies attributing extremely negative characteristics to the material world, and that is exactly what Irenaeus wants to refute. According to the Gnostic teachings the original imperfection of man that led to his fall would imply such a creator who is not actually characterized by divine creative omnipotence and goodness but, rather a creator who manifests his impotence, i.e. his creative imperfection[10].

---

[8] R. M. Grant, Theophilus of Antioch to Autolycus, HThR 40/4 (1947) 227–256; R. Rogers, Theophilus of Antioch, ET 120/5 (2009) 214–224; N. Z.-V. Vorst, La création de l'homme (Gn 1, 26) chez Théophile d'Antioche, VigChr 30/4 (1976) 258–267.

[9] AH 4.38.3: SC 100, p. 956–957. English transl. ANF 1, p. 522: "Now it was necessary that man should in the first instance be created (*fieri*, γενέσθαι); and having been created, should receive growth (*augeri*, αὐξῆσαι); and having received growth, should be strengthened (*corroborari*, ἀνδρωθῆναι); and having been strengthened, should abound (*multiplicari*, πληθυνθῆναι); and having abounded, should recover [from the disease of sin] (*convalescere*, ἐνισχῦναι); and having recovered, should be glorified (*glorificari*, δοξασθῆναι); and being glorified, should see (*videre*, ἰδεῖν) his Lord".

[10] According to Steenberg's interpretation, the understanding held by H. Jonas and many others that overemphasizing knowledge in the context of soteriology is a key feature of Gnosticism is actually wrong: "That which might unite the various groups called 'Gnostic', which are in a proper sense hardly homogenous at all, is, if anything, their attitude towards creation and not their conception of knowledge vis-à-vis redemption". M. C. Steenberg, Of God and Man. Theology as Anthropology from Irenaeus to Athanasius (London 2009) 30. Cf. M. Widmann, Irenäus und seine theologischen Väter, ZThK 54/2 (1957) 156–173.

Theophilus' and Irenaeus' understanding of man's initial imperfection was quite different. They attributed this imperfection to the novelty of human existence and not to human nature itself. They state the reasons why, in their opinion, Adam and Eve were not created as perfect. According to their argument, it is simply not possible for newly created beings to possess perfection, because there is an ontological difference in the mode of existence between the creation and the Creator. However, the absence of perfection is not the same as the presence of sin and evil in human nature. Hypothetically, in the abovementioned words of Irenaeus:

> It was possible for God Himself to have made man perfect from the first, but man could not receive this [perfection], being as yet an infant[11].

Adam and Eve simply functioned as infantile beings at the very beginning of his existence, with insufficiently acquired experience and practice in perfect obedience to God. The reason for this should be sought solely in the fact that he exists as a created being[12]. The basic argument of both Theophilus and Irenaeus is that perfection is the result of a long process, and this argument should also work adequately both in the interpretation of the Fall as well as the existence and life of Christians who are susceptible to sin even after a new birth or Baptism. Consequently, Theophilus and Irenaeus viewed Adam and Eve as not fully mature and adult people from the very beginning but as children who should progress further in the future. Their fall was caused primarily by weakness, inexperience and immaturity, and not by a deliberate, premeditated, perfidious act of personal decision. It follows from this that Adam and Eve could not have fallen into sin if they had been completely perfect from the beginning. If they had not been in the state of childhood, they would have confronted the existential dilemma in which they found themselves in a moment of temptation in a significantly different way. Their free will, in that case, would then be in perfect harmony with their cognitive and experiential insights. That, however, was not the case.

---

[11] AH 4.38.1: SC 100, p. 942–949. English transl. ANF 1, p. 521.
[12] In order to substantiate this position, Irenaeus draws a parallel between Adam and Christ (see n. 25), who also went through the phase of childhood, most likely following the verses from Hebrews 5:8–9. Cf. G. Wingren, Man and the Incarnation. A Study in the Biblical Theology of Irenaeus, transl. R. Mackenzie (Philadelphia 1959) 79–113; A. N. S. Lane, Irenaeus on the Fall and Original Sin, in: R. J. Berry, T. A. Noble (eds.), Darwin, Creation and the Fall. Theological Challenges (Nottingham 2009) 130–148.

Therefore, in accordance with the teachings of Theophilus and Irenaeus, there seems to be absolutely no ontological reason to claim that the world was created as completely perfect in the very beginning. In this regard, it is, however, necessary to unequivocally distinguish between what is good and what is perfect. Namely, something or someone that is in the process of development can be good in all particular stages of its development and yet still imperfect in its manifestations and acts. Such a distinction speaks in favor of the thesis of Theophilus and Irenaeus that Adam and Eve were in the stage of childhood just before their fall[13].

It seems self-evident that one may rightfully ask what this actually meant. Is it about describing primarily physical infantilism, that is, the assumption that Adam and Eve were physiologically unformed and anatomically underdeveloped like small children? Or perhaps is it primarily a matter of describing their psychological, cognitive, experiential immaturity given the supposedly relatively short period of time that elapsed between their creation and their fall? In other words, does this concept imply that no ontological implications regarding the goodness of creation can be deduced from its use and that it simply describes what that term usually does when we speak of human individuals in the stage of childhood? In such a case, of course, we do not want

---

[13] As for the question of how soon the Fall occurred after the creation of the world and man it is certainly impossible to give a reliable answer. In all probability, the event described in the Book of Genesis seems to have occurred relatively soon after the creation of man. One of the reasons why we should assume that Adam and Eve were in the age of children, is Irenaeus' remark that they had yet to reach the capacity of sexual reproduction. It was necessary for them to grow up first and only then to reproduce: "having been strengthened, should abound (*multiplicari*, πληθυνθῆναι)" (AH 4.38.3: SC 100, p. 956–957. English transl. ANF 1, p. 522). Irenaeus analyzes this topic in more detail in the following section: "And even as she, having indeed a husband, Adam, but being nevertheless as yet a virgin (for in Paradise 'they were both naked, and were not ashamed,' inasmuch as they, having been created a short time previously, had no understanding of the procreation of children: for it was necessary that they should first come to adult age, and then multiply from that time onward) [...]" (AH 3.22.4: SC 211, p. 440–441. English transl. A. Roberts, J. Donaldson, ANF 1 [Grand Rapids 1953], p. 455). Cf. also: Epid. 14: SC 406, p. 102. English transl. J. Smith, St. Irenaeus: Proof of the Apostolic Preaching, ACW 16 (New York 1952), p. 56: "And Adam and Eve (for this is the name of the woman) *were naked and were not ashamed*, for their thoughts were innocent and childlike (*infantilis*), and they had no conception or imagination (*cogitare*, ἐννοέω) of the sort that is engendered in the soul by evil, through concupiscence, and by lust. For they were then in their integrity, preserving their natural state, for what had been breathed into their frame was the spirit of life; now, so long as the spirit still remains in proper order and vigour, it is without imagination or conception of what is shameful. For this reason they *were not ashamed*, as they kissed each other and embraced with the innocence of childhood". By the way, the very dilemma as to whether they were both sexually and reproductively mature does not play a decisive role in the context of the topic in this paper.

to say that something is wrong or bad in relation to the stage in which children temporarily are, that they lack something in the physiological sense, nor that their potentials are in any way debatable. What we want to say is simply that at this particular stage of development they are not sufficiently capable, neither physically nor psychologically, to bear full responsibility for their discernments and actions. After all, this is a generally accepted cultural norm as well as an integral part of the civilized legal regulations for the life of minors.

Consequently, recognizing the rational capacities that Adam possessed from the beginning does not mean that they were fully realized and exercised. In the same manner, it is possible to say that any completely healthy child is rational i.e. endowed with cognitive capacities but that does not mean that it is capable of using those capacities fully in that life's phase (for example, for abstract theoretical thinking, mathematical computing etc.). Irenaeus actually speaks in several instances about this category of concepts, attributing to Adam the capacities that he possesses but which were not fully realized. This is the case, for example, when he spoke about Adam as an icon and likeness of God[14]. Doing this Irenaeus intends primarily to strongly emphasize the radical otherness of man in relation to God and to emphasize the incompleteness that characterizes man as a created being[15]. This notion of man as an incomplete being, autonomously observed, is one of the most important anthropological insights in Irenaeus' theology.

In any case, it seems that Theophilus and Irenaeus did not have a metaphorical use in mind, but that notion of infancy functioned in a strictly descriptive sense in their theological anthropology. When they say that Adam is a child, they simply mean that they are describing his age, which does not contain any negative connotations[16]. It is simply about his current disposition, that is, about a specific developmental phase in his existence as a human being. In other words, it is only natural for Adam to be in the phase of childhood before he reaches the full maturity of an adult human being. Anyhow, the

---

[14] E.g., AH 3.18.1: SC 211, p. 342–345 (English transl. ANF 1, p. 445–446); AH 3.23.1-2: SC 211, p. 444–451 (English transl. ANF 1, p. 455–456); AH 4.38.3-4: SC 100, p. 952–961 (English transl. ANF 1, p. 521–522); Epid. 97: SC 406, p. 214–217 (English transl. ACW 16, p. 107–108).

[15] See: AH 3.8.3: SC 211, p. 94–97 (English transl. ANF 1, p. 421–422); AH 3.18.2: SC 211, p. 344–347 (English transl. ANF 1, p. 446); AH 4.16.4: SC 100, p. 568–571 (English transl. ANF 1, p. 481–482); AH 5.1.1: A. Rousseau, SC 153 (Paris 1969), p. 16–21 (English transl. ANF 1, p. 526–527); Epid. 18: SC 406, p. 106–109 (English transl. ACW 16, p. 58); Epid. 31: SC 406, p. 126–129 (English transl. ACW 16, p. 67–68).

[16] In Steenberg's view: "references to Adam and Eve as νήπιοι appear directly descriptive [...]" M. C. Steenberg, Children in Paradise, 6.

reasonable assumption that emerges is that Irenaeus would find it difficult to resort to a figurative interpretation of the Genesis' text, because this is exactly the approach that was characteristic of the Gnostics who approached the text with a tendency to excessive allegorization and mythologizing[17]. In the light of his anti-Gnostic polemic, Irenaeus would certainly approach the text with an emphasized desire to enable literary interpretation whenever the text itself allowed it. Moreover, as Steenberg rightly observes, Irenaeus emphasizes that reliable faith and relevant theology can only be built in the context of what he denotes as "faith rests upon reality" and what really is, as it is which requires a "true perception of reality"[18]. Another question is certainly what specifically he wanted to explain by using this notion of infancy in a theological context.

By all accounts, the essence of this insight of both Theophilus and Irenaeus refers primarily to the fact that Adam and Eve were immature like children in the ethical, spiritual, and intellectual sense of the word. They needed to progress gradually over time, to mature, and what actually happened to them was that they prematurely and unprepared entered a sphere of independence that led in the wrong direction and left them on a path that was not originally planned for them by God[19]. Since he was immature and infantile, Adam was relatively easy to deceive and mislead. This therefore means that Adam was created as an initially weak being that was practically at the very beginning of his long process of perfection. In accordance with this thinking, one could draw the conclusion that the fall of man into sin was caused not so much by a fully conscious decision, but rather by the manifestation of certain tendencies that were inherent in man as a newly created being. From there the manifestation of Adam's inability to face the seriousness of the existential situation in which he found himself originated[20].

---

[17] AH 2.27.1: A. Rousseau, L. Doutreleau, SC 294 (Paris 1982), p. 264–267 (English transl. ANF 1, p. 398); AH 2.28.2: SC 294, p. 270–273 (English transl. ANF 1, p. 399); AH 1.9.1–4: A. Rousseau, L. Doutreleau, SC 264 (Paris 1979), p. 137–151 (English transl. ANF 1, p. 329–330); AH 5.35.2: SC 153, p. 442–453 (English transl. ANF 1, p. 565–566). Cf. N. Brox, Die biblische Hermeneutik des Irenäus, ZAC 2/1 (1998) 26–48.

[18] Epid. 3: SC 406, p. 86–87: [...] *fidem autem veritas adquirere facit* (περιποιέω), *nam fides super vere* (ἀληθῶς) *exsistentes stat res, (ita) ut his quae sunt, sicut sunt, credamus, et creden<tes his> quae sunt, sicut sunt, semper (eam quae) ad illa (est) adsensionem* (πεισμονή) *firmiter custodiamus* (διαφυλάσσω). *Igitur, quoniam salutis nostrae continens* (συνεκτικός) *fides est, multam diligentiam-curae* (ἐπιμέλια) *huic oportet-et-convenit facere, et eorum quae sunt adprehensionem* (κατάληψις) *habeamus veram*. English transl. ACW 16, p. 49–50. This reflection on the context for the authentic theology Irenaeus develops in the section in which his *regula fidei* emerges as a normative interpretive milieu.

[19] A. N. S. Lane, Irenaeus on the Fall and Original Sin, 130–148.

[20] A. M. McCoy, The Irenaean Approach, 160–172.

Christological focus

However, although it is true that in Irenaeus' theology, soteriology, i.e. the salvation of creation in Christ, is much more important and prominent than Adam's Fall and the consequences that the Fall had for humanity, it would be wrong to conclude that the Fall itself is a minor episode that could be eliminated from his theological reflections. Man's sin was possible from the very beginning and it represents, by God's permission, an aspect of the existence of the created world which God allows in order to achieve greater good that is the eschatological salvation of the world in the incarnate Christ. This view of Irenaeus perhaps represents a reason why he was actually uninterested in creating some grandiose, all-permeating theological narrative about the Fall or original sin.

In order to avoid any confusion on Irenaeus' position, it is unequivocal that he clearly understood Adam's disobedience to God as a Fall and that he described this disobedience in accordance with the later Christian Tradition as an event that disturbed the creation and changed its movement toward future perfection making it more receptive to the reign of death and decay[21]. Irenaeus also describes the consequences of Adam's Fall as moving the creation away from the goal that God originally intended for it[22]. Nevertheless, Irenaeus does not develop a complex theology of original sin in the way that, for example, Augustine later did. Instead, he writes about sin basically in the context of a reflection on what God has revealed in the incarnate Christ. In other words, he always places man's sin within the framework of the theological understanding of the process of salvation of creation, which was fulfilled by Christ. It seems that a very significant implication could be drawn from this point of view. This conception of sin is quite consistent with his refusal to separate the Old and New Testaments in any way, because his primary goal is to show, contrary to Gnostic speculations, that they are an inseparable part of the same divine economy of salvation. In the context of this implication, it is clear that for Irenaeus there is an inseparable connection between the historical events that took place at the very beginning of the life of creation and

---

[21] AH 5.5.1: SC 153, p. 61–67. English transl. ANF 1, p. 530–531.
[22] AH 4.39.3: SC 100, p. 969–971. English transl. ANF 1, p. 523: "The skill of God, therefore, is not defective, for He has power of the stones to raise up children to Abraham but the man who does not obtain it, is the cause to himself of his own imperfection (*suae imperfectionis est causa*, ἑαυτῷ τῆς ἰδίας ἀνεργασίας αἴτιος) [...]. Those persons, therefore, who have apostatized from the light given by the Father, and transgressed the law of liberty, have done so through their own fault, since they have been created free agents, and possessed of power over themselves".

the subsequent eschatological events that were inaugurated by Christ's incarnation and resurrection. The connection between history and eschatology in the context of Irenaeus' theology is always within one and the same divine economy of salvation[23].

However, this approach to the original sin doesn't provide a mechanism for Irenaeus to ignore the subsequent phenomenon of sin that is present in the creation, nor the very event of Adam's Fall. He simply points to the absolute priority of the event of Christ's incarnation and the possibility that man, after the Incarnation, has to gain all that he lost in Adam, but also to be fully realized and perfected as an image and likeness of God[24]. However, it would be completely wrong to conclude on the basis of this theological view of Irenaeus that he perceived sin as something that is "natural", that is, as an immanent aspect of man's created nature. Irenaeus' strong insistence on the recapitulation (ἀνακεφαλαίωσις) that was realized in Christ irrevocably confirms the goodness of the created world from the very beginning of its existence, because Christ recapitulates the entire history of the world in himself. In order to strengthen his position that the recapitulation includes Adam personally, Irenaeus repeatedly speaks about the fact that Christ went through all the chronological phases of human life, including childhood[25]. When the

---

[23] Cf. Cullmann's comment on this subject: "Judaism and Christianity could only find acceptance in Gnosticism when they were disrobed of this their specific uniqueness, that is, when they were de-historicized [...] No one knew this more fully than Irenaeus. So he carried on his impassioned fight against Gnosticism, for the connection of the Old Testament with the New, for the economy of salvation, for salvation history. Christianity emerged victorious from that decisive crisis because it preserved the only thing that kept it from ruin, namely, the idea of salvation in history". O. *Cullmann*, Salvation in History, transl. S. G. Sowers (New York 1967) 26–27. Cf. also: A. *Bengsch*, Heilsgeschichte und Heilswissen. Eine Untersuchung zur Struktur und Entfaltung des theologischen Denkens im Werk 'Adversus haereses' des Hl. Irenaeus von Lyon (Leipzig 1957) 55, and A. M. *McCoy*, The Irenaean Approach, 160–172.

[24] AH 5.36.3: SC 153, p. 460–467. English transl. ANF 1, p. 567: "First-begotten Word, should descend to the creature (facturam, ποίημα), that is, to what had been moulded (*plasma*, πλάσμα), and that it should be contained by Him; and, on the other hand, the creature should contain the Word (*factura iterum capiat Verbum*, ποίημα πάλιν χωρῇ τὸν Λόγον), and ascend to Him, passing beyond the angels, and be made after the image and likeness of God".

[25] AH 2.22.4: SC 294, p. 220–223. English transl. ANF 1, p. 391: "He therefore passed through every age, becoming an infant for infants (*infantibus infans factus*), thus sanctifying infants; a child for children (*paruulis paruulus*), thus sanctifying those who are of this age [...] a youth for youths (*iuuenibus iuuenis*) [...] So likewise He was an old man for old men (*senior in senioribus*) [...]". See also: AH 3.21.10: SC 211, p. 426–430 (English transl. ANF 1, p. 454); Epid. 31–33: SC 406, p. 127–131 (English transl. ACW 16, p. 67–69). Compare the concise interpretation given by de Andia: "Et pour que l'homme, dans cet état d'enfance,

passages about Adam as a child are read in the broader context of important topic of the ontological distance between God and man, then the Christological context of Irenaeus' soteriology also appears in much sharper contours. The only complete and accomplished man for Irenaeus is Jesus Christ. Only he is the perfect image of God and only communion with him enables man to reach his fulfillment, that is, his own maturity[26]. In this context, Adam as a child stands in opposition to Adam as a fully grown and complete man who achieved his perfection in Christ[27]. Here, in fact, is the key to Irenaeus' dynamic anthropology.

Protological or Eschatological Emphasis?

In aforementioned sense, one can ask whether it is possible to understand Irenaeus' teaching on ἀνακεφαλαίωσις[28] as a teaching that primarily highlights the topic of protological restoration. If that were the case, it would practically mean that Christ "restores" man and returns him to the state as it was at the historical beginning of man's existence. This would further mean that man returns to a state of imperfection and immaturity or to a state in which it would be possible for man to fall into sin again. Hypothetically speaking, man could then again choose to disobey God, which would mean that in such circumstances Christ is obviously not "all, and in all" as the Apostle Paul puts it (Col. 3:3–11). The whole story of the fall from the Book of Genesis could be then restaged and lead to its repetition. This would indicate that the victory of Christ, realized on the Cross and confirmed by the Resurrection, was not final at all.

---

puisse recevoir Dieu, le Verbe, dit magnifiquement Irénée, s'est fait ‹co-enfant› (νηπιάζων) avec Adam-enfant". Y. *de Andia*, Adam-Enfant chez Irénée de Lyon, in: ead., Le Fruit de l'Esprit. Etudes sur Irénée de Lyon (Paris 2021) 101–113, 110.

[26] See AH 5.6.1: SC 153, p. 61–67. English transl. ANF 1, p. 530–531.

[27] AH 5.16.2: SC 153, p. 216–217. English transl. ANF 1, p. 544: "For in times long past, it was said that man was created after the image of God, but it was not [actually] shown; for the Word was as yet invisible, after whose image man was created. Wherefore also he did easily lose the similitudes. When, however, the Word of God became flesh, he confirmed both these: for He both showed forth the image truly (*imaginem enim ostendit veram*, εἰκόνα ἔδειξεν ἀληθῶς), since He became himself what was his image; and He re-established the similitude after a sure manner (*similitudinem firmans restituit*, ὁμοίωσιν βεβαίως ἀποκατέστησεν), by assimilating man to the invisible Father through means of the visible Word".

[28] AH 5.21.1: SC 153, p. 260–265 (English transl. ANF 1, p. 548–549); AH 5.29.2: SC 153, p. 366–371 (English transl. ANF 1, p. 558).

Another crucial insight that emerges from Irenaeus' theology is that the materiality of human existence inextricably connects Adam with time and with the flow of history. In this sense, Adam is imperfect at the very beginning not only because he was created by God and because he is ontologically different from Him. Adam is imperfect precisely because he is in the initial stage of the course of human history[29]. His progress and development of all his potentials represent a phenomenon that takes place within history and whose fulfillment is connected with the future and ultimately with the Eschaton. Adam's material, i.e. bodily existence is firmly connected to history, and it is precisely the briefness of elapsed time of his existence within history that makes him a child. To rephrase it, and this is another crucial implication, Adam was a child before the fall simply because he had a body as an inseparable and constitutive aspect of his (good) being[30]. The material aspect of human existence simply requires a process of growth, maturation and adaptation to the rest of the created world within history[31]. In this sense, man possesses the so-called "preventive limitation: it is materiality that binds him to time and time that limits the capabilities of his knowledge and receptivity of his body"[32]. Man was in a state of childhood because his existence was new and young.

Irenaeus' insistence on the idea of the historical progression of man to the eschatological perfection for which he was destined from the beginning is not surprising at all. It is precisely in his affirmation of the material aspect of the creation that he sees as essential point of his critique of Gnostic "spiritualism" and their contempt for embodied material existence. Irenaeus had to defend both the original goodness of creation and the goodness of providence that God has for creation. He had to show that the appearance of a certain "relative" evil is not incompatible with God's providence because it does not represent the final destiny of the created world and will be eventually defeated and God's οἰκονομία will be fulfilled. Irenaeus resorts to notions of the progressive nature of creation and the soteriological adaptation of God to the historical movement of his creation, precisely to explain that sin and evil can appear in a creation that is said to be good and the work of a good God[33]. In this way, Irenaeus indicates that evil can play a role in God's providence for the world

---

[29] *M. A. B. Castellanos*, Salvación del ser humano como proceso histórico de plasmación en Ireneo de Lyón, CuestTeol 45/104 (2018) 357–381.
[30] *M. C. Steenberg*, Children in Paradise, 18.
[31] *M. C. Steenberg*, Irenaeus on Creation. The Cosmic Christ and the Saga of Redemption (Leiden 2008) 118–139.
[32] *M. C. Steenberg*, Children in Paradise, 1–22, 20.
[33] *J. Vives*, Pecado original y progreso evolutivo del hombre en Ireneo, EE 43 (1968) 561–589.

that incomprehensibly transcends the negative elements that are present in its historical path.

Moreover, another significant implication of Irenaeus' theology is that he understands matter as a reality characterized by adaptability and the ability of transformation[34]. The limitations that belong to the material world due to its created mode of existence are transcended by the action of the Holy Spirit. In this context, the term νήπιος, and anthropology in general, is inevitably associated with pneumatology. After all, this is where the capacity for the mystery of the Incarnation is to be found[35].

Eschatological Fulfillment—Anthropological Dynamism

As already mentioned, according to Irenaeus' understanding, salvation does not simply mean restoration to the prelapsarian state, but recapitulation, that is, the creation of a new man in Christ. The reason for this is that the original way of existence of Adam and Eve implied childish innocence and naivety rather than perfection. In this context, the eschatological fulfillment of humanity is something much greater than the restoration to the original state of the ancestors. Consequently, one can speak of the dynamic approach that Irenaeus employs when contemplating God's acts of creation and salvation of the world. Irenaeus, therefore, does not view the man as a static reality, but as a reality to which God intended development and growth, with the goal of making it incomparably more perfect and sublime than it was in the beginning[36]. Christ leads man to his perfection and attainment of perfection in the Eschaton, while simultaneously renewing all the original capacities that man had before the Fall.

In contemporary theological thought, however, the themes of growth, i.e. the progress, and the themes of protological renewal or restoration in the context of Irenaeus' teaching on recapitulation are sometimes inadequately viewed as mutually inconsistent, that is as theological themes with a certain

---

[34] This concrete insight represents an intriguing and relevant starting point for a dialogue with modern science in its various disciplines.

[35] AH 5.10.1: SC 153, p. 122–127 (English transl. ANF 1, p. 536); AH 2.19.6: SC 294, p. 192–195 (English transl. ANF 1, p. 386-387). Cf. H. Boersma, Redemptive Hospitality in Irenaeus: A Model for Ecumenicity in a Violent World, ProEccl 11/2 (2002) 207–226, 211; S. Zañartu, La salvación de la carne según Ireneo en ADV. HAER. V,1–14: Breve presentación de conjunto. «Fructus autem operis spiritus est carnis salus» (V,12,4,77s), TyV 54 (2013) 43–78.

[36] AH 4.38.3: SC 100, p. 956–957. Cf. E. Falque, God, the Flesh, and the Other. From Irenaeus to Duns Scotus, transl. W. C. Hackett (Evanston 2015) 138–139.

mutual tension[37]. As a result of this inadequate juxtaposition of progress and renewal, sometimes disproportionately more attention is paid to the topic of protological renewal with a tendency to neglect the meaning of eschatological connotations that the term recapitulation implies in Irenaeus' theology. It seems that this is about postulating an actually non-existent tension between Irenaeus' two soteriologies. Namely, having in mind Irenaeus' cosmology and anthropology, it is clear that for him the notion of recapitulation had primarily eschatological connotations, and not connotations of protological restoration or return to the state that existed in the so-called prelapsarian state. What Christ really recapitulates is not primarily the original human condition of Adam's infancy and immaturity but his orientation and designation in the context of God's providence about his future eschatological fulfillment.

The dynamism of human nature, which is in the function of God's designation of man and his progress towards the eschatological perfection or deification represents therefore the very foundation of Irenaeus' anthropology and soteriology. Precisely because of infant Adam's initial imperfectness, Christ revealed the fullness of man's adult, mature character, that is, the fullness of the image of God towards which Adam and his descendants should continually progress. Moreover, after the Incarnation, man's growth and maturation continues because the act of recapitulation did not represent some sudden act that would end the process of salvation with an abrupt and magical metamorphosis. Even after the Incarnation, man's dynamic movement does not stop. It continues in order to gain cosmological proportions and actively engage in the process of salvation of the whole of the created world[38]. The soteriological theme of human maturation and growth is not unique to the theology of Irenaeus of Lyons. However, this insight is found in a completely unique form in the context of his teaching about Adam and Eve in the state of infancy before the Fall.

Concluding Remarks—Relevance for Contemporary Theological Anthropolgy

The tragedy of the Fall, exemplified in theologies of Theophilus of Antioch and Irenaeus of Lyon, is shown primarily in the reorientation of human movement

---

[37] R. F. *Brown*, On the Necessary Imperfection of Creation: Irenaeus' Adversus Haereses IV,38, SJTh 28/01 (1975) 17–25; J. *Hick*, Evil and the God of Love (New York ⁵2010) 201–240.

[38] The term ἀνακεφαλαίωσις had comprehensive cosmological meaning already in Ephesians 1:10.

and inclination. From the potential to progress towards its own perfection in communion with the Holy Trinity after the Fall man turned in a direction that is not in harmony with God's providence. This kind of alienation from one's own destiny, that is, from maintaining communion with God, results in the experience of death and sin, which affect every aspect of human existence. In this context, it could be said that the theology of Theophilus and Irenaeus implies that progress in itself is not a desirable quality if the direction and movement of man no longer takes place in the coordinates of communion with God but outside them. The theology of recapitulation primarily implies the renewal and construction of a perfect *community between man and God* and of all connotations that this community implies, primarily in its eschatological fulfillment. This is one of the most important aspects of Irenaeus' anthropology and his teaching on the fall. The eschatological perfection of the whole creation and man should be understood as a *relational* phenomenon and not as an individualistic endeavor.

In this context, Theophilus' and Irenaeus' ontology has crucial *sacramental and eccesial connotations*. The potential for progressing and reaching eschatological maturity certainly represents one aspect of the goodness of creation, but this potential can only be fully accomplished and realized through the establishment of an unbreakable sacramental, that is, Eucharistic communion with God the Father and his "two hands", with the Son and the Holy Spirit. In the context of Theophilus' and Irenaeus' theology, progress is an anthropological phenomenon that inevitably requires an ecclesial context for its realization[39].

Irenaeus' insistence on understanding that the Fall was a historical event and that, accordingly, the God's soteriological work, which entails the entry of the God into the matrix of history, implies the *affirmation of temporality and history* as a context in which human potential is realized. In this way, Irenaeus holds the viewpoint of the biblical theology of history with its complete affirmation of man's historical existence and resolute *resistance to* any tendency of *escapism* in theology. This in turn implies the need for a stronger and more visible presence of the Church in the world and culture. On the other hand, we should not lose sight of Irenaeus' view that Adam and Eve actually represent all of humanity, the entire historical course of the human species, but also their eschatological fulfillment. This idea of representing the entire human race is deeply rooted in Irenaeus' theology of history. Namely,

---

[39] As far as one can tell the well-known saying of Irenaeus: "But our opinion is in accordance with the Eucharist, and the Eucharist in turn establishes our opinion" can certainly function explanatory in this sense (AH 4.18.5: SC 100, p. 610–613. English transl. ANF 1, p. 486).

having in mind the anti-gnostic context of his thought, Irenaeus does not separate Adam's capacity to symbolize and represent the entire human race from Adam's true presence in history. For a person or event to be able to symbolize a future historical or eschatological event, it must itself be rooted in true history.

Additionally, one of the significant implications that stems from Theophilus' and Irenaeus' teaching about Adam as a child is the so-called *ethical apophaticism* as one important aspect of the topic of the relationship between Christian anthropology and ethics. Namely, just as Adam's Fall is seen in the context of his immaturity in dealing with dilemmas that have ontological consequences, it is possible to take a similar attitude towards the actions of people with whom we share historical and cultural space. It is enough to at least allow that, when thinking about the actions of other people, we take into account the possibility that their actions were not always defined by a completely clear understanding of the complex existential situations they were confronted with.

The enumerated concluding remarks represent only one part of the theological heritage entrusted to us in the context of Theophilus' and Irenaeus' teachings on Adam and Eve as infants at the beginning of their historical existence. The capacities arising from this ancient teaching for considering topics concerning the relationship between *theology and modern science* are quite likely the subject of intensive research in the field of theological anthropology in the near future as well. This is especially true when it comes to motives such as the adaptability and dynamism of matter and created nature, as well as the cosmological connotations of Irenaeus' recapitulation theory of the atonement.

Ysabel de Andia, Paris (France)

Eve *causa mortis* et Marie *causa salutis*. Désobéissance d'Adam et d'Eve et obéissance du Christ et de Marie

Introduction

C'est dans le cadre d'une réflexion sur le péché originel que j'ai choisi d'examiner la relation des deux Adam et d'Eve et de Marie selon la récapitulation de la désobéissance des premiers, Adam et Eve, par l'obéissance des seconds, le Christ, nouvel Adam, et Marie, nouvelle Eve.

Dans un premier moment, il s'agira de définir le péché comme transgression du commandement divin, qui entraîne la mort de l'homme, avant de voir la *récapitulation* de la désobéissance d'Adam par le Christ, nouvel Adam, et le retournement, la «*recirculatio*» de Marie, *causa salutis*, à Eve, *causa mortis*, ce qui nous conduira à l'affirmation d'une «*nouvelle naissance*» ou d'une «*nouvelle génération*» de l'homme par la foi dans l'incarnation du Verbe.

I. Transgression et mort

Irénée ne parle pas de «péché originel», mais d'une transgression qui a entraîné la mort[1].

1. Satan

Cette transgression est due à Satan, «l'ange apostat». Dans son commentaire sur les tentations du Christ, par Satan, au désert, Irénée écrit :

---

[1] Cf. *Y. de Andia*, Ch. III. Le péché et la mort, in : Y. de Andia, Homo vivens. Incorruptibilité et divinisation de l'homme selon Irénée de Lyon (Paris 1986) 109–125.

Eve causa mortis et Marie causa salutis.

> A l'origine, il avait persuadé à l'homme de *transgresser le commandement du Créateur* et l'avait ainsi réduit sous son pouvoir, car son pouvoir consiste *dans la transgression et l'apostasie,* et c'est précisément par celles-ci qu'il avait enchaîné l'homme. [...] Aussi fallait-il qu'il fût à son tour vaincu par le moyen de l'Homme, afin que l'homme, ainsi libéré pût revenir à son Seigneur, en laissant à celui-là les liens par lesquels il avait été enchaîné, à savoir *la transgression*[2].

L'homme, en transgressant le commandement divin, tombe sous le pouvoir de Satan.

Et le Christ libère l'homme en enchaînant Satan : « Car c'est l'enchaînement de celui-là qui fut la libération de l'homme ». Il est cet «*homme fort*» de la parabole[3] qu'il faut enchaîner pour «*entrer dans sa maison et s'emparer de ses meubles*» (Mt 12, 29).

> Le Verbe *l'enchaîna* hardiment comme son propre transfuge et *s'empara de ses meubles,* c'est-à-dire des hommes qu'il détenait sous son pouvoir[4].

Or l'homme qui avait été enchaîné par le diable, Irénée dit qu'«il a été fait dans la transgression».

2. L'homme fait dans la transgression

«L'homme a été fait dans la transgression» (*homo factus est in transgressione*), cette affirmation qui revient deux fois dans le livre V de l'*Adversus haereses* ne signifie pas que l'homme a été «créé» ainsi, mais que tout homme, après la faute d'Adam, naît dans la transgression :

> Et parce que, en cette chair modelée selon Adam, l'homme était tombé (avait été fait) dans la transgression (*Et quoniam in illa plasmatione quae secundum Adam fuit in transgressione factus homo*) et avait besoin du bain de régénération, le Seigneur dit à l'aveugle-né, après lui avoir enduit les yeux de boue : « Va te laver à la piscine de Siloé» (Jn 9, 7)[5].

Par la transgression, les hommes sont devenus (*ont été faits*) les «ennemis de Dieu» :

---

[2] *Irénée de Lyon,* Adv. haer. V, 21, 3. La traduction française de l'*Adversus hæreses* est donnée d'après : A. *Rousseau,* Irénée de Lyon. Contre les hérésies. Dénonciation et réfutation de la gnose au nom menteur (Paris ²1985).
[3] Cf. Mc 3, 27 ; Lc 1, 78.
[4] *Irénée de Lyon,* Adv. haer. V, 21, 3.
[5] *Irénée de Lyon,* Adv. haer. V, 15, 3.

C'est précisément de lui [le Créateur] que, pour avoir transgressé son commandement, nous étions devenus les ennemis (*cuius et praeceptum transgredientes inimici facti sumus eius* – Τὴν ἐντολὴν παραβάντες ἐχθροποιήθημεν πρὸς αὐτόν)[6].

Cette transgression est une « apostasie » :

> Les meubles et la maison du diable, c'était nous-mêmes quand nous étions dans l'apostasie (*cum essemus in apostasia*), car il se servait de nous comme il voulait et l'esprit impur habitait en nous. Ce n'est pas, en effet, contre celui qui l'enchaînait et pillait sa maison qu'il était *fort*, mais bien contre les hommes dont il disposait à son gré pour avoir fait apostasier leurs pensées à l'égard de Dieu[7].

Elle est aussi une « aliénation » :

> Car il [Jean-Baptiste] préparait un peuple en annonçant d'avance à ses compagnons de servitude la venue du Seigneur et en leur prêchant la pénitence, afin que, lorsque le Seigneur serait présent, ils fussent en état de recevoir son pardon, pour être revenus à Celui auquel ils s'étaient rendus étrangers par leurs péchés et leurs transgressions (*propter transgressionem abalienati*), selon ce que dit David : « Les pécheurs se sont rendus étrangers dès le sein maternel, ils se sont égarés dès leur conception » (Ps 57, 4)[8].

La citation du Psaume 57, 4 affirme une « aliénation » dès le « sein maternel », un « égarement » dès leur conception. Cette parole du psaume fonde la transmission du péché dans la conception même de l'homme.

L'affirmation d'une « aliénation » « dès le sein maternel » se retrouve, au livre V, avec l'idée d'un « héritage de la mort par la naissance antérieure » à partir d'Adam, opposée à l'« héritage de la vie » par la naissance nouvelle du Fils de l'homme. Nous reviendrons sur ce texte qui s'appuie sur saint Paul : « De même que tous sont morts en Adam, ainsi tous seront vivifiés dans le Christ (*Et sicut in Adam omnes moriuntur, ita et in Christo omnes vivificabuntur*) » (1 Co 15, 22).

3. « Nous sommes tous morts en Adam »

La conséquence de la transgression de l'homme est sa mort. Tombant sous le pouvoir de Satan, il est tombé sous le pouvoir de la mort :

---

[6] *Irénée de Lyon*, Adv. haer. V, 17, 1.
[7] *Irénée de Lyon*, Adv. haer. III, 8, 2.
[8] *Irénée de Lyon*, Adv. haer. III, 10, 1.

Eve causa mortis et Marie causa salutis.

Il fallait donc que Celui qui devait tuer le péché (*occidere peccatum et mortis reum redimere hominem*) et racheter l'homme digne de mort se fît cela même qu'était celui-ci, c'est-à-dire cet homme réduit en esclavage par le péché et retenu sous le pouvoir de la mort (*id est hominem qui a peccato quidem in servitium tractus fuerat*), afin que le péché fût tué par un homme et que l'homme sortît ainsi de la mort.

Car, de même que par la désobéissance d'un seul homme, qui fut le premier modelé à partir d'une terre vierge, *beaucoup ont été constitués pécheurs* et ont perdu la vie, ainsi fallait-il que, *par l'obéissance d'un seul homme* qui est le premier-né de la Vierge, *beaucoup soient justifiés et reçoivent le salut*[9].

Plus loin, Irénée oppose « Adam (qui) a été fait principe de ceux qui meurent » et le Seigneur qui est *« le premier-né d'entre les morts »* (Col 1, 18).

Car le Seigneur, en devenant le *Premier-né des morts*, et en recevant dans son sein les anciens pères, les a fait renaître à la vie de Dieu, devenant lui-même le *Principe des vivants* (Col 1, 18), parce qu'Adam était devenu le principe des morts (*Adam initium morientium factus est*). C'est pourquoi aussi Luc a commencé sa généalogie par le Seigneur pour la faire remonter jusqu'à Adam, indiquant par là que ce ne sont pas les pères qui ont donné la vie au Seigneur, mais lui, au contraire, qui les a fait renaître dans l'Évangile de vie[10].

C'est ce même mouvement de la fin – « le Seigneur », « principe des vivants » – au commencement – « Adam », « principe des morts » – qui est celui de la récapitulation du premier Adam par le second et d'Eve par Marie.

II. Désobéissance et Obéissance

1. La récapitulation du premier Adam par le second Adam

La « récapitulation » (ἀνακεφαλαίωσις, *recapitulatio*) signifie reprendre le commencement (le premier Adam) dans la fin (le second Adam), à partir d'un seul chef (κεφαλή, *caput*) qui est le Christ, nouvel Adam. Cette récapitulation se fait dans le Christ. Ce qui est « récapitulé », c'est la désobéissance du premier par l'obéissance du second. Alors que la désobéissance d'Adam a introduit la mort dans le monde, l'obéissance du Christ produit des « fruits de vie ».

---

[9] Irénée de Lyon, Adv. haer. III, 18, 7.
[10] Irénée de Lyon, Adv. haer. III, 22, 4.

C'est donc aussi l'ouvrage modelé à l'origine qu'il a récapitulé en lui-même (*Et antiquam plasmationem in se recapitulatus est*). En effet, de même que, par la désobéissance d'un seul homme, le péché a fait son entrée et que, par le péché, la mort a prévalu, de même, par l'obéissance d'un seul homme, la justice a été introduite et a produit des fruits de vie chez les hommes qui autrefois étaient morts[11].

La récapitulation suppose une similitude entre les deux Adams. Cette similitude est d'abord celle de la naissance virginale et, ensuite, celle de «l'économie du bois», la tentation du premier Adam par le fruit de l'arbre et la crucifixion sur le bois du Second.

a. La naissance virginale

Le Premier Adam a été formé directement par Dieu à partir d'une terre vierge et le Christ est né d'une Vierge. La récapitulation d'Adam par le Christ exige une même naissance virginale.

> Et de même que ce premier homme modelé, Adam, a reçu sa substance d'une terre intacte et vierge encore [...], de même, récapitulant en lui-même Adam, lui, le Verbe, c'est de Marie encore Vierge qu'à juste titre il a reçu cette génération qui est la récapitulation d'Adam[12].

Le parallèle entre la «terre vierge» et «Marie encore Vierge» manifeste l'absence de père dans les deux cas.

> Si donc le premier Adam avait eu pour père un homme et était né d'une semence d'homme, ils auraient raison de dire que le second Adam a été aussi engendré de Joseph. Mais si le premier Adam a été pris de la terre et modelé par le Verbe de Dieu, il fallait que ce même Verbe, effectuant en lui-même la récapitulation d'Adam, possédât la similitude d'une génération identique[13].

La récapitulation d'Adam par le Christ exige «la similitude d'une génération identique», c'est-à-dire une naissance virginale. A l'objection : «Pourquoi alors, Dieu n'a-t-il pas pris de nouveau du limon» de la terre pour modeler le second Adam ? –, Irénée répond :

> Pour qu'il n'y eut pas un autre ouvrage modelé et que ce ne fut pas un autre ouvrage qui fut sauvé, mais que celui-là même fut récapitulé, du fait que serait sauvegardée *la similitude* en question[14].

---

[11] Irénée de Lyon, Adv haer. III, 21, 10.
[12] Irénée de Lyon, Adv haer. III, 21, 10.
[13] Irénée de Lyon, Adv haer. III, 21, 10.
[14] Irénée de Lyon, Adv. haer. III, 21, 10.

Eve causa mortis et Marie causa salutis.

La récapitulation suppose qu'il n'y ait pas un «autre» ouvrage modelé (*plasma*), mais «celui-là même» que Dieu a formé du limon de la terre.

b. L'économie du bois
Comme il y a une similitude dans la naissance virginale des deux Adams, de même il y a une similitude entre l'arbre de la connaissance du bien et du mal et l'arbre de la Croix. C'est ce qu'Irénée appelle l'«économie du bois»:

> Pour détruire la désobéissance originelle de l'homme, qui s'était perpétrée sur le bois, «*il s'est fait obéissant jusqu'à la mort et la mort sur une croix*» (Ph 2, 8), guérissant ainsi par son obéissance sur le bois la désobéissance qui s'était accomplie sur le bois. Or il ne serait pas venu détruire au moyen des mêmes choses, la désobéissance commise à l'égard de celui qui nous avait modelés, s'il avait annoncé un autre Père[15].

Irénée donne ici la raison de la similitude du bois: le Christ ne serait pas venu «détruire» la désobéissance «*au moyen des mêmes choses*», le bois, si le Créateur n'était pas «le même» que le Père de N.S.J.C. et non «*un autre Père*», comme le pensent Marcion et les gnostiques.

> Mais en fait, *c'est par ces mêmes choses*, par lesquelles nous avions été désobéissants à Dieu et indociles à sa parole, qu'il a réintroduit l'obéissance à Dieu et la docilité à sa parole: par là, de la façon la plus claire, *il fait voir ce Dieu même* que nous avions offensé dans *le premier Adam* et avec qui nous avons été réconciliés dans *le second Adam*, en devenant obéissants jusqu'à la mort; car nous n'étions les débiteurs de nul autre que de celui dont nous avions transgressé le commandement à l'origine (*et praeceptum transgressi fueramus ab initio*)[16].

C'est le «même Dieu» que nous avions offensé et avec qui nous avons été réconciliés, le même dont nous étions devenus les ennemis et avec lequel le Seigneur nous a rétablis dans l'amitié:

> C'est de lui que, pour avoir transgressé son commandement, nous étions devenus les ennemis (*transgredientes inimici facti sumus ejus*). Et c'est pourquoi, dans les derniers temps, le Seigneur nous a rétablis dans l'amitié par le moyen de son incarnation: devenu «*médiateur de Dieu et des hommes*» (1 Tm 2, 5), il a fléchi en notre faveur [*propitians*] son Père contre qui nous avions péché et l'a consolé [*consolatus*] de notre désobéissance par son obéissance, et il nous a accordé la grâce de la conversion et de la soumission à notre Créateur[17].

---
[15] *Irénée de Lyon*, Adv. haer. V, 16, 3.
[16] *Irénée de Lyon*, Adv. haer. V, 16, 3.
[17] *Irénée de Lyon*, Adv. haer. V, 17, 1.

La «médiation» du Christ apporte la «consolation» au Père et la «grâce de la conversion» aux hommes. Là encore, ce n'est pas «un autre dont nous avions transgressé les commandement», et «un autre qui dit ‹ *Tes péchés te sont remis* ›», mais c'est le même Père juste et bon.

> Comment les péchés nous eussent-ils été vraiment remis, à moins que celui-là même contre qui nous avions péché ne nous en eût accordé la rémission, «*par les entrailles de la miséricorde de notre Dieu, en lesquelles celui-ci nous a visités*» (Lc 1, 78) par son Fils?[18].

L'opposition entre le péché d'Adam et la «rémission des péchés» par le Christ se retrouve dans celle d'Eve, «cause de mort» par son péché et de Marie, «cause de salut» par son obéissance.

2. Eve, *causa mortis*, et Marie, *causa salutis*

Irénée oppose Eve, comme *causa mortis*, et Marie, comme *causa salutis*, aux livres III et V de l'*Adversus haereses* et il reprend cette opposition dans la *Démonstration apostolique*. Nous examinerons ces trois textes.

a. Adv. III, 22, 4 : Eve, *causa mortis*, et Marie, *causa salutis*

Au livre III de l'*Adversus haereses*, Irénée commence par souligner la virginité d'Eve et de Marie, toutes deux «vierges» et «destinées à un mari», Adam ou Joseph.

Adam et Eve n'avaient pas de notion de la procréation, «il leur fallait d'abord grandir» pour se multiplier. Cette présentation de l'enfance d'Adam et d'Eve, montre que, pour Irénée, l'acte de procréation n'est pas peccamineux. Pour Irénée, Adam et Eve sont encore des enfants[19] au paradis, alors que, pour Thomas d'Aquin, Adam est créé dans la plénitude de son humanité.

Il y a donc une similitude entre Eve et Marie : toutes les deux sont vierges, mais l'une a désobéi, alors que l'autre a obéi.

> De même donc qu'Eve, en désobéissant, devint *cause de mort* pour elle-même et pour tout le genre humain, de même Marie, ayant pour époux celui qui lui avait été destiné par avance, et cependant Vierge, devint, en obéissant, *cause de salut* pour elle-même et pour tout le genre humain[20].

---

[18] Irénée de Lyon, Adv. haer. V, 17, 1.
[19] Cf. Y. de Andia, Adam enfant chez Irénée de Lyon, in : Y. de Andia, Le Fruit de l'Esprit. Études sur Irénée de Lyon (Paris 2021) 101–113.
[20] Irénée de Lyon, Adv. haer. III, 22, 4.

Eve causa mortis et Marie causa salutis.

Par sa désobéissance, Eve est devenue «*cause de mort*» et, par son obéissance, Marie est devenue «*cause de salut* pour elle-même et pour tout le genre humain». L'obéissance de l'une a corrigé ou réparé la désobéissance de l'autre.

Irénée explicite cette réparation, dans la suite du texte, par l'image du dénouement des «boucles de nœuds»:

> C'est pour cette raison que la Loi donne à celle qui est fiancée à un homme, bien qu'elle soit encore vierge, le nom d'«*épouse*» de celui qui l'a prise pour fiancée, signifiant de la sorte le retournement qui s'opère de Marie à Eve (*a Maria in Euam recirculationem significans*). Car ce qui a été lié ne peut être délié (*quod colligatum est solueretur*) que si l'on refait en sens inverse les boucles du nœud, en sorte que les premières boucles soient défaites grâce à des secondes et qu'inversement les secondes libèrent les premières: il se trouve de la sorte qu'un premier lien est dénoué par un second et que le second tient lieu de dénouement à l'égard du premier[21].

Irénée ne parle de «*récapitulation*» que pour le Christ, qui est le seul «chef», pour Marie, il parlera de «*recirculatio*», de retournement. La «recirculation» qui s'opère de Marie à Eve est un «retournement» de la seconde à la première, de la fin au commencement, de telle sorte que Marie «délie» ou «dénoue» les «boucles du nœud» du péché jusqu'à ce premier nœud qu'est le péché d'Eve.

b. *Adv. haer.* V, 19, 1: Marie avocate d'Eve

Au livre V de l'*Adversus haereses*, Irénée ajoute l'idée que c'est par son obéissance que Marie est devenue «l'avocate» d'Eve.

> Et de même que celle-là avait été séduite de manière à désobéir à Dieu, de même celle-ci se laissa persuader d'obéir à Dieu, afin que, de la vierge Eve, la Vierge Marie devînt **l'avocate**; et, de même que le genre humain avait été assujetti à la mort par une vierge, il en fut libéré par une Vierge, la désobéissance d'une vierge ayant été contrebalancée (*aequa lance*) par l'obéissance d'une Vierge (*et sicut illa [Eva] seducta est ut <non> obaudiret Deo, sic et haec suasa est obaudire Deo, uti virginis Evae virgo Maria fieret advocata; et quemadmodum astrictum est morti genus humanum per virginem, solutum est per virginem, aequa lance disposita virginali inobaudientia per virginalem obaudientiam*)[22].

Voici que, par son obéissance, Marie devient l'«avocate» d'Eve qui a désobéi. Elle «libère» le genre humain de l'assujettissement à la mort.

---

[21] Irénée de Lyon, Adv. haer. III, 22, 4.
[22] Irénée de Lyon, Adv. haer. V, 19, 1.

> Si donc le Seigneur est venu d'une manière manifeste dans son propre domaine;
> s'il a été porté par sa propre création, qu'il porte lui-même; s'il a *récapitulé par son obéissance sur le bois, la désobéissance qui avait été perpétrée par le bois*; si cette séduction dont avait été misérablement victime Eve, vierge destinée à un mari, a été dissipée par la bonne nouvelle de vérité magnifiquement annoncée par l'ange à Marie, elle aussi vierge destinée à un mari – car, de même que celle-là avait été séduite par le discours d'un ange, de manière à se soustraire à Dieu en transgressant sa parole, de même celle-ci fut instruite de la bonne nouvelle par le discours d'un ange, de manière *à porter Dieu* en obéissant à sa parole; et de même que celle-là avait été séduite de manière à désobéir à Dieu, de même celle-ci se laissa persuader d'obéir à Dieu, afin que, **de la vierge Eve, la Vierge Marie devînt l'avocate**; et, de même que le genre humain avait été *assujetti* à la mort par une vierge, il en fut *libéré* par une Vierge, la *désobéissance d'une vierge ayant été contrebalancée* (aequa lance) *par l'obéissance d'une Vierge*; si donc, encore une fois, le péché du premier homme a reçu guérison par la rectitude de conduite du Premier-né, si la prudence du serpent a été vaincue par la *simplicité de la colombe* (Mt 10, 16) et si par-là ont été brisés ces liens qui nous assujettissaient à la mort, (19, 2) ils sont stupides tous les hérétiques et ignorants de l'économie de Dieu[23].

La création «*porte Dieu*», qui l'a créée par sa parole, et Marie «*porte Dieu*» en obéissant à sa parole. L'obéissance de Marie «contrebalance» (*aeque lance*) la désobéissance d'Eve. Cette fois-ci l'idée est celle d'une «équivalence» ou d'un «contre balancement» dans la suppression de la faute de l'une par l'obéissance de l'autre.

c. *Démonstration apostolique* 33

Le thème de Marie «avocate» d'Eve se retrouve dans la *Démonstration apostolique* (33).

Pour que la récapitulation d'Adam par le Verbe soit parfaite il fallait que la création de l'un et la naissance de l'autre soient semblables. Adam a été modelé directement par Dieu, à partir d'une «terre vierge» «pour qu'il soit le point de départ de l'humanité»[24]. Et le Verbe s'est fait chair d'une femme vierge.

> Comme c'était cet homme même qu'il récapitulait en lui, le Seigneur reçut une chair formée selon la même «économie» que celle d'Adam, en naissant d'une Vierge par la volonté et la sagesse de Dieu, afin de montrer lui aussi une chair formée d'une manière semblable à celle d'Adam et de se faire cet homme dont il est écrit qu'il était à l'origine «*à l'image et à la ressemblance de Dieu*» (Gn 1, 26)[25].

---

[23] Irénée de Lyon, Adv. haer. V, 19, 1–2.
[24] Irénée de Lyon, Dem. 32.
[25] Ibid.

Eve causa mortis et Marie causa salutis.

Nous retrouvons les thèmes de la similitude de la naissance virginale, de l'identité de la chair modelée (*plasma*) et de la récapitulation de la désobéissance d'Eve par l'obéissance de Marie.

> Et de même que, par le fait d'une *vierge désobéissante*, l'homme tomba et mourut, de même, par le fait d'une *Vierge obéissante* à la parole de Dieu, l'homme fut ranimé et recouvra la vie. Car le Seigneur vint pour chercher la brebis qui était perdue, et cette brebis perdue était l'homme. Et c'est pourquoi il ne se fit pas autre chair modelée, mais < en naissant > de celle-là qui était la descendante d'Adam, il garda la similitude de la chair modelée : car il fallait qu'Adam fut récapitulé dans le Christ, afin que ce qui était mortel fut englouti par l'immortalité, et il fallait qu'Eve le fut aussi en Marie, afin qu'une Vierge, en se faisant *l'avocate* d'une vierge, détruisit la désobéissance d'une vierge par l'obéissance d'une Vierge[26].

Par la désobéissance d'Eve, l'homme, c'est-à-dire l'humanité, « tomba et mourut » et par l'obéissance de Marie, « l'homme fut ranimé et recouvra la vie ».

Irénée ne dit pas : par sa mort, le Christ a vaincu la mort, mais « ce qui était mortel a été englouti par l'immortalité » du Verbe. L'accent est mis ici sur l'immortalité du Verbe. Les deux verbes employés pour exprimer la victoire sur la mort sont « *engloutir* » et « *détruire* ».

> Et la transgression qui s'était perpétuée *par le moyen du bois* fut détruite par l'obéissance qui s'accomplit par le moyen du bois, cette obéissance par laquelle le Fils de l'homme obéit à Dieu lorsqu'il fut *cloué au bois*, abolissant par là la science du mal et procurant la science du bien : car le mal c'était de désobéir à Dieu, de même qu'obéir à Dieu était le bien[27].

La transgression s'est faite par le « moyen du bois » et l'obéissance lorsque le Fils fut « cloué au bois ». L'arbre de la connaissance du bien et du mal, planté au milieu du paradis, est mis en parallèle avec l'arbre de la Croix. L'arbre de la Croix est maintenant l'arbre planté au milieu du paradis de l'Église ; la Croix donne la science du bien, comme le fruit de l'arbre du paradis donnait la science du bien et du mal.

Sur le plan invisible, « le Verbe de Dieu soutient la création toute entière, sa largeur et sa longueur, sa hauteur et sa profondeur » et « est imprimé en forme de croix dans l'univers, afin de révéler, par sa posture visible de crucifié, son action invisible ».

---

[26] *Irénée de Lyon*, Dem. 33.
[27] Ibid.

III. La nouvelle naissance et l'héritage de la vie

Pour recevoir cette nouvelle génération dans le nouvel Adam et la nouvelle Eve, il faut la foi dans l'incarnation du Verbe. Les Ébionites qui refusent l'incarnation du Verbe de Dieu et pensent que le Christ n'est qu'un homme, refusent par là même l'idée d'une « nouvelle génération » et demeurent « dans *le vieux levain* de leur naissance ».

> Vains aussi les Ébionites. Refusant d'accueillir dans leurs âmes, par la foi, l'union de Dieu et de l'homme, ils demeurent dans *le vieux levain* (1 Co 5, 7) de leur naissance. Ils ne veulent pas comprendre que l'Esprit Saint est survenu en **Marie** et que *la puissance du Très-Haut l'a couverte de son ombre*, à cause de quoi *ce qui est né d'elle est saint et est le Fils du Dieu Très-Haut* (Lc 1, 35), le Père de toutes choses ayant opéré l'incarnation de son Fils et ayant fait apparaître ainsi une naissance nouvelle, afin que, comme nous avions **hérité de la mort** par la naissance antérieure (*per priorem generationem mortem hereditavimus*), **nous héritions de la vie par cette naissance-ci**. Ils repoussent donc le mélange du vin céleste et ne veulent être que l'eau de ce monde, n'acceptant pas que Dieu se mélange à eux, mais demeurant en cet Adam qui fut vaincu et chassé du Paradis[28].

Irénée oppose la « génération antérieure » d'Adam, par laquelle nous avons « hérité de la mort », à la « nouvelle génération » à partir du Christ par laquelle nous « héritions de la vie ».

La transmission de la mort ou de la vie est une « hérédité ». La foi est nécessaire pour « hériter » de la nouvelle naissance dans le nouvel Adam.

> [...] ainsi, à la fin, le Verbe du Père et l'Esprit de Dieu en s'unissant à l'antique substance de l'ouvrage modelé, c'est-à-dire Adam, ont rendu *l'homme vivant* et parfait, capable de comprendre le Père parfait, afin que, comme nous **mourrons** tous dans *l'homme animal*, ainsi nous soyons tous **vivifiés** dans *l'homme spirituel* (1 Co 15, 22)[29].

Comme nous mourrons tous dans *l'homme animal*, ainsi nous soyons tous vivifiés dans *l'homme spirituel*. Cette affirmation d'Irénée se fonde sur l'Épître aux Corinthiens :

> *En effet, puisque la mort est venue par un homme, c'est par un homme aussi que vient la résurrection des morts : comme tous meurent en Adam, en Christ, tous recevront la vie, mais chacun à son rang*[30].

---

[28] Irénée de Lyon, Adv. haer. V, 1, 3.
[29] Irénée de Lyon, Adv. haer. V, 1, 3.
[30] 1 Co 15, 22-23.

Eve causa mortis et Marie causa salutis.

> Il en est ainsi pour la résurrection des morts : semé corruptible, le corps ressuscite incorruptible, semé méprisable, il ressuscite éclatant de gloire, semé dans la faiblesse, il ressuscite plein de force, semé corps animal, il ressuscite corps spirituel. S'il y a un corps animal, il y a aussi un corps spirituel. C'est ainsi qu'il est écrit : *le premier homme Adam fut un être animal doué de vie* (Gn 2, 7), *le dernier Adam est un être spirituel donnant la vie* (Jn 6, 63 ; 2 Co 3, 6–17). Mais ce qui est premier, c'est l'être animal, ce n'est pas l'être spirituel : il vient ensuite. *Le premier homme tiré de la terre est terrestre. Le second homme, lui vient du ciel*[31].

L'opposition entre le premier Adam « *l'homme animal* » et le dernier Adam, « *l'homme spirituel* » montre que la mort n'affecte que l'homme animal qui est terrestre, alors que l'homme spirituel, vient du ciel.

> Si donc la mort, en s'emparant de l'homme, a expulsé de lui la vie et a fait de lui un mort, à bien plus forte raison la vie, en s'emparant de l'homme, expulsera la mort et rendra l'homme vivant pour Dieu […]. Or la première vie a été expulsée, parce qu'elle avait été donnée par le moyen d'un simple souffle et non par le moyen de l'Esprit. Car autre chose est le « *souffle de vie* » (Gn 2, 7), qui fait l'homme psychique, et autre chose « *l'Esprit vivifiant* » (1 Co 15, 45), qui le rend spirituel[32].

« L'homme vivant pour Dieu » vit de la vie de l'Esprit que lui a communiquée « l'homme céleste », le Christ.

Conclusion

Irénée ne parle jamais du « péché originel », mais de la « transgression » du commandement divin par Adam et il dit que : « en cette chair modelée selon Adam, l'homme était tombé (avait été fait) dans la transgression » (*quoniam in illa plasmatione quae secundum Adam fuit in transgressione factus homo*)[33]. Cela ne signifie pas qu'Adam a été créé dans la transgression, mais que tout homme après lui ou en lui est « fait » dans la transgression et que cette transgression entraîne la mort : *in Adam omnes moriuntur*.

Irénée ne parle pas d'« hérédité » du péché, mais d'hérédité de la mort[34].

Irénée ne parle pas de « salut » ou de « rédemption », mais de « récapitulation », c'est-à-dire de reprise ou de refondation du commencement, le premier Adam, dans la fin eschatologique, le second Adam.

---

[31] 1 Co 15, 42–47.
[32] *Irénée de Lyon*, Adv. haer. V, 12, 1–2.
[33] *Irénée de Lyon*, Adv. haer. V, 15, 3 ; *Irénée de Lyon*, Adv. haer. V, 17, 1
[34] *Irénée de Lyon*, Adv. haer. V, 1, 3.

De même le péché d'Eve, *causa mortis*, a été réparé par l'obéissance de Marie, *causa salutis*, qui dénoue les liens qu'Eve a noués par son péché : c'est un retournement (*recirculatio*) de l'une à l'autre, mais non une « récapitulation » que seul le Christ, « tête » (*caput*), peut opérer.

La « récapitulation » du premier Adam par le second suppose une « similitude » de l'un et de l'autre. Cette similitude est celle de leur naissance virginale, tous les deux sans père : l'un à partir de la terre vierge, l'autre à partir de la Vierge Marie.

La naissance virginale du Christ appelle la « nouvelle naissance » de l'homme dans le Christ. Celle-ci ne peut se faire que par la foi dans l'incarnation du Verbe dans le sein de la Vierge Marie. C'est pourquoi les Ébionites qui refusent l'idée d'une « nouvelle génération » du Verbe fait chair[35] demeurent dans le « vieux levain » de leur naissance.

C'est seulement par la FOI dans l'incarnation du Verbe que l'homme est devenu un « homme vivant », que l'« homme animal » est devenu un « homme spirituel ».

Eve, causa mortis, Maria, causa salutis. Deux vierges, deux femmes qui engendrent, l'une pour la mort, l'autre pour la vie. Marie a engendré virginalement le Christ, et c'est dans la foi en l'incarnation du Verbe que l'homme renaît.

---

[35] Ibid.

Tomasz Stępień, Warsaw (Poland)

The Sin of Embodiment in the Platonic Tradition

Abstract
Throughout the entire course of Greek philosophy and especially the Platonic tradition, we can observe two opposite views of human nature and relations between body and soul. The first one, which was called Olympic, perceives the body in a positive way, as a natural part which brings no negative consequences for the soul's desire of perfection. The second view was influenced by Orphic claims of the divine soul which is diminished and limited by the negatively perceived body. The negative perception of the body, expressed in the myth of Dionysius/Zagreus, was present in the early dialogues of Plato, who demonstrated the immaterial nature of the soul and claimed that its proper place is in the noetic reality. Therefore the soul's goal is to get rid of the influences of the body and completely detach itself from it in order to take its proper place among gods. But Plato himself was not consistent in his position since in his late dialogues he presents a more positive attitude to the body.

This inconsistency was noticed and commented by the Neoplatonics and therefore they also presented two opposite views of human body. Plotinus himself was probably the philosopher who had the most negative attitude to the body. Discussing the descent of the soul into matter he perceived it as a double sin. The first sin is the very descent, which is simultaneously voluntary and compulsory, and the second sin is committed by the soul already influenced by matter, which is submission to bodily desires. Iamblichus is the best example of the positive attitude to the body in the Platonic tradition. Thanks to theurgical rites he sees matter as a place where the soul must bring about order and beauty of the noetic realm. This is the mission of the soul which is willed by gods since the soul by such activity can partake in the creative process of constructing the cosmos. Therefore for Iamblichus embodiment is natural and only in certain cases can be perceived in a negative way.

Although the perception of embodiment in the Platonic tradition is not consistent, there are some elements which are common. Those elements make it possible to draw some conclusions at the end of the paper and make a brief comparison between the Platonic and Christian views.

Diogenes Laertius, in his *Life of Eminent Philosophers* discussing the origin of philosophy in the proper sense, divides it into two schools. The first one is called the Ionian school, and it dates back to Anaximander, while the second, called the Italian school, dates back to Pythagoras[1]. It is significant that for the most famous ancient historian of philosophy none of those schools seems more prominent or more important for the shaping of early philosophical thought. Moreover, Diogenes does not say that one of them appeared earlier than the other; for him they rose simultaneously and independently. What is even more important, the division is not only based on geographical origin, but there are significant differences between the groups of problems discussed in those two schools and their views of the universe and man.

Modern scholars very early recognized that difference, and the best example of exploiting Diogenes' division is F. M. Cornford, who refers to it in his classical study *From Religion to Philosophy*[2]. Cornford notices that those two philosophical schools were backed by more general traditions, which he calls Olympism and Orphism:

> Behind Anaximander stands the Ionian Homer, with his troop of luminous Olympians; behind Pythagoras we discern the troubled shapes of Orpheus and Dionysus[3].

In those two traditions Cornford sees the influence of two types of the Greek religion—Olympic and Orphic, which differ mainly as regards their opinion about the sensual world. While the Olympians perceive the natural beauty of the material cosmos and have a positive attitude to it, the Orphics see the matter as the source of corruption and destruction of what is divine.

Although nowadays we think of many of Cornford's conclusions as being too general and outdated, especially since he based his opinion of the Orphic religion on Emile Durkheim's discussion, I think that he managed to highlight the problem which was addressed by the thinkers throughout the course of ancient Greek philosophy. Regardless of whether there were indeed two types of Greek religion, there certainly were two types of philosophy, which was noticed already in the ancient era by Diogenes. The main difference between those two schools lied not only in the view of the cosmos and matter, but primarily in their perception of man, his destiny and role in the universe.

---

[1] *Diogenes Laertius*, Vitae Philosophorum I, 13–14: M. Markovich, BS GR 1316, vol. 1 (Berlin – Boston 2011), p. 12,8–23.

[2] F. M. *Cornford*, From religion to philosophy. The Study of the Origin of Western Speculation (New York 1957) VI–VIII.

[3] Ibid., VII.

The Ionian philosophers generally thought of the human soul as the principle of movement which is material. Therefore, there was no conflict between body and soul: they were the parts of the same material universe in which man should find his fulfillment and happiness. The Italians thought of the soul as having its origin in the divine reality and being in a fundamental conflict with the body. Orphism contributed to philosophy the concept of the immortal and divine soul, which in such meaning was absent in the poems of Homer and Hesiod. The conflict between the good soul and the evil material body was expressed in the myth of Zagreus, Zeus' son who was identified with Orphic Dionysus.

This myth is of special interest to us since it is the most important part of the Orphic corpus, but also because of its impact on the Neoplatonic philosophy[4]. We must omit here the complicated history of the versions of the myth,[5] to concentrate on its meaning for philosophers. Zagreus/Dionysus was the son of Zeus and Persephone/Kore, who was declared by his father to be the king of gods. But the Titans were jealous of the child and therefore they distracted him with a mirror and other toys and while he was playing they killed him and tore his body into pieces. The Titans not only killed him and dismembered his body, but also ate his flesh. The remaining parts of the body of Dionysus were collected by Apollo and deposited in Delphi. His heart was saved by Athena, and thanks to it his father made Dionysus reborn. Finally, Zeus killed the Titans using his thunderbolt and from the ashes of their bodies humankind was born[6]. Because of that, humans are composed of two elements. The soul is divine and good, because it has its origin in the divine body of Dionysus devoured by the Titans. The human body is evil and corrupted like the body of wicked Titans. The myth then expresses the fundamental conflict between body and soul, and in this collision, soul is immortal and good, while body is mortal and evil. This clash of elements is then the basis of human nature, which always vacillates between the spiritual and the material.

The Orphic doctrine depicted by this story had a fundamental impact on the Platonic philosophy since the times of Plato. We suspect that the Orphic doctrine of the soul had some meaning in shaping the Platonic concept of the soul as a super-sensual and noetic entity. However, for Plato such a conviction was no longer the object of myth and religion, since he was the first who presented proof for it. Because the soul is capable of conceiving the ideal reality

---

[4] This myth was widely quoted by Neoplatonists: cf. *W. K. C. Guthrie*, Orpheus and the Greek Religion. A Study of the Orphic Movement (Princeton 1993) 107.
[5] Ibid., 107–120.
[6] Ibid., 82–83.

of forms, it must have a nature similar to them. Therefore it is non-material and immortal. In the early dialogues it becomes a basis which backs up the Orphic understanding of the soul. It was inevitable that with Orphic influences the concept of the conflict in human nature came along. Since the soul belongs to the noetic reality, the body becomes an obstacle which does not allow it to see the ideas, and a barrier which must be removed for the soul to return to the place where it belongs.

In the early Socratic dialogues we find many places where the body is perceived in a negative way. The body is like a prison to the soul, which would rather like to see the ideal forms free of its influence[7]. In the passage of *Phaedrus* probably referring to Eleusinian mysteries[8], to which we will come back below, the soul's proper place is among the gods where it enjoys full potential of its nature. Plato says that in this time of being among the gods and celebrating true mysteries:

> We were surrounded by rays of pure light, being pure ourselves and untainted by this object we call a "body" and which we carry around with us now, imprisoned like shellfish[9].

In *Phaedo* we read that this poor state of the soul can be reverted only by getting rid of the body, and even after death the fate of the soul depends on how much it has made itself similar to the body[10]. Therefore the practice of philosophy can make the soul closer to the sphere where it truly belongs, and it is the cultivation (or meditation) of death (μελέτη θανάτου)[11], since it gives the soul the opportunity to focus on the noetic world and get rid of the sensual influences. Similarly, in *Phaedrus* the soul can be saved from the many cycles of metempsychosis only by the philosophy which reestablishes the link with the true reality. This passage was of special importance to Plato's successors, as in one of his speeches Socrates presents the myth of the chariot with two horses and describes the happiness of the soul dwelling with the gods before embodiment. The very act of descent into a body is presented as losing of the

---

[7] Cf., *Plato*, Phaed. 82de: I. Burnet, Platonis Opera I (Oxford 1901).
[8] W. *Buckert*, Greek Religion. Archaic and Classical, transl. J. Raffan (Blackwell 1955) 285–290.
[9] *Plato*, Phaedr. 250c: I. Burnet, Platonis Opera II (Oxford 1901). English transl. R. Waterfield, Plato. Phaedrus (Oxford 2002), p. 34. In this passage the term ἀσήμαντος translated by ... as "untainted" can be also translated as "unentombed in". This is probable a reference to the Orphic teaching which was expressed in the saying: σῶμα σῆμα. Cf. See the note of R. Waterfield, p. 93.
[10] Cf. *Plato*, Phaed. 78d–80b.
[11] *Plato*, Phaed. 81a.

wings which allowed the soul to dwell in the divine reality. The body is described not only as something evil in the sense that it distracts the soul from seeing the true reality, but as something evil in a moral sense. For Plato what is divine is also morally good, and therefore the wings depict what makes the soul good, i.e. virtues and good deeds. Therefore Plato writes:

> Anything divine is good, wise, virtuous, and so on, and so these qualities are the best source of nourishment and growth for the soul's wings, but badness and evil and so on cause them to shrink and perish[12].

The wings of the soul can no longer sustain it in its primal state, since it makes the body alive, and its fall is not only ontological but also moral. The consequences of the fall on earth also depend on the degree of being close to the true vision of ideas in the life among the gods. Therefore more illuminated souls fall in their first incarnation into the bodies of philosophers and they have the best chances to return to the previous bodiless and happy state[13].

Those fragments of the dialogues certainly exerted the greatest influence on the Platonic tradition of negative approach to the body which limits the divine nature of the soul. We can also observe how Plato, thanks to the discovery of the nature of the noetic realm, gives the philosophical (rational) basis for the Orphic teaching on the body-soul relations. Thus, for his successors the body with its irrational influences will always be an obstacle to the soul and will be treated in a suspicious way. But as we well know, in the later dialogues Plato himself tended to question his earlier opinions and this involves also his negative attitude to the human body. Especially in *Timaeus*, it seems evident that he no longer treats the body as something that endangers the true vision and philosophy, but rather becomes a natural part of the human being which also serves well in the philosophical investigation. Let us recall only one passage where the eyes of the body are no longer prison bars but rather the tools which are necessary to get a true vision of ideas:

> Sight, then, in my judgment is the cause of the highest benefits to us in that no word of our present discourse about the universe could ever have been spoken, had we never seen stars, Sun, and sky. But as it is, the sight of day and night, of months and the revolving years, of equinox and solstice, has caused the invention of number and bestowed on us the notion of time and the study of the nature of the world; whence

---

[12] Plato, Phaedr. 246de. English transl. R. *Waterfield*, p. 29.
[13] Plato, Phaedr. 248bc.

we have derived all philosophy, than which no greater boon has ever come or shall come to mortal man as a gift from heaven[14].

In the late dialogues Plato seems to change his mind and the Olympic tradition with its positive attitude towards the sensual world becomes clearly visible. It is significant that centuries later when Neoplatonism was born the scholars who learned philosophy by reading Plato's entire *corpus*, clearly saw inconsistencies in his attitude to the body. The best example is Plotinus who, when discussing the descent of the souls into the bodies, evokes first the opinions of various philosophers. When it comes to discussing Plato he writes:

> Well, it will be plain that he does not say the identical thing in every instance, so that one might easily discern his intention, but granting in all cases scant respect for the sensible world, and blaming the soul for its association with the body, he declares that the soul is "in bondage" and has buried itself within it, and that "the pronouncement made in secret rites is a great one", to the effect that the soul is "in prison" here. And his "Cave", like the cavern of Empedocles, is to be taken, it seems to me, to be referring to this universe, seeing as the "release from the shackles" and the "ascent" from the Cave he declares to be the journey towards that which is intelligible. And in *Phaedrus* he identifies "moulting of feathers" as the cause of its arrival in the sensible world; and "periodic cycles" bring the soul which has ascended back down here, and judgements send others down here, and lots, chances, and necessities.
>
> But then again, while in all these passages he has blamed the soul for its arrival in the body, in *Timaeus*, in speaking of this universe, he commends the cosmos and declares it to be a "blessed god", and that the soul was bestowed by the Demiurge in his goodness so as to render this universe intelligent, since it had to be intelligent, and this could not come about without soul.
>
> The soul of the universe, then, was sent down into it by the god for this purpose, while the soul of each one of us was sent to ensure its perfection; since it was necessary for the identical genera of living being in the intelligible world also to exist in the sensible world[15].

---

[14] *Plato*, Tim. 47ab: I. Burnet, Platonis Opera IV (Oxford 1922). English transl. F. MacDonald Cornford, Plato's Cosmology. The Timaeus of Plato (Indianapolis 1997), p. 157–158.
[15] *Plotinus*, Enn. IV, 8, 1, 27–50: P. Henry, H. R. Schwyzer, Plotini Opera, vol. 2 (Oxford 1977), p. 166–167. English transl. L. P. Geson, Plotinus. The Enneads (Cambridge 2018), p. 513.

This passage is very important for the further Neoplatonic teaching on the soul's relation to the body. For Plotinus Plato's wavering between Orphic and Olympic influences is intentional and serves the aura of mystery and hiding the true intention of the Divine Master. But in this passage we also see the characteristic features of Plotinus' view. It seems that the passages of *Timaeus* which he recalls only add new elements to the Orphic view of earlier dialogues. The body is still a negative and restrictive element for the soul, but since the material universe also must have a soul, the individual souls should be discussed from the point of view of the cosmic Soul. The universal being is always more perfect than the specific one, so the material world will always be a shadowy copy of the original, but also in the intellectual world the Soul is primarily general and becomes fully individual only by its contact with the body. Another important aspect of Plotinus' passage is the necessity of assuming the body by the Soul of the Universe and individual souls. The universal Soul and individual ones are sent down by the will of god (i.e. the One). Therefore the soul cannot avoid it, and the connection with the body is natural and indispensable because this is the only way in which the material universe can become intelligent. That is why in the following passage Plotinus writes that the prime topic of investigation is to understand how the soul: "acquired a natural impulse to associate itself with the body" (πῶς ποτε κοινωνεῖν σώματι πέφυκε)[16]. The connection with the body is then willed by god and necessary, but this does not exclude the possibility of asking the second question of whether it is voluntary or compulsory (ἑκοῦσα εἴτε ἀναγκασθεῖσα)[17], which is one of the most interesting questions regarding the fate of the soul.

The nature of the soul is twofold. Since it is intellectual it naturally unites with the Soul understood here as the third hypostasis of Plotinus' system[18]. But simultaneously it is drawn to assume the body, with all negative consequences thereof, and the fundamental question is why does it happen. Why does the soul abandon the perfect world and assume the body? Plotinus does not give a clear answer. Since united with the hypostasis of the Soul it is only a part of the whole, it has a certain desire of being the individual soul of the particular body. The united soul has a part in ruling the material world and bringing order to it, but it wants to bring order and rule also in a much more

---

[16] *Plotinus*, Enn. IV, 8, 2, 3-4: Plotini Opera, vol. 2, p. 167. English transl. L. P. Geson, p. 513.
[17] *Plotinus*, Enn. IV, 8, 2, 5: Plotini Opera, vol. 2, p. 167.
[18] Cf. *Plotinus*, Enn. IV, 8, 3: Plotini Opera, vol. 2, p. 169-170.

direct sense to the specific part of this world[19]. Therefore this desire is based on the necessity which for Plotinus is naturally connected with the procession of all hypostases from the One. Each lower hypostasis wants to imitate the One in the creative process and the soul's part in this process relies on bringing an intellectual order to the chaos of matter[20]. Therefore the first part of the answer is natural necessity, and Plotinus clearly points out that the soul is: "necessitated eternally by a law of nature" (ἀναγκαῖον ἀιδίως φύσεως νόμῳ) because it was god who has sent it down[21].

The human soul, however, is also drawn by its own desire and therefore is responsible for the act of embodiment[22]. Therefore Plotinus writes about two kinds of moral error/sin (ἁμαρτία), and two dimensions of the soul being tainted or contaminated. The first comes from the very contact with the body, which makes the soul diminished and limits its natural cognitive and voluntary powers, and this very limitation is the punishment for the embodied soul. The second error of the already embodied soul is the commitment of wicked deeds for which the punishment is to be confined in the cycles of reincarna-

---

[19] *Plotinus*, Enn. IV, 8, 4, 12–20: Plotini Opera, vol. 2, p. 171. English transl. L. P. Geson, p. 516–517: "When the soul actually does this over a period of time, and shunning the totality of things and standing apart in self-distinction, it ceases to look towards the intelligible; having become a part, it falls into isolation and weakness, and busies itself with trivialities and takes a partial view, and due to its separation from the whole, it fastens upon some individual body and shuns the rest of the totality, coming and directing itself towards that one individual; battered as it is in every way by the totality of things, it severs itself from the whole and turns to administering the particular with all the trouble that involves, fastening now upon this and putting itself in thrall to externals through its presence in it, and plunging itself deep into the interior of it".

[20] Cf. *Plotinus*, Enn. IV, 8, 5, 24–29: Plotini Opera, vol. 2, p. 173. English transl. L. P. Geson, p. 518–519: "In this way, then, though soul is a divine being and derives from the places above, it comes to be encased in a body, and though being a god, albeit of low rank, it comes thus into this world by an autonomous inclination and at the bidding of its own power, with the purpose of bringing order to what is inferior to it".

[21] *Plotinus*, Enn. IV, 8, 5, 11–15: Plotini Opera, vol. 2, p. 172–173. English transl. L. P. Geson, p. 518: "But when the doing and experiencing of these things becomes necessitated eternally by a law of nature, that soul which unites itself to a body in descending from a world superior to the human, accommodating itself to the needs of another—if one says that it is a god who has sent it down, one would not be in contradiction either with the truth, or with oneself".

[22] *Plotinus*, Enn. IV, 8, 5, 9–10: Plotini Opera, vol. 2, p. 172: Πᾶν μὲν γὰρ ἰὸν ἐπὶ τὸ χεῖρον ἀκούσιον, φορᾷ γε μὴν οἰκείᾳ ἰὸν πάσχον τὰ χείρω ἔχειν λέγεται τὴν ἐφ' οἷς ἔπραξε δίκην. English transl. L. P. Geson, p. 518: "After all, every process towards the worse is involuntary, but if something goes there by its own motion, in suffering the worse it is said to suffer punishment for its actions".

tion, and for the more serious sins the punishment is ordained by demons[23]. We can see, then, that for Plotinus the very contact with matter is a sin of the soul, so he clearly speaks of the sin of embodiment. This sin is inevitable for every man and even to some extent it is good, because its consequences, while negative or even catastrophic to the soul, can be beneficial by bringing an intellectual order to the material reality. Since this fate of the soul is unavoidable and all human souls commit the sin of embodiment, this concept is to some extent similar to the Christian teaching of the original sin, since nobody is free form its negative consequences which last in human nature.

One of the consequences of Plotinus's doctrine for the further development of Neoplatonism is the strengthening of the conviction of the negative influence of the body on the soul. The proper or natural state of the soul is always noetic, and embodiment in a specific body is only temporary. Therefore for Plotinus the soul never descends into the body fully; there is always a part of it which stays untainted and untouched by matter[24]. Although embodiment is necessary for the proper functioning and order of the material universe, and thus willed by gods, this does not change the negative attitude to the material world and the negative consequences which the body brings about to the soul. Therefore, as we know from Porphyry's account, Plotinus was even "embarrassed about having a body" and was constantly refusing to sit for a portrait or sculpture of him[25].

Looking forward into the Neoplatonic tradition we can observe that the negative view of the body was not always supported to such a wide extent.

---

[23] *Plotinus*, Enn. IV, 8, 5, 16–24: Plotini Opera, vol. 2, p. 173: Διττῆς δὲ τῆς ἁμαρτίας οὔσης, τῆς μὲν ἐπὶ τῇ τοῦ κατελθεῖν αἰτίᾳ, τῆς δὲ ἐπὶ τῷ ἐνθάδε γενομένην κακὰ δρᾶσαι, <δίκη> ἡ μὲν ἔστιν αὐτὸ τοῦτο, ὃ πέπονθε κατελθοῦσα, τῆς δὲ τὸ ἔλαττον εἰς σώματα ἄλλα δῦναι καὶ θᾶττον ἐκ κρίσεως τῆς κατ' ἀξίαν—ὃ δὴ θεσμῷ θείῳ γιγνόμενον διὰ τοῦ τῆς κρίσεως ὀνόματος δηλοῦται— τὸ δὲ τῆς κακίας ἄμετρον εἶδος μείζονος καὶ τῆς δίκης ἠξίωται ἐπιστασίᾳ τινυμένων δαιμόνων. English transl. L. P. Geson, p. 518: "Now, accepting that there are two stages of moral error, the one connected with the cause of the initial descent, the other with whatever vicious deeds one might commit when down here, the first is punished precisely by that very thing, what it experiences in the initial descent, while the nature of the second, when less serious, causes it to enter one body after another and the more quickly to proceed to judgement according to its due—the fact that it indeed comes about by divine ordinance is indicated by its very name, 'judgement'—while the immoderate type of vice merits punishment of a more serious nature, under the supervision of avenging daemons".

[24] *Plotinus*, Enn. IV, 8, 8, 2, 4: Plotini Opera, vol. 2, p. 176; IV, 9, 2, 5: Plotini Opera, vol. 2, p. 179; III, 4, 3, 24–27: Plotini Opera, vol. 1 (Oxford 1964), p. 286; IV, 3, 12, 1–3: Plotini Opera, vol. 2, p. 27; V, 1, 10, 13–19: Plotini Opera, vol. 2, p. 200; VI, 4, 14, 16–22: Plotini Opera, vol. 3 (Oxford 1983), p. 133; VI, 7, 5, 26: Plotini Opera, vol. 3, p. 189.

[25] Cf. *Porphyry*, Vita Plotini I, 1–10: Plotini Opera, vol. 2, p. 1. English transl. L. P. Geson, p. 17.

The Orphic influence was not established once and for all, and the Olympic tradition also played its role in the last period of pagan Greek philosophy. It was Iamblichus who seems to be the most important figure in this case. In his philosophy we observe much greater Aristotelian influences up to the point that for him the soul is the act (ἐντελέχεια) of the body. Therefore, contrary to Plotinus, he was convinced that the soul descends fully into the body and man is naturally composed of body and soul[26]. Discussing the same problem which we have seen in the *Enneads* of the causes of the soul's descent, he states that this is a fully natural process caused by the Demiurge—the creator of the cosmos. Thus in a standard situation there is no sin or guilt of embodiment as such, but its consequences depend on the reason why the embodiment took place:

> Furthermore, I actually think that the purposes for which souls descend are different and that they thereby also cause differences in the manner of the descent. For the soul that descends for the salvation, purification, and perfection of this realm is immaculate in its descent. The soul, on the other hand, that directs itself about bodies for the exercise and correction of its own character is not entirely free of passions and was not sent away free in itself. The soul that comes down here for punishment and judgment seems somehow to be dragged and forced[27].

For Iamblichus the negative consequences of contact with the body occur only when the soul comes down for punishment. When it descends to fulfill its cosmic duty it stays untainted, so not every descent is evil as some philosophers maintained with whom Iamblichus disagrees[28]. However, he realized that such teaching about the good descent and deep acceptation of the Peripatetic tradition caused the soul to become mortal after embodiment. Thus special means were necessary to free the soul from the grasp of the body. Those special means were theurgical rites—religious or even magical rituals which relied on using the material object, which, thanks to the cosmic sympathy were filled with the presence and powers of gods. During the ritual the soul of the philosopher-theurgist was uplifted by this power helping the soul to regain its immortal status. Another outcome of this rituals was the ability to wield the power of gods, which served the above-mentioned goal of the descent, i.e. introducing the intellectual order to the chaos of the material reality.

---

[26] Cf. G. Shaw, Theurgy and the Soul. Neoplatonism of Iamblichus (Pennsylvania 1995) 95.
[27] *Iamblichus*, De anima 29: J. Finamore, J. Dillon, Iamblichus' De Anima. Text, Translation, and Commentary (Leiden – Boston – Köln 2002), p. 56,17–24.
[28] Ibid., p. 56,25–28.

Such a positive attitude to matter and body as natural parts of the cosmos, which is "filled with gods", does not change the fate of the soul after death. In another preserved passage of *De anima*, Iamblichus presents various opinions of his predecessors and analyses the interpretations of the description of Hades made by Plato. But he seems to accept the opinion that the soul after death has a place with the angels (ἀγγελικῷ ἐνὶ χώρῳ) and receives the duty of care for the unanimated material world[29]. Notwithstanding the place where the good soul dwells after death one thing is clear: it is the soul in its proper state, which is without the body.

An analysis of the most material-friendly Neoplatonic philosopher allows to sum up the elements common to the Platonic tradition. As we have seen, the philosophical successors of Plato seemed to be, like their "divine teacher", under the influence of both the Orphic and the Olympic traditions with various attitudes to matter and body assumed by the soul. Not all of them saw the embodiment as such as a sin; such opinions obviously betrayed sympathies with the Orphic tradition. However, in spite of their various attitudes towards the sensual reality one thing remains constant: even the most Peripatetic and Olympic inclined Neoplatonist—Iamblichus—thought about the state of happiness after death as being without the body. The soul properly belongs to the kind of immortal gods, and it cannot be happy being united to the body which limits its ability to see the ideal reality. Even Plato's statements from *Timaeus* could not change the common conviction that the soul is in the body only temporarily performing its hard and tormenting duty of making order out of the material chaos. Even for Iamblichus the best way of punishment for the soul is to expose it to the draws of sensuous lusts. So there is a natural discord between those two and the body disturbs the soul's true purpose, true vision, and true happiness.

Thanks to pointing out the common elements in the Platonic tradition as a whole we can finally briefly look at the differences between the Platonic and Christian views of the soul-body relations. First of all, there is a field of agreement between the Orphism-influenced Neoplatonic philosophy and Christianity. In both cases there is a conviction about some kind of disagreement between body and soul which we can observe in the present human state. This is understood as a kind of a crack in human nature which occurs in the soul-body relations and results in diminishing the soul's cognitive abilities and making the will prone to bodily sensual pleasures. Such a view is a simple

---

[29] Cf. *Iamblichus*, De anima 47–53: Iamblichus' De Anima, p. 73–75; also commentary, 207–211.

recognition of a conflict in human nature which can be observed by a simple analysis of moral behavior, in which there are two opposite attractions: the desire of moral excellency, which comes from the soul which sees the true good, and a draw to taste sensual pleasures, which comes from the body. The second common element is the conviction about the need of salvation and getting out of such state to achieve perfection and happiness.

In my opinion those two are only common elements, because Platonism and Christianity differ fundamentally as regards the causes of the conflict in human nature and the possible ways to overcome it. For ancient Christian writers, the body itself is not the obstacle for the soul, since the material world was created along with the spiritual one, the soul is created like the body, and it is no longer an eternal being belonging to the ranks of gods. What makes a human being immersed in sensual desires and lusts is not the initial contact of the soul with the body, but rather that a man already composed of the body and the soul committed a sin with such devastating consequences. This of course involves a different conception of how an individual human being was made. While for the Platonists the soul existed eternally or was created long before embodiment, the Christian tradition rooted in the Bible did not confirm the eternity of the soul or (with some exceptions) its long dwelling in the noetic reality before assuming the body. This anthropological background harmonizes with two different causes of corruption of the soul. As we have seen above for Plotinus the cause of corruption was the contact of the soul with the body which caused the second guilt of moral sin. So embodiment is in a sense a moral error or sin, which causes a further fall. In the Christian tradition the body as such is not conflicted with the soul, but the conflict is the effect of the sin. So there is no place here for embodiment in the Platonic sense and the body is no longer to blame. But this puts Christianity in need to explain the current condition of human nature in another way. Therefore we could say that some kind of the concept of the original sin is needed to fill this gap and explain why in the present state there is a conflict which originally did not exist.

Jana Plátová, Olomouc (Czech Republic)

Sündenlehre bei Clemens von Alexandria[1]

Abstract:
Der Aufsatz konzentriert sich auf die Sündenlehre bei Clemens von Alexandria, die dieser in einem Exkurs über die christlichen Tugenden im zweiten Buch der Stromata *am systematischsten behandelt. Anhand von Aristoteles' Klassifizierung des freiwilligen und unfreiwilligen Handelns in der Nikomachischen Ethik setzt sich Clemens mit eindeutiger Verurteilung der Sünde im Sinne eines freiwilligen Handelns in Hebr 10,26–27 auseinander und versucht, die falsche Auslegung von Röm 7,19–20 zu korrigieren, die die Anhänger von Valentinus und Basilides für ihre Lehre von Seelenanhängseln missbrauchten. Zu diesem Zweck nutzt Clemens den aristotelisch-stoischen Begriff* τὸ ἐφ' ἡμῖν *(„das, was von uns abhängt").*

Dass Clemens gerade das freie Handeln eines Christen hervorhebt, hat praktische Konsequenzen und findet auch an anderen Stellen der Stromata *Anwendung, z. B. im dritten Buch, wo sich der Autor auf eine Polemik mit den Verfechtern einer kompletten sexuellen Enthaltsamkeit einlässt, oder im vierten Buch, wo er in einer Diskussion mit Basilides den Sinn des Märtyrertums überlegt.*

Einleitung

Clemens von Alexandria formulierte seine Lehre im 2. Jahrhundert einerseits mit Hinblick auf seine gebildeten Leser, zu denen Christen oder am Christentum Interessierte gehören, und andererseits als Teil einer Polemik mit unterschiedlichen heterodoxen Gruppen, v.a. mit der valentinianischen Gnosis. Er ordnet seine Gedanken nicht zu systematischen Abhandlungen, sondern lässt sie eher frei fließen; seine Themen sind lose aneinandergereiht, überschneiden sich und ergänzen sich gegenseitig. Seine Überlegungen untermauert Clemens textuell durch eine große Zahl von Autoritäten – durch die Schrift, durch Werke der Klassiker oder seiner Zeitgenossen, die ihn inspirieren oder die er ablehnt, und nicht zuletzt durch Texte, die heutzutage als heterodox oder apokryph bezeichnet werden. Diese charakteristische Schreibweise gilt v.a. für

---

[1] Diese Studie entstand im Rahmen des Projekts "Continuity – Discontinuity – Progression" (IGA_CMTF_2021_009), Palacký University Olomouc.

Clemens' wichtigstes und umfangreichstes Werk – die *Stromata*, die in ihrem Stil an einen orientalischen Teppich (also an ein Patchwork) erinnern sollen.

I. Clemens' Sündenlehre im Kontext seiner Tugendlehre in *Strom.* II

Clemens' stellt seine Überlegungen über die Sünde hauptsächlich in dem zweiten Buch der *Stromata* in den Kontext seiner Ausführungen über die Tugenden. Als ein Christ, der darüber hinaus über Kenntnisse der griechischen Philosophie verfügt, versucht er die bisherige stoische (oder stoisch-platonische) Ordnung der Tugenden zu innovieren[2]. Der Anfang jeder Tugend sei für einen Christen der Glaube. Um den Begriff des Glaubens einem gebildeten Leser näher zu bringen und ihn von bloßem Aberglauben zu trennen, gelangt Clemens zu einer komplizierten Definition, die durch die stoische Epistemologie angeregt ist. Der Glaube, der in seiner Sicht im Unterschied zu den Gnostikern (den Valentinianern und Basilidianern) einer freien vernünftigen Entscheidung obliegt (προαίρεσις ἔμφρων)[3], ist eine Art „Annahme aus freiem Entschluss" (πρόληψις ἑκούσιος), „eine zustimmende Anerkennung der Gottesfurcht" (θεοσεβείας συγκατάθεσις)[4], die dem Menschen einen „unumstößlichen Maßstab" (κριτήριον ἀμετάπτωτον) der Wahrheit zur Verfügung stellt[5]. Aus diesem Grund kann der Glaube als Fundament der wahren Erkenntnis verstanden werden[6].

Neben dem Glauben präsentiert Clemens die Furcht (φόβος) als eine zweite Säule der Erkenntnis. Das stellt ihn vor die intellektuelle Herausforderung, die Furcht (φόβος) *per definitionem* den Tugenden zuzuordnen. Nach der stoischen Auffassung gehört nämlich φόβος zusammen mit Trauer (λύπη), Verlangen (ἐπιθυμία) und Wonne (ἡδονή) zu den vier Grundleidenschaften (πάθη), die sonst als irrationale Regungen der Seele beschrieben und somit als eindeutig unerwünscht aufgefasst wurden. Clemens, der die Philosophie mit

---

[2] Vgl. Clemens' Ordnung der Tugenden in *Clem. Alex.*, Strom. II, 6, 31, 1: GCS 52 (Berlin [4]1985), p. 129,16-19: καὶ δὴ ἡ πρώτη πρὸς σωτηρίαν νεῦσις ἡ πίστις ἡμῖν ἀναφαίνεται, μεθ' ἣν φόβος τε καὶ ἐλπὶς καὶ μετάνοια σύν τε ἐγκρατείᾳ καὶ ὑπομονῇ προκόπτουσαι ἄγουσιν ἡμᾶς ἐπί τε ἀγάπην ἐπί τε γνῶσιν; vgl. auch Strom. II, 1, 1, 1 und 9, 45, 1: GCS 52, p. 113,9-11 und p. 136,23-26.
[3] Vgl. *Clem. Alex.*, Strom. II, 2, 9, 2 und 3, 11, 1: GCS 52, p. 117,15-18 und p. 118,21-29; etc. Zur Lehre der Valentinianer und Basilidianer vgl. Strom. II, 3, 10, 1-3: GCS 52, p. 118,11-21.
[4] Vgl. *Clem. Alex.*, Strom. II, 2, 8, 4: GCS 52, p. 117,9.
[5] Vgl. *Clem. Alex.*, Strom. II, 2, 7, 2; 2, 9, 6 und 4, 12, 1: GCS 52, p. 116,17; p. 118,4-7 und p. 119,6.
[6] Vgl. *Clem. Alex.*, Strom. II, 2, 9, 3: GCS 52, p. 117,19-21. Vgl. auch ganze Passage Strom. II, 4, 12, 1-6, 31, 3: GCS 52, p. 119-129.

der biblischen Tradition verbindet, steht hier also vor der Aufgabe zu erklären, in welchem Sinn die Furcht den Anfang der Weisheit bilden könnte (laut Spr 1,7). Zu diesem Zweck unterscheidet er zwei Formen von φόβος. Die erste Form ist ein gewöhnliches Entsetzen (ἔκπληξις), das auch die Stoiker beschreiben. Eine zweite Form ist eine den Glauben begleitende Tugend, der die „Philosophen" eher den Namen „Vorsicht" (εὐλάβεια) beilegen[7]. Und gerade diese Form des φόβος verteidigt Clemens als den Weg, der in Verbindung mit dem Glauben, mit dem Bedauern über die Sünde und mit Hoffnung zu einer vollkommeneren Haltung, nämlich der Liebe zu Gott führt[8].

Nicht jeder Mensch rückt jedoch auf seinem geistigen Weg von der Furcht zur Liebe vor. Einige Christen kennen, so Clemens, bis jetzt weder eine Freundschaft mit Gott, noch bezeichnen sie sich selbst als Gottessöhne, sondern bleiben auf dem Niveau eines Dieners, der Gott als seinen Herren fürchtet[9]. In dieser frühen Phase des geistigen Aufstiegs ist die rationale Furcht (Respekt vor den göttlichen Bestimmungen) nützlich, meint Clemens, denn sie hilft dem Menschen, sich von dem Bösen abzuwenden. Und nur derjenige, der sich für immer von der Schlechtigkeit abwendet, ist zu einer liebevollen Beziehung zu Gott imstande. Wie soll es aber zu dieser Wandlung kommen? In erster Linie dadurch, dass diese Furcht vor Gott, die im Grunde eine Ehrfurcht vor ihm ist und in sich bereits (wenn auch bisher unvollkommene) Spuren von Liebe trägt[10], den Menschen zur Reue über die begangene Sünde und zur Hoffnung, oder anders gesagt einer „hoffnungsfrohen Erwartung von Gutem" bringt[11]. Während sich die Reue bzw. Buße (μετάνοια) auf die Vergangenheit bezieht, verweist die Hoffnung (ἐλπίς) auf die Zukunft[12].

Wie bereits bei der Furcht (φόβος), ist es auch bei der Reue (μετάνοια) für Clemens' Zeitgenossen keineswegs selbstverständlich, dass es sich um eine positive Gemütsregung handele. Denn eine übermäßige Reuigkeit (Schwermut) ist nach Aristoteles Zeichen der fehlenden Menschen[13] und nach den Stoikern

---

[7] Vgl. *Clem. Alex.*, Strom. II, 7, 32, 1-4; 8, 40, 1-3 und 12, 53, 4: GCS 52, p. 130,1-15; p. 134,7-15 und p. 142,7-10); Paed. I, 9, 87, 1-2: GCS 12 (Berlin ³1972), p. 140,29-141,8.
[8] Vgl. vor allem Kap. 9-12 (*Clem. Alex.*, Strom. II, 9, 41, 1-12, 55, 6: GCS 52, pp. 354-364).
[9] Vgl. Beschreibung des geistigen Wegs in *Clem. Alex.*, Strom. I, 27, 173, 6 und II, 9, 45, 3: GCS 52, p. 107,23-30 und p. 136,29-137,1; VII, 11, 62, 7 und 13, 82, 7; Ecl. proph. 19, 1: GCS 17, p. 45,11-14 und p. 59,7-11; p. 142,3-7.
[10] Wir müssen uns nämlich nicht nur davor fürchten, dass Gott unsere Sünde bestraft, sondern auch davor, dass wir durch unsere Sünde Gott, der uns liebt, beleidigen werden (vgl. *Clem. Alex.*, Strom. II, 12, 53, 2-5: GCS 52, p. 142,3-13).
[11] *Clem. Alex.*, Strom. II, 9, 41, 1: GCS 52, p. 134,17.
[12] Vgl. *Clem. Alex.*, Strom. II, 12, 53, 1: GCS 52, p. 141,25-142,2.
[13] Vgl. *Aristoteles*, Eth. Nic. IX, 4, p. 1166b14-29.

ist die Reue eine Emotion, die mit dem Bild eines Weisen vollkommen unvereinbar sei[14]. Clemens muss daher zuerst erklären, in welchem Sinn Reue eine Tugend ist. Er geht dabei von der Etymologie des Wortes im Griechischen sowie von der Aufforderung zur Buße im *Hirten des Hermas* aus. Während eine Prophezeiung eine Art „Weissagung" (*pro-gnósis*) sei[15], stelle Buße eine Art „erst hintennach kommende Erkenntnis" dessen dar, was passiert war (*meta-noia*); kurz gesagt eine verspätete Erkenntnis (βραδεῖα γνῶσις)[16]. Bereits deswegen hat sie zentrale Bedeutung für einen Gnostiker als Christen, der um die wahre Erkenntnis bemüht ist. Auch wenn eine „Erkenntnis gleich von vorne" (πρώτη γνῶσις) freilich besser wäre, ist auch eine verspätete Erkenntnis (μετάνοια) bei jemandem, der gesündigt hat, erwünscht[17]. Der *Hirte des Hermas* drückt es, so Clemens, treffend aus: er bezeichnet die Buße als „eine tiefe Einsicht" (σύνεσις μεγάλη) und meint, dass der Büßende „seiner Seele [...] Gutes [tut]"[18]. Buße (μετάνοια) ist daher eine Tugend genauso wie die Tugend der Furcht, die ihr vorangeht, sowie der Hoffnung, die sie begleitet.

II. Sündenlehre zwischen Hebr 10,26–27 und der *Nikomachischen Ethik* von Aristoteles

Eine auf diese Weise aufgefasste Buße für die Sünden, die man in der Zeit des vorangehenden heidnischen Lebens (d. h. eines Lebens im Unwissen) beging, hat eine feste Stelle bei der Bekehrung, dem Beginn des christlichen Lebenswegs. Diese wird durch die Taufe besiegelt, bei der alle bisherigen Sünden vergeben werden. Die Reue über die begangenen Sünden bei der Taufe ist einmalig und unwiederholbar[19], Clemens gesteht aber zu, dass man auch ein zweites Mal bereuen könnte[20]. Keinesfalls sei Reue jedoch ein Prozess, den man unzählige Male wiederholen könne[21]. Clemens zitiert dazu eine Passage aus dem Brief an die Hebräer:

---

[14] Vgl. *Cicero*, Pro Mur. 61; SVF (von Arnim) I, 53–54.
[15] Vgl. *Clem. Alex.*, Strom. II, 12, 54, 1: GCS 52, p. 142,13.
[16] Vgl. *Clem. Alex.*, Strom. II, 6, 26, 5: GCS 52, p. 127,14.
[17] Vgl. *Clem. Alex.*, Strom. II, 6, 26, 5–27, 1: GCS 52, p. 127,10–19.
[18] *Past. Herm.*, Mand. IV, 2, 2 in *Clem. Alex.*, Strom. II, 12, 55, 6: GCS 52, p. 143,10–13. Zu Clemens' Auffassung der *metanoia* vgl. K. *Schmöle*, Gnosis und Metanoia, TThZ 82 (1974) 304–312.
[19] Vgl. *Clem. Alex.*, Strom. II, 13, 56, 1: GCS 52, p. 143,15–20 und Paed. I, 6, 30, 1: GCS 12, p. 108,4–5.
[20] Vgl. *Clem. Alex.*, Strom. II, 13, 57, 2: GCS 52, p. 143,29–32 und QDS 42: GCS 17 (Berlin ²1970), p. 187,27–191,13.
[21] Zur Problematik der Buße bei Clemens vgl. A. *Méhat*, „Pénitence seconde" et „péché involontaire" chez Clément d'Alexandrie, VigChr 8 (1954) 225–233.

Sündenlehre bei Clemens von Alexandria 89

Denn wenn wir mit Willen sündigen, nachdem wir die volle Erkenntnis der Wahrheit erlangt haben, so bleibt uns kein Opfer für Sünden mehr übrig, sondern wir haben ein schreckliches Gericht und brennendes Feuer zu erwarten, das die Widersacher verzehren soll[22].

Eine häufig wiederholte Reue helfe nicht, sich von der Sünde zu befreien, sondern treibe diese eher an[23]. Ein um Vollkommenheit bemühter Christ muss sich große Mühe geben, muss asketisch leben und nicht selten kämpfen, um den Tugenden gemäß zu handeln und Sünden zu vermeiden[24]. Das ist deswegen notwendig, weil der Mensch erstens durch irrationale verderbliche Kräfte – sogenannte Leidenschaften – beeinflusst wird, die in ihm einfach angelegt sind[25], zweitens, weil ein Versucher da ist, der den Menschen absichtlich von der Tugend abzubringen trachtet[26].

In den nachfolgenden Kapiteln setzt sich Clemens mit den drohenden Folgen auseinander, die laut des zitierten Briefes von Paulus diejenigen erwarten, die nach der Bekehrung wieder freiwillig sündigen. Angeregt durch eine Reihe von Zitaten aus dem Buch der Psalmen und Sprüche zur Gerechtigkeit und Barmherzigkeit Gottes[27], formuliert Clemens einige subtile Ausführungen, in denen er mit Hilfe der aristotelischen Terminologie zu erklären versucht, welche Art des schlechten Handelns/der Sünde überhaupt als freiwillig und somit als dem „schrecklichen Gericht" und „verzehrenden Feuer" obliegend bezeichnet werden können[28].

Zuerst befasst er sich mit dem Teil der aristotelischen Lehre, der das unfreiwillige Handeln (τὸ ἀκούσιον) bespricht. Ein Mensch, der das Schlechte unfreiwillig tut, kann nicht verurteilt werden, meint Clemens. Grundlegend ist für ihn die von Aristoteles durchgeführte Trennung von zwei Arten des unfreiwilligen Handelns: das Handeln aus Unkenntnis (μετ' ἀγνοίας) und das Handeln unter Zwang (ἀνάγκῃ)[29]. Für das unfreiwillige Handeln führt Cle-

---

[22] Hebr 10,26-27 in *Clem. Alex.*, Strom. II, 13, 57, 2: GCS 52, p. 143,29-32; Clemens glaubte, daß Paulus der Autor des Briefes an die Hebräer ist.
[23] Vgl. *Clem. Alex.*, Strom. II, 13, 58, 3: GCS 52, p. 144,19-20.
[24] Vgl. *Clem. Alex.*, Strom. II, 9, 45, 7; VI, 15, 121, 3: GCS 52, p. 137,9-13; p. 492,28-34; VII, 3, 19, 2-3: GCS 17, p. 14,5-14; u. a.
[25] Vgl. *Clem. Alex.*, Strom. II, 13, 59, 6: GCS 52, p. 145,5-6.
[26] Vgl. *Clem. Alex.*, Strom. II, 13, 56, 2: GCS 52, p. 143,20-25. Zur Figur des Teufels bei Clemens vgl. P. Karavites, Evil, Freedom and the Road to Perfection, Suppl. to VigChr 49 (Leiden – Boston 1999) 43-46.
[27] Vgl. Prov 11,5; Ps 102/103,13; 125/126,5; 127/128,1; 48/49,17 und 5,8-9 in *Clem. Alex.*, Strom. II, 13, 59, 2-5: GCS 52, p. 144,24-145,2.
[28] Vgl. *Clem. Alex.*, Strom. II, 14, 60-17, 77: GCS 52, p. 145-153.
[29] Vgl. *Aristoteles*, Eth. Nic. III, 1-3 in *Clem. Alex.*, Strom. II, 14, 60, 1: GCS 52, p. 145,10-12.

mens anschließend eine Reihe von Beispielen an, die sich jedoch ausschließlich auf die erste Art – das unfreiwillige Handeln aus Unkenntnis – beziehen[30]. Danach widmet er sich dem freiwilligen bösen Handeln, also der Sünde im heutigen Sinne. Nach dem Vorbild von Aristoteles klassifiziert er drei Arten dieser Handlung: Erstens die Sünde (ἁμάρτημα), die aus einem schlechten Begehren begangen wird, zweitens der Irrtum (ἀτύχημα), den man aufgrund einer falschen Entscheidung begeht, und drittens das Verbrechen (ἀδίκημα), das auf einem schlechten Vorhaben/einer schlechten Absicht fußt[31]. Auch diese Unterscheidung illustriert er durch einige Beispiele[32]. Gleich danach kehrt er jedoch zu der Frage der Freiwilligkeit zurück: ist die Grenze zwischen einem freiwilligen und unfreiwilligen Handeln überhaupt klar? Während ein Irrtum, der aufgrund einer falschen Entscheidung entsteht, für einen unwillkürlichen, unvorhersehbaren Fehler (παράλογός [...] ἁμαρτία) gehalten werden kann, der demnach ein reines Versehen ist, geht es bei einem auf schlechter Absicht fußenden Verbrechen fast immer um eine beabsichtigte Schlechtigkeit (ἑκούσιος κακία). Wie verhält es sich aber bei einer Sünde, die aus falschem Begehren begangen wird? Man kann seinem Begehren unterliegen, aber dies geschieht unfreiwillig, gegen den eigenen Willen. In solchem Fall handelt es sich nicht um eine freiwillige Sünde, sondern eine unfreiwillig begangene schlechte Tat (ἀκούσιος ἀδικία)[33].

Nach dieser komplexen Unterscheidung, die von der aristotelischen Ethik ausgeht, führt Clemens eine Reihe alt- sowie neutestamentlicher Stellen an, die allerdings letztendlich nur wenig Licht in die Problematik bringen[34]. Vielleicht wurden sie nur angegeben, um zu zeigen, dass die christlichen Texte zum Thema des schlechten Handelns im Vergleich zu Aristoteles ebenfalls etliches zu bieten haben. Die einzelnen Verweise machen jedoch eher den Eindruck freier Assoziationen als dem ernsthaften Versuch, die Klassifikation von Aristoteles zu bestätigen oder zu entkräften. Während man die zitierten Psalmen mit gutem Willen als Beleg für die aristotelische dreistufige Klassifikation ansehen kann, ist der Zusammenhang der anderen zitierten Textstellen (zum Beispiel 1Joh 5,16–17) mit der aristotelischen Ethik nur sehr oberflächlich.

---

[30] Vgl. *Clem. Alex.*, Strom. II, 14, 60, 2–7: GCS 52, p. 145,12–146,2.
[31] Vgl. *Aristoteles*, Eth. Nic. III, 4 in *Clem. Alex.*, Strom. II, 15, 62, 1: GCS 52, p. 146,17–19. Zur aristotelischen Vorlage vgl. *E. Clark*, Clement's Use of Aristotle (New York – Toronto 1977) 45–65.
[32] Vgl. *Clem. Alex.*, Strom. II, 15, 62, 2: GCS 52, p. 146,19–21.
[33] Vgl. *Clem. Alex.*, Strom. II, 15, 62, 3–64, 3: GCS 52, p. 146,22–147,20.
[34] Vgl. Ps 31/32,1–2; Jes 44,22; 1Petr 4,8; Mt 5,28; Jer 27,20.44 (LXX); 1Joh 5,16–17 und Ps 1,1 in *Clem. Alex.*, Strom. II, 15, 65, 1–68, 1: GCS 52, p. 148,3–149,15.

Sündenlehre bei Clemens von Alexandria 91

III. Eine irrige Exegese des Röm 7,11–25 und Clemens' Korrektur mit Hilfe des aristotelisch-stoischen Begriffs τὸ ἐφ' ἡμῖν

Spannender als diese wörtlichen Zitate erscheinen die versteckten Anspielungen auf den Römerbrief, vor allem auf die Kapitel 6–8, in denen über die Befreiung vom Gesetz zu einem neuen Leben gesprochen wird. Wie interpretiert Clemens nun diese Textstelle? Es könnte am Relevantesten scheinen, wenn er bei seinen Überlegungen über die Freiwilligkeit oder Unfreiwilligkeit der Sünde sich zuerst Röm 7,14–25 zuwenden würde, wo der innere Kampf des Menschen beschrieben wird:

> Denn ich tue nicht das Gute, das ich will, sondern das Böse, das ich nicht will, das vollbringe ich. Wenn ich aber das tue, was ich nicht will, dann bin nicht mehr ich es, der es bewirkt, sondern die in mir wohnende Sünde (οἰκοῦσα ἐν ἐμοὶ ἁμαρτία)[35],

sagt hier Paulus. Obwohl Clemens an anderen Stellen die Briefe von Paulus (inklusive des Römerbriefs) gerne zitiert, scheint er an dieser Stelle sehr vorsichtig zu sein. Bereits davor konstatiert er, dass die Sünde eine „unbeabsichtigte Verfehlung" (ἀκούσιος ἀδικία) sei und fährt hier nun fort, indem er Paulus unauffällig korrigiert: ἔστιν οὖν ἡ μὲν ἁμαρτία ἐμὸν ἀκούσιον (mit Betonung auf dem Possessivpronomen „meine"). Das heißt: Wenn ich sündige, ist es zwar eine unbeabsichtigte Verfehlung, jedoch *meine eigene*[36]. Es ist nicht schwer zu erraten, warum Clemens den Satz von Paulus, in dem das ungewollte Handeln auf die inne „wohnende Sünde" zurückgeführt wird, vermeidet. Er will verhindern, dass die Gläubigen der Verantwortung entgehen. Die Gefahr einer solchen Interpretation sah Clemens offensichtlich bei den Gnostikern, bei den Anhängern des Basilides und Valentinus, über deren irrige Meinungen er in der zweiten Hälfte desselben Buches berichtet. Die Basilidianer seien gewohnt die Leidenschaften als Anhängsel (προσαρτήματα) zu bezeichnen und halten sie für eine Art unreine Geister, die an einer vernünftigen Seele haften blieben[37]. Ähnliches berichtet Clemens auch über die Lehre der Valentinianer:

---

[35] Röm 7,19–20.
[36] *Clem. Alex.*, Strom. II, 15, 64, 3: GCS 52, p. 147,19–20.
[37] Vgl. *Clem. Alex.*, Strom. II, 20, 112, 1: GCS 52, p. 174,6–7. Vgl. Kommentar von W. A. Löhr, Basilides und seine Schule. Eine Studie zur Theologie- und Kirchengeschichte des zweiten Jahrhunderts, WUNT 83 (Tübingen 1996) 78–101.

die vielen Geister, die in [der Seele] wohnen, lassen es nicht rein sein, vielmehr vollführt jeder einzelne von ihnen seine eigenen Werke, indem sie durch ihre ungeziemenden Begierden der Seele alle mögliche Schmach antun[38].

Eine solche Vorstellung halten weder Clemens, noch selbst Isidor, der Sohn von Basilides, für gelungen, denn sie gewährt denjenigen Menschen eine Ausflucht, die nach einer Ausrede suchen:

„Mir ist Gewalt geschehen, ich wurde hingerissen, wider meinen Willen habe ich es getan, ohne zu wollen habe ich gehandelt", während sie doch selbst mit der Begierde nach dem Schlechten begonnen und gegen die Kräfte der Anhängsel nicht angekämpft haben[39],

meint Isidor und Clemens pflichtet ihm bei.

Sünde ist zwar für Clemens eine unfreiwillige Tat, es ist aber *meine* unfreiwillige Tat, das heißt, die Verantwortung dafür tragen keine fremden Leidenschaften, keine fremden Geister oder sogar eine Sünde, die in mir wohnen würde als eine fremde Entität, sondern nur ich selbst. Aus diesem Grund vermeidet Clemens Röm 7,19–20 und wendet lieber den aristotelisch-stoischen Begriff τὸ ἐφ' ἡμῖν an[40]. Ob ich einer Sünde unterliege oder nicht, „hängt von mir ab", anders gesagt, die Sünde liegt in meiner Macht: und zwar nicht als einmaliges Versagen, sondern vielmehr als starker Entschluss ihr nicht zu unterliegen.

---

[38] Vgl. *Clem. Alex.*, Strom. II, 20, 114, 4: GCS 52, p. 175,4–6. Vgl. Kommentar von *Ch. Markschies*, Valentinus Gnosticus? Untersuchungen zur Valentinianischen Gnosis mit einem Kommentar zu den Fragmenten Valentins, WUNT 65 (Tübingen 1992) 54–82. Ich zitiere die Übersetzung von *O. Stählin*, Clemens von Alexandrien ausgewählte Schriften (München 1934).

[39] *Clem. Alex.*, Strom. II, 20, 113, 3–4: GCS 52, p. 174,21–28; mit dem Zitat aus der Schrift Isidors *Über die angewachsene Seele*.

[40] Vgl. vor allem *Aristoteles*, Eth. Nic. III, 3–7: p. 1111–1114. Die Verbindung ἐφ' ἡμῖν (ἐστι) kommt laut TLG (Thesaurus Linguae Graecae) bei Aristoteles noch an zehn anderen Stellen in Eth. Eud. und zwölfmal in Mor. Mag. vor; bei Platon findet sie sich dagegen nur in Resp. 398b5; im Neuen Testament gar nicht. Clemens benutzt diese Wendung ziemlich häufig, am meisten findet man sie gerade in den Passagen der *Stromata*, wo die Persönlichkeit des Gnostikers beschrieben wird, am häufigsten in dem zweiten Buch (vgl. *Clem. Alex.*, Strom. II, 6, 26, 3; 7, 35, 5; 12, 55, 6; 13, 59, 6; 15, 62, 4; 15, 69, 2; 17, 76, 1–2; 23, 140, 1: GCS 52, p. 127,5; p. 131,26; p. 143,13–14; p. 145,7; p. 146,25–26; p. 149,29–150,2; p. 152,29–153,2). Zu dem aristotelischen Begriffsinhalt in Eth. Eud. vgl. *A. Kenny*, Aristotle's Theory of the Will (London 1979) 3–12 und *F. Karfík*, τὸ ἐφ' ἡμῖν mezi Aristotelem a stoiky, in: idem, Duše a svět. Devět studií z antické filosofie (Praha 2007) 129–149.

[...] in unserer Macht (ἐφ' ἡμῖν) steht sowohl, daß man sich unserer Lehre anschließt, als auch, daß man gegen die Gebote gehorsam ist[41],

so Clemens. Die Akzentuierung der Freiheit der menschlichen Entscheidung ist bei Clemens unübersehbar[42].

An der Spitze von allem steht also das Wollen; denn die Kräfte des Verstandes sind ihrer Natur nach dazu bestimmt, Dienerinnen des Wollens zu sein[43],

meint er und schließt seine Ausführungen über die Sünde und die Genesung von deren Folgen mit der Paraphrase eines Satzes des Evangeliums, in dem Jesus zu einem Kranken spricht: „Wolle! und du wirst können"[44]. In einem Nachsatz stellt er im Anschluss daran fest, dass bei einem wahren Gnostiker der Wille (βούλησις), die Urteilskraft (κρίσις) und die Zucht (ἄσκησις) eins seien[45]. Bei einem rational denkenden Menschen, der sich entschließt, nicht mehr zu sündigen, gibt es also nach Clemens keinen inneren Widerspruch zwischen dem Wollen, dem Urteil und dem Handeln.

IV. Praktische Konsequenzen: die Polemik über die komplette sexuelle Enthaltsamkeit in *Strom.* III und die Frage nach dem Sinn des Märtyrertums in *Strom.* IV

Diese (vielleicht viel zu) optimistische Theorie schwingt auch in weiteren Ausführungen von Clemens mit, in denen er einige heikle Themen des alexandrinischen Christentums diskutiert. Im dritten Buch der *Stromata* polemisiert Clemens zum Beispiel mit einigen Christengruppen, die sich zu der Lehre der völligen sexuellen Enthaltsamkeit von Julius Cassianus bekannten[46]. Für diese Christen, die die Schöpfung, die Geburt und die Sexualität verachten, führt

---

[41] *Clem. Alex.*, Strom. II, 15, 62, 4: GCS 52, p. 146,24-26: ἀλλ' ἐφ' ἡμῖν γε ἥ τε πρὸς τὴν παιδείαν ἡμῶν παράστασις ἥ τε πρὸς τὰς ἐντολὰς ὑπακοή. Vgl. auch Strom. II, 13, 59, 6: GCS 52, p. 145,6-8: ἡ δ' ἀπόστασις καὶ ἔκστασις καὶ ἀπείθεια ἐφ' ἡμῖν, ὥσπερ καὶ ἡ ὑπακοὴ ἐφ' ἡμῖν· διὸ καὶ τὰ ἑκούσια κρίνεται, und Strom. II, 15, 69, 2: GCS 52, p. 149,29-150,1: πάλιν ὁ κύριος δείκνυσιν ἄντικρυς ἐφ' ἡμῖν καὶ τὰ παραπτώματα καὶ τὰ πλημμελήματα [...].
[42] Vgl. M. Havrda, Grace and Free Will According to Clement of Alexandria, JECS 19/1 (2011) 21-48.
[43] *Clem. Alex.*, Strom. II, 17, 77, 5: GCS 52, p. 153,21-22: προηγεῖται τοίνυν πάντων τὸ βούλεσθαι· αἱ γὰρ λογικαὶ δυνάμεις τοῦ βούλεσθαι διάκονοι πεφύκασι.
[44] *Clem. Alex.*, Strom. II, 17, 77, 5 (mit Anspielung auf Joh 5,6 bzw. Mk 1,40; GCS 52, p. 153,22-23): "θέλε," φησί, "καὶ δυνήσῃ".
[45] Vgl. *Clem. Alex.*, Strom. II, 17, 77, 5: GCS 52, p. 153,23-24: τοῦ γνωστικοῦ δὲ καὶ ἡ βούλησις καὶ ἡ κρίσις καὶ ἡ ἄσκησις ἡ αὐτή.
[46] Vgl. *Clem. Alex.*, Strom. III, 13, 91, 1-92, 2: GCS 52, p. 238,9-26.

Clemens einige Bibelverse an, die vielleicht zu einer entsprechend irrigen Interpretation verführen können, und rückt sie ins rechte Licht[47]. Nachdem er die folgenden Stellen als Beispiel zitiert hat: „Verflucht sei der Tag, an dem ich geboren wurde!" oder „Warum ist denn meiner Mutter Schoß nicht mein Grab geworden?" und „Niemand ist rein von Schmutz, auch wenn sein Leben nur einen Tag währte?"[48], verlangt er ironisch:

> Sie sollen uns sagen, wo das neugeborene Kind Unzucht getrieben hat, oder wie das Kind, das noch nichts getan hat, unter den Fluch Adams gefallen ist[49].

Danach erklärt er, wie die Worte des Psalms 50/51,7 zu verstehen sind: „In Sünde wurde ich gezeugt, und in Unrecht hat mich meine Mutter empfangen". Es ist wichtig, meint Clemens, dass hier David mit „Mutter" Eva meint, die zwar als „Mutter der Sünde" und als „Todesursache"[50] bezeichnet wird, aber ebenfalls als das „Leben" (*Zóé*) und als solche als Mutter alles Lebenden anzusehen ist. Aufgrund dieser Ambivalenz lohne sich das Risiko, neue Nachkommen in die Welt zu setzen, sagt Clemens und fügt noch hinzu:

> wenn auch [ein Mensch] in Sünde erzeugt wurde, so ist er doch nicht selbst in Sünde und ist auch nicht selbst Sünde[51].

An keiner anderen Stelle seines Werks geht er auf die Bedeutung des Ps 50/51,7 mehr ein; die Frage der Sündenübergabe bei der Zeugung/der Geburt gehörte offensichtlich nicht zu seinen Prioritäten.

---

[47] Vgl. *Clem. Alex.*, Strom. III, 14, 94, 1–17, 104, 5: GCS 52, p. 239,8–244,20.
[48] Jer 20,14; 4Esr 5,35; Ijob 14,4–5 in *Clem. Alex.*, Strom. III, 16, 100, 1–4: GCS 52, p. 242,3–12.
[49] *Clem. Alex.*, Strom. III, 16, 100, 5: GCS 52, p. 242,12–14: λεγέτωσαν ἡμῖν ποῦ ἐπόρνευσεν τὸ γεννηθὲν παιδίον, ἢ πῶς ὑπὸ τὴν τοῦ Ἀδὰμ ὑποπέπτωκεν ἀρὰν τὸ μηθὲν ἐνεργῆσαν.
[50] Vgl. Gen 3,20. Clemens lässt sich da durch Philons Interpretation inspirieren, Quis rerum div. her. 52; Leg. alleg. II, 40; De opif. 156; De spec. leg. III, 179. Dazu vgl. A. van den Hoek, Clement of Alexandria and His Use of Philo in the Stromateis (Leiden – Boston 1988).
[51] *Clem. Alex.*, Strom. III, 16, 100, 7: GCS 52, p. 242,17–20: καὶ ὅταν ὁ Δαβὶδ εἴπῃ "ἐν ἁμαρτίαις συνελήφθην καὶ ἐν ἀνομίαις ἐκίσσησέν με ἡ μήτηρ μου", λέγει μὲν προφητικῶς μητέρα τὴν Εὕαν, ἀλλὰ "ζώντων Εὕα μήτηρ" ἐγένετο, καὶ εἰ ἐν ἁμαρτίᾳ συνελήφθη, ἀλλ' οὐκ αὐτὸς ἐν ἁμαρτίᾳ οὐδὲ μὴν ἁμαρτία αὐτός. Zur Symbolik von „Eva" vgl. auch Strom. III, 9, 65, 1 und 12, 80, 2: GCS 52, p. 225,29–226,1 und p. 232,15–17.

Sündenlehre bei Clemens von Alexandria 95

Im vierten Buch der *Stromata* kehrt Clemens jedoch im Kontext seiner Abhandlung über den Sinn des Leidens zu der Frage nach der Sündhaftigkeit kleiner Kinder zurück. Diese Abhandlung ist Teil von Clemens' Überlegungen zum Märtyrertum. Wieder als Reaktion auf Basilides[52], der verkündete, dass ein kleines Kind (Säugling) zwar nicht aktiv sündigen könne (ἐνεργῶς μὲν οὐχ ἡμαρτηκὸς οὐδέν), aber die Sünde in sich trage (ἐν ἑαυτῷ [τῷ] δὲ τὸ ἁμαρτῆσαι ἔχον)[53], macht Clemens darauf aufmerksam, dass bereits die Voraussetzung von Basilides, Seelen hätten in einem früheren Leben gesündigt und würden hier (in diesem Leben) nur ihre Strafe abbüßen, falsch ist. Die Seelen der Auserwählten sollen laut Basilides nämlich durch ein Märtyrertum gereinigt werden, die Seelen der Anderen aber durch Strafe[54].

> Wie kann aber dies wahr sein, da es doch in unserer Macht (ἐφ' ἡμῖν) steht, zu bekennen und bestraft zu werden oder nicht?[55]

protestiert hier Clemens und widerspricht dem Gedanken von Basilides vehement: Märtyrertum ist in seiner Sicht weder Vergeltung, noch Strafe, weil wir es freiwillig für unseren Glauben auf uns nehmen. Und nur so können wir den Begriffen des Glaubens, der Gottesliebe und unserer freiwilligen Entscheidung für Gott gerecht werden[56].

Die Betonung der Entscheidungsfreiheit und der eigenen Verantwortung hängt mit dem großen Vertrauen zusammen, das Clemens in den *Stromata* der Persönlichkeit des wahren Gnostikers schenkt. Ein fortgeschrittener Christ soll Vorbild für andere (Ungläubige und Anfänger in Sachen des Glaubens) sein; diese ahmen sein Handeln nach. Laut Clemens fasste es z. B. der Apostel Matthias treffend zusammen, dem in der Überlieferung folgender Satz zugesprochen wird:

---

[52] Vgl. *Clem. Alex.*, Strom. IV, 12, 81, 1–88, 5: GCS 52, p. 284,5–287,8. Der Text enthält ein umfangreiches Zitat aus der Schrift Bibelerklärungen (Exegetica) des Basilides; vgl. W. Löhr, Basilides und seine Schule, 122–159.
[53] *Clem. Alex.*, Strom. IV, 12, 82, 1: GCS 52, p. 284,15–22: εἶθ' ὑποβὰς πάλιν ἐπιφέρει· "ὡς οὖν τὸ νήπιον οὐ προημαρτηκὸς ἢ ἐνεργῶς μὲν οὐχ ἡμαρτηκὸς οὐδέν, ἐν ἑαυτῷ [τῷ] δὲ τὸ ἁμαρτῆσαι ἔχον, ἐπὰν ὑποβληθῇ τῷ παθεῖν, εὐεργετεῖται [τε], πολλὰ κερδαῖνον δύσκολα, οὑτωσὶ δὴ κἂν τέλειος μηδὲν ἡμαρτηκὼς ἔργῳ τύχῃ, πάσχῃ δέ, ὃ ἂν πάθῃ, τοῦτο ἔπαθεν ἐμφερῶς τῷ νηπίῳ· ἔχων μὲν <γὰρ> ἐν ἑαυτῷ τὸ ἁμαρτητικόν, ἀφορμὴν δὲ πρὸς τὸ ἡμαρτηκέναι μὴ λαβὼν οὐχ ἥμαρτανεν. ὥστ' οὐκ αὐτῷ τὸ μὴ ἁμαρτῆσαι λογιστέον [...]".
[54] Vgl. *Clem. Alex.*, Strom. IV, 12, 83, 2: GCS 52, p. 285,3–8.
[55] *Clem. Alex.*, Strom. IV, 12, 83, 2: GCS 52, p. 285,6–7: καὶ πῶς τοῦτο ἀληθὲς ἐφ' ἡμῖν κειμένου τοῦ ὁμολογῆσαι καὶ κολασθῆναι ἢ μή;
[56] Vgl. *Clem. Alex.*, Strom. IV, 12, 85, 2–3: GCS 52, p. 285,27–286,3.

Wenn der Nachbar eines auserwählten Mannes sündigte, so sündigte der Auserwählte; denn wenn dieser sein Leben so geführt hätte, wie es das göttliche Wort gebiete, so hätte im Blick auf dieses Leben auch sein Nachbar sich davor gehütet zu sündigen[57].

Gerade ein Gnostiker sollte diese Worte des Matthias verinnerlichen. Denn ein Gnostiker, der zu „Gottes Tempel" wird (vgl. 1Kor 3,16), ist als solcher „göttlich und bereits heilig; er trägt Gott in sich und wird selbst von Gott getragen," ergänzt Clemens den Apostel Matthias[58]. Einem Gnostiker sei es vollkommen fremd zu sündigen, so Clemens[59]. An einer anderen Stelle gelangt er dann zu der Formulierung, dass ein vollkommener Gnostiker „nie in Sünden verfällt"[60]. Damit ist sicher nicht gemeint, dass ein Gnostiker nicht sündigen kann, sondern vielmehr, dass er in dem Zustand von *apatheia* lebt, d. h. dass sein Leben frei von Leidenschaften ist und er sich somit nicht zur Sünde verführen lässt. Darüber hinaus erlaubt ihm die Nähe (Liebe) zu Gott nicht zu sündigen.

Zusammenfassung

Clemens' Überlegungen über die Sünde sind in den Kontext seiner Ausführungen über die Tugenden eingesetzt; das sind in Clemens' Auffassung in erster Linie Glaube, Furcht, Buße, Hoffnung und Liebe, die sich zusammen zur Erkenntnis verbinden, wie man an der Persönlichkeit eines vollkommenen Christen, d. h. des wahren Gnostikers beobachten kann. Der Autor, der

---

[57] Die Traditionen des Matthias, Fr. 3 in *Clem. Alex.*, Strom. VII, 13, 82, 1: GCS 17, p. 58,20–23: Λέγουσι δὲ ἐν ταῖς Παραδόσεσι Ματθίαν τὸν ἀπόστολον παρ' ἕκαστα εἰρηκέναι ὅτι "ἐὰν ἐκλεκτοῦ γείτων ἁμαρτήσῃ, ἥμαρτεν ὁ ἐκλεκτός· εἰ γὰρ οὕτως ἑαυτὸν ἦγεν, ὡς ὁ λόγος ὑπαγορεύει, κατῃδέσθη ἂν αὐτοῦ τὸν βίον καὶ ὁ γείτων εἰς τὸ μὴ ἁμαρτεῖν". Zu anderen Fragmenten dieser Schrift, die nur bei Clemens Alexandrinus erhalten sind, vgl. W. *Schneemelcher*, NT Apokryphen, I (Tübingen ⁶1990) 306–309. Den Apostel Matthias hebt Clemens als Vorbild auch in Strom. IV, 17, 105, 1-2: GCS 52, p. 294,18–25 hervor.
[58] *Clem. Alex.*, Strom. VII, 13, 82, 2: GCS 17, p. 58,23–26: τί τοίνυν περὶ αὐτοῦ τοῦ γνωστικοῦ φήσαιμεν <ἄν>; "ἢ οὐκ οἴδατε", φησὶν ὁ ἀπόστολος, "ὅτι ναός ἐστε τοῦ θεοῦ;" θεῖος ἄρα ὁ γνωστικὸς καὶ ἤδη ἅγιος, θεοφορῶν καὶ θεοφορούμενος.
[59] Vgl. *Clem. Alex.*, Strom. VII, 13, 82, 3: GCS 17, p. 58,26–28: αὐτίκα τὸ ἁμαρτῆσαι ἀλλότριον παριστᾶσα ἡ γραφὴ τοὺς μὲν παραπεσόντας τοῖς ἀλλοφύλοις πιπράσκει· "μὴ ἐμβλέψῃς" δὲ "πρὸς ἐπιθυμίαν ἀλλοτρίᾳ γυναικί" λέγουσα, ἄντικρυς ἀλλότριον καὶ παρὰ φύσιν τοῦ ναοῦ τοῦ θεοῦ τὴν ἁμαρτίαν λέγει.
[60] *Clem. Alex.*, Strom. VII, 12, 74, 6: GCS 17, p. 53,21–24: οὐ γάρ ἐστιν ὅπως ὑπὸ τοιούτων παιδευθείη ποτ' ἂν ὁ γνωστικὸς ἢ τερφθείη, ἐκ προαιρέσεως καλὸς καὶ ἀγαθὸς εἶναι συνασκήσας καὶ ταύτῃ ἄτεγκτος ἡδοναῖς γενόμενος· οὔποτε ὑποπίπτων ἁμαρτήμασιν [...]. Vgl. auch Strom. VII, 3, 14, 2; 12, 73, 1 und 12, 80, 2: GCS 17, p. 11,4; p. 52,23–24 und p. 57,11).

sich selbst in der Rolle eines Lehrers des christlichen Lebens sieht, interessiert sich weniger für die Frage, woher die Sünde in den Menschen gelangt, als eher dafür, wie man sie vermeiden kann: im Vordergrund stehen bei ihm die Fragen der Askese, die Möglichkeit der Buße und der Vergebung. Im Einklang mit Hebr 10,26–27 lehnt er die Sünde im Sinne eines freiwilligen Handelns eindeutig ab. Clemens' Formulierungen entstehen dabei einerseits aus seiner Inspiration durch die griechische Philosophie (in diesem Fall v.a. durch Aristoteles und die Stoiker), andererseits durch seine Bemühungen, sich von den Lehren der Gnostiker abzugrenzen, die die Sünder genauso wie den Glauben für eine Art Gegebenheit hielten und sich dabei auf ausgewählte Bibelverse (unter anderem Ps 50/51,7 und Röm 7,14–25) stützten. Clemens will dagegen zeigen, dass die Sünde, obwohl wir sie manchmal „unfreiwillig" begehen (da wir in der Tugend noch nicht genügend geübt sind), letztendlich immer von unserem Willen abhängt (ἐφ' ἡμῖν ἐστι). Entsprechend unserer wachsenden Verbundenheit mit Gott sollte sie daher vollkommen aus unserem Leben verschwinden.

Alexey Morozov, Fribourg (Suisse)

La notion du libre arbitre dans l'héritage littéraire de Méthode d'Olympe

Abstract :
In this paper, the author analyses three dialogues of a writer of the late third and early fourth centuries, Methodius of Olympus : On Free Will, On Resurrection and The Symposium. The first part of the article focuses on the question of free will as Methodius of Olympus' response to the existence of evil. The second part is devoted to the development of the fall of the first man and its consequences.

« Si l'on en juge d'après les œuvres qui nous sont parvenues », cet auteur « apparaît comme l'un des auteurs chrétiens anciens les plus intéressants. Il est pourtant aussi l'un des plus mystérieux »[1]. Cette caractéristique, attribuée par Emanuela Prinzivalli à Méthode d'Olympe, est absolument vraie, car, à part quelques éléments contradictoires, donnés dans la notice du traité de Jérôme *Sur les hommes illustres*, nous n'en savons rien de plus. Selon lui, Méthode était évêque d'Olympe en Lycie (Asie Mineure), puis de Tyr et il est mort lors des dernières persécutions (311–312)[2]. C'est à l'héritage de cet auteur anténicéen que sera consacrée cette contribution.

Le thème, lié au libre arbitre de l'homme et au péché originel[3], même si le péché originel n'apparaît nulle part comme terme dans les textes conservés du corpus méthodien, est traité en détail dans le dialogue, intitulé *De autexusio*.

---

[1] E. Prinzivalli, Méthode d'Olympe, in : B. Pouderon (dir.), Histoire de la littérature grecque chrétienne des origines à 451. Vol. III. De Clément d'Alexandrie à Eusèbe de Césarée (Paris 2017) 399–412, ici 399.
[2] Hieron. Strid., Vir. ill. 83 : E. C. Richardson, TU 14 (Leipzig 1896), p. 43–44. Pour plus de détails sur les sources anciennes et les hypothèses modernes relatives à la vie et à l'héritage littéraire de Méthode, voir : *A. Morozov*, Le De Resurrectione de Méthode d'Olympe : édition critique, traduction, commentaire. Partie I. Étude, Thèse de doctorat, Sorbonne Université et Université de Fribourg (thèse en cotutelle) (Paris - Fribourg 2023) 16–72.
[3] Ces sujets sont aussi traités, par exemple, dans : *J. Farge*, Les idées morales et religieuses de Méthode d'Olympe (Paris 1929) 100–116 ; *T. Badurina*, Doctrina S. Methodii de Olympio de peccato originali et de eius effectibus (Roma 1942) ; *R. Franchi*, Appendice V. Una difficile questione : Metodio et la dottrina sul peccato originale, in : R. Franchi, Metodio di Olimpo : Il libero arbitrio, Letture cristiane del primo millenio 53 (Milano 2015) 382–388.

Ce texte nous est parvenu grâce aux longs fragments grecs et à la traduction vieux-slave qui remonte au Xe s.[4] Son texte grec, ainsi que la version slavonne ont été édités en 1930 par André Vaillant[5] dont nous utiliserons l'édition et la traduction française.

Le deuxième traité dans lequel Méthode d'Olympe examine aussi ces questions, est intitulé *Contre Aglaophon, sur la résurrection*. Ce texte du début du IVe s.[6] est dirigé contre la conception origénienne de la résurrection des morts. Il est composé en trois livres sur le modèle des dialogues platoniciens. Rédigé initialement en grec, son texte complet ne nous est parvenu que grâce à sa traduction vieux-slave datant du même siècle que le traité précédent, tandis que d'importants fragments grecs de ce dialogue nous sont conservés par quelques auteurs postérieurs, comme Épiphane de Salamine, Photius, Jean Damascène, et par quelques florilèges. L'édition des textes grec et vieux-slave du *De resurrectione*, ainsi que sa traduction en français, ont été préparées par nous[7].

Enfin, le dernier traité que nous exploiterons dans notre contribution est le *Symposium*, texte conservé dans toute sa totalité en grec et dont la traduction vieux-slave a aussi été découverte par nous en 2019[8]. Le texte grec de ce dialogue, accompagné d'une traduction française, a été édité en 1963 dans la collection des «Sources chrétiennes»[9], cependant, en 2017, une nouvelle édition de ce texte a été proposée dans le cadre d'une thèse de doctorat par J. Sieber[10].

---

[4] A. Vaillant, Introduction, in : A. Vaillant, Le De Autexusio de Méthode d'Olympe. Version slave et texte grec édités et traduits en français, PO 22.5 (Paris 1930) 717–719.

[5] A. Vaillant, Le De Autexusio de Méthode d'Olympe. Version slave et texte grec édités et traduits en français, PO 22.5 (Paris 1930).

[6] M. Mejzner – M. B. Zorzi, Introduzione, in : M. Mejzner – M. B. Zorzi, Metodio di Olimpo. La risurrezione (Roma 2010) 25.

[7] A. Morozov, Le De Resurrectione de Méthode d'Olympe : édition critique, traduction, commentaire. Partie II. Édition critique, Thèse de doctorat, Sorbonne Université et Université de Fribourg (thèse en cotutelle) (Paris – Fribourg 2023); *idem*, Le De Resurrectione de Méthode d'Olympe : édition critique, traduction, commentaire. Partie III. Traduction, Thèse de doctorat, Sorbonne Université et Université de Fribourg (thèse en cotutelle) (Paris – Fribourg 2023).

[8] Voir : A. Morozov, Pour une édition critique du De Resurrectione de Méthode d'Olympe : enjeux et problèmes, in : M. Vinzent – K. Künzl (éds.), Papers presented at the Eighteenth International Conference on Patristic Studies held in Oxford 2019. Volume 23: Apocrypha et Gnostica; Ignatius of Antioch—The Mysterious Bishop; The Second and Third Centuries, Studia Patristica CXXVI (Leuven 2021) 397–406, ici 401.

[9] H. Musurillo – V.-H. Debidour, Méthode d'Olympe. Le Banquet, SC 95 (Paris 1963). C'est cette traduction française que nous utiliserons dans notre contribution.

[10] J. Sieber, Das Symposium des Methodius von Olympus. Überlieferung, Edition, Übersetzung und Erläuterungen. Inauguraldissertation zur Erlangung des Doktorgrades der Philosophie an der Ludwig-Maximilians-Universität München und UZH Zürich (München – Zü-

Quant à la traduction vieux-slave du *Banquet*, son édition est actuellement en préparation.

C'est sur ces trois textes que nous établirons notre analyse de la notion du libre arbitre et du thème de la chute du premier homme dans l'héritage littéraire de Méthode d'Olympe. Pour ce faire, nous procéderons en deux temps. Premièrement, nous aborderons la question du libre arbitre comme réponse à l'existence du mal ; deuxièmement, nous examinerons le développement proposé par Méthode concernant la chute ancestrale et ses conséquences.

I. Libre arbitre et existence du mal

1. Existence du mal

Le problème, posé par l'existence du mal et celle de Dieu, est une question à la fois philosophique et théologique qui a fait couler beaucoup d'encre au cours de l'histoire[11]. Méthode d'Olympe ne fait pas exception et il y consacre un de ces traités. Il s'agit du *De autexusio* dans lequel ce problème est traité comme point de départ pour la réflexion méthodienne relative à la notion du libre arbitre.

Cette question est introduite par le premier hétérodoxe du dialogue, identifié dans la tradition de la transmission de ce texte comme le représentant de la doctrine gnostique (en particulier, celle de Valentin)[12]. Pour ne pas reprocher à Dieu la création du mal[13], ce personnage propose une solution fondée sur une des théories relatives au principe de la constitution de l'univers : à savoir

---

rich 2017), p. 48–199. URL : https ://edoc.ub.uni-muenchen.de/22522/1/Sieber_Janina.pdf.
[11] Voir, par exemple : *Ch. Meister – P. K. Moser*, The Cambridge Companion to the Problem of Evil (Cambridge 2017).
[12] Une telle attribution est donnée dans le *Dialogue d'Adamantius*, pour plus de détails et d'autres hypothèses concernant l'identification des adversaires de ce traité, voir : A. Vaillant, Introduction, 639–643.
[13] *Méth. Olymp.*, Autex. III, 6–7 : PO 22.5, p. 740–741 : Τοσούτων τοίνυν καὶ τοιούτων θεατὴς γενόμενος ἐγὼ πόθεν ταῦτα ἀναζητεῖν ἠρχόμην, τίς δὲ καὶ ἡ τῆς κινήσεως αὐτῶν ἀρχή, καὶ τίς ὁ τοσαῦτα κακὰ ἀνθρώπων μηχανησάμενος, πόθεν τε ἡ εὕρεσις αὐτῶν, καὶ τίς ὁ τούτων διδάσκαλος. Καὶ τὸν μὲν θεὸν ποιητὴν τούτων λέγειν τολμᾶν οὐχ οἷός τε ἤν, ἀλλὰ μὴν οὐδὲ ἐξ αὐτοῦ τὴν ὑπόστασιν ἔχειν οὐδὲ τὴν τοῦ εἶναι σύστασιν. Πῶς γὰρ οἷόν τε ἦν ταῦτα περὶ θεοῦ ἐννοεῖν ; […] Καὶ πῶς οὐκ ἄτοπον ἦν τὸν θεὸν τούτων λέγειν δημιουργόν, τὸν ταῦτα παραιτούμενον ; Trad. : « Témoin de tant de crimes, j'entreprenais d'en chercher l'origine : je me demandais quel est leur principe moteur, quel être a inventé tout ce mal chez les hommes, où ils en ont fait la découverte et qui le leur a enseigné. Lui donner Dieu comme créateur, je ne me sentais pas l'audace de le faire, encore moins d'admettre qu'il a en Dieu sa substance ou sa réalisation. Comment en effet concevoir de Dieu ces idées ? […] Et comment ne serait-il pas absurde de faire de Dieu le créateur du mal, lui qui le réprouve ? ».

que l'univers est issu de la matière coexistant éternellement à Dieu ou bien de Dieu tout seul[14].

Quant à l'idée de la création *ex nihilo*, défendue par Méthode d'Olympe, elle est rejetée par son interlocuteur, puisque, selon ce dernier, elle peut aboutir à la conclusion d'après laquelle c'est Dieu qui est le créateur du mal. En effet, selon la logique hétérodoxe, exposée dans ce traité, l'adhésion à cette théorie a comme conséquence inévitable la responsabilité divine dans la création du mal, car soit c'est Dieu lui-même qui a laissé exister le mal, tiré par lui du néant, soit il se complaisait jadis dans le mal, alors que maintenant ce n'est plus le cas. Comme toutes ces explications sont impossibles à appliquer à Dieu, l'interlocuteur de Méthode propose de prendre comme fondement la théorie de la coexistence éternelle de la matière à partir de laquelle le mal tire son origine lorsque Dieu commence à façonner la matière « en en séparant les bons des éléments mauvais »[15].

En réfutant cette théorie hétérodoxe, Méthode avance comme contrargument la nécessité de l'existence du troisième incréé en tant que séparateur,

---

[14] *Méth. Olymp.*, Autex. II, 9 : PO 22.5, p. 735-737 : ἀλλὰ τὸ λοιπὸν ὅθεν ταῦτα τὴν σύστασιν ἔχει ζητεῖν ἠρχόμην, πότερον ἔκ τινος συνόντος ἀεὶ τῷ θεῷ ἢ ἐξ αὐτοῦ καὶ μόνου, συνυπάρχοντος αὐτῷ οὐδενός. Τὸ γὰρ ἐξ οὐκ ὄντων πεποιηκέναι οὐδὲ σκοπεῖν μοι καλῶς ἐδόκει, τέλεον ἀπίθανον <τοῖς πολλοῖς> ὑπάρχοντος τοῦ λόγου· τὰ γὰρ γινόμενα ἐξ ὄντων πέφυκε τὴν σύστασιν ἔχειν. Trad. : « J'entreprenais maintenant de chercher le principe de la constitution de cet univers, s'il tire son origine de quelque chose qui coexistait éternellement à Dieu ou bien de Dieu seul, sans rien de coexistant à lui. En effet, que Dieu l'ait créé du néant, c'est une hypothèse qu'il ne me semblait pas même à propos de discuter, car elle est jugée complètement invraisemblable par la plupart des philosophes : c'est une loi que rien ne vient de rien ».

[15] *Méth. Olymp.*, Autex. III, 8-9 : PO 22.5, p. 741-743 : ἢ εἰ τοῦτο, ἀνάγκη λέγειν ὡς ἦν ποτε καιρὸς ὅτε τοῖς κακοῖς ἔχαιρεν ὁ θεός, νῦν δὲ οὐκέτι, ὅπερ ἀδύνατον εἶναί μοι δοκεῖ λέγειν τοῦτο περὶ θεοῦ· ἀνοίκειον γὰρ αὐτοῦ τῆς φύσεως τοῦτο προσαρμόζειν αὐτῷ. Διόπερ ἔδοξέ μοι συνυπάρχειν τι αὐτῷ ᾧ τοὔνομα ὕλη, ἐξ ἧς τὰ ὄντα ἐδημιούργησε τέχνῃ σοφῇ διακρίνας καὶ διακοσμήσας καλῶς, ἐξ ἧς καὶ τὰ κακὰ εἶναι δοκεῖ. ὁποίου γὰρ καὶ ἀσχηματίστου οὔσης αὐτῆς, πρὸς δὲ τούτοις καὶ ἀτάκτως φερομένης, δεομένης τε τῆς τοῦ θεοῦ τέχνης, οὐκ ἐφθόνησεν οὗτος οὔτε διὰ παντὸς καταλιπεῖν αὐτὴν οὕτως φέρεσθαι, ἀλλὰ δημιουργεῖν ἤρχετο καὶ ἀπὸ τῶν χειρίστων αὐτῆς τὰ κάλλιστα διακρίνειν ἤθελεν. Trad. : « Si toutefois on doit concéder que quelque chose puisse naître de rien – en disant que Dieu créateur a créé aussi le mal. Car celui qui l'aurait fait sortir du néant ne l'y ferait pas rentrer dans la suite. Ou sinon, il faut admettre qu'il y a eu un temps où Dieu se complaisait dans le mal, tandis qu'il ne s'y complaît plus maintenant : hypothèse qu'il me parait impossible de formuler à propos de Dieu, ce changement qu'on lui attribuerait étant contraire à sa nature. Pour ces raisons, je crus devoir admettre que quelque chose coexistait à Dieu, ce qu'on nomme la matière, dont son art savant a fait l'univers en en séparant les éléments et l'ordonnant d'une façon heureuse : c'est de cette matière que le mal doit tirer son origine. Sans qualités et sans forme, et en outre agitée d'un mouvement désordonné, elle réclamait l'industrie de Dieu. Il ne s'y refusa pas et voulut bien ne pas l'abandonner éternellement à cette agitation confuse : il entreprit de la façonner et se proposa d'en séparer les bons éléments des éléments mauvais ».

afin que les deux incréés, Dieu et la matière, puissent être distingués l'un de l'autre, ce qui provoquerait ainsi l'existence du nombre infini des incréés pour qu'ils puissent séparer chaque incréé des autres[16].

Après l'avoir fait, l'auteur du dialogue entreprend aussi la démonstration de l'incohérence de la deuxième théorie proposée, d'après laquelle Dieu a fait sortir la matière pour la création de ce monde à partir de lui-même. Pour cette hypothèse, Méthode d'Olympe présente deux développements possibles : soit c'est Dieu qui résidait dans la matière, soit c'est la matière qui était placée en Dieu. D'après Méthode, la conséquence de la première hypothèse revient à accepter le caractère limité et circonscrit de Dieu qui subit des mouvements désordonnés, ce qui est absolument impossible[17]. Concernant la deuxième hypothèse, si on suppose que la matière est placée en Dieu comme les oiseaux dans l'air, on introduit la division en Dieu, tandis que si c'est à l'image de

---

[16] *Méth. Olymp.*, Autex. V, 1–4 : PO 22.5, p. 747-749 : Ὅτι μὲν ὑπάρχειν ἀδύνατον ἀγένητα δύο ἅμα […], τῷ πάντως ἐξ ἀνάγκης τὸ ἕτερον δεῖν λέγειν, ἢ ὅτι κεχώρισται τῆς ὕλης ὁ θεὸς, ἢ αὖ πάλιν ὅτι ἀμέριστος αὐτῆς τυγχάνει. Εἰ μὲν οὖν ἡνῶσθαί τις αὐτὸν εἰπεῖν ἐθέλοι, ἓν τὸ ἀγένητον λέξει· ἕκαστον γὰρ τούτων μέρος ἔσται τοῦ πλησίον, ἀλλήλων δὲ μέρη τυγχάνοντα οὐκ ἔσται ἀγένητα δύο, ἀλλ᾽ ἓν ἐκ διαφόρων συνεστώς. […] Εἰ δὲ κεχωρίσθαι φήσει τις, ἀνάγκη εἶναί τι τὸ ἀνὰ μέσον ἀμφοτέρων, ὅπερ καὶ τὸν χωρισμὸν αὐτῶν δείκνυσιν· ἀδύνατον γὰρ ἐν διαστάσει ἐξετάζεσθαί τι ἀπό τινος οὐκ ὄντος ἑτέρου καθ᾽ ὃ ἡ διάστασις ἑκατέρου γίνεται. Ὅπερ οὐ μέχρι τούτου ἵσταται καὶ μόνου, ἀλλὰ καὶ πλείστων ὅσων· ὃν γὰρ ἐπὶ τῶν δύο ἀγενήτων εἴπαμεν λόγον, τοῦτον ἐξ ἀνάγκης ὁμοίως προχωρεῖν, εἰ τὰ ἀγένητα δοθείη τρία. Trad. : « Qu'il ne puisse pas exister deux incréés à la fois […]. Car il faut, de toute nécessité, dire de deux choses l'une : qu'entre Dieu et la matière il y a séparation, ou bien indivision. Or si l'on se prononce pour l'union, on affirme que l'incréé est un : chacun d'eux sera partie du tout de l'autre, et étant mutuellement parties d'un même tout, ils ne constitueront pas deux incréés, mais un seul, composé de parties diverses. […] Mais si l'on prononce que Dieu est séparé de la matière, il faut qu'il y ait quelque être dans l'intervalle qui marque leur séparation. On ne peut pas en effet observer qu'une chose est distante d'une autre en dehors de l'existence d'un troisième élément qui fasse mesurer cette distance entre les deux choses. Et ce n'est pas la seule conclusion à laquelle aboutisse l'argument : son développement est illimité. Car le raisonnement que nous avons appliqué aux deux incréés vaudra également, de toute nécessité, pour le cas où on admet trois incréés ».

[17] *Méth. Olymp.*, Autex. VI, 1–2 : PO 22.5, p. 750-751 : ἐὰν τόπον τοῦ θεοῦ τὴν ὕλην εἴπωμεν, ἐξ ἀνάγκης αὐτὸν καὶ χωρητὸν λέγειν δεῖ καὶ πρὸς τῆς ὕλης περιγραφόμενον. Ἀλλὰ μὴν καὶ ὁμοίως αὐτὸν τῇ ὕλῃ ἀτάκτως φέρεσθαι δεῖ, μὴ ἵστασθαι δὲ μηδὲ μένειν αὐτὸν ἐφ᾽ ἑαυτοῦ ἀνάγκη, τοῦ ἐν ᾧ ἐστιν ἄλλοτε ἄλλως φερομένου. Πρὸς δὴ τούτοις καὶ ἐν χείροσι γεγονέναι τὸν θεὸν εἰπεῖν ἀνάγκη […]. Trad. : « Si nous disons que la matière était le lieu de Dieu, il faut dire nécessairement du même coup que Dieu était limité par un contenant et qu'il était circonscrit par la matière. D'autre part, il devait être agité comme elle d'un mouvement désordonné, sans connaître l'immobilité ni la permanence, puisque son contenant se mouvait tantôt d'un côté tantôt de l'autre. En outre, nous voilà forcés également d'admettre que Dieu a séjourné dans un milieu bien inférieur […] ».

La notion du libre arbitre dans l'héritage littéraire de Méthode d'Olympe 103

l'eau dans la terre, on introduit ainsi la confusion et le mal en Dieu[18] ; toutes ces conséquences sont donc aussi impossibles à imaginer.

Ayant réfuté les deux solutions données par son interlocuteur, Méthode d'Olympe propose de considérer encore une fois la théorie de la coexistence éternelle de la matière en faisant la distinction aristotélicienne entre la substance (οὐσία) et les qualités (ποιότης). D'après lui, même si on accepte l'idée de la coexistence, il faudra, quand même, reconnaître que c'est Dieu qui a formé la matière première en lui donnant différentes qualités, qui sont, quant à elles, tirées du néant[19].

Pour Méthode d'Olympe, le mal est à la fois un accident (συμβεβηκός) et une qualité qu'il définit comme l'acte d'un être agissant :

> Eh bien, si la substance est une essence corporelle, si l'essence corporelle ne réclame pas l'existence d'une autre essence dans laquelle se réaliser, si le mal existe comme acte d'un être agissant, si les actes réclament l'existence d'un être agissant dans lequel ils se réalisent, le mal ne sera pas une substance. Si le mal est une substance, et si le meurtre est un mal, le meurtre sera une substance. Mais en fait le meurtre n'est que l'acte d'un être agissant : le meurtre n'est donc pas une substance [...]. Nous nommons l'homme tantôt un méchant, tantôt un homme de bien : mais c'est à cause des crimes ou au contraire des bonnes actions qu'il accomplit, et ces qualifi-

---

[18] *Méth. Olymp.*, Autex. VI, 4–5 : PO 22.5, p. 752–753 : Εἰ δὲ τὴν ὕλην ἐν τῷ θεῷ εἶναί τις λέξει, ὁμοίως ἐξετάζειν δεῖ, πότερον ὡς διϊσταμένου αὐτοῦ ἀφ' ἑαυτοῦ, καὶ ὥσπερ ἐν ἀέρι ζῴων ὑπάρχει γένη, διαιρουμένου καὶ μεριζομένου αὐτοῦ εἰς ὑποδοχὴν τῶν γινομένων ἐν αὐτῷ· ἢ ὡς ἐν τόπῳ, τουτέστιν ὥσπερ ἐν γῇ ὕδωρ. Εἰ μὲν γὰρ εἴποιμεν ὡς ἐν ἀέρι, μεριστὸν ἀνάγκη τὸν θεὸν εἰπεῖν. Εἰ δ' ὥσπερ ἐν γῇ ὕδωρ, ἣν δὲ ἄτακτος ἡ ὕλη καὶ ἀκόσμητος, πρὸς δὴ τούτοις ἔχουσα καὶ κακά, τὸν θεὸν λέγειν ἀνάγκη τόπον εἶναι τῶν ἀκοσμήτων καὶ τῶν κακῶν. Trad. : « Si l'on dit que c'est la matière qui était en Dieu, il faut également examiner les deux façons de l'entendre : prétend-on que Dieu était discontinu et que la matière était en lui comme sont les espèces animales dans l'air, qui s'écarte et se partage pour recevoir ce qui naît en son sein, ou bien que la matière était en Dieu comme dans un lieu, c'est-à-dire comme l'eau dans la terre ? Si nous répondons : comme les animaux dans l'air, il faut nécessairement dire que Dieu était divisé. Si nous répondons : comme l'eau dans la terre, puisque la matière était dans le désordre et la confusion, et qu'en outre elle portait en elle le mal, nous sommes forcés de dire de Dieu qu'il était le lieu de la confusion et du mal ».

[19] *Méth. Olymp.*, Autex. VII, 4 : PO 22.5, p. 754–755 : Οὐκοῦν εἰ μήτε ἐξ ὑποκειμένων ποιοτήτων τὰς ποιότητας ἐδημιούργησεν ὁ θεός, μήτε ἐκ τῶν οὐσιῶν ὑπάρχουσιν, τῷ μηδὲ οὐσίας αὐτὰς εἶναι, ἐκ μὴ ὄντων αὐτὰς ὑπὸ τοῦ θεοῦ γεγονέναι ἀνάγκη εἰπεῖν· ὅθεν περιττῶς ἐδόκεις μοι λέγειν ἀδύνατον εἶναι δοξάζειν ἐξ οὐκ ὄντων γεγονέναι τι πρὸς τοῦ θεοῦ. Trad. : « Eh bien, si d'une part Dieu n'a pas formé les qualités en en prenant la matière dans des qualités préexistantes, et si d'autre part elles ne sont pas issues des substances, n'étant pas substances elles-mêmes, il faut nécessairement dire que Dieu les a tirées du néant. C'est pourquoi tes déclarations sur l'impossibilité de penser que Dieu ait créé quelque chose de rien m'apparaissaient tout à l'heure superflues ».

catifs qu'on attache à la substance ne représentent que ses accidents, qui ne sont pas la substance elle-même[20].

Grâce à cette distinction entre la substance et les qualités, l'auteur du traité démontre de nouveau que la théorie de la coexistence éternelle de la matière n'aide pas à préserver Dieu de la responsabilité de l'existence du mal. Car, «si le mal était une qualité de la substance, si la matière était sans qualités, si Dieu est le créateur des qualités, [...], Dieu sera aussi l'auteur du mal»[21].

C'est à cette conclusion de Méthode d'Olympe que répond le deuxième hétérodoxe du dialogue en proposant de considérer la matière comme «pourvue de qualités de toute éternité»[22]. Cependant, cette solution ne peut pas aider non plus à préserver Dieu de toute accusation, car il s'ensuit nécessairement : soit que Dieu a transformé des qualités premières de la matière en qualités mauvaises, soit qu'il n'a pas pu transformer ces qualités mauvaises de la matière première à cause de son refus de le faire ou bien à cause de son impuissance :

> Eh bien, si le mal est une qualité de la matière, et si Dieu a modifié les qualités de la matière dans le sens du bien, il faut chercher d'où vient le mal. En effet, les qualités n'ont pas gardé leur nature primitive. Alors, de deux choses l'une : s'il n'y avait pas au début de qualité du mal, et si tu prétends que c'est la transformation des qualités originelles opérée par Dieu qui a pourvu la matière d'une qualité de cette sorte, la cause du mal sera Dieu, qui aura transformé en qualités mauvaises des qualités qui ne l'étaient pas. Ou bien tu admets que la qualité du mal n'a pas subi de modification, et que ce sont uniquement les autres qualités, celles qui étaient indifférentes au bien et au mal, que Dieu a modifiées dans le sens du bien pour ordonner l'univers [...]. Eh bien, en disant que Dieu a laissé sans changement la qualité du mal, comment

---

[20] *Méth. Olymp.*, Autex. VIII, 9–11 : PO 22.5, p. 760–761 : Οὐκοῦν εἰ ἡ οὐσία σωματική τίς ἐστι σύστασις, ἡ δὲ σωματικὴ σύστασις οὐ δεῖταί τινος, ἐν ᾧ γενομένη τὸ εἶναι λήψεται· τὰ δὲ κακὰ ἐνέργειαι ὑπάρχουσί τινος, αἱ δὲ ἐνέργειαι δέονταί τινος, ἐν ᾧ γενόμεναι τὸ εἶναι λαμβάνουσιν, οὐκ ἔσονται οὐσίαι τὰ κακά. Εἰ δὲ οὐσίαι τὰ κακά, κακὸν δὲ ὁ φόνος, οὐσία ἔσται ὁ φόνος. [...] λέγομεν δὲ τὸν ἄνθρωπόν ποτε μὲν κακὸν διὰ τὸ φονεύειν, ποτὲ δ' αὖ πάλιν διὰ τὸ εὐεργετεῖν ἀγαθόν· καὶ πέπλεκται ταῦτα τὰ ὀνόματα τῇ οὐσίᾳ ἐκ τῶν συμβεβηκότων αὐτῇ, ἅτινα οὐκ ἔστιν αὐτή.
[21] *Méth. Olymp.*, Autex. VIII, 7 : PO 22.5, p. 757 : εἰ τὰ κακὰ ποιότητες ὑπάρχουσιν οὐσιῶν, ἡ δὲ ὕλη ἄποιος ἦν, τῶν δὲ ποιοτήτων ποιητὴν [...] τὸν θεὸν εἶναι, ἔσται καὶ τῶν κακῶν δημιουργὸς ὁ θεός.
[22] *Méth. Olymp.*, Autex. IX, 3 : PO 22.5, p. 765 : [...] ἡ ὕλη ποιότητας ἀνάρχως ἔχειν δοκεῖ· οὕτως γὰρ καὶ τὰ κακὰ ἐκ τῆς ἀπορροίας αὐτῆς εἶναι λέγω, ἵνα τῶν κακῶν ὁ μὲν θεὸς ἀναίτιος ᾖ, τούτων δ' ἁπάντων ἡ ὕλη αἰτία. Trad. : «[...] la matière est de toute éternité pourvue de qualités. Cette thèse me permet d'expliquer le mal comme une émanation de la matière, afin que la responsabilité de l'existence du mal ne tombe pas sur Dieu, mais sur la matière, cause du mal sous toutes ses formes».

La notion du libre arbitre dans l'héritage littéraire de Méthode d'Olympe 105

l'entends-tu ? Admets-tu qu'il pouvait la détruire comme les autres, mais qu'il ne l'a pas voulu, ou bien estimes-tu qu'il n'en avait pas le pouvoir ? Si tu dis qu'il le pouvait, mais qu'il ne l'a pas voulu, il te faut convenir que c'est lui le responsable du mal, puisqu'il a toléré que le mal subsistât alors qu'il pouvait le supprimer[23].

Dans sa réponse à ce deuxième interlocuteur, l'auteur du dialogue introduit aussi un nouvel élément important. Il s'agit du choix de l'être agissant[24], car, selon lui, aucun acte ne peut être mal par nature, mais il devient mauvais « du point de vue de l'usage qu'on en fait ». Pour illustrer sa thèse, Méthode d'Olympe propose d'analyser cinq crimes, à savoir l'adultère, la fornication, le meurtre, le vol et l'idolâtrie :

> Le terme d'adultère désigne les relations entre un homme et une femme. Mais si un homme a des rapports avec sa femme en vue de la procréation et pour perpétuer sa race, ces relations sont une chose bonne. Si un autre délaisse le commerce de son épouse légitime pour faire outrage aux droits conjugaux d'autrui, il commet une action mauvaise. L'acte charnel est le même dans les deux cas, mais le mode d'usage en est différent < : le premier de ces deux hommes s'assure une paternité incontestée, le second rend la paternité douteuse>[25].

---

[23] Méth. Olymp., Autex. XI, 1–3 : PO 22.5, p. 770-771 : Οὐκοῦν εἰ ποιότητες ὕλης τὰ κακά, τὰς δὲ ποιότητας αὐτῆς εἰς τὸ κρεῖττον ἔτρεψεν ὁ θεός, πόθεν τὰ κακὰ ζητεῖν ἀνάγκη. Οὐ γὰρ ἔμειναν αἱ ποιότητες ὁποῖαί ποτε ἦσαν τῇ φύσει. Ἢ εἰ μὲν πρότερον οὐκ ἦσαν αἱ ποιότητες κακαί, ἐκ δὲ τοῦ τραπῆναι πρὸς τοῦ θεοῦ τὰς πρώτας τοιαύτας περὶ τὴν ὕλην γεγονέναι ποιότητας φῇς, αἴτιος ἔσται τῶν κακῶν ὁ θεός, τρέψας τὰς οὐκ οὔσας ποιότητας κακὰς εἰς τὸ εἶναι κακάς· ἢ τὰς μὲν κακὰς ποιότητας εἰς τὸ κρεῖττον οὐ δοκεῖ σοι τρέψαι τὸν θεόν, τὰς δὲ λοιπὰς καὶ μόνας, ὅσαι ἀδιάφοροι ἐτύγχανον, τῆς διακοσμήσεως ἕνεκα πρὸς τοῦ θεοῦ τετράφθαι [...]. Πῶς τοίνυν αὐτὸν τὰς τῶν φαύλων ποιότητας ὡς εἶχον καταλελοιπέναι λέγεις; Πότερον δυνάμενον μὲν κἀκείνας ἀνελεῖν, οὐ βουληθέντα δέ, ἢ τὸ δύνασθαι μὴ ἔχοντα; Εἰ μὲν γὰρ δυνάμενον λέξεις, οὐ βουληθέντα δέ, αὐτὸν αἴτιον τούτων εἰπεῖν ἀνάγκη, ὅτι δυνάμενος ποιῆσαι μὴ εἶναι κακὰ συνεχώρησεν αὐτὰ μένειν ὡς ἦν.

[24] Méth. Olymp., Autex. XIII, 5 : PO 22.5, p. 782-783 : Εἰ δὲ οὐδ' ὁπότερον τούτων εἰπεῖν ἐθέλοις, πρᾶξιν ἀρχὴν τοῦ εἶναι λαμβάνει. Πρὸς δὲ τούτοις οὐδὲν ἕτερον παρὰ ταῦτα τὸ κακὸν εἰπεῖν ἔχεις· ποίαν γὰρ πρᾶξιν κακὴν ἑτέραν παρὰ τὰ ἐν ἀνθρώποις δεικνύειν ἔχεις; Ὅτι γὰρ ὁ ἐνεργῶν οὐ κατὰ τὸν τῆς οὐσίας λόγον ὑπάρχει κακία, κατὰ δὲ τὸν τῆς προαιρέσεως τρόπον, τοιαῦτα πράττειν ἐπαναιρούμενος ἐξ ὧν τοῦ κακὸς λέγεσθαι τὴν προσηγορίαν λαμβάνει, προλαβὼν ἔδειξα τῷ λόγῳ. Trad. : « Mais tu peux repousser les deux thèses à la fois, et concevoir les manifestations du mal chez les hommes comme des produits de l'activité d'un Mal agissant. Alors tu dénonces le mal comme créé, car l'activité d'un être agissant a un commencement ; et d'autre part tu ne peux faire du mal rien de plus que ses manifestations chez les hommes, car quel produit d'une activité mauvaise as-tu à indiquer en dehors des actions humaines ? Nous avons vu en effet que l'être agissant n'est pas méchanceté en tant que substance, mais d'après la façon dont il se conduit volontairement, et en tant qu'il choisit d'accomplir les actes qui lui valent l'appellation de méchant : c'est une des prémisses que j'ai établies dans ma démonstration ».

[25] Méth. Olymp., Autex. XV, 1 : PO 22.5, p. 788-789 : Τὸ τῆς μοιχείας ὄνομα κοινωνίας ἐστὶν ἀνδρὸς καὶ γυναικὸς σημαντικόν. Ἀλλ' ἐὰν κοινωνῇ τις τῇ γυναικὶ παιδοποιίας ἕνεκα καὶ τῆς

Ainsi, pour Méthode, le mal doit être défini comme une qualité qui résulte de l'intention d'un être agissant qui accomplit cet acte. Une telle définition fait surgir une autre question : d'où vient cette mauvaise attitude de l'homme ?

- S'agit-il de l'impulsion vers le mal, située dans les hommes eux-mêmes et qui les pousse à inventer le mauvais usage ?
- Ou bien, est-ce par nature que les hommes agissent, étant créés ainsi par Dieu ?
- Ou encore, y a-t-il un autre qui les incite ?

2. Fatalité et libre arbitre

C'est dans ce cadre que Méthode introduit la notion du libre arbitre en rejetant chacune des trois réponses proposées par son interlocuteur. Cependant, avant de passer à la définition que l'auteur du dialogue donne à ce terme, il nous paraît nécessaire d'évoquer aussi quelques arguments, développés par lui en vue de la réfutation d'une autre réponse possible à cette question, à savoir la fatalité. L'auteur en parle dans son autre traité, *Symposium*.

Il s'agit d'une doctrine, répandue à l'époque de Méthode dans le milieu païen selon laquelle le destin des hommes serait dicté par le mouvement des astres. Parmi les différents arguments avancés dans ce traité, il y en a deux que nous aimerions évoquer et qui sont aussi liés à la question de l'existence du mal et de la responsabilité de Dieu.

Premièrement, Méthode d'Olympe souligne le fait que si on accepte que les «nécessités inévitables d'un destin et ses arrêts non écrits» gouvernent l'homme, on doit accuser Dieu de la création du mal, car c'est lui qui a créé et qui gouverne les astres déterminant la présence des vertus et des vices dans l'homme :

τοῦ γένους διαδοχῆς, ἀγαθή τις ἡ κοινωνία γίνεται· εἰ δέ τις καταλιπὼν τὴν νομίμην κοινωνίαν ἐνυβρίζοι γάμοις ἀλλοτρίοις, ἔργον πράττει κακόν. Καὶ ἡ μὲν κοινωνία ἡ αὐτή, ὁ δὲ τῆς χρήσεως τρόπος οὐχ ὅμοιος· <ὃ μὲν γὰρ γνήσιος γίνεται πατήρ, ὃ δ' ἄγνωστον ποιεῖ τὸν τεκόντα>.

Poser que l'homme n'a pas de libre arbitre, prétendre qu'il est gouverné par les nécessités inévitables d'un destin et par ses arrêts non écrits, c'est outrager Dieu lui-même en faisant de lui la source et l'auteur du péché humain. Car si c'est lui qui dirige toute la révolution circulaire des astres, harmonieusement, par son ineffable et inconcevable sagesse, tenant ferme le gouvernail de l'univers, et si ce sont les astres qui déterminent dans notre vie les modalités du vice et de la vertu, en y enchaînant les hommes par des liens de nécessité, alors ces gens-là font apparaître Dieu comme cause responsable et comme dispensateur des maux. Mais Dieu n'est cause d'aucun dommage pour personne[26].

Deuxièmement, il s'agit de l'argument qui s'appuie sur l'existence des lois dans ce monde. En effet, s'il existe une fatalité, elle exclut inévitablement les lois, car elles ne peuvent pas empêcher l'homme, destiné déjà par cette fatalité, à commettre des crimes, mais les lois existent, de même que Dieu donne aussi des commandements à l'homme :

> Et puis, si c'est sa naissance qui voue fatalement un homme à s'ensanglanter les mains d'un meurtre, tandis que la loi le lui interdit, alors, en châtiant les criminels et en faisant obstacle par ses menaces à l'accomplissement des décrets de la fatalité, tels qu'injustices, adultères, vols, empoisonnements, la loi va contre la fatalité de naissance ; car ces actes que la fatalité a déterminés, la loi les empêche tous, et tous ceux que la loi empêche, la fatalité contraint à les commettre : donc la loi fait la guerre à la fatalité. Et si elle lui fait la guerre, les législateurs, si l'on se place dans la perspective fataliste, ne sont pas des législateurs, puisque ceux qui prennent des décrets en contradiction avec la fatalité sapent la fatalité. Ainsi donc, ou bien il y a fatalité de naissance, et il ne devrait pas y avoir de lois, ou bien il y a des lois et elles contreviennent à la fatalité[27].

---

[26] *Méth. Olymp.*, Symp. VIII, 16, 220–221 : SC 95, p. 248–249 : Οἱ διοριζόμενοι μὴ εἶναι τὸν ἄνθρωπον αὐτεξούσιον, ἀλλ' ἀνάγκαις ἀφύκτοις εἱμαρμένης λέγοντες οἰακίζεσθαι καὶ ἀγράφοις προστάγμασιν, εἰς αὐτὸν ἀσεβοῦσι τὸν θεὸν παρεκτικὸν τῶν ἀνθρωπίνων αὐτὸν κακῶν καὶ ποιητὴν εἰσηγούμενοι. Εἰ γὰρ τὴν τῶν ἀστέρων ἅπασαν κυκλικὴν κίνησιν ἐμμελῶς αὐτὸς ἀφράστῳ σοφίᾳ καὶ ἀνεννοήτῳ διέπει κατευθύνων τὸν οἴακα τῆς οἰκουμένης, οἱ δὲ ἀστέρες τὰς ποιότητας τῆς κακίας καὶ τῆς ἀρετῆς ἐκτελοῦσι τῷ βίῳ ἀνάγκης δεσμοῖς τοὺς ἀνθρώπους ἕλκοντες εἰς ταῦτα, αἴτιον τῶν κακῶν τὸν θεὸν ἀποφαίνονται καὶ δότην. Ἀλλ' ἀναίτιος πᾶσι πάσης βλάβης ὁ θεός.
[27] *Méth. Olymp.*, Symp. VIII, 16, 224–225 : SC 95, p. 252–253 :Ἔτι εἰ τὸ ἀνελεῖν τινα καὶ φόνῳ τὰς χεῖρας αἱμάξαι γένεσις ἐργάζεται, τοῦτο δὲ νόμος κωλύει κολάζων τοὺς ἀλάστορας καὶ δι' ἀπειλῆς ἀπείργων τὰ τῆς γενέσεως δόγματα, οἷον τὸ ἀδικῆσαι, μοιχεύσασθαι, κλέψαι, φαρμακεῦσαι, ἐναντίον ἄρα νόμος γενέσει. Ὅσα μὲν γὰρ γένεσις ὥρισε, ταῦτα νόμος κωλύει, ὅσα δὲ νόμος κωλύει, ταῦτα γένεσις ποιεῖν βιάζεται. Πολέμιον ἄρα γενέσει νόμος. Εἰ δὲ πολέμιον, οὐκ ἄρα κατὰ γένεσιν οἱ νομοθέται νομοθέται· τὰ γὰρ ἐναντία δογματίζοντες γενέσει γένεσιν λύουσιν. Ἤτοι οὖν γένεσις ἔστι καὶ οὐκ ἐχρῆν εἶναι νόμους, ἢ εἰσὶ νόμοι καὶ οὐκ εἰσὶ κατὰ γένεσιν.

Ainsi, l'hypothèse, selon laquelle la mauvaise attitude de l'homme est dictée par la fatalité, est aussi rejetée par Méthode d'Olympe, comme les trois autres réponses que nous avons déjà évoquées. Selon lui, c'est seulement l'homme lui-même qui est responsable de ses crimes à cause du libre arbitre qu'il possède.

3. Définition du libre arbitre

Quant à la définition de cette notion importante dans le système théologique de Méthode, il la donne de nouveau dans son traité *De autexusio* :

> Le premier homme a été créé maître de ses actes, c'est-à-dire libre, et que les continuateurs de l'espèce ont hérité de lui la même liberté. Oui, je prétends que l'homme est né libre, et je n'accepte pas d'en faire un esclave. C'est même, dis-je, la plus haute faveur que Dieu lui ait faite, parce qu'en effet, hors de lui, tout doit exécuter servilement les ordres de Dieu[28].

Dans cette définition du libre arbitre, l'auteur emploie l'adjectif grec αὐτεξούσιος qu'il comprend comme équivalent de la notion de liberté (ἐλεύθερος et ἐλευθερία) : le premier homme en est doté dès sa création et le transmet, même après sa transgression, à toute sa descendance. Ce don unique, offert par Dieu à l'homme et aux anges, lui donne le droit d'avoir un « avantage supplémentaire » de la part de son Créateur[29].

---

[28] *Méth. Olymp.*, Autex. XVI, 2-3 : PO 22.5, p. 794-795 : αὐτεξούσιον δὲ τὸν πρῶτον ἄνθρωπον γεγονέναι […], τουτέστιν ἐλεύθερον, ἀφ' οὗ καὶ οἱ διάδοχοι τοῦ γένους τὴν ὁμοίαν ἐλευθερίαν ἐκληρώσαντο. Φημὶ τοιγαροῦν ἐλεύθερον γεγονέναι τὸν ἄνθρωπον, δουλεύοντα δὲ αὐτὸν οὐ βούλομαι. Τοῦτο γὰρ αὐτῷ καὶ μέγιστον πρὸς τοῦ θεοῦ κεχαρίσθαι λέγω, ὅτι τὰ μὲν γὰρ ἄλλα πάντα ἀνάγκη δουλεύει τῷ θείῳ προστάγματι.

[29] *Méth. Olymp.*, Autex. XVI, 5 : PO 22.5, p. 796-797 : Ἄνθρωπος δὲ τὴν ᾧ βούλεται πείθεσθαι προσέλαβεν ἐξουσίαν ἑαυτὸν δουλαγωγῶν, οὐκ ἀνάγκῃ τῆς φύσεως κρατούμενος οὐδὲ τῆς δυνάμεως ἀφαιρούμενος· ὅπερ αὐτῷ τῶν κρειττόνων ἕνεκα κεχαρίσθαι φημί, ἵνα τι πλεῖον ὧν ἔχει προσλάβῃ παρὰ τοῦ κρείττονος, ὅπερ αὐτῷ ἐκ τῆς ὑπακοῆς προσγίνεται καὶ ὡς ὀφειλὴν ἀπαιτεῖ παρὰ τοῦ πεποιηκότος. Trad. : « Mais l'homme a obtenu la faculté d'obéir à qui il veut et de se choisir lui-même son maître, sans être asservi à une fatalité naturelle ni privé du pouvoir d'agir. Et je dis que c'est là une faveur qu'il a reçue pour son profit, afin de lui permettre d'obtenir de son maître quelque avantage en plus de ceux qu'il possède, avantage supplémentaire qu'il retire de son obéissance et qu'il réclame comme un dû à son créateur ».

En ce qui concerne les commandements que Dieu établit pour l'homme, il ne s'agit pas de la suppression de la liberté de choix dont l'homme est doté par son Créateur lui-même, mais plutôt des conseils, susceptibles d'être soit rejetés, soit acceptés par l'être libre qu'est l'homme : lorsqu'il leur obéit, il a l'accès au « bien supérieur »[30], c'est-à-dire, à l'incorruptibilité éternelle, perdue au moment de la chute ancestrale :

> Car Dieu ne voulait pas faire ainsi un don, celui de l'incorruptibilité éternelle, sans raison : le don aurait été fait sans raison s'il avait été accordé sans justice, et ce n'aurait pas été un don juste, si celui qui le recevait n'avait pas eu le double pouvoir : d'obéir aux commandements de Dieu, et aussi <de ne pas y obéir> s'il ne le voulait pas[31].

II. Péché originel et ses conséquences

1. Chute du premier homme

Dès sa création, l'homme, ignorant encore le mal, possède pourtant, grâce au libre arbitre dont il est doté par Dieu, la responsabilité de son choix : obéir ou désobéir à son Créateur. Quant à l'apparition du mal, elle a lieu, d'après Méthode d'Olympe, lors de la réception du premier précepte divin : c'est la

---

[30] *Méth. Olymp.*, Autex. XVI, 7-9 : PO 22.5, p. 797-799 : τὸ μὲν γὰρ δύνασθαι πάρεστιν αὐτῷ, κἂν τὴν ἐντολὴν λαμβάνῃ, τὴν δὲ τοῦ δύνασθαι προαίρεσιν εἰς τὸ κρεῖττον τρέπειν ὁ θεὸς παραινεῖ. Ὥσπερ γὰρ πατὴρ παιδὶ παραινῶν, ἐξουσίαν ἔχοντι ἐκμανθάνειν τὰ μαθήματα, καὶ μᾶλλον ἔχεσθαι τῶν μαθημάτων, ὅτι κρεῖττον τοῦτο μηνύων, οὐ τὴν τοῦ δύνασθαι τοῦ παιδὸς ἐξουσίαν ἀφαιρεῖ, κἂν μὴ ἑκὼν μανθάνειν βούληται, οὕτω μοι καὶ τὸν θεὸν οὐ δοκεῖ προτρέποντα τὸν ἄνθρωπον πείθεσθαι τοῖς προστάγμασιν ἀφαιρεῖν αὐτοῦ τὴν ἐξουσίαν τῆς προαιρέσεως, τῷ δύνασθαι καὶ μὴ ὑπακούειν τοῖς προστάγμασιν. Καὶ γὰρ τὴν ἀρχὴν τὸ οὕτως παραινεῖν ὅτι <μὲν> μὴ ἀφεῖλε τὴν ἐξουσίαν μηνύει· προστάττει δὲ ἵνα τῶν κρειττόνων ἄνθρωπος ἀπολαύειν δυνηθῇ· τοῦτο γὰρ ἕπεται τῷ πεισθῆναι τῷ τοῦ θεοῦ προστάγματι. Trad. : « L'homme conserve son pouvoir d'agir, même en recevant les instructions de Dieu ; Dieu ne fait que lui conseiller d'orienter vers le bien le libre usage de ce pouvoir. C'est comme quand un père conseille à son enfant, qui a la possibilité de bien apprendre les sciences, de s'appliquer davantage encore à cette étude, en lui en montrant l'utilité : l'enfant n'est pas privé par là de sa liberté d'agir, même s'il n'a pas de lui-même la volonté d'étudier. J'estime de même que Dieu, en pressant l'homme d'obéir à ses commandements, ne lui enlève pas son libre vouloir, puisque l'homme garde le pouvoir de ne pas obéir à ses prescriptions. Car, en lui-même, le fait que Dieu lui donne ainsi des conseils prouve bien qu'il ne lui a pas ôté sa liberté ; et si Dieu ordonne, c'est pour permettre à l'homme de jouir du bien supérieur, bien qui résulte de l'obéissance à l'ordre de Dieu ».

[31] *Méth. Olymp.*, Autex. XVI, 10 : PO 22.5, p. 798 : [Old Church Slavonic text]

désobéissance à ce commandement qui est présentée par l'auteur comme mal lui-même, cause principale de la chute ancestrale[32].

Cependant, le mal n'est pas une caractéristique innée de la nature de l'homme créé, mais celui-ci l'a acquis par l'apprentissage : Méthode le démontre par les paroles que Dieu prononce après la transgression du premier commandement commise par les ancêtres : «[…] Voilà que l'homme est devenu comme l'un de nous par la connaissance du bien et du mal» (Gn 3, 22)[33].

Le mal est enseigné à l'homme par l'intermédiaire d'un maître qui est le serpent :

> Eh bien, celui qui le lui enseigne est le Serpent, créé par Dieu même; et il le lui enseigne dans l'intention de l'empêcher d'atteindre au bien supérieur. Si tu veux encore en savoir la cause, c'est qu'il porte envie à l'homme. Et si tu demandes aussi l'origine de cette envie, c'est parce qu'il n'a pas reçu les mêmes honneurs que

---

[32] *Méth. Olymp.*, Autex. XVII, 1-2 : PO 22.5, p. 800-801 : Αὐτεξούσιον δέ φημι τὸν ἄνθρωπον γεγονέναι· οὐχ ὡς προϋποκειμένου τινὸς ἤδη κακοῦ, οὗ τὴν ἐξουσίαν τοῦ ἑλέσθαι, εἰ βούλοιτο, ὁ ἄνθρωπος ἐλάμβανεν, ἀλλὰ τὴν τοῦ ὑπακούειν τῷ θεῷ καὶ μὴ ὑπακούειν αἰτίαν μόνην· τοῦτο γὰρ τὸ αὐτεξούσιον ἐβούλετο. Καὶ γενόμενος ὁ ἄνθρωπος ἐντολὴν λαμβάνει παρὰ τοῦ θεοῦ, καὶ ἐντεῦθεν ἤδη τὸ κακὸν ἄρχεται· οὐ γὰρ πείθεται τῷ θείῳ προστάγματι. Καὶ τοῦτο καὶ μόνον ἦν τὸ κακόν, ἡ παρακοή, ἥτις τοῦ εἶναι ἤρξατο. Οὐδὲ <γὰρ> ἀγένητον ταύτην τις εἰπεῖν ἔχει, τοῦ ποιήσαντος αὐτὴν ὄντος γενητοῦ. Trad. : « Je dis que l'homme a été créé pourvu du libre arbitre; non que j'admette un mal déjà préexistant pour lequel l'homme aurait reçu le pouvoir d'opter s'il le voulait, mais il recevait seulement la responsabilité de l'obéissance ou de la désobéissance à Dieu : c'est à cela en effet que répondait l'octroi du libre arbitre. L'homme, une fois créé, reçoit un ordre de Dieu, et dès lors le mal commence, l'homme refusant d'obéir à la prescription divine. Et c'était cela uniquement qui constituait le mal, la désobéissance à Dieu, qui a eu un commencement : car personne n'ira dire qu'elle était incréée, puisque son auteur était créé ».
[33] *Méth. Olymp.*, Autex. XVII, 3-4 : PO 22.5, p. 800-801 : Πάντως δὲ πόθεν τὸ παρακοῦσαι ζητήσεις. Ἀλλὰ κεῖται σαφῶς ἔν τινι θείᾳ γραφῇ, ὅθεν οὐδὲ τοιοῦτον τὸν ἄνθρωπον πρὸς τοῦ θεοῦ γεγονέναι φημί, κατὰ δὲ τήν τινος διδασκαλίαν τοῦτο πεπονθέναι λέγω· οὐδὲ γὰρ τοιαύτην <ἣν> φύσιν εἰληφὼς ὁ ἄνθρωπος· εἰ γὰρ οὕτως εἶχεν, οὐκ ἂν αὐτῷ κατὰ διδασκαλίαν τοῦτο προσεγένετο, τῆς φύσεως αὐτῆς οὕτως ἐχούσης. Λέγει δέ τις θεία φωνὴ μεμαθηκέναι τὸν ἄνθρωπον τὰ πονηρά· διδάσκεσθαι δ' αὐτόν φημι τὸ παρακούειν θεοῦ· τοῦτο γὰρ καὶ μόνον ἐστὶ τὸ κακόν, ὃ παρὰ τὴν τοῦ θεοῦ προαίρεσιν γίνεται. Trad. : « Mais tu vas sûrement demander d'où est venue cette désobéissance. L'explication se trouve dans un certain livre divin, et c'est ce qui m'autorise à dire que l'homme n'a pas été créé par Dieu pourvu de ce penchant, mais qu'il n'en a été affecté que parce que quelqu'un le lui a enseigné : l'homme, en effet, n'avait pas pu le recevoir comme trait de sa nature, ou sinon ce penchant ne se serait pas développé en lui comme une chose apprise, puisque sa nature elle-même l'aurait comporté. Une certaine parole divine déclare que l'homme « a appris le mal »; et je dis que ce qui lui est enseigné, c'est de désobéir à Dieu, car cela seul est le mal qui arrive contre le désir de Dieu ».

l'homme. En effet, l'homme seul a obtenu d'être créé « à l'image et à la ressemblance » de Dieu[34].

Cependant, si l'apprentissage du mal se déroule sous la tutelle du diable, représenté par le serpent, lui-même ignorait encore à cet instant ce qui est le mal[35], ainsi que ce en quoi consistait le mal dans la désobéissance au précepte de Dieu : il ne l'a déduit que grâce aux menaces que Dieu avait adressées à l'homme :

> Il persuada l'homme de transgresser l'ordre de Dieu, sans savoir encore en quoi résidait le mal dans cette action. Puis il s'aperçut que Dieu blâmait l'homme d'avoir désobéi à son ordre et qu'il le dépouillait comme un condamné, et il comprit alors, non du fait de sa nature antérieure, mais par les menaces de Dieu, en quoi le mal consistait[36].

C'est ainsi, d'une manière détaillée et suivie, que Méthode décrit le déroulement de la transgression des ancêtres, ainsi que l'apparition du mal au sein de la création divine, originellement dépourvue de tout mal. Le point de départ de cette histoire est l'envie (φθόνος), éprouvée par le diable vis-à-vis de l'homme et de l'honneur, reçu par ce dernier : lui seul est créé « à l'image et à la ressemblance » divines[37]. Concernant le mal, il consistait dans la transgres-

---

[34] *Méth. Olymp.*, Autex. XVII, 4–5 : PO 22.5, p. 802–803 : Оучии же оуво єсть змии, ѿт самого бога сътворенъ оучить же ѿка съдрьжоути хотѧ ѿт вышнаго. Аци аи нєфоу хоџішиевьти забиѧть єсть помжєюу. Аци ани забиѧти пытаєшиѿтоудоу, єгоже дѣана такожє саноучитъ єдино ѿка по юразоу ипо подобиоу полоучишти бого[у].

[35] *Méth. Olymp.*, Autex. XVIII, 1–2 : PO 22.5, p. 802–804 : нѣкоуже не оумоу зѣ, ѿт коудоу измии єжє диаволъ нариєѧ, вьѣжие зало. Противоу же се добрьмаготѣсѧ тако диаволъ се зло разумѣеш прѣслоушити бога тѣм же и ни се оустрами ѿка. Trad. : « s'il n'y avait pas de mal préexistant, d'où est venue au Serpent, que j'appelle le diable (le fauteur de discorde), la connaissance du mal ? Voici la bonne réponse à faire à cette objection : le diable s'est aperçu que le mal consistait dans la désobéissance à Dieu ; et c'est pourquoi il a incité l'homme à désobéir ».

[36] *Méth. Olymp.*, Autex. XVIII, 5 : PO 22.5, p. 806 : прѣстрѣаѣти зановѣдъ божиѧ, не еци вѣмини иж есть зло маѣикѧже посаѣже бога покумашь ѣка сѿкже прѣстѫпа заповѣдъ его и корить юсужени вѣдмиѧ, не ѿт дрѣнаго естьства, ни ѿт прѣштѣаѣти божиѧ тогда разумѣкаю есть зло.

[37] Voir aussi : *Méth. Olymp.*, Res., I, 37, 3 : A. Morozov, Partie II, p. 79 : ἀλλ' οἱ μὲν λοιποὶ ἐφ' οἷς αὐτοὺς ἐποίησε καὶ διέταξεν ὁ θεὸς ἔμειναν, ὁ δὲ ἐνύβρισε καὶ πονηρὸς περὶ τὴν τῶν πεπιστευμένων ἐγένετο διοίκησιν, φθόνον ἐγκισσήσας καθ' ἡμῶν, ὥσπερ καὶ οἱ μετὰ ταῦτα σαρκῶν ἐρασθέντες καὶ ταῖς τῶν ἀνθρώπων εἰς φιληδονίαν ἐνομίλησαντες θυγατράσιν. Trad. : A. Morozov, Partie III, p. 72 : « Mais, tandis que le reste des anges est resté sur les postes pour lesquels Dieu les avait créés et placés, le diable fut pris d'orgueil et devint pervers dans l'administration de ce qui lui était confié. Il conçut une jalousie envers nous, comme le firent ceux qui, plus tard, tombèrent amoureux des créatures charnelles et eurent commerce, pour le goût du plaisir, avec les filles des hommes ».

sion (παράβασις) du précepte de Dieu, suivie de la condamnation visant à la fois Adam, Ève et le serpent.

Cependant, il faut faire la distinction entre le fait de manger de l'arbre de la connaissance, acte qui ne représente pas en soi le mal, et le même acte, mais accompli contre la volonté de Dieu. C'est uniquement cette dernière condition qui applique la qualité du mal à l'acte humain[38].

À la fin de sa réflexion relative au chapitre 3 de la Genèse, l'auteur reprend la définition du mal en tant que qualité et accident, liés à l'intention de celui qui agit, afin de l'appliquer aussi à ce récit biblique de la chute ancestrale :

> Quant au mal, j'entends la désobéissance, ce n'est pas comme une substance préexistante, je l'ai déjà dit, qu'il est venu à la connaissance du diable, mais comme un des accidents de la substance qui résulte de l'usage de la volonté. Voilà pourquoi j'affirme que l'homme reçoit la juste punition de ses actes : car c'est volontairement qu'il se livre à l'enseignement du diable, et il s'écarte de ses leçons de lui-même, quand il le veut. Il a en effet la faculté de vouloir ou de ne pas vouloir, ce qui a pour conséquence le pouvoir de faire ce qu'il veut[39].

2. Concupiscence

Cette chute des ancêtres a deux conséquences principales : la concupiscence et la mort. Pourtant, elle ne modifie point la nature humaine dotée du libre arbitre : l'homme continue à avoir sa liberté de choix même dans sa condition postlapsaire. Méthode d'Olympe en parle dans un passage du *Symposium* :

---

[38] *Méth. Olymp.*, Autex. XVIII, 8 : PO 22.5, p. 808–809 : Τὴν μὲν οὖν ἀρχὴν τοῦ κακοῦ τὸν φθόνον εἶπον ἔγωγε, τὸν δὲ φθόνον ἐκ τοῦ κρείττονι τιμῇ κατηξιῶσθαι τὸν ἄνθρωπον πρὸς τοῦ θεοῦ· τὸ δὲ κακὸν ἡ παρακοή, ἐκ τοῦ προστίμῳ περιπεσεῖν τὸν ἄνθρωπον ὑπερβάντα τὴν τοῦ θεοῦ ἐντολήν, <ὅθεν καὶ> πολλάκις, εἰ καὶ τὰ μάλιστα τὸ γινόμενον τῇ φύσει φαῦλον οὐκ ἔστιν, ἀλλά γε δὴ διὰ τὸ μὴ βούλεσθαι τὸν θεὸν γίνεσθαι αὐτὸ <когда же бго пѡдъпти ꙗко тѧхрити, еже прїк.ѡшпти токмо бога пѣк.иземкшимоу бытн звоу>. Trad. : « Ainsi j'ai dit que la cause première du mal était l'envie, et que l'envie résultait de ce que Dieu a jugé l'homme digne d'un honneur plus grand. Et le mal consiste dans la désobéissance, du fait que l'homme, en transgressant l'ordre de Dieu, a encouru le châtiment que comportait sa faute. <Si bien qu'>il arrive souvent qu'une action, encore qu'elle ne soit pas mauvaise en elle-même, se trouve cependant être mauvaise parce que Dieu ne voulait pas qu'elle s'accomplît <, et qu'il a indiqué le moment où il convenait de l'accomplir, et uniquement du fait que son auteur, qui était> exactement <renseigné, a désobéi à Dieu>».

[39] *Méth. Olymp.*, Autex. XVIII, 11–12 : PO 22.5, p. 810–812 : Зѡ же рѣи̑ прїк.ѧѫшнїс, къ такоже сѫтавькъмидркъе сѫ нѫ выдѣніе рїѧкъ имѣти дїаволоу, но тако ничто семеиалирѧ самемлюціи иземлишлоу рекст тѣм же оуко ⱋно итинноую прїимлтн казнъ ѡнѧжъ техрить, самохотъи во сама оученїе подлетъ, ѡтлетъ же саѹ еніи тогда ѥгда самъ хоцітъ. Хотѣнѧ во иматъ и нехотѣнѧ блⷭ̏ть, последѫтвоутъ же емоу и еже мошн техрити еже хоⷰ̏тъ.

Car il nous appartient de donner préférence et préséance aux biens supérieurs sur les biens terrestres, puisque l'entendement que nous avons reçu est libre de toute autorité et détermination extérieures, échappant à toute contrainte qui l'empêcherait d'être son propre maître en choisissant ce qui lui plaît ; il n'est esclave ni du destin ni des hasards[40].

Malgré la préservation du libre arbitre après sa transgression, l'homme devient cependant victime des assauts de la concupiscence, sujet que Méthode d'Olympe aborde au début du livre II de son dialogue *De resurrectione* (*Res.* II, 1–8). Toute sa réflexion autour de ce sujet est fondée sur l'interprétation d'un des versets pauliniens : « et moi, jadis, sans la Loi, je vivais ; mais quand le commandement est venu, le péché est devenu vivant » (Rm 7, 9).

Selon Méthode, l'expression « jadis, sans la Loi, je vivais » se réfère à la vie des ancêtres avant leur chute, tandis qu'après l'apparition du mal dans le monde, causée par la transgression du premier précepte divin, l'homme est devenu l'objet des attaques continuelles de la concupiscence (ἐπιθυμία) :

> Nous passions notre vie hors de la concupiscence, n'ayant aucune connaissance des attaques de la concupiscence dénuée de raison qui, avec les distractions attirantes des plaisirs, nous pousse avec violence à l'intempérance[41].

En même temps, la concupiscence, elle-même, est présentée par Méthode comme conséquence inévitable de l'interdiction : sans cette condition la concupiscence ne pourrait même pas exister :

> Car le fait de convoiter ne s'applique pas à ce qui est présent et se trouve en notre pouvoir, mais à ce qui est présent, mais pas en notre pouvoir. Comment peut-on convoiter et désirer vivement ce qui n'est pas interdit et dont on n'a pas besoin ? De là précisément vient : « Je n'aurais pas connu la concupiscence, si la loi n'avait pas dit : Tu ne convoiteras pas »[42].

---

[40] *Méth. Olymp.* Symp., VIII, 13, 208 : SC 95, p. 236–237 : Ἡμέτερον προκρίνειν γὰρ τὰ κρείττω καὶ προτάσσειν πρὸ τῶν γηγενῶν, αὐτοκράτορα καὶ αὐτεξούσιον τὸν λογισμὸν εἰληφότας καὶ πάσης ἀνάγκης ἐκτὸς εἰς τὸ αὐτοδεσπότως αἱρεῖσθαι τὰ ἀρέσκοντα, οὐ δουλεύοντας εἱμαρμένῃ καὶ τύχαις.

[41] *Méth. Olymp.* Res., II, 1, 1 : A. Morozov, Partie II, p. 159 : ἐκτὸς δὲ ἐπιθυμίας διήγομεν, οὐ γινώσκοντες ὅλως ἐπιθυμίας ἀλόγου προσβολάς, βιαζομένης ἡμᾶς ἑλκτικαῖς ἡδονῶν περιαγωγαῖς πρὸς ἀκρασίαν. Trad. : A. Morozov, Partie III, p. 143.

[42] *Méth. Olymp.* Res., II, 1, 3 : A. Morozov, Partie II, p. 159 : τὸ γὰρ ἐπιθυμῆσαι οὐκ ἐπὶ τῶν παρόντων καὶ ὑποκειμένων ἐν ἐξουσίᾳ πίπτει, ἀλλ' ἐπὶ τῶν παρόντων μέν, μὴ ὄντων δὲ ἐν ἐξουσίᾳ. πῶς γὰρ οὐ μὴ κεκώλυταί τις μηδὲ ἐνδεής ἐστι, τούτου ἐπιθυμεῖ καὶ ἐρᾷ ; ὅθεν διὰ τοῦτο «τὴν ἐπιθυμίαν οὐκ ᾔδειν», <ἔφη,> «εἰ μὴ ὁ νόμος ἔλεγεν, οὐκ ἐπιθυμήσεις». Trad. : A. Morozov, Partie III, p. 144.

Dans ce dialogue *De resurrectione*, comme aussi dans le *De autexusio*, Méthode souligne le fait qu'après avoir compris que c'est la transgression du précepte de Dieu qui est le mal, le diable s'en est servi afin de faire chuter l'homme de son état prélapsaire :

> En effet, une fois le précepte donné, le diable a pu produire en moi, par l'intermédiaire du précepte, de la concupiscence, après m'avoir excité et m'avoir invité habilement à tomber dans le désir de ce qui est interdit[43].

Cependant, ces commandements divins ne sont pas destinés à faire tomber l'homme, mais ils lui ont été donnés comme exhortation « en vue de la vie et de l'incorruptibilité »[44]. En même temps, Méthode met un accent sur le fait que lorsqu'il s'agit de la concupiscence, inspirée de l'extérieur, le libre arbitre reste actif dans l'homme, même si ce dernier est incapable de s'empêcher de méditer sur des pensées mauvaises :

> En effet, ce n'est pas de méditer ou non sur ce qui est insolite qui dépend entièrement de nous, mais d'user ou non de ces pensées. Car empêcher les pensées, inspirées de l'extérieur pour nous éprouver, nous ne le pouvons pas, mais ne pas leur obéir ou ne pas en user, nous le pouvons[45].

Méthode présente ce pouvoir du diable d'inspirer les pensées insolites à l'homme, impuissant devant de tels assauts, comme conséquence directe de la transgression du premier homme :

> C'est ainsi d'abord qu'une dissension est tombée sur nous et nous avons été remplis d'agitations et de pensées qui ne nous sont pas familières. Nous avons été vidés de l'inspiration divine, et nous sommes remplis d'un désir matériel que le serpent aux milles détours nous a inspiré, parce que nous avions rapidement quitté la sphère du précepte de Dieu[46].

---

[43] *Méth. Olymp. Res.*, II, 2, 1 : A. Morozov, Partie II, p. 161 : Δοθείσης γὰρ τῆς ἐντολῆς ἔσχε λαβὴν διὰ τῆς ἐντολῆς ὁ διάβολος κατεργάσασθαι ἐν ἐμοὶ τὴν ἐπιθυμίαν, παρορμήσας με καὶ προσκαλεσάμενος ἐντέχνως εἰς ὄρεξιν καταπεσεῖν τῶν κεκωλυμένων. Trad. : A. Morozov, Partie III, p. 145.
[44] *Méth. Olymp. Res.*, II, 2, 4 : A. Morozov, Partie II, p. 161 : εἰς ζωὴν καὶ ἀφθαρσίαν. Trad. : A. Morozov, Partie III, p. 146.
[45] *Méth. Olymp. Res.*, II, 3, 1 : A. Morozov, Partie II, p. 165 : Οὐ γὰρ ἐφ' ἡμῖν ὅλως τὸ ἐνθυμεῖσθαι ἢ μὴ ἐνθυμεῖσθαι κεῖται τὰ ἄτοπα, ἀλλὰ τὸ χρῆσθαι ἢ μὴ χρῆσθαι τοῖς ἐνθυμήμασι. κωλῦσαι μὲν γὰρ μὴ ἐμπίπτειν εἰς ἡμᾶς τοὺς λογισμοὺς οὐ δυνάμεθα, πρὸς δοκιμὴν ἡμῶν ἔξωθεν εἰσπνεομένους, μὴ πεισθῆναι μέντοι ἢ μὴ χρῆσθαι αὐτοῖς δυνάμεθα. Trad. : A. Morozov, Partie III, p. 149.
[46] *Méth. Olymp. Res.*, II, 6, 2 : A. Morozov, Partie II, p. 175 : οὕτως γὰρ πρῶτον στάσις ἐνέπεσε σφαδασμῶν τε καὶ λογισμῶν ἀνοικείων ἐπληρώθημεν, κενωθέντες μὲν τοῦ ἐμφυσήματος

La notion du libre arbitre dans l'héritage littéraire de Méthode d'Olympe 115

À part ces pensées « qui ne nous sont pas familières » et qui sont inspirées par le diable de l'extérieur, il existe aussi d'autres causes du péché. Il s'agit des habitudes, de l'éducation, des passions de l'âme et des désirs du corps : leur liste est donnée dans un autre dialogue méthodien, *Symposium*[47]. Cependant, l'homme déchu reste capable de lutter contre les différentes causes des péchés, y compris contre le diable :

> La lignée des sages a dit que notre vie est comme un festival dramatique ; nous y sommes entrés comme sur un théâtre pour tenir notre rôle dans la présentation du drame de Vérité – c'est-à-dire de la justice – et nos adversaires et rivaux de scène, ce sont le diable et les démons ; il nous faut donc, lever haut la tête et prendre notre essor vers le ciel, il nous faut fuir, plus que ceux des sirènes d'Homère, les charmes de leurs belles voix et de leurs attitudes – tous attraits qui n'ont qu'un fard superficiel de continence[48].

3. Mort

S'agissant de la deuxième conséquence de la transgression, la mort, elle est aussi décrite par l'auteur dans le premier discours « orthodoxe » du *De Resurrectione* (*Res.* I, 36–46). En effet, Méthode exprime l'interdépendance entre la chute ancestrale et la mort de cette manière :

τοῦ θεοῦ, πληρωθέντες δὲ ἐπιθυμίας ὑλικῆς, ἣν ὁ πολύπλοκος ἐνέπνευσεν εἰς ἡμᾶς ὄφις, βραχυπορησάντων ἡμῶν τῆς παραγγελίας τοῦ θεοῦ τὸν κύκλον. Trad. : A. Morozov, Partie III, p. 158.

[47] *Méth. Olymp. Symp.*, VIII, 16, 227–228 : SC 95, p. 254–257 :Ἤτοι ἀνατροφαὶ καὶ τὰ ἔθη τῶν ἁμαρτημάτων εἰσὶν αἴτια, ἢ τὰ πάθη τῆς ψυχῆς καὶ αἱ διὰ σώματος ἐπιθυμίαι. Ὁπότερον δ' ἂν τούτων ᾖ τὸ αἴτιον, ὁ θεὸς ἀναίτιος. Εἰ κρεῖσσόν ἐστι τὸ δίκαιον εἶναι τοῦ ἀδίκου, διὰ τί τοιοῦτος αὐτόθεν ὁ ἄνθρωπος ἀπὸ τῆς γενέσεως οὐ γίνεται ; Εἰ δὲ ὕστερον, ὅπως ἀμείνων γενηθῇ, σωφρονίζεται μαθήμασι καὶ νόμοις, ὡς αὐτεξούσιος ἄρα σωφρονίζεται καὶ οὐχ ὡς ἐκ φύσεως ὢν κακός. Trad. : « Au vrai, ce sont l'éducation et les habitudes qui sont causes des péchés, ou les passions de l'âme et les désirs du corps. Mais qu'il s'agisse d'une cause ou de l'autre, Dieu n'est point ici cause responsable. S'il vaut mieux être juste qu'injuste, pourquoi l'homme ne l'est-il pas d'emblée, dès sa venue au monde ? Et si ensuite, pour le rendre meilleur, on lui donne des enseignements et des lois qui l'assagissent, c'est comme être libre qu'il est capable de s'assagir, et non pas comme être naturellement pervers ».
[48] *Méth. Olymp. Symp.*, VIII, 1, 171–172 : SC 95, p. 202–203 :Ἐπειδὴ γὰρ πανήγυριν τὸν βίον ἡμῶν εἶναι σοφῶν παῖδες εἰρήκεσαν, ἡμᾶς δὲ τὸ δρᾶμα τῆς ἀληθείας τὴν δικαιοσύνην ἥκειν ὡς εἰς θέατρον ἐπιδειξομένους, ἀντιτεχνούντων ἡμῖν καὶ ἀνταγωνιζομένων τοῦ διαβόλου καὶ τῶν δαιμόνων, ἀνανεύοντας ἄνω δεῖ καὶ ἀνιπταμένους μετεωρίζεσθαι καὶ φεύγειν τὰ θέλγητρα τῆς καλλιφωνίας αὐτῶν καὶ τὰ σχήματα ἔξωθεν φαντασίᾳ σωφροσύνης ἐπικεχρωσμένα, <μᾶλλον> ἢ τὰς Σειρῆνας [μᾶλλον] τὰς Ὁμηρικάς.

C'est l'ennemi du bien qui est survenu et l'a ensorcelé, par l'envie, alors qu'il avait été créé avec le libre arbitre pour choisir le bien et avait reçu cette loi. « Car Dieu a créé l'homme pour l'incorruptibilité, il a fait de lui une image de sa propre éternité »[49]. En effet, « Dieu n'a pas fait la mort, il ne se réjouit pas de voir mourir les êtres vivants »[50], « mais par l'envie du diable, la mort est entrée dans le monde[51], comme en témoigne aussi la Sagesse par l'intermédiaire de Salomon[52].

Selon lui, l'introduction de la mort après la transgression a comme but non pas le châtiment de l'homme, mais elle est présentée comme moyen de sa conversion[53], ou plutôt un remède contre la maladie qui est l'emprise du diable sur l'homme déchu :

> De ce fait, lorsque l'homme fut sali et souillé, s'étant révolté contre le décret de Dieu, et qu'il reçut les empreintes des taches d'une méchanceté considérable que le prince des ténèbres, père de la tromperie, avait enfantées, « ayant conçu la douleur »[54], selon l'Écriture, afin qu'il puisse toujours inspirer à l'homme l'injustice et l'y inciter. Dieu le Tout-puissant, voyant que l'homme était devenu un méchant immortel par suite d'un complot du diable, puisque c'était aussi le diable qui l'a trompé, il prépara les tuniques de peau, en le revêtant d'une sorte de mortalité, afin que, à travers la suppression du corps, tout le mal apparu en lui puisse mourir[55].

---

[49] Sg 2, 23.
[50] Sg 1, 13.
[51] Sg 2, 24.
[52] *Méth. Olymp.* Res., I, 36, 2 : A. Morozov, Partie II, p. 75 : γενόμενον αὐτεξούσιον πρὸς τὴν αἵρεσιν τοῦ καλοῦ καὶ τοῦτον τὸν θεσμὸν εἰληφὸς ὁ μισόκαλος ἐπιστὰς ἐβάσκανε φθόνῳ. «ὁ γὰρ θεὸς ἔκτισε τὸν ἄνθρωπον ἐπὶ ἀφθαρσίᾳ καὶ εἰκόνα τῆς ἰδίας ἀιδιότητος ἐποίησεν αὐτόν». καὶ γὰρ «ὁ θεὸς θάνατον οὐκ ἐποίησεν οὐδὲ τέρπεται ἐπ' ἀπωλείᾳ ζώντων»· «φθόνῳ δὲ διαβόλου θάνατος εἰσῆλθεν εἰς τὸν κόσμον», καθάπερ καὶ ἡ σοφία διὰ Σολομῶνος μαρτυρεῖ. Trad. : A. Morozov, Partie III, p. 69.
[53] *Méth. Olymp.* Res., I, 38, 1 : A. Morozov, Partie II, p. 81 : ὁ δὲ θάνατος πρὸς ἐπιστροφὴν ηὑρέθη, καθάπερ καὶ τοῖς ἀρτιμαθέσι γραμμάτων παιδίοις πρὸς ἐπανόρθωσιν αἱ πληγαί. οὐδὲν γὰρ ἄλλο ὁ θάνατος ἢ διάκρισις καὶ διαχωρισμὸς ψυχῆς ἀπὸ σώματος. Trad. : A. Morozov, Partie III, p. 73 : « quant à la mort, elle fut conçue pour la correction, tout comme les coups de fouet furent conçus pour corriger les enfants qui viennent d'apprendre à lire. Car la mort ne représente rien d'autre que la décomposition et la séparation de l'âme du corps ».
[54] Ps 7, 15.
[55] *Méth. Olymp.* Res. I, 38, 5 : A. Morozov, Partie II, p. 83 : ὅθεν ἐπειδὴ κατερρυπώθη καὶ κατεμιάνθη τῆς ἀποφάσεως ἀποστατήσας ὁ ἄνθρωπος τοῦ θεοῦ καὶ κηλίδας ἐναπεμάξατο κακίας πολλῆς, ἃς ὁ ἄρχων τοῦ σκότους ἀπεκύησε καὶ πατὴρ τῆς πλάνης, πόνον κατὰ τὴν γραφὴν συλλαβών, ἵνα τὸν ἄνθρωπον φαντάζειν ἀεὶ πρὸς ἀδικίαν ἔχῃ καὶ κινεῖν, ὁ θεὸς ὁ παντοκράτωρ ἀθάνατον κακὸν ἐξ ἐπιβουλῆς τοῦ διαβόλου ἰδὼν αὐτὸν γεγενημένον, καθάπερ καὶ ὁ διάβολος πλάνος ἦν, τοὺς δερματίνους χιτῶνας διὰ τοῦτο κατεσκεύασεν, οἱονεὶ νεκρότητι περιβαλὼν αὐτὸν ὅπως διὰ τῆς λύσεως τοῦ σώματος πᾶν τὸ ἐν αὐτῷ γενηθὲν κακὸν ἀποθάνῃ. Trad. : A. Morozov, Partie III, p. 75.

Ainsi, la mortalité, indiquée dans le texte biblique, selon l'interprétation méthodienne, par l'expression des « tuniques de peau », a comme but d'empêcher l'homme de se transformer en mal immortel et de le sauver : la mort du corps doit déraciner le mal qui y a trouvé sa demeure au moment de la chute ancestrale. C'est le concept du péché originel qu'exprime l'auteur en parlant de « l'empreinte des taches de la grande méchanceté ».

Au terme de notre analyse, nous pouvons dire que pour Méthode d'Olympe le troisième chapitre de la Genèse est une description de l'apparition du mal en tant que qualité et accident qui résulte de l'intention d'un être agissant qui accomplit cet acte, car l'homme est, dès sa création, doué du libre arbitre. Pourtant, avant la transgression, ni l'homme, ni le diable lui-même ne connaissaient encore ni ce qui est le mal, ni ce en quoi consistait le mal dans la transgression du précepte divin, c'est seulement au moment de la transgression même qu'ils l'apprennent.

En même temps, cette transgression ancestrale n'a pas anéanti le don le plus précieux de Dieu à l'homme, le libre arbitre, mais elle a seulement donné lieu à la concupiscence, exprimée aussi par la possibilité d'infuser dans l'homme des pensées mauvaises. Le diable a reçu une telle possibilité grâce à « l'empreinte des taches de la grande méchanceté » laissée sur l'homme après sa chute. L'homme est impuissant face à cette infusion des pensées mauvaises, mais il reste quand même capable de décider à propos de leur mise en pratique grâce à ce libre arbitre. Quant à la mort, la deuxième conséquence de la transgression, elle est introduite comme moyen de guérir l'homme de ce mal qui réside en lui après la transgression.

Mariya Horyacha, L'viv (Ukraine)

Adam's Inheritance: Macarian Teaching on Indwelling Sin[1]

Abstract:
The question of the inheritance that Adam left to the human race received variety of answers among the Church Fathers. One such answer was given by the author of the Macarian corpus in the 4th century. Based on the Pauline theology of sin, he developed his teaching on indwelling sin, which became a reality for the human race after the Fall. The consideration of the Macarian teaching on the origin of evil and the consequences of Adam's transgression for his descendants, as well as the analysis of the essential characteristics of indwelling sin have shown that Macarian hamartiology belongs to the pre-mature stage of theological thought and does not easily agree with the later doctrine of original sin. Therefore, in order to be reconciled with the later terminology of sin Macarian hamartiology needed some revision.

Keywords: Adam's transgression, death, evil, indwelling sin, Macarius, Messalianism, Satan.

Introduction

"Surely I was sinful at birth, sinful from the time my mother conceived me" (Ps 50:5). These words of the Scriptures confirm that from the very moment of conception man appears sinful and somehow linked with sin. The fall of Adam has brought a radical change in human nature, which is now marked by weakness, sufferings and mortality/death. Through the history of Christian thought there have been various attempts to explain what actually happened in the Garden of Eden to Adam and the nature of the transgression of our forefather and how it affected human beings in the postlapsarian age. In the East, the doctrine of Ancestral (or generational) Sin (προπατορικὸν ἁμάρτημα, προγονικὴ ἁμαρτία) was developed. In the West, a firm conviction in the need to baptize infants to give them access to the heavenly kingdom finally resulted in the doctrine of original sin (*peccatum originale*), developed

---

[1] This paper is the abridged version of a part of my study, published in Ukrainian: M. Горяча, Подорож у серці. Динамічна антропологія преподобного Макарія, Витоки християнства 5: Дослідження 3 (Львів 2019).

Adam's Inheritance: Macarian Teaching on Indwelling Sin 119

by Augustine in the 5th century. Still the meaning of Adam's sin and the question of how it affected his descendants were subject to various interpretations in the writings of the Church Fathers. In this paper, I would like to draw attention to the teaching of indwelling sin (ἐνοικούση ἁμαρτία, cf. Rom 7:17), as developed by the anonymous ascetic of the 4th century, whose collections of parenetic discourses are known as the Macarian corpus. This author, whom we would simply name Macarius, being in line with Eastern Fathers, anticipated Augustine's idea of the radical presence of evil within man and human inability to be freed from it by one's own efforts. Drawing upon the Pauline theology of sin and his personal experience of evil and grace, he developed an original teaching on sin that can hardly be incorporated into any theological system except his own. Therefore, in order to understand his approach correctly we need to master his specific vocabulary and resist any temptation to approach his ideas through the prism of already formed theological presuppositions. We will consider Macarius' teaching concerning the origins of evil, his understanding of the Pauline key-text on consequences of Adam's sin for his descendants in Rom 5:12 and discuss the nature of indwelling sin, as it is presented in the corpus[2].

Origin of Evil

Before making any attempt to discuss the Macarian idea of sin, it is necessary to examine his teaching concerning the origins of evil. When the homilist speaks of evil and sin (both in the world and in the human soul), he usually refers to Satan and to the transgression of Adam.

First of all, he speaks of Satan whom he associates with sin itself, appealing to the words of the Apostle: *For until the law sin was in the world* (Rom 5:13)[3]. Though here Paul speaks of human sinfulness before the Law of Moses, Macarius interprets these words allegorically. For him, this law was not that

---

[2] The references to the Macarian corpus will be given through the following abbreviations: B = Collection I: *H. Berthold* (ed.), Makarios / Symeon. Reden und Briefe; die Sammlung I des Vaticanus Graecus 694 (B), Teil I: Einleitung und Tabellen. Die Logoi B 2–29; Teil II: Die Logoi B 30–64, GCS 55 (Berlin 1973); H = Collection II: *H. Dörries, E. Klostermann, M. Kroeger* (eds.), Die 50 geistlichen Homilien des Makarios, PTS 4 (Berlin 1964); C = Collection III: *E. Klostermann, H. Berthold* (eds.), Neue Homilien des Makarios/Symeon aus Typus III, TU 72 (Berlin 1961); or: *V. Desprez*, Pseudo-Macaire. Les œuvres spirituelles. Homélies propres à la Collection III, SC 275 (Paris 1980). The English translation of Collection II (H) is by *G. A. Maloney*, Pseudo-Macarius. The Fifty Spiritual Homilies and the Great Letter, CWS (New York 1992). The English translation of other texts, if not indicated otherwise, is my own.
[3] B 2:2 (2); B 2:3 (7).

of Moses but God's *commandment for life* (Rom 7:10), given to Adam in Paradise, while sin was considered to be Satan himself. It is about Satan that the Scriptures say: *darkness was over the face of the deep* (Gen 1:2)[4]. Macarius believes that Satan fell even before the creation of the world and human beings, when *the earth was* still *unsightly and unfurnished* (Gen 1:2)[5].

At the beginning Satan was a great and glorious angel but by his own malicious will he became hostile to God. He wanted to become a god himself and "rebelled against the divine glory, as it was written: *An unrighteous judge wants to be a god*"[6]. Because of this he was cast down to the earth together with like-minded demons who were obedient to him. Cut off from the higher land of the living, Satan became a dark spirit, worldly and deceitful, the progenitor and the founder of sin[7]. However, after his fall Satan was not immediately condemned to Gehenna but was set free for some time in order to perform a great act: according to God's providence, he was to become God's educational means for the training of humankind[8].

Though expelled from heaven, Satan still had the possibility to return to God. Nevertheless, he did not repent but added the murder of man to his misdeeds[9]. Since Adam was made according to the image of God (Gen 1:26) and the ruler of the whole world, Satan maliciously intended to steal this human dignity. Therefore, he approached man and deceived him through the promise that he would become a god because of the fruit of the tree of knowledge (Gen 3:6). He stripped Adam of his glory, subdued him to himself and made him a sinner[10]. In the second fall Satan managed to steal the dignity of Adam, assume his power and become the prince of this world.

---

[4] B 2:3 (11).
[5] There is also a direct indication that Satan had sinned even before the creation of Adam. See B 2:2 (2–4).
[6] B 2:2 (2–4). The citation is not identified. Berthold refers to 2 Thes 2:4: *who opposes and exalts himself against every so-called god or object of worship, so that he takes his seat in the temple of God, proclaiming himself to be God.* See H. Berthold (ed.), Makarios / Symeon. Reden und Briefe, 4. Dunaev tried to establish the citation from the inner evidence of the Macarian corpus. He notices that the expression "unrighteous judge" occurs twice in the corpus: once—in the *Great Letter* (as a synonymic paraphrase of Lk 18:6: *Hear what the unrighteous judge says*, and the second time—in B 61:1 (3–4). Dunaev does not exclude the use of an apocryphal source. See A. *Dunavio, V. Desprez* (eds.), Sancti patris nostri Macarii Aegyptii (Symeonis Mesopotamitae) Sermones ascetici et epistulae. Collectio I (Sancti montis Athou – Moscvue 2015) 705, note 71.
[7] B 2:2 (2–4).
[8] B 2:2 (7–8); B 2:3 (19).
[9] B 2:2 (5).
[10] B 2:2 (6).

If pride was the motive of his first fall, it was envy and hatred of man that brought him to the second fall (cf. Wis 2:24). Through the first fall, when Satan fell from heaven, evil came into existence in the world; in the second fall, when Satan deceived Adam, evil found its place in the human soul. Macarius makes a clear-cut distinction between the sinful state of Satan before the fall of Adam and after it. After Adam's fall "sin (that is, the devil) became *exceedingly sinful* (Rom 7:13) because of the animosity towards man, insidiousness and envy"[11]. The transgression of Adam became a landmark not only in the history of Satan's disgrace but also in the history of humankind.

Rethinking the story of Adam's fall (Gen 3), Macarius develops the dynamic idea of Satan's recurrent coming into man's heart and human history. Presenting Satan as the tempting word, he shows how the cosmic drama of Adam's fall is performed today in every human soul. Today this cunning serpent appears as "the creeping passion to pleasure that through fellowship crawls into [our heart] and entices us to taste from the [forbidden] tree, namely from the worldly worry"[12]. The worldly deceitful spirit of the sinful darkness acts through the energy of passions in man with the mind set on the flesh (Rom 8:6–7) in which it feeds and dwells[13].

Adam's Inheritance for His Descendants

The fall brought Adam into a new reality of spiritual death. He found himself under the sentence of wrath and his soul died a grievous death. It was abandoned by God, cast out from the delights of Paradise to this world, and sent into captivity and shame[14]. Though Adam visibly continued to live, since he died after 930 years (Gen 5:5), his soul was killed by the evil passions that entered it after the fall. Adam's transgression also determined the course of the whole history of the human race[15]. Because by his sin not only Adam became prey to the darkness of passions but this evil inheritance of passions passed to all his descendants[16]. As a participant of this drama Macarius says:

---

[11] B 2:2 (2–4).
[12] B 36:1 (3).
[13] B 22:1 (10).
[14] H 48:5.
[15] Macarius so often speaks of Adam's transgression that it is sometimes difficult to distinguish between his expressions which refer directly to the fallen state of Adam and those phrases in which he speaks generally of the fallen state of the human race.
[16] B 29:2 (8).

We believe that everything that happened to him in a visible way, as it is said, can be recognised in the innermost part of every soul, for the heart is surrounded by the dark veil of the worldly fiery spirit that does not allow the mind to approach God and prevents the soul from praying as it wishes, from believing as it wishes, and from loving the Lord as it wishes[17].

The entire offspring of Adam incurs the consequences of his fall. Every soul has become affected by the same depravity of passions, which infiltrated into the whole human race due to Adam's transgression.

There are several important passages found in the corpus, where this transmission of the evil inheritance from Adam to all people is considered. One of these passages is Macarius' answer to the question as to why the serpent lifted up by Moses in the wilderness (Num 21:8) was a type and symbol of the Saviour (Jn 3:14)[18]. In his answer Macarius refers to Rom 5:12:

> The death was bitter to man who came under its power because of the former transgression, for the whole human race died and suffered due to the transgression of one. *Wherefore, as by one man,* as the Apostle says, *sin entered into the world, and death by sin; and so death passed upon all men, for that all have sinned* (δι' ἑνὸς ἀνθρώπου ἡ ἁμαρτία εἰς τὸν κόσμον εἰσῆλθε, καὶ διὰ τῆς ἁμαρτίας ὁ θάνατος, οὕτως εἰς πάντας ἀνθρώπους ὁ θάνατος διῆλθεν, ἐφ' ᾧ πάντες ἥμαρτον, Rom 5:12). So the whole of humankind became bitter and through sins and passions became similar to the venom and evil of the ancient serpent…[19]

It is not all together clear from this passage how Macarius understands the Pauline words in Rom 5:12. The meaning of the relative clause "ἐφ' ᾧ πάντες ἥμαρτον" is subject to interpretation. Depending on the choice of which term of the main clause the expression "ἐφ' ᾧ" is taken to refer to, three variant readings are possible[20]:

1. The Latin translator of the New Testament interpreted "ἐφ' ᾧ πάντες ἥμαρτον" as "*in quo omnes peccaverunt*", referring the expression "ἐφ' ᾧ" to "one man" (ἑνὸς ἀνθρώπου) and meaning that all sinned in Adam. Such a translation presupposes the idea of hereditary guilt: since all people were in Adam's loins when he committed sin, they all are responsible for his transgression. Following the Latin translation, Augustine of Hippo understood this passage precisely in this sense

---

[17] B 2:3 (13).
[18] B 2:12 (1–9).
[19] B 2:12 (2).
[20] See И. Мейендорф, Введение в святоотеческое богословие: конспекты лекций, Пер. с англ. Ларисы Волохонской (Киев ⁴2002) 206–208.

and from this interpretation developed his doctrine of original sin[21]. However, it should be pointed out that Greek grammar does not admit such a translation, since the pronoun "ᾧ" is too remote from the noun "ἀνθρώπου" (that is Adam) to be understood as referring to him. Moreover, the preposition "ἐπί" does not mean "in" but expresses causality or sequence.

2. If "ἐφ' ᾧ" refers to the whole main clause, then it should be translated "because" and the relative clause will be "death came to all men, because all sinned", meaning that as Adam had sinned and died, so all people die because they have sinned individually.

3. If "ἐφ' ᾧ" refers to the subject of the main clause "ὁ θάνατος", then the complete sentence should be translated as follows: "death passed upon all men, for that all have sinned". After Adam's transgression death came into the world as a personal and cosmic reality that brought mortality to all Adam's descendants. Most of the Eastern Church Fathers endorsed this interpretation and spoke of the aftermath of the fall in terms of hereditary death and not in terms of hereditary guilt.

However, the understanding of death and its transition to the whole of humanity still varied considerably from one Church Father to an another. The Apostolic Fathers (Ignatius of Antioch, Barnabas, Hermas) interpreted death as a spiritual disease. Irenaeus of Lyon explained it as the loss of holiness or a sinful state. Origen spoke of double death: the privation of divine life and the inevitably ensuing physical death. The Cappadocian Fathers understood death as the rupture of the former intimate relations with God and the loss of the Holy Spirit[22]. John Chrysostom proposed the following understanding: Adam's disobedience marred all things, for through his sin death passed to all people and prevailed over them. All became mortal, for that all have sinned. Inhered mortality caused fear of death, which led people to struggle for their survival and, finally, to sin[23].

---

[21] *Augustinus Hipponensis*, Expositio quarundam propositionum ex epistola ad Romanos 5, 27–30: PL 35, 2067–2068. See also P. Gorday, Principles of Patristic Exegesis: Romans 9–11 in Origen, John Chrysostom, and Augustine, Studies in the Bible and Early Christianity 4 (New York – Toronto 1983) 160; E. TeSelle, Augustine the Theologian (New York 1970) 159.
[22] *Origenes*, Commentarium in Epistolam B. Pauli ad Romanos 4, 9–12: PG 14, 993B–1003A. See also P. Gorday, Principles of Patristic Exegesis, 65–66; M. Hauke, Heilsverlust in Adam: Stationen griechischer Erbsündenlehre: Irenäus – Origenes – Kappadokier, Konfessionskundliche und kontroverstheologische Studien 58 (Paderborn 1993) 704.
[23] *Joannes Chrysostomos*, Homiliae in epistulam ad Romanos 9, 1–2; 10, 1: PG 60, 467–468 and 473–476. See also P. Gorday, Principles of Patristic Exegesis, 116.

In the Macarian corpus, the passage quoting Rom 5:12 does not give much possibility for an interpretation of the words of St Paul, as the passage itself is concerned more with the question of atonement than that of ancestral sin. To understand in what sense Macarius uses these words and what meaning he gave to them we have to examine other passages of the corpus.

Marcus Plested, for example, argues that the Macarian usage of the legal term "τὸ ἔγκλημα" (charge or accusation, incurred at the fall) implies an element of inherited guilt: "the Lord cancels 'the legal right arising from the disobedience' (τὸ δικαίωμα τῆς παρακοῆς) held by the devil over us by taking upon himself the charges (τὰ ἐγκλήματα) against us"[24]. Yet, Adam's descendants did not inherit his guilt but only the responsibility for the evil dwelling in them. They were not responsible for the fact that evil inhabited them but for their personal response to this indwelling evil. If the descendants are guilty of anything, their guilt does not lay in the very inheritance of evil but rather in their carelessness and negligence due to which evil grew and gained control over them. That the entire human race is infected by the sin of Adam is its misfortune rather than its guilt. The entire sinful human race is condemned not because of the sin of Adam but every person receives his or her condemnation interiorly and personally, when he/she follows the wiles and wishes of the Evil One[25].

Macarius also considers Adam as the type of all sinners. He often expresses this idea through the use of the name "the whole Adam" (ὅλος Ἀδάμ) as a collective name for the whole of sinful humankind. In his allegorical interpretation of the Scriptures, he explains that what happened to Adam in Paradise in a visible way now occurs invisibly to every human soul[26]. Adam, expelled from Paradise, personifies all people, separated from God due to their own sins. The way, in which Adam fell, is repeated again and again by his descendants. Such a typology might give the impression that Macarius understands Rom 5:12 in the second sense: "because all sinned". However, this idea does not exhaust the meaning of Adam's transgression for his descendants in the Macarian corpus. People would not know evil, if the leaven of passions had not entered them through Adam's transgression. Adam came to fall from the

---

[24] M. Plested, The Macarian Legacy: The Place of Macarius-Symeon in the Eastern Christian Tradition, Oxford Theology and Religion Monographs (Oxford 2004) 77, 79–80. See B 37:6. I would translate rather: "he tore the handwritings of disobedience" (ἔσχισε τὸ τῆς παρακοῆς χειρόγραφον). Here Macarius clearly makes an allusion to *the handwriting of ordinances that was against us* (Col 2:14). Compare also B 53:3 (2).
[25] B 48:1 (6–7); H 5:3.
[26] B 36:1 (2).

blessed state but his descendants find themselves already in the state of slavery. From the very beginning they are already endowed with this inherited evil and it is impossible to separate them from it. The whole human race has, by participation (κατὰ μετοχήν), shared in this leaven of evil passions[27]. The homilist compares this evil inheritance with one ounce of evil in every person, which people by their volition brought to perfection in their propensity for evil and developed in different ways: some to ten ounces of evil, others—to one hundred, the third ones to one thousand, and finally, wickedness was multiplied into a talent of evil[28]. Such an image of spreading evil in human history shows that despite evil inherited from Adam, each person is responsible for their own sins and not for that of Adam. Though the passions cannot be extirpated, they can still be resisted by everyone and maintained at the level of this one ounce.

Referring to Adam's transgression, Macarius also speaks of the inheritance of death that has passed to all people and has made them sin. It is precisely at that point that he sheds light on the query as to how the consequences of Adam's fault were transmitted to all his descendants. However, his answer to this question varies from one passage to another. At one time he says that death reigned over all humankind and destroyed the whole world through the body of Adam[29]. In another place Macarius says that it is primarily in the soul, wherein death found its shelter and from where "it flows throughout, sending roots into all the other members"[30]. Consequently, the entire body also fell victim to passions and corruption, so that not a single part of the soul or the body was immune from the passions of sin that are dwelling in us[31]. These two statements can be finally reconciled if we take into account that Macarius never considers body and soul separately: for him, the soul does not exclude corporality and the body is the dwelling place of the soul. He can easily interchange the notions of body and soul, meaning in fact the same reality: death entered and defiled both soul and body together[32] and the whole of human nature became dead and infertile[33].

Taking into account Macarius' holistic anthropology and his idea of death as a spiritual reality, we can now clarify his understanding of Rom 5:12.

---

[27] H 24:2.
[28] B 42:4–5.
[29] B 53:3 (5); B 4:30 (10). Compare H 52:2; H 30:8; C 21:3.
[30] H 15:48 (46).
[31] H 2:4.
[32] B 2:5 (1–2).
[33] H 52:3. Compare C 18:1.

Though acknowledging that the curse of Adam lies upon all people, Macarius understands it in terms of the common alienation from God, the privation of grace, and the acquisition of passions. In some points his theology resembles that of Augustine, especially with regard to the persistence of radical evil, which cannot be uprooted by man alone. However, concerning the transmission of this evil, his approach is distinct from Augustine's. Since Macarius understands death as a spiritual reality and identifies it with sin, he never confronts the dilemma of the Pelagian controversy, that is whether Adam transmitted to his children only physical death or also sin. For him, Adam transmitted both at the same time and by the same causality, and he did this by way of generation, when he begot his children in a natural way.

The teaching of Macarius is more in line with the Eastern Patristic thought, in which death was a key issue concerning the topic of the ancestral sin, although he still preserves his originality. Just as in the case of the comparison with Augustine, his thought also differs from that of John Chrysostom. While John Chrysostom emphasises death as the physical reality that causes fear and makes people struggle for their survival, Macarius sees death as the spiritual reality, associated with Satan, passions, and indwelling sin or evil. Though Macarius often varies his expressions concerning the elements of human nature that are affected by death, he in fact always has the same thing in mind: the whole human being is captured by death and sin. However, the question still remains: what exactly does that reality of death mean to Adam's descendants? How did it affect the human race? How does sin operate in the children of Adam? To answer these questions, we have to consider the nature of that sin, as it is presented in the corpus.

Vocabulary and Imagery of Sin in the Macarian Corpus

The large vocabulary Macarius employs to denote the reality of sin includes several dozen different terms and expressions, underlining one or another characteristic feature of sin. He can easily replace the notion of sin with Satan himself. The term "sin" (ἁμαρτία) can signify the fallen state of humanity; it can also be used in the more precise meaning of personal sin.

Macarius often speaks of indwelling sin (τῆς ἐνοικούσης ἁμαρτίας)[34], or uses the language of mixing (μῖξις) and blending (κρᾶσις) of the soul with

---

[34] B 38:1 (2). Compare Rom 7:5.

evil[35]. He says that the serpent is so intimately connected and mixed with the soul like a second soul with the real soul[36], that the *old leaven* (1 Cor 5:7) of darkness entered in and *leavened the whole* Adam (1 Cor 5:6), and to some degree Adam himself was mingled with vice[37]. Yet, he points out that the Evil One blends (συνεκράθη) with us not like a mixture (μῖξιν) of wine with water. It is more like wheat and the tares in the same field but independent of each other. It is like a robber in one part of the house and the owner in another[38]. It is clear that Macarius does not imply a confusion but a simple mechanical combination of evil with the soul. This happens when the soul mixes its natural movements with the wicked passions of the Evil One[39]. This mixture has to be understood as a kind of contamination with evil, which can be presented in the image of a spring that pours forth pure water and yet has mud lying under it, or gold mixed with mud in the earth[40].

Sometimes Macarius decribes this mixture in terms of contact or association. His favorite image is that of consorting with evil. It is like a young maid, seduced by a young man working in the household. When she commits for-

---

[35] The Stoics elaborated the technical terminology that became standard for language describing mixing. They distinguished between two kinds of mixture: that of distinct elements which retained their identity and could be separated (μῖξις of two kinds: παράθεσις and κρᾶσις) and that which produced a compound of uniform appearance (σύγχυσις). The word "παράθεσις" referred to the simple juxtaposition of elements (for example, a mixture of various kinds of grains), κρᾶσις—the most common term for the complete mutual coextension of elements (κρᾶσις δι' ὅλων), which came together to form a compound while retaining their inherent quality and allowing for separation (usually used for mixtures of moist elements, the classical example of wine and water), the word "σύγχυσις" (blending) was used for the fusion of elements whereby a new substance was created through the destruction of the original quality of the constituent elements. The term "μῖξις" was less precise. It served as a catch-all for any kind of mixture or blending (as for example, the blending of fire and iron) but only the term "σύγχυσις" entailed the loss of the distinction between two elements. See C. Stewart, 'Working the Earth of the Heart'. The Messalian Controversy in History, Texts, and Language to A.D. 431, Oxford Theological Monographs (Oxford 1991) 172–173; A. Dunavio, V. Desprez (eds.), Sancti patris nostri Macarii Aegyptii (Symeonis Mesopotamitae) Sermones ascetici et epistulae. Collectio I (Sancti montis Athou – Moscvue 2015) 726–728, note 490.
[36] B 33:1 (6), H 15:35. Literally: "intertwined or plaited with the soul" (συμπέπλεκται μετὰ τῆς ψυχῆς).
[37] B 4:30 (6).
[38] B 45:1 (1–2); H 16:1. In this concrete example, Pseudo-Macarius shows more precisely that the evil that inhabits the human soul is there as a stranger, a robber, as someone who does not belong there, while the human person is the owner of the house. See G. A. Maloney, Pseudo-Macarius. The Fifty Spiritual Homilies, 280, note 59. See also B 46:1 (11) – 2 (1); H 16:6.
[39] B 25:1 (13).
[40] B 46:1 (3); H 16:2; B 21:6; B 53:1 (6); H 11:3. Compare B 14:18.

nication, she loses her purity and is expelled. Similarly, the terrible serpent of sin is always present in the soul, enticing and provoking it. If the soul consents, it communicates with the incorporeal evil of the serpent (that is, spirit converses with spirit) and thereby commits adultery in the heart[41]. For this imagery Macarius relies on 1 Cor 6:16: *who clings to the harlot is one body with her*[42].

To describe how sin affected the spiritual sight of man Macarius appeals to different metaphors of darkness such as the veil of evil lying on our hearts, the dark veil of the worldly spirit, the veil of sin, the kingdom of darkness that infiltrated the city of the soul as well as several other images [43].

A number of expressions in the corpus underline the state of human captivity and slavery to sin. Macarius characterises sin as the hidden barren boulder, lying on the earth of the heart, the fetters of sin, the walls of evil, the palisade of evil, a dark prison of evil, a heavy yoke of sinful passions[44].

That sin is not natural to human nature is expressed by different terms for illness and death such as the incurable wound of evil passions, the mortality of passions, the scab and leprosy of sin, the illness of virtues, the misery of passions, the bitter poison of death, darkness and sin, the garment of death[45].

Macarius also uses numerous expressions to emphasise the alien nature of evil. Sin is described as the dark nightly second crop, the admixture of the foreign worldly spirit, the tares or weeds of sin, the bitter tree that the enemy planted within the soul, the robber that entered the household[46].

The reality of sin often appears in the corpus in the image of the serpent that lives in the human mind and thoughts, digs itself deeply into the secret chambers of the soul, sets up its nest there[47], creeps around the heart, and entices man with pleasure[48]. Davids also points out that Macarius applies similar epithets not only to the image of the serpent but also to the general descriptions

---

[41] B 32:8 (15); H 15:28.
[42] B 46:1 (3); H 16:2. Compare B 22:1 (16).
[43] B 26:12 (compare 2 Cor 3:15: B 35:3; B 22:2 (7), H 40:2); B 2:3 (13); B 14:11 (see also B 14:11; compare H 43:7, 35:3–5); B 15:2 (4), H 9:12; and B 2:5 (1); B 2:6 (7); H 16:12.
[44] B 3:3 (10) (compare C 3:1); B 22:2 (9); H 50:3; C 11; B 22:2 (9) (compare C 26:8); B 22:2(11).
[45] B 12:2 (3), H 20:5l (compare H 30:8); B 28:1 (4); H 44:3 (compare H 44:4; H 48:3; B 50:1 (6) (compare C 27:2); C 25:5; C 18:1 (see also B 2:12 (6)); B 28:1 (4).
[46] B 3:6 (4); C 18:1; B 18:4 (1), H 28:3; Mt 13:25; B 18:4 (1); B 32:3 (2).
[47] B 16:3 (7), H 17:15. See E. A. Davids, Das Bild vom Neuen Menschen: Ein Beitrag zum Verständnis des Corpus Macarianum, Salzburger Patristische Studien 2 (Salzburg – München 1968) 50.
[48] B 36:2 (1), H 37:1.

Adam's Inheritance: Macarian Teaching on Indwelling Sin

of sin[49]. So he speaks not only of the creeping and enticing serpent but also of the creeping desire of pleasure, of the evil power that appeals to reason and entices the soul, of sin with its filthy thoughts that "settles down and creeps over the thoughts of the heart along with an infinite number of demons"[50].

These few examples of Macarius' expressions for sin do not exhaust the rich arsenal of terms and images of the corpus but some of them shed light on the nature of sin and offer some insights into its essential characteristics.

Nature of Adam's Legacy: Indwelling Sin

1. Macarius always links sin to the special power of Satan over the human race. It is in the power of Satan over human nature that the root and cause of sin lie. Due to this power the whole race of Adam was seduced to evil and wickedness. The human nature of Adam's descendants is injured by the action of Satan who sows evil thoughts in the human heart and educates man in vice from the very moment of his birth. Macarius defines sin as "a certain power of Satan of a spiritual and intellectual nature" (λογική τις οὖσα καὶ νοερὰ δύναμις τοῦ σατᾶν)[51], or as "a sort of power and intellectual creation of Satan" (δύναμίς τις οὖσα λογικὴ τοῦ σατανᾶ καὶ οὐσία)[52], which dwells and operates within human nature. Davids points out that such definitions should be placed in a proper context[53]. On the one hand, the Macarian concept of sin as a spirit (πνεῦμα)[54] is connected with his interpretation of Jesus' words to Mary (Lk 10:38) as such that "were in-breathing (πνεῦμα) and of a certain power"[55]. Macarius believes that an alien power (divine or demonic) can penetrate the human soul and become like a second soul in the human soul. It happens when the soul listens to the spiritual or tempting word. On the other hand, the Macarian usage of such terminology as spirit and power can be explained by his view of the soul as "an intellectual and spiritual being" (νοερὰ καὶ λογικὴ οὐσία)[56]; or this language can be based on the Pauline understanding of "the spirit of

---

[49] See E. A. Davids, Das Bild vom Neuen Menschen, 50.
[50] B 36:1 (3); H 42:3; H 43:7.
[51] H 24:3.
[52] H 15:49. Compare B 4:29 (12). See also other expressions: C 1:3; B 14:14, B 18:1 (2), compare H 41:1; H 32:10, B 2:5 (2), B 22:1 (10), B 44:1. Compare Col 1:13.
[53] See E. A. Davids, Das Bild vom Neuen Menschen, 53.
[54] B 46:2 (6), H 16:7; H 16:10.
[55] H 12:16.
[56] B 52:1 (2). See also B 9:2 (8), H 1:7; B 32:8 (8), H 15:22.

the world" (πνεῦμα τοῦ κόσμου)⁵⁷. This last connection deserves special attention. Since Macarius often appeals to the Pauline definition of death as *the mind set on the flesh* (τὸ φρόνημα τῆς σαρκὸς, Rom 8:7), he also describes sin as the source of fleshly reasoning, contrasting this with the mind under the guidance of the Spirit. For him, sin is the unclean fountain of the evil thoughts of the soul⁵⁸, the breeding ground of passions that never cease pouring out. Due to this power of arousing evil thoughts, sin always ambushes and shackles the soul⁵⁹, and thereby impeding it from entering the life of the kingdom⁶⁰.

Macarius teaches that Satan accompanies man from within throughout his entire life. He surpasses man many times both in experience and knowledge, he knows his weak points, secret desires and thoughts; he can foresee human actions and behaviour, attack and threaten the soul as well as conceal himself and temporarily remain inactive in order to mislead the soul into self-conceit⁶¹. With such characteristics Satan seems to have an overwhelming power over man. However, by means of such descriptions Macarius principally wants to emphasise that man cannot escape the demonic temptation. Sooner or later Satan will certainly come with his tempting words and wicked suggestions, and man has no power to restrict or avoid this activity of evil.

2. Macarius also teaches that after Adam's transgression sin had been firmly established in human nature and from that time onward it operates in the fallen human race as an objective reality. This statement has to be clarified in two points. First, the author of the corpus does not say that evil exists by itself (ἐν ὑποστάσει)⁶², he only stresses that in us it "works on its own (ἐνυπόστατον) with full power, especially, in our senses, suggesting all sorts of obscene desires"⁶³. Evil has become an objective reality within human nature, which acts in all members of soul

---

[57] H 4:7, 1 Cor 2:12 ("Now we have received, not the spirit of the world, but the spirit which is of God; that we might know the things that are freely given to us of God"). Compare H 9:8.
[58] B 12:2 (2), H 20:5.
[59] C 3:1. Compare C 11:1.
[60] B 27:2 (7).
[61] B 7:6 (1); 8:1 (2). See also a detailed consideration of this passage in *H. Dörries*, Symeon von Mesopotamien. Die Überlieferung der messalianischen "Makarios"-Schriften, TU 55/1 (Leipzig 1941) 107–108.
[62] See the anti-Manichean statement of Macarius in B 46:1 (1), H 16:1.
[63] B 46:1 (1–2); H 16:1.

and body. Second, while confirming the real (ὑποστατική)[64] power of sin, Macarius does not say that evil is essential to human nature. When he speaks of sin, he always refers to the transgression of Adam as a cause due to which evil achieved its reality within human nature. By saying that evil is ἐνυπόστατον within the human being, the homilist simply acknowledges that sin is so imbedded in human nature, that it can be uprooted only by divine power[65]. It is impossible to separate sin from the soul by means of human efforts: "For just as the sun shines and the wind blows together, each having its own body and nature, yet no one can separate the wind from the sun unless God alone who can calm the wind so it blows no more, similarly sin is also mixed with the soul even though each has its own nature"[66]. Therefore, Macarius speaks of indwelling sin as "the very sin" (αὐτὴ ἡ ἁμαρτία)[67] or "the root of evil" (ἡ ῥίζα τῆς κακίας)[68], which is inaccessible to man.

3. One of the distinguishing features of indwelling sin is that it tends to expand and grow, as the darkness or fog thickens, and as the leaven grows[69]. Its influence does not finish at the point where it has darkened and veiled the spiritual sight of man so that man cannot see the Lord[70] but it has become in him the cause of all other evils: paralysis, fever, sickness, concupiscence, evil thoughts and passions—all flow from it. Macarius defines sin as a pastureland, a predisposition (πρόληψις)[71] and a strong habit, growing up with each person from infancy and instructing him in vices[72], as the mother of all faults and evil deeds[73]. As soon as sin flourishes, it produces vices and draws man to many sins[74], for "just as a house, full of smoke, belches it out into the outside air, so also the evil that abounds in the soul is poured outside and produces its own

---

[64] B 4:29 (10).
[65] H 3:4.
[66] H 2:2. Compare B 50:1 (9).
[67] B 34:14.
[68] B 4:29 (10). Compare H 15:46 (48).
[69] B 34:14.
[70] B 7:13 (2).
[71] Πρόληψις is a Stoic term. In Macarius it means simply the inveterate habit of sin that arises from the habituation to evil and disposes one to sin all the more. See M. Plested, The Macarian Legacy, 99. See B 22:2 (1); H 4:8.
[72] B 18:1 (3).
[73] B 34:14.
[74] B 14:12; B 27:1 (12).

kind of evil"[75]. Due to this capacity for expanding, sin, this leaven of evil passions, "has grown and increased so that in man the sinful passions have developed into fornications and debaucheries and idolatries and murders and other absurdities until mankind is permeated with the leaven of evil"[76]. Consequently, the entire world has gradually been lost in iniquity, and evil became something habitual. It grows together with man and educates him in evil[77].

4. Indwelling sin has also a special manner of acting. It operates secretly and does not want to be unmasked[78]. In general, it works in two main ways. One way of acting is with those who do not believe and another way—with those who believe. Within the unbelievers, this opposing power of darkness works in such a manner that these do not even suspect its actions. Macarius describes this as follows:

> For the world evident to your gaze, from kings to the weakest, is all in tumult, confusion, and battle, and no one knows the cause of it, nor do they understand that it is an unveiling of the evil which entered in through Adam's disobedience, *the sting of death* (1 Cor 15:56). It works in a hidden manner in the inner man and in the mind and contends with the thoughts. However, men are unaware that they are being moved by a certain foreign power when they do these things, but they think this is done naturally and that they do them with a certain self-determination. But those who have the peace of Christ in their mind and are enlightened by him know from whence these actions come[79].

Since it is impossible for this opposing power to remain completely unknown and hidden from those who believe in God and partake in divine grace, it fights against them pretending to be grace. Though grace acts in the believers, sin still remains inside and suggests to them to imagine that they are rich and need no more so that they may cease their work; and then sin builds up and takes over within. It captures the pasturelands of the soul, robs it secretly, and leads it away from God[80]. In many cases, Satan struggles against the believers by pretended good thoughts. Through a cunning suggestion such as "In this way you can please God",

---
[75] H 16:12.
[76] H 24:2. Compare B 53:2.
[77] B 4:29 (13).
[78] B 4:29 (12). H 32:10; C 21:1,2; C 25:1.
[79] H 15:49.
[80] B 34:14.

he leads a person astray to subtle and half-truths, and the person, being unable to detect that he (or she) is secretly being seduced, *falls into the snare and perdition of the devil* (1 Tm 6:9)[81].

5. One important characteristic of sin is that it is unrestrained evil. Macarius characterises it as follows: "It is continually bubbling up like a centre of a fountain"[82], or: "Just as the water runs through a pipe, so too sin runs through the heart and the thoughts"[83]. It troubles and harasses the soul constantly, besets and attacks it from all sides. The homilist usually presents this feature of sin by the image of Satan in his indomitableness: he is never quieted; he utterly hates humans and never stops waging war against man[84]; he is intractable and unbridled, so that neither prophets, nor apostles, nor the Scriptures could restrain him and bring him under control, only God alone can do this[85]. Therefore, nobody, even the perfect ones, can live totally in security. As long as man lives in this world and wears the flesh, he is always in a state of anxiety and subject to attack[86].

It should be pointed out that Macarius applies these general characteristics of sin to all people, regardless of whether they are baptised or not. Such a view alludes to the Messalian ideas about the indwelling demon that persists within the human soul[87]. One polemical passage in the corpus seems to explicitly bear testimony to such a similarity. Macarius argues as follows:

> But if you insist that through the coming of Christ sin was condemned and that after baptism evil has no more power of suggestion within the human heart, then you ignore the fact that from the coming of the Lord up to this day the many who have been baptized, have they not thought evil things at some time? Have not some of them turned to vain desire for glory, to fornication, or to gluttony? Moreover, are all those who live in the Church, men of the world, are they endowed with a pure and blameless heart? Or do we not find after baptism that many commit many sins

---

[81] B 7:6 (7–8); H 26:12 (with slight difference).
[82] H 15:46 (48); B 6:3 (2). Compare C 11.
[83] B 32:8 (6), H 15:21. See also B 6:9 (2–3), H 26:21; B 2:5 (1–2).
[84] B 32:7, H 15:18–19.
[85] C 21:2.
[86] B 7:7 (1), H 26:14; H 16:12.
[87] On the Messalian teaching concerning indwelling demons, see B. Dehandschutter, Demons among the Messalians, in: N. Vos, W. Otten (eds.), Demons and the Devil in Ancient and Medieval Christianity, Supplements to Vigiliae Christianae 108 (Leiden – Boston 2011) 183–191.

and many live in error? So even after baptism the thief has a foot hold (νομήν) and can freely enter and do what he pleases.[88]

Yet, however similar to the Messalian propositions the Macarian thoughts might sound, they cannot be regarded as Messalian, for they differ from them on a decisive point: while acknowledging the significance of prayer, Macarius never claims that prayer can release man from evil. On the contrary, he affirms that it is impossible to separate the soul from sin, so that neither prayer, nor all human efforts suffice unless God comes and turns back this evil wind. Man is unable to purify himself by his own strength. He can only resist the attacks of the Evil One and work the earth of his heart. It is God alone who can heal man from sin and dry up the fountain of evil thoughts as he once healed the woman afflicted with an issue of blood[89].

The passage cited above also clearly shows that baptism does not suffice to remove indwelling sin from the human heart[90]. The elimination of indwelling sin is associated in the corpus not with baptism but with the state of perfection. Since baptism does not immediately provide perfection but only gives the potential to obtain it, sin is still present in the soul even after baptism. Ultimately, indwelling sin can only be removed by the coming of the Lord: either in this life, when one attains the state of perfection and acquires the Holy Spirit in all assurance and perception, or at the moment of death, when God rewards everyone according to one's deeds.

This makes clear that the term "indwelling sin" does not imply original sin but describes rather the unavoidability of temptations and the lack of divine protection against them. Through Adam's transgression evil received access to the human heart and became able to act through the thoughts. It is the loan

---

[88] B 32:3 (2), H 15:14. Maloney's translation is modified.
[89] B 12:1–2, H 20:4.
[90] On the Macarian teaching on baptism see: H. *Dörries*, Symeon von Mesopotamien, 202–205 and 235–237; A. J. M. *Davids*, Der Grosse Brief des Makarios. Analyse einer griechischer Kontroversschrift, in: T. Michels (ed.), Heuresis. Festschrift für Andreas Rohracher 25 Jahre Erzbischof von Salzburg (Salzburg 1969) 78–90, 109; K. *Ware*, The Sacrament of Baptism and the Ascetic Life in the Teaching of Mark the Monk, Studia Patristica 10 (1970) 441–452; O. *Hesse*, Markos Eremites und Symeon von Mesopotamien, Untersuchung und Vergleich ihrer Lehre zur Taufe und zur Askese (Göttingen 1973) 45–121; M. *Kniewasser*, Deux homélies inédites du Pseudo-Macaire sur la 'subtilité' physique de l'Esprit, Istina 19 (1974) 343–349; M.-J. *Le Guillou*, Remarques sur la notion macarienne de «subtilité», Istina 19 (1974) 339–342; H. *Dörries*, Die Theologie des Makarios/Symeon, Abhandlungen der Akademie der Wissenschaften in Göttingen, Philologisch-Historische Klasse, Dritte Folge 103 (Göttingen 1978) 426–434; V. *Desprez*, Le baptême chez le Pseudo-Macaire, Ecclesia Orans 5 (1988) 121–155. See also the analysis of the scholarly discussion in: М. Горяча, Подорож у серці. Динамічна антропологія преподобного Макарія, 217–226.

of or entrance to the pastureland of the human heart which Satan gained to and now can enter and sow the seeds of all evils. One image can help understand this idea:

> Take the example of a garden having fruit-bearing trees and other sweet-scented plants, in which all is well cultivated and beautifully laid out. It also has a small wall before a ditch to protect it. Should it so happen that a fast-moving river passed that way, even though only a little of the water dashes against the wall, it tears away the foundation. It digs a course and gradually dissolves the foundations. It enters and tears away and uproots all the plants and destroys the entire cultivation and renders it fruitless. So it is also with man's heart. It has the good thoughts, but the rivers of evil are always flowing near the heart, seeking to bring it down and draw it to its own side. If the mind should be turned ever so little toward frivolity and yield to unclean thoughts, look out—the spirits of error have roamed the pastureland and have entered and have overturned there the beautiful things. They have destroyed good thoughts and devastated the soul.[91]

Man cannot change the course of the river. The only thing he can do is to fortify the wall, thus protecting the garden. In baptism man receives all the necessary equipment to provide this fortification. Yet, he still has to work hard and struggle with the flow of evil thoughts, and even doing so, he is not able to stop this river or to turn its watercourse. This belongs to God alone. It is only when man achieves union with God that he becomes protected by divine power, and the river can bring him no harm, though it still continues to flow. As long as the soul is in union with God, it is inaccessible to the tempting words of Satan. However, even then man cannot live in security, for grace can withdraw at any moment, and then he again becomes disposed to the temptations by this unrestrained evil. This example shows that Macarius understands the indwelling sin in terms of temptation, which is unavoidable till the very end of human life.

What is important in his teaching concerning sin is not the distinction between the transgression of Adam and its consequences, but the awareness of a radical presence of evil within the human heart, which man experiences in his daily life and spiritual struggle, regardless of how this evil found its place there: either through the inheritance of Adam's transgression, or by way of education in a perverted milieu, or by means of a personal decision and agreement with evil thoughts and desires after baptism. This persistent evil reaches far beyond the human grasp and efforts and therefore unconditionally necessitates the coming of the Saviour in order to liberate man from its tyranny.

---

[91] H 43:6.

Conclusion

Macarius shares with other early Church Fathers the conviction in the solidarity of the whole human race with the first Adam and in his fate after the fall. He teaches that through Adam's transgression evil passed to all humanity and gained access to the human heart. Referring to Adam's inheritance to his descendants, Macarius describes this reality of evil in different terms and images such as death, the leaven of passions, blindness, captivity, slavery, illness etc. Most often he speaks of indwelling sin, which he defines as the spiritual power of Satan, firmly established in human nature, so that nobody can remove it save God alone. It operates there even after baptism and seeks the consent of human will. In the Macarian corpus, the notion of indwelling sin does not correspond to the idea of original or ancestral sin, which is removed by baptism, but rather has a psychological and moral connotation, implying the human vulnerability with regard to the evil attacks. It covers a wide range of different experiences of evil, among which personal sins are only the tip of the iceberg. Much more remains invisible and scarcely comprehensible, hidden somewhere in the deepest reaches of the human heart and coming out from somewhere in our subconscious. Macarius can personify indwelling sin with the images of Satan, demons, a serpent, wild beasts, or describe it impersonally as the desire for pleasure within the human heart but, in fact, he always means the same thing—the experience of the impossibility for man to be free from evil suggestions and attacks. This activity of evil is experienced both before and after baptism, both in the state of grace and in the state of sin.

The development and refinement of the theological terminology of sin in the following generations took a direction, in which the Macarian idea of indwelling sin could hardly find a place. Consequently, it was reconsidered and reworked by two Orthodox ascetics of the 5th century: Mark the Monk and Diadochus of Photice. In the light of this critical revision, it is evident that hamartiology of Macarius can be properly understood only in the framework of his own spiritual teaching.

Pablo Argárate, Graz (Austria)

"Sin was planted in our father Adam and in our mother Eve on the day they sinned. It entered and lived in all their children" (*LG* 19, 3) Evil and Sin in the Syriac *Liber Graduum*

Abstract:
The Book of Steps (Liber Graduum) offers a non-systematic but narrative approach to the question of sin and evil. In order to understand its contribution to those themes, we need to refer to the context of Syriac (ascetic) theology. For the communities addressed by the Book of Steps, it is crucial to provide an explanation to the question about why evil and sin remain indwelling in the depth of human heart, even after baptism.

The *Liber Graduum*

The *Liber Graduum* (=LG)[1] is a collection of 30 *memre* by an anonymous author, preceded by a prologue by the Syriac editor of the work. It is not mentioned in the Vatican manuscripts until 1719. The work, discovered by Kmosko in 1901 among the manuscripts of the British Museum, was edited by himself in 1926 with an extensive introduction (*Praefatio*), a Latin translation[2], a dossier on the development of Messalianism and a detailed index[3]. This publication will strongly determine the directions of research for many years. In addition, Kmosko mentions three key areas of research in his introduction, namely the dating of the *LG*, its placement within the Messalian movement and its relation to the underlying text of the *Diatessaron*.

---

[1] Cf. P. *Argárate*, Das Ktābā dmasqātā oder Liber Graduum. Ein Überblick über den Forschungsstand, in: D. Bumazhnov, E. Grypeou, T. B. Sailors, A. Toepel (eds.), Bibel, Byzanz und Christlicher Orient. Festschrift für Stephen Gerö zum 65. Geburtstag (Leuven 2011) 239–258.
[2] In addition to this one, as far as I know there is only one published translation into modern languages: the English translation by R. A. Kitchen, M. F. G. Parmentier, The Book of Steps. The Syriac Liber Graduum (Kalamazoo, MI 2004).
[3] M. *Kmosko* (ed.), Liber Graduum, Patrologia Syriaca I.3 (Paris 1926).

In the edition of the *Patrologia Syriaca* by Kmosko, the text of the *LG* takes 460 columns. The edition is based on two manuscripts[4] that contain all the *memre* and 13 containing only some of them. The title, *Ktābā dmasqātā*, cannot be attributed to the author. Furthermore, it occurs in only seven manuscripts and clearly refers to *memre* (=M) 19–20 and not to the entire work. Neither an ascending gradation as in the case of John Climacus is to be found in the *LG*. Wickham, on the other hand, claims that the original title was: "On the Way of Life of Perfection and the Discernment of the Commandments of Our Lord"[5].

The author of the prologue expresses that the author of the *LG* explicitly wishes to remain anonymous and that nothing is known about his life and times. He adheres only to traditions that portray the author as one of the last disciples of the apostles. The editor assumes that he was one of the first teachers to write in Syriac. Furthermore, he calls him "blessed" (*tubana*). Therefore even the editor of the *LG* does not know much about its author. Recently, B. Colless unsuccessfully suggested that Adelphios of Edessa was the author of the *LG*[6]. On the contrary, almost all specialists today agree on a deliberate anonymity. Moreover, the author sees himself as a charismatic interpreter of the Bible. In addition, from the content of the work it can be inferred that the author is the spiritual leader of a pre-monastic Christian community in a time of upheaval[7].

As for the dating of our work, Baumstark in 1922 dated it to the 6th century and, at the same time, attributed it to Severus of Antioch[8]. This was, however, soon rejected. Instead, Kmosko suggested the first half of the 4th century[9]. Hausherr[10], on the other hand, advocates a date around 400, which is usually accepted. What tends to be overlooked, however, is the fact that Hausherr's finding is dependent on the *LG*'s relation to Messalianism. If this relation is called into cause, the justification of that dating becomes problematic. Today,

---

[4] Syrus 201 (a) from the Bibliothèque nationale de France and Syrus 180 (R) from the Monastery of St. Mark in Jerusalem. The first manuscript comes from the 12th century, while the second one from the 7th–8th centuries.
[5] L. Wickham, The "Liber Graduum" Revisited, in: R. Lavenant (ed.), Symposium Syriacum (Roma 1994) 179.
[6] B. Colless, Unpublished paper at the VII Symposium Syriacum in Sydney (2000).
[7] R. A. Kitchen, Becoming Perfect: The Maturing of Asceticism in the Liber Graduum, Journal of the Canadian Society for Syriac Studies 2 (2002) 31.
[8] A. Baumstark, Geschichte der syrischen Literatur (Bonn 1922) 165.
[9] Cf. M. Kmosko, Liber Graduum. Praefatio, CXLIX–CLX.
[10] I. Hausherr, Quanam aetate prodierit „Liber Graduum"?, OCP 1 (1935) 502: "Librum Graduum certo ante annum 435, certo non ante tria ultima decennia quarti, probabilius nec multo ante nec multo post annum 400 elucubratum esse".

the work is situated in the second half of the fourth century, primarily during the persecutions of Christians under Shapur II in the years 339-379. Based on the mention of the Cappadocians and Evagrios in the prologue, the year 400 is given as the *terminus ad quem*. Information about the place remains extremely meagre. Based on a mention of the small river Zab[11], the *LG* is to be placed within the Persian Empire in Mesopotamia in the Adiabene, in present-day northern Iraq[12]. Close to its home, there is a hilly region with frost in winter near the Roman Empire, where Latin fragments are being used.

The various *memre* are diverse in scope and genre. M 19 is the longest, while M 6 is the shortest *memra*. There is hardly any order[13]. Wickham[14] presents a special division of the work. R. Kitchen, on the other hand, proposes the following structure: a) Basic Commandments (M 1-9), b) Advanced Perfection (10-24), c) Last Period and Redemption of the Righteous (25-30). In terms of genre, one finds in the *LG* a rule for the congregation, long biblical expositions, sermons, tracts on the controversy over the role of the contemporary church and also on sexuality and marriage, brief juxtapositions of the righteous and the perfect, a justification and encouragement of the spiritual office of the righteous[15]. Above all, Kitchen sees in the *LG* a "sect-canon" which serves the needs of the community[16]. This canon: 1. legitimizes the members of the sect and describes what they must do, 2. explains the internal structure of the Church, 3. constitutes a declaration of resistance against the world, 4. Is an evidence of conflict and persecution by outsiders, 5. delineates the iden-

---

[11] LG 30, 14.
[12] Differently L. *Wickham*, Teaching about God and Christ in the Liber Graduum, in: H. Brennecke (ed.), Logos. FS Luise Abramowski (Berlin 1993) 488: "The work probably comes from the fourth century; its milieu is West, rather than East, Syria".
[13] Cf. L. *Wickham*, The „Liber Graduum" Revisited, 184: "The collection of 30 *memre* is a congeries of different works of varying kinds, put together sometimes in the wrong order; Kmosko's division, *pars didactica/pars polemica* may correctly indicate the reasoning behind the present arrangement".
[14] Ibid., 184: "Within the 30 I discern: (a) A treatise in probably at least two *memre* 'On the mode of life of full maturity and on the discrimination of Our Lord's commandments' = I/IX, XIII/XIV, XVI/XX, 15. (b) A group of *memre* dealing with sin and repentance: XXI, XXIII-XXVI; perhaps a single *memra*, perhaps in the order: XXVI, XXI, XXIII-XXV. (c) An address to a beginner: XXVII. (d) Two sermons: XII and XXIX (?). (e) A digest of (a): XXX. (f). Independent or disconnected essays dealing with particular themes: X, XI, XV, XX, 16 to end, XXII, XXVIII".
[15] R. A. *Kitchen*, Becoming Perfect: The Maturing of Asceticism, 31.
[16] R. A. *Kitchen*, The Gattung of the Liber Graduum, Implications for a Sociology of Asceticism, in: H. J. W. Drijvers (ed.), IV Symposium Syriacum, 1984: Literary Genres in Syriac literature (Roma 1987) 175.

tity of the sect, 6. develops an eschatology, a theology of the final goal of the community[17].

From the literary perspective, Böhlig has seen in the *LG* a certain influence of Greco-Roman rhetoric[18]. While Juhl disputes this statement[19], Wickham perceives, nevertheless, a mastery of cultivated rhetorical skills[20]. There is little, if any, reception and impact of the *LG*. In fact, the basic distinction between the righteous and the perfect only appears in Philoxenos of Mabbug, but in a different context. Since we do not have a translation in other languages, it can be assumed that the *LG* did not transcend the boundaries of the Syriac Church. On the contrary, the *LG* Church remains an isolated, short-lived and local phenomenon. It will not survive the internal and external fierce conflicts and upheavals. On the one hand, this kind of Christianity is strongly rooted in the archaic peculiarities of the Syriac Church and can be classified in the succession of the itinerant missionaries of the *Acts of Thomas* and the Pseudo-Clementine *De virginitate*[21]. On the other hand, however, this form of Christianity remains an unsolved mystery. Nevertheless, according to Vööbus, the *LG* has inestimable value.

> It is one of the most ancient works which has come to us from ancient Syriac literature devoted to the subject of spiritual life and asceticism. As such it is a very precious source about the very archaic spirituality in Christendom in Mesopotamia. It unfolds pneumatic mysticism, characteristic of the archaic Syrian spirituality indigenous to Mesopotamian Christianity. It is an exceptional opportunity to be permitted to here so deeply a glimpse into such an important phase in the history of spirituality in the lands washed by the Tigris and the Euphrates—in a document whose

---

[17] Ibid.
[18] R. A. *Kitchen*, The Gattung of the Liber Graduum, 173–182. A. *Böhlig*, Zur Rhetorik im Liber Graduum, in: A. Böhlig (ed.), Gnosis und Synkretismus, 1. Teil (Tübingen 1989) 305: "An Hand dieser Beispiele glaubte ich, zeigen zu können, dass die Sermonen des Liber Graduum nach rhetorischen Formen aufgebaut sind. Das *genus deliberativum* scheint dabei mitunter in das *genus demonstrativum* überzugehen".
[19] D. *Juhl*, Die Askese im Liber Graduum und bei Afrahat. Eine vergleichende Studie zur frühsyrischen Frömmigkeit (Wiesbaden 1996) especially 25–27: "Es ist also an Einflüsse griechisch-römischer Rhetorik ebensowenig zu denken wie an Einflüsse hellenistischer Theologie, denn das Zwei-Stufen-Schema des anonymen Autors ist mit dem Dualismus nicht gleichzusetzen".
[20] L. *Wickham*, Teaching about God and Christ in the Liber Graduum, 487–488.
[21] Cf. D. *Caner*, Wandering, begging monks: spiritual authority and the promotion of monasticism in late antiquity (Berkeley, CA 2002). See also V. *Desprez*, Le monachisme primitif: des origines jusqu'au concile d'Éphèse (Bégrolles-en-Mauges 1998) 485.

antiquity and content make it an incomparable source, valuable beyond price for its contribution to our knowledge of archaic Syrian spirituality[22].

A topic already mentioned by Kmosko concerns the biblical sources of the *LG*. Here Kmosko's remark proves to be correct. Our work is indeed based on the *Diatessaron*, as Rücker later confirmed[23]. According to Kerschensteiner, the *Corpus Paulinum*[24] is based on a pre-Peshitta form[25]. This, however, is relativized by Baker[26].

Beyond the canonical writings, certain other writings such as the Book of Jesus Sirach[27], the *Acts of Thecla*, the *Didache*, the *Shepherd of Hermas* and the *Gospel of Thomas* become visible in our work. Due to the discovery of the Nag Hammadi library, the relationship of the *LG* to other writings was intensively researched in the 1960s. In particular, the relationship of the *LG* to the *Gospel of Thomas* was discussed. Opinions differed on this. While Ménard and Quispel find a dependence, Baker denies a direct quotation[28]. According to him, the common property of the *LG* and the *Gospel of Thomas* can be explained in such a way that "they seem to be heirs of a similar tradition, though they apply it differently"[29]. Poirier expresses the relationship of Aphrahat to the *Gospel of Thomas* in a similar way[30]; he denies a direct dependence[31]. A decade later

---

[22] A. Vööbus, History of Asceticism in the Syrian Orient, III (Leuven 1988) 17.
[23] A. Rücker, Die Zitate aus dem Matthäusevangelium im syrischen „Buche der Stufen", Byzantinische Zeitschrift 20 (1932) 342-354.
[24] Regarding Paul in the *LG*, see M. Westerhoff, Zur Paulus-Rezeption im Liber Graduum, in: M. Tamcke (ed.), Syriaca (Münster 2002) 259.
[25] J. Kerschensteiner, Der Altsyrische Paulustext (Leuven 1970).
[26] A. Baker, The Significance of the New Testament Text of the Syriac Liber Graduum, in: F. L. Cross (ed.), Studia Evangelica 5 (Berlin 1968) 171-175.
[27] Cf. W. Strothmann, Jesus-Sirach-Zitate bei Afrahat, Ephraem und im Liber Graduum, in: R. H. Fischer (ed.), A Tribute to A. Vööbus. Studies in early Christian literature and its environment, primarily in the Syrian East (Chicago 1977) 153-158.
[28] A. Baker, The "Gospel of Thomas" and the Syriac "Liber Graduum", New Testament Studies 12 (1965/1966) 55: "G.T. in general is gnostic, whereas L.G., at least in its practical application, is not gnostic at all. But they seem to be heirs of a similar tradition, though they apply it differently. It is possible by their joint help to elucidate the logia they have assumed".
[29] A. Baker, The "Gospel of Thomas", 55.
[30] A. Poirier, L'Évangile selon Thomas (log. 16 et 23) et Aphraate (Dém. XVIII, 10-11), in: R.-G. Coquin (ed.), Mélanges Antoine Guillaumont (Genève 1988) 18: "L'enracinement syriaque de Thomas, tant sur le plan des idées que sur celui du lexique et de la syntaxe".
[31] A. Baker, Early Syrian Asceticism, Downside Review 88 (1970) 403: "a direct dependence remains unproved. It is equally possible and, in my opinion, much more probable to explain the relation by saying that our authors (scil. Aphraates and *Liber Graduum*) picked up stray logia which also happen to appear in the *Gospel of Thomas*".

Englezakis[32] again discusses the question of the parallelism between the *LG* and the *Gospel of Thomas*.

A fundamental element of the *LG* is to be seen in its strong biblical approach[33]. Although it is not primarily an exegetical work, it is filled with over 1200 biblical quotations[34]. In addition, there are countless allusions and ultimately the entire horizon of thought of the work.

Main Argument of the *LG*

According to the author of the *LG*, Adam and Eve, our first parents, were created by God in the state of perfection. Deceived by Satan, who convinces them to desire becoming God, they fell from that perfection. Having eventually repented of having followed the Evil one in his rebellion, God will statue the state of uprightness and with Christ will reopen the way to perfection[35]. The *LG* is unique in distinguishing Christians into perfects and upright ones[36], who have different ways, tasks, and even commandments. Perfect are required to carry out a life of full renunciation, neither working nor possessing nor marrying nor judging their brethren but forgiving and loving everybody, especially the evil-doers and praying for them, strongly based on the ethics of the Mount Sermon[37]. The upright ones live in the world, work, possess and marry. In

---

[32] B. *Englezakis*, Thomas Logion 30, NTS 25 (1979) 262–272.

[33] Cf. *M. Westerhoff*, Zur Paulus-Rezeption im Liber Graduum, 253–254: "Der *LG* entfaltet keinen Gedanken ohne Berufung auf die Heilige Schrift und hier insbesondere auf ‚alles was unser Herr und der Apostel (…) ihren Jüngern befohlen haben' (5,5 [108]). Die Herrenworte entstammen der Bergpredigt und der Spruchtradition der Synoptiker insgesamt, weniger dem Johannesevangelium".

[34] Kitchen can affirm: "Virtually all his illustrations and allusions are biblical—with the exception of Memra Six […]" (*R. A. Kitchen, M. F. G. Parmentier* (eds.) The Book of Steps. The Syriac Liber Graduum [Kalamazoo, MI 2004] LXIII). On general preaching in Syria, cf. *H. O. Old*, The Reading and Preaching of the Scriptures in the Worship of the Christian Church, II: The Patristic Age (Grand Rapids, MI 1998) 247–295. Cf. also *L. Wickham*, Teaching about God and Christ in the Liber Graduum, 487: "The work is certainly learned in its scriptural exegeses and wealth of biblical quotations especially from the gospels and the Pauline corpus inclusive of Hebrews (without Revelation, 2 Peter, Jude and the small Johannines, though James is not cited either)".

[35] Cf. *P. Argárate*, The Perfect and Perfection in the Book of Steps, in: *K. S. Heal, R. A. Kitchen* (eds.), Breaking the Mind. New Studies in the Syriac "Book of Steps" (Washington D.C. 2014) 156–172.

[36] As stated, only Philoxenos will follow into this distinction, understanding it, however, in a different way.

[37] Cf. *P. Argárate*, 'Love Whoever Hates You and Persecutes You': The Reception of the Mount Sermon in a Fourth-Century Anonymous Work, The Syriac Annals of the Romanian Academy [SARA] 1 (2020–2021) 129–148.

such a way, they can be saved even if they cannot attain perfection, which would require perfectly imitating Christ and the original couple in their state of perfection. In addition to these main groups there are several other which as a matter of fact find themselves in deep violent conflicts.

Evil

In my presentation, I will focus upon the evil par excellence, Satan, and then I will delve into sin, first of our forefathers, presenting and analyzing the detailed account of that primaeval transgression and eventually examine the consequences of that event for their children. In this regard, I will discuss if there is or even could be in the *LG* an inherited sin.

First of all, in the *LG* Satan gains precise contours, becoming its most impressive and colorful character[38]. Again and again he appears through the pages of the *LG* under different names and characterizations. He is chiefly the Evil one, but also the Prince of the demons, the Tempter, the Teacher, the Tree[39], the Murderer, the Denier, the Enemy[40], the Corrupter, the one who upset creation through his evil teaching[41], and blinded Adam and Eve[42], the Shrew one, the Deceiver, the one who fights against humans and "kills the people who obey him"[43]. He is even called "the god of this world", who "wished to become a god in heaven"[44] and "on earth"[45]. Highly relevant is, however, his characterization as "the Rebel". In this regard, as we will see, in the concrete context of the first temptation, Eve, who interestingly plays the role of messenger between Satan and Adam, back and forth, refers to the former, precisely as the Rebel. Indeed, she tells Adam: "hat rebel advised us well, if as much because he preceded us and is older than us, he knows". This short passage is rich in nuances. Satan is not only the one who had rebelled against God but

---

[38] G. Fuchs, Auflehnung und Fall im syrischen Buch der Stufen (Liber Graduum). Eine motiv- und traditionsgeschichtliche Untersuchung (Wiesbaden 2012) 311: "Das Fascinosum des Bösen (*malum*) umgibt besonders seine Verkörperung, den Satan, die eindrucksvollste, nuancenreichste und am farbigsten geschilderte Gestalt des *Liber Graduums*".
[39] LG 21, 1: "Because God had only taught what is good to Adam and Eve when he created them, they did not know evil until they had obeyed Satan and he taught them evil. Because of this Satan is called the 'Tree', through which Adam and Eve knew evil and good".
[40] LG 23, 3. I follow the English translation of R. A. Kitchen, M. F. G. Parmentier, The Book of Steps.
[41] LG 23, 4.
[42] LG 21, 10.
[43] LG 22, 8.
[44] LG 23, 5.
[45] LG 23, 8.

also regarded at least by Eve as somebody who knows, given his age, and in this regard he seems qualified to advise the first couple what to do. We observe also in this short passage that will be analyzed in detail below, that Satan argues, although in the *LG* not directly with Adam, but with his companion. He eventually will persuade and trick not only Eve but also the first father. Satan is on the one hand the intellectual, sophistic deceiver ("Adam and Eve supposed that everything that the evil one had taught them would come to be"[46]). The other key characterization is of Satan the Rebel (*maruda*) par excellence, who has rebelled to God and would be eventually overthrown by him. This polarity between rebellion and subsequent fall is central in the *LG*'s account of Satan[47], but also of the first couple.

In the M 23, the *LG* in drawing a parallel with Judas, summarizes its teaching on Satan: created in high honor by God, he freely became his opponent and "wicked ruler". His rebellion is motivated by his desire to become God and had as a consequence his fall and transformation into the "son of darkness", "a dweller of darkness". Indeed, it is summarily stated: "The worst of all of this [...] he sought to become a god, but he was defeated and fell"[48] and again: "Satan desired to become a god on earth"[49]. We will later see, how that desire to become God or at least "as God" will eventually allure the first couple, who will ally with the Rebel.

> Now God did not make anything that is an opponent, but God did create this one who today is an opponent. [God had created him] as one of the higher powers and made him [sit at his] right hand, as he had raised up Iscariot on his right. By his own will, however, [Judas] crossed over to the left side; so also this wicked ruler, under the pretext that God had given him power like the angels, and [that God] had promoted him and placed him on [his] right, yet he acted wickedly with his authority, and desired to become God. The Lord cast him down from heaven to earth and light departed from him and he became the son of darkness. His power was cast out from the light and he became a dweller in the darkness[50].

The *LG* will constantly stress the voluntary character of that original transgression, as it will do it again and again not only with Adam and Eve's but also with our own sin.

---

[46] LG 15, 1.
[47] Cf. G. *Fuchs*, Auflehnung und Fall, 313.
[48] LG 23, 5.
[49] LG 23, 8.
[50] LG 23, 1.

Sin

Having briefly sketched the *LG*'s views on Satan, it is time to focus on Adam's (and eventually on our) sin. It has been referred above that that "original" sin had as its most catastrophic consequence the loss of the state of perfection, although God would eventually devise another way back, the one of "justice" or "uprightness". In any case, Adam and Eve's sin is understood as a transgression. Indeed, in referring to that, our author uses mainly two verbs: *htt* (fail, sin) and *'bar* (transgress). The first one is negatively used in order to describe the initial situation of Adam "before sinning", the one which preceded sin, whereas the following stage is presented as postlapsarian, the one after the sin of our forefathers. As stated, this sin is understood as a transgression of God's commandment, i.e. the law, the word received by Adam at the beginning.

> [J]ust as the heart of our father Adam was pure before he transgressed against the commandment[51].

This first sin is frequently described with some other verbs. First, with *napl* (fall). It is the fall from a "primitive form (*dmuta*)" or simply from perfection, from heaven. Also frequently connected to Adam's fall is the verb *'askel* (be deceived, err, sin), which is also close to *htt*.

A highly-relevant question that has always drawn attention is the one about the nature of that sin. In this regard, the *LG* is very clear. Adam and Eve's sin is pride. Indeed through sin they entered into the "form (*dmiruta*) of pride". As referred before in relation to Satan, the verb to rebel (*mrad*) takes a singular place. Following the advice of the Rebel, Adam and Eve "were persuaded and turned their minds to the earth and descended from heaven and their mind was on the earth like their bodies"[52].

It is useful to listen to the particular and detailed presentation of Adam and Eve's sin in the account of the *LG*[53]. Behind it, it is Satan who takes the initiative by deceiving and seducing the first couple. In that account, we could also see how our author expands or even departs from the biblical text, in following different Syriac traditions. The first piece of advice is, upon the background of Syriac pre-monastic asceticism, to abandon poverty and, on the contrary, to

---

[51] LG 20, 1.7.
[52] LG 21, 10.
[53] Other presentations refer in addition to the tree (for instance LG 20, 1) and to the serpent (LG 21, 17) of the biblical narrative.

possess[54], to acquire and to rule as a king. Possession and power, as appears in the narrative of Jesus' temptations, come here to the foreground. Adam will answer to Eve that God had commanded them neither to work nor to possess. Also here, perfection is tied to the absence of work and possessions. The final promise of the Devil is the one which had moved him himself. In the end, they will become like God, and in attaining this status, God will have no power upon them. Satan, on the contrary, already knows that this had not worked with himself but still allures the couple that believes that he cares for them and he knows what he is talking about.

> But when the deceitful one approached Eve and Adam through his deception, he seduced them as he would have seduced Jesus, and said to the Creator of the Universe, 'Look, see how the earth is attractive with its possession and its kingdoms. Listen to me and take possession and rule and you will not become poor and empty yourself and become a stranger on the earth'. Our Lord said to him, 'Go behind me, Satan'. Immediately, his battle and temptation wasted away and he was overthrown and vanished. In this way he also seduced Adam with deceit and approached him as someone concerned [for him] and a bearer of [his] burden and he counseled Eve to advise Adam and commanded her to speak to Adam so that he might acquire wealth and become a king. 'Look, gold and silver are on the earth and all sorts of pleasures. Possess and enjoy yourself; rule, increase, and multiply', the evil one counseled. 'Cast off from yourself asceticism and renunciation and holiness, also lowliness, and know evil as well as good things and grow and become like God who created you'. Eve advised Adam, 'That rebel advised us well, if as much because he preceded us and is older than us, he knows'. Adam said to Eve, 'Go back and say to him, 'Our Creator commanded us not to obey you, nor eat from [the tree], nor be united with earthly things'; that is, we should not labor or possess anything on the earth'. The tongue [of the evil one] again persuaded [Eve], 'Because [God] did not wish and was not content that you become like him'. Adam said, 'If he does not desire that we become like this, will he not punish us because we have dared [to do this]?' The evil one said, 'When you become like him, what can he do to you?'[55].

As already shown, the author of the *LG* consistent with Early Syriac traditions stresses the freedom of Adam's fall[56]. That freedom (*heruta*) is regarded as a gift from God to our forefathers that distinguished them from the rest of

---

[54] Cf. LG 25, 5: "[The evil one] deluding the Perfect one, says the following, 'It is virtuous that you should acquire a little [wealth] through Uprightness, sufficient for your own comfort and for whomever comes to you. Build for yourself a dwelling that is just adequate for strangers to come and rest in it'".
[55] LG 21, 9.
[56] A. *Kowalski*, Perfezione e giustizia di Adamo nel Liber Graduum (Roma 1989) 123-124: "La libertà di Adamo e la sua libera volontà potevano essere dedotte dallo stesso racconto della

creation. Being free, the first parents disobeyed God with a free act of their will. The voluntary character of sin and the full consciousness of the sinner is underlined again in the following passage, which considers that sin a rebellion:

> Adam and Eve desired all these things but were humbled through the mediation of the evil one and they abandoned heaven and the heavenly wealth and loved the earth and all that is in it. However, Adam and Eve were naked without this visible clothing in this world. Adam and Eve had been like this before they had sinned, and it was not that they did not know they had sinned by their rebellion[57].

Negatively expressed, "Adam had a will, and if he had not so desired, the evil one would not have oppressed him"[58]. Also from the Pharaoh, who in the M 23 is parallelized with Satan, and the Israelites it is explicitly stated that they "sinned by their own [choice, for] the Lord did not compel them"[59]. On the contrary, "if we or they had stood by them, Satan might have been defeated"[60].

The first couple was deceived and seduced by the Rebel and their attitude towards him is described by some verbs expressing obedience (*sm'* and *pys*) to the Evil One, and also Satan's persuasion (*mlak*). In this way, the LG underscores Satan's rebellion and opposition to God and, what is very important, the association of humankind being in that rebellion.

It has been already referred as how Satan suggests and allures Adam to desire becoming "like gods" (*'alahe*). This reading bases on Gen 3:5 according to the *Peshitta* version, which in its turn follows the LXX θεοί. Indeed, according to the *LG*'s account, Satan asks Eve to encourage Adam to become like God and, afterwards, Satan argues that God did not want them to eat from the tree "because [He] did not wish and was not content that you become like him"[61]. Satan attempts to expand his own rebellion by sharing his deep desire of becoming god. Indeed, "Adam desired, with the advice of Satan, to become a

---

Genesi, ma indubbiamente questo non è stato l'unico fattore che ha causato la formulazione del tema (presente del resto anche nella patristica greca). Bisogna prendere in considerazione l'insistenza sulla libertà umana che è una delle caratteristiche della tradizione siriaca. La libertà è presente nella vita paradisiaca escatologica, anche quella già anticipata nella Chiesa, va perciò attribuita pure agli abitanti del paradiso primitivo che peccarono volontariamente e coscientemente. Ed è proprio questo il tema sviluppato dall'autore del *LG*, il quale usa il termine heruta principalmente nel contesto della storia di Adamo".

[57] LG 21, 11.
[58] LG 21, 10.
[59] LG 23, 1.
[60] LG 22, 7.
[61] LG 21, 9.

god"[62]. This ancient desire comes in the following paragraph in the perspectives of Satan, Adam and Christ:

> In this they, however, were foolish for they had hoped to become like God. They erred because there is nothing that is able to become like the Creator of all the worlds, that one who is the Creator, and who is our Lord Jesus Christ [...]. Because of this the apostle said, 'Christ did not by force desire to become the equal of God like Adam, but he emptied himself, even from this thing that Adam loved and sought to become God through earthly wealth [...]. For nothing brought down Adam on the day he fell, except the pride by which he desired to become the equal of God in his majesty. Too much [pride] forced him to depart from the Paradise of the Kingdom and humbled him down to earth'[63].

The first sin is essentially a sin of pride; pride of becoming like God. Few paragraphs before Satan had asked Eve to suggest Adam to "grow and become like God who created you"[64]. On account of the pride of Adam, God closed the doors of Paradise before him, that is, the doors of heaven[65].

On the other hand, it is clear that that first sin is neither concupiscence nor sexual. Neither before nor during temptation there is concupiscence. This is, on the contrary, one of the consequences of the fall, together with the desire for conjugal union. Indeed,

> After he had sinned and was censured, a law was established for him, inferior to that first [law]. By this same law [God] permitted him to marry. Because he had desired to become physical and not spiritual, that is, earthly and not heavenly, it was then that carnal desire came to exist in him, for Adam desired intercourse as a result of the teaching of the evil one who had plotted to make him fall from the sanctity of the angels and imitate wild beasts[66].

And again, "[t]hey went on to desire [conjugal] union and to give birth like the animals"[67]. On the contrary, "Adam and Eve had no lust while they had not yet sinned"[68]. This came only after sin and it will disappear when perfection is attained again:

---

[62] LG 23, 7.
[63] LG 21, 11.
[64] LG 21, 9.
[65] LG 12, 10.
[66] LG 15, 1.
[67] LG 21, 1.
[68] LG 15, 2.

Just as from the [moment] sin existed in the heart of Adam and Eve, and they desired intercourse. God allowed them to marry—the instinct and lust of intercourse being in them; [...] [When they kill sin inside them and ascend to the desire of God] then God will command that lust be removed from the heart and the instinct from the body completely[69].

Most important is also another consequence of sin: the strong desire to possess (and to rule), which is very characteristic of the *LG*. In any case, Adam and Eve, unlike Satan[70], will eventually repent of that sin. God will react to that conversion by introducing another way, the one of "justice"[71] promising the return to previous perfection:

[This spirit] was promised also to Adam when he wept and prayed and made supplication, 'I will come and perfect those who pursue love and Perfection' from which he had fallen[72].

Satan and the First Couple

At this stage, we could draw a comparison between Satan and Adam. This connection is not original of our author but is preceded by Jewish as well as earlier Syriac traditions, in the last case to be found in works such as the *Cave of Treasures* and the *Vita Adae*. The *LG* is, nevertheless, original in its strong emphasis of that parallelism. According to our author, Satan and Adam are united through the same crime (*sura'ta*) and the same fall (*npal*) from Heaven. *Sura'ta* is the equivalent for Adam's fall, being both committed out of free will (*b-sebjana*). Adam shares Satan's rebellion and fall caused by their desire to become God[73]. The fall of the first couple is the same fall of Satan and motivated by the same desire to become God.

---

[69] LG 15, 3.
[70] LG 21, 18.
[71] A. Kowalski, Perfezione e giustizia, 160: "Così il motivo della penitenza di Adamo, sconosciuto nella Bibbia, ma molto diffuso nella tradizione, è servito al nostro autore per spiegare le ragioni che hanno indotto Dio a dare all umanità un altra possibilità di salvezza, introducendo la legge della giustizia".
[72] LG 15, 8.
[73] Cf. G. Fuchs, Auflehnung und Fall, 314.

> Because [Satan] rebelled and God overthrew him, Satan became the son of darkness by his own will. However, [God] turned away and did not kill him because of his patience, yet [Satan] did not repent on account of his stubbornness and rebellion, because he had not worked for the Lord as our Lord had said, "It is written: you shall worship the Lord your God and you shall work and pray to him only." However, [he did] the opposite of this, alluring other creatures encouraging rebellion, as he had taught the serpent and Adam and Eve to rebel. Adam fell from heaven with that [same] fall by which the Rebel slipped and fell. For, the idea came upon the Rebel to become God. When he was ruined he came to allure Adam so that he might slip and fall to become his son and disciple. But God did not give him rest according to what he had thought, but had pity upon Adam and Eve on account of their repentance, and established a law for them on earth, for if a person does it he will be saved thereby[74].

Satan's fall is the model of Adam and Eve's own, or, expressed in a different way, the first couple follows into the Evil's steps. They, and to some extent its children, become, at least for some time, his disciples[75]. The *LG* introduces, however, some slight differences between both Satan and the couple. Whereas Satan is overthrown, Adam falls. While Satan "wanted to be God in Heaven"[76], Adam had the hope "to become great as God" *('ajk 'alaha)*[77]. The main opposition lies, however, in the fact that Satan unlike Adam did not convert and his fall and transformation was permanent.

Sin in the Children of Adam

First of all, and as is it is strongly stressed within the Syriac ascetic tradition, even after baptism sin is still present and active in the lives of Christians. Our book attempts to portray the spectrum of sin's presence by recurring to Paul's notion of pledge *(urbana)*. In the current situation after the sin of the forefathers, there are at least three possible situations for human beings: those who have the pledge of sin and are, consequently, devoid from the pledge of the Spirit, the ones that possess the fullness of the Spirit, and, finally and perhaps the most common, women and men in whom both God and Satan act through the pledges of the Spirit and of sin, causing the human being to carry out both good and evil deeds.

---

[74] LG 21, 18.
[75] Cf. ibid.
[76] LG 23, 4.
[77] LG 15, 2.

> There is a category of people who are devoid of the pledge of the Spirit. They are rejected because they do not have the Spirit of God at all. The Apostle said this, '[...] if the Spirit of God is in you. And if not, you are rejected'. There is another category of people in whom there is something from God and something from Satan. They do good works because of the pledge of the Holy Spirit that is in them, and they sin and do evil works because of the pledge of sin that is in them. The pledge of the Holy Spirit admonishes them constantly to quit the evil and to do good works and to crucify themselves for the Evil One in order to conquer him. If they conquer him, they become Upright, and if they are prepared to raise themselves further, they will become Perfect; whereas if they remain as they were, then on the Day of Judgment they will receive the reward of their bad and good works, or they will receive mercy, be delivered, and saved.
>
> There is yet another category of people who have cleansed themselves from the pledge of Satan and are full of the Spirit of God every moment of their entire lifetime. Our Lord said this to him who takes up his cross in imitation of himself, 'See I send you the Paraclete to be with you until the end of the world'. The people of this category belong to our Lord continually, and our Lord is in them. But the person who does not even do one good work, neither in his body nor in his heart, and who never meditates on honorable things, that person is devoid of God and his grace[78].

The presence and energy of both pledges in human heart causes the inner battle for the heart, the task of gradually uprooting sin, "wrestle with Satan and overthrow him as our Lord has overthrown him"[79]. In this struggle, we need to overcome first all external sins. After doing this, we ought to focus upon the most difficult battle against internal sin. Satan (and the Spirit as well) intervene in this battle chiefly through thoughts.

> As evil thoughts exist in the heart through the mediation of Satan, in the same way good thoughts exist in it and good works has something from God and something from Satan inside himself[80].

Satan devises those evil thoughts in our hearts and they dwell internally. The *LG* does not refer, however and unlike the doctrine attributed to Messalianism, to a substantial presence of Satan in the soul after baptism, which could only be expelled through intensive prayer, causing in this way the arrival of the Spirit in a sensitive way. Prayer is important in the *LG*, nevertheless in a different way and is Christologically grounded in the following passage

---

[78] LG 3, 11.
[79] LG 6.
[80] LG 3, 12.

So now, let us leave behind everything visible because it is transitory, and let us turn away from external sins. When we cut off all our visible sins we shall rise up in the struggle against the Sin that dwells in us internally, because they are the evil thoughts that Sin devises in the heart. With power may we pursue the struggle that is set before us and let us do battle with prayer just as our Lord did before us. He showed us that with a mighty groan and many tears Jesus offered a petition to him who delivered him from death. He was heard and made perfect [...]. But until we are afflicted in prayer like him and shed tears as he shed and powerfully implore as he implored, we will not be rescued from the sin that dwells in the heart, or from the evil thoughts that we inwardly think[81].

The complexity of the deep reality of sin is portrayed under the typical image of an evil plant or a tree that needs to be not only trimmed in its leaves, shoots and branches, but to be totally uprooted. This uprooting is significant in the Syriac context. Messalians seem to have suggested that while baptism cuts off sin, it does not uproot it, calling in this way into cause the efficacy of baptism. This is, however, not the position of the *LG*. As we have seen that uprooting is often presented also under the military image of an inner battle. In the meantime, there is a distinction between external and internal indwelling sin, through which Satan engages us in the most ferocious battle. Another recurring image, which gave the name to the whole *LG*, is the one of ascents and, especially, steps. Indeed, in this battle we come to the last step.

'This step is difficult because through it a person does battle against sin, and if he does climb this step he will enter the house of our Lord. Ardently and defiantly, [sin] stands in front of him: either it kills or is killed [...]. While you have not yet cut off the leaves of a withered tree, its shoots and its branches, you have not yet approached the root, nor do you know how difficult it will be to uproot it.' That is, while you have not yet conquered even the visible sins, which are the leaves and shoots and branches of sin, when you reach its root, then you will see murder and the battle by which sin and the powers of Satan engage you, as it is written, 'A battle outside and fear within'. Externally, the powers of Satan do battle and internally sin attacks. Therefore, all the difficulty of this step lies in that a person uproots the hidden death, which Adam experienced in the transgression of the commandment, [as well as] all the [evil] thoughts of sin [...][82].

Often the *LG* uses the terminology of indwelling of sin[83]; terminology that is central not only in the Messalian controversy but in the entire Syriac theology. From this text it results that Satan, remaining external, operates internally

---

[81] LG 18, 3.
[82] LG 20, 4.
[83] Cf. for instance LG 20, 11: "sin still resides within us".

Evil and Sin in the Syriac Liber Graduum

through sin and through evil thoughts inside the human heart. This becomes clear in the subsequent paragraph:

> Sin will not be rooted up from our heart nor will the evil thoughts and their fruits pass away unless we pray as our Lord and all of his preachers prayed[84].

In the two following passages, which are highly significant for our topic, the author traces a link between the sin of our first parents and their children's. In this context, he speaks about three steps, being the first two the reconciliation with one's enemies and not working in order to divest oneself of everything.

> But these three [steps] are especially hard and this is the last step: when a person has kept all of the commandments, he uproots all sin, its [evil] thoughts and fruits from the heart, *that [very] sin that was planted in our father Adam and in our mother Eve on the day they sinned. [Sin] entered and lived in all their children.* This is the most difficult step. The nearer one comes to the city of our Lord, the harder and steeper [the road] becomes, so that no one is able to climb it except with difficulty[85].

The key notion in it is the notion of (im)plantation. While sin was planted into Adam, it entered into its children and lives in them. In the meantime, the text proclaims the universality of sin. This passage could seem to suggest an understanding that would not be far from a sort of inherited sin. However, there is no explicit reference to inheritance. Let us bring this passage into relation with another text:

> For there is no one among the sons of Adam, who has not in the first place sinned and subsequently been justified. *This inclination was implanted in Adam on the day he transgressed the command. From then on it was implanted in all of his offspring from their mother's womb.* As soon as they had come to know themselves, they struggled to overcome it and be justified, or they were overcome and defeated by it and started acting impiously. 'You wicked servant', it is written, 'should you not have spared your fellow-servant as I had mercy on you?' 'So', it is written also, 'my father in heaven will do to anyone of you who does not from this heart forgive his brother his transgressions'[86].

---

[84] LG 18, 4.
[85] LG 20, 3.
[86] LG 5, 14.

This passages starts by asserting, as the text quoted before, universality of sin (and of justification as well). Significantly, it does not speak of sin but of inclination, which is implanted in human beings from their own conception. This nuance is highly relevant since it seems to indicate that not sin itself but a certain inclination to sin is acquired by human beings, in following the first couple after they sinned, from the very start of their lives.

On the other hand, the idea of an inherited sin, transmitted from generation to generation would go against the basic tenet of the *Liber Graduum* that, in following Syriac tradition, again and again stresses human (and even Satan's) free will and own choice when they sin.

Conclusions

The *LG* offers a non-systematic but narrative approach to the question of sin and Evil. In order to understand its contribution to those themes, we need to refer to the context of Syriac (ascetic) theology. For the communities addressed by the *LG*, it is crucial to provide an explanation to the question about why evil and sin remain indwelling in the depth of human heart, even after baptism. Indeed we find inside ourselves the pledge of sin beside the one of the Spirit, "having something from God and something from Satan inside"[87]. Sin or evil thoughts (the author does not produce a sharp distinction between different notions, often remaining imprecise) indwell in the depth of human heart. In two passages, as we have seen, an explicit connection between the sins of the first couple and the one of their children is established. That connection is, nevertheless, neither further detailed nor related to inheriting. In addition to this, in both passages discussed above the key terms (sin and inclination) are different. If we add that sin is always the result of free choice, we cannot find in the *LG* a doctrine of inherited sin[88].

The book's author, following different Syriac exegetical traditions but also being innovative, sees as consequence of Adam's sin not only death and the loss of Paradise but the fall from the primaeval state of perfection, in which the first couple was created and established. Having they repented of having fol-

---

[87] LG 3, 12.
[88] Cf. G. Fuchs, Auflehnung und Fall, 314–315: "Ein Sündenbegriff nach Art einer ‚Erbsünde', die von Generation zu Generation übertragen, ‚vererbt' würde, kennt der ‚Selige' nicht: Der Gedanke an ein unentrinnbares Verhängnis, ein peccatum hereditarium, das die Menschheit zu einer massa damnationis macht, ist ihm fremd. Auch die Auffassung, dass der Mensch willentlich sündigen muß (*non posse non peccare*), liegt unserem Autor ganz fern; denn das Axiom von der Autonomie des menschlichen Willens schließt ‚die Lehre von der totalen Sündhaftigkeit des Menschen' ganz und gar aus".

lowed the Evil one it his rebellion, God established the possibility of attaining uprightness and re-opened with Christ the way to perfection. Christ shows not only the true countenance of Adam and Eve[89] but also perfection itself. Attaining perfection requires in the *Book of Steps* an extreme asceticism[90] that entails of course uprooting sin and full renunciation of the world in all its forms. Nevertheless, the goal of this asceticism is the configuration with the humble and suffering Christ and his all-embracing love.[91] In becoming servants not only of the good but especially of the evil ones, the enemies, and even of their own murderers[92]. Perfects are called to reflect upon the world—like God's sun—the unlimited compassion of the Father[93].

---

[89] Cf. LG 23, 1: "Our Lord showed us through his person the creation of Adam and how Adam became like the heavenly angels [...]. According to that image of [Adam], our Lord was born. For by the imitation of Adam, our Lord came in order to show people their original nature [and] how they were created".

[90] Regarding asceticism in the *Book of Steps*, see R. A. *Kitchen*, Becoming Perfect, 30–43 and D. *Juhl*, Askese im Liber Graduum.

[91] See A. *Guillaumont*, Situation et signification, 313: "Les vertus du parfait sont avant tout l'humilité, le pardon, la douceur. Il s'applique à faire la paix parmi les hommes, à les enseigner avec humilité, à les corriger s'il le faut, mais en s'abstenant de les juger: aussi bien il s'estime inférieur à tous les hommes, bons ou pécheurs".

[92] Cf. P. *Argárate*, "Ktābā dmasqātā, 257–258: "Aus den 30 Mēmrē resultiert ein faszinierendes Bild einer asketisch charismatisch geprägten Gemeinde. Mitten in den verschiedenen und sogar komplexen Verfolgungen werden die Christen aufgerufen, ihren leidenden, armen und gedemütigten Herrn nachzuahmen. Auf diesem Weg werden sie durch die steigernde Präsenz und Wirksamkeit des Geistes zu einer mystique pneumatique bewegt. Ziel des Weges ist die Stadt Gottes, der Garten von Eden, die Wiedererlangung des verlorenen Paradieses".

[93] Cf. LG 25, 7: "But he is not able to attain Perfection unless he has abandoned the earth according to what our Lord has commanded him and has taken up the cross, has emptied and lowered himself and become celibate; and has become like a servant in his obedience, and not like a lord in his supervision. Let him have compassion on the sinners and the righteous; and let him love to give himself up for the evil ones, as [did] our Lord and his apostles. Then he will comprehend the height and the depth, the length and the width along with the saints, these who have understood the Holy One in everything he has shown them, with compassion and love and peace for all people, good and bad". Also LG 19, 33: "This is the Perfect road: If you love only the one who loves you and you greet only your brothers, what is your righteousness? Because even tax-collectors and heathen and sinners act in this way. But love whoever hates you and persecutes you, and your peace will increase toward the good and the evil, and you shall be imitating the Father in heaven who makes his sun shine and his rain fall upon them equally". Cf. P. *Argárate*, The Perfect and Perfection in the Book of Steps.

Johannes Arnold, Frankfurt am Main (Deutschland)

Zur Frage nach dem Ursprung des Bösen im Menschen bei Origenes vor dem Hintergrund mittelplatonischer Philosophie

Abstract:
Instead of an inherited 'original sin', Origen seems to assume that an individual decision distancing oneself from God is made by each human soul before its union with an earthly body. This article takes up the current discussion on the doctrine of preexistence attributed to Origen and its compatibility with the biblical narrative of original sin (Gen 3). It also looks at the contemporary philosophical background.

Während die Frage, ob Origenes eine Erbsündenlehre vertritt[1], umstritten und – angesichts der unvollständigen Überlieferung seiner Werke – schwer zu beantworten ist[2], scheint klar zu sein: Wenn Origenes erklären wollte, dass der Mensch vom Beginn seiner irdischen Existenz an in Schuld verstrickt ist, war er nicht auf eine Erbsündenlehre angewiesen, sofern er eine Präexistenz der menschlichen Seelen und eine schon vor dem irdischen Leben stattfindende individuelle Entscheidung gegen Gott annahm. Ob bzw. in welcher Weise Origenes eine Präexistenzlehre vertritt, ist allerdings ebenfalls umstritten und angesichts der Quellenlage nicht leicht zu beantworten. Ohne den Anspruch, endgültige Lösungen zu präsentieren, bietet der vorliegende Beitrag einzelne Beobachtungen und Überlegungen zu folgenden Fragen: Ist auszuschließen, dass Origenes eine Entscheidung der menschlichen Seele gegen Gott vor der irdischen Existenz des Menschen voraussetzt? Inwieweit wäre eine solche Präexistenzlehre mit zeitgenössischer Philosophie kompatibel – und inwieweit eine Erbsündenlehre? Und wie verhält sich, falls Origenes eine Präexistenzlehre vertrat, dazu seine Deutung der Sünde Adams? Ich werde mich weitgehend darauf beschränken, Elemente der aktuellen Diskussion dieser Fragen aufzugreifen und durch Anmerkungen zu ergänzen.

---

[1] Vgl. im vorliegenden Band L. *Karfíková*, Hereditary Sin? Augustine and Origen.
[2] Vgl. bereits M. *Hauke*, Heilsverlust in Adam. Stationen griechischer Erbsündenlehre: Irenäus – Origenes – Kappadozier (Paderborn 1993) 427.

I. Zur Frage nach einer Entscheidung gegen Gott vor der irdischen Existenz

Dass Origenes den Ursprung des Bösen in einer Entscheidung vernunftbegabter Geschöpfe gegen Gott sieht, ist nicht zu bezweifeln. An erster Stelle nennt er in diesem Zusammenhang den „Teufel und seine Engel"[3]. Auch bei jedem Menschen ist „der Wille Ursache für die Bosheit, die in ihm selbst existiert"[4]. In welcher Weise aber trifft der Mensch seine Entscheidung? Im ersten der Anathematismen des Jahres 543 wird Origenes bekanntlich die Lehre zugeschrieben,

> die Seelen der Menschen hätten präexistiert (προϋπάρχειν), indem sie früher Geister (νόας) und heilige Kräfte gewesen seien, sie seien aber der göttlichen Anschauung satt geworden (κόρον δὲ λαβούσας)[5], hätten sich zum Schlechteren (πρὸς τὸ χεῖρον) gewandt, seien deshalb in der Liebe zu Gott erkaltet (ἀποψυγείσας), aus diesem Grund Seelen (ψυχάς) genannt und zur Strafe (τιμωρίας χάριν) in Körper hinabgesandt worden (καταπεμφθείσας)[6].

Dass die Position des Origenes durch eine solche Darstellung korrekt wiedergegeben sei, ist bestritten worden[7]. Nach manchen Interpreten kann Origenes

---

[3] Vgl. *Orig.*, Cels. IV, 65: M. Borret, SC 136 (Paris 1968), p. 346,25–26. Übers. C. Barthold, FC 50/3 (Freiburg u.a. 2011), p. 799: „Und niemand wird ‚den Ursprung des Bösen erkennen' können, der sich nicht zuvor mit der Lehre vom sogenannten Teufel und seinen Engeln befasst hat [...]." In Cels. VI, 43 sagt Origenes über den Ursprung (ἀρχή) und die Entstehung (γένεσις) der Bosheit (κακία), dass sie „von gewissen (Wesen) stammt (ὑπέστη ἀπό τινων), die ihre Flügel verloren haben (πτερορρυησάντων) und dem gefolgt sind, der als Erster die Flügel verloren hat" (vgl. unten bei Anm. 65). Deutsche Übers. hier und überall, wo nicht anders angegeben, vom Verf. Vgl. auch Cels. VI, 44 (unten Anm. 80).

[4] *Orig.*, Cels. IV, 66: SC 136, p. 348,10–11: Τὸ γὰρ ἑκάστου ἡγεμονικὸν αἴτιον τῆς ὑποστάσης ἐν αὐτῷ κακίας ἐστίν.

[5] Wie M. Harl (*M. Harl*, Recherches sur l'origénisme d'Origène: la „satiété" [κόρος] de la contemplation comme motif de la chute des âmes, StudPatr VIII/2, TU 93 [Berlin 1966] 373–405; Nachdruck in: *M. Harl*, Le déchiffrement du sens. Études sur l'herméneutique chrétienne d'Origène à Grégoire de Nysse [Paris 1993] 191–223) gezeigt hat, verstand Origenes unter κόρος/*satietas* im vorliegenden Zusammenhang ein schuldhaftes Nachlassen des Verlangens und der Ausrichtung nach dem Guten, nicht aber „Überdruss".

[6] Edikt des Kaisers Justinian an Patriarch Menas von Konstantinopel, veröffentlicht auf der Synode von Konstantinopel 543 n.Chr.: E. Schwartz, ACO III (Berlin 1940), p. 213–214. Übers. (mit Änderungen) nach H. Denzinger – P. Hünermann, Kompendium der Glaubensbekenntnisse und kirchlichen Lehrentscheidungen (Freiburg u.a. [45]2017) Nr. 403. Als Zeugen gegen Origenes werden hier zitiert: Cyrill von Alexandrien [vgl. unten Anm. 31], Basilius von Caesarea, Gregor von Nazianz, Gregor von Nyssa, Johannes Chrysostomus, Peter von Alexandrien, Athanasius von Alexandrien, Theophil von Alexandrien.

[7] Vgl. z.B. *M. Harl*, La préexistence des âmes dans l'œuvre d'Origène, in: L. Lies (Hg.), Origeniana Quarta (Innsbruck – Wien 1987) 238–258, 238; *M. Edwards*, Origen against Plato

gar keine Präexistenz der menschlichen Seele vor einem körperlichen Dasein vertreten haben. So zeigt sich der Patrologe Mark Edwards (Oxford) in einem 2019 veröffentlichten Disput mit seinem Kollegen Peter W. Martens (St. Louis) davon überzeugt, dass

> Origenes sicher seine eigene Meinung zum Ausdruck brachte, wenn er in *De principiis* erklärte, dass nichts ohne einen Körper subsistieren könne außer den drei Personen der Trinität, und wenn er die Meinung vertrat, dass der Terminus ‚unkörperlich' nur in einem nicht strengen Sinn von geschaffenen Geistwesen ausgesagt werden kann[8].

Nach Edwards setzt Origenes voraus, dass die menschliche Seele nie ohne einen Körper ist, dass nur die Art ihres Körpers sich wandelt (vom ‚ätherischen' zum ‚fleischlichen' Körper und umgekehrt)[9]. Martens weist in seiner Response zu Edwards' Artikel darauf hin, dass sich zu der eben genannten Aussage aus Rufins Übertragung von *De principiis* kein griechisches Pendant erhalten hat und dass sie mit anderen Aussagen im Werk des Origenes in Spannung steht[10].

Konzentriert man sich nun auf die in griechischer Sprache überlieferten Texte, findet man einerseits Passagen, die tatsächlich von einer Verwandlung der Eigenschaften des menschlichen Körpers[11], andererseits aber auch solche, die doch von einer körperlosen Seele sprechen. So heißt es im zweiten Buch von Origenes' *Kommentar zum Johannesevangelium* – entstanden vor 232, al-

---

(Burlington 2002) 89–97.

[8] M. *Edwards*, Origen in Paradise: A Response to Peter Martens, ZAC 23 (2019) 163–185, 176: „[...] he was certainly expressing his own opinion [...] when he asserted in *De principiis* [I, 6, 4; Anm. J. A.] that nothing can subsist without a body except the three persons of the Trinity and maintained that the term ‚incorporeal' can be predicated only in a loose sense of created spirits". Der Beitrag reagiert auf P. W. *Martens*, Origen's Doctrine of Pre-Existence and the Opening Chapters of Genesis, ZAC 16 (2012) 516–549.

[9] M. *Edwards*, Origen against Plato, 94, 105, 160; M. *Edwards*, Origen's Platonism: Questions and Caveats, ZAC 12 (2008) 20–38, 34. Ähnlich bereits L. *Lies*, Origenes und Reinkarnation, ZKTh 121 (1999) 139–158; vgl. M. *Harl*, Préexistence, 245.

[10] P. W. *Martens*, Response to Edwards, ZAC 23 (2019) 186–200, 190.

[11] Siehe z.B. Orig., Cels. III, 41: SC 136, p. 96,13–98,19: Wenn die von Griechen vertretene Lehre vernünftig (ὑγιῆ) ist, dass die im eigentlichen Sinn eigenschaftslose Materie sich „mit den Eigenschaften bekleidet, mit denen der Schöpfer sie ausstatten will", und häufig „die früheren ab[legt], um bessere und davon verschiedene anzunehmen [...], was ist dann verwunderlich daran, dass durch die Vorsehung Gottes, der es so wollte, die Eigenschaft ‚sterblich' am Leib Jesu in eine ätherische und göttliche Eigenschaft verwandelt wurde (μεταβαλεῖν)?" Übers. C. Barthold, FC 50/2 (Freiburg u.a. 2011), p. 585; vgl. dort Anm. 192 (Lit.). Vgl. auch unten Anm. 18.

so etwa zur gleichen Zeit wie *De principiis* –, „dass die Seele des Johannes [...] älter als sein Körper ist und schon vorher da war"[12]. Und kurz danach:

> Wenn aber die allgemeine Lehre über die Seele (ὁ καθόλου περὶ ψυχῆς λόγος) Geltung hat (κρατῇ), dass sie nicht zusammen mit dem Körper ausgesät wurde, sondern vor ihm da war[13] und aus vielfältigen Ursachen mit Fleisch und Blut bekleidet wurde, scheint das ‚von Gott gesandt' nicht mehr nur speziell von Johannes gesagt zu werden[14].

Man könnte fragen, in welchem Maß Origenes sich mit der genannten ‚Lehre von der Seele' identifiziert. Zu dieser Frage sei auf eine weitere Stelle hingewiesen, die in der aktuellen Diskussion vernachlässigt zu werden scheint. In seiner *Exhortatio ad martyrium* – entstanden um 235 n.Chr., also nicht lange nach den ersten Büchern des *Johannes-Kommentars* und somit auch nicht lange nach *De principiis* – erklärt Origenes, dass die „vernunftbegabte Seele (λογικὴ ψυχή) etwas mit Gott Verwandtes" habe, denn beide seien „geistig (νοερά) und unsichtbar (ἀόρατα) und, wie die herrschende Lehre (ὁ ἐπικρατῶν λόγος) zeigt, unkörperlich (ἀσώματα)"[15].

Auch hier stimmt Origenes der genannten Lehre zwar nicht explizit zu. Die eben zitierte Aussage ist aber in Verbindung mit zwei weiteren Passagen aus der *Exhortatio* zu sehen. Kurz nach Beginn des Werkes spricht Origenes von den Menschen, die ihre „mit ganzer Seele (ὅλῃ ψυχῇ) auf Gott gerichtete Liebe" nach Kräften dadurch bewiesen, dass sie „das irdene Gefäß" (τοῦ ὀστρακίνου σκεύους) verachtet haben[16]. Origenes fährt fort:

> Mit ganzer Seele aber (ὅλῃ δὲ ψυχῇ) wird Gott [...] von denen geliebt, die [...] ihre Seele nicht nur vom irdischen Körper (τοῦ γηΐνου σώματος) losreißen und trennen (ἀποσπώντων καὶ διϊστάντων), sondern sogar *von jedem Körper* (ἀλλὰ καὶ ἀπὸ παντὸς σώματος)[17].

---

[12] *Orig.*, In Ioh. comm. II, 30, 181: C. Blanc, SC 120 (Paris 1966), p. 330,5–7: πρεσβυτέραν οὖσαν τὴν Ἰωάννου ψυχὴν τοῦ σώματος καὶ πρότερον ὑφεστῶσαν.
[13] Vgl. *Platon*, Leges X, 896c: ψυχὴ [...] πρεσβυτέρα σώματος οὖσα.
[14] *Orig.*, In Ioh. comm. II, 30, 182: SC 120, p. 330,10–14: Ἐὰν δὲ κρατῇ ὁ καθόλου περὶ ψυχῆς λόγος ὡς οὐ συνεσπαρμένης τῷ σώματι ἀλλὰ πρὸ αὐτοῦ τυγχανούσης καὶ διὰ ποικίλας αἰτίας ἐνδουμένης σαρκὶ καὶ αἵματι, τὸ «ἀπεσταλμένον ὑπὸ θεοῦ» οὐκέτι δόξει ἐξαίρετον εἶναι περὶ Ἰωάννου λεγόμενον. Vgl. auch *Orig.*, In Ioh. comm. I, 17, 96–97: SC 120, p. 110,3–15: Die Heiligen führten zuerst ein „ganz immaterielles und körperloses Leben" (ἄυλον πάντῃ καὶ ἀσώματον ζωήν).
[15] *Orig.*, Exh. 47: P. Koetschau, GCS 2 (Orig. 1) (Leipzig 1899), p. 42,30–43,1.
[16] *Orig.*, Exh. 2: GCS 2 (Orig. 1), p. 4,16–18; Übers. nach M.-B. v. Stritzky, Orig.WD 22 (Berlin u.a. 2010), p. 33.
[17] *Orig.*, Exh. 3: GCS 2 (Orig. 1), p. 4,19–22; vgl. Übers. M.-B. v. Stritzky, p. 33.

Soll man diese Aussage so verstehen, dass Origenes die Trennung der Seele z.B. auch von einem „ätherischen Körper" für möglich hält und propagiert?[18] An einer dritten Stelle der *Exhortatio*[19] vergleicht Origenes die beiden potentiellen Märtyrer, denen das Werk gewidmet ist, mit Paulus, der von sich sagt, er sei „in den dritten Himmel", „in das Paradies entrückt worden" (2 Kor 12,2.4). Die Worte „ob im Körper oder ohne den Körper – ich weiß es nicht" (2 Kor 12,3) übergeht Origenes hier. Von den beiden Adressaten aber heißt es: Wenn sie das Kreuz auf sich nähmen und Christus nachfolgten, würden sie „sofort eine noch größere Erkenntnis" als Paulus erlangen und nicht, wie er, aus dem dritten Himmel wieder herabsteigen, sondern „die Himmel und ihre Geheimnisse überschreiten". In Gott selbst seien noch größere Gegenstände der Betrachtung (θεάματα), die keine Natur derer, die sich in einem Körper befinden (οὐδεμία φύσις τῶν ἐν σώματι), in sich aufnehmen (χωρῆσαι) kann, wenn sie nicht vorher *jeden Körper abgelegt* hat (ἀπαλλαγεῖσα παντὸς σώματος). Ist hier nur in einem ‚nicht strengen Sinn' von Körperlosigkeit die Rede? Auch wenn Henri Crouzel mit Recht darauf hinweist, dass die Freiheit von einem Körper bei Origenes einen „moralischen", „asketischen Sinn" haben kann[20], stellt sich angesichts der Anspielung auf die Lehre von der vor einem Körper existierenden Seele, der Rede vom Ablegen eines jeden Körpers[21] und von der Verwandtschaft der ihrem Wesen (οὐσία) nach körperlosen Vernunftseele – offenbar auch dessen, der noch „das (irdische) Leben liebt" (φιλοζωεῖ)[22] – mit dem körperlosen Gott die Frage, ob Origenes hier nicht doch mit der Möglichkeit geistiger Geschöpfe ohne Körper rechnet, die sich in der Präexistenz gegen Gott entscheiden und nach dem Wiederaufstieg gerade aufgrund der wiedererlangten nicht nur asketischen Freiheit vom Körper die göttlichen Geheimnisse wieder schauen können[23].

---

[18] In den folgenden Sätzen wird nur der „Körper der Erniedrigung" (τὸ τῆς ταπεινώσεως σῶμα) erwähnt, den die, die Gott von ganzer Seele lieben, „abzulegen" (ἀποθέσθαι) vermögen, wenn sie im Augenblick des (physischen) Todes „den Körper des Todes ausziehen" (ἐκδύσασθαι τὸ σῶμα τοῦ θανάτου). Zum ‚Körper des Todes' s.a. *Orig*., Exh. 3: GCS 2 (Orig. 1), p. 4.26–27.30. Im Unterschied zum ‚Ablegen (ἀποθέσθαι) des Körpers der Erniedrigung' vgl. die Rede von seiner ‚Umgestaltung' (μετασχηματίζειν) nach Phil 3,21 in *Orig*., Cels. VII, 50 und In Mt. comm. XIII, 21.
[19] *Orig*., Exh. 13: GCS 2 (Orig. 1), p. 13,15–27.
[20] H. *Crouzel*, La doctrine origénienne du corps ressuscité, BLE 81 (1980) 175–200 und 241–266, 188–189.
[21] Crouzel selbst (ibid., 189 Anm. 62) bezeichnet diesen Gedanken aus Exh. 3 als für seine Argumentation „plus difficile".
[22] *Orig*., Exh. 47: GCS 2 (Orig. 1), p. 42,29.
[23] Zu dieser Position vgl. A.-C. *Jacobsen*, Origen on body and soul, in: B. Bitton-Ashkelony u.a. (Hgg.), Origeniana Duodecima (Leuven u.a. 2019) 589–601.

Außerdem: Selbst wer davon überzeugt ist, dass Origenes sich keine Seele ohne irgendeinen Körper vorstellen konnte, ist mit Aussagen konfrontiert, die eine Entscheidung des Menschen vor seiner Geburt voraussetzen: Nach *De principiis* darf angenommen werden, dass Jakob „auf Grund von Verdiensten eines früheren Lebens (*ex praecedentis* [...] *vitae meritis*) von Gott mit Recht geliebt wurde, so dass er auch nach Verdienst dem Bruder vorgezogen wurde"[24]. Die Gerechtigkeit Gottes erscheine

> erst dann genügend deutlich, wenn man von jedem himmlischen, irdischen oder unterirdischen Wesen sagt, es habe in sich selbst (*in semet ipso*) für die Verschiedenheit Ursachen, welche der körperlichen Geburt vorausgehen (*praecedentes nativitatem corpoream*)[25].

Nach Edwards ist aus dieser Aussage zwar auf eine „prä-natale Wahl" zu schließen, nicht aber zwingend auf eine Wahl vor der irdischen Existenz[26]. Er verweist auf rabbinische Interpreten, nach denen Jakob noch im Mutterleib Verdienste erwarb, und darauf, dass Origenes schon dem Embryo eine voll entwickelte Seele zuschreibt[27]. Allerdings lässt sich im erhaltenen Werk des Origenes kein Indiz dafür finden, dass er selbst eine Position in der Art der rabbinischen vertreten hätte[28]. In *De principiis* ist von „voraufgehenden Ursachen" die Rede, die schon vor jeder körperlichen Existenz Jakobs und Esaus gegeben waren[29]. Dass Origenes zumindest in seinen früheren Jahren eine Entscheidung der menschlichen Seele gegen Gott schon vor der Empfängnis für möglich hielt – sei es, dass die Seele bereits in einem ‚feineren' als

---

[24] *Orig.*, Princ. II, 9, 7: H. Görgemanns, H. Karpp, TzF 24 (Darmstadt ³1992), p. 414–415 (Ed. und Übers.). Vgl. L. Karfíková, Is Romans 9,11 Proof for or against the Pre-Existence of the Soul?: Origen and Augustine in Comparison, in: B. Bitton-Ashkelony u.a. (Hgg.), Origeniana duodecima (Leuven u.a. 2019) 627–642.
[25] Vgl. *Orig.*, Princ. II, 9, 7: TzF 24, p. 416–417 (Ed. und Übers.).
[26] M. Edwards, Origen in Paradise, 171: „[...] justice requires that this should be the consequence of some ante-natal choice. Nevertheless, the causes of Esau's subjection to Jacob are not related either to paradise or to a fall from heaven". Vgl. M. Edwards, Origen's Platonism, 35–37.
[27] M. Edwards, Origen's Platonism, 33.
[28] So auch M. Edwards, Origen's Platonism, 36.
[29] *Orig.*, Princ. III, 1, 22 (nach der Philokalie): TzF 24, p. 548–551 (Ed. und Übers.): „Wenn wir [...] einmal dem Gedanken Raum geben, dass es gewisse voraufgehende Ursachen (πρεσβυτέρας αἰτίας) für das ‚Gefäß der Ehre' und das ‚Gefäß der Unehre' gibt, ist es dann abwegig, [...] daran zu denken, dass es voraufgehende Ursachen dafür gab, dass Jakob geliebt und Esau gehasst war, bevor noch Jakob einen Körper annahm (πρὸ τῆς ἐνσωματώσεως) und bevor noch Esau in den Schoß Rebekkas einging (πρὸ τοῦ εἰς τὴν κοιλίαν τῆς Ῥεβέκκας γενέσθαι)?"

dem irdischen Körper war, sei es ohne jeden Körper – wird man wohl weiterhin nicht ausschließen können[30].

II. Zum philosophischen Hintergrund

Cyrill von Alexandrien macht Origenes den Vorwurf, er sei in der Ablehnung einer Auferstehung des Fleisches, die im Zusammenhang mit seinen Lehren von der Präexistenz der Seelen und vom Ursprung des Bösen gesehen wird, „dem unnützen Geschwätz der Griechen" (ταῖς Ἑλλήνων φλυαρίαις) gefolgt[31] – eine sehr pauschale Behauptung angesichts der Vielfalt philosophischer Positionen, die zur Zeit des Origenes vertreten werden, ganz speziell in der Frage nach dem Ursprung des Bösen oder allgemeiner des Übels. Wenn Origenes sich in dieser Frage außer an der Heiligen Schrift auch an Philosophen orientieren wollte[32], musste er sich entscheiden.

So wird der epikureische Verzicht auf eine Vorsehung von Origenes mehrfach ausdrücklich abgelehnt[33]. Auch die stoische Meinung, letztlich sei ein einziger Ursprung für alles, auch für das Übel, verantwortlich[34], kann ihm

---

[30] In anderen Werken bringt Origenes die Bevorzugung Jakobs eher mit Gottes Vorherwissen in Verbindung. Vgl. *M. Harl*, Préexistence, 251: „Dans les textes de sa maturité, lorsqu'il prend en compte le sens théologique de l'Épître aux Romains qui cite l'exemple de Jacob et d'Esaü (Rm 9,10–13 avec la citation de Ml 1,2 s.), il ne parle plus de ,causes antérieures' mais seulement, me semble-t-il, de la prescience divine" (es folgen Verweise auf *Orig.*, Comm. in Rom. VII, 15 [zu Röm 9,9–13], fr. in Rom. 1, enthalten in Philoc. XXV [zu Röm 1,1], Orat. 5 und 6); vgl. ibid., 242.

[31] *Cyrill von Alexandrien*, Ep. 81 (Ad monachos in Phua constitutos): E. Schwartz, ACO III (Berlin 1940), p. 201,20–202,17: Als Origenes die Auferstehung des Fleisches ablehnte, „dachte er nicht christlich, sondern folgte dem Geschwätz der Griechen und ist so irregeführt worden. Der Ursprung seiner Verirrung kam ihm von folgender Meinung: Er behauptete, dass die Seelen vor den Körpern existieren (προϋπάρχουσιν), dass sie von einem Zustand der Heiligkeit abgewichen sind und sich von bösem Verlangen und sich von Gott entfernt haben. Aus diesem Grund hat Gott sie verurteilt und mit Körpern versehen (ἐσωμάτωσεν), und sie sind im Fleisch wie in einem Gefängnis." Vgl. *D. Pazzini*, La critica di Cirillo Alessandrino alla dottrina origenista della preesistenza delle anime, Cristianesimo nella storia 9 (1988) 237–279, 239 und 252; *M.-O. Boulnois*, La résurrection des corps selon Cyrille d'Alexandrie: une critique de la doctrine origénienne?, Adamantius 8 (2002) 83–113, 84.

[32] Zum (vorrangigen) Einfluss biblischer Texte (und Philos von Alexandrien) im vorliegenden Kontext vgl. *G. Bostock*, The Sources of Origen's Doctrine of Pre-Existence, in: L. Lies (Hg.), Origeniana Quarta (Innsbruck – Wien 1987) 259–264; *M. Harl*, Préexistence, 243–244; *R. Roukema*, L'origine du mal selon Origène et dans ses sources, RHPhR 83 (2003) 405–420; *P. W. Martens*, Embodiment, Heresy, and the Hellenization of Christianity: The Descent of the Soul in Plato and Origen, HThR 108 (2015) 594–620.

[33] Siehe z.B. *Orig.*, Cels. I, 10.13; IV, 75; V, 3.

[34] Siehe etwa Zenon von Kition nach *Tatian*, Orat. 3: H. von Arnim, SVF I (Leipzig 1905), Nr. 159: ὁ θεὸς κακῶν ἀποδειχθήσεται [...] ποιητής.

nicht akzeptabel erscheinen: Mit den Platonikern des 2. und 3. Jahrhunderts stimmt er darin überein, dass Gott gut ist und nicht die Ursache des κακόν sein kann[35]. Mit einigen ihrer sehr unterschiedlichen Antworten auf die Frage nach der Herkunft des Übels (und des Bösen) ist seine Position dagegen nicht vereinbar. So lehnt er die von Kelsos angedeutete Erklärung entschieden ab, das Übel sei mit der Materie gegeben, es „hafte" ihr „an" (ὕλῃ δὲ προσκεῖται)[36]. Auch ein dualistischer Ansatz (wie er z.B. in Plutarchs *De Iside et Osiride* zum Ausdruck kommt), wäre für Origenes nicht akzeptabel[37]. Eine gewisse Nähe zu ihm weisen Autoren auf, die den freien Willen der menschlichen Seele als Ursprung von Übeln hervorheben. Der in der zweiten Hälfte des zweiten Jahrhunderts wirkende Maximos von Tyros etwa erkennt in seiner 41. *Dissertatio* eine zweifache Schlechtigkeit (μοχθηρία), aus der die unterschiedlichen irdischen Übel (κακά) resultieren. Diese μοχθηρία beruht einerseits auf der Fehlerhaftigkeit (πλημμελές) der Materie, derer der gute Schöpfer sich bedient, andererseits auf dem freien Willen der Seele (ἡ ψυχῆς ἐξουσία).

In freier Anlehnung an Platons Gleichnis vom Seelenwagen (*Phaedr.* 246bc) führt Maximos in derselben *Dissertatio* aus:

> Gott [...] setzte die Seele über einen irdischen Körper (γηΐνῳ σώματι) wie den Lenker über einen Wagen (ἅρματι), übergab der Lenkerin die Zügel und ließ sie losfahren,

---

[35] *Orig.*, Princ. II, 9, 6; Cels. IV, 66; vgl. *Plutarch*, De Iside et Osiride 45: J. G. Griffiths, Plutarch's De Iside et Osiride (Cardiff 1970), p. 190,17: „Das Gute (τἀγαθόν) kann wohl keinen Anlass für Übles (αἰτίαν δὲ κακοῦ) geben"; *Apuleius*, De Platone I, 12: G. Magnaldi, Apulei opera philosophica (Oxford 2020), p. 49: „Man wird Gott nicht die Ursache für irgendein Übel (*ullius mali causa*) zuschreiben können"; *Kelsos*, Alethes Logos fr. IV, 65: SC 136, p. 344,3: „Übel (κακά) stammen nicht von Gott (ἐκ θεοῦ)"; *Alkinoos*, Didaskalikos 10, 3: J. Whittaker, Alcinoos. Enseignement des doctrines de Platon (Paris ²2002), p. 23,31-37. Übers. nach O. F. Summerell – Th. Zimmer, Alkinoos, Didaskalikos, Lehrbuch der Grundsätze Platons (Berlin 2007), p. 27: „Der erste Gott (ὁ πρῶτος θεός) ist [...] das Gute (ἀγαθόν). [...] Und er ist das Gute, weil er alles, so weit wie möglich, gut bewirkt (εὐεργετεῖ), da er Verursacher alles Guten (παντὸς ἀγαθοῦ αἴτιος) ist"; *Maximos von Tyros*, Dissertatio 41, 3: G. L. Koniaris (Berlin – New York 1995), p. 486,52-55. Übers. O. Schönberger – E. Schönberger, Maximos von Tyros, Philosophische Vorträge (Würzburg 2001), p. 182-183: „Was sind Quellen und Ursprung der Übel? Von wo gehen sie aus und kommen zu uns? Von Äthiopien wie die Pest? Aus Babylon wie Xerxes? Aus Makedonien wie Philippos? Bestimmt nicht vom Himmel, beim Zeus, nicht vom Himmel!" Vgl. auch *Platon*, Respublica II 379b. Übers. R. Rufener, Platon, Der Staat. Politeia (Düsseldorf – Zürich 2000), p. 171: „So ist also das Gute (τὸ ἀγαθόν) nicht Ursache von allen Dingen. Es ist wohl Ursache von dem, was sich gut verhält, an dem Schlechten aber ist es unschuldig (τῶν δὲ κακῶν ἀναίτιον)."

[36] *Kelsos*, Alethes Logos fr. IV, 65: SC 136, p. 344,3-346,4; vgl. *H. Lona*, Die ‚Wahre Lehre' des Kelsos (Freiburg u.a. 2005) 257 Anm. 311 (mit Hinweisen auf Numenios, Harpokration, Attikos und Maximos von Tyros). *Orig.*, Cels. IV, 66: SC 136, p. 348,6, bezeichnet die These des Kelsos als nach christlichem Verständnis „nicht wahr" (οὐκ ἀληθές).

[37] Vgl. *Orig.*, Princ. I, 8, 2; II, 4-5.

wobei sie von Gott die Kraft (ῥώμην) erhielt, kunstvoll zu fahren, freilich auch die Freiheit (ἐξουσίαν), nicht kunstvoll zu fahren[38].

Die Wahlfreiheit der menschlichen Seele betont auch Alkinoos in seinem ‚Platon-Handbuch' *Didaskalikos*[39]. Auf dieses Werk verweist Jean Daniélou, als er nach den Quellen der Origenes zugeschriebenen Lehre vom Abstieg und Aufstieg der Seele fragt[40]. Es wäre zwar kühn, hier eine direkte Abhängigkeit zu postulieren[41]. Einzelne Parallelen sind aber nicht zu übersehen: Nach Alkinoos „sandte der Demiurg des Weltalls" die menschlichen Seelen „auf die Erde", weil „er und die von ihm abstammenden Götter um die menschliche Gattung [...] Sorge (φροντίς) hatten, da sie ja den Göttern am meisten verwandt ist"[42]. Ziel der irdischen Existenz des Menschen ist es, sich durch ein Leben auf dem Weg des Rechts (δίκῃ) zu bewähren und die Möglichkeit zum Wiederaufstieg zu erhalten.

Weitere mittelplatonische Quellen, die von einem Abstieg und Aufstieg der Seele sprechen, wären zu nennen[43]. Obwohl durchaus Unterschiede zwischen den Denkmodellen festzustellen sind, konnte Origenes, wenn er eine Präexistenz der Seele voraussetzte, bei Platonikern seiner Zeit verwandte Vorstellungen finden, bei manchen von ihnen vielleicht auch ansatzweise mit Verständnis rechnen.

An dieser Stelle sei darauf hingewiesen, dass im Platonismus des 2. und 3. Jahrhunderts auch Positionen vertreten werden, an die eine Erbsündenlehre hätte anknüpfen können: Plutarch setzt sich in seiner Schrift *Über die spä-*

---

[38] *Maximos von Tyros*, Diss. 41, 5: G. L. Koniaris, p. 494,151–154. Übers. nach O. Schönberger – E. Schönberger, Maximos von Tyros, p. 185. Kurz nach diesen Worten, in der Beschreibung der Reaktionen der unterschiedlichen Pferde, bricht der erhaltene Text ab.

[39] *Alkinoos*, Didaskalikos 26, 2: J. Whittaker, Alcinoos, p. 51,10–52,13: Ἀδέσποτον οὖν ἡ ψυχὴ καὶ ἐπ' αὐτῇ μὲν τὸ πρᾶξαι ἢ μή· καὶ οὐ κατηνάγκασται τοῦτο, τὸ δὲ ἑπόμενον τῇ πράξει καθ' εἱμαρμένην συντελεσθήσεται [...]. „Ohne einen Herrn nun ist die Seele, und es liegt bei ihr zu handeln oder nicht. Und das unterliegt keiner Notwendigkeit; was aber dem Handeln folgt, wird entsprechend dem Schicksal vollendet werden [...]."

[40] J. *Daniélou*, Message évangélique et culture hellénistique aux IIe et IIIe siècles (Tournai u.a. 1961) 389: „La doctrine de la descente des âmes dans les corps et de leur retour à l'unité initiale est sûrement platonicienne – et plus directement issue du Moyen-Platonisme et en particulier d'Albinos [= Alkinoos; Anm. J.A.] (*Epit.*, XVI, 2; *Contre Celse*, IV, 40). De même aussi la possibilité éternelle des rechutes, le caractère éducatif du châtiment, la finitude nécessaire du mal."

[41] In den erhaltenen Schriften des Origenes wird Alkinoos nicht erwähnt. Zudem lässt der *Didaskalikos* sich bisher nicht genauer als auf das 1. bis 3. Jahrhundert datieren.

[42] *Alkinoos*, Didaskalikos 16, 2: J. Whittaker, Alcinoos, p. 36,2–37,7.

[43] Z.B. *Plutarch*, De genio Socratis 22; De sera 22–33; vgl. auch *Numenios*, frr. 30–35, 37 und Orac. Chald. frr. 61, 99, 110, 164.

te Strafe der Gottheit (*De sera numinis vindicta*) mit einem Vers des Euripides auseinander, in dem dieser kritisiert, dass „die Götter das, was die Eltern falsch gemacht haben, auf die Nachkommen abwälzen" (τοὺς θεοὺς τὰ τῶν τεκόντων σφάλματ᾽ εἰς τοὺς ἐγγόνους τρέποντας)[44]. Nach Plutarch kann es sein, dass spätere Generationen mit Recht an der Bestrafung ihrer Vorfahren Anteil erhalten. Dies gelte zum Beispiel für Menschen, die zu unterschiedlichen Zeiten derselben Polis angehören: Wenn die „ganze Bewohnerschaft einer Stadt" von einem Strafgericht heimgesucht werde, liege „der Rechtsgrund (τὸν τοῦ δικαίου λόγον) auf der Hand"[45]. Die Stadt sei nämlich

> ein einheitliches (ἕν), zusammenhängendes (συνεχές) Ding wie ein Lebewesen [...]. Es trägt für alles, was es als Kollektivwesen (κατὰ τὸ κοινόν) tut oder getan hat, die Schuld (αἰτίαν) und das Verdienst (χάριν), solange die Gemeinsamkeit (κοινωνία), welche die Einheit schafft und durch ihre Verflechtungen zusammenknüpft, diese Einheit aufrechterhält.

Wie bei einem Menschen hält Plutarch es bei einer Stadt für „richtig", dass sie

> dieselbe bleibt und weiterhin mit den Vorwürfen belastet ist (ἐνέχεσθαι τοῖς ὀνείδεσι), die von früheren Generationen (τῶν προγόνων) herrühren – mit demselben Recht, wie sie deren Ruhm und Macht genießt[46].

Wie eine Stadt sieht Plutarch auch ein Geschlecht (γένος) als ein „einheitliches und zusammenhängendes Ding". Denn ein Geschlecht ist

> in einem einzigen Ursprung (ἀρχῆς μιᾶς) verankert, von welchem eine Art Kraftwirkung (δύναμιν), ein alles durchziehendes Einheitsmoment (κοινωνίαν διαπεφυκυῖαν) ausgeht, das immer wieder in Erscheinung tritt[47].

Hier kommt nun auch das Motiv der ‚Vererbung' ins Spiel: „Das, was gezeugt wurde" (τὸ γεννηθέν), ist, so Plutarch,

> nicht wie ein handwerkliches Produkt vom Erzeuger (τοῦ γεννήσαντος) losgelöst; denn es ist aus ihm geworden, nicht von ihm gemacht; es besitzt und trägt also ein Stück von ihm in sich, und es ist ganz in der Ordnung, dass es dafür sowohl Strafe als auch Anerkennung erhält (κολαζόμενον προσηκόντως καὶ τιμώμενον).

---

[44] Plutarch, De sera 12 (eigene Übers.); vgl. *Euripides*, fr. 980 Nauck. Aus welchem Werk der Vers stammt, ist nicht bekannt (vgl. *H. Görgemanns*, Plutarch. Drei religionsphilosophische Schriften [Düsseldorf ²2009] 373 Anm. 2).
[45] Plutarch, De sera 15. Übers. H. Görgemanns, Plutarch, p. 93, auch für das Folgende; die griechischen Zitate, wenn nicht anders angegeben, nach der Edition von M. Pohlenz, Plutarchi moralia III (Leipzig 1929; Repr. 1972), p. 394–444.
[46] Plutarch, De sera 15. Übers. H. Görgemanns, Plutarch, p. 95.
[47] Plutarch, De sera 16. Übers. H.Görgemanns, Plutarch, p. 95, auch für das Folgende.

In den Kindern böser Menschen sei

> von Geburt her der Wesenskern der Väter mit anwesend (τὸ κυριώτατον ἐμπέφυκε καὶ πάρεστι μέρος), nicht wirkungslos schlummernd, sondern als Triebkraft des Lebens (ζῶσιν αὐτῷ [wörtlich: „sie leben dadurch"]), des Wachstums (τρέφονται), der Lebensplanung (διοικοῦνται), des Denkens (φρονοῦσι); und daher ist es nicht anstößig und auch nicht absurd, dass sie als deren Kinder auch ihr Erbe antreten (οὐθὲν δεινὸν οὐδ' ἄτοπον, ἂν ἐκείνων ὄντες ἔχωσι[48] τὰ ἐκείνων)[49].

Dass die κακία vererbt werden kann[50], bedeutet aber nicht, dass sie sich zwangsläufig auch in der nächsten Generation auswirkt. So wie die Kinder kränklicher Eltern nach Plutarch die Möglichkeit haben, eine Veranlagung zu „verdrängen" (ἐξωθεῖν), wenn sie sie rechtzeitig durch umsichtiges Verhalten beeinflussen[51], so vermag die menschliche Natur den „angeborenen Makel der Bosheit (ἐγγεννῆ κηλῖδα τῆς κακίας) ganz zu tilgen und ihm zu entrinnen, indem sie sich unter den Einfluss von Gewohnheiten, theoretischen Lehren und Gesetzen begibt" und so „das Schlechte versteckt und das Gute nachahmt"[52].

Es kommt vor, dass einem guten Menschen, der von einem schlechten abstammt, von Seiten der Götter „die Sühne des Geschlechts (τῆς τοῦ γένους ποινῆς) erlassen wird, so als ob durch Adoption in eine andere Familie die Bindung an die Bosheit (κακίας) beseitigt wäre"[53]. So wurden manche Söhne, die zwar von bösen Vätern stammten, selbst aber gut waren, nicht für ihre Väter zur Rechenschaft gezogen; dagegen wurden „Menschen, deren Natur das Ererbte (τὸ συγγενές [wörtlich: „das Angeborene"]) willkommen hieß und aufnahm", wegen der „Ähnlichkeit im Bösen (τὴν ὁμοιότητα τῆς κακίας) von der Gerechtigkeit ereilt".

Wenn ein Mensch „in ähnliche Eigenschaften zurückfällt, wie sein verderbtes Geschlecht sie zeigte", ist es in Plutarchs Augen

---

[48] ἔχωσι: Görgemanns] πάσχωσι: Pohlenz.
[49] Plutarch, De sera 16. Übers. H. Görgemanns, Plutarch, p. 97.
[50] Siehe Plutarch, De sera 20: ἐγγενῆ κηλῖδα τῆς κακίας. Vgl. 19: κακίας δ' ὁμοιότητα συγγενικήν; 20: τὸ συγγενὲς ἦθος.
[51] Plutarch, De sera 19.
[52] Plutarch, De sera 20. Übers. verändert gegenüber Görgemanns. Allerdings kann angeborene κακία des Menschen auch lange Zeit einfach verborgen bleiben und dann (wieder) ausbrechen (ibid.). Gott, der die Veranlagung (διάθεσιν) und Natur (φύσιν) des Menschen kennt, beseitigt die κακία bei manch einem, der zu Vergehen neigt, durch Strafmaßnahmen schon vor ihrem Ausbrechen (ibid.).
[53] Plutarch, De sera 21. Übers. nach H. Görgemanns, Plutarch, p. 111, auch für das Folgende.

doch gewiss angemessen, dass er gleichsam die mit der Erbschaft verbundenen Schulden (χρέα κληρονομίας) übernimmt, das heißt die Sühnung der Schlechtigkeit[54].

Ob Origenes Plutarchs Werk *De sera numinis vindicta* kannte, ist nicht feststellbar[55]. Die Diskussion darüber, ob Veranlagungen und eine bestimmte ‚Natur' vererbt werden können, die nicht nur in diesem Werk geführt wurde, kann ihm durchaus bekannt gewesen sein[56]. In jedem Fall entwickelt Origenes seine Überlegungen zum Ursprung der κακία, die das irdische Leben von Beginn an prägt, vor dem Hintergrund eines bunten Fächers philosophischer Positionen, die sowohl für die Theorie einer Entscheidung in der Präexistenz als auch für eine Erbsündenlehre Ansatzpunkte bieten.

III. Präexistenzlehre und Adams Sünde

Wenn Origenes eine Präexistenzlehre vertrat, bleibt zu klären, ob bzw. wie diese mit seiner Interpretation von Gen 1–3 vereinbar ist. Diese vielfach diskutierte Frage[57] ist der Hauptgegenstand der schon erwähnten Auseinandersetzung zwischen Mark Edwards und Peter Martens. Nach Martens sieht Origenes in Gen 1–3 eine symbolische, allegorische Darstellung. Demnach stehen diese Kapitel, „die die Schöpfung des Kosmos, die Erschaffung von Menschen

---

[54] Ibid. Wie körperliche Eigenschaften kann nach Plutarch auch eine Naturanlage zum Guten oder zum Bösen bei der einen Generation verborgen bleiben, sich aber bei einer späteren wieder Bahn brechen (ibid.).
[55] Ein expliziter Hinweis auf Plutarch und seine „Bücher über die Seele" (περὶ ψυχῆς) findet sich in *Orig.*, Cels. V, 57.
[56] Vgl. *Aristoteles*, fr. 94 Rose (= Stob. flor. 88, 13): ἐκ τοῦ Ἀριστοτέλους περὶ εὐγενείας) zur Vererbbarkeit der Tugend (ἀρετή) eines adligen γένος. Dazu *G. Dietze-Mager*, Das Konzept des sozialen Friedens und seine Widersprüche: ein Beitrag zu Aristoteles' argumentativer und historischer Glaubwürdigkeit, Histos 15 (2021) 52–87, 66: „[...] gute Geburt, d.h. Adel, leitet sich aus der Tugend her, die durch die Zugehörigkeit zu einem *genos* zwangsläufig gegeben ist" (mit Verweis auch auf *Aristoteles*, Rhet 2.15, 1390b22 und Pol 3.13, 1283a38–39). In Cels. I, 24: M. Borret, SC 132 (Paris 1967), p. 140,44, erwähnt Origenes die „vermeintliche edle Geburt" (νομιζομένην εὐγένειαν).
[57] Siehe bereits *G. Bürke*, Des Origenes Lehre vom Urstand des Menschen, ZKTh 72 (1950) 1–39; *G. Sfameni Gasparro*, Doppia creazione e peccato di Adamo: fondamenti biblici e presupposti platonici dell'esegesi origeniana, in: H. Crouzel – A. Quacquarelli (Hgg.), Origeniana Secunda (Rom 1980) 57–67 (Nachdruck: *G. Sfameni Gasparro*, Origene. Studi di antropologia e di Storia della tradizione [Rom 1984] 101–138); *M. Harl*, Préexistence, v.a. 244–247; *P. Pisi*, Peccato di Adamo e caduta dei NOES nell'esegesi origeniana, in: L. Lies (Hg.), Origeniana Quarta (Innsbruck – Wien 1987) 322–335; *C. P. Bammel*, Adam in Origen, in: R. Williams (Hg.), The Making of Orthodoxy. Essays in honor of Henry Chadwick (Cambridge 1989) 62–93.

und ihren anschließenden Fall sowie ihre Ausweisung aus dem Paradies schilderten", in den Augen des Origenes für das

> Drama der ursprünglichen (*primordial*) Schöpfung unkörperlicher vernunftbegabter Geistwesen, für ihre Betrachtung Gottes und dafür, wie diese ins Stocken geriet, was für viele zur Folge hatte, dass sie einen Körper erhielten und in die körperliche Welt versetzt wurden[58].

Diese Interpretation wird in Mark Edwards' *Response* von 2019 einer detaillierten Kritik unterzogen und – im selben Jahr – von Peter Martens wiederum verteidigt. Im Folgenden konzentriere ich mich auf die Argumente, die unmittelbar mit Origenes' Verständnis der Sünde Adams und ihrer Folgen zu tun haben.

Im Zentrum dieser Auseinandersetzung steht eine Passage aus Origenes' Spätwerk *Contra Celsum*. Nach Origenes werden

> diejenigen Adam und seine Sünde in philosophischer Weise betrachten (φιλοσοφήσουσιν), die erkannt haben, dass ‚Adam' in der griechischen Sprache ἄνθρωπος (Mensch) heißt, und dass Mose dort, wo er über Adam zu sprechen scheint, allgemeine (‚naturphilosophische') Aussagen über die Natur des Menschen macht (φυσιολογεῖ Μωϋσῆς τὰ περὶ τῆς τοῦ ἀνθρώπου φύσεως). Denn „in Adam sterben alle", wie die Schrift sagt (1 Kor 15, 22), und „in Entsprechung zur Übertretung Adams" (Röm 5, 14) wurden alle verurteilt; das Wort Gottes trifft diese Feststellungen nicht so sehr über einen einzelnen Menschen als vielmehr über die gesamte Menschheit. Denn obwohl dies von einem einzelnen Menschen gesagt wird, ergibt sich aus dem Kontext, dass die Verfluchung Adams allen gilt. Und das gegen die Frau Gesagte bezieht sich ausnahmslos auf jede Frau[59].

---

[58] *P. Martens*, Origen's Doctrine, 518: „I will argue that in these chapters that depicted the creation of the cosmos, the making of humans, and their subsequent fall and dismissal from paradise, Origen saw a narrative symbolic of his corresponding drama of beginnings." Ibid., 516: „Origen's doctrine of pre-existence—the drama of a primordial creation of incorporeal rational minds, their contemplation of God, and how this activity faltered, resulting in subsequent embodiment for many and placement in the corporeal world [...]."

[59] *Orig.*, Cels. IV, 40: SC 136, p. 288,10–20: καὶ περὶ τοῦ Ἀδὰμ καὶ περὶ τῆς ἁμαρτίας αὐτοῦ φιλοσοφήσουσιν οἱ ἐγνωκότες ὅτι καθ' ἑλλάδα φωνὴν ὁ Ἀδὰμ ἄνθρωπός ἐστι, καὶ ἐν τοῖς δοκοῦσι περὶ τοῦ Ἀδὰμ εἶναι φυσιολογεῖ Μωϋσῆς τὰ περὶ τῆς τοῦ ἀνθρώπου φύσεως. Καὶ «γὰρ ἐν τῷ Ἀδάμ», ὥς φησιν ὁ λόγος, «πάντες ἀποθνήσκουσι», καὶ κατεδικάσθησαν ἐν «τῷ ὁμοιώματι τῆς παραβάσεως Ἀδάμ», οὐχ οὕτως περὶ ἑνός τινος ὡς περὶ ὅλου τοῦ γένους ταῦτα φάσκοντος τοῦ θείου λόγου. Καὶ γὰρ ἐν τῇ τῶν λεγομένων ὡς περὶ ἑνὸς ἀκολουθίᾳ ἡ ἀρὰ τοῦ Ἀδὰμ κοινὴ πάντων ἐστί· καὶ τὰ κατὰ τῆς γυναικὸς οὐκ ἔστι καθ' ἧς οὐ λέγεται. Übers., geringfügig verändert, nach FC 50/3, p. 749.

Auch wenn hier keine präexistenten Seelen erwähnt werden, weist schon diese „allegorische Auslegung von Adams Sünde" nach Peter Martens „stark auf Origenes' Darstellung der Präexistenz hin", in der „nicht einfach eine einzelne Person (oder ein Paar) gefallen ist, sondern vielmehr ‚das gesamte Menschengeschlecht'"[60]. Origenes setzt seine Ausführungen fort:

> Auch der aus dem Paradies vertriebene Mensch zusammen mit der Frau, bekleidet mit Gewändern aus Fell (Gen 3, 21), die Gott wegen der Übertretung der Menschen für die Sünder angefertigt hatte, enthält eine nicht in Worte fassbare und geheimnisvolle Lehre, die erhabener ist als der Abstieg der Seele nach Platon, der Seele, die ihre Flügel verliert und hierher (zur Erde) fällt, bis sie etwas Festes ergreifen kann[61].

Aus dieser Aussage zieht Martens den Schluss, die „Sünde Adams im Garten" werde als der Sündenfall des Menschengeschlechts in der Präexistenz interpretiert[62]. Edwards dagegen sieht hier keinen Hinweis auf eine Präexistenz menschlicher Wesen. Er erinnert an eine weitere Stelle in *Contra Celsum*, an der Origenes auf das anspielt, „was Ezechiel über den Pharao, über Nebukadnezar und den Herrscher von Tyrus sagt", und „auf die Klagen über den König von Babylon bei Jesaja"[63]. Aus diesen Worten, die sich nach Origenes auf den Teufel beziehen[64], kann man, so stellt der Alexandriner fest,

> nicht wenig über die Bosheit (περὶ τῆς κακίας) lernen, nämlich: welchen Ursprung und welche Entstehung (ποίαν ἀρχὴν καὶ γένεσιν) sie hatte, und dass das Vorhandensein der Bosheit auf bestimmte Wesen zurückgeht, die ihre Flügel verloren und dem gefolgt sind, der als Erster seine Flügel verlor[65].

---

[60] *P. Martens*, Origen's Doctrine, 534: „Origen confirms his suspicion that Genesis is narrating the fall not of an individual person, but ‚of the whole human race' [...]." – „[His] allegorical interpretation of Adam's sin strongly points to Origen's account of pre-existence, where it is not simply one person (or couple) who fell, but rather ‚the whole human race'."
[61] *Orig.*, Cels. IV, 40: SC 136, p. 288,20–290,26: Καὶ ὁ ἐκβαλλόμενος δὲ ἐκ τοῦ παραδείσου ἄνθρωπος μετὰ τῆς γυναικός, τοὺς «δερματίνους» ἠμφιεσμένος «χιτῶνας», οὓς διὰ τὴν παράβασιν τῶν ἀνθρώπων ἐποίησε τοῖς ἁμαρτήσασιν ὁ θεός, ἀπόρρητόν τινα καὶ μυστικὸν ἔχει λόγον, ὑπὲρ τὴν κατὰ Πλάτωνα κάθοδον τῆς ψυχῆς, πτερορρυούσης καὶ δεῦρο φερομένης, «ἕως ἂν στερεοῦ τινος λάβηται».
[62] *P. Martens*, Origen's Doctrine, 540; vgl. bereits 534: „Adam's sin in the garden is, thus, rendered as the fall of the primordial human race."
[63] *Orig.*, Cels. VI, 43; vgl. *M. Edwards*, Origen in Paradise, 182.
[64] Vgl. *Orig.*, Princ. I, 5, 4; *M. Edwards*, Origen in Paradise, 183.
[65] *Orig.*, Cels. VI, 43: M. Borret, SC 147 (Paris 1969), p. 286,37–40: [...] ἀφ' ὧν οὐκ ὀλίγα τις ἂν μανθάνοι περὶ τῆς κακίας, ποίαν ἔσχεν ἀρχὴν καὶ γένεσιν, καὶ ὅτι ἀπό τινων πτερορρυησάντων καὶ κατακολουθησάντων τῷ πρώτῳ πτερορρυήσαντι ὑπέστη ἡ κακία.

Edwards schließt aus dieser Aussage, die „Lehre, die derjenigen Platons weit überlegen ist", betreffe also das „Mysterium der ersten Übertretung", die „nicht von einem menschlichen Akteur begangen wurde"⁶⁶ (sondern vom Teufel und den ihm folgenden Engeln).

Tatsächlich ist an der zuletzt zitierten Stelle zumindest nicht explizit von Menschen die Rede. Wenn es aber zuvor (in Cels. IV, 40) hieß, dass der aus dem Paradies vertriebene Mensch *selbst* eine geheimnisvolle Lehre impliziere, die der Lehre Platons überlegen sei, stellen sich weiterhin zwei Fragen:

Erstens: Was verbindet nach Origenes' Ansicht den Menschen mit der Übertretung und dem Fall des Teufels?

Zweitens: In welchem Verhältnis steht das Paradies, aus dem Adam vertrieben wurde, zu dem ‚Ort' oder Status, aus dem der Teufel abstürzte?

Zunächst zur zweiten Frage. Im Kontext des zuletzt angeführten Zitats aus *Contra Celsum* (VI, 43) ist einerseits „von dem bösen Wesen" die Rede (περὶ τοῦ πονηροῦ τούτου), das „aus den himmlischen Regionen gestürzt wurde" (ἐκπέσοντος τῶν οὐρανίων), andererseits von der „Vertreibung" des Menschen „aus dem göttlichen Paradies" (ἐκβληθῆναι τοῦ θείου παραδείσου); kurz danach wird der ursprüngliche Ort Satans vor seinem Fall als „Paradies Gottes" bezeichnet⁶⁷. Sofern das „göttliche Paradies" bei Origenes für den ursprünglichen Ort oder Zustand präexistenter Wesen steht, also für die ‚himmlischen Regionen', mag die Vermutung plausibel erscheinen, dass die Erzählung von Gen 1–3 den Urstand und den Sturz der präexistenten Seelen symbolisch darstellen soll⁶⁸. In manchen Schriften des Origenes finden sich allerdings Aussagen, die ein anderes Verständnis nahelegen.

1) So scheint er zwischen einem (außer-irdischen) Paradies und dem Himmel zu unterscheiden, wenn er an der bereits zitierten Stelle aus dem Kommentar zum Johannesevangelium sagt, Johannes der Täufer sei gesandt worden „aus dem Himmel *oder* (ἤ) aus dem Paradies oder (ἤ) von welchem anderen Ort auch immer als dem hier auf der Erde"⁶⁹.

---

⁶⁶ M. *Edwards*, Origen in Paradise, 183: „The ‚doctrine far superior to Plato's' thus concerns the mystery of the first transgression, which was not committed by a human agent."
⁶⁷ Orig., Cels. VI, 43–44: SC 147, p. 284,5–6.8 und 288,32–33.
⁶⁸ Vgl. bereits G. *Sfameni Gasparro*, Doppia creazione, 63 (= G. *Sfameni Gasparro*, Origene, 117): „Sembra [...] che per Origene la situazione paradisiaca di Adamo sia figura dello *status* iniziale di purezza ed integrità della *natura rationabilis*, al quale pone fine quella caduta che, espressa altrove in termini di ‚negligenza' o ‚trascuratezza' del bene, è ora descritta, sulla base del testo biblico relativo alla trasgressione dei protoplasti, con l'immagine di un desiderio o indebito bisogno di gustare il frutto dell'albero proibito."
⁶⁹ Orig., In Ioh. comm. II, 29, 176: C. Blanc, SC 120 (Paris 1966), p. 326.

2) In der *Exhortatio ad martyrium* verspricht Origenes seinen Adressaten, nicht nur wie Paulus in das Paradies bzw. in den dritten Himmel entrückt zu werden, sondern sogar „die Himmel" zu „überschreiten" (ὑπερβαίνοντες [...] καὶ οὐρανούς), sofern sie ihr Kreuz auf sich nehmen und Jesus nachfolgen[70]. Hier scheint das Paradies nicht die letzte Station des Aufstieges zu sein.

3) Auch wenn ausdrücklich von einem Paradies *auf Erden* die Rede ist, kann dies als Etappe des Weges beschrieben werden. In *De principiis* heißt es:

> Ich glaube [...], dass alle Heiligen, wenn sie aus diesem Leben scheiden, an einem Ort auf der Erde weilen, den die Heilige Schrift ‚Paradies' nennt, gleichsam an einer Stätte der Erziehung (*velut in quodam eruditionis loco*) und sozusagen in einem Hörsaal, einer Schule der Seelen (*auditorio vel schola animarum*)[71].

Erst von diesem Ort aus, an dem die Heiligen unter anderem über das „noch Folgende und Zukünftige" (*de consequentibus et futuris*) belehrt werden, steigt der, der Fortschritte macht,

> zum Bereich der Luft auf und gelangt ins Reich der Himmel durch die verschiedenen Regionen [...], die die Griechen als ‚Sphären' bezeichnen, die heilige Schrift aber als ‚Himmel'[72].

Auch wenn Origenes den Terminus ‚Paradies' in seinem Werk nicht einheitlich gebraucht, stellt sich die Frage: Kann das in Gen 1–3 beschriebene Paradies den Urzustand vor jedem Sündenfall darstellen oder symbolisieren, wenn Origenes in den zitierten Texten sowohl beim Abstieg als auch beim Aufstieg der Seele eine Durchgangsstation als ‚Paradies' bezeichnet? Wenn die Regel gelten soll, dass das Ende dem Anfang entspricht[73], scheint sich für diese Texte eine andere Interpretation näherzulegen. Schon von Marguerite Harl und Caroline Bammel wurde die Meinung vertreten, dass Adams Sünde in Gen 3 nach Origenes nicht die allererste Sünde ist, sondern eine Sünde auf einer Etappe des Weges der Seele zur Erde, der sich „allmählich" (*paulatim*)

---

[70] Orig., Exh. 13: GCS 2 (Orig. 1), p. 13,24.
[71] Orig., Princ. II, 11, 6: TzF 24, p. 452–453 (Ed. und Übers.).
[72] Ibid., p. 455.
[73] Orig., Princ. III, 5, 3.

vollzieht⁷⁴. Auch wenn Origenes das Paradies nicht explizit als Ort der ‚Strafe' bezeichnet⁷⁵: Sah er vielleicht schon das Paradies in den ersten Kapiteln des Buches Genesis als ‚Schule', in der der Mensch sich bewähren oder (wieder) scheitern konnte?⁷⁶ Dass die Bedeutung der Sünde Adams von Origenes geradezu relativiert werden konnte, zeigt seine 16. *Predigt über Jeremia* (entstanden um 240 n.Chr.). Hier geht der Alexandriner beiläufig darauf ein, dass Adam sich vor dem Angesicht Gottes verbarg, als er nach der Übertretung des göttlichen Gebots die Stimme des Herrn hörte, der am Abend im Paradies wandelte. Im Anschluss an Philo stellt Origenes zunächst fest, dass es die schlechten Menschen sind, die sich vor dem Angesicht Gottes verbergen. Aber:

> Auch wenn Adam gesündigt hat, beging er nicht eine übermäßig schwere Sünde. Deswegen *verbarg* er sich (nur) vor dem Angesicht Gottes. Ein größerer Sünder als er aber, und der gottloseste, Kain, der Brudermörder, was hat er getan? „Er *ging* vom Angesicht Gottes *weg*"⁷⁷.

Bleibt noch die Frage nach der Verbindung des Menschen mit dem Fall des Teufels. In der *Exhortatio ad martyrium* ist von potentiellen Märtyrern die Rede, die im letzten Moment versagen und dadurch „vom himmlischen Martyrium abgefallen sind" (ἀπὸ τοῦ οὐρανίου μαρτυρίου καταπεπτωκόσιν)⁷⁸. Ein Christ, so Origenes, der in dieser Situation fällt, ist „durch seine Verleugnung

---

⁷⁴ So nach *Hieronymus*, C. Ioh. Hieros. 19: J.-L. Feiertag, CCL 79A (Turnhout 1999), p. 31,45. Nach *M. Harl*, Préexistence, 246, ist die Sünde Adams eine Imitation oder Reproduktion des Falls in der Präexistenz. Vgl. *C. P. Bammel*, Adam in Origen, 83: „If we wish to systematize Origen's scattered hints and tentative suggestions, we must think in terms of the story of Adam (the first event in human history) as having taken place subsequent to and at a lower level than the fall of rational creatures from their original state of contemplation, also of individual souls having descended through more than one level before their entry into human life."
⁷⁵ Vgl. *M. Edwards*, Origen in Paradise, 168.
⁷⁶ Nach *M. Harl*, Préexistence, 245–246, betrachtet Origenes das irdische Paradies („paradis de *kosmos*"), in dem Adam sich aufhält, als „son lieu de correction-éducation". Vgl. auch *Iren.*, Adv. haer. IV, 37, 7 – 38, 4.
⁷⁷ *Orig.*, In Ier. hom. 16, 4: P. Nautin, SC 238 (Paris 1977), p. 142,52–56: Ὁ μὲν οὖν Ἀδὰμ εἰ καὶ ἥμαρτεν, οὐκ εἰς ὑπερβολὴν χαλεπὴν ἁμαρτίαν ἥμαρτεν· διὰ τοῦτο 'ἐκρύβη ἀπὸ προσώπου τοῦ θεοῦ'· ὁ δὲ ἁμαρτωλότερος αὐτοῦ Κάϊν καὶ ἀσεβέστατος ὁ ἀδελφοκτόνος τί πεποίηκεν; «Ἐξῆλθεν ἀπὸ προσώπου τοῦ θεοῦ». Die Fortsetzung (ibid. 142,57–59) lautet: ὥστε συγκρίσει κακῶν ἔλαττον εἶναι τὸ κρυβῆναι ἀπὸ προσώπου τοῦ θεοῦ· καὶ γὰρ οὗτος κρύπτεται οὐκ ἀπερυθριῶν, ἀλλ' αἰδούμενος τὸν θεόν. „So ist es ein vergleichsweise geringeres Übel, sich vor Gottes Angesicht zu verbergen. Jener [sc. Adam] verbirgt sich ja auch nicht aus Dreistigkeit, sondern weil er sich vor Gott schämt."
⁷⁸ *Orig.*, Exh. 18: GCS 2 (Orig. 1), p. 17,11–12.

dem Teufel ähnlich geworden" (διαβόλῳ διὰ τῆς ἀρνήσεως ὡμοιωμένον)[79] – besonders wenn dieser Christ in der Gemeinde ‚geglänzt' hat. So lassen sich mehrere Worte aus dem 14. Kapitel des Propheten Jesaja auf ihn beziehen, zum Beispiel, dass sein Ruhm „hinabfuhr (κατέβη) in die Unterwelt" (Jes 14, 11). Von ihm heißt es auch: „Wie wurde der Morgenstern vom Himmel herabgestürzt [...]?" (Jes 14, 12: Πῶς ἐξέπεσεν ἐκ τοῦ οὐρανοῦ ὁ ἑωσφόρος [...];) und: „Du wirst im Gebirge hingeworfen werden (ῥιφήσῃ)" (Jes 14, 19). Durch eine freie Entscheidung gegen Gott kann der einzelne Mensch demnach in seinem irdischen Leben den Fall des Teufels unmittelbar nach- und mitvollziehen[80].

Von Adams Sündenfall ist hier nicht die Rede. Welche Rolle er für die Menschheit spielt, wird in einem (nur in der lateinischen Übersetzung des Rufin erhaltenen) Abschnitt von Origenes' *Kommentar zum Römerbrief* betrachtet, konkret zur Aussage von Röm 5, 18, „durch die Übertretung eines einzigen" sei es „für alle Menschen zur Verurteilung gekommen". Das Ergebnis der Verurteilung Adams, an der alle Menschen teilhaben, ist hier die Vertreibung aus dem Paradies auf diese Erde. Wie aber gelangten *alle* Menschen auf diese Erde? Zwei Möglichkeiten werden formuliert:

> [...] sei es, dass alle, die aus Adam geboren wurden, in seinen Lenden waren und auf gleiche Weise wie er zusammen mit ihm vertrieben wurden; sei es, dass jeder auf irgendeine Weise, die nicht in Worte gefasst werden kann und Gott allein bekannt ist, aus dem Paradies gestoßen worden zu sein und eine Verurteilung empfangen zu haben scheint[81].

Wenn jeder seine eigene Verurteilung für eine eigene Entscheidung gegen Gott empfangen hat, sind die Sünde Adams im Paradies und sein Fall aufs Neue relativiert. Insofern Adam von Origenes als historische Person gesehen wird[82],

---

[79] Ibid., p. 18,1.
[80] Vgl. *Orig.*, Cels. VI, 44: M. Borret, SC 147 (Paris 1969), p. 288,24–29. Übers., geringfügig verändert, nach FC 50/4, p. 1099: „Jeder, der sich für die Bosheit und ein von ihr bestimmtes Leben entschieden hat, handelt im Gegensatz zur Tugend und ist damit ein ‚Satanas', d.h. ein ‚Widersacher' des Sohnes Gottes, der die Gerechtigkeit, Wahrheit und Weisheit ist. Der Widersacher im eigentlichen Sinn aber ist das Wesen, das als erstes von allen, die ein friedvolles und glückseliges Leben führen, seine Flügel verloren hat (πτερορρυήσας) und aus der Glückseligkeit gestürzt worden ist (ἐκπεσών)." Nach Origenes (ibid., p. 290,42–45) gehört Kelsos selbst zu denen, „deren Seele durch den bösen Daimon von Gott und von seiner rechten Erkenntnis und von seinem Logos herabgezogen und herabgezerrt worden ist (καθελκομένων καὶ κατασπωμένων)".
[81] *Orig.*, In Rom. comm. V, 4, 3: C. P. Hammond Bammel, SC 539 (Paris 2010), p. 432,7–10: [...] *sive quod in lumbis Adae fuerunt omnes, qui ex eo nascuntur et cum ipso pariter eiecti sunt, sive alio quolibet inenarrabili modo et soli Deo cognito unusquisque de paradiso trusus videtur et excepisse condemnationem.*
[82] Vgl. *Orig.*, Princ. II, 3, 4; III, 2, 1; IV, 3, 7 u.ö.

wäre er der erste von zahllosen Menschen, die sich gegen Gott entschieden haben und entsprechend gefallen sind. Insofern Adam symbolisch für die ganze Menschheit steht, würde anhand seiner Person erzählt, was für jeden einzelnen Menschen aufgrund persönlicher Entscheidung gilt.

Ob Origenes, wenn der zuletzt zitierte Text von ihm stammt, nur die zweite darin erwähnte Möglichkeit vertrat oder auch die erste für denkbar hielt, ist umstritten[83]. Diese Frage wäre im Kontext der umfassenderen Frage zu diskutieren, ob Origenes (auch) eine Erbsündenlehre vertreten hat. Aber die sollte hier nicht gestellt werden.

---

[83] Vgl. *P. Martens*, Origen's Doctrine, 534, und *M. Edwards*, Origen in Paradise, 177.

Latin Tradition

Alexey Fokin, Moscow (Russia)

Tertullian's doctrine of the "original vice" (*vitium originis*) and its contradictory nature

Abstract:
The article shows that Tertullian can be counted as the first Western theologian who touched upon the whole set of questions about the fall of the first man and its consequences for all mankind. According to Tertullian, though Adam's sin was his personal act of transgression of God's commandment, its consequences can be divided into three classes: natural, judicial, and moral. The first includes mortality, the irrational element of the soul and the "law of sin". Death was imputed not only to Adam personally, but to all humanity. Besides, an irrational and passionate element (anger and lust) appeared in human soul as its "natural evil", and a "second nature", corrupted and marked by the "law of sin", which affected the entire human nature, making it unclean and source of all sins. The judicial consequences of the Adam's fall consist of the offence to God and enmity between Him and all the humans, which implies a certain collective responsibility of all mankind before God. The moral consequences of Adam's fall could be seen in viewing Adam's sin as an example of habit of disobedience towards God. The way of inheriting of the consequences of Adam's fall is rendered as a natural way of propagation of souls: every human soul is generated from Adam's soul through the mediation of its parents, and inherits his nature, corrupted by sin. Certain difficulties are noted in understanding the inherited nature of Adam's sin in Tertullian, caused by his views on baptism of infants and on the goodness of human nature, preserving in itself the "seed of good" and the full power of free will. The negative consequences of Adam's fall could be eliminated by means of the due satisfaction afforded to God and reconciliation with Him through repentance. The authors concludes that Tertullian's doctrine of Adam's sin and its inherited nature is marked by an ambiguity, that was not peculiar to Tertullian alone, but was a common feature of many of his Christian contemporaries, as well as of the most of later Greek Fathers of the Church.

I. Introduction

Tertullian was the first Western theologian who touched upon the whole set of questions concerning the fall of the first man and its consequences for all mankind. In fact, as many scholars have noted, in Tertullian we find an anticipation of the later Western (or Latin) doctrine of "original sin" (*peccatum originale*) as both an inherited corruption of human nature, and the guilt in offending God, which was developed later by Augustine in his polemics with Pelagians and subsequently became a traditional doctrine of the Catholic Church[1]. Indeed, Tertullian speaks of Adam's sin not only as the "first sin" (*primum delictum*), but also as the "vice of origin" (*vitium originis*), the "vice of substance" (*vitium substantiae*), the "corruption of nature" (*corruptio naturae*), and even as the "natural evil" (*malum naturale*), that was inherited by all mankind. At the same time Tertullian does not go so far as to deny the natural goodness of man and his free will after Adam's fall, which could serve as a counter-balance to his idea of the *vitium originis*. To prove this in what follows I will consider Tertullian's statements concerning Adam's sin and its consequences, referring to some key passages, scattered among his works, such as *Adversus Marcionem, De anima, De resurrectione carnis, De baptismo, De patientia, De paenitentia* and several others, where this doctrine is developed by him in a very unsystematic way.

II. The original state of man and the circumstances of his fall

I will start from Tertullian's views on the original state of man and from the circumstances of his fall. Adam was created by God in a very special way: not merely by His commanding word (*imperiali verbo*), but by the very friendly hand of God (*familiari manu*) he was created in "the image and likeness" of God and animated by His Spirit, so that he was dignified to inhabit this world created especially for his sake[2]. God placed the first man above all His creatures as the "*dominus universitatis*" in order that he might use them, rule over them, and through them understand his Creator[3]. Furthermore, God be-

---

[1] See: R. E. Roberts, The Theology of Tertullian (London 1924) 165; N. P. Williams, The Ideas of the Fall and of Original Sin (London 1927) 233; A. Gaudel, Art. Le péché originel, in: DThC 12 (Paris 1933) 365; H. Rondet, Le péché originel dans la tradition patristique et théologique (Paris 1966) 74; J. N. D. Kelly, Early Christian Doctrines (London 1968) 175-176; P. F. Beatrice, Tradux peccati: Alle fonti della dottrina agostiniana del peccato originale (Milano 1978) 267; G. L. Bray, Holiness and the will of God: Perspectives on the theology of Tertullian (London 1979) 81; E. Osborn, Tertullian, First Theologian of the West (Cambridge 1997) 163; J. Leal, La antropología de Tertuliano. Estudio de los tratados polémicos de los años 207-212 d. C. (Roma 2001) 124.

[2] See: *Tertullian*, Adv. Marc. I, 13, 2: E. Kroymann, CCL 1 (Turnhout 1954), p. 454; II, 4, 3-4: ibid., p. 478-479; II 8, 2: ibid., p. 484; De resurr. 5, 6-8: J. G. Ph. Borleffs, CCL 2 (Turnhout 1954), p. 927.

[3] Adv. Marc. II, 9, 7: CCL 1, p. 485; De resurr. 9, 1: CCL 2, p. 932.

stowed man with the opportunity to spend his life in various pleasures, placing him in Paradise—the "more pleasant region" of the world (*in amoenioribus*), and also provided for Adam a relevant helper, similar to him, but of the opposite sex, that is Eve[4]. In Paradise the first man was close to God as His friend; he was innocent and dwelled in integrity[5]. Like the angels, man was originally good (*bonus*), but this goodness belonged to him not by nature (*natura*), but by the "institution" (*institutione*)[6], because he received this institution or condition, including the power of free choice, that is to freely choose and follow the good, from a good Institutor and Creator of all goods, who alone is good by nature[7]. Thus, according to Tertullian, from the beginning man was bestowed with freedom of will, enabling him both to choose good, and to avoid evil, to which he had sufficient strength to resist. In doing so, goodness would belong to man as his "own property" (*bonum suum, bonum proprium*), and "as if his nature" (*quodammodo natura*)[8]. At the same time, God gave Adam "the law" (*lex*) for exercising his obedience, so that the first man, as a rational creature endowed with powers of understanding and knowledge (*animal rationale, intellectus et scientiae capax*), might remain in an intimate spiritual union with God, restraining himself to the limits of rational freedom (*libertate rationali*) and freely submitting himself to God, who has subjected all creatures to him[9].

The necessity of imposing of this law was due to the fact that God created man not merely to live like other living beings, but to "live rightly" (*ad recte vivendum, recte vivere*), that is, to live in harmony with God and His will by giving him "counsel to obey the law" (*admonito in legis obsequium*)[10]. In doing so, God warned man in advance that his failure to obey the law of God, i.e. the transgression of it (*transgressio*), would inevitably result in death and expulsion from Paradise as *punishment* for this transgression (*poena transgressionis*); so that the injunction to prevent sin (*non delinquendi*) was strengthened by the "threat of death" (*comminatione moriendi*)[11]. It follows, that man

---

[4] Adv. Marc. II, 4, 4-5: CCL 1, p. 479.
[5] See: De patien. 5, 13: J. G. Ph. Borleffs, CCL 1 (Turnhout 1954), p. 304; De resurr. 26, 12: CCL 2, p. 955.
[6] On the term *institutio* in Tertullian's theology see: R. Braun, Deus Christianorum. Recherches sur le vocabulaire théologique de Tertullien (Paris 1977) 393-394.
[7] Adv. Marc. II, 6, 4: CCL 1, p. 481.
[8] Adv. Marc. II, 6, 5-6: CCL 1, p. 481-482.
[9] Adv. Marc. II, 4, 5: CCL 1, 479; cf. De jejun. 3, 2: A. Reifferscheid, CCL 2 (Turnhout 1954), p. 1259.
[10] Adv. Marc. II, 8, 1: CCL 1, p. 483-484.
[11] See: Adv. Marc. II, 4, 6: CCL 1, p. 479; 9, 8: ibid., p. 486. Cf. De anima 52, 2; De jejun. 3, 2; De patien. 5, 11, etc. In one passage Tertullian on the contrary calls the commandment

would not ever die, if he had kept the law given to him by God[12]. Besides, the law itself confirmed man's status as a free and autonomous being (*liberum et sui arbitrii et sui potestatis, arbitrii sui libertate et potestate signatus*), which, according to Tertullian, is what mainly reflected the image and likeness of God in man; the law thus did not exclude, but rather certified human freedom through free obedience or free contempt of it[13]. Although God foresaw that man would make bad use of his freedom of choice, nevertheless He did not want to deprive man of His most precious gift[14].

In full agreement with a literal understanding of the biblical narrative of Genesis, ch. 3, Tertullian teaches that the first man and woman, Adam and Eve, failed to resist the devil's temptation and freely broke God's commandment not to eat from the tree of knowledge[15]. This was exactly the "fall of man" (*hominis ruina*)[16], which Tertullian also calls the "sin of Adam" (*Adae delictum*)[17], the "sin of [the first] man" (*delictum hominis*)[18], the "first sin" (*primum delictum*)[19], the "sin of transgression" (*delictum transgressionis*)[20], or simply the "transgression"[21]. Adam committed this sin of transgression because he chose his own opinion over God's commandment[22]. He was impatient with God's admonition, which he failed to keep, and succumbed to the temptation of the devil, which he failed to reject[23]. In doing so Adam also

---

not to eat from the tree of knowledge "the law of life" (*legem vivendi*), probably because it protected man from death; see: Scorpiac. 5, 11: A. Reifferscheid, CCL 2 (Turnhout 1954), p. 1078.

[12] Adv. Marc. II, 9, 9: CCL 1, p. 486. Cf. Adv. Marc. II, 8, 2; IV, 41, 1; De anima 52, 2; Scorpiac. 5, 12, etc.

[13] Adv. Marc. II, 5, 5-7: CCL 1, p. 480-481; 6, 3-7: ibid., p. 481.

[14] Adv. Marc. II, 7, 2-4: CCL 1, p. 482-483; 9, 9: ibid., p. 486.

[15] See: De patien. 5, 5-15; De jejun. 3, 2; Adv. Marc. I, 22, 8; II, 2, 7; 5, 1-2; 8, 2; 10, 4-6; 25, 1-5; De cultu fem. I, 1, 1-2; De exhort. cast. 2, 3-5; Scorpiac. 5, 11-13, etc.

[16] Adv. Marc. II, 6, 8: CCL 1, p. 482.

[17] Adv. Marc. II, 2, 7: CCL 1, p. 477; De exhort. cast. 2, 5: E. Kroymann, CCL 2 (Turnhout 1954), p. 1017.

[18] Adv. Marc. II, 9, 9: CCL 1, p. 486; 11, 1: ibid., p. 488.

[19] De cultu fem. I, 1, 1: E. Kroymann, CCL 1 (Turnhout 1954), p. 343.

[20] De resurr. 26, 12: CCL 2, p. 955.

[21] See: Adv. Marc. II, 5, 4; V, 18, 13; De resurr. 34, 1; De anima 16, 1; Scorpiac. 5, 12, etc. As a synonym for Adam's sin Tertullian sometimes uses another judicial term: *crimen* (see: De patien. 5, 8-13: CCL 1, p. 304), which also means "guilt", "fault", "culpability". It should be noted that Tertullian never uses the biblical term *peccatum* ("sin") for the crime committed by Adam as well as for that which was inherited from him by his descendants and which later in the Latin theological tradition came to be called "original sin" (*peccatum originale*). See: P. F. Beatrice, Tradux peccati, 269; J. Leal, La antropología de Tertuliano, 119.

[22] See: Adv. Marc. II, 2, 7: CCL 1, p. 477; 9, 8: CCL 1, p. 486.

[23] De patien. 5, 11: CCL 1, p. 304.

violated the rule of abstinence (*abstinentiam*), which had been prescribed to him by God[24], and succumbed to gluttony, thereby "selling his salvation for gluttony" (*gula*)[25].

Tertullian supposes that Adam's sin was committed as much by the impulse of the soul driven by lust (*animae instinctu ex concupiscentia*) as by the act of the flesh that ate from the forbidden tree (*carnis actu ex degustatione*)[26]. He also insists that the guilt (*culpa, reatus*) for this sin lies not with God, who gave man freedom of choice, but with man himself, since he used it in an improper way (*non ut debuit*)[27]. According to Tertullian, the devil also cannot be blamed for Adam's sin because he was not directly responsible for his crime, for he did not put the "will to sin" (*voluntatem deliquendi*) in man, but only provided the occasion for exercising of such a will (*materiam voluntati*)[28]. Moreover, the "evil of transgression" (*malum transgressionis*), committed by the first man at the instigation of the devil, should not be considered as natural, since it was completely alien to man's nature and immaterial (*tam non naturale quam nec materiale*)[29]. We may say, then, that Adam's sin, which consisted in transgressing the commandment or the law of God, was his *own personal act of transgression and personal fault* (*delictum transgressionis, crimen, culpa*)[30], due only to his own free choice and deliberate deviation from his original institution, given to him by God, which included natural inclination to good, into the opposite direction, that is to evil and sin, against God's will[31].

III. Natural consequences of Adam's sin

Let us now consider what are the consequences of Adam's sin, both for him personally and for humanity as a whole. From Tertullian's point of view, it would seem that these consequences can be divided into three classes: 1) *natural* consequences, that concern entire human nature; 2) *judicial*, that concern

---

[24] Scorpiac. 5, 12: CCL 2, p. 1078.
[25] De jejun. 3, 2: CCL 2, p. 1259. As D'Alès correctly pointed out, Adam's sin combined various genres of evil: impatience, disobedience, gluttony, incontinence, etc.; see: A. D'Alès, La théologie de Tertullien (Paris 1905) 265.
[26] De resurr. 34, 1: CCL 2, p. 964; cf. Adv. Marc. II, 9, 8; De bapt. 4, 5.
[27] Adv. Marc. II, 9, 8-9: CCL 1, p. 486; cf. ibid. II, 10, 6.
[28] De exhort. cast. 2, 5: CCL 2, p. 1017.
[29] De anima 21, 3: J. H. Waszink, CCL 2 (Turnhout 1954), p. 813.
[30] On these and other terms designating both Adam's sin, and other sins, see: J. Leal, La antropología de Tertuliano, 121-125.
[31] See: Adv. Marc. II, 2-10; De anima 21; De patien. 5, etc.

relationship between God and all mankind; and 3) *moral*, that concern moral deterioration of human beings.

It seems that all the *natural* consequences of Adam's sin mentioned by Tertullian can be reduced to the three fundamental ones: *mortality*, the *irrational (passionate) element* of human soul, and the *"law of sin"*. Indeed, according to Tertullian, Adam and Eve's transgression of God's commandment made all humans mortal so that death became a part of human nature or human condition[32]:

> Man ... has brought upon himself the danger of death. He had received from his own Lord, as from a physician, the salutary enough rule to live according to the law, that he should eat of all indeed [that the garden produced] and should refrain from only one little tree which in the meantime the Physician Himself knew as an inopportune one (*importunam*). He gave ear to him whom he preferred, and broke through self-restraint. He ate what was forbidden (*illicitum*), and, satiated with the trespass (*transgressione saturatus*), suffered indigestion tending to death; and certainly fully deserved to perish his life totally (*in totum perire*) the one who wished to do so[33].

Elsewhere, Tertullian contrasts the "status of life", that is, the natural power to live, which Adam received from God, with the "status of death", which he gained both for himself and for all his descendants through his transgression:

> As, therefore, God designed for man a condition of life (*vitae statum*), so man brought on himself a state of death (*mortis statum*); and this, too, neither through infirmity nor through ignorance, so that no blame can be imputed to the Creator[34].

In this way Adam became the "author of death" (*auctor mortis*) for all his descendants, making them mortal in their bodies, for "in Adam [...] all die fleshly" (*omnes [...] in Adam carne moriuntur*, cf. 1 Cor. 15, 22)[35]. In this connection Tertullian frequently states that death was a result of the personal fault (*culpa*) of the first man, as it is clear from this passage of the *De anima*:

---

[32] See: De test. anim. 3, 2; De resurr. 34, 1; Adv. Marc. I, 22, 8; II, 4, 6; II, 8, 2; II, 9, 8-9; II, 25, 4; IV, 41, 1; Scorpiac. 5, 11-12; De paenit. 2, 3; De patien. 5, 9-11; De jejun. 3, 2; De anima 52, 2, etc.

[33] Scorpiac. 5, 11-12: CCL 2, p. 1078. Transl. by S. Thelwall, in: A. Roberts, J. Donaldson, A. Cleveland Coxe (eds.), ANF 3 (Buffalo, NY 1885) 638. Slightly modified.

[34] Adv. Marc. II, 8, 2: CCL 1, p. 484; transl. by P. Holmes, in: A. Roberts, J. Donaldson, A. Cleveland Coxe (eds.), ANF 3 (Buffalo, NY 1885) 303.

[35] De resurr. 48, 8-9: CCL 2, p. 988. Besides bodily death Tertullian also mentions *the spiritual death* of man (Adam), which is the ignorance of God (*ignorantia Dei*), see: De resurr. 19, 3-7: CCL 2, p. 944–945; 37, 9: CCL 2, p. 970. However, Tertullian here rather ascribes this opinion to the Gnostics and Docetists, who denied a literal understanding of both death and bodily resurrection.

We know what was man's origin, and we boldly assert and persistently maintain that death happens not by way of natural consequence to man, but owing to a fault and defect which is not itself natural (*non ex natura* [...] *sed ex culpa, ne ipsa quidem naturali*) [...]. If man had been directly appointed to die as the condition of his creation, then of course death must be imputed to nature. Now, that he was not thus appointed to die (*non in mortem institutum*), is proved by the very law which made his condition depend on a warning, and death result from man's arbitrary choice (*arbitrio hominis addicens mortis eventum*). Indeed, if he had not sinned, he certainly would not have died (*si non deliquisset, nequaquam obiisset*). That cannot be nature which happens by the exercise of volition (*accidit per voluntatem*) after an alternative has been proposed to it, and not by necessity—the result of an inflexible and unalterable condition[36].

Thus, according to Tertullian, death appeared as *an accidental property* or *new condition* of human nature, contrary to its original "vital" status; it is the result both of Adam's *personal act of free will*, and of God's *punishment* for his transgression (*poena transgressionis*)[37]. Another punishment was the expulsion from Paradise, which deprived both Adam and Eve and all their descendants of the opportunity to keep friendly union with God and enjoy the fruits of the tree of life and the other paradisiac delicious, and condemned them to the burdens of earthly life[38].

Another important consequence of Adam's sin was a change in the structure of the human soul. Indeed, according to Tertullian, the human soul, created by God in His "image and likeness", although much less perfect than its Creator, resembles Him in that it is totally rational, and its Creator is also rational and creates only that which is consistent with reason[39]. Therefore, the soul's original nature possesses only the higher rational part, whereas its lower irrational part was joint to it later as a consequence of Adam's fall:

It is the rational element (*rationale*) which we must believe to be soul's natural condition (*naturale*), impressed upon it from its very first creation (*animae a primordio sit ingenitum*) by its Author, who is Himself rational (*a rationali auctore*). For how should that be other than rational, which God produced on His own prompting; nay more, which He expressly sent forth by His own *afflatus* or breath? The irrational element (*irrationale*), however, we must understand to have accrued later, as hav-

---

[36] De anima 52, 2: CCL 2, p. 858; transl. by P. Holmes, in: A. Roberts, J. Donaldson, A. Cleveland Coxe (eds.), ANF 3 (Buffalo, NY 1885) 229. Cf. Adv. Marc. II, 8, 2; II, 9, 9; Scorpiac. 5, 11-12, etc.
[37] Adv. Marc. II, 4, 6: CCL 1, p. 479.
[38] See: Adv. Marc. I, 22, 8; II, 10, 6; II, 5, 4; De paenit. 2, 3; De patien. 5, 14, etc.
[39] See: Adv. Marc. I, 13, 2; II, 9, 3-7; De anima 16, 1-2.

ing proceeded from the instigation of the serpent (*acciderit ex serpentis instinctu*)—the very achievement of the first transgression (*transgressionis admissum*)—which thenceforward became inherent in the soul, and grew with its growth, assuming the manner by this time of a natural development (*ad instar iam naturalitatis*), happening as it did immediately at the beginning of nature (*in naturae primordio accidit*)[40].

Thus Tertullian considers the origins of an irrational (passionate) element of human soul together with its two powers—*angry* (*indignativum*) and *lust* (*concupiscentivum*)[41]—as a result of Adam's sin, so that, in his opinion, this irrational element, which is no longer under the control of human reason, does not belong to "that nature which is the production of God, but to that which the devil brought in" (*ex illa [natura] quam diabolus induxit*), being a "property of the second, later, and deteriorated nature" (*proprietatem naturae alterius [...] posterioris et adulterae*)[42]. He also calls this irrational element "the evil of soul" (*malum animae*) and "the corruption of nature" (*naturae corruptio*), which became, so to speak, its "another nature" (*alia natura*):

> The evil, which exists in the soul (*malum animae*), other than that which built upon it from by the visitation of the wicked spirit, is antecedent [to particular evil actions], being derived from the fault of our origin (*ex originis vitio antecedit*), and is in a certain manner natural (*naturale quodammodo*). For, as we have said, the corruption of [our] nature is another nature (*naturae corruptio alia natura est*) having a god and father of its own, namely the author of that corruption (*corruptionis auctorem*)[43].

---

[40] De anima 16, 1: CCL 2, p. 802; transl. by P. Holmes, in: A. Roberts, J. Donaldson, A. Cleveland Coxe (eds.), ANF 3 (Buffalo, NY 1885) 194. On "lust" (*concupiscentia*) as an impetus for Adam's sin, see also: De pudicit. 6, 15; De resurr. 34, 1.

[41] See: De anima 16, 3-7.

[42] De anima 16, 7: CCL 2, p. 803. It should be noted that in the same treatise *De anima* Tertullian agrees that in the Gospels the two irrational powers of the soul, *anger* and *lust*, together with the rational element, are also attributed to Jesus Christ as constituting parts of His human soul. Moreover, God put in Adam and Eve (and thus in all other humans) the desire to eat, commanding them to eat from every tree in Paradise except the tree of knowledge; finally, a justified and appropriate usage of anger and lust directed to something good is also approved by the Apostle Paul. In order to resolve this problem, Tertullian, it seems, inclines to distinguish between *two kinds* of anger and lust: the first kind is *properly irrational and secondary* (*irrationale indignativum*), which is not controlled by reason and belongs to the irrational element of the soul, arising from the instigation of the devil and the transgression of God's commandment; the second kind is *rational and natural* (*rationalis concupiscentia, rationalis indignatio, proprie naturalis concupiscentia*), which is controlled by reason and belongs to the rational element of the soul and the original condition of human nature; see: De anima 16, 4-7; 38, 3.

[43] De anima 41, 1: CCL 2, p. 844; transl. by N. P. Williams, The Ideas of the Fall, 239; slightly modified. On "original corruption" of human nature see also: De anima 41, 4: CCL 2, p. 844

This "original vice" or "original fault" (*vitium originis*) of human nature, or the "vice of substance" (*vitium substantiae*)[44], Tertullian, following the Apostle Paul (cf. Rom. 7, 23; 8, 2), sometimes calls "sin" (*peccatum*)[45] and the "law of sin" (*lex delinquentiae*), which dwells in the members of human body and possesses its own "sinful power" (*virtus delinquentiae*) or "power of sin acting against will" (*ipsam vim delinquendi contra voluntatem*), or against the "law of the mind" (*militantem adversus legem animi sui*)[46]. This "law of sin" affected all human nature, both soul and body, making them unclean and "sinful" (*peccatrix*), that is, the sources of sin, though not equally, since the body is but an instrument or servant of the soul in the fulfillment of its desires, and the soul is its mistress[47]. Thus, when discussing the qualities of the flesh of Jesus Christ, Tertullian explicitly points out that human flesh itself is also sinful in its very nature:

> Christ was in the likeness of sinful flesh, not, however, as if He had taken on Him the likeness of the flesh, in the sense of a semblance of body instead of its reality; but the Apostle means us to understand likeness to the flesh which sinned, because the flesh of Christ, which itself was sinless (*non peccatrix caro Christi*), was equal to that flesh to which sin belonged (*eius fuerit par, cuius erat peccatum*)—being equal to it in its general nature, but not in the corruption (*genere, non vitio adaequanda*). Whence we also affirm that there was in Christ the same flesh as that whose nature in man is sinful (*cuius natura est in homine peccatrix*). In the flesh, therefore, we say that sin (*peccatum*) has been abolished, because in Christ that same flesh is maintained without sin, which in man was not maintained without sin (*in homine sine peccato non habebatur*)[48].

Thus Adam's sin, being originally the result of his free choice and personal act of will, became a natural condition or "sinful status" of human nature, so that

---

(*corruptio pristina*); Adv. Marc. II, 16, 4: CCL 1, p. 493 (*in homine corruptoriae condicionis habentur huiusmodi passiones*); V, 17, 10: CCL 1, p. 517 (*apparet communi naturae omnium hominum et delicta et concupiscentias carnis, et incredulitatem, et iracundiam reputare, diabolo tamen captante naturam, quam et ipse iam infecit delicti semine inlato*); De resurr. 51, 6: CCL 2, p. 994 (*aculeus autem mortis delinquentia, haec erit corruptela*).
[44] Adv. Marc. V, 14, 2: CCL 1, p. 705.
[45] See: Adv. Marc. V, 14, 1-2: CCL 1, p. 705.
[46] See: De resurr. 46, 10-12: CCL 2, p. 984; 51, 6: CCL 2, p. 994; cf. De pudicit. 17, 9-10; Adv. Marc. V, 14, 1-2; De carn. Chr. 16, 3-4.
[47] See: De anima 40, 1-4; De carn. Chr. 16, 2-4; De resurr. 16, 1-13; 46, 13-14; De bapt. 4, 5; De pudicit. 6, 15, etc.
[48] De carn. Chr. 16, 3-4: CCL 2, p. 902-903; transl. by P. Holmes, in: A. Roberts, J. Donaldson, A. Cleveland Coxe (eds.), ANF 3 (Buffalo, NY 1885) 535; slightly modified. Cf. ibid. 16, 2; De pudicit. 6, 15. See also: H. Rondet, Le péché originel, 73.

all the natural consequences of Adam's fall, such as the mortality of the body, the irrational element of the soul, and the "law of sin", affecting both human soul and body, were propagated to all human race.

IV. Judicial consequences of Adam's sin

Let us now consider *judicial* consequences of Adam's sin, affecting relationships between God and humans, in which their solidarity with the first man, Adam, is apparent. Indeed, Tertullian mentions, that after the fall Adam lost both his ability to comprehend God (*Deo sapere*), and his connection with the heavenly world (*caelestia sustinere*)[49]. Adam also lost the participation to the Spirit of God, whom he received in the very moment of his creation through the divine inflation (*de adflatu eius*), but lost because of his sinful act (*amiserat per delictum*)[50]. Moreover, failing to keep God's commandment and to resist the devil's advice Adam committed the sin of impatience and disobedience, which made God angry and offended:

> Hence, whence the origin of sin (*delicti origo*), arose the first origin of judgment (*prima judicii*); hence, whence man was induced to offend (*offendere homo inductus*), God began to be angry (*irasci exorsus*). Whence came the first indignation in God (*indignatio prima*), thence came His first patience; who, content at that time with malediction only, refrained in the devil's case from the instant infliction of punishment[51].

Elsewhere, Tertullian in a similar way speaks of an offence to God committed by all mankind and resulted in the enmity ("war", *bellum*) between Him and all humans:

> Grace and peace are not only His who had them published, but His likewise to whom offence had been given (*qui fuerit offensus*). For neither does *grace* (*gratia*) exist, except after offence (*offensae*); nor *peace* (*pax*), except after war (*belli*). Now, both the people [of Israel] by their transgression of His laws, and the whole race of mankind (*omne hominum genus*) by their neglect of natural duty, had both sinned and rebelled against the Creator[52].

---

[49] De patien. 5, 13: CCL 1, p. 304.
[50] De bapt. 5, 7: CCL 1, p. 282; cf. De anima 41, 4.
[51] De patien. 5, 11-12: CCL 1, p. 304; transl. by S. Thelwall, in: A. Roberts, J. Donaldson, A. Cleveland Coxe (eds.), ANF 4 (Buffalo, NY 1885).
[52] Adv. Marc. V, 5, 3-4: CCL 1, p. 676; transl. by P. Holmes, in: A. Roberts, J. Donaldson, A. Cleveland Coxe (eds.), ANF 3 (Buffalo, NY 1885) 438-439.

Although from this passage it is not quite clear, whether there is a connection between Adam's own offence to God, and that of the rest of mankind, but there is no doubt that it was Adam who was the cause not only of mortality for all humans, but also of their *common condemnation* by the Divine justice, which is passed on from him to all his descendants:

> In the beginning man was deceived [...] by the angel of malice, the source of error, the corrupter of the whole world, so that he overstepped the commandment of God. Wherefore man was given over to death (*propterea in mortem datus*), and has made the whole of his race, drawing contamination from his seed, a stock stained with his own condemnation (*totum genus de suo semine infectum suae etiam damnationis traducem fecit*)[53].

As Norman Williams correctly comments, the last phrase "might easily be interpreted as meaning that every member of the race is born subject to the judicial sentence pronounced against Adam"[54]. This impression is strengthened by the following words of Tertullian:

> When the Lord says that He is come to save that which was lost, what are we to understand by "that which was lost"? Undoubtedly man. Is man "lost" as a whole, or only In part? Surely as a whole, seeing that the transgression, which is the cause of man's ruin (*transgressio [...] perditionis humanae causa*), was committed both by an impulse of the soul, that is through concupiscence, and also by an action of the flesh, that is through the testing [of the forbidden fruit], has branded the whole man with the sentence of his transgression (*totum hominem elogio transgressionis inscripsit*), and therefore has deservedly filled him with perdition[55].

According to Williams, the term *elogium* here, which literally means "judicial record" of sin of Adam, "seems to be understood as binding his posterity also"[56]. It is true not only because all individuals, from all nations, Jews and Gentiles alike, offended God in a manner similar to Adam, but because both the "guilt" or "crime" (*culpa, reatus, crimen*) of Adam, and the divine "judgment" (*damnatio, judicium, elogium, sententia Dei*) were imposed on all humans due to Adam's sin. This presupposes a kind of *collective responsibility* of all mankind before God, as is clearly stated by Tertullian in the following famous passage:

---

[53] De test. anim. 3, 2: CCL 1, p. 178; transl. by N. P. *Williams*, The Ideas of the Fall, 240; slightly modified.
[54] N. P. *Williams*, The Ideas of the Fall, 241.
[55] De resurr. 34, 1: CCL 2, p. 964; transl. by N. P. *Williams*, The Ideas of the Fall, 240; slightly modified.
[56] N. P. *Williams*, The Ideas of the Fall, 240.

We have indeed borne "the image of the earthy man" (*imaginem choici*, cf. 1 Cor. 15, 47-48), by our sharing in his transgression (*per collegium transgressionis*), by our participation in his death (*per consortium mortis*), by our banishment from Paradise (*per exilium paradisi*)[57].

As A. Gaudel notes, it is clear from this passage that "une telle solidarité dans la corruption a pour raison une certaine participation à la transgression"[58]. In this connection Tertullian often refers to Adam as the "originator of our race and our sin" (*princeps et generis et delicti*)[59], and the "originator of the human race, and of human offense against the Lord" (*et stirpis humanae et offensae in Dominum princeps Adam*)[60], who made the whole human race undergo his condemnation (*damnatio*)[61].

The same is true of Eve as well, for, according to Tertullian, every woman feels *personal responsibility* for the Eve's deed, and therefore she has to strive with all her efforts

> in order that by every garb of penitence she might the more fully expiate that which she derives from Eve (*id quod de Eua trahit*),—the ignominy, I mean, of the first sin (*ignominiam primi delicti*), and the odium [attaching to her as the cause] of human perdition (*invidiam perditionis humanae*) [...]. The sentence of God (*sententia Dei*) on this sex (cf. Gen. 3, 16) is alive in this age; thus the guilt (*reatus*) must also be alive[62].

V. Traducianism and the inheritance of the consequences of Adam's sin

To prove the possibility of inheriting the consequences of Adam's sin Tertullian refers to the stoic[63] doctrine of *traducianism*[64] concerning the way of

---

[57] De resurr. 49, 6: CCL 2, p. 991; transl. by P. Holmes, in: A. Roberts, J. Donaldson, A. Cleveland Coxe (eds.), ANF 3 (Buffalo, NY 1885) 582. Cf. Adv. Marc. I, 22, 8.
[58] A. Gaudel, Le péché originel, 364.
[59] De exhort. cast. 2, 5: CCL 2, p. 1017; cf. De paenit. 2, 3.
[60] De paenit. 12, 9: CCL 1, p. 340.
[61] De test. anim. 3, 2: CCL 1, p. 178 (see above).
[62] De cultu fem. I, 1, 1-2: CCL 1, p. 343; transl. by S. Thelwall, in: A. Roberts, J. Donaldson, A. Cleveland Coxe (eds.), ANF 4 (Buffalo, NY 1885) 14; slightly modified.
[63] On the stoic origins of Tertullian's traducianism see: M. Spanneut, Le stoïcisme des Pères de l'Église (Paris 1957) 178-179, 181-188.
[64] The majority of scholars agreed that Tertullian did explain the "mechanism" of the transmission of Adam's sin by means of traducianism; see, for example: A. D'Alès, La théologie de Tertullien, 265-266; R. E. Roberts, The Theology of Tertullian, 165; N. P. Williams, The Ideas of the Fall, 231-238, 242; A. Gaudel, Le péché originel, 364; E. Testa, Il peccato di Adamo nella Patristica (Gerusalemme 1970) 152; P. F. Beatrice, Tradux peccati, 261-263, 267-268; J. Leal, La antropología de Tertuliano, 126-127, etc.

propagation of human souls: every human soul is generated from the first man's soul through the mediation of the parents in the same time and the same way as the body, for there is a seed of soul (*semen animae, semen animale*), which simultaneously with the seed of a body enters into a woman's womb[65]. Thus, from one man, Adam, comes all the multitude of human souls (*ex uno homine tota haec animarum redundantia agitur*)[66]. That is why Tertullian insists that every human soul, descended through the parents from the progenitor Adam and possessing his nature, is impure (*immunda*) and sinful (*peccatrix*), as is the flesh, with which it is inseparably united:

> Every soul is enumerated as being in Adam (*in Adam censetur*), until that moment when it is re-enumerated as being in Christ (*in Christo recenseatur*); and it is unclean (*immunda*) until it is so re-enumerated. But the soul is sinner (*peccatrix*), because it is unclean, taking disgrace from its alliance with the flesh (*recipiens ignominiam et carnis ex societate*)[67].

As bishop Irenei Steenberg rightly comments on this passage, "Tertullian has introduced a notion of inherited *sinfulness* into his anthropological framework. All are not merely 'in Adam', but thereby 'unclean' and therefore 'actively sinful'"[68]. Indeed, according to Tertullian, all the descendants of Adam and Eve are sinners[69], and only Jesus Christ, who was conceived and born by the Virgin Mary without intercession of masculine semen and free from carnal coitus[70], is absolutely sinless both in His Divine and in His human nature[71], consisting of soul and flesh:

---

[65] See: De anima 9, 8; 27, 3-8; 36, 1-4; De resurr. 45, 4-5, etc.
[66] De anima 27, 9: CCL 2, p. 824; cf. ibid. 19, 6: CCL 2, p. 811 (*hominis, cujus anima velut surculus quidam ex matrice Adam in propaginem deducta*); 41, 3: CCL 2, p. 844 (*unum omnes animae genus*).
[67] De anima 40, 1-2: CCL 2, p. 843; transl. by N. P. Williams, The Ideas of the Fall, 240; slightly modified. See also: De anima 41, 3: CCL 2, p. 844 (*nulla anima sine crimine*); De carn. Chr. 16, 2-4; De resurr. 16, 1-13; 46, 13-14, etc. As A. Rondet correctly points out, the above quotation from the *De anima* "a été souvent apporté comme preuve de la doctrine du péché originel en nous"; and although the Latin text allows two different interpretations concerning relationships between human soul and flesh, it nevertheless means that Tertullian "enseigne que l'âme infusée à toute chair vient d'Adam, portant la marque du premier péché", see: H. *Rondet*, Le péché originel, 72.
[68] M. C. *Steenberg*, Impatience and humanity's sinful state in Tertullian of Carthage, VigChr 62 (2008) 111.
[69] See: De pudic. 22, 3; De cult. fem. I, 1, 1-2, etc.
[70] See: De carn. Chr. 16, 5; 17, 3; 18, 1, 3; 19, 2-4; De resurr. 49, 3, etc.
[71] See: De anima 41, 3; De carn. Chr. 16, 3-4; Adv. Marc. V, 14, 1-3, etc.

> He who was going to consecrate a new order of birth, must Himself be born after a new fashion (*nove nasci*) [...]. This is the new nativity (*nativitas nova*); a man is born in God. And in this man God was born, taking the flesh of an ancient origin, without the help, however, of the ancient seed (*carne antiqui seminis suscepta sine semine antiquo*), in order that He might reform it with a new seed, that is, with a spiritual one, and cleanse it by the removal of all its ancient stains (*ut novo semine, id est spiritali, reformaret exclusis antiquitatis sordibus expiatam*)[72].

Moreover, it seems that many of Tertullian's texts imply that all the descendants of Adam by way of natural propagation inherit not only his corrupted *nature*, but also his *guilt* and the divine *punishment* for it. It clearly follows from a passage of *De testimonio animae* quoted above, that Adam "has made the whole his race, drawing contamination from his seed, a stock stained with his own condemnation"[73]. However, it is not quite clear how a person by his or her physical birth may inherit the *personal guilt* of his or her progenitor, which should rather be imputed to every person *individually* than transmitted to all humans *naturally*. One possible explanation might be that Tertullian endorses an Old Testament notion of the "guilt of the fathers" (*reatus patrum*), which is imputed by God to their children as well, so that, in his words, "through the whole race runs both grace and guilt" (*per totum genus et gratia decurreret et offensa*)[74]. Bishop Irenei proposes a possible solution of this, saying that "one can still speak of a guilt passed on from one generation to the next—not because children are held accountable for their parents crimes, but because in the distorted economy the children realise the fundamental crimes of their ancestors"[75]. However, following Tertullian's own logic, we should rather speak of a certain *collective judicial and moral responsibility* of all the descendants of Adam and Eve for the transgression of their ancestors, and of a *solidarity* with them not only in corrupted human nature, but also in the common guilt of offending God.

---

[72] De carn. Chr. 17, 2-3: CCL 2, p. 904; transl. by P. Holmes, in: A. Roberts, J. Donaldson, A. Cleveland Coxe (eds.), ANF 3 (Buffalo, NY 1885) 536; slightly modified. On the relation between Christ's sinlessness and His "seedless conception" see also: H. Rondet, Le péché originel, 73; P. F. Beatrice, Tradux peccati, 268; J. Leal, La antropología de Tertuliano, 126. It means at least that Tertullian has already anticipated Ambrosian-Augustinian views on human (sexual) procreation as a channel of transmission of the "original sin".
[73] See above, De test. anim. 3, 2. See also: A. D'Alès, La théologie de Tertullien, 265-266; A. Gaudel, Le péché originel, 364; J. Leal, La antropología de Tertuliano, 126, etc.
[74] Adv. Marc. II, 15, 2: CCL 1, p. 492.
[75] M. C. Steenberg, Impatience and humanity's sinful state, 114.

VI. The sacrament of baptism and the forgiveness of sins

Furthermore, additional difficulties for our understanding of the transmission of Adam's sin arise from Tertullian's views on the sacrament of baptism, and, more precisely, on the forgiveness of sins. On the one hand, Tertullian insists that in baptism God not only forgives us all our *personal* sins (*delicta*)[76], but also takes away the "veil of the ancient corruption" (*detracto corruptionis pristinae aulaeo*)[77]. Moreover, according to Tertullian, in baptism "death is destroyed by washing away of sins" (*deleta morte per ablutionem delictorum*), because here each individual's *guilt* (*reatus*)—probably inherited from Adam—is removed along with *the punishment* (*poena*) for it in the form of death[78]. On the other hand, Tertullian was convinced that only adult persons are in need of baptism, while infants are innocent, and therefore should wait until they grow up to be baptized:

> According to the circumstances and disposition, and even age, of each individual, the delay of baptism is preferable; principally, however, in the case of little children (*praecipue tamen circa parvulos*) [...] Let them come, then, while they are growing up; let them come while they are learning, while they are learning whither to come; let them become Christians when they have become able to know Christ. Why does the innocent period of life hasten to the remission of sins (*quid festinat innocens aetas ad remissionem peccatorum*)? More caution will be exercised in worldly matters: so that one who is not trusted with earthly things is trusted with divine! Let them know how to ask for salvation, so that you may seem to have given *to the one who asks* (cf. Luke 6, 30)[79].

This famous passage seems to be an obstacle for our understanding of the hereditary nature of Adam's sin, which we have found in Tertullian's other texts. Although here Tertullian obviously refers to the *personal sins* (*peccata*)[80] of children, which could be committed only *deliberately* and absolved in baptism, it is very strange that nothing is said here about Adam's sin and its consequences, including death and guilt in offending God. Moreover, in his trea-

---

[76] See: De bapt. 1, 1; 4, 5; 5, 6; 6, 1: CCL 1, p. 277, 280, 282. The term *delictum* in Tertullian usually means personal sin or trespass: both of Adam, and all the other humans.
[77] De anima 41, 4: CCL 2, p. 844. Cf. De carn. Chr. 17, 3: CCL 2, p. 904 (*exclusis antiquitatis sordibus*).
[78] De bapt. 5, 6: CCL 1, p. 282.
[79] De bapt. 18, 4-5: CCL 1, p. 293; transl. by P. Holmes, in: A. Roberts, J. Donaldson, A. Cleveland Coxe (eds.), ANF 3 (Buffalo, NY 1885) 678; slightly modified.
[80] This is a common opinion of the majority of scholars, see, for instance: A. D'Alès, La théologie de Tertullien, 266; A. Gaudel, Le péché originel, 364; J. Leal, La antropología de Tertuliano, 119-121, etc.

tise *De anima* Tertullian, on the one hand, considers all the children of pagan parents unclean by birth (*nulla nativitas munda, immundi*), and, on the other hand, he calls the children of Christian parents (or those born of mixed marriages) "saints" (*sanctos*), because they have the "privilege of [Christian] blood" (*ex seminis praerogativa*) and are sanctified by Christian education (*ex institutionis disciplina*)[81]. At the same time, in *De anima*, Tertullian, as we have shown, expressly states that every soul descended from Adam—most probably the souls of children born of Christian parents as well—is impure (*immunda*) and sinful (*peccatrix*) until it is reborn in Christ[82]. Perhaps Tertullian was simply unaware that some of his statements are mutually incompatible, so that his views on Adam's sin and its consequences, considered before, seem to be contradictory to his own views on the sacrament of baptism. Moreover, his opinions concerning the original goodness of human nature, and freedom of will after Adam's fall are also in contradiction with his own claims about the corruption of human nature and the "law of sin", that makes his doctrine even more obscure and ambiguous.

VII. The preservation of the original goodness of human nature and of the power of free will

Indeed, Tertullian believes that in spite of the corruption of human nature as a result of Adam's sin, all humans preserve the "natural goodness" (*bonum naturale*) which was "inserted" into human nature in its very beginning:

> Still there is a portion of good in the soul, of that original, divine, and genuine good (*bonum* [...] *illud principale, illud divinum atque germanum*), which is its proper nature (*proprie naturale*). For that which is derived from God is rather obscured than extinguished. It can be obscured, indeed, because it is not God; extinguished, however, it cannot be, because it comes from God. As therefore light, when intercepted by an opaque body, still remains, although it is not apparent, by reason of the interposition of so dense a body; so likewise the good in the soul, being weighed down by the evil (*bonum in anima a malo oppressum*), is, owing to the obscuring character thereof, either not seen at all, its light being wholly hidden, or else only a stray beam is there visible where it struggles through by an accidental outlet[83].

---

[81] De anima 39, 3-4: CCL 2, p. 842-843.
[82] De anima 40, 1-2: CCL 2, p. 843; the full quotation see above.
[83] De anima 41, 1-2: CCL 2, p. 844; transl. by P. Holmes, in: A. Roberts, J. Donaldson, A. Cleveland Coxe (eds.), ANF 3 (Buffalo, NY 1885) 220.

Further Tertullian points out that since the souls all form but one genus (*unum genus*), even in the worst there is something good (*aliquid boni*), and in the best there is something bad (*nonnihil pessimi*); and as there is no soul without crime (*nulla anima sine crimine*), so there is no soul without "the seed of good" (*nulla sine boni semine*)[84]. The "original goodness" (*bonum prius*) given to the soul by God, is not only preserved in it, but is often manifesting itself in the natural knowledge of God (*conscientia Dei*), available to all men, even to pagans; it becomes even more clear after receiving baptism, when, free from the "veil of ancient corruption", the soul beholds the divine light in all its brightness (*totam lucem suam*)[85].

In addition, Tertullian clearly asserts that after Adam's fall human free will remains untouched. For, according to him, even "now" (*hodie*) every man possesses the "same substance of soul" (*eamdem substantiam animae*) and the same "free status" as Adam (*eumdem Adae statum*), since he can fully exercise his free will and power of free choice (*eadem arbitrii libertas et potestas*), that could make him strong enough to resist the temptations of the devil, if he would freely obey the laws of God[86]. God's commandments and laws, forbidding bad things and prescribing good ones, have been given to all humans to observe, on the basis of their freedom of choice and decision of their own will[87]. Tertullian was convinced, that when a person commits a sin that offends God[88], he could "expiate" it (*satisfacere*) and return to God through his

---

[84] See: De anima 41, 3: CCL 2, p. 844.
[85] See: De anima 41, 3-4: CCL 2, p. 844; cf. De test. anim. 2-6; De resurr. 3-5; Apol. 17; Adv. Marc. I, 10.
[86] See: Adv. Marc. II, 8, 3; II, 10, 6; De pudic. 9, 16; De exhort. cast. 2, 3-7; Scorpiac. 6, 1; De paenit. 7, 7-10, etc
[87] See: Adv. Marc. II, 5, 7; De exhort. cast. 2, 3-6; De monog. 14, 6-7, etc.
[88] In Tertullian we can find quite a "Pelagian" understanding of how Adam's sin could be transmitted to the posterity, that is, if a person commits a sin, he or she follows the "bad example" of Adam, especially of his disobedience, stemming from his impatience. In fact, in his treatise De patientia, Tertullian regards impatience (*inpatientia*) exhibited by Adam and Eve as the "source" and "root" (*matrix*) of all other human sins: "Impatience conceived of the devil's seed, produced, in the fecundity of malice, anger as her son; and when brought forth, trained him in her own arts. For that very thing which had immersed Adam and Eve in death, taught their son, too, to begin with murder [...]. And how great were the new augmentations of impatience! And no wonder, if it has been the first delinquent (*prima deliquit*), it is a consequence that, because it has been the first, therefore it is also the only parent stem of every delinquency (*sola sit matrix in omne delictum*), pouring down from its own source various veins of crimes (*defundens de suo fonte varias criminum venas*)"—De patien. 5, 14-18: CCL 1, p. 304-305; transl. by P. Holmes, in: A. Roberts, J. Donaldson, A. Cleveland Coxe (eds.), ANF 3 (Buffalo, NY 1885) 710; slightly modified. I suppose, that in this kind of "bad example" of Adam consist the *moral consequences* of his sin, which I will not discuss in this paper.

repentance (*paenitentia*), which is a "price" (*pretium*) settled by God for forgiveness of sin and restoration of the innocence[89]. According to Tertullian, in this way God becomes our "debtor" (*debitor*), and is obliged to reward us for our good deeds, which we have done by the power of our free will, as well as to punish us for our evil deeds, done by the bad exercise of the same power[90]. Moreover, Adam himself, though he was the first who offended God, was restituted to Paradise through his repentance (*Adam exomologesi restitutus in paradisum suum*)[91]. Having accepted Adam's repentance, God, in Tertullian's own words, returned to "His original mercy" (*ad suam misericordiam*), thus showing in Himself a perfect example of repentance: He rescinded the "sentence of His first wrath" (*sententia irarum pristinarum*) and promised forgiveness (*ignoscere pactus*) to man as His own work and image[92]. This is, however, a strong testimony that Tertullian does not see any substantial difference between Adam (both before and after the fall), and the rest of mankind regarding the exercise of free will and power to choose and to fulfill the good, which "seed" in human nature is preserved untouched, that in Tertullian serves as a counter-balance to his ideas concerning the inheritance both of Adam's sin and guilt, and the "natural evil" and the "law of sin"[93]. Regarding all these difficulties, we may rightly say, that Tertullian's doctrine of Adam's sin and the "original vice" (*vitium originis*) is marked by an ambiguity and has a contradictory nature, since along with the recognition of fundamental corruption of human nature and the guilt in offending God imputed to all Adam's descendants, Tertullian preserves the original goodness of human nature and its free will, capable to choose both good and evil and making a person possible to acquire merits before God. Nevertheless, such an ambiguity in the question of Adam's fall and its consequences was not peculiar to Tertullian alone,

---

[89] See: De paenit. 6, 4-5; 7, 14; 8, 8-9; 9, 2; De cultu fem. I, 1, 1; De pudic. 9, 16, etc.

[90] See: De paenit. 2, 11. On importance of human merits in man's salvation according to Tertullian, see: K. H. *Wirth*, Der Begriff des meritum bei Tertullian (Leipzig 1892) passim; A. *D'Alès*, La théologie de Tertullien, 268-272; J. *Leal*, La antropología de Tertuliano, 133-144.

[91] De paenit. 12, 9: CCL 1, p. 340. By Adam's return to Paradise here Tertullian most likely means the state of innocence; but we cannot exclude the influence of the apocryphal literature, where we could find some texts, describing Adam and Eve's return to the "earthly paradise" (see: C. *Munier*, Commentaire, in: SC 316 (Paris 1984) 239-240). In addition, Tertullian sometimes understands by the "Paradise" the Church of God where Adam was placed immediately after his creation (*translatus in paradisum, iam tunc de mundo in Ecclesiam*, Adv. Marc. II, 4, 4: CCL 1, p. 479) and probably returned to it through his repentance. On Adam's repentance and his forgiveness by God, see also: Adv. Marc. II, 2; 10; 25: CCL 1, p. 477, 487, 503-504.

[92] De paenit. 2, 3: CCL 1, p. 322.

[93] Cf. R. E. *Roberts*, The Theology of Tertullian, 165; P. F. *Beatrice*, Tradux peccati, 270.

but was a common feature of many of his Christian contemporaries, such as Clement of Alexandria, Origen, Cyprian of Carthage, as well as of the most of later Greek Fathers of the Church.

Gregor Emmenegger, Freiburg (Schweiz)

Der verdorbene Samen.
Traduzianismus und dessen naturphilosophische Grundlagen bei Tertullian und Augustinus

Abstract:
Traducianism was widespread among physicians and Stoics in antiquity. It is the doctrine that the animating soul emanates from the father and is transmitted to the child through the seed. This idea played a special role for Tertullian, who used it to defend aspects of a Christian anthropology: the soul did not exist independently of the body before conception. Rather, God breathed the breath of life into Adam, and this animating soul is passed on to all subsequent human beings. Augustine was also sympathetic to this doctrine, although he did not want to commit himself to the question of ensoulment. For both authors, it was clear that a Traducianism based on a dualistic doctrine of procreation, with a male-active, fertilising principle and a female-receiving, nurturing principle, was the most appropriate to the biblical evidence. If one accepts these biological theories, it becomes understandable why the evil that began with the fall of Adam and Eve affects all human beings. Only Jesus Christ is exempt because of his virgin birth.

Wie eine Weinranke, so gehe bei der Zeugung die Seele eines Kindes aus der Seele des Vaters hervor. Die Lehre des Traduzianismus (von *tradux*, „Weinranke"), die Tertullian von Stoikern[1] und Medizinern[2] übernommen hat, baut er in seine christliche Weltsicht ein und folgert, dass jede menschliche Seele ein Schössling (*surculus*) aus der sündhaften Seele Adams sei.[3]

---

[1] Vgl. das bei Eusebius überlieferte Fragment, das die Seelenlehre des Zenon von Kition, des Begründers der Stoa zusammenfasst: Sperma sei „ein losgerissener Seelenteil und ein Gemenge von Samen der Vorfahren". Vgl. Anm. 19. Die Lehren sind allerdings nicht einheitlich: Manche Autoren gehen davon aus, dass im Embryo zunächst die pflanzliche Seele wirke und erst bei der Geburt die menschliche Seele gebildet werde.
[2] Vgl. *A. E. Hanson, M. H. Green*, Soranus of Ephesus: Methodicorum Princeps, in: ANRW II, 37, 2 (1994) 1006.
[3] Vgl. *Tertullian*, De Anima 19, 6: *J. H. Waszink*, CCL 2 (1947) 276.

Bei der Frage nach der Herkunft der augustinischen Lehre zum *Peccatum originale* kommt die Rede früher oder später auf Tertullian und dessen Traduzianismus.[4] Unbestritten ist, dass Augustinus diese Lehre kennt und sie in adaptierter Form in seinem Werk eine gewisse Rolle spielt.[5] Im folgenden Artikel stehen die naturphilosophischen Grundlagen im Fokus, die beim Traduzianismus stets mitschwingen.

I. Tertullian

Ein zentraler Unterschied zwischen Augustinus und Tertullian besteht im Fokus: Tertullian fragt nicht nach der Sünde, sondern nach der Seele. Der streitbare Apologet greift so das meist diskutierte Thema antiker Anthropologie überhaupt auf. Ist die Seele präexistent? Hat sie somit eine eigene Geschichte jenseits des Körpers – wie es Platon postuliert? Oder ist sie, so Aristoteles, mit dem Körper verschränkt? Von dieser Frage hängt viel ab: Welchen Status hat die Materie, woher kommt sie, wie sind die Menschen mit dem Göttlichen verbunden?

Tertullian ist ein entschiedener Christ. Er orientiert sich an der Heiligen Schrift und an kirchlichen Glaubenssätzen: Gott hat dem Menschen Leben eingehaucht; die menschliche Seele ist unsterblich. Doch darüber hinaus bleibt die damalige christliche Lehre vage. Das führt zu Unsicherheiten und heftigen Debatten: Was geschieht, wenn der Schöpfer dem Adam den Lebensatem (πνοὴν ζωῆς) ins Angesicht bläst und er eine lebende Seele wird (Gen 2, 7 LXX)? Was geht konkret vor sich, wenn das heilige Pneuma über Maria kommt, und die Kraft des Höchsten sie überschattet (Lk 1, 35)? Was ereignet sich nach dem Tod mit der Seele? Diese Fragen bieten zahlreiche Möglichkeiten, um mit Hermogenes, Markion, den Valentinianern und anderen zu streiten – und bei dieser Gelegenheit der eigenen christlichen Leserschaft alternative Thesen vorzustellen. Tertullians Werke über die Seele (*De Anima, De testimonio animae, De censu animae*) sind keine magistralen Abhandlungen, sondern polemische Klarstellungen, die sich gegen bestimmte Gegner richten.

---

[4] Vgl. *P. F. Beatrice*, The Transmission of Sin (Oxford 2013) 223–240 und *D. J. Billy*, Traducianism as a Theological Model in the Problem of Ensoulment, in: IThQ 55 (1989) 18.
[5] Augustinus verweist ablehnend auf Tertullians Lehre. Vgl. *M. Lamberigts*, Art. Peccatum originale, in: AL 4 (2018) 600.

1. Die Rolle der Medizin bei Tertullian

Um sich nicht in endlosen Diskussionen mit Häretikern zu verheddern, greift Tertullian gelegentlich auch zum verbalen Zweihänder und trennt den gordischen Knoten, indem er die Debatte auf eine Metaebene verlagert. Bekannt ist seine diesbezügliche Argumentation im Werk *De praescriptione haereticorum*, wo er auf eine juristische Beweisführung ausweicht und konstatiert: Die Häretiker haben zum vornherein und de jure gar kein Recht, mit den Christen über die Schrift zu diskutieren, weil die Bibel Eigentum und ausschliesslicher Erbbesitz der Kirche ist. Auch die Debatte über die Seele kürzt der Nordafrikaner gleichermassen ab. Er schreibt zu Beginn von *De Anima*:

> Ich weiss sehr gut, wie ausgedehnt der Wald dieser Materie bei den Philosophen ist, schon im Hinblick auf die blosse Zahl derjenigen, die sie erörtert haben: wie viele verschiedene Ansichten gibt es, wie zahlreich sind die Kampfplätze der Meinungen, wie gross die Zahl der aus den Problemen hervor gehenden Fragen, wie zahlreich die Verwicklungen bei den Lösungen! Auch mit der Medizin habe ich mich noch hierfür beschäftigt, der Schwester der Philosophie, wie man sagt, die gleichfalls für sich diese Aufgabe beansprucht – wie sollte sie auch nicht? –, da wegen ihrer Sorge für den Körper das Studium der Seele sie noch mehr zu betreffen scheint. Daher widersetzt sie sich auch öfters ihrer Schwester, weil sie die Seele dadurch, dass sie diese gleichsam im unmittelbaren Kontakt in ihrer eigenen Behausung behandelt, auch besser kennt.[6]

Tertullian weicht auf die Medizin aus. Das bietet ihm mehrere Vorteile: Die grossen Ärzte seiner Zeit stehen der Stoa nahe und sind von Aristoteles beeinflusst. Ihr Materialismus bietet dem Christen eine tragfähige Grundlage, um gegen die Spekulationen der Gnostiker vorzugehen. Deren Lehre einer präexistenten Seele führt dazu, dass der Leib und dessen Erschaffung abgewertet und die Verbindung von Leib und Seele als widernatürlich konnotiert werden. Geht man aber mit den Medizinern davon aus, dass die individuelle Seele erst bei der Fortpflanzung entsteht, so wird bei der Zeugung ein ganzer Mensch reproduziert. Gegen die Gnostiker lässt sich so zeigen, dass die Verbindung von Leib und Seele gut ist und dem Schöpferwillen entspricht.

---

[6] Tertullian, De Anima 19, 6: *J. H. Waszink*, CCL 2 (1947) 4: „Nec ignoro, quanta sit silua materiae istius apud philosophos pro numero etiam ipsorum commentatorum, quot uarietates sententiarum, quot palaestrae opinionum, quot propagines quaestionum, quot implicationes expeditionum. Sed et medicinam inspexi, sororem, ut aiunt, philosophiae, sibi quoque hoc negotium uindicantem. Quidni? ad quam magis animae ratio pertinere uideatur per corporis curam. Vnde et plurimum sorori refragatur, quod animam quasi coram in domicilio suo tractando magis norit."

So kommt es, dass ein Arzt die argumentative Basis von *De Anima* liefert: Es ist der Methodiker Soran von Ephesus[7], genauer dessen Werk über die Seele (Περὶ ψυχῆς). Auf ihn dürfte angespielt sein, wenn Tertullian zu Beginn des Werkes schreibt, dass er sich mit der Medizin beschäftigt habe. Zu Soran bemerkt er in *De Anima*:

> Deshalb beansprucht auch Soran selbst, der sehr ausführliche Erläuterungen über die Seele in vier Büchern gibt und sich mit allen Ansichten der Philosophen auseinandergesetzt hat, für die Seele eine körperliche Substanz, wenn er sie auch der Unsterblichkeit beraubte: nicht allen ist gegeben zu glauben, was den Christen gehört.[8]

In diesem kurzen Zitat kommen zwei Haltungen Tertullians Soran gegenüber zum Vorschein: Seine Bewunderung für diesen Arzt und dessen gelehrtes Werk, und sein Bedauern, dass dieser kein Christ sei und die Unsterblichkeit der Seele leugne. Sorans Bücher Περὶ ψυχῆς sind leider verloren. Dennoch konnten Karpp, Waszink und Polito in ihren Arbeiten nachweisen, dass der Mediziner Referenz und Gewährsmann war: Tertullian scheint der Argumentation des Arztes dessen Περὶ ψυχῆς in seinem eigenen Werk *De Anima* über weite Strecken zu folgen.[9]

2. Traduzianismus bei Tertullian

Tertullians Traduzianismus ist damit mehr eine medizinische denn eine philosophische Angelegenheit, und antike medizinische Literatur spielt eine wichtige Hilfe zum Verständnis. Doch hier liegt auch die Schwäche von Tertullians Lehre zur Weitergabe der Seele: Er hat die naturphilosophischen Lehren der Stoiker und des Arztes Soran rezipiert und nach christlichen Standpunkten ausgerichtet. Diese Neuausrichtung ist nicht in allem geglückt, wie wir sehen

---

[7] Soran von Ephesus war um 100 n. Chr. in Rom tätig. Er war der berühmteste Vertreter der methodischen Ärzteschule. Erhalten ist von ihm u.a. ein Standardlehrbuch der Gynäkologie, worin Ausführungen zur Embryologie, Geburtshilfe und Säuglingspflege enthalten sind. Vgl. A. E. Hanson, M. H. Green, Soranus of Ephesus: Methodicorum Princeps, in: ANRW II, 37, 2 (1994) 968–1075.
[8] *Tertullian*, De Anima 19, 6: *J. H. Waszink*, CCL 2 (1947) 8: „Ita etiam ipse Soranus plenissime super anima commentatus quattuor uoluminibus et cum omnibus philosophorum sententiis expertus corporalem animae substantiam uindicat, etsi illam immortalitate fraudauit."
[9] Vgl. *H. Karpp*, Sorans vier Bücher Περὶ ψυχῆς und Tertullians Schrift De Anima, in: ZNW 33 (1934) 31–47; *J. H. Waszink*, CCL 2 (1947) 26–28; *R. Polito*, I quattro libri sull'anima di Sorano e lo scritto "De Anima" di Tertullian, in: Rivista di Storia della Filosofia 49 (1994) 423-468.

werden. Sich ergebende Widersprüche führen dazu, dass Tertullian in seiner Bearbeitung nicht konsistent bleibt.

Soran ist nicht der einzige Ideengeber für Tertullian. Karpp[10] hat darauf hingewiesen, dass valentinianische Gnostiker schon vor Tertullian von einer „Seelenranke" sprachen – und Tertullian davon wusste. Denn er skizziert in seinem Buch gegen die Valentinianer deren Lehre, dass der Äon Sophia einen „tradux animae" in Adam versteckte.[11] Theologische Ansichten mit biologischen Argumenten zu stützen, ist keine Besonderheit von Tertullian und ebenso selbstverständlich wie der Rückgriff auf pagane philosophische Argumente. Dass Tertullian dabei eine ähnliche Terminologie wie die Valentinianer verwendet, darf nicht über die grundsätzliche Diskrepanz zwischen beiden hinwegtäuschen: ihre differierenden Seelenlehren.

Beginnen wir deshalb mit dem wichtigsten Element: Was ist überhaupt eine Seele? Tertullian definiert in *De Anima 22*:

> Definimus animam dei flatu natam, immortalem, corporalem, effigiatam, substantia simplicem, de suo sapientem, varie procedentem, liberam arbitrii, accidentiis obnoxiam, per ingenia mutabilem, rationalem, dominatricem, divinatricem, ex una redundantem.
>
> Wir bestimmen die Seele als aus Gottes Hauch geboren, unsterblich, körperlich, gestaltet, der Substanz nach einheitlich, durch eigene Kraft denkend, in verschiedenen Arten sich entwickelnd, dem Willen nach frei, äusseren Einflüssen ausgesetzt, in ihren Anlagen wandelbar, vernünftig, herrschend, zur Vorahnung befähigt und aus einer einzigen Seele hervorströmend.[12]

Die wichtigsten Punkte in dieser Definition sind:[13]

dei flatu natam: Der Häretiker Hermogenes hatte behauptet, dass die Seele des Menschen aus der Materie stamme und nicht aus Gott komme. Er sah sich zu dieser Position gezwungen, weil sonst eine aus Gott stammende, aber zur Sünde fähige Seele die absolute Gutheit des Schöpfers in Frage stellen würde. Genau dieses Argument führt Markion an, um zu beweisen,

---

[10] Vgl. *H. Karpp*, Probleme altchristlicher Anthropologie (Gütersloh 1950) 41–46.
[11] Vgl. *Tertullian*, Adversus Valentinianos 25: *J.-C. Fredouille, J.P. Mahé, V. Lukas*, FC 84 (2019) 96–99.
[12] *Tertullian*, De Anima 19, 6: *J. H. Waszink*, CCL 2 (1947) 31.
[13] Zur Terminologie vgl. *J.-C. Fredouille*, Observations sur la terminologie anthropologique de Tertullien: constantes et variations, in: *V. Boudon-Millot, B. Pouderon* (Ed.), Les Pères de l'Eglise face à la science médicale de leur temps (Paris 2005) 321–334; *H. Karpp*, Probleme altchristlicher Anthropologie (Gütersloh 1950) 41–46; *G. Esser*, Die Seelenlehre Tertullians (Paderborn 1893).

dass der Erschaffer der Menschen ein Demiurg gewesen sei – und nicht ein gänzlich guter Gott.[14] Tertullian seinerseits trennt zwischen der menschlichen Seele und dem göttlichen Pneuma. Die Seele entstammt zwar dem Hauch Gottes (*[af-]flatus*, πνοή), ist aber nicht identisch mit dem göttlichen Pneuma. So bleibt Gott absolut gut, doch sein Geschöpf ist zur Sünde fähig.

corporalem: Tertullian folgt der stoischen Lehre von einer körperlichen Seele. Sie hat Ausdehnung und Gewicht, und ist – zumindest für Gott – sichtbar. Die Bezeichnung *körperlich* charakterisiert nicht nur die Materie der Seele, sondern die Seele an und für sich.[15]

substantia simplicem: Die Seele hat keine verschiedenartigen Teile oder Partien und ist homogen. Tertullian unterscheidet nur zwischen der Substanz der Seele und ihren Bewegungen (*spiritus*, *mens* und πνεῦμα).

per ingenia mutabilem, rationalem: weist auf die Fähigkeiten der Seelensubstanz. Sie betreffen sowohl die sinnliche Wahrnehmung als auch die geistige Erkenntnis. Beide Tätigkeiten richten sich zwar auf unterschiedliche Objekte, sind aber ein und dieselbe Aktion.

dominatricem: Die Seele hat ein leitendes Prinzip und ist fähig, zu herrschen und zu bewegen. Sitz dieses ἡγεμονικόν, des Zentralorgans der Seele, ist das Herz.[16]

In Tertullians Definition der Seele sind stoische Ansichten und christliche Elemente (unsterblich, von Gottes Hauch) verwoben. Diese Verbindung ist gelegentlich unausgegoren, was ihm aber offenbar nicht auffiel. So argumentiert er, dass die Seele nur unsterblich sein könne, wenn sie unteilbar sei. Alles, was teilbar ist, zerfällt irgendwann. Der Mensch stirbt, wenn Leib und Seele getrennt werden. Der Körper zersetzt sich anschliessend, aber die Seele ist unteilbar und bleibt damit erhalten.

---

[14] Vgl. P. Kitzler, Ex uno homine tota haec animarum redundantia, in: VigChr 64 (2010) 357.
[15] Der Begriff Corpus ist bei Tertullian generell weit gefasst, so dass er schreiben kann: „Alles, was existiert, ist ein Körper von jeweils eigener Art, nichts ist unkörperlich." – „Omne quod est corpus est sui generis. Nihil est incorporale, nisi quod non est." *Tertullian*, De carne Christi 11, 4: *J.-C. Fredouille, J.P. Mahé, V. Lukas*, FC 84 (2019) 210–211.
[16] Vgl. *Tertullian*, De Anima 15: *J. H. Waszink*, CCL 2 (1947) 18–19.

> Weiter fordert die Unteilbarkeit der Seele, die aus ihrer Unsterblichkeit folgt, dass wir auch den Tod als unteilbar betrachten, nicht der Unsterblichkeit, sondern der Unteilbarkeit der Seele wegen, zu der im ungeteilten Zustand der Tod hinzutritt. Umgekehrt wird der Tod ebenfalls geteilt, wenn auch die Seele geteilt wird, weil ja der Rest der Seele doch zu irgendeinem Zeitpunkt sterben muss; so wird ein Teil des Todes mit dem Teil der Seele übrig bleiben.[17]

Es gibt nur den einen Tod, bei welchem Körper und Seele getrennt werden, eine weitere Teilung und damit einen weiteren Tod gibt es nicht. Diese Unteilbarkeit müsste aber auch zur Folge haben, dass ein Vater kein Seelenteil an sein Kind weitervererben könnte. Damit wäre jede Generationstheorie und folglich die Lehre vom Traduzianismus logisch unmöglich.

Kapitel 27 von *De Anima* dreht um die Frage des gleichzeitigen Entstehens von Körper und Seele. Tertullian bringt dabei zwei zentrale Ereignisse zusammen: Die Empfängnis des Menschen generell – und die Erschaffung Adams. In *De carne Christi* kommt noch ein dritter Aspekt hinzu: Die Empfängnis Christi im Schoss Marias. Grundsätzlich geht Tertullian davon aus, dass in allen drei Fällen dieselben Mechanismen wirken. Ich werde zunächst die Empfängnis des Menschen generell skizzieren, um dann auf die Erschaffung Adams sprechen zu kommen. Den dritten Aspekt behandle ich nur als Referenz für die beiden andern.

Die antiken Lehren zur Empfängnis des Menschen basieren auf Annahmen, die hier kurz erläutert werden sollen. Nach Meinung der massgeblichen Autoritäten – Aristoteles, Soran, Galen – unterscheiden sich Männer nicht grundsätzlich von Frauen. Alle Körperteile (inklusive Geschlechtsteile), welche Männer haben, haben Frauen auch – nur in energetisch weniger hochstehender Ausführung.[18] Männer wie Frauen haben Samen – bei den Männern das heisse Sperma, das aus Blut gekocht wird, bei den Frauen das kühlere Blut der Menstruation. Ein Kind entsteht, wenn das Sperma des Vaters im Blut der Mutter eine Gerinnung auslöst. Tertullian erläutert diese Theorie bezüglich der Empfängnis Christi gegen die Doketen:

---

[17] *Tertullian*, De Anima 51, 5: *J. H. Waszink*, CCL 2 (1947) 69: „Ceterum anima indiuisibilis, ut immortalis, etiam mortem indiuisibilem exigit credi, non quasi immortali, sed quasi indiuisibili animae indiuisibiliter accidentem. Diuidetur autem et mors, si et anima, superfluo scilicet animae quandoque morituro; ita portio mortis cum animae portione remanebit."

[18] Vgl. *Galen*, De usu partium corporis humani 14, 6: *G. Helmreich*, BiTeu (1968) 299. Vgl. *G. Emmenegger*, Wie die Jungfrau zum Kind kam (Freiburg 2014) 70–72.

Der verdorbene Samen 203

> „Wenn der Vers [Joh 1, 13] aber auch negierte, dass er aus dem Willen des Fleisches geboren wurde, weshalb negierte er damit nicht auch, dass er aus der Substanz des Fleisches geboren wurde?" Weil er, da er eine Geburt aus dem Blut negierte [i.e. das Sperma des Vaters], nicht auch die Substanz des Fleisches [Mariens] ablehnte, sondern die Materie des Samens, welche bekanntlich ein erhitzter Zustand des Blutes ist, welcher durch eine Art von Überschäumen zur Gerinnung des Blutes der Frau übergeht. Denn ebenso besteht das Lab im Käse aus derjenigen Substanz, welche es dadurch, dass es sie benetzt, gerinnen lässt, das heisst: aus Milch.[19]

Wie Lab die Milch, so lässt der männliche Samen das Fleisch des Kindes im Blut der Mutter klumpen. Was genau diese Gerinnung auslöst, darüber streiten sich die Gelehrten. Aristoteles und mit ihm Galen sind der Meinung, dass es nur auf die formende Hitze ankommt, wobei die Materie des männlichen Samens ein blosser Trägerstoff für diese immaterielle Hitze darstellt. Diese Hitze setzt Aristoteles mit dem ersten Seelenteil gleich, der Ernährungsseele.[20] Aristoteles schreibt:

> Und nur der Körper (des werdenden Embrios) stammt vom Weibchen, die Seele aber vom Männchen.[21]

Während die übrigen Seelenteile später hinzutreten, so kommt der erste Seelenteil doch stets vom Zeuger. Aristoteles folgert daraus, dass, wenn die Menschheit einen Anfang gehabt hat, der erste Mensch wie bei einfachen Lebewesen als Made oder Ei durch Urzeugung seinen Anfang genommen hat.[22] Von diesem ersten Menschen muss die Nährseele auf alle Menschen übergegangen sein. Lesky zeigte, dass Aristoteles bei der Vererbung eine Trennung von Merkmalen der Art und jenen des Individuums vornahm.[23] Während die Art nur vom Zeuger stammt, kommen individuelle Merkmale durch die Ein-

---

[19] *Tertullian*, De carne Christi 11, 4: *J.-C. Fredouille, J.P. Mahé, V. Lukas*, FC 84 (2019) 242–245: „‹Negans autem ex carnis quoque voluntate natum, cur non negavit etiam ex substantia carnis?› neque enim quia ex sanguine negavit substantiam carnis renuit, sed materiam seminis quam constat sanguinis esse calorem ut despumatione mutatum in coagulum sanguinis feminae: nam ex coagulo in caseo eius est substantiae quam medicando constringit, id est lactis."
[20] Vgl. *G. Emmenegger*, Wie die Jungfrau zum Kind kam (Freiburg 2014) 97.
[21] *Aristoteles*, De generatione animalium III (738b25): *H. J. Drossaart Lulofs*, OCT (1972) 165: „ἔστι δὲ τὸ μὲν σῶμα ἐκ τοῦ θήλεος ἡ δὲ ψυχὴ ἐκ τοῦ ἄρρενος".
[22] Vgl. *G. Emmenegger*, Wie die Jungfrau zum Kind kam (Freiburg 2014) 111.
[23] Vgl. *E. Lesky*, Die Zeugungs- und Vererbungslehre der Antike und ihr Nachwirken, in: AAWLM.G 19 (1950) 1233. 1372–1375 und 1413.

wirkung des weiblichen Samens zustande.[24] Sonst würden alle Kinder dem Vater vollständig gleichen und stets männlich sein.

Die Stoiker sehen nicht in der immateriellen Seelenhitze, sondern im warmen, materiellen Pneuma des Samens die Keimkraft. Der Grund für diesen Unterschied liegt im grösseren philosophischen Kontext, in welchem sie diesen Vorgang deuten: Das universelle Pneuma umfasst alle gestaltenden Kräfte, die es aus sich heraus entlässt. Diese λόγοι σπερματικοί verwirklichen die konkreten Zeugungen und werden deshalb auch Absenker des Weltpneumas genannt. Sie sind vernunftbegabt und walten gemäss des Logos der Natur. Von Zenon von Kition, dem Begründer der Stoa, überliefert Eusebius von Caesarea folgendes Fragment:

> Zenon sagt: Das Sperma, das der Mensch entlässt, sei Pneuma an Flüssiges gebunden, ein losgerissener Seelenteil und ein Gemenge von Samen der Vorfahren, eine Mischung, die von [allen] Seelenteilen zusammengekommen ist; denn dieses Sperma enthalte eben dieselben vernünftigen Kräfte [λόγους] wie das Ganze; wenn es in die Gebärmutter gelangt sei, werde es von einem anderen Pneuma, einem Teil der weiblichen Seele, aufgenommen, werde (mit diesem) eins und wachse im Verborgenen, wobei es bewegt und erregt werde von jenem [Pneuma] und immerfort die Feuchtigkeit an sich reisse und aus ihr sich vermehre.[25]

Manche Stoiker unterscheiden mit Soran im Sperma ein körperliches und ein seelisches Element. Das körperliche Element wird vom ganzen väterlichen Leib und seinen Säften gebildet. Das seelische Element im Samen ist eine heisse, luftige Substanz und entsteht durch „Abtröpfelung" der väterlichen Seele (*ex anima destillatione*). Tertullian folgt dieser Meinung in *De Anima*[26] und schreibt bezüglich der Schlaffheit des Mannes nach der Samenabgabe:

---

[24] Aristoteles, De generatione animalium III, 20 (768b15): *H. J. Drossaart Lulofs, OCT (1972)* 165.
[25] Vgl. Das Fragment des Areios Didymos bei *Eusebius von Cäsarea*, Praeparationes evangelicae 15, 20, 2: *E. Des Places, SC 338 (1987) 322*: „ τὸ δὲ σπέρμα φησὶν ὁ Ζήνων εἶναι ὃ μεθίησιν ἄνθρωπος πνεῦμα μεθ᾽ ὑγροῦ, ψυχῆς μέρος (καὶ) ἀπόσπασμα καὶ τοῦ σπέρματος τοῦ τῶν προγόνων κέρασμα καὶ μίγμα τῶν τῆς ψυχῆς μερῶν συνεληλυθός· ἔχον γὰρ τοὺς λόγους τῷ ὅλῳ τοὺς αὐτοὺς τοῦτο, ὅταν ἀφεθῇ εἰς τὴν μήτραν, συλληφθὲν ὑπ᾽ ἄλλου πνεύματος μέρος ψυχῆς τῆς τοῦ θήλεος καὶ συμφυὲς γενόμενον κρυφθὲν τε φύει κινούμενον καὶ ἀναρριπιζόμενον ὑπ᾽ ἐκείνου, προσλαμβάνον ἀεὶ εἰς τὸ ὑγρὸν καὶ αὐξόμενον ἐξ ἑαυτοῦ."
[26] In *De carne Christi* scheint er eher die klassische Lehre von Galen und Aristoteles zu belegen, wonach der väterliche Beitrag nur die Seele ist, welche die Gerinnung im mütterlichen Blut auslöst. Auf diese Weise wird Christus ganz Gott und ganz Mensch.

Der verdorbene Samen

Endlich – um eher die Schamhaftigkeit als den Beweis in Gefahr zu bringen –, eben in jener Glut der höchsten Lust, in der die Zeugungsflüssigkeit hinausgedrängt wird, fühlen wir da nicht, dass auch die Seele einen Verlust erleidet, ja werden wir da nicht erschlafft und unter Schädigung der Sehkraft geschwächt? Das dürfte der seelische Samen sein, der geradewegs aus einem Abtröpfeln der Seele kommt, wie auch jene Flüssigkeit, der Same des Körpers, aus einer Absonderung des Fleisches entsteht.[27]

Auf die logische Inkonsequenz, dass eine unteilbare Seele nicht *destillieren* – „abtröpfeln" kann, habe ich schon hingewiesen. Tertullian rechnet – vielleicht deshalb – beim ganzen Vorgang mit göttlicher Hilfe:

Den ganzen Vorgang aber, der darin besteht, den Menschen in die Gebärmutter zu säen, dort aufzubauen und auszubilden, reguliert jedenfalls irgendeine dem göttlichen Willen dienstbare Macht, was auch immer jene Regel sein mag, nach der sie zu handeln bestimmt ist.[28]

Beide Samenteile im väterlichen Sperma sind wegen der unterschiedlichen Ausgangsstoffe (Körper und Seele) wesensverschieden, aber ebenso wie die Ausgangsstoffe aneinandergebunden und gleichzeitig tätig. Die Zeugung lässt ein Fötus entstehen, dem nichts fehlt, was den Menschen ausmacht. Der Vater ist das *principium seminale* des Erzeugten, das Kind ein Absenker aus seiner Substanz.

Für die Stoiker stellt das Samenpneuma eine Mischung (*confusio*; σύγχυσις) dar, wobei wie bei der Legierung Elektron aus Gold und Silber ein neuer, unteilbarer, einheitlicher Stoff entsteht: Dieses Samenpneuma setzt sich aus vielfältigen Pneumaströmen zusammen, die vom Herzen als Sitz der Seele zu den einzelnen Organen fliessen und dort die entsprechenden Funktionen ausführen. Darum ist das Samenpneuma ebenfalls eine *confusio* mit Anteilen aus verschiedenen Seelenströmen.

---

[27] *Tertullian*, De Anima 27, 6: *J. H. Waszink*, CCL 2 (1947) 39: „Denique ut adhuc uerecundia magis pericliter quam probatione, in illo ipso uoluptatis ultimae aestu quo genitale uinis expellitur, nonne aliquid de anima quoque sentimus exire atque adeo marcescimus et deuigescimus cum lucis detrimento? Hoc erit semen animale, protinus ex animae destillatione, sicut et uirus illud corporale semen ex carnis defaecatione."

[28] *Tertullian*, De Anima 37, 1: *J. H. Waszink*, CCL 2 (1947) 53: „Omnem autem hominis in utero serendi struendi fingendi paraturam aliqua utique potestas diuinae uoluntatis ministra modulatur, quamcumque illam rationem agitare sortita."

In der stoischen Erblehre übermittelt das Samenpneuma dem werdenden Embryo die Merkmale der Eltern und der Vorfahren. Man geht davon aus, dass nur das männliche Samenpneuma keimfähig ist. Das weibliche Samenpneuma tritt in der Gebärmutter hinzu, mischt sich mit dem männlichen und beide sorgen so, je nach Stärke, für Ähnlichkeiten mit den Vorfahren beider Seiten. Die Verbindung der beiden πνεύματα formt den Körper des Kindes aus dem feuchten Samenteil des Vaters. Im Augenblick der Geburt wandelt sich das Pneumagemisch infolge des Kontakts mit der kalten Luft in eine kühle Seele (ψυχή), wovon Letztere ihren Namen habe (ψυχρός = kalt).

Hier greift Tertullian ein: Er reduziert den weiblichen Zeugungsanteil auf eine nährende Funktion – die auch von einem Ackerboden übernommen werden kann. Die Seele kann zudem nicht erst durch Abkühlung bei der Geburt entstehen. Der Fötus muss ab Zeugung ein beseeltes Wesen, ein *animal* sein, ab der Ausbildung der körperlichen Gestalt auch Mensch – *homo*.[29] Da die Erschaffung Adams für ihn paradigmatische Bedeutung hat, müssen die medizinischen Vorgänge bei einem werdenden Kind analog zum Schöpfungsbericht gedeutet werden.

> Am zuverlässigsten sind die Vorbilder des Uranfangs: aus dem Lehm entstand das Fleisch, das zu Adam wurde. Was ist Lehm anderes als fettige Feuchtigkeit? Von da wird die Zeugungsflüssigkeit stammen. Aus Gottes Hauch entstand die Seele. Was ist Gottes Hauch anderes als ein Wehen des Lebensodems? Von da wird das kommen, was wir mit jener Feuchtigkeit aushauchen. Als also im Anfang zwei verschiedene und getrennte Stoffe, Lehm und Odem, sich zu einem Menschen zusammengefunden hatten, da haben die beiden vermengten Substanzen auch ihre Samen vermischt und damit das Fortpflanzungsprinzip dem Menschengeschlecht überliefert, so dass auch jetzt noch beide, wenn auch verschieden, dennoch vereint, zugleich abfliessen. Wenn sie gleichermassen in die für sie bestimmte Furche und ihren Acker eingedrungen sind, lassen sie gleichzeitig den Menschen aus den beiden Substanzen keimen. In diesem wiederum befindet sich nach seiner Gattung sein eigener Same, so wie es für jeden Zeugungsakt im voraus festgesetzt worden ist.[30]

---

[29] Vgl. *Tertullian*, De Anima 37, 2: *J. H. Waszink*, CCL 2 (1947) 53.
[30] *Tertullian*, De Anima 27, 7–9: *J. H. Waszink*, CCL 2 (1947) 39: „Fidelissima primordii exempla. De limo caro in Adam. Quid aliud limus quam liquor opimus? Inde erit genitale uirus. Ex afflatu dei anima. Quid aliud afflatus dei quam uapor spiritus? Inde erit quod per uirus illud efflamus. Cum igitur in primordio duo diuersa atque diuisa, limus et flatus, unum hominem coegissent, confusae substantiae ambae iam in uno quoque sua miscuerunt atque exinde generi propagando formam tradiderunt, ut et nunc duo, licet diuersa, etiam unita pariter effluant pariterque insinuata sulco et aruo suo pariter hominem ex utraque substantia effruticent, in quo rursus semen suum insit secundum genus, sicut omni condicioni genitali praestitutum est."

Der verdorbene Samen

Die Seelensubstanz wird vom Vater auf das Kind verdoppelt. Bekannt ist sein Vergleich mit dem Ableger (*surculus*) einer Weinranke (*tradux*), wenn er vom „*tradux animae*" und „*surculus quidam ex matrice Adam*" redet.[31] Wie die unteilbare und nicht vermehrbare väterliche Seele sich absenken kann, damit das Kind schliesslich eine gleiche Menge an Seelensubstanz hat wie der Erzeuger, das präzisiert Tertullian mit dem Ausdruck „*quod per virus illud efflamus*" – „*was wir mit jener Feuchtigkeit aushauchen*". So wie Gott sein Ebenbild mit seinem Lebensatem anhauchte und belebte – ohne dass er von seiner Substanz verlor, so haucht der werdende Vater im Zeugungsakt seinem Kind Seele ein. Augustinus wird später das Bild des Lichts verwenden: „*tamquam lucerna de lucerna accendatur*".[32] Wie die Kerzenflamme weitergegeben wird, so verteilt sich die Seele. Jede Flamme entsteht neu, doch nur mit Hilfe einer Vorangehenden. Ob Tertullian mit diesem Bild einverstanden wäre, wissen wir nicht. Die spärlichen Ausführungen zeigen, dass der später so scharf formulierte Antagonismus von Kreatianismus und Traduzianismus für Tertullian noch keine Problematik war, die er hätte klären müssen. Denn auch Aristoteles, Galen und die Stoiker bewegen sich zwischen diesen beiden Extremen.

Hat man erst eine solche immer gleich bleibende Seelensubstanz postuliert, ist der Weg zu einer Generationsthese nicht mehr weit. Schon Aristoteles hatte die These aufgestellt, dass, wenn die Menschheit einen Anfang hat, ein erster Mensch nur dadurch entstanden sein kann, dass göttliches Pneuma über fetten Schlamm gestrichen sei, der die erste Nahrung für den Fötus enthielt. In der Terminologie des Aristoteles wird diese Verbindung von nahrungsreichem Schlamm und erstem Pneuma „Made" genannt, die sich anschliessend zum Menschen weiterentwickelt und schliesslich fortpflanzt:

Daher könnte man auch bei der Entwicklung der Menschen und Vierfüssler annehmen, falls sie wirklich einmal der Erde entsprosst sind, wie manche behaupten, dass dies auf eine von zwei Weisen geschehen sein müsse: Entweder muss sich der erste Keim aus einer Made [σκώληξ] oder aus einem Ei entfaltet haben. Denn entweder mussten sie die Nahrung für das erste Wachstum schon in sich tragen (ein solcher Keimling ist aber eine Made), oder sie mussten sie anderswoher beziehen, und dies wieder entweder aus der Mutter oder einem Teil des Keimes; und da die eine dieser letzten Möglichkeiten ausscheidet, weil aus der Erde die Nahrung nicht so zuströmen kann, wie aus der Mutter, so muss die Nahrung einen Teil des Keimes liefern. Eine solche Entstehungsweise nennen wir die aus einem Ei. Man sieht also, dass, wenn alle Geschöpfe einen Ursprung ihrer Entwicklung gehabt haben müssen, ganz natürlich nur eine dieser beiden in Frage kommt. Die geringere Wahrscheinlichkeit

---

[31] Vgl. *Tertullian*, De Anima 19, 6 und 36, 4: *J. H. Waszink*, CCL 2 (1947) 31 und 52.
[32] Vgl. *Augustinus*, Epistula 190 ad Optatum 190, 4: *A. Goldbacher*, CSEL 57 (1911) 149.

spricht für die Entstehung aus Eiern, da wir eine solche Entwicklung bei keinem Tier beobachten, sondern immer die andere, bei den aufgeführten Bluttieren und bei den Blutlosen.[33]

Tertullians Traduzianismus ist eine christlich-stoische Adaption:

> Mithin stammt aus einem einzigen Menschen diese ganze Unzahl von Seelen, indem die Natur den Ausspruch Gottes befolgt: „Wachset und mehret euch."[34]

Die Seelensubstanz ist ab Zeugung vollständig im Fötus da. Sie wächst nicht, sie ist unteilbar und sie wird nicht kleiner – aber sie kann wie ein Klumpen Gold bearbeitet werden: Das Schmuckstück entfaltet sich, und das Ergebnis ist grösser und schöner als der ursprüngliche Klumpen. Im Grunde bleibt aber dieselbe Substanz in derselben Menge bestehen.[35] Diese Ausfaltung der Seele ist im vierzehnten Lebensjahr abgeschlossen, denn dann erlangt die Seele ebenso wie der Körper die Reife. Es ist anzunehmen, dass bei dieser Bearbeitung väterliche und mütterliche Pneumata eine Rolle spielen – Pneuma hier im Sinne Tertullians als Wirken der jeweiligen Seele an der Seelensubstanz des Kindes. Obwohl Tertullian im Kontext einer allgemeinen Embryologie darüber nichts sagt, so sind es die Tätigkeiten von Adam und Eva, welche die Seelensubstanz verdorben und korrumpiert haben. Soran weist darauf hin, dass besonders im Zeitraum von der Zeugung bis zur Geburt die zarten Seelen werdender Föten nachhaltig verändert werden – und rät Frauen von hässlichen Ehemännern, edle Stauten zu betrachten, damit trotz der väterlichen Vorbelastung schöne Kinder entstehen.[36] Für eine antike Leserschaft mit me-

---

[33] Aristoteles, De generatione animalium III, 11 (762b28–763a7): H. J. Drossaart Lulofs, OCT (1972) 161: „διὸ καὶ περὶ τῆς τῶν ἀνθρώπων καὶ τετραπόδων γενέσεως ὑπολάβοι τις ἄν, εἴπερ ἐγίγνοντό ποτε γηγενεῖς ὥσπερ φασί τινες, δύο τρόπων τούτων γίγνεσθαι τὸν ἕτερον· ἢ γὰρ ὡς σκώληκος συνισταμένου τὸ πρῶτον ἢ ἐξ ᾠῶν. – ἀναγκαῖον γὰρ ἢ ἐν αὑτοῖς ἔχειν τὴν τροφὴν εἰς τὴν αὔξησιν (τὸ δὲ τοιοῦτον κύημα σκώληξ ἐστίν) ἢ λαμβάνειν ἄλλοθεν, τοῦτο δ' ἢ ἐκ τῆς γεννώσης ἢ ἐκ μορίου τοῦ κυήματος· ὥστ' εἰ θάτερον ἀδύνατον, ἢ ἐκ τῆς γῆς ὥσπερ ἐν τοῖς ἄλλοις ζῴοις ἐκ τῆς μητρός, ἀναγκαῖον ἐκ μορίου λαμβάνειν τοῦ κυήματος· τὴν δὲ τοιαύτην ἐξ οὗ λέγομεν εἶναι γένεσιν. – ὅτι μὲν οὖν, εἴπερ ἦν τις ἀρχὴ τῆς γενέσεως πᾶσι τοῖς ζῴοις, εὔλογον τοῖν δυοῖν τούτοιν εἶναι τὴν ἑτέραν φανερόν· ἧττον δ' ἔχει λόγον ἐκ τῶν ᾠῶν· οὐδενὸς γὰρ τοιαύτην ὁρῶμεν ζῴου γένεσιν ἀλλὰ τὴν ἑτέραν, καὶ τῶν ἐναίμων τῶν ῥηθέντων καὶ τῶν ἀναίμων."

[34] Tertullian, De Anima 27, 9: J. H. Waszink, CCL 2 (1947) 39: „Igitur ex uno homine tota haec animarum redundantia, obseruante scilicet natura dei edictum: crescite et in multitudinem proficite."

[35] Vgl. Tertullian, De Anima 37, 7: J. H. Waszink, CCL 2 (1947) 54.

[36] Vgl. Soran, Gynaeikeia 1, 12: P. Burguière, D. Gourevitch, Y. Malinas, CUFr (1990) 35. Tertullian selbst macht verschiedene ähnliche Beispiele, etwa die lügenden Kreter oder die Hautfarbe der Äthiopier. Augustinus übernimmt diese Argumentation und verweist auf Soran, Vgl. Augustinus, Contra Iulianum V, 51: PL 44, 794.

dizinischer Bildung ist die dauerhafte Korrumpierung einer Seele durch einen einschneidenden Sinneseindruck durchaus glaubwürdig. Auf die Frage nach dem Verhältnis zwischen der Schuld Adams und der Verderbtheit der Nachkommen muss Tertullian folglich nicht weiter eingehen. Gegen die Gnostiker besteht er darauf, dass Gott nicht Urheber, und der Leib nicht Träger der Befleckung sein kann. Letztere kann nur einem Ding zukommen, das Verstand und freien Willen hat. Zur Weitergabe des Übels drängt sich die im Samen weitergegebene Seele auf, da sie alle Menschen mit Adam verbindet.

> [Es ist der Satan …], durch den der Mensch beim Uranfang umgarnt wurde, so dass er das Gebot Gottes übertrat und deswegen dem Tod übergeben wurde, infolgedessen er seine ganze Nachkommenschaft durch seinen Samen befleckte und diese zur Übermittlerin seiner eigenen Verdammnis machte.[37]

Die Sünde Adams pflanzt sich als „Verdunkelung" und „Verderbtheit" auf der Seele fort – denn was von Gott kommt, kann nicht ausgelöscht, sondern nur durch freien Willen pervertiert werden. So wie bei Pflanzen es immer dieselben Samen sind, die aber unterschiedliche Charakteristiken weitergeben, so wird die Seele geprägt: Es sind alle Samen betroffen, aber dies wirkt sich unterschiedlich aus[38] – genau wie die Kreter alle Lügner sind, mehr oder weniger, und die Äthiopier schwarze Hautfarbe haben.[39]

> Deutlich wird, wie zahlreich die Einflüsse sind, welche die einheitliche Natur der Seele in so verschiedene Fassungen versetzt haben, so dass sie meistens zu dieser Natur gerechnet werden. Dabei sind sie doch keine Arten, sondern durch Zufälligkeiten entstandene Eigenschaften einer einzigen Natur und Substanz, und zwar derjenigen, die Gott dem Adam verlieh, und die er zur Stammmutter aller Seelen machte.[40]

---

[37] *Tertullian*, De testimonio animae, 3, 2: *R. Willems*, CCL 1 (1954) 180: „Satanam denique in omni uexatione et aspernatione et detestatione pronuntias, quem nos dicimus malitiae angelum, totius erroris artificem, totius saeculi interpolatorem, per quem homo a primordio circumuentus, ut praeceptum dei excederet, et propterea in mortem datus exinde totum genus de suo semine infectum suae etiam damnationis traducem fecit."

[38] *Tertullian*, De Anima 41, 3: *J. H. Waszink*, CCL 2 (1947) 57: „Sic pessimi et optimi quidam, et nihilominus unum omnes animae genus; sic et in pessimis aliquid boni et in optimis nonnihil pessimi." – „Deshalb sind einige Menschen sehr schlecht und einige sehr gut und nichtsdestoweniger alle Seelen einer Art; deshalb ist auch in den schlechtesten etwas Gutes und in den besten etwas Schlechtes".

[39] Vgl. *Tertullian*, De Anima 20: *J. H. Waszink*, CCL 2 (1947) 28–29.

[40] *Tertullian*, De Anima 20, 6: *J. H. Waszink*, CCL 2 (1947) 29: „Apparet quanta sint quae unam animae naturam uarie collocarint, ut uulgo naturae deputentur, quando non species sint, sed sortes naturae et substantiae unius, illius scilicet quam deus in Adam contulit et matricem omnium fecit; [atque adeo sortes erunt, non species substantiae unius, id est uarietas ista moralis, quanta nunc est, tanta non fuerit in ipso principe generis Adam.]"

Gott hat am Anfang mit seinem Hauch die menschliche Seele entstehen lassen. Nun haucht der Teufel den „von Ungeduld infizierten Geist" der Seele ein und korrumpiert sie so.[41] Erst die zweite Geburt in der Taufe lässt diesen ererbten „Vorhang der früheren Verderbnis fallen", denn ein neuer Geist heilt die alte Prägung.

Es wird also jede Seele so lange in Adam geboren, bis sie in Christus neugeboren wird; sie ist so lang unrein, bis sie neugeboren wird. Sündhaft aber ist die Seele, weil sie unrein ist und auch die Schande des Fleisches infolge ihrer Verbindung mit demselben auf sich lädt.[42]

Obwohl Tertullians Lehre eine Reihe von Fragen offenlässt, wurde sie breit rezipiert: Hieronymus zufolge bekannte sich zu seiner Zeit der grösste Teil der Okzidentalen zum Traduzianismus.[43] Die Gründe dafür hängen auch mit der Medizin zusammen: Tertullian präsentiert diese Lehre als glaubwürdig, denn sie kollidiert nicht mit allgemein bekannten medizinischen Erkenntnissen.

II. Augustinus

1. Die Frage nach der Herkunft der Seele

Der Traduzianismus beschäftigt Augustinus durch die ganze Zeit seines Wirkens. Dabei lassen sich drei Phasen unterscheiden:[44] Die erste Zeit tastender Versuche (bis 395), jene von 395 bis zum Beginn des pelagianischen Streits (412) und die folgenden Jahre bis zu seinem Tod 430. Über die erste Zeit bis 395 lässt sich nichts Genaues sagen. Augustinus scheint, geprägt von seinen

---

[41] Eben diese Ungeduld ist die Wurzel jeder Sünde, denn das Böse ist nur die Ungeduld im Verhältnis zum Guten. Vgl. *Tertullian*, De patientia 5, 9 und 5, 21: J.-C. Fredouille, SC 310 (2011) 74: „Conuenta statim illi (sc. Diaboli) mulier, non temere dixerim, per conloquium ipsum eius adflata est spiritu inpatientia infecto : usque adeo numquam omnino peccasset, si diuino interdicto patientiam praeseruasset!" Vgl. *M. C. Steenberg*, Impatience and Humanity's Sinful State in Tertullian of Carthage, in: VigChr 62 (2008) 107-132.
[42] *Tertullian*, De Anima 40, 1: J. H. Waszink, CCL 2 (1947) 56: „Ita omnis Anima eo usque in Adam censetur, donec in Christo recenseatur, tamdiu immunda, quamdiu recenseatur, peccatrix autem, quia immunda, recipiens ignominiam et carnis ex societate."
[43] Vgl. *Hieronymus*, Epistula 126 (= Epistula 165 von Augustinus) an Marcellinus und Anapsychia: I. Hilberg, CSEL 56 (1918) 143: „[…] an certe ex traduce, ut Tertullianus, Apollinaris et maxima pars occidentalium autumat, ut, quomodo corpus ex corpore, sic anima nascatur ex anima […]" – „[…] oder, wie Tertullian, Apollinaris und der grösste Teil des Okzidents sagen, dass, in der Weise wie Leib aus Leib, so auch die Seele aus der Seele geboren wird […]".
[44] J. Gross macht diese drei Phasen in der Frage nach der Weitergabe der Erbschuld aus. Ich adaptiere sie hier analog zur Frage nach dem Traduzianismus. Vgl. *J. Gross*, Entstehungsgeschichte des Erbsündendogmas von der Bibel bis Augustinus (München 1960).

Der verdorbene Samen 211

manichäischen Jahren und der Lektüre von Neuplatonikern wie Plotin der platonischen Auffassung eines Seelenepos zuzuneigen: Die Geistseelen sind präexistent, haben sich aber von Gott entfernt und sind in die materielle Welt gefallen. Hieraus erklärt sich ihre Sündhaftigkeit. Die Körper dagegen entstehen durch eine zweite, schlechte Leibseele, die sich durch Ableger weiter verbreitet.[45] Der Umstand, dass die Geistseelen in der Materie des Körpers gefangen sind, belegt ihre schuldhafte Abkehr von Gott.

Mit *De librio arbitrio* aus dem Jahr 395[46] überdenkt Augustinus seine Position bezüglich der Frage nach der Beseelung und der Ursache der Korrumpierung des menschlichen Willens. Er stellt die vier grundsätzlichen Möglichkeiten vor. Die erste These lautet:

> Dann, wenn eine einzige Seele geschaffen wurde, aus der alle Menschen geboren werden, wer kann sagen, dass er nicht gesündigt hat, wenn der erste Mensch gesündigt hat?[47]

Der Traduzianismus erklärt also die Sündhaftigkeit aller Menschen einsichtig. Die drei übrigen Hypothesen erfordern deutlich mehr Erklärung, weil die Transmission der Korruption nicht auf der Hand liegt. Es ist dies die Vorstellung, dass jedes Neugeborene eine eigens geschaffene individuelle Seele bekommt – was später Kreatianismus genannt werden wird. Eine weitere These ist die Annahme eines Seelentresors bei Gott, woraus Seelen zugeteilt werden, und schliesslich das Seelenepos mit der Postulierung, dass präexistente gefallene Seelen jeweils einen Körper annehmen. Augustinus bewertet die vier Positionen so:

> Von diesen vier Meinungen über die Seele sollte man jedoch keine leichtfertig behaupten. Denn entweder wurde diese Frage noch nicht von den katholischen Kommentatoren der göttlichen Bücher aufgrund ihrer Dunkelheit und Verwirrung an-

---

[45] Die Manichäer scheinen diesbezüglich die valentinianische Lehre zu teilen, die Tertullian beschreibt. Augustinus bekämpft später die These einer guten Geistseele und einer bösen Fleischseele in *De duabus Animabus*, die er den Manichäern vorwirft. Vgl. *C. G. Scribona*, The doctrine of the soul in Manichaeism and Augustine, in: NHMS 74 (2010) 377–418.
[46] Das erste Buch dieses Werkes stammt aus dem Jahr 387/388. Die weiteren Bücher, woraus im Folgenden zitiert wird, sind aus den Jahren 391–395. Vgl. *V. H. Drecoll*, Zur Chronologie der Werke, in Augustin Handbuch, UTB 4187 (2014) 254.
[47] *Augustinus*, De librio arbitrio 3, 20, 56: *W. M. Green*, CCL 29 (1970) 307: „Deinde si una anima facta est ex qua omnium hominum trahuntur nascentium, quis potest dicere non se peccasse cum primus ille peccauit?". Vgl. *M. Lamberigts*, Julian and Augustinus on the origin of the soul, in: Augustiniana 46 (1996) 250.

gemessen behandelt und geklärt, oder wenn dies bereits geschehen ist, sind solche
Schriften noch nicht in unsere Hände gelangt.[48]

Fest steht für ihn: Der freie Wille unterwirft die Menschen der Konkupiszenz.
Letztere kann nicht von Gott stammen, weil Gott nichts Mangelhaftes schafft.
Folglich spielt die Adamssünde eine zentrale Rolle. Sie erklärt, warum wir in
Unwissenheit, Ohnmacht und Sterblichkeit geboren werden. Um das Jahr 420
wird Augustinus sein Urteil zur Überlegenheit des Traduzianismus bekräftigen:

> Die Verteidiger der Meinung, die Seelen würden bei der Geburt neu eingehaucht,
> und nicht von den Eltern hergeleitet, sollen sich deshalb auf alle Art vor jedem der
> vier Punkte, die ich oben erwähnt habe, in acht nehmen. Das heisst:
> Sie sollen nicht sagen, dass die Seelen von Gott her durch die fremde Ursprungssünde sündig werden.
> Sie sollen nicht sagen, dass die Kinder, die ohne Taufe gestorben sind, zum ewigen Leben und zum Himmelreich gelangen können, nachdem die Ursprungssünde
> durch irgendetwas anderes nachgelassen wurde.
> Sie sollen nicht sagen, die Seelen hätten irgendwo vor ihrer Fleischwerdung gesündigt und seien durch dieses Missverdienst in das sündige Fleisch verwiesen worden.
> Sie sollen nicht sagen, dass Sünden, die sich in ihnen nicht vorfanden, mit Recht
> bestraft worden seien, weil sie vorausgewusst waren, [und dies,] obwohl sie nicht
> die Erlaubnis erhielten, in dieses Leben zu gelangen, wo sie diese [Sünden] hätten
> begehen können.[49]

Der Traduzianismus vermeidet einige theologische Irrtümer, welche den übrigen Thesen zur Herkunft der Seele anhaften. Dennoch wagt Augustinus nicht,
ein eindeutiges Urteil darüber zu fällen. Denn auch der Traduzianismus weist
Aporien auf, aufgrund derer namhafte Theologen ihn deswegen ablehnen. Hilarius von Poitiers etwa schreibt, dass Gott jedem werdenden Menschen eine
Seele zuteile, auch Christus, weil sonst (also beim Traduzianismus) Christus
von seiner Mutter Fleisch und eine korrumpierte Seele erhalten hätte.[50]

---

[48] *Augustinus*, De libero arbitrio 3, 21, 59: *W. M. Green*, CCL 29 (1970) 309: „Harum autem quatuor de anima sententiarum […] nullam temere adfirmare oportebit. Aut enim nondum ista quaestio a diuinorum librorum catholicis tractatoribus pro merito suae obscuritatis et perplexitatis euoluta atque in lustrata est, aut si iam factum est nondum in manus nostras huiuscemodi litterae peruenerunt."
[49] *Augustinus*, De anima et eius origine = De natura et origine animae 1, 19, 34: *C. F. Vrba; J. Zycha*, CSEL 60 (1913) 333,27–334,8.
[50] *Hilarius*, De trinitate 10, 20 und 10, 22: *P. Smulders*, CCL 62A (1980) 474.

Der verdorbene Samen

Beide Zitate zeigen, wie eng bei Augustinus die Frage nach der Beseelung mit der Frage nach der Sündhaftigkeit des Menschen verbunden ist. Wie bei Tertullian lassen sich drei Ebenen unterscheiden: erstens die Frage nach der Beseelung von Adam; zweitens die Frage nach der Weitergabe der Seele an die folgenden Menschen; und drittens die Frage nach der Seele Christi. Dabei steht für Augustinus fest, dass Gott dem ersten Menschen eine perfekte Seele eingehaucht hat, dass zweitens die Kinder von Adam und Eva die erste Sünde bzw. die Sündenfolge erben, und dass drittens Jesus davon ausgenommen ist. Diese enge Verknüpfung der beiden Fragen ist auch der Grund, warum das Problem mit dem pelagianischen Streit ab 412 deutlich akzentuiert wird. In den folgenden Ausführungen steht nicht die Erbsündenlehre des Augustinus im Fokus, sondern Augustinus' Auffassungen von der Beseelung, der Weitergabe des Lebens und die dabei mitschwingenden biologischen Lehren.

2. Traduzianismus als Konsequenz naturphilosophischer Grundannahmen

Im Unterschied zu Tertullian schreibt Augustinus für ein Publikum, das keine Bestätigung der Glaubwürdigkeit des Christentums mehr erwartet – schon gar nicht durch einen heidnischen Mediziner. Dennoch spielen bei ihm nicht nur philosophische und biblische Argumente eine Rolle, sondern auch medizinische Vorstellungen, die als gemeinsame Basis für die Argumentationen dienen. Im Werk von Augustinus spiegeln sich folglich die medizinischen Lehren seiner Zeit – doch der Bischof von Hippo beschäftigt sich deutlich weniger mit diesen Themen, als es Tertullian tat.[51] Das zeigt sich u. a. daran, dass Augustinus bezüglich der menschlichen Fortpflanzung gerne auf alte agrarische Analogien zurückgreift: Der Mann ist der Sämann und die Frau der zu bestellende Acker. Gegen Julian von Aeclanum führt er aus, dass vor dem Sündenfall alles perfekt eingerichtet war:

> Die Menschen im Paradies konnten auf den fruchtbaren Feldern der Frauen durch die Geschlechtsorgane der Männer gesät werden, wie Getreide auf den Feldern der Bauern gesät wird, so dass keine Lust auf das Säen des Menschen hinweist, wie kein Schmerz auf das Gebären des Menschen drängt.[52]

---

[51] Zur Rolle der Medizin vgl. *I. Bochet*, Art. Medicina, medicus, in: AL 3 (2011) 1230-1234.
[52] *Augustinus*, Contra Iulianum opus imperfectum 5, 14 (responsio Augustini): *M. Zelzer*, CSEL 85, 2 (2004) 187: „… ita in paradiso potuisse seminari homines in arvis genitalibus feminarum per membra genitalia masculorum, sicut frumenta in terris agricolarum manibus seminantur, ut sic ad hominem serendum stimulus nullus libidinis incitaret, quemadmodum ad hominem pariendum dolor nullus urgeret."

Er übernimmt zwar die Terminologie der Mediziner[53] und schreibt, dass Männer wie Frauen Samen haben, und der männliche Samen bzw. das mit ihm übertragene Pneuma die Gerinnung im weiblichen Samen auslöst.[54] Doch in seinen Augen stellt die werdende Mutter mit ihrem Samen, dem Menstruationsblut, nur die notwendige Nahrung für den Fötus bereit. Das Wesentliche kommt einzig vom Vater: das eine menschliche Samenkorn, das in der Mutter gedeiht und wächst. Obwohl Galen oder die Stoiker von einem Mitwirken des mütterlichen Samens bei der Zeugung ausgehen,[55] ignoriert Augustinus diese Erkenntnis aus theologischen Gründen. Er schreibt gegen Julian:

> Ein Kind hat zwar zwei Eltern; aber um geboren zu werden, zeugt ihn einer durch Samen, die andere bringt ihn durch Geburt zur Welt. Daher ist offensichtlich, wem die Haupt- oder erste Generierung zugeschrieben werden soll, damit du aufhörst, nachdem die Dinge ins Licht gerückt wurden, Nebel der Geschwätzigkeit zu verbreiten.[56]

Der väterliche Same, der zu einem Menschen wird, ist wie bei den Pflanzen dafür alleine ausreichend. In ihm ist alles Notwendige angelegt. Folglich entsteht Samenkorn aus Samenkorn. Deshalb ergibt sich zwangsläufig eine Art Generationalismus, der sich bis auf die Schöpfung zurückführen lässt:

> Denn aus einem einzigen [Samen] können tatsächlich nach ihrer Natur entweder Getreidefelder von Getreidefeldern oder Wälder von Wäldern oder Herden von Herden oder Völker von Völkern über Jahrhunderte hinweg verbreitet werden, so dass kein Blatt oder keine Haarsträhne in dieser so zahlreichen Nachfolge ist, deren Ursprung nicht in diesem ersten und einzigen Samen liegt.[57]

---

[53] Vgl. *J.-P. Rassinier*, Le vocabulaire médical de saint Augustin, in: G. Sabbah, Le latin médical (Saint-Etienne 1991) 379–395.
[54] *Augustinus*, De nuptiis et concupiscentia 2, 13, 26: C.F. Urba; J. Zycha, CSEL, 42 (1902) 279: „utrum autem utriusque sexus semina in muliebri utero cum uoluptate misceantur, uiderint feminae quid in secretis uisceribus sentiant" – „Ob jedoch die Samen beider Geschlechter im weiblichen Uterus mit Lust vermischt werden, mögen die Frauen sehen, was sie in ihren geheimen Eingeweiden fühlen."
[55] Vgl. *E. Lesky, J. H. Waszink*, Art. Embryologie, in: RAC 2 (1959) 1230.
[56] *Augustinus*, Contra Iulianum opus imperfectum 3, 88 (responsio Augustini): M. Zelzer, CSEL 85, 1 (1974) 415: „Natus quidem duos parentes habet; sed ut nascatur, unus eum serendo gignit, altera edendo parit. Unde satis apparet, cui sit potissimum uel cui primum generatio tribuenda, ut desinas rebus in luce positis nebulas loquacitatis offundere."
[57] *Augustinus*, De vera religione 42: K.-D. Daur, CCL 32 (1962) p. 240: *De uno quippe possunt secundum suam naturam uel segetes segetum uel siluae siluarum uel greges gregum uel populi populorum per saecula propagari, ut nullum folium sit uel nullus pilus per tam numerosam successionem, cuius non ratio in illo primo et uno semine fuerit.*

Diese veraltete Konzeption ermöglicht es Augustinus auch, die Kritik des Hilarius am Traduzianismus zu parieren. Dessen Einwand bezüglich der Seele Christi gilt nur, wenn man wie Hilarius von paritätischen Zeugungsanteilen der Eltern ausgeht: Dann nimmt Christus von Maria auch Seele auf. Wenn die Mutter jedoch nur für die Nahrung des Keimes zuständig ist, hat Jesus von Maria nichts angenommen, das von Adam herrührt, denn er ist nicht aus einem Samen entstanden, was, so Augustinus, Joh 1, 13 auch bestätigt.[58]

Der Same spielt im Denken Augustins eine zentrale Rolle. Er unterscheidet dabei den Seelensamen, der die Seele (*spiritus*) entstehen lässt, und den Leibessamen mit dessen Lebenskraft (*vita seminalis*).[59] Letzterer stammt zweifelsfrei von Adam, beim Ersteren will sich der Bischof von Hippo nicht festlegen.[60] Diese stufenweise Beseelung des Menschen vertreten zahlreiche Mediziner und Naturphilosophen wie Aristoteles, die Stoiker und Galen.[61] Dabei wird der Zeitpunkt des Eintritts der Geistseele unterschiedlich gesetzt – mit Tertullian ist Augustinus überzeugt, dass beide Seelenteile von Anfang an da sind.

Im Jahr 418 nimmt Augustinus an einer Synode in Cäsarea in Mauretanien teil. Dort zeigt man ihm den Brief eines sonst nicht bekannten Bischofs namens Optatus.[62] Dieser votiert darin zugunsten des Kreatianismus und gegen den Traduzianismus. Im Brief 190 protestiert Augustinus und erklärt, warum er sich in dieser Frage nie festgelegt habe – und dass der Kreatianismus meist mit der Leugnung der Erbsünde einhergehe. Er verwendet das berühmte Bild der Flamme, die von Lampe zu Lampe weitergegeben wird. Dabei diskutiert er das Zusammenspiel von Seelensamen und Leibessamen:

> Aber wenn man anfängt zu überlegen und zu untersuchen, was gesagt wird, ist es erstaunlich, ob irgendein menschlicher Verstand begreifen kann, auf welche Weise das geschieht. Wie eine Lampe von einer anderen Lampe entzündet wird und ohne Schaden ein anderes Feuer daraus entsteht, so wird die Seele von der Seele eines Elternteils im Nachkommen geboren oder in den Nachkommen übertragen. Ob das

---

[58] Vgl. *Augustinus*, De genesi ad litteram 10, 18, 32: *I. Zycha*, CSEL 28, 1 (1970) 319.
[59] Vgl. *G. O'Daly*, Art. Anima, animus, in: AL 1 (1994) 315–340.
[60] R. Ferwerda hat vermutet, dass dies auf die manichäische Zweiseelenlehre zurückgeführt werden könnte, M. Lamberigts widerspricht ihm. Vgl. *R. Ferwerda*, Two Souls. Origen's and Augustine's Attitude towards the two Soul doctrine, in: VigChr 37 (1983) 360–378 und *M. Lamberigts*, Julian and Augustinus on the origin of the soul. Augustiniana 46 (1996) 252.
[61] Eine Zusammenstellung bietet *J. H. Waszink*, Art. Beseelung, in: RAC 2 (1954) 177–180.
[62] Zum Kontext von Ep. 190 und dem Werk De anima et eius origine vgl. *A. Zumkeller*, Entstehungsgeschichte der Schrift „Natur und Ursprung der Seele", in: ders., Schriften gegen die Pelagianer 3, Würzburg 1977, 42–62 und ders., Art. Anima et eius origine, in: AL 1 (1994) 340–350.

immaterielle Samenkorn der Seele auf geheimem und unsichtbarem Weg getrennt vom Vater zur Mutter fliesst, wenn die Empfängnis in der Frau stattfindet? Oder ob es, was noch unglaublicher ist, im Samen des Körpers verborgen ist? Wenn jedoch Samen ohne jede Empfängnis vergeblich fliessen, ob die Seele nicht gleichzeitig austreten kann? Ob sie mit höchster Geschwindigkeit und im Bruchteil einer Sekunde, von wo sie ausgegangen ist, zurückkehrt? Oder ob sie vergeht? Und wenn sie vergeht, auf welche Weise ist dann die Seele, deren Samen sterblich ist, unsterblich? Ob sie Unsterblichkeit erhält, wenn sie geformt wird, um zu leben, so wie Gerechtigkeit geformt wird, um zu verstehen? Auf welche Weise formt Gott sie im Menschen, selbst wenn die Seele als Samen aus der Seele gezogen wird? So wie er im Menschen die Körperteile formt, obwohl der Körper als Samen aus dem Körper gezogen wird? […] Aber es ist zu untersuchen, ob dies aus der einen Seele des ersten Menschen geschieht, so wie das Angesicht einzelner Menschen aus dem einzigen Körper des ersten Menschen gebildet ist.[63]

Wie bei Aristoteles trägt nach Augustinus der Same nicht nur die Merkmale des Individuums. Letzteres kann, wenn die Kreatianisten recht haben, auch von aussen kommen. Wichtiger ist, dass der von Adam überkommene Samen die Natur der ganzen menschlichen Art enthält – und bereits am Anfang korrumpiert worden ist, wie es die heiligen Schriften bezeugen. Noch in seinem letzten, unvollendeten Werk gegen Julian schreibt Augustinus:

Von Natur aus ist der Same gut, aber der Same wird [in Adam] verdorben, und durch den verdorbenen Samen wird auch die Verderbnis fortgepflanzt.[64]

---

[63] *Augustinus*, Epistula 190 ad Optatum 190, 4: *A. Goldbacher*, CSEL 57 (1911) 149: „sed cum considerari et pertractari coeperit, quid dicatur, mirum, si ullus sensus comprehendit humanus, quonam modo, tamquam lucerna de lucerna accendatur et sine detrimento alterius alter inde ignis existat, sic anima de anima parentis fiat in prole uel traducatur in prolem, utrum incorporeum semen animae sua quadam occulta et inuisibili uia seorsum ex patre currat in matrem, cum fit conceptus in femina, an, quod est incredibilius, in semine corporis lateat; cum autem fluunt inrita sine ullis conceptibus semina, utrum semen animae non simul exeat, an summa celeritate atque atomo temporis, unde exierat, recurrat, an pereat; et si perit, quo modo ipsa, cuius mortale semen est, inmortalis est anima, an inmortalitatem tunc accipit, quando formatur, ut uiuat, sicut iustitiam, quando formatur, ut sapiat; et quo pacto deus eam fingat in homine, etiamsi anima seminaliter trahatur ex anima, sicut fingit in homine corporis membra, quamuis corpus seminaliter trahatur ex corpore. […] sed quaeritur, utrum ex una anima hominis primi, sicut fingit singillatim facies hominum ex uno tamen corpore hominis primi."
[64] *Augustinus*, Contra Iulianum opus imperfectum 2, 123: *E. Kalinka; M. Zelzer*, CSEL 85, 1 (1974) 254: „Natura bona sunt semina, sed uitiantur et semina eis que uitiatis propagantur et uitia."

Der verdorbene Samen

Dass es eine Vererbung der Leibseele geben muss, das ist für Augustinus aus biologischen Gründen gegeben. Dieser Vorgang bietet eine plausible Erklärung, wie die Sünde tradiert wird: über die Weitergabe des männlichen Samens. Für den Seelensamen dagegen ergeben sich zwei Möglichkeiten: Entweder er ist wie der Leibessamen in Adam korrumpiert worden und ist in der Folge wie dieser weitervererbt worden. Oder aber der Seelensamen kommt von aussen, ist als Gottes Geschöpf unverdorben, wird aber beim Kontakt mit dem Fleisch korrumpiert.

> Da sowohl die Seele als auch der Körper gleichermassen bestraft wurden, muss das [Kind], das geboren wird, durch die Wiedergeburt [der Taufe] gereinigt werden. Zweifellos entsteht entweder beides verderbt aus dem Menschen, oder das eine wird im anderen wie in einem verdorbenen Gefäss korrumpiert – hier liegt das Geheimnis der Gerechtigkeit des göttlichen Gesetzes vor. Welches von beiden wahr ist, erfahre ich lieber, als dass ich es ausspreche, damit ich nicht wage, das zu lehren, was ich nicht weiss. Aber dies weiss ich, dass unter diesen [Optionen] jene wahr ist, die nicht als falsch widerlegt, was der wahre, alte, katholische Glaube glaubt und behauptet, dass die Erbsünde existiert.[65]

Julian von Aeclanum, überzeugter Kreatianist und ausgestattet mit einem ausgeprägten Sensorium für die Schwachstellen seines Gegners, hält mit spitzer Feder fest: Augustinus ist ein treuer Schüler der Manichäer und Anführer der Traduzianerschar, denn er verurteilt den Geschlechtsverkehr von Eheleuten, weil da sich die Sünde auf ein schuldloses Kind weiterverpflanzt. Damit ist er schlimmer als die Heiden, denn er stellt so die Gerechtigkeit Gottes in Frage.[66]

Augustinus reagiert auf diese Kritik unwirsch. Zum Vorwurf der Pelagianer, er würde die Fortpflanzung der Seele mit jener der Sünde in Verbindung bringen, meint er nur, dass er nicht wisse, wo sie das gelesen hätten. Ganz klar sei nach den heiligen Schriften, dass es eine Ursprungssünde gegeben habe, die in der Taufe abgewaschen werden müsse. Jede Seelenlehre, die dem widerspreche, könne nicht wahr sein.[67]

---

[65] *Augustinus*, Contra Iulianum V,17: PL 44, 794: „Ut ergo et anima et caro pariter utrumque puniatur, nisi quod nascitur, renascendo emundetur; profecto aut utrumque uitiatum ex homine trahitur, aut alterum in altero tanquam in uitiato uase corrumpitur, ubi occulta iustitia diuinae legis includitur. quid autem horum sit uerum, libentius disco quam dico, ne audeam docere quod nescio. hoc tamen scio, id horum esse uerum, quod fides uera, antiqua, catholica, qua creditur et asseritur originale peccatum, non esse conuicerit falsum."

[66] Vgl. *Augustinus*, Contra Iulianum opus imperfectum 1, 27, 6–1, 29, 9 (= Julian von Aeclanum, Ad florum Liber primus): *E. Kalinka; M. Zelzer*, CSEL 85, 1 (1974). Vgl. V. Müller, Julian von Aeclanum, Ad florum liber primus, in: SVigChr 175 (2022) 260.

[67] *Augustinus*, Contra duas epistulas Pelagianorum 111, 26: *C. F. Vrba*, CSEL 60 (1913) 519.

III. Schlussbetrachtung

Im Rahmen der Frage zur Herkunft der Seele kritisiert Augustinus Tertullian wiederholt. Doch die Kritik zielt nicht auf den Traduzianismus selbst ab, sondern auf dessen stoische Grundlagen und insbesondere auf die Stofflichkeit der Seele. Im Brief 190 an Optatus schreibt er:

> Manche sagen, die Seelen stammten von der einen ab, die Gott dem ersten Menschen gab, und kämen somit von den Eltern. Falls diese sich die Meinung Tertullians zu eigen machen, so behaupten sie, dass die Seelen keine Geister, sondern Körper sind und aus körperlichem Samen entstehen. Kann man etwas Verkehrteres sagen? Es ist nicht verwunderlich, dass Tertullian dies erträumt hat, er, der sogar glaubt, dass der Schöpfergott selbst nur ein Körper ist.[68]

Dieser Aussage haftet freilich zu Lebzeiten des Augustinus keine revolutionäre Bedeutung an, den mit Galen und dem dominierenden Neuplatonismus ist Augustins Ansicht, dass die Seele immateriell sei, längst zur Selbstverständlichkeit geworden.

Auf die theologischen Differenzen zwischen Tertullians und Augustins Lehre bezüglich des Traduzianismus möchte ich hier nicht ausführlich eingehen.[69] Erwähnt sei nur die unterschiedliche Qualität des über den Samen weitergegeben Übels: Tertullian spricht nie von Sünde und denkt eher an eine Verderbtheit der Natur, die vererbt wird. Die These einer Erbsünde hätte er wohl abgelehnt.

Im Rahmen meiner Fragestellung sei vielmehr auf die Rolle der antiken Medizin bei beiden Autoren hingewiesen: Für Augustinus wie für Tertullian steht fest, dass ein Traduzianismus auf der Basis einer dualistischen Zeugungslehre mit einem männlich-aktiv befruchtenden und einem weiblich-aufnehmenden, ernährenden Prinzip dem biblischen Befund am ehesten gerecht wird. Wenn man diese biologischen Thesen teilt, wird die Weitergabe des Übels, das bei Adam seinen Anfang nahm, aber auch Jesu Sündlosigkeit aufgrund der jungfräulichen Empfängnis einsichtig. Beide präferieren jene biologischen Theorien, die zu ihren theologischen Standpunkten passen. Auffällig

---

[68] *Augustinus*, Epistula 190 ad Optatum, 4: A. Goldbacher, CSEL 57 (1911) 147–148: „nam et illi, qui animas ex una propagari adserunt, quam deus homini primo dedit, atque ita eas ex parentibus trahi dicunt, si Tertulliani opinionem sequuntur, profecto eas non spiritus sed corpora esse contendunt et corpulentis seminibus exoriri, quo peruersius quid dici potest? neque hoc Tertullianum somniasse mirandum est, qui etiam ipsum creatorem deum non esse nisi corpus opinatur."

[69] Darauf geht Beatrice ausführlich ein: Vgl. P. F. *Beatrice*, The Transmission of sin, Oxford 2013, 231–233.

Der verdorbene Samen

ist die unterschiedliche Gewichtung: Tertullian bemüht sich, die christliche Wahrheit ins Konzert der Philosophen und Mediziner einzufügen. Augustinus dagegen argumentiert auf Basis einer medizinischen Allgemeinbildung, die er voraussetzt. Im Kontext der Frage nach der Erbsünde erwähnt er nur ein einziges Mal einen Mediziner als Referenz: Es ist wiederum der Methodiker Soran.[70] Für die Plausibilität von theologischen Kernaussagen spielen medizinische Lehren eine wichtige Rolle. Doch die Naturphilosophie ist eine treulose Verbündete, und ewige Wahrheiten mit sich immer wieder wandelnden medizinischen Erkenntnissen zu legitimieren, ist eine heikle Angelegenheit.

Aus diesem Grund zeichnet sich in der Spätantike eine allmähliche Trennung von theologischen Fragestellungen und den damit verbundenen medizinischen Aspekten ab. Sie lassen sich auch bei anderen Themen wie etwa der Jungfrauengeburt beobachten.[71] Papst Anastasius II. setzt im Jahr 498 dem Traduzianismus ein Ende, als er ihn in einem Brief verurteilt. Biologische Argumente spielen dabei keine Rolle mehr.[72]

---

[70] Vgl. *Augustinus*, Contra Iulianum V, 51: PL 44, 794. Das dort angeführte Argument bezüglich der Weitervererbung von körperlichen Merkmalen über die Seele verwendet auch Tertullian in *De Anima*, vgl. FN 40. Zu weiteren Medizinern im Werk Augustins vgl. *I. Bochet*, Art. Medicina, medicus, in: AL 3 (2011) 1230-1234.
[71] Vgl. *G. Emmenegger*, Wie die Jungfrau zum Kind kam (Freiburg 2014) 87–196.
[72] Vgl. Anastasius II., Bonum atque iucundum an die Bischöfe Galliens, 23. August 498: Thiel 1868. Vgl. *H. Denzinger; P. Hünermann*, Enchiridion symbolorum, definitionum et declarationum de rebus fidei et morum = Kompendium der Glaubensbekenntnisse und kirchlichen Lehrentscheidungen (Freiburg 1991) Nr. 360–361.

Giuseppe Caruso, Roma (Italia)

Il peccato di Adamo in Girolamo

Abstract:
La colpa di Adamo, nella riflessione teologica cristiana, ha avuto conseguenze sull'umanità intera, intesa come sua posterità. Ma quali sono state esattamente queste conseguenze? Se Agostino d'Ippona considera la concupiscenza un doloroso prodotto del peccato originale Girolamo, suo contemporaneo, manifesta posizioni più sfumate: i progenitori, con la loro disobbedienza, hanno prodotto per la posterità un destino di mortalità e di sofferenza, ma non immediatamente di debolezza davanti alla tentazione; questa, infatti, viene ritenuta dallo Stridonense come qualcosa di connaturato con la condizione umana. In questo contributo verrà analizzato il trattamento riservato, lungo tutta la vasta produzione geronimiana, al tema del peccato adamitico e delle sue ricadute sul destino dell'umanità.

Nell'epistolario di Paolo, sia in 1 Cor 15, 21–22 che in Rom 5, 12–19, viene istituito un paragone tra Adamo e Cristo: dal primo l'umanità ha ricevuto un destino di morte mentre dal secondo gli è venuta una vita rinnovata. Agostino, raccogliendo e organizzando suggestioni e spunti che, da Paolo in poi, hanno costellato gli scritti cristiani dei primi secoli, giunge alla formulazione compiuta della dottrina del peccato originale il cui punto di forza consiste nel ritenere che se tutti gli uomini muoiono come Adamo e in conseguenza del suo peccato, in qualche modo devono essere ritenuti colpevoli insieme a lui. Queste idee, che verranno vieppiù radicalizzate nel corso della controversia pelagiana, sono poi divenute patrimonio comune della teologia cattolica. Il presente intervento si propone di indagare se e fino a che punto la dottrina del peccato originale, nella forma classica qui appena delineata, trovi riscontro nell'opera di Girolamo; per fare ciò si passeranno in rassegna, in ordine cronologico, i riferimenti geronimiani al progenitore e alle conseguenze della sua colpa.

I. I primi scritti

Nel 377 Girolamo si trova nel deserto di Calcide, non lontano da Antiochia, per dare attuazione al suo progetto di intraprendere la vita eremitica. Mal-

Il peccato di Adamo in Girolamo 221

grado il suo proposito di astrarsi dal mondo, in quel torno di tempo egli intrattiene un intenso scambio epistolare con diversi corrispondenti residenti in Italia: tra le missive di questo periodo si colloca l'*Epistula* 10, indirizzata a Paolo di Concordia, un uomo ultracentenario. In essa lo Stridonense afferma che il peccato del primo uomo in quanto ha comportato per tutti i suoi discendenti il passaggio dall'immortalità primigenia alla mortalità; l'accrescersi dei peccati ha fatto poi in modo che la vita degli esseri umani diventasse sempre più breve e pertanto il fatto che i bambini, ai quali evidentemente non si possono imputare peccati personali, muoiano prematuramente è segno che il mondo si spinge sempre più avanti nel vizio[1]. In questa lettera si stabilisce una stretta correlazione tra il peccato – non però solo quello dei progenitori! – e la morte contrapposti alla santità e alla vita; però nel corso della missiva lo stesso Girolamo attenua il parallelismo tra vita buona e vita longeva affermando che Dio può elargire la buona salute ai buoni come anche il diavolo ai cattivi (salta quindi la stretta associazione tra la longevità, che della buona salute è conseguenza, e la santità)[2]; resta però inteso che il peccato di Adamo ha avuto la nefasta conseguenza di assoggettare ogni essere umano alla morte. La tendenza a peccare, invece, non viene ritenuta un perverso lascito di Adamo e viene connessa semplicemente alla condizione creaturale dell'uomo: di ciò si legge nell'*Epistula* 21 che tra il 382 e il 383 lo Stridonense invia a papa Damaso per presentargli la spiegazione della parabola del figliol prodigo (Lc. 15, 8-10). L'esegesi principale proposta da Girolamo vede rispettivamente nel figlio maggiore e minore l'immagine degli ebrei e dei pagani; accanto a questa ne propone anche una seconda che ritiene i due fratelli la rappresentazione del giusto e del peccatore, rendendosi però conto che questa interpretazione ingenera un problema: se il figlio maggiore è «giusto», come può provare un sentimento di rancorosa invidia? Si risponde che è possibile perché nemmeno il giusto è immune da difetti in quanto la santità perfetta si addice solo a Dio[3]; in tutte le creature, invece, sia umane che angeliche, si trova il peccato e a sostegno di ciò si citano diversi passaggi delle scritture: Iob 15, 15 (*Sidera non sunt munda in conspectu eius*), Iob 4, 18 (*Contra angelos suos perversum quid intellexit*), Ps. 133, 2 (*Non iustificabitur in conspectu eius omnis vivens*). Tale diffusa peccaminosità viene spiegata facendo riferimento al libero arbitrio – che è proprio la prerogativa che rende l'uomo a immagine e somiglianza di Dio! – cioè alla possibilità concessa agli esseri razionali di scegliere il bene

---

[1] Hier., Ep. 10, 1: I. Hilberg, CSEL 54 (Wien 1996), p. 35
[2] Hier., Ep. 10, 2: I. Hilberg, CSEL 54 (Wien 1996), p. 37.
[3] Hier., Ep. 21, 39: I. Hilberg, CSEL 54 (Wien 1996), p. 137-138.

o il male: tutti almeno qualche volta, attuano la seconda opzione[4]; il peccato universale è dunque frutto di scelte personali, sia delle creature angeliche che di quelle umane: non sembra quindi esserci un nesso con la colpa dei progenitori che, in ogni caso, non dovrebbe aver avuto nessuna conseguenza per gli angeli.

L'assunto appena enunciato con tanta chiarezza torna a farsi nebuloso e confuso nell'*Epistula* 22, la famosa istruzione indirizzata alla vergine consacrata Eustochio. Nell'esortare la sua discepola a un regime alimentare frugale e semplice, Girolamo fa riferimento alla colpa del progenitore presentandola come un peccato di gola. A prescindere dall'evidente forzatura che simile interpretazione esercita sul testo genesiaco è opportuno, in questo contesto, mettere in evidenza un punto di specifico: Adamo, per aver obbedito al proprio ventre piuttosto che a Dio, è stato precipitato «in questa valle di lacrime»[5], in altri termini, l'allontanamento dal paradiso l'inserimento in una condizione certamente più infelice è stato una conseguenza della sua colpa; non viene invece chiarito se il fatto che i discendenti di Adamo si trovino a vivere anch'essi fuori dal paradiso sia dovuto alla colpa dell'antenato comune o a peccati personali. Tra le conseguenze del peccato di Adamo si annovera, nella medesima lettera, anche l'istituzione delle nozze; Girolamo spiega infatti che il comando di crescere e moltiplicarsi (Gen 1, 28) è stato dato agli esseri umani solo dopo la cacciata dal paradiso, quando gli uomini erano ormai rivestiti delle «tuniche di pelle», che sono immagine non tanto della corporeità quanto delle gravose fatiche della condizione postlapsaria[6]; si deve per altro osservare che in questo argomentare Girolamo non rispetta la successione del racconto genesiaco che pone il comando di crescere e moltiplicarsi prima dell'espulsione dal giardino dell'Eden.[7]

II. Gli scritti di Betlemme

Tra il 387 e il 389, dopo il suo definitivo trasferimento a Betlemme, Girolamo pose mano alla composizione di alcuni commentari paolini: *Ad Philemonem*, *Ad Galatas*, *Ad Ephesios* e *Ad Titum*, trattati esegetici fortemente debitori, sia

---

[4] Hier., Ep. 21, 40: I. Hilberg, CSEL 54 (Wien 1996), p. 140.
[5] Hier., Ep. 22, 10: I. Hilberg, CSEL 54 (Wien 1996), p. 157.
[6] Hier., Ep. 22, 18-19: I. Hilberg, CSEL 54 (Wien 1996), p. 168-170.
[7] Per ulteriori dettagli su questo tema: G. *Sfameni-Gasparro*, Enkrateia e antropologia. Le motivazioni protologiche ed escatologiche della continenza e della verginità nel cristianesimo dei primi secoli e nello gnosticismo (Roma 1984) 293-295.

pur non senza sfumature, alla lezione di Origene[8]. Il progenitore viene menzionato nei *Commentarii ad Galatas* quando si deve spiegare Gal 4, 1–2, un testo in cui l'Apostolo afferma che l'erede durante la sua minorità è in tutto assimilato ai servi. Per Girolamo l'erede al quale non vengono riconosciute ancora le sue prerogative di signoria è l'intero genere umano fino alla venuta di Cristo o, addirittura, fino alla fine del mondo: il brano allude quindi alla progressività della rivelazione. In tutto questo viene però inserito un riferimento a 1 Cor 15, 22, brano che pone in forte evidenza la profonda solidarietà di tutti gli uomini che in Adamo muoiono, anche se nati dopo di lui, e in Cristo ricevono la vita, benché vissuti prima[9]. Non è del tutto chiaro di quale morte si stia parlando; probabilmente Girolamo fa riferimento alla morte fisica che, come si vide, egli ritiene (ma non sempre!) una conseguenza della colpa di Adamo.

Nei medesimi anni in cui si dedica al commento degli scritti paolini sopra menzionati, Girolamo inaugura la sua attività di esegeta dell'Antico Testamento con il *Commentarius in Ecclesiasten*, opera che, al pari dei commentari paolini, è ampiamente compilativa nel senso che in essa Girolamo riporta le opinioni di altri esegeti senza però distinguerle sempre e con chiarezza dal suo sentire[10]. Indubbiamente geronimiano è il vigoroso rigetto del traducianesimo: l'idea che l'anima dei figli derivi, al pari della carne, da quella dei genitori è per lo Stridonense ridicola: l'anima, infatti, viene data agli uomini direttamente da Dio[11]. Nei *Commentarioli in Psalmos*, di poco posteriori, il traducianesimo viene di nuovo condannato negando esplicitamente che in Adamo fossero contenute le anime di tutti i suoi discendenti, dal momento che Dio plasma singolarmente ciascuna anima[12]. Negli anni tra il 389 e il 392, dunque in contemporanea con la composizione dei *Commentarioli in Psalmos*, Girolamo inizia il commento ai libri profetici, fatica che lo accompagnerà fino alla fine dei suoi giorni.

Nei *Commentarii in Habacuc*, composti in quel torno di tempo, quando deve spiegare i versetti in cui il profeta paragona il pressante fiscalismo dei Caldei all'azione di un pescatore che cattura i pesci con la rete (Hab 1, 15), Girolamo interpreta il testo in senso spirituale e fa riferimento alla pesca con cui il diavolo cattura le anime: Adamo abboccò al suo amo dal momento che, tratto

---

[8] Si veda in proposito, F. Bucchi, Introduzione, in: F. Bucchi, CCL 77C (Turnhout 2003) VII–IX.
[9] *Hier.*, CGal. 2, 4, 1–2: G. Raspanti, CCL 77A (Turnhout 2006), p. 104
[10] Si veda in proposito F. Cavallera, Saint Jérôme, vol. I (Louvain – Paris 1922) 135–137.
[11] *Hier.*, In Eccl. 12, 6–8: M. Adriaen, CCL 72 (Turnhout 1959), p. 356–357.
[12] *Hier.*, CPs. 32: G. Morin, CCL 72 (Turnhout 1959), p. 204.

in inganno dai suoi discorsi fallaci – proprio come se fosse stato imprigionato dalla rete di un pescatore – commise peccato. La colpa del progenitore sembra aver avuto conseguenze anche per la sua posterità dal momento che a causa sua tutti sono stati costituiti peccatori (Rom 5, 19) e in lui, infatti, tutti gli uomini sono morti (c'è un'allusione a 1 Cor 15, 22) inoltre tutti i santi sono stati cacciati «allo stesso modo insieme a lui» (*cum illo pariter*) dal paradiso. Il brano non è di facile interpretazione: poiché Girolamo si premura di specificare che quelli scacciati con Adamo erano santi, si può interpretare il suo pensiero in questi termini: a causa del peccato del progenitore tutta l'umanità ha ereditato la morte e l'esilio dalla condizione paradisiaca; non sembra che però che una colpevolezza ereditaria sia parte di questo gravoso lascito[13].

In diversi brani dei *Commentarii in Micheam* Girolamo, facendo riferimento ad Adamo, presenta una protologia di grande interesse e problematicità. Il testo di Mich 1, 16 (*Decalvare et detondere super filios deliciarum tuarum, dilata calvitium tuum sicut aquila, quoniam captivi ducti sunt ex te*) non è di facile comprensione; Girolamo spiega che quell'espressione si può intendere come rivolta ad Adamo, da identificarsi con la Gerusalemme celeste, che a sua volta è intesa come immagine dell'anima umana che è stata precipitata dalle altezze paradisiache nella prigionia babilonese; questa interpretazione però non si può *sic et simpliciter* ritenere espressiva del pensiero dello Stridonense che afferma di averla trovata in commentari di altri autori[14]. Non è difficile riconoscere in questa lettura il classico tema origeniano della preesistenza e caduta delle anime che ritorna anche poco dopo. In effetti, quando commenta l'oracolo minaccioso pronunciato contro gli Israeliti divorati dall'avidità (Mich 2, 1–5) e ai quali è preannunciata la deportazione assira, Girolamo offre del brano una triplice lettura: la prima lo intende come una severissima reprimenda morale; la seconda lo attualizza e ne fa il rimprovero rivolto a Israele che non ha accolto Cristo; la terza ed ultima, di carattere «spirituale», lo riferisce all'anima umana passata da una condizione paradisiaca alla prigionia di questo mondo. Ripresentando le tre interpretazioni, dopo averle esposte prima più diffusamente, Girolamo le riassume in breve: l'interpretazione «spirituale» viene riassunta dicendo che ogni uomo «è precipitato dal paradiso insieme ad Adamo» (*de paradiso cum Adam cecidit*)[15]. Si deve osservare che a una più attenta lettura la spiegazione «spirituale» e il suo sunto appaiono alquanto diverse. La prima proviene evidentemente da Origene, che Gi-

---

[13] Hier., CHab. 1, 1–15–17: S. Mantelli, CCL 76–76A bis I (Turnhout 2018), p. 26.
[14] Hier., CMich. 1, 1, 16: M. Adriaen, CCL 76 (Turnhout 1969), p. 438,540–550.
[15] Hier., CMich. 1, 2, 1–5: M. Adriaen, CCL 76 (Turnhout 1969), p. 442,125–133.

rolamo dice apertamente di aver tenuto presente nella composizione del suo commento[16]; il sunto invece, nel quale probabilmente lo Stridonense si sente più libero dal suo modello – posto che qui Adamo non può essere interpretato come simbolo di ogni anima anche della celeste Gerusalemme – sembra fare riferimento all'umanità in qualche modo solidale con il progenitore e pertanto decaduta insieme a lui.

III. La polemica con Gioviniano

Nel 393, Girolamo pose mano a uno scritto polemico contro il monaco Gioviniano che criticava duramente l'idea che l'ascetismo, soprattutto esercitato attraverso la rinuncia alle nozze e il digiuno, potesse garantire a chi ne avesse fatto la propria scelta di vita un più alto grado di gloria ultraterrena in quanto la salvezza ultima è legata alla santità che si ottiene attraverso il battesimo e una vita coerentemente cristiana. Per ribadire, contro ogni esaltazione eccessiva della consacrazione verginale, il valore delle nozze Gioviniano si serviva di un lungo elenco di personaggi biblici vissuti nel matrimonio. Girolamo, nel suo all'*Adversus Iovinianum*, passa in rassegna questo elenco e riguardo ai progenitori, che erano censiti in prima posizione, sottolinea che prima del peccato essi vivevano nella verginità, dal momento che le nozze sono iniziate dopo la cacciata dal paradiso[17], quasi fossero una conseguenza della primordiale caduta. Ancora poco dopo torna a parlare di Adamo – che egli interpreta come «uomo» – dicendo che in lui erano compresi entrambi i sessi; ma in effetti nel progenitore è in qualche modo contenuta tutta la sua posterità. Ciò si deduce dal fatto che Girolamo continua la sua argomentazione introducendo un eloquente *nos*, che fa riferimento a tutta l'umanità, creata da Dio in una condizione di bontà e rettitudine e che in seguito per sua colpa è piombata in una situazione deteriore in cui si è corrotto ciò che aveva di buono. Si sta ovviamente parlando della condizione verginale che, conservata nel paradiso, è venuta meno dopo il peccato. In effetti, Girolamo si rende conto che anche prima del peccato c'era la differenziazione sessuale tra l'uomo e la donna e questo potrebbe suggerire che le nozze erano in qualche modo parte del progetto di Dio, ma non si rassegna ad ammetterlo; ritiene infatti che non sia noto a nessuno quel che sarebbe avvenuto se non ci fosse stato il primo peccato e

---

[16] Hier., CMich. 2, Prol.: M. Adriaen, CCL 76 (Turnhout 1969), p. 473,226–230.
[17] Hier., Adv. Iov. 1, 16: PL 23, 246A.

resta per lui indubitabile che i rapporti sessuali appartengono alla condizione postlapsaria[18].

Con la sua seconda proposizione Gioviniano affermava che quanti hanno ricevuto «con piena fede» (*plena fide*) il battesimo non possono essere «travolti» dal diavolo; in termini forse più perentori che essi non possono essere tentati[19]. Girolamo sottolinea a questo proposito che il peccato è una realtà universalmente condivisa: radunando una panoplia di citazioni evidenzia che tutti hanno peccato in molti modi (Iac 3, 2) e nessuno è puro dal peccato, anche se la sua vita è di un solo giorno (Iob 14, 4–5 LXX); pertanto nessuno si può vantare di avere il cuore puro (Prov 20, 9) in quanto tutti sono ritenuti colpevoli a somiglianza della colpa di Adamo (Rom 5, 14)[20]. La citazione del testo paolino suggerisce che tutti quelli che sono colpevoli lo sono in quanto hanno imitato Adamo, però non si spiega come abbiano potuto far ciò gli eventuali infanti morti prematuramente; in ogni caso di questo collage geronimiano, che fece molta impressione ad Agostino si dovrà parlare ancora.

L'idea che il matrimonio sia in qualche modo connesso alla condizione postlapsaria è ribadita quando Girolamo vuole difendere, contro le posizioni minimaliste di Gioviniano, la prassi dell'astensione dai cibi: Adamo aveva ricevuto il comando di «digiunare» dai frutti di un solo albero: finché persevererò in quel digiuno, rimase in paradiso e vergine; quando invece si fu saziato, venne allontanato dal paradiso e diede inizio alla prassi matrimoniale[21]. La colpa del protoplasto per Girolamo è stata un avvenimento carico di spiacevoli conseguenze: la morte, come si è già visto, l'allontanamento dal paradiso e l'inizio delle nozze (ovviamente questo tema va letto in considerazione dello specifico contesto polemico); sembra però estranea al sentire dello Stridonense l'idea che quel peccato dei progenitori abbia alterato la natura umana: un punto da tenere presente anche nel seguito della presente ricerca.

L'*Epistula* 60 risale al 396; si tratta di un testo indirizzato da Girolamo all'amico Eliodoro dopo la morte del nipote Nepoziano. Nella missiva si riconoscono gli elementi caratteristici di uno scritto consolatorio cristiano in cui il rammarico per la recente perdita è contemperato dalla speranza. Lo Strido-

---

[18] Hier., Adv. Iov. 1, 29: PL 23, 262A–263C. La connessione tra le nozze e la condizione postlapsaria dell'uomo non costituisce una novità, né tra i padri in genere, né nella riflessione di Girolamo in specie; si veda su questo tema G. *Sfameni-Gasparro*, Enkrateia e antropologia. Le motivazioni protologiche ed escatologiche della continenza e della verginità nel cristianesimo dei primi secoli e nello gnosticismo (Roma 1984) 290–300.

[19] La prima forma della proposizione si legge: Hier., Adv. Iov. 1, 3: PL 23, 2224B; la seconda in: Adv. Iov. 2, 1: PL 23, 295A.

[20] Hier., Adv. Iov. 2, 2: PL 23, 296C–297A.

[21] Hier., Adv. Iov. 2, 15: PL 23, 319B–319C.

Il peccato di Adamo in Girolamo 227

nense si rivolge direttamente al Salvatore e lo ringrazia per aver ucciso la morte, definita «adversarius potens»; proprio il perdurante terrore suscitato dalla consapevolezza di dover morire rattristava l'esistenza di ogni persona umana dandole come unica prospettiva la morte. Sembra che qui si faccia riferimento alla morte fisica, conseguenza della colpa adamitica: lo suggerisce la citazione di Rom 5, 14. Subito dopo, però, si afferma che, prima della venuta di Cristo, anche i santi patriarchi della Prima Alleanza erano negli inferi in quanto erano ritenuti colpevoli del peccato di Adamo: sembra quindi che, oltre alla morte fisica, quell'antica disobbedienza abbia prodotto per tutti l'esclusione dal regno dei cieli, almeno fino a Cristo; resta inteso che dopo quell'evento salvifico per i santi del Primo Testamento le porte del paradiso saranno riaperte, mentre resteranno ermeticamente chiuse per quanti si sono volontariamente volti a opere di malvagità[22]. La colpa di Adamo sembra dunque aver avuto due conseguenze: la morte fisica, che tutti raggiunge, e l'esclusione dal regno dei cieli con conseguente imprigionamento agli inferi dei defunti (ma quest'ultima, con la redenzione, è venuta meno per i buoni).

Sempre nel 396 Girolamo pone mano al commento *In Ionam*. Quando deve spiegare i versetti che parlano della penitenza dei Niniviti, Girolamo, notando che tutti, senza distinzione di età, si diedero alle opere di penitenza (Ion 3, 5), conclude che ciò avvenne perché nessuno è immune da peccato, neppure colui la cui vita dura un giorno solo (Iob 15, 15 LXX); Girolamo rincara poi la dose osservando che se nemmeno le stelle, stando al dettato biblico (Iob 25, 5), sono pure agli occhi di Dio, a maggior ragione non lo saranno quanti sono ritenuti colpevoli per il peccato dell'offensore Adamo (*hi qui peccato offendentis Adam tenentur obnoxii*)[23]. Lo Stridonense sta forse alludendo a una condizione di colpevolezza ereditata dal progenitore? In effetti quest'idea non è abituale nei suoi scritti, come si è visto fin qui, mentre invece ritorna molte volte l'idea che, in seguito alla colpa di Adamo, i suoi discendenti si vengono a trovare in una situazione di gran lunga peggiore di quella che il progenitore sperimentò all'inizio: forse solo in questo senso essi sono ritenuti colpevoli e trattati come tali; in ogni caso di questo specifico testo sarà necessario parlare ancora.

Nel commento *In Zachariam*, assegnato al 406, Girolamo spiega gli effetti redentivi della risurrezione di Cristo: il Salvatore, infatti, ha liberato quanti erano tenuti prigionieri nell'inferno, trattenuti dai peccati di Adamo, come altri pensano, dai legacci di un errore radicato o della morte (*hi qui peccatis*

---

[22] Hier., Ep. 60, 3: I. Hilberg, CSEL 54 (Wien 1996), p. 551–552.
[23] Hier., CIon. 3, 5: M. Adriaen, CCL 76 (Turnhout 1969), p. 405–406.

Adam, sive, ut quidam volunt, erroris inoliti, ac mortis vinculis tenebantur)[24]. Si è già visto in precedenza che, per Girolamo, la chiusura del paradiso (e quindi la necessità di scendere agli inferi per i defunti) e la stessa morte sono conseguenza della colpa del progenitore e pertanto possono essere ritenuti «vincoli» dovuti al suo peccato; resta però da spiegare a che cosa faccia riferimento l'espressione «error inolitus», cioè un errore che è cresciuto mettendo radici e sviluppandosi: forse si vuole alludere all'esemplarità della colpa adamitica che ha trovato vasto seguito nei suoi discendenti.

Nel secondo libro del commentario *In Oseam*, anche questo terminato nel 406, Girolamo si ritrova ad affrontare, sia pure incidentalmente, il tema della colpa di Adamo e delle conseguenze che questa ha avuto sui suoi discendenti; ciò avviene quando deve commentare le parole con cui Dio rimprovera gli Israeliti perché, come Adamo, anch'essi lo hanno offeso con la trasgressione di quanto pattuito (Os 6, 6-7). Lo Stridonense spiega che gli uomini hanno fatto sulla terra quello che il progenitore ha fatto in paradiso e questo potrebbe semplicemente essere interpretato nell'ottica dell'imitazione che si è vista, sia pure nebulosamente, poco sopra; però la spiegazione continua dicendo che anche in paradiso tutti hanno peccato a somiglianza del peccato di Adamo (*et ibi, hoc est in paradiso, omnes prevaricati sunt in me, in similitudine praevaricationis Adam*) e si aggiunge che non deve stupire che sia condannato nei figli quel che prima era avvenuto nel genitore (*non enim mirum si quod in parente praecessit, etiam in filiis condemnetur*)[25]. Non è facile spiegare come e in che senso gli uomini, in paradiso, hanno peccato; si potrebbe pensare a una dipendenza dall'idea origeniana della preesistenza e caduta degli esseri intellettuali; del resto, Girolamo si era servito del commentario origeniano ad Osea[26]. D'altra parte, stupisce non poco che lo Stridonense, a così pochi anni dall'infuriare della controversia origeniana sia così pronto a seguire il suo antico maestro su un punto tanto insidioso. Non si può nemmeno ritenere che gli uomini abbiano peccato, in paradiso, perché solidali con Adamo e, in qualche modo, «inclusi» in lui: il testo parla infatti di quanti hanno peccato non «in Adamo» ma «a somiglianza di Adamo». Pur tenendo presente questa difficoltà, non risolta, il testo sembra genericamente andare nella direzione di una cattiva esemplarità offerta dal progenitore ai suoi discendenti: l'uno e gli altri hanno peccato similmente e similmente sono puniti. Di ben più agevole comprensione il brano in cui si commentano le parole con cui Dio pronuncia

---

[24] Hier., CZach. 2, 9, 11-12: M. Adriaen, CCL 76A (Turnhout 1970), p. 831-832,287-289.
[25] Hier., COs. 2, 6, 6-7: M. Adriaen, CCL 76 (Turnhout 1969), p. 66, 152-157.
[26] Si veda: M. C. Pennacchio, Propheta insaniens. L'esegesi patristica di Osea tra profezia e storia (Roma 2002) 165.

parole minacciose contro la morte (Os 13, 14-15): Girolamo ne vede la realizzazione in Cristo in quanto la redenzione da lui realizzata ha liberato tutti gli uomini dall'antica condanna per la quale tutti gli uomini muoiono (*quia in Adam omnes morimur*)[27]. Vi è un chiaro riferimento a 1 Cor 15, 22; l'idea soggiacente, per altro già vista, è quella che il peccato di Adamo ha comportato per tutti gli uomini la mortalità.

IV. La controversia con Pelagio

Probabilmente nei primi mesi del 410 Girolamo inizia a comporre i *Commentarii in Ezechielem*. Proprio mentre egli attende a questa nuova impresa esegetica, intorno al 411, giunge in Palestina Pelagio. Il monaco britannico, com'è noto, si era già fatto banditore di una prassi cristiana rigorosa e incline all'ascetismo insegnando che ciascuno, se si fosse impegnato fortemente, sarebbe riuscito a evitare tutti i peccati in quanto l'uomo è stato creato e resta sempre libero di scegliere se agire bene o male. Tale predicazione aveva già suscitato la preoccupazione di Agostino e non lascia tranquillo nemmeno Girolamo che denunzia Pelagio come l'eretico sorto per dare continuità agli errori del defunto e tuttavia ancora aborrito Rufino (alla faccia del *parce sepulto!*)[28].

Nel corso di questo lavoro esegetico, quando deve commentare il brano in cui il profeta descrive la visione dell'acqua scaturita dal tempio (Ez 47, 1-5), lo Stridonense offre al lettore diverse interpretazioni di quelle mistiche acque, che possono significare la predicazione di Cristo ma anche la dottrina ecclesiale e infine le acque del battesimo, acque che introducono in percorso di crescita spirituale che viene ben espresso attraverso le tappe del guado del torrente meticolosamente descritte dal profeta. Si osserva che non è facile pervenire ai fastigi della santità in quanto il cuore dell'uomo, sin dall'infanzia, è proclive al male (Gen 8, 21) tanto che lo stesso Davide confessa di essere stato concepito nell'iniquità e nei peccati (Ps 50, 7); Girolamo si premura si specificare che non si tratta dell'iniquità della madre – e quindi di un peccato ereditato – né di quella di Davide – cioè di un peccato personale – bensì dell'iniquità connessa alla condizione umana (*in iniquitatibus humanae conditionis*); proprio questa iniquità spiega il testo famoso di Rom 5, 14, quello secondo il quale la

---

[27] *Hier.*, COs. 3, 13, 14-15: M. Adriaen, CCL 76 (Turnhout 1969), p. 148-149,291-294.
[28] *Hier.*, CEz. 6, Prol.: F. Glorie, CCL 75 (Turnhout 1964), p. 223. Per notizie relative al passaggio di Pelagio in Palestina e la sua identificazione con la «nuova Idra», germogliata dal «serpente» (così viene chiamato Rufino!) si veda J. N. D. Kelly, Jerome (London 1975) 309-311.

morte ha regnato, a partire da Adamo, anche su quelli che non hanno peccato a somiglianza del progenitore: come a dire che il fomite al peccato è in qualche modo insito nella natura umana[29].

L'*Epistula* 128, scritta nel 413, ha come tema l'educazione di una bambina. La piccola Pacatula era stata consacrata a Dio dai genitori e Girolamo si affretta a offrire ai suoi familiari consigli utili per la sua formazione spirituale. Introducendo il tema delle precauzioni che si devono porre in atto per custodire la castità della fanciulla la «tunica di pelle» (Gen 3, 21) viene interpretata come un simbolo delle nozze con le quali Adamo fu rivestito all'atto della sua espulsione dal paradiso della verginità (*Adam eiectus de paradiso virginitatis*)[30]. Ancora una volta, come nella polemica contro Gioviniano, Girolamo torna a sostenere che il matrimonio appartiene all'economia postlapsaria; in questo frangente, considerato il contesto di promozione dell'ascetismo, il paradiso è assimilato alla condizione in cui l'uomo nasce, in quanto vergine, e che poi perde; il ruolo del progenitore sembra qui rinchiuso nella sfera della semplice esemplarità.

La figura di Adamo ritorna, ma anche questa volta in modo incidentale, nell'*Epistula* 129, assegnata all'anno 414. Scrivendo a Dardano, che aveva chiesto spiegazioni sul senso, storico o metastorico, da assegnare all'espressione biblica «terra promessa». Girolamo spiega il senso dell'espressione «terra dei vivi» (*terra viventium*) che si legge in Ps 59, 10 dicendo che questa è il paradiso nel quale, prima dell'incarnazione, nemmeno i patriarchi dell'Antico Testamento riuscirono a entrare; questo però è stato finalmente riaperto dal sangue di Cristo, che ne è la chiave (*sanguis Christi clavis paradisi est*); proprio lui ha riacquistato e restituito agli uomini quella terra colma di ricchezze e di doni divini che Adamo aveva perduto (*primus Adam perdidit et secundus invenit, immo ab illo perdita iste restituit*)[31]. Il brano suggerisce che la colpa del progenitore ha avuto come conseguenza l'esclusione dal paradiso per lui e per tutti i suoi discendenti, anche per quelli che si segnalavano a causa di una sovreminente santità, almeno fino alla redenzione operata da Cristo.

Poco sopra si è fatto un sia pur rapido cenno alla controversia che vide Girolamo e Agostino alleati contro Pelagio. Proprio nel contesto di questa polemica acquisirà sempre maggior importanza, soprattutto nell'elaborazione teologica di Agostino, il peccato di Adamo e le conseguenze che questo ha avuto

---

[29] Hier., CEz. 14, 47, 1-5: F. Glorie, CCL 75 (Turnhout 1964), p. 711-712,1039-1047.
[30] Hier., Ep. 128, 3: I. Hilberg, CSEL 56/1 (Wien 1996), p. 158,14-16.
[31] Hier., Ep. 129, 2: I. Hilberg, CSEL 56/1 (Wien 1996), p. 165,5-8.

Il peccato di Adamo in Girolamo 231

sui discendenti del progenitore; ciò avrà delle ricadute anche sul pensiero di Girolamo, come si metterà presto in evidenza. Proprio nel corso della controversia pelagiana il vescovo di Ippona e il monaco di Betlemme ripresero lo scambio epistolare che avevano interrotto molti anni prima[32]; nel 415 infatti, latore Orosio, giunsero dall'Africa in Palestina due missive, le *Epistulae* 131 e 132 (nella collezione delle lettere di Agostino sono la 166 e 167). La prima di queste è di grande interesse per il tema che qui si tratta. Marcellino, lo sfortunato tribuno che tanto si era battuto contro lo scisma donatista, intorno al 411 aveva rivolto a Girolamo alcune domande sul tema dell'origine dell'anima e lo Stridonense gli aveva risposto con l'*Epistula* 126, consigliandogli allo stesso tempo di farsi istruire sul tema da Agostino; nella sua missiva a Girolamo l'Ipponense confessa invece di avere sulla questione idee tutt'altro che chiare. Egli è infatti profondamente convinto che ogni anima viene al mondo già macchiata dal peccato e deve essere purificata mediante il battesimo e si chiede come questo fatto possa conciliarsi con l'opinione creazionista di Girolamo, secondo la quale Dio crea di volta in volta le anime degli uomini che vengono al mondo; l'ipotesi traducianista che tutte le anime derivano da quella del primo uomo, il peccatore Adamo, spiegherebbe in modo alquanto più semplice la colpevolezza universale. Nel corso di questa lettera Agostino fa riferimento all'interpretazione geronimiana di Iob 14, 4–5 LXX che, come si è visto in precedenza, si legge nell'*Adversus Iovinianum* e nell'*In Ionam*; l'Ipponense si riferisce proprio a questo commentario per osservare che anche Girolamo ritiene i bambini colpevoli del peccato di Adamo e per questo bisognosi di penitenza[33]; malgrado ciò non risulta affatto evidente che le parole di Girolamo indichino una sua totale conformità al pensiero di Agostino. In effetti l'idea che si può legittimamente ricavare dalla lettura dell'*In Ionam*, cioè quella dell'esistenza di una colpa passata per ereditarietà da Adamo a tutta l'umanità, non sem-

---

[32] Agostino e Girolamo, tra il 394 e il 405, si erano già scambiati 12 lettere (7 di Agostino e 5 di Girolamo); il carteggio, che era stato avviato per iniziativa dell'Ipponense, fu condotto faticosamente tra ritardi nella consegna delle missive, incomprensioni e malintesi. Si veda in proposito: F. Cavallera, Saint Jérôme, vol. I, 297–306 ed anche in *J. N. D. Kelly*, Jerome, 263–272. Per le questioni relative alla cronologia della corrispondenza tra Girolamo e Agostino si veda F. Cavallera, Saint Jérôme, vol. II, 47–50. Alla seconda fase della corrispondenza tra Girolamo ed Agostino, databile tra il 415 e il 419 – cioè mentre infuriava la controversia con Pelagio – appartengono 7 lettere superstiti, 3 di Agostino e 4 di Girolamo. Per i rapporti tra Girolamo e Agostino si consulti: *A. Fürst*, Art. Hieronymus, in: Augustinus-Lexikon 3 (Basel – Stuttgart 2005) 317–336.

[33] Hier., Ep. 131, 6: I. Hilberg, CSEL 56/1 (Wien 1996), p. 207. I riferimenti sono ad *Adv. Iov.* 2, 2 e *CIon.* 3, 5.

bra essere ben acclimatata nella riflessione di Girolamo, almeno fino a questo punto del suo percorso.

Con l'*Epistula* 133 Girolamo, assegnata al 414, prende vigorosamente posizione contro la dottrina di Pelagio, anche se il nome di quest'ultimo non viene mai menzionato nella missiva; i suoi errori sono invece illustrati e redarguiti a vantaggio di Ctesifonte, il destinatario della lettera, che si era rivolto allo Stridonense proprio per avere chiarimenti riguardo a uno dei temi più cari alla predicazione pelagiana, quello dell'impeccanza, cioè della possibilità per l'uomo di vivere senza peccato. In questo scritto di grande impegno polemico, il nome di Adamo compare solo una volta, ma in un contesto ben diverso da quello che ci si potrebbe attendere: Girolamo, traendo profitto da una panoplia di citazioni paoline, lascia intendere infatti – come già altre volte – che è la corporeità, con le sue irrefrenabili pulsioni, il fomite che costantemente induce gli uomini a peccare tanto che questi, una o l'altra volta, finiscono con il peccare effettivamente[34]. Non si deve però per questo cadere nell'errore manicheo di ritenere malvagia la corporeità: la carne è debole perché così è stata creata e nessuno ha il diritto di chiedere a Dio perché ha inserito nella costituzione della creatura umana un elemento così fragile e al contempo indocile. A chi osasse porre queste domande inopportune Girolamo si affretta a opporre il riferimento all'imperscrutabilità della volontà di Dio, che nessuno deve pretendere di sondare dal momento che molte cose restano per l'uomo oscure; tra queste quella che suscitava la curiosità di Porfirio, cioè il motivo per cui Dio ha sopportato che i pagani, da Adamo fino a Cristo, perissero ignorano la legge e i comandamenti[35]. In questo contesto il progenitore è menzionato solo come *terminus a quo* per indicare la creazione, che si pone ben prima della rivelazione mosaica (che però aveva dato la Legge solo agli Ebrei) e ancor più di quella cristiana, che si è rivolta anche ai pagani prima esclusi: non viene posta invece nessuna correlazione tra la sua colpa e la condizione non felicissima dei suoi discendenti, divisi tra il desiderio di evitare il male e l'impossibilità di riuscirci.

Il *Dialogus adversus Pelagianos*, di poco posteriore all'*Epistula* 133, è una più ampia risposta a quelli che Girolamo percepiva come gli errori di Pelagio

---

[34] Hier., Ep. 133, 8: I. Hilberg, CSEL 56/1 (Wien 1996), p. 252–254.
[35] Hier., Ep. 133, 9: I. Hilberg, CSEL 56/1 (Wien 1996), p. 254–256.

Il peccato di Adamo in Girolamo 233

e dei suoi sodali[36]. Esso si può macroscopicamente suddividere in tre parti[37]: la prima parte riprende gli argomenti già trattati nell'*Epistula* 133 integrandoli con la confutazione di alcune proposizioni tratte dal *Testimoniorum liber* di Pelagio[38]; la seconda è costituita da un ampio *excursus* scritturistico con cui Girolamo intende dimostrare, Bibbia alla mano, che l'uomo non può essere senza peccato; la terza parte dell'opera consiste infine nell'approfondimento di alcuni temi già trattati in precedenza e nella proposizione di tematiche nuove, quali quelle connesse al battesimo e ai suoi effetti; proprio qui si troveranno alcuni spunti interessanti per il tema affrontato in questo contributo.

Intanto già nella seconda parte, per comprovare che anche i giusti non sono privi di qualche colpa sia quando ancora si trovano nel grembo materno (e qui si cita Ps 57, 4) che dal momento della nascita si menziona Adamo facendo un riferimento a Rom 5, 14: tutti gli esseri umani, a somiglianza della prevaricazione di Adamo (*in similitudinem praevaricationis Adae*), sono stato sottomessi al peccato[39]. Purtroppo, non viene spiegato da che cosa dipenda questa diffusa peccaminosità: in ogni caso Girolamo non la connette esplicitamente al peccato di Adamo. Subito dopo viene citato Ex 13, 2; 34, 1 (*Omnis qui aperit vulvam, sanctus vocabitur Domino*) e si spiega che questo versetto deve essere inteso solo di Cristo, nato verginalmente da Maria; insorge dunque il sospetto che una certa colpevolezza sia da connettersi alla generazione sessuata, circostanza che non riguarda Cristo, il santo per eccellenza.

Nel corso della terza parte il peccato di Adamo torna ancora nel momento in cui si tratta un tema particolarmente difficile, cioè quello della relazione tra la prescienza di Dio e la libertà dell'uomo; si chiede infatti se, dal momento che Dio conosceva in anticipo e da sempre che Adamo, Saul e Giuda avrebbero

---

[36] A. Canellis, La composition du Dialogue contre les Lucifériens et du Dialogue contre les Pélagiens de saint Jérôme. A la recherche d'un canon de l'altercatio, REA 43 (1997) 250–255, ha difeso l'ipotesi che il titolo dell'opera geroniminiana doveva essere *Altercatio* (o, meno probabilmente, *Dialogus*) *Attici et Critobuli*. Sul *Dialogus* in genere si veda B. Jeanjean, Le Dialogus Attici et Critobuli de Jérôme et la predication pelagienne, in: A. Cain, J. Lössl (eds.), Jerome of Stridon. His life, writings and legacy (Farnham – Burlington 2009) 59–71; per il problema del titolo originale p. 64, n. 19. Malgrado ciò, si continuerà ad usare qui la titolazione ormai vulgata.
[37] La suddivisione qui proposta è solo parzialmente coincidente con quella in tre libri e si articola come segue: CoPelag. 1, 1–33 (prima parte); CoPelag. 1, 33–2, 40 (seconda parte) e CoPelag. 3 (terza parte).
[38] Il *Testimoniorum Liber* era costituito da una serie di affermazioni di Pelagio corroborate da citazioni scritturistiche. Si veda in proposito: G. Caruso, Il Testimoniorum liber di Pelagio tra Girolamo e Agostino, in: A. Bartolomei Romagnoli, U. Paoli, P. Piatti (eds.), Hagiologica. Studi per Réginald Grégoire, vol. I (Fabriano 2012) 357–373.
[39] Hier., CoPelag. 2, 4: C. Moreschini, CCL 80 (Turnhout 1990), p. 57,22–27.

peccato, le azioni di questi possano davvero ritenersi libere. Girolamo spiega che Dio, pur conoscendo in anticipo le scelte dell'uomo, non per questo le determina: in altre parole, il Creatore sa quello che la creatura farà *sua sponte*, senza essere condizionata dalla prescienza divina[40].

Nella terza parte del *Dialogus*, avviandosi alla conclusione del suo scritto, Girolamo introduce il tema del battesimo dei bambini correlandolo a quello della colpa ereditata da Adamo. Quando Critobulo, cioè il pelagiano, afferma che gli infanti sono senza peccato perché incapaci di peccare, Attico, il portavoce di Girolamo, gli risponde che lo sono solo i bambini battezzati e solo per un dono della grazia senza la quale sarebbero, ne consegue, colpevoli[41]. Ma di quale colpa? Girolamo a questo punto dichiara a chiare lettere che essi sono ritenuti colpevoli del peccato commesso da Adamo in paradiso: da cui i pargoli nel battesimo vengono liberati solo da questo peccato, mentre per gli adulti si devono aggiungere all'antica colpa i peccati personali[42].

Duval ritiene con ottime ragioni che l'introduzione di questo specifico tema nel contesto antipelagiano sia stato suggerito a Girolamo dalla lettura degli scritti antipelagiani di Agostino intrapresa quando la composizione del *Dialogus* era già a buon punto; in effetti si deve osservare che la tematica pedobattesimale è assente in tutti gli altri scritti geronimiani che è possibile datare a prima del *Dialogus*[43]. Del resto, nella conclusione del suo scritto dialogico, Girolamo chiama esplicitamente in causa l'Ipponense elencando alcuni scritti composti da quello in opposizione a Pelagio: si tratta del *De peccatorum meritis et remissione et de baptismo parvulorum*, indirizzato a Marcellino, e della *Lettera* 157 a Ilario di Siracusa; inoltre afferma di aver anche sentito parlare di un altro testo scritto contro Pelagio, che però non è in suo possesso: si tratta probabilmente del *De natura et gratia*[44].

I *Tractatus in Psalmos* furono restituiti all'attenzione degli studiosi, nel passaggio tra il XIX e il XX secolo, dal dotto benedettino Germain Morin che ne pubblicò 59 nel 1897 (insieme ad altre omelie di argomento diverso)[45] e poi, nel 1903, diede alle stampe altre 15 omelie[46].

---

[40] *Hier.*, CoPelag. 3, 6: C. Moreschini, CCL 80 (Turnhout 1990), p. 105,40–42.
[41] *Hier.*, CoPelag. 3, 17: C. Moreschini, CCL 80 (Turnhout 1990), p. 121, 15–19.
[42] *Hier.*, CoPelag. 3, 18: C. Moreschini, CCL 80 (Turnhout 1990), p. 122, 4–14.
[43] Y.-M. Duval, Saint Augustine et le Commentaire sur Jonas de Saint Jérôme, REA 12 (1966) 9–40; si vedano particolarmente le pagine 14 e 21.
[44] *Hier.*, CoPelag. 3, 19: C. Moreschini, CCL 80 (Turnhout 1990), p. 123–124.
[45] *Hier.*, Tractatus sive homiliae in Psalmos, in Marci evangelium aliaque varia argumenta: G. Morin, Anecdota Maredsolana III, 2 (Maredsoli - Oxoniae 1897), p. 1–316.
[46] *Hier.*, Tractatus sive homiliae in Psalmos quattuordecim: G. Morin, Anecdota Maredsolana III, 3 (Maredsoli - Oxoniae 1903), p. 1–94. Entrambe le serie di omelie sui salmi, insieme

Secondo Morin – la cui tesi ha fatto scuola – Girolamo predicò queste omelie a Betlemme, nella sua comunità monastica, tra il 401 e il 410[47]; Alessandro Capone ha ampliato, con sagaci osservazioni, questa finestra temporale portandola almeno dal 389 fino a dopo il 410[48]: a chi scrive sembra che, almeno per qualche omelia, si debba necessariamente proporre una datazione posteriore proprio in relazione al modo in cui viene trattato il tema del peccato adamitico, come si vedrà nel seguito.

Commentando per il suo uditorio il Salmo 78 Girolamo afferma di desiderare il ritorno nel paradiso dal quale Adamo è stato scacciato e, insieme a lui, tutti gli uomini (*in Adam omnes nos de paradiso eiecti sumus*)[49]; se le modalità dell'allontanamento forzoso del progenitore sono agevoli da comprendere, lo sono molto meno quelle dei i suoi discendenti. Nell'*Omelia sul Salmo 81* l'idea torna, ma con un supplemento di spiegazione; commentando in versetto 7 di quel componimento (*vos autem sicut homines moriemini*), facendo anche riferimento al testo ebraico da lui ritenuto preferibile e nel quale si menziona il progenitore (*vos autem sicut Adam moriemini*), Girolamo sembra stabilire una connessione tra la cacciata dal paradiso e la condizione di mortali, quasi che la seconda sia l'interpretazione della prima[50]; di contro, quando commenta il Salmo 114, lo Stridonense afferma che tutti gli uomini erano stati posti,

---

ad altri testi omiletici, si possono leggere in: *Hier.*, Tractatus sive homiliae in Psalmos, in Marci evangelium aliaque varia argumenta: G. Morin, CCL 78 (Turnholti 1958). Morin ha affermato e dimostrato la paternità geronimiana delle omelie, addirittura prima della loro pubblicazione (per la prima serie: G. *Morin*, Les monuments de la prédication de saint Jérôme, Revue d'histoire et de littérature religieuses 1 (1896) 393–434; per la seconda: G. *Morin*, Quatorze nouveaux discours inédits de saint Jérôme sur les Psaumes, Revue bénédictine 19 (1902) 113–144. Invece V. *Peri*, Omelie origeniane sui salmi. Contributo all'identificazione del testo latino (Città del Vaticano 1980), ritiene che esse siano traduzioni, sia pure riadattate, di omelie origeniane; del medesimo parere è stato il primo traduttore delle stesse in italiano: G. *Coppa*, Origene-Girolamo, 74 omelie sul libro dei salmi (Milano 1993). La tesi di Peri è stata contrastata da P. *Jay*, Jérôme à Bethléem: les Tractatus in psalmos, in: Y.-M. Duval (ed.), Jérôme entre l'Occident et l'Orient. XVI centenaire du départ de saint Jérôme de Rome et de son installation à Bethléem (Paris 1988) 367–380 e definitivamente confutata da A. *Capone*, «Folia vero in verbis sunt»: parola divina e lingua umana nei Tractatus in psalmos attribuiti a Gerolamo, Adamantius 19 (2013) 437–456, anche in seguito alla felice scoperta di Marina Molin Pradel che nel 2012 ha rinvenuto, nel codice *Monac. Gr.* 314, il testo delle *Omelie sui salmi* di Origene (per queste si veda: L. Perrone, M. Molin Pradel, E. Prinzivalli, A. Cacciari, Origenes Werke. XIII. Die neuen Psalmenhomilien. Eine kritische Edition des Codex Monacensis Graecus 314, GCS N.F. 19 (Berlin – München – Boston 2015).

[47] G. Morin, Les monuments, 409.
[48] A. Capone, Girolamo. 59 omelie sui Salmi (1–115). Omelia sul Salmo 41 ai neofiti (Roma 2018) 13–14.
[49] *Hier.*, Tr59Ps. 78, 11: G. Morin, CCL 78 (Turnhout 1958), p. 75,34–36.
[50] *Hier.*, Tr59Ps. 81, 7: G. Morin, CCL 78 (Turnhout 1958), p. 86–87.

insieme ad Adamo, nel paradiso (*omnes cum Adam in paradiso posuit*) e che ne sono stati scacciati per una scelta personale di ciascuno (*nostro arbitrio a beatitudine illa cecidimus*)[51]; in questo caso sembra che la condizione paradisiaca si perda in ragione delle colpe personali e quindi non risulta più chiaro più quali conseguenze abbia avuto il peccato di Adamo sulla sua posterità.

Con quanto fin qui detto concorda un'affermazione che si legge nella *series altera* dei *Tractatus* geronimiani, cioè in quelli che furono scoperti e pubblicati nel 1903. Commentando il Salmo 88 Girolamo afferma che gli uomini sono stati scacciati dal paradiso a causa della colpa di Adamo[52], quasi che tutti siano stati solidali con il progenitore, anche se non si dice se questa solidarietà sia stata deliberata o in qualche misura subita. Nel *Tractatus* sul Salmo 89, invece, si dice a chiare lettere che tutti gli uomini hanno suscitato l'ira di Dio con i peccati personali (*quia iram tuam per peccata meruimus*), ma che in Adamo, cioè in conseguenza della sua colpa, hanno perso l'immortalità (*immortalitatem quam dederas perdidimus in Adam*) e che in qualche modo naturale, per diritto di eredità, è stato trasmesso a tutti il suo peccato (*a quo nobis quasi naturaliter peccatum ereditario iure dimissum est*)[53]. L'idea di un peccato ereditato da Adamo, come si è visto, non è comune in Girolamo e fa la sua prima comparsa nel *Dialogus adversus Pelagianos* (precisamente in 3, 18), dopo che lo Stridonense ha letto gli scritti di Agostino: non sembra pertanto impossibile sostenere che anche il *Tractatus in Psalmum* 89 della *series altera* sia posteriore al 415.

Resta inteso che anche se per Girolamo la colpa del protoplasto ha avuto delle conseguenze per i suoi discendenti, primo fra tutti la mortalità, l'idea di un peccato trasmesso dal progenitore alla posterità – che compare molto tardi e raramente nei suoi scritti – sembra essere mutuata dalla riflessione dell'Ipponense.

---

[51] *Hier.*, Tr59Ps. 114, 7: G. Morin, CCL 78 (Turnhout 1958), p. 237.
[52] *Hier.*, TrPs. 88, 6: G. Morin, CCL 78 (Turnhout 1958), p. 409,53-58.
[53] *Hier.*, TrPs. 89, 7: G. Morin, CCL 78 (Turnhout 1958), p. 417.

Franz Mali, Freiburg (Schweiz)

„Die zerrissene Tunica der Unsterblichkeit wurde von Christus wieder zusammengenäht". Zur Erlösung von Adams Sünde durch Christus im *Opus imperfectum in Matthaeum*

Abstract:
The author of the Opus imperfectum in Matthaeum *emphasises the fact that human was created good by God. It is only through the penetration of evil that the good or good substance diminishes, causing human to lose his immortality and mortality to enter. The devil's temptation was first followed by Eve and then by Adam: through this transgression of God's commandment resp. this sin, the good in human diminished. This inferior state resulting the arch-parents' sin is shown in the subsequent* corruptibilitas *and* mortalitas *of the flesh (*caro*) of the human being, which is passed on to all descendants. Only through the baptism of Christ is it possible for all who descend into the baptismal waters as "carnal children of Adam the sinner" to ascend as "spiritual children of God". It is Christ who sewed the tunic of immortality back together.*

Vorspann

Dieses Werk eines unbekannten Autors mit dem üblichen Titel *Opus imperfectum in Matthaeum* wird in den mittelalterlichen Handschriften immer Johannes Chrysostomus zugeschrieben. Obwohl es der umfangreichste lateinische Kommentar zum Matthäusevangelium aus patristischer Zeit ist, ist er entweder nur unvollständig verfasst oder nur teilweise überliefert. Er dürfte wohl in der ersten Hälfte des 5. Jahrhunderts von einem arianischen Autor verfasst worden sein. Lokalisiert wird der Verfasser von den meisten Forschenden in den römischen Donauprovinzen oder auf dem nördlichen Balkan.

Einleitung

Manlio Simonetti, einer der berühmten Kenner des *Opus imperfectum in Matthaeum*, hält in einem umfangreichen Beitrag 1969 fest:

Aber nirgends im *Opus in Mt.* wird ausdrücklich Adam für den gegenwärtigen Zustand des Fleisches verantwortlich gemacht, das so anfällig für das Böse und die Sünde ist; niemals wird dieses Merkmal des Menschen als eine Folge der Sünde des Stammvaters betrachtet[1].

Joseph Hugh Crehan geht in einem Artikel aus dem Jahr 1970 noch deutlich weiter und stellt lapidar fest, dass der Autor, wer auch immer er war, engen Kontakt zu den Pelagianern gehabt haben muss, weil ihm jede Idee von der Erbsünde beinahe gänzlich fehle[2].

Und Joop van Banning, wohl der beste Kenner des *Opus imperfectums in Matthaeum*, schreibt in seiner im Jahr 1983 abgeschlossenen und bisher nur in Teilen publizierten Dissertation zusammenfassend, dass alle Autoren bis anhin mit dieser Meinung Crehans übereinstimmen[3]. Er selber aber widerspricht Crehan und Simonetti, wenn er schreibt:

> Contrary to the view of several scholars, Original Sin (*sic*) is recognized by the *Opus Imp.* in many places[4].

Und er widmet dieser Frage einen kleinen Abschnitt, der sehr aufschlussreich ist. Allerdings, so denke ich, kann man dieser Frage noch gründlicher nachgehen und mehrere Anspielungen des Verfassers des *Opus imperfectums* untersuchen, mit deren Hilfe sich ein differenziertes Bild erstellen lässt. Auch wenn sich der Ausdruck „*peccatum originale*" bei unserem Verfasser nirgends findet, werden wir sehen, dass er sehr wohl ein Verständnis davon hat. Zu klären ist allerdings, inwieweit man von „inherited sin", also von „ererbter Sünde" reden kann.

---

[1] M. *Simonetti*, Note sull'Opus imperfectum in Mathaeum, StMed 3. Ser. 10/1 (1969) 117–200, hier 150: „Conseguenza del peccato di Adamo è stata la preclusione del regno dei cieli per l'uomo fino alla venuta di Cristo e la perdita della immortalità, che l'uomo riacquisterà soltanto alla fine del mondo: 659d, 812b, 925d. Ma in nessun punto dell'*Opus in Mt.* viene riportata esplicitamente alla responsabilità di Adamo l'attuale condizione della carne così propensa al male ed al peccato; mai questo carattere dell'uomo viene considerato conseguenza del peccato del progenitore. Tutt'al più il peccato di Adamo è considerato come prototipo, paradigma di ogni peccato (669a); e Adamo come modello dell'uomo peccatore".

[2] J. H. *Crehan*, Sinful Marriage in the Pseudo-Chrysostom, in: P. Granfield – J. A. Jungmann (Hgg.), Kyriakon. Festschrift für Johannes Quasten, Vol I (Münster 1970) 490–498, hier 491: „What no one seems to have observed is that the writer, whoever he was, must have had close contacts with the Pelagians, for he is almost completely lacking in an idea of Original Sin".

[3] J. H. A. *van Banning*, The Opus imperfectum in Matthaeum: Its provenance, theology and influence, D. Phil. Thesis (Oxford 1983) 229: „All the authors up to now have agreed with Father Crehan on the point that our work is ‚completely lacking in an idea of Original Sin'".

[4] Ibid., 6.

I. Der Mensch ist unsterblich geschaffen bzw. nach dem unvergänglichen Bild seines Schöpfers

1. Die Welt ist von Gott als gute Welt geschaffen

Trotz der recht pessimistischen Sicht des Autors des *OIM*, hält er fest, dass die Welt von Gott als gute Welt geschaffen worden ist:

> Denn die Welt selbst gehört nicht von Natur aus dem Teufel, sondern aufgrund von Verführung; nicht von Beginn an machte der Teufel diese Welt, sondern Gott. Später wurde sie durch Verführung zum Eigentum des Teufels. Also gehört die Welt selbst Gott; die Verführung aber gehört zur Welt des Teufels. [...] Soweit wir jetzt leben, leben wir in der Welt Gottes; so weit wird aber sündigen, sündigen wir in der Welt des Teufels[5].

Der Verfasser des *OIM* sieht zunächst den Urstand der Welt als gut, da diese Welt von Gott als gute erschaffen ist. Erst in einem zweiten Schritt (*postea*) gerät ein Teil dieser guten Welt durch die Verführung des Teufels unter dessen Herrschaft, die eine Parallelwelt darstellt. Somit lebt der Mensch seit dem ersten Sündenfall in einem Miteinander von Welt Gottes, der das Leben ist und gibt, und Welt des Teufels, der das Gute vernichtet und das Leben nimmt.

2. Die Gottebenbildlichkeit des Menschen ist unzerstörbar

In der Auslegung des Dialogs Jesu über die kaiserliche Steuer überträgt der Verfasser des *OIM* den Vergleich mit dem Bild des Kaisers auf die Gottebenbildlichkeit des Menschen:

> Das Bild Gottes ist nicht in Gold gezeichnet, sondern in Menschen dargestellt. Die Münze des Kaisers ist Gold, die Münze Gottes ist der Mensch. Auf den Solidi sieht man den Kaiser, in den Menschen wird Gott erkannt[6].

---

[5] *OIM*, hom. 29: PG 56, 786: *Nam et ipse mundus non natura diaboli est, sed corruptione. Nec ab initio fecit hunc mundum diabolus, sed Deus: postea corruptione factus est diaboli. Ergo mundus quidem ipse Dei est: corruptio autem mundi diaboli est. [...] Nunc quod vivimus, in Dei mundo vivimus: quod autem peccamus, in diaboli mundo peccamus.* Die deutsche Übersetzung des *OIM* ist unsere eigene.

[6] *OIM*, hom. 42: PG 56, 867: *Imago Dei non est in auro depicta, sed in hominibus figurata. Numisma Caesaris, aurum est: numisma Dei, homo. In solidis Caesar videtur, in hominibus Deus agnoscitur.*

Dieses Bild Gottes im Menschen ist unvergänglich: der Mensch soll dieses Bild seines Schöpfers durch die Pflege der Tugenden und durch das Vermeiden der Laster unvergänglich erhalten[7].

Und dieses Ebenbild Gottes im Menschen ist ohne Schuld bzw. unschuldig; diese Unschuld ist im Gewissen des Menschen angesiedelt, denn unser Verfasser ruft dazu auf, diese „*innocentia*" zu bewahren: „Bewahrt für Gott als einzige die Unschuld eures Gewissens, in der Gott erscheint"[8].

Der Mensch trägt die unsterbliche Seele, die von Gott geschaffen ist, als „himmlischen Schatz" in sich und die „himmlische Weisheit in einem irdenen Gefäss" (cf. 2 Kor 4, 7). Wegen dieses Schatzes versucht der Teufel den Menschen zu verführen und zu korrumpieren, um ihm das „Heil seiner Seele und das wohlgefällige Wesen seines Herzens" zu zerstören[9].

3. Der Mensch ist im Anfang gut geschaffen

Für unseren anonymen Autor ist klar, dass alles von Gott Geschaffene gut ist und deshalb Substanz ist:

> Jedes Gute ist lebendige Substanz, und ist Leben, das Leben aber ist Christus. Jedes Böse hingegen ist ohne Substanz, und ist nichts. Was auch immer also lebendig geschaffen worden ist auf der Erde, lebt aus dem Leben. Und nichts kann nämlich lebendig sein, in dem nicht der Geist des Lebens ist[10].

Der lebendige Mensch ist von Anfang an gut geschaffen, denn Gott hat ihn auf die Erde gestellt, damit er „aus dem Leben lebe", denn alles von Gott Geschaffene, das lebt, hat den Lebensgeist in sich. Da das Böse keine Substanz ist,

---

[7] OIM, hom. 42: PG 56, 868: *Ita qui vitare horrenda exitia cupit, incorruptam studeat auctoris sui imaginem conservare, quatenus cum suam, quam formavit, requisierit Deus imaginem, salvam et immunem ab inimici infectionibus cernens, suo collocet gremio, angelorumque choris admiscens, perpetuis faciat caelorum gaudiis perfrui.*
[8] OIM, hom. 42: PG 56, 867: *Deo autem conscientiae vestrae solam innocentiam reservate, ubi Deus videtur.*
[9] OIM, hom. 27: PG 56, 774: *Sic et diabolus videns hominem habentem in se thesaurum caelestem, id est, animam immortalem a Deo creatam, sapientiam caelestem in arca terrena positam, ideo ostendit illi aurum et argentum [...] ut per hoc subjugans eum voluptatibus suis, auferat salutem animae ejus, et corrumpat gratiam cordis ipsius.*
[10] OIM, hom. 41: PG 56, 859: *Omne bonum viva substantia est, et vita est, vita autem est Christus. Omne autem malum sine substantia est, et nihil est. Ita quidquid vivum creatum est super terram, ex vita vivit. Nec enim potest esse aliquid vivum, in quo non sit spiritus vitae* (cf. Röm 8, 2).

kann aus dem Bösen auch nichts entstehen[11]. Das Böse selbst kann auch nichts verlieren, sondern es verringert und vernichtet das Gute, in dem es wohnt:

> Von jener Sache, in der Böses ist, zieht sich das Gute ab, weil in ihr Böses wohnt. Und wenn so das Gute weniger wird, bewegt sich die Sache zum Nichts hin (*res vadit ad nihilum*). Eine Sache also, in der nur Gutes ist, ist lebendig und unsterblich (*viva et immortalis*)[12].

Der Mensch ist demnach ursprünglich, d.h. so wie Gott ihn im Ursprung vollkommen gut geschaffen hat und bevor Böses in ihn eingedrungen ist, in vollem Sinne „lebendig und unsterblich" (*vivus et immortalis*).

Erst nachdem Böses in das Gute eindringt, verringert sich das Gute in dieser Sache und die Endlichkeit oder Sterblichkeit zieht ein: Unser Autor schreibt weiter:

> Eine Sache, in der allerdings sowohl Gutes als auch Böses wohnt, lebt zwar eine Zeitlang, weil in ihr Gutes wohnt, sie stirbt aber, weil in ihr Böses wohnt, und sie ist eine sterbliche Sache, wie der Mensch[13].

Mit dem Einzug des Bösen vermindert sich das Gute, und die Unsterblichkeit geht verloren. Diese Sache wird sterblich. Als Beispiel nennt er den Menschen, der sterblich ist.

Doch unser Verfasser zieht aus dieser Tatsache sogleich einen moralischen Schluss, wenn er daraus folgt:

> Der Mensch ist also aus Gutem und Bösem geschaffen (*creatus*), damit er nach der Versuchung durch das Böse dem Guten folgt, und dadurch den Lohn der Erwählung erhält[14].

---

[11] OIM, hom. 41: PG 56, 859: *Ex malo autem nulla res esse potest. Cum vero ipsum malum nihil sit, quomodo potest facere rem aliquam esse?* Diese Feststellung kann auch als eine polemische Spitze gegen den Manichäismus verstanden werden.

[12] OIM, hom. 41: PG 56, 859: [*Tamen perdere potest, sed non ipsum malum perdet rem, sed*] *de illa re, in qua est malum, subtrahit se bonum propter inhabitans malum in ea: et sic bono recedente, res vadit ad nihilum. Ergo res, in qua solum bonum est, viva et immortalis est.*

[13] OIM, hom. 41: PG 56, 859: *in qua* [*re*] *autem et bonum et malum habitat, vivit quidem, tamen pro tempore propter inhabitans bonum, moritur autem propter inhabitans malum, et est res mortalis, sicut homo.*

[14] OIM, hom. 41: PG 56, 859: *Homo autem ideo ex bono et malo creatus est, ut contempto malo, sequatur bonum, et per hoc habeat electionis mercedem.* [*Quod si contempto bono, sequutus fuerit malum, suscipiet eum aeternus interitus. Si autem, dimisso malo, sequutus fuerit bonum, in morte natura carnis ejus solvetur ab omni malo: et cum resurrectio facta fuerit sanctorum, tunc suscipiet eum sola vita, quae est Christus, et mortalitatem ejus in sua immortalitate absorbebit*] (cf. 1 Kor 15, 55).

Aus dem Vorangegangenen geht klar hervor, dass unser Verfasser nicht annimmt, dass der Mensch aus einem bösen und einem guten Prinzip heraus entstanden ist oder aus einer guten und einer bösen Substanz zusammengesetzt ist, sondern dass im Menschen die Möglichkeit zur Verminderung des Guten angelegt ist, wenn sein Wille der Versuchung durch das Böse nachgibt, d.h. die Verringerung des Guten akzeptiert und dadurch an guter Substanz einbüsst.

Aus dieser neuplatonischen Lehre vom Bösen als Nicht-Sein folgt auch der Gedankengang für das Ende:

> Wenn er (der Mensch) in Missachtung des Guten dem Bösen gefolgt ist, wird ihn der ewige Untergang empfangen[15].

Dem Bösen zu folgen heisst also, konsequent die Verringerung bzw. die Vernichtung des Guten voranzutreiben, bis nichts mehr bleibt bzw. alles im buchstäblichen Sinn vernichtet ist.

Diese Möglichkeit zur Verringerung sieht unser Autor im Fleisch angesiedelt, wenn er zwischen dem Ziel der Schöpfung von Fleisch und Seele unterscheidet:

> Das Fleisch ist uns zur Versuchung geschaffen, die Seele hingegen zum Heil[16].

Auf seine Art folgt unser Verfasser der Unterscheidung gemäss der Anthropologie des Johannesevangeliums:

> Wenn jemand nicht aus dem Wasser und dem Geist geboren wird, kann er das Reich Gottes nicht erben. Was aus dem Fleisch geboren ist, das ist Fleisch; was aus dem Geist geboren ist, das ist Geist[17].

Insofern ist die Erklärung des *OIM* weniger eine Aussage über den Urstand des Menschen, als vielmehr eine Auslegung der Verse des Johannesevangeliums über den Weg zum Heil[18].

---

[15] OIM, hom. 41: PG 56, 859: *Quod si contempto bono, sequutus fuerit malum, suscipiet eum aeternus interitus.*
[16] OIM, hom. 12: PG 56, 695: *caro ad tentationem nobis creata est, anima autem ad salutem.*
[17] Joh 3, 5–6.
[18] Vgl. auch Paulus: 1 Kor 15, 50: „Fleisch und Blut können das Reich Gottes nicht erben; das Verwesliche erbt nicht das Unverwesliche".

II. Adam und Eva haben gesündigt

1. Adam und Eva haben sich zur Sünde verführen lassen

In der Auslegung der Perikope von der Frau des Zebedäus, die für ihre beiden Söhne Jakobus und Johannes um die Plätze links und rechts von Jesus in seinem Reich bittet (Mt 20, 20–28), kommt unser Verfasser auf die Rolle der Frauen zu sprechen. Er unterstreicht, dass der Teufel nicht mittels der Jünger Jesus bedrängen wollte, sondern mittels der „bewährten Waffe der Frauen", durch die er auch schon Adam seinerzeit blossgestellt hatte[19]: Denn auch im Paradies schaffte es der Teufel nicht, Adam zu verführen. Nicht Adam, sondern Eva wurde durch den Teufel verführt, sie,

> die, als sie vom Baum kostete, allein verführt wurde und den Tod gebar. Adam aber nahm nicht an dieser Verführung durch den Teufel teil; nicht als einer, der vom Teufel verführt worden war, sündigte er, sondern weil er der Frau zugestimmt hatte[20].

Der Verfasser des *OIM* hebt hervor, dass in diesen beiden Fällen es Frauen sind, die zunächst der Verführung durch den Teufel erliegen, um dann für die nächste Verführung instrumentalisiert zu werden.

Doch in der Erklärung von Mt 24, 23 über die Versuchungen der Endzeit unterstreicht unser Verfasser,

> dass der Teufel die Art der Versuchung nicht in den Menschen hineinträgt, sondern dass er den Wunsch eines jeden betrachtet, und aus dem, was er den Menschen sich wünschen sieht, entnimmt er die Gelegenheit zur Versuchung: […] Adam und Eva verführte er durch das Versprechen der Göttlichkeit, als er sah, dass sie die Liebe zum Göttlich-Sein hatten[21].

---

[19] OIM, hom. 35: PG 56, 826–827: *Vidit enim diabolus, quia per illos ipsos adversus eos agere non valebat; contulit se ad consueta arma mulierum, ut sicut Adam per mulierem spoliavit [diabolus], ita et istos separaret per matrem.*

[20] OIM, hom. 1: PG 56, 634: *Sicut enim tunc mulier gustans de ligno, sola seducta est, et peperit mortem; Adam autem non fuit particeps in seductione illius; non enim a diabolo seductus peccavit, sed quia consensit mulieri.*

[21] OIM, hom. 49: PG 56, 915: *[Aliquoties diximus,] quod diabolus non ingerat genus tentationis in hominem, sed desiderium uniuscujusque considerat, et secundum quod viderit hominem desiderantem aliquid, ex eo accipit occasionem tentandi. Unde et Christum cum esurientem sensisset, tentavit in fame. Et Adam et Hevam cum vidisset divinitatis amorem habentes, divinitatis promissione seduxit.*

Der Mensch, Adam, ist nach dem *OIM* ins Paradies gesetzt gewesen, um es zu pflegen und zu bearbeiten. Da aber Adam das unterlassen hat, wurde er aus dem Paradies hinausgeworfen[22].

2. Die Vergänglichkeit (*corruptibilitas*) und Sterblichkeit (*mortalitas*) geht auf alle Kinder Adams über, erben alle Kinder Adams

Wie schon oben erwähnt, geht durch die Vermengung von Gutem und Bösem die Unvergänglichkeit verloren – Dinge werden vergänglich. So auch der Mensch.

In der Kommentierung der Taufperikope Mt 3, 13ss (hom. 4) nennt unser Autor alle Täuflinge „Söhne Adams, des Sünders".

> Alle nämlich, die als fleischliche und Söhne/Kinder Adams, des Sünders, ins Wasser hinuntergestiegen sind, steigen sofort aus dem Wasser herauf als geistliche Menschen, die zu Söhnen/Kindern Gottes gemacht geworden sind[23].

Alle Menschen sind Kinder Adams und deshalb auch Sünder. Jene, die sich taufen lassen, steigen zwar als Sünder ins Wasser hinab, steigen aber daraus herauf als Kinder Gottes.

In der Auslegung der Versuchungen Jesu (Mt 4, 1ss.) legt unser Verfasser dar, dass er fünf Arten von Taufe kennt: die Taufe im Wort, die Taufe im Wasser, die Taufe im Geist, die Taufe im Feuer und die Taufe im Tod[24]. Für jede Art zitiert er einen biblischen Beleg. Für die Taufe im Tod gibt er Röm 6, 7 an: „Wer nämlich gestorben ist, ist gerechtfertigt von der Sünde"[25]. Und er setzt fort:

---

[22] OIM, hom. 34: PG 56, 817: *Adam enim positus est in paradiso, colere et operari eam: sed quia neglexit eam, projectus est de ea.*
[23] OIM, hom. 4: PG 56, 658: [*Puto autem factum Christi ad mysterium pertinere omnium qui post modum fuerant baptizandi: ideo dixit, Confestim, et non dixit, Egressus est, sed Ascendit: quia omnes, qui digne secundum omnia membra justitiae formati et consummati baptizantur in Christo, confestim de aqua ascendunt: id est, proficiunt ad virtutes, et ad dignitatem sublevantur caelestem.*] *Qui enim ingressi fuerant in aquam carnales et filii Adam peccatoris, confestim de aqua ascendunt spirituales filii Dei facti.*
[24] OIM, hom. 5: PG 56, 661: *Constat in nobis quinque baptismata esse. Unum in verbo* […]. *Secundum in aqua,* […]. *Tertium in spiritu* […]. *Quartum vere in igne* […]. *Quintum in morte* […].
[25] Röm 6, 7: *Qui enim mortuus est, justificatus est a peccato.*

Welche Sünde aber im Tod vergeben wird, weiss derjenige, der versteht, für welche Sünde der Tod eingeführt worden ist. Denn, wenn der Mensch an der Sünde stirbt, wird er ohne Zweifel davon erlöst, woran er stirbt[26].

Aus diesen beiden Stellen geht hervor, dass der Autor des *OIM* in jedem Menschen das Erbe Adams, des Sünders, erkennt: einerseits ist dies die Fleischlichkeit, d.h. die Sündhaftigkeit des Menschen, und andererseits ist dies die Sterblichkeit, die alle Menschen vom ersten Elternpaar geerbt haben, bzw. der Tod, dem alle Menschen unterliegen.

Nach Joop van Banning ist diese die einzige Stelle im *OIM*, die von der Erbsünde bzw. vom *peccatum originale* Adams explizit spricht[27].

III. Die ganze Welt steht unter der Macht des Bösen (1 Joh 5, 19)

Der Verfasser des *OIM* hat an vielen Stellen eine sehr negative Sicht der Welt, obwohl er – wie wir gesehen haben – bekräftigt, dass die Welt von Gott gut geschaffen worden ist. Aber die „*corruptio*", die Verführung durch den Teufel, hat so überhandgenommen, dass unser Autor zur Überzeugung gelangt, dass die ganze Welt dem Bösen unterworfen ist, wie er es dem ersten Johannesbrief (1 Joh 5, 19) entnimmt.

1. Vorstellung (*offerre*) der neugeborenen Kinder

In der Deutung der Perikope von der Segnung der Kinder durch Jesus (Mt 19, 13–15) kommt unser Verfasser zum Schluss, dass

> diese Stelle alle Eltern lehrt, ihre Kinder unaufhörlich den Priestern zu zeigen (*offerre*): Wenn sie sie nämlich den Priestern zeigen, zeigen sie sie Christus. Nicht der Priester nämlich legt die Hände auf, sondern Christus, in dessen Namen die Hände aufgelegt werden[28].

---

[26] OIM, hom. 5: PG 56, 661: *Quale autem peccatum in morte remittitur, scit qui intelligit pro quali peccato introducta est mors. Nam si propter peccatum moritur homo, sine dubio solvitur propter quod moritur.*

[27] J. H. A. van Banning, The Opus imperfectum in Matthaeum: Its provenance, theology and influence, D. Phil. Thesis (Oxford 1983) 188 n. 31: „This is the only point in the *Opus Imp.* where Original Sin is explicitly mentioned. It does not play a major role".

[28] OIM, hom. 32: PG 56, 805: *Praesens locus instruit omnes parentes, ut filios suos indesinenter sacerdotibus offerant: quia si sacerdotibus offerunt, offerunt Christo. Non enim sacerdos manus imponit, sed Christus, in cujus nomine manus imponitur.*

Und das *OIM* bemüht den Vergleich mit den Speisen, die vor dem Verzehr Gott vorgestellt werden müssen, damit sie „durch Gottes Wort und das Gebet" (1 Tim 4, 4–5) von jedem Makel gereinigt und geheiligt werden: „Um wieviel mehr müssen Knaben Gott vorgestellt und geheiligt werden?"[29].
Unser Autor schliesst daraus, dass auch die neugeborenen Kinder wie die Speisen unrein, d.h. mit Makel versehen sind, von denen sie „durch Gottes Wort und Gebet" gereinigt werden müssen. Seine Begründung für diese Anweisung bietet ihm der erste Johannesbrief (1 Joh 5, 19): *„Die ganze Welt ist dem Bösen unterworfen"*.

> Also ist auch jede körperliche Sache, weil sie Teil der Welt ist, dem Bösen unterworfen, und deshalb muss sie geheiligt werden. Folglich sind auch kleine Kinder, wenn sie geboren werden, und, insofern sie dem Fleisch angehören, dem Bösen unterworfen: weil eben jedes Fleisch als Teil der Welt dem Bösen unterworfen ist. Deshalb müssen die Kinder vorgestellt (Gott dargebracht) werden, damit über sie inständig das Gebet gesprochen wird[30].

Schon neugeborene Kinder unterliegen dem Gesetz, dass diese Welt dem Bösen unterworfen ist. Deshalb bedürfen sie der Reinigung und der Heiligung durch das Wort Gottes und das Gebet.

An dieser Stelle nennt unser Verfasser zwar nicht Adam als Auslöser für diese Wirkung des Bösen auf die Menschen, sondern er übernimmt die Argumentation der johanneischen Tradition, die einen theologischen Gegensatz zwischen „dieser Welt" und „nicht von dieser Welt" einführt.

2. Die fleischliche Natur des Menschen ist sündig

Für unseren Verfasser ist die fleischliche Natur, die *caro* des Menschen, Teil der Welt, die unter der Macht des Bösen steht. Diese ist gefangen in den Lei-

---

[29] OIM, hom. 32: PG 56, 805: *Si enim qui escas suas per orationem non offert Deo, coinquinatas eas manducat, secundum quod de illis ait Apostolus:* Quoniam omnis creatura Dei bona, et nihil rejiciendum, quod cum gratiarum actione percipitur: sanctificatur enim per verbum Dei, et orationem; *dicens enim,* Sanctificatur per verbum Dei et orationem (1. Tim. 4. 4.5), *ostendit, quia maculata est, nisi per orationem fuerit omnis esca mundata et sanctificata: quanto magis pueros offerri Deo et sanctificari necesse est?*
[30] OIM, hom. 32: PG 56, 805: *Ergo et omnis res corporalis, quoniam mundi est pars, in maligno est posita, et ipsam propterea oportet sanctificari. Consequenter et infantes, quando nascuntur, et ipsi quantum ad carnem in maligno sunt positi: quoniam et omnis caro, quasi pars mundi, in maligno posita est. Propterea necesse est offerri pueros, ut assidue super eos oratio fiat.*

denschaften; die Seele hingegen ist frei und steht unter der Herrschaft Gottes und unterliegt nicht der Gefangenschaft des Teufels[31].

Dies unterstreicht das *OIM* auch in der Auslegung der Bergpredigt (Mt 5, 23): „Wenn aber dein Auge krank ist, dann wird dein ganzer Leib finster sein". Das *OIM* deutet die „Finsternis" als „die fleischlichen, böswilligen und üblen Sinne, die immer wünschen, was zur Dunkelheit gehört und nicht zum Licht"[32]. Diese Sinne sind ein Charakteristikum der fleischlichen Natur, die immer Sünderin ist:

> Wie wir oben gesagt haben, ist die fleischliche Natur immer dunkel, weil sie immer Sünderin ist; auch wenn sie nicht sündigt, weil ihr die Seele widerspricht, wird sie dennoch mit Recht Sünderin und dunkel genannt, weil das Fleisch immer den Vorsatz hat zu sündigen: so beschleicht dieser oft auch eine gerechte Seele, damit diese macht, was es (das Fleisch) will. Wer ist denn so zuverlässig, der niemals mindestens zum Teil vom Fleisch besiegt worden ist? Auch wenn es das gibt, dann selten[33].

Im Unterschied zur Seele im Menschen ist das Fleisch immer Sünderin, weil in ihm der Wunsch zum Sündigen fest verankert ist.

In der Auslegung der Taufperikope unterstreicht das *OIM*, dass Christus die Taufe nicht nötig hatte, weil er ja ohne Sünde war. Er kam, um geheiligte Wasser zu hinterlassen für jene, die nach ihm getauft würden. Aber auch damit er, der die menschliche Natur angenommen hat, das ganze Mysterium der menschlichen Natur erfülle[34].

> Obwohl er selbst nämlich kein Sünder war, hat er dennoch die sündige Natur angenommen; auch wenn er selbst der Taufe nicht bedurfte, benötigte die fleischliche Natur sie dennoch[35].

---

[31] OIM, hom. 13: PG 56, 702: *quoniam anima libera est, et sub principatu Dei est; caro autem captiva est, et sub principatu diaboli est, sicut et mundus qui in maligno positus est, quoniam et ipsa caro de mundo est.*

[32] OIM, hom. 15: PG 56, 721: *Sensus carnales, malevoli et iniqui, qui semper desiderant quae sunt tenebrarum, et non lucis.*

[33] OIM, hom. 15: PG 56, 721: *Sicut supra diximus, tenebrosa est semper carnalis natura, quia semper peccatrix est, etsi non peccet, contradicente sibi anima, tamen recte peccatrix et tenebrosa vocatur, quia semper habet caro peccandi propositum, ut frequenter etiam justae animae surrepat, ut quod suum est agat. Quis enim est ita fidelis, qui numquam vel ex parte est a carne victus? Et si est, rarus est.*

[34] Vgl. OIM, hom. 4: PG 56, 657: *Deinde venit ad baptismum, non ut ipse remissionem peccatorum acciperet per baptismum, sed ut sanctificatas aquas relinqueret postmodum baptizandis. Adhuc autem, ut qui humanam suscepit naturam, totum humanae naturae inveniatur implesse mysterium.*

[35] OIM, hom. 4: PG 56, 657: *Nam quamvis ipse non erat peccator, tamen naturam susceperat peccatricem: propterea etsi ipse baptismate non egebat, tamen carnalis natura opus habebat.*

Wieder finden wir die Feststellung, dass die menschliche Natur *peccatrix* ist, selbst jene, die Christus angenommen hat, weil die menschliche Natur der reinigenden und erlösenden Taufe bedurfte. Damit hat Christus aber auch das Verlangen zum Sündigen angenommen (vgl. oben), aber dieser Neigung nicht nachgegeben.

Zunächst will Johannes Jesus nicht taufen. Diesem Widerstand Johannes' des Täufers hält Jesus entgegen, dass Johannes und er „die Gerechtigkeit ganz erfüllen" (Mt 3, 15) sollen.

Und der Kommentator fragt:

> Wie hat Christus die Gerechtigkeit der Taufe erfüllt? Ohne Zweifel gemäss dem Heilsplan (Ökonomie) der menschlichen Natur: Die Taufe ist nämlich für die Menschen notwendig, die entsprechend der fleischlichen Natur alle Sünder sind[36].

Neuerlich unterstreicht der Verfasser des *OIM*, dass die Sündhaftigkeit schon in der fleischlichen Natur aller Menschen verankert ist. Deshalb ist die Taufe heilsnotwendig, folgert der anonyme Verfasser.

IV. Die einzigartige Rolle Christi in Bezug auf die Sünde Adams bzw. die „sündige Natur des Fleisches"

1. Einzig Christus öffnet den Himmel für alle

Nicht nur für Christus öffnete sich der Himmel im Moment der Taufe (Mt 3, 16), sondern für alle Menschen[37]. Vor der Ankunft Christi gab es wohl schon einzelne Gerechte, denen sich der Himmel öffnete, aber er verschloss sich anschliessend sogleich wieder[38].

---

[36] OIM, hom. 4: PG 56, 658: *Quomodo implevit baptismi justitiam Christus? Sine dubio secundum dispensationem humanae naturae: hominum enim est opus habere baptismatis, qui secundum naturam carnalem omnes sunt peccatores.* [*Sicut ergo implevit justitiam baptismi, sic implevit et justitiam nascendi et crescendi, manducandi et bibendi, dormiendi et lassandi: sic et suscipiendae tentationis, sic et timoris, et fugae, et tristitiae: sic et passionis, et mortis, et resurrectionis implevit justitiam: id est, secundum dispensationem quam suscepit humanae naturae, omnes justitias istas implevit*].

[37] Vgl. OIM, hom. 4: PG 56, 659: *Aperti sunt ei caeli, id est, propter eum, gratia ejus. Aperti sunt autem caeli, non solum ei, sed omnibus propter eum.*

[38] Vgl. OIM, hom. 4: PG 56, 659: *Vis autem manifeste scire, quoniam ante Christum caeli si aperiebantur, iterum claudebantur. Nam justi quidem forsitan ascendebant in caelum, peccatores autem nequaquam. Ideo autem dixi, forsitan, ne quibusdam placeat etiam ante Christi adventum justorum animas ascendere potuisse in caelum.*

Aber keiner konnte damals so gerecht sein, dass er würdig gewesen wäre, die Pforten des Himmels für den Einzug aller Menschen zu öffnen[39].

Nach der Taufe der sündigen fleischlichen Natur Christi öffnet sich ihm der Himmel: seinetwegen und dank ihm[40] für uns alle[41].

Weil der Himmel bisher für alle verschlossen war und keine Seele in den Himmel aufsteigen konnte, stieg Christus in das Totenreich hinab:

> Übrigens meine ich, dass keine Seele vor Christus in den Himmel aufgestiegen ist, weil Adam gesündigt hat, und ihr die Himmel verschlossen worden sind, vielmehr alle (Seelen) in der Unterwelt festgehalten worden sind, deretwegen er auch zu den Toten hinabstieg[42].

Christus stieg zu den Toten hinab, um diese zu befreien, weil er auch für sie die Pforten des Himmels geöffnet hat, die bisher verschlossen waren.

Wieder zeigt sich die Auswirkung der Sünde Adams bzw. der Erzeltern, dass für alle Generationen bis Christus der Himmel verschlossen war. Vielleicht lässt sich sogar sagen, dass alle Nachkommens Adams den verschlossenen Himmel *geerbt* haben, bis Christus ihn für alle wieder öffnete.

2. Christus näht die Tunica der Unsterblichkeit wieder zusammen

In der Erklärung zum Dialog Jesu über Reichtum und Nachfolge bzw. über die Frage, wie kann jemand „das Reich Gottes gewinnen" oder „in das Himmelreich kommen" (Mt 19, 16–30), geht unser Autor auf die unterschiedlichen Voraussetzungen ein, die Juden und Heiden mitbringen, wenn sie in das Himmelreich kommen möchten. Dabei vergleicht Jesus diesen Zugang mit einem Nadelöhr, das kaum zu durchschreiten ist.

So taten die Heiden zwar viele gute Werke, aber sie vollbrachten sie nicht wegen Gott, sondern wegen des menschlichen Ansehens, oder damit man ihrer in zukünftigen Generationen gedenkt, oder einfach deshalb, weil Gutes tun gut ist.

---

[39] OIM, hom. 4: PG 56, 659: [*Etsi in singulis quibusque generationibus erant justi, quibus aperirentur, tamen iterum caeteris peccatoribus claudebantur:*] *et nullus poterat esse tam justus, ut dignus esset aperire portas caelorum ad introitum omnium hominum.*
[40] OIM, hom. 4: PG 56, 659: *propter eum, gratia ejus.*
[41] OIM, hom. 4: PG 56, 659: Ei *aperti sunt caeli, id est, propter eum nobis aperti sunt.*
[42] OIM, hom. 4: PG 56, 659–660: *Alioqui nullam animam ante Christum arbitror ascendisse in caelum, ex quo peccavit Adam, et clausi sunt ei caeli: sed omnes in inferno detentas propter quas etiam descendit ad inferos.*

Doch dieser ihr Umgang zerstörte die fleischliche Natur nicht, weil dieses Gute, das für irgendetwas Eitles (*vanum*) getan wird und nicht wegen Gott, gemäss dem Fleisch und gemäss dem Willen der fleischlichen Natur ist, und nicht das Gegenteil zur fleischlichen Natur: deshalb zerstört es (dieses Gute) sie (die fleischliche Natur) nicht[43].

Alle diese guten Werke der Heiden bewirken nicht, dass die sündige fleischliche Natur zerstört würde. Die Nähnadel, durch dessen Öhr die Heiden und die Juden in das Himmelreich eintreten können, ist Christus. So schreibt unser Autor:

> Die Nadel ist das Wort Gottes, das der Sohn Gottes selber ist, dessen erster Teil dünn und spitz ist. Dünn ist sie aufgrund seiner eigenen Göttlichkeit, spitz aber aufgrund seiner Inkarnation. Gänzlich gerade und ohne jede Krümmung oder ohne das geringste Gewicht ist sie, durch dessen Leidenswunde die Heiden schon in das ewige Leben eingegangen sind; er, der allein die Wunden vernähen kann, von dem das Kleid der Unsterblichkeit genäht worden ist, das einst über Adam zerrissen worden war. Diese Nähnadel ist es, die das Fleisch mit dem Geist zusammennäht, das sich danach nicht mehr abtrennen kann. Diese Nähnadel verband zugleich das jüdische Volk und das der Heiden[44].

Der Sohn Gottes, Christus, ist die Nähnadel, die und der das entzweigerissene Kleid der Unsterblichkeit Adams wieder zusammennäht, der auch Fleisch und Geist unwiderruflich wieder miteinander vernäht und Juden und Heiden miteinander verbindet.

Auch hier kommt zum Ausdruck, dass die Sünde Adams, die sein Kleid der Unsterblichkeit seinerzeit zerrissen hat, ihre Auswirkung bis auf Jesus hat, der es wieder zusammennäht.

---

[43] OIM, hom. 33: PG 56, 812: [*Gentiles autem etsi bona opera faciebant, tamen quia non propter Deum faciebant, sed aut propter aestimationem humanam, aut propter futuram nominis memoriam, aut propter hoc solum, quia bonum facere, bonum est:*] *ipsa conversatio ipsorum non dissipabat naturam carnalem, quia hoc ipsum bonum, quod propter vanum aliquid fit, et non propter Deum, secundum carnem est, et secundum voluntatem naturae carnalis, et non est contrarium naturae carnali, propter quod nec dissipat eam.*

[44] OIM, hom. 33: PG 56, 812: *Acus autem est verbum Dei, quod est Filius Dei ipse: cujus prima pars subtilis est, atque acuta. Subtilis secundum causam divinitatis ipsius, acuta autem secundum causam incarnationis ejus. Tota recta, et nullam habens deflexionem, aut scrupulum, per cujus vulnus passionis Gentes jam ingressae sunt vitam aeternam, qui vulnera consuere solus potest, a quo consuta est immortalitatis tunica, quae olim conscissa erat super Adam. Ipsa est acus, quae spiritui consuit carnem, ulterius separare se non potentem. Haec acus Judaicum populum junxit simul et Gentium.*

V. Zusammenfassung

Zum Schluss will ich versuchen, sehr kurz (und etwas undifferenziert) zusammenzufassen:

Ich bin überzeugt, dass man im *OIM* von einer Lehre des der „Erbsünde" – „Inherited sin" sprechen kann, auch wenn der Fachausdruck nicht vorkommt. Weil die gesamte Schöpfung von Gott gut geschaffen worden und Substanz ist, besteht das Böse nur in der Negation des Guten bzw. in seiner Verminderung.

Die Sünde der Erzeltern hat Auswirkungen auf die ganze Menschheit und alle Nachkommen „erben" sie und ihre Auswirkungen:

die Konsequenzen dieser Ursünde sind die Verringerung des Guten im Menschen und die Verankerung des Bösen in dessen Fleisch: dadurch verliert der Mensch die Unsterblichkeit. Die Nachkommen erben diese *„corruptibilitas"* und *„mortalitas"*, d.h. die Todesverfallenheit, die „eingefleischte" Neigung zur Sünde – für das *OIM* das sündige Fleisch – und die unheilbaren Wunden.

Dieser Verlust der Unsterblichkeit ist wie ein zerrissenes Kleid, das erst durch Christus wieder zusammengenäht wurde. Seit der Verstoßung aus dem Paradies ist der Himmel für die Menschen – abgesehen von einigen individuellen kurzzeitigen Ausnahmen – verschlossen, der erst durch Christus wieder dauerhaft für alle Menschen geöffnet wurde.

Alle diese Einschränkungen werden einzig durch den sündelosen Christus geheilt: Sein Heil empfängt der gläubige Christ durch die Taufe, in der er oder sie Kind Gottes wird. In Vollendung und Fülle allerdings erhält der gläubige Christ das Heil erst in der Taufe „im Tod", wenn die Sterblichkeit von der Unsterblichkeit verschlungen werden wird.

Paul Mattei, Lyon (France)

Quid habes, o homo, quod non accepisti ? Remarques sur l'état de l'homme après la chute selon saint Ambroise

Introduction

Première mesure

Dans le domaine du péché originel comme dans celui de la grâce, Augustin, à bien des reprises, contre Pélage, Julien et les Provençaux, se prévaut de l'enseignement d'Ambroise. Les modernes ont souvent cherché à vérifier ce jugement et, souvent aussi, en conséquence, ils n'ont envisagé l'évêque de Milan que comme un précurseur, il est vrai parfois décevant à leur goût, de l'évêque d'Hippone : avec de tels présupposés, favorables ou non, Ambroise n'est pas étudié pour lui-même. J'entends ici, en quelque sorte, me défaire d'Augustin ; de ce point de vue, je ne me livrerai pas, dans le corps du travail, au comparatisme : je désire observer Ambroise dans ce qu'il dit et ce qu'il ne dit pas, et déterminer pourquoi il le dit ou ne le dit pas.

Orientation d'ensemble

En règle générale, traiter du péché d'origine signifie non pas seulement porter le regard, d'une manière que l'on dirait négative, sur la chute d'Adam et, selon une contagion restant à définir, l'état qui en est résulté pour lui et pour sa descendance, mais aussi, positivement, évaluer en la globalité de ses aspects la situation de l'homme blessé (peut-être à mort), et considérer le secours divin qui le guérit (le ramène à la vie). La faute ne saurait se séparer du relèvement, et l'examen de l'une ne saurait aller sans l'étude de l'autre. C'est l'application de cet axiome à Ambroise qui commande la perspective et le contenu du présent travail.

Limites et objectif du présent travail

Vu le temps imparti, je ne renverrai pas à tous les textes ambrosiens disponibles : je m'en tiendrai à ceux qui m'ont semblé les plus *parlants*[1]. Et je limiterai la bibliographie au minimum : j'ai fourni tous les titres nécessaires touchant l'anthropologie ambrosienne (et, partant, le thème de la chute et de la grâce) dans un article qui paraîtra dans les *Mélanges* Marie-Anne Vannier et auquel je renvoie[2]. Le verset biblique en surtitre ne formera qu'implicitement le fil directeur de l'étude, même si, d'emblée, il pose la prévalence du don divin[3]. Nous dégagerons pleinement l'idée de cette prévalence, et avec toutes les nuances idoines, en conclusion.

L'enquête sera systématique[4], selon une démarche combinant progrès linéaire et approches convergentes. Elle sera également problématique. À la réflexion, étant donné ce qu'avancé plus haut («Orientation d'ensemble»), le plan que l'on verra que j'ai choisi n'impose pas à la pensée d'Ambroise un carcan arbitraire. Tout à l'inverse : son caractère opératoire se trouvera validé,

---

[1] J'ai néanmoins cru devoir faire une large place au volumineux commentaire qu'Ambroise a consacré au Psaume 118 : les renseignements que l'on trouve dans cet écrit se révèlent tout particulièrement abondants et riches.

[2] P. *Mattei*, Genèse 1, 26a selon saint Ambroise. Coup d'œil à partir des derniers *Sermons de l'Hexaemeron*. – Je ne donnerai dans les notes qui suivent que des indications bibliographiques ponctuelles. – Je cite Ambroise, le plus fréquemment, dans les éditions publiées au CSEL. Mais quand s'en offre l'opportunité, j'utilise celles qui existent dans la coll. Sources chrétiennes : en ce cas, je l'indique expressément.

[3] Il s'agit de 1 Co 4, 7. La banque de données «Biblindex», réalisée par les Sources chrétiennes, relève dans Ambroise 9 citations ou souvenirs de ce verset : Cain et Ab. I, 7, 27 : K. Schenkl, CSEL 32/1 (Vindobonae 1896/1897), p. 362 ; Exh. uirg. VI, 41 : PL 16, 348B ; Hex. VI, 8, 51 : K. Schenkl, CSEL 32/1 (Vindobonae 1896/1897), p. 243 ; In Psalm. CXVIII 15, 30 : M. Petschenig, CSEL 62 (Vindobonae 1913), p. 346 ; 18, 7 : CSEL 62, p. 400 ; Iob. I, 6, 19 : K. Schenkl, CSEL 32/2 (Vindobonae 1897), p. 224 ; Ios. 9, 50 : K. Schenkl, CSEL 32/2 (Vindobonae 1897), p. 107 ; Obit. Theod. 22 : O. Faller, CSEL 73 (Vindobonae 1955), p. 382 ; Paen. 2, 6, 41 : O. Faller, CSEL 73 (Vindobonae 1955), p. 181. Sur les deux pôles entre lesquels se structure, en réalité, sa signification plénière, voir *infra*, n. 24. – Sur d'autres versets, ou groupes de versets, relatifs à la grâce, à savoir Rm 7, 25 ; Rm 8, 29–30 ; Ep 1, 5, et les relevés qu'en fait «Biblindex», voir *infra* n. 26 et 27. – Précision que j'ai omis de fournir dans l'article nommé n. préc. : la même banque de données permet de constater que Gn 1, 26 fait l'objet de 86 citations ou allusions, réparties sur 23 œuvres d'Ambroise.

[4] Cela revient à dire que j'utilise la documentation ambrosienne sans me préoccuper de la chronologie, au demeurant toujours hypothétique, des œuvres. On compensera ce qui, dans la perspective qui est la mienne, n'est pas un manque, en se rapportant au livre bien connu de G. *Visonà*, Cronologia Ambrosiana – Bibliografia Ambrosiana, Sancti Ambrosii Mediolanensis opera omnia, SAEMO 25/26 (Milan – Rome 2004). Que la présente étude soit thématique implique qu'on n'y trouvera pas non plus, sauf exception, d'enquête d'ordre lexicologique (sur le vocabulaire ambrosien du péché, et en particulier du péché originel).

in fine, par sa capacité à mettre à nu, une fois de plus (car, pour ma part, je l'ai déjà fait ailleurs), par-delà les incertitudes de la doctrine, le cœur du projet ambrosien.

❦

I. Peccatum (le péché d'origine)

1. Peccatum originans[5]

Je n'ai pas à brosser un portrait d'Adam *ante lapsum* selon Ambroise. J'attirerai seulement l'attention sur deux traits capitaux pour la suite :

- Adam fut créé enfant, c'est-à-dire immature dans sa connaissance des commandements (cf. *In Psalm*. 118, 19, 44) : Ambroise reprend là un vieux thème attesté, comme on le sait, dès le IIe siècle, chez Théophile d'Antioche et Irénée de Lyon[6].

- Adam connaissait la loi *perfunctorie* : « superficiellement » (le mot, sous sa forme adjective ou adverbiale, connaît au moins trois occurrences dans le *De paradiso* : 6, 30 [*perfunctoria scientia*, bis] ; 7, 36 [*perfunctorie*]).

Adam était donc appelé à un approfondissement dans la sagesse et à un progrès dans la vertu, s'il obéissait aux préceptes, et spécialement à l'injonction de ne pas goûter au fruit de l'arbre de la connaissance du bien et du mal. Mais il se montra trop pressé. Par orgueil (comme d'ailleurs le démon : *In Psalm*. 118, 7, 8-9), il ne crut pas devoir s'astreindre aux longs apprentissages qui l'auraient rendu docile aux préceptes et à la grâce. Le premier couple a usurpé ce qu'il ignorait, et s'est imaginé pouvoir emprunter des raccourcis (*In Psalm*. 118, 8, 31).

---

[5] Il va de soi que les expressions *peccatum originans* et *peccatum originatum* employées dans cette section sont anachroniques. On a une idée de la variété du lexique ambrosien en matière de nomination du péché d'origine selon ses deux aspects dans les textes d'*Exs. Sat.* et *Ap. proph. Dauid* que je rapporte plus bas.

[6] Sur ce thème chez ces deux auteurs, toutes premières indications dans : P. Mattei, L'anthropologie de Novatien. Affinités, perspectives et limites, REAug 38 (1992) 235-259, spéc. 251.

2. Peccatum originatum. L'état de l'homme déchu

La faute d'Adam introduit en l'homme déchéance physique et morale. Cf. *In Luc.* 7, 234. Voir aussi *Ep.* 1 e.c. (Mauristes 41), 7 : l'homme est désormais propriété du démon. Plus exactement, la faute des premiers parents a deux conséquences :

- L'homme est soumis à la mort (cf. *De bono mortis* 1, 2 ; 4, 15).

- L'âme, qui a perdu l'image en refusant de se soumettre à Dieu (nous y reviendrons), voit la chair se rebeller contre elle : alors qu'elle était forte par grâce, elle est désormais sous la tyrannie de la chair, laquelle est faible par nature ; elle est en proie à un désordre qui fait qu'elle ne domine plus ni le corps ni véritablement les autres êtres animés ; car seule la soumission à Dieu lui garantissait une telle domination : voir e.g. *In Psalm.* 118, 4, 4.6.

3. Une qualification délicate

Cette déchéance ou ce désordre sont-ils, à proprement parler, un péché ? Deux textes probants à cet égard :

> J'ai failli en Adam, j'ai été chassé du Paradis en Adam, je suis mort en Adam ; comment pourra-t-il me rappeler, s'il ne me trouve en Adam, soumis à la faute et voué à la mort en lui et, en proportion, justifié en Christ[7] (trad. PM).

Il ne s'agit pas seulement de chute (*lapsus*) et de mort (*mortuus*) en Adam ; il est question, plus précisément, de faute (*culpa*) en Adam et de justification (*iustificatus*) en Christ.

> Avant notre naissance déjà la contagion nous souille et avant de jouir de la lumière nous contractons l'injustice qui vient de notre origine elle-même. C'est dans l'iniquité que nous sommes conçus – il (*scil.* David) n'a pas précisé si c'est celle de nos parents ou la nôtre, et c'est dans les fautes que chacun de nous est mis au monde par sa mère – mais ici non plus il n'a pas précisé si c'est dans ses propres fautes qu'une mère enfante ou s'il n'y a pas déjà certains péchés chez le nouveau-né. Mais prends garde, il se pourrait qu'il faille comprendre l'un et l'autre. L'être conçu n'est pas exempt d'iniquité, car ses parents aussi ne sont pas sans faute.

---

[7] *Exc. Sat.* 2, 6 : O. Faller, CSEL 73 (Vindobonae 1955), p. 254 : *Lapsus sum in Adam, de paradiso eiectus in Adam, mortuus in Adam ; quomodo reuocet, nisi me in Adam inuenerit, ut in illo culpae obnoxium, morti debitum, ita in Christo iustificatum.*

Et si même l'enfant qui n'a qu'un jour n'est pas sans péché combien plus les jours où la mère a conçu ne sont pas sans péché[8].

Texte remarquable dont nous retiendrons deux traits : (1) quoique sous une forme encore dubitative, il évoque un péché de chacun dès la conception ; (2) non sans obscurité ni hésitation, il met en rapport ce péché avec le péché des parents, en particulier dans l'acte de chair (d'une manière corrélative, il semble, selon *In Psalm.* 118, 6, 13, que c'est précisément la conception virginale qui préserve l'humanité du Christ)[9].

II. *Imago* (l'impuissance de l'homme)

1. Préliminaire : L'image originelle et sa perte

Les composantes de l'image. J'ai mentionné plus haut, en Introduction, l'article que j'ai consacré à l'iconologie d'Ambroise. Je me contenterai ici de formaliser la structure suivante, en une sorte de tableau :

(1) Origine. Le Christ est Image, l'homme est à l'image : d'emblée, il est à noter que l'économie supralapsaire est centrée sur le Christ.

(2) Nature. L'image est grâce (nous verrons plus bas qu'Ambroise, au début du *De Iacob*, parle de *gratia creaturae*). Plus encore, elle est grâce du Christ : le *De paradiso* ne cesse de revenir sur ce thème que les biens dont nos premiers parents jouissaient en Éden, les secours divins dont ils abondaient, leur venaient du Christ.

---

[8] Ap. proph. Dauid 11, 56 : P. Hadot, M. Cordier, SC 239 (Paris 1977), p. 150-151 (texte et trad.) : *Antequam nascimur maculamur contagio, et ante usuram lucis originis ipsius excipimus iniuriam. In iniquitate concipimur – non expressit* (scil. *David*) *utrum parentum an nostra – et in delictis generat unumquemque mater sua. Nec hic declarauit utrum in delictis suis mater pariat an iam sint aliqua delicta nascentis. Sed uide ne utrumque intellegendum sit. Nec conceptus exors iniquitatis est, quoniam et parentes non carent lapsu. Et si nec unius diei infans sine peccato est* (cf. Jb 14, 4-5 LXX), *multo magis nec illi materni conceptus dies sine peccato sunt.*

[9] L'hésitation d'Ambroise s'explique d'autant mieux que, dans ce texte, il dépend d'Origène, *Hom. in Luc.* 14, 5, qui hésitait lui aussi. Cf. P. Hadot, *l.c.*, n. 82-83.

(3) Lieu et caractéristiques de l'image. Quant à son lieu, l'image s'imprime dans l'âme. Quant à ses caractéristiques, l'image veut dire : (a) action dans la vertu, pour parvenir à la parfaite ressemblance (Ambroise ne distingue pas image et ressemblance) ; (b) domination sur le monde conférée par Dieu ; (c) contemplation du monde conduisant à Dieu.

L'image est perdue dans le péché : la «vieille grâce», *uetus gratia*, disparaît (*In Psalm.* 118, 11, 18). Ayant perdu l'image du céleste, Adam et Ève revêtent l'image du terrestre, ce que représentent les «tuniques de peau» de Gn 3, 21 (*In Psalm.* 118, 11, 14).

Cette phénoménologie de la perte de l'image fait difficulté. La ressemblance vertueuse est ruinée par le péché. L'image est-elle donc totalement détruite ? Mais l'homme demeure un être qui domine l'univers et déploie sa curiosité pour en acquérir la science. Subsiste-t-il alors quelque chose de l'image ? Cela revient à s'interroger sur les forces qui restent à l'homme pour accomplir sa destinée morale. En termes équivalents, c'est le problème des vertus des païens.

2. Les vertus des païens

Une comparaison : feuilles et fruits. Tous ceux qui, dans l'économie présente, n'ont pas reçu le baptême et sont étrangers à l'Église catholique, c'est-à-dire, nommément, les païens, et qui néanmoins pratiquent les vertus, sont comme des arbres qui portent des feuilles sans produire aucun fruit. La similitude semble aimée d'Ambroise ; je l'ai trouvée à bien des reprises – soit, pour donner quelques références, sans exhaustivité : *De paradiso* 13, 6 ; *In Luc.* 7, 10 ; *In Psalm.* 1, 41 ; *In Psalm.* 118, 12, 8.13, 26.

Valeur de la comparaison. Les vertus des païens sont *matériellement* de vraies vertus : en ce sens elles ne sont pas des péchés. Cependant elles n'emportent aucun mérite : elles sont vaines pour le salut, et (s'il est permis d'employer un mot étranger à Ambroise comme à toute la patristique) *surnaturellement* les païens sont des morts (*In Psalm.* 118, 5, 1).

La chute n'a certes pas éteint le libre arbitre de l'homme ; en ce sens, la raison subsiste et tout homme reste *rationis capax* (*In Psalm.* 118, 2, 13). Néanmoins c'est une raison superficielle et, en fin de compte, dévoyée. Le païen, ou le pécheur, a perdu le Verbe, donc la raison ; il est pareil à une bête, et ne retrouve la dignité humaine qu'en récupérant l'image (*In Psalm.* 118, 13, 20) : car l'être rationnel qu'est l'homme n'a plus, sans le Christ, qu'une apparence de raison (cf. *In Psalm.* 118, 14, 23). La vraie vertu ne se sépare pas de la connaissance actuelle de Dieu (*In Psalm.* 118, 10, 43; 118, 11, 12) et la parfaite raison, qui va de pair avec la sainteté, consiste dans le respect des préceptes, reconnus comme tels, c'est-à-dire émanant d'une source transcendante, et extrinsèque, qui est divine (cf. *In Psalm.* 118, 9, 15, à propos des bons anges).

Ainsi, la raison dont usent les païens et la moralité dont ils font preuve peuvent bien en imposer : cette frondaison est spécieuse. On en a un bon exemple avec les sages de ce monde, philosophes et savants profanes; leur intelligence est creuse (*phalerata*) et non véritable (*uera*) : cf. *In Psalm.* 118, 22, 9–10[10]; c'est qu'ils estiment être en mesure de mépriser la grâce (*In Psalm.* 118, 10, 21) et, à l'instar de Socrate, ne manifestent aucune humilité (*In Psalm.* 118, 16, 11).

3. Un pas de plus dans le questionnement

Cependant, ce jugement sévère une fois posé, et compte tenu de l'ambivalence que malgré tout il recèle, le problème « rebondit », comme on dit aujourd'hui volontiers. D'une part, en effet, quoique la grâce originelle, entendue comme puissance salvifique, n'opère plus, il n'est pas interdit pour autant de conjecturer que, même chez les païens, subsiste d'elle au moins un souvenir; elle demeurerait comme en creux, ou pareille à une ombre qui, à l'occasion, garderait une certaine capacité à s'animer. Dieu sait approuver le Gentil, l'aimer et l'estimer, si celui-ci sait se montrer humble, comme le publicain de l'Évangile (*In Psalm.* 118, 3, 41 renvoyant à Lc 18, 10–14)[11]. Même, la rémanence de la grâce originelle, je crois (mais dans un passage dont la forte couleur métaphorique ne facilite pas l'exégèse), pourrait s'analyser comme désir du salut

---

[10] Sur la position, très critique, d'Ambroise à l'égard de la philosophie, voir la thèse, classique à mon sens, de G. *Madec*, Saint Ambroise et la philosophie, Coll. des Études Augustiniennes. Série Antiquité 61 (Paris 1974).

[11] Les termes dont use Ambroise sont nets, en l'occurrence : In Psalm. CXVIII 3, 41 : CSEL 62, p. 63 : […] *(S)i publicanus se humiliauerit, exaltabitur. Audi quem diligat et non pro nihilo habeat Deus. Quicumque sanctus est, qui sine macula uiuit, ueritatem custodit, non appetiuit proximum suum* […] *talis etiam si sit gentilis, deuotione humilitatis a Deo comprobatur. Superbi autem, uelut pharisaeus, arrogantia sua pro nihilo ab eo aestimantur. Denique gentilitas non est : deuotio autem manet in aeternum.* / «[…] Si le publicain s'humilie, il est exalté. Apprends qui Dieu aime et ne tient pas pour rien. Quiconque est saint, mène une vie sans tache, garde la vérité, n'a pas convoité le bien de son prochain […] un tel homme, même s'il est un Gentil, Dieu, du fait de l'empressement de son humilité, l'approuve complètement. Mais les orgueilleux, comme le pharisien, sont estimés par lui pour rien. De fait, la qualité de Gentil n'existe pas : mais son empressement demeure pour l'éternité» (trad. PM).

(*In Psalm.* 118, 1, 5)¹². Il est vrai que le publicain prie dans le Temple, et qu'il semble, d'après le second des passages cités, que la grâce originelle soit stimulée par une connaissance plus ou moins floue des promesses prophétiques : comme si, en toute hypothèse, le réveil de ce qui fut conféré au commencement ne se produisait que sous l'influence de la révélation biblique.

Il y a davantage encore, peut-être. Lors de sa venue au monde, tout homme est potentiellement éclairé par la lumière (*lucerna*) qu'est le Verbe de Dieu (*In Psalm.* 118, 14, 5, par réminiscence de Jn 1, 9¹³). Faudrait-il en conclure que cette lumière continue, même après la chute, de « recharger » ce qui n'est pas éteint de la lueur primitive ?

Seulement, d'autre part, quelque suggestives que semblent être les conjectures à l'instant ébauchées à propos de deux ou trois textes, et même si, dans une formule au demeurant générale, Ambroise certifie que « le Seigneur n'a pas coutume de refuser sa faveur à qui l'en supplie »¹⁴ (trad. PM), quand bien même, enfin et surtout, les deux économies, avant comme après la faute d'Adam, sont enracinées *in Christo*, il ne paraît pas que le Milanais se soit soucié d'élaborer un « modèle » pleinement théorisé qui expliciterait comment la grâce du Verbe incarné et rédempteur vient s'articuler sur la trace, quelle qu'elle soit, de grâce originelle, ou, en d'autres termes, et pour formuler la question dans le cadre qui est celui de la présente sec-

---

¹² Comme ce texte n'est quand même pas, je le reconnais, d'une portée bien assurée, je crois devoir en citer quelques formules, pour qu'on juge de l'interprétation que je propose : In Psalm. CXVIII 1, 5 : CSEL 62, p. 7 : […] *(I)ntellige mihi carnem illam, quae madefacta fuerat in Adam serpentis ueneno, quae criminum marcebat fetore, quae procedebat in filiabus Sion alta ceruice et nutibus oculorum* […] *eamdem tamen plurimis edoctam oraculis quod uenturus esset qui, serpentis illecebris exclusis, sancti Spiritus infunderet gratiam, ut omnis caro uideret salutare Dei, omnis caro ad Deum ueniret, inarsisse desiderio* […]. / « Considère-moi cette chair, qui avait été arrosée en Adam du venin du serpent, qui était flétrie par l'infection des vices, qui avançait parmi les filles de Sion la tête haute et l'œil impérieux […], la même cependant, instruite par d'innombrables oracles que viendrait celui qui, écartant les séductions du serpent, répandrait la grâce de l'Esprit saint, afin que toute chair voie le salut de Dieu, que toute chair vienne à Dieu – considère-la brûlant de désir […] » (trad. PM). Si c'est bien des païens aussi qu'il s'agit dans cette brillante variation à partir de Ct 1, 1 (mais noter *in filiabus Sion* : sommes-nous face à Jérusalem l'infidèle, ou à Babylone la prostituée ?), lesdits païens auraient une certaine connaissance des prophéties : résurgence du motif traditionnel, si présent chez Ambroise (et cardinal dans sa critique de la philosophie), du larcin de philosophes ?
¹³ Dans cette réminiscence, Ambroise lit *uenientem*. Comme partout ailleurs à une exception peut-être (Fug. 3, 16 : *ueniens*, selon la dernière éditrice, C. Gerzaguet, SC 576 [Paris 2015], p. 314–315).
¹⁴ Fug. 6, 36 : SC 576, p. 262, l. 2–3 : *non* […] *solet bonum datum deprecantibus dominus denegare*.

tion de cet article, comment le vestige de l'image oblitérée servirait de point d'accroche à sa restauration.

III. *Gratia* (la nécessité de la grâce)

1. Préliminaire. Universalité du péché

Personne ne doit oser assurer qu'il est pur de péchés (*In Psalm*. 118, 2, 13). Même après le sacrement du baptême (*post suscepta baptismi sacramenta*) nul n'est sans péché (*In Psalm*. 118, 5, 39), à l'exception, bien sûr, du Christ, qui était indemne du péché, mais que le Père a fait péché pour nous (*In Psalm*. 118, 6, 21). Le thème de l'universalité du péché est récurrent : cf. *In Psalm*. 118, 15, 32 (*omnes sub peccato sumus* / «nous sommes tous sous le coup du péché»); 22, 27 (*nemo sine peccato; negare hoc, sacrilegium est; solus enim Deus sine peccato est* / «personne n'est sans péché; nier cela est un sacrilège; car Dieu seul est sans péché» [trad. PM]).

2. La grâce (1). Seul le Christ sauve : Le Christ et la Loi, ou : effort humain et grâce du Christ selon le *De Iacob et uita beata*, livre I

Une surprise attend le lecteur au seuil du *De Iacob* : Ambroise y affirme avec tranquillité, et plusieurs fois, que c'est par l'effort de sa propre volonté que l'homme peut régler ses passions («métriopathie» qui ne prétend pas éteindre les passions, à la façon de l'ancien stoïcisme, mais les redresser et les contenir, selon ce que prêchait le Moyen Portique et toute la tradition platonicienne); de la sorte l'homme serait par lui-même en capacité d'acquérir la vertu et de se composer une vie morale, et qui ouvre au bonheur. Le Christ, la grâce semblent absents des toutes premières lignes du *De Iacob*. Voir, par exemple, dès l'attaque du traité (1, 1, 1) :

> Une bonne parole pleine de prudence est nécessaire à l'instruction de tous, et l'esprit attaché à la raison ouvre la voie aux vertus, réprime les passions [...][15].

---

[15] Iac. I, 1, 1 : G. Nauroy, SC 534 (Paris 2010), p. 348–349 (texte et trad.) : *Necessarius ad disciplinam bonus sermo omnibus plenus prudentiae, et mens rationi intenta praecurrit uirtutibus, passiones coercet* [...].

Comparer quelques lignes plus loin :

> [...] ou bien la libre impulsion de notre affectivité nous entraîne à l'erreur ou bien notre volonté, en suivant la raison, nous en détourne[16].

Toutefois, très vite, la pensée se révèle plus complexe. Dès 1, 1, 2, et sans transition, « le pouvoir de retrancher une défaillance du corps », comme on taille le figuier stérile (cf. Lc 13, 7-9, cité *ad loc.*), se trouve attribué au « Maître » (*dominus*) de l'arbre. L'homme peut atteindre à la vertu par ses efforts – mais la grâce indispensable du « Seigneur » (*dominus* a d'évidence, en réalité, ce sens) n'est pas oubliée.

Il est à se demander si ce schéma décrivant le rapport entre effort libre de l'homme et don divin concerne l'homme en général, en clair le païen aussi, non touché par la révélation biblique (ce que laisserait penser la globalité du propos), ou, spécifiquement, celui qui ressortit à cette révélation, sous la Loi ou sous l'Évangile, étant entendu que les justes de l'Ancien Testament furent des chrétiens *ante litteram*, prophétiquement éclairés et soutenus par le Christ (l'exemple du « saint David » développé en 1, 1, 3 tendrait à corroborer cette seconde supposition[17]). Néanmoins, dans le premier des deux cas, si c'est par le don, imparti dès l'origine, de l'empire exercé par l'esprit rationnel sur les pulsions que l'homme doit se conduire, ce don, qui demeure dans la mouvance du Seigneur qui l'a conféré, doit de toute manière se comprendre, à la lettre, comme une grâce – celle de la création (*gratia creaturae*, 1, 1, 4) : jamais, intègre ou non, la nature que l'homme a reçue au commencement n'échappe à l'ascendant de celui qui l'a formée.

La loi positive donnée à Moïse vient éclairer la conscience : car, de toute manière, la vertu s'enseigne. Les préceptes, ainsi considérés, sont une aide (*ibid.*). La Loi cependant ne permet pas d'atteindre à la vertu : elle est impuissante, ainsi que l'explique Paul aux Romains, car elle édicte ce qu'il faut faire, sans donner la force de le faire. Voir 1, 4, 13 :

> La Loi a dénoncé le péché, mais dans une condition encline au mal, elle n'a pu l'empêcher tout à fait[18].

---

[16] Ibid., p. 348-351 : [...] *nos aut liber affectus ad errorem trahit aut uoluntas reuocat rationem secuta.*
[17] Que David eût vécu déjà selon le Christ est un motif récurrent dans l'*In Psalm.* 118.
[18] Iac. I, 4, 13 : SC 534, p. 368-369 (texte et trad.) : *Lex* [...] *peccatum denuntiauit, sed in condicione lubrica penitus cohibere non potuit.*

Même – et en l'occurrence Ambroise paraphrase Paul avec une rigoureuse fidélité –, provoquant la conscience du péché, sans apporter de remède, la Loi n'en immerge que davantage dans le péché :

> J'ai connu le péché que j'ignorais, j'ai connu que la concupiscence était un péché, et à l'occasion de cette prise de conscience du péché ma dette s'est accrue, parce que le péché, qui auparavant à cause de mon ignorance était mort, a revécu en moi : je suis mort de la blessure du péché [...][19].

Là intervient la grâce de l'Évangile, qui achève la Loi, en donnant de mettre en pratique les préceptes moraux qu'elle contient (il n'est plus question de grâce primitive) :

> Qu'y a-t-il que le Seigneur ne t'ait accordé ? Il a donné la Loi, il a ajouté la grâce[20].

Le Christ se soumet l'homme et, en se le soumettant, le rend libre. Dès lors, le bonheur (dont l'obtention constitue le sujet du *De Iacob*), c'est le Christ – ou plus exactement c'est «suivre Jésus» (1, 7, 28), jusqu'au milieu des épreuves (1, 7, 27). Le matériel lexical, tout à fait stoïcien, qui forme le revêtement de cette méditation ne doit pas tromper[21].

3. La grâce (2) : la grâce du Christ prévient

Quoi qu'il en soit, empreinte du don fait à Adam ou pas, le Milanais, en plusieurs rencontres, avance *apertis uerbis* que la grâce est nécessaire, même pour commencer (l'équivalent de ce que l'on appellera plus tard *initium fidei* ou *initium bonae uoluntatis*). L'homme ne peut trouver la *voie* si le Seigneur ne le *précède* sur cette voie :

---

[19] Ibid. : *Cognoui [...] peccatum quod nesciebam, cognoui concupiscentiam esse peccatum, et hac occasione cognitionis peccati aera cumulata sunt, quia peccatum quod ante per ignorantiam meam mortuum uidebatur, in me reuixit : ego autem mortuus sum sub peccati uulnere [...]*.
[20] Ibid. (lignes d'ouverture de tout le §, qui en donnent comme la clé) : *Quid autem est quod tibi non contulit Dominus? Legem dedit, adiunxit gratiam.*
[21] Ajouter qu'en 1, 5, 17, qui ouvertement revient aux considérations du début de l'ouvrage, dont nous avons fait état (SC 534, p. 374–375 : [...] *ut ad exordia sermonis huius reuertamur* [...]. / «[...] pour en revenir au début de mon discours [...]»), Ambroise précise : *Mens[...] bona, si rationi intendat, sed parum perfecta, nisi habeat gubernaculum Christi.* / «(L)'esprit est bon, s'il s'attache à la raison, mais par trop imparfait sans le gouvernail du Christ» (ibid., l. 11–13). Où l'on pourrait apercevoir une allusion à ce que l'évêque pense des vertus des Gentils. Et une réflexion sur la *mens* aussi bien païenne que chrétienne, mais s'imaginant pouvoir *fare da se*.

J'ose [...] même dire pour ma part que l'homme ne peut s'engager dans une voie s'il n'a le Seigneur pour l'y précéder. Aussi est-il écrit : 'Tu marcheras à la suite du Seigneur ton Dieu' [...]. Tu vois bien que partout la puissance du Seigneur collabore avec les efforts humains, en sorte que personne ne peut construire sans le Seigneur, personne garder sans le Seigneur, personne entreprendre quoi que ce soit sans le Seigneur [...][22].

Affirmation directe de la grâce prévenante : *Dominum praeuiantem*; *nemo quidquam possit incipere sine Domino*. La prévenance de la grâce est à entendre au sens strict : c'est Dieu même qui fait naître les pensées bonnes :

Tout ce que tu penses de saint, cela est don de Dieu, inspiration de Dieu, grâce de Dieu[23] (trad. PM).

La prévenance de la grâce a pour corollaire qu'elle est donnée gratuitement : *In Luc*. 7, 27 – en particulier la phrase :

Dieu appelle ceux qu'il juge bon d'appeler, et il rend fidèle celui qu'il veut rendre fidèle[24].

Voir de même *In Psalm*. 118, 1, 18. En *In Psalm*. 118, 4, 3, dans une image magnifique, il est stipulé qu'Adam ne peut se relever de la poussière si la Croix du Christ ne se lève sur lui. La grâce antécédente est nécessaire : *In Psalm*. 118, 13, 2. Le Christ est la source de toutes les vertus (*omnium origo uirtutum*, *In Psalm*. 118, 14, 5). En un mot, dans l'ordre de la création comme dans celui de la rédemption, tout est grâce, et si le Milanais évoque la « dot de la nature » (*naturae dos* : *In Psalm*. 118 15, 18), ou, avec plus de netteté encore, déclare que le Christ « recrée la nature » (*naturam reformat* : ibid. 14, 42), on ne se méprendra pas sur le vocable *natura*, qui, au moins dans le premier des deux morceaux signifie exactement, je crois, l'état conféré à Adam lors de sa

---

[22] In Luc. 2, 84 : G. Tissot, SC 45bis (Paris [2]1971), p. 111 (texte et trad., retouchée PM) : *Audeo [...] etiam ego dicere quod homo uiam non possit adoriri, nisi Dominum habeat praeuiantem. Vnde scriptum est : 'Post dominum tuum ambulabis'* (Dt 13, 4) [...] *Vides utique quia ubique Domini uirtus studiis cooperatur humanis; ut nemo possit aedificare sine Domino, nemo custodire sine Domino* (cf. Ps 126, 1), *nemo quidquam incipere sine Domino* [...].
[23] Cain et Ab. I, 9, 45 : CSEL 32/1, p. 376 : *Quidquid autem sanctum cogitaueris hoc Dei munus est, Dei inspiratio, Dei gratia*.
[24] In Luc. 7, 27 : G. Tissot, SC 52bis (Paris [2]2006), p. 18 (texte et trad., retouchée PM) : *Deus quos dignatur uocat, et quem uult religiosum facit*; idée identique en *In Luc*. 1, 10; voir aussi *Exh. uirg*. 7, 43, qui souligne avec force que la collation de la grâce ne relève pas des œuvres de l'homme, mais de la seule volonté souveraine de Dieu

naissance : confirmation de ce que j'ai allégué plus haut sur la portée dudit vocable[25].

4. Points aveugles

L'affirmation que la grâce est nécessaire n'empêche pas qu'il faille, *en même temps*, noter ceci.

1. Relativement à la grâce à conférer, Dieu donne *gratis*, sans regarder au mérite, mais en considérant la foi et la volonté de chacun. L'homme doit commencer par ouvrir son cœur : *In Psalm.* 118, 8, 59; *Exh. uirg.* 7, 43 mentionné ci-dessus est clair : la gratuité de la grâce ne requiert que la foi. Mais, même dans ce texte, il ne paraît pas qu'Ambroise s'interroge trop sur l'émergence même de la foi – sur le *comment* de cette émergence : il ne semble pas loin d'en faire une pure initiative humaine, quoi qu'il dise ailleurs. En bien des passages, la grâce paraît seulement venir seconder la liberté : e.g. *Fug.* 5, 30; *In Psalm.* 118, 14, 25[26].

2. Relativement à la grâce une fois donnée, l'homme y coopère librement. Il s'acquiert par là des mérites subséquents : le mérite consiste à s'abandonner à faire volontairement ce que veut le Christ (*In Psalm.* 118, 14, 25). Mais il ne paraît pas qu'Ambroise parle franchement du mérite comme fructification de la grâce reçue, sous la motion de cette grâce.

---

[25] Il est remarquable que 1 Co 4, 7 (*supra*, n. 3) soit utilisé, en *Hex.* 6, 8, 51, pour dire les bienfaits temporels de Dieu et, en *Paenit.* 2, 6, 41, pour souligner la gratuité du salut. Sur la nécessité de la grâce il convient de mentionner l'usage significatif que fait Ambroise de Rm 7, 25 («Biblindex» relève 17 citations et allusions, réparties sur 12 œuvres : on en trouvera la liste *ad loc.*, évidemment à vérifier quant au bien-fondé de la références). On notera surtout la forme exclusive qu'il donne du verset dans ses citations (e.g. Iac. 1, 4, 16 : SC 534, p. 372 : *Infelix ego homo, quis me liberabit de corpore mortis huius? Gratia Dei per Iesum Christum Dominum nostrum*) et le sens que cette forme impose s'agissant des mots *gratia Dei* (litt. «Malheureux homme que je suis, qui me libèrera du corps de cette mort? La grâce de Dieu par Jésus-Christ notre Seigneur»). Comme on le sait, cette forme (avec le sens induit) n'est pas propre à Ambroise : elle est celle de la tradition latine à peu près unanime et la leçon de la Vulgate; on sait aussi qu'elle joue un grand rôle chez Augustin; le grec, à peu d'exceptions près (dont celle, notable, du *Codex Bezae*), porte une formule qui signifie «Grâces soient rendues à Dieu, etc.» (voir *E. Nestle, K. Aland*, NT Graece et Latine (Stuttgart [22]1963) app. *ad loc.*).

[26] Il y a ici une difficulté, dont la formulation ne fait que rejoindre, et redoubler, ce que j'ai conjecturé plus haut, dans la deuxième partie de cette contribution, à partir du début de *Iac.* Voir aussi plus bas, n. 30.

3. Relativement à la distribution de la grâce, sa nécessité et surtout sa gratuité n'empêche pas qu'Ambroise ne s'appesantit pas, sauf erreur, sur le problème, qui reste à l'arrière-plan, de la prédestination[27]. En revanche, il insinue (cf. *In Psalm.* 118, 8, 41) qu'aucun pécheur, si injuste (*nequissimus*) et détestable (*detestabilissimus*) soit-il, n'est exclu du salut; le Christ appelle tous les hommes, même ceux qui ne le cherchent pas, et la miséricorde du Seigneur s'étend sur toute chair (cf. *In Psalm.* 118, 20, 29).

---

[27] En m'aidant de «Biblindex» j'ai mené une rapide enquête sur les citations que fait Ambroise de Rm 8, 29-30 (VVLG : [29]*Nam quos praesciuit et praedestinauit conformes fieri imaginis Filii sui, ut sit ipse primogenitus in multis fratribus.* [30]*Quos autem praedestinauit hos et uocauit, et quos uocauit hos et iustificauit, quos autem iustificauit illos et glorificauit*) et Ep 1, 5 (VVLG : *qui praedestinauit nos in adoptionem filiorum per Iesum Christum in ipsum secundum propositum uoluntatis suae*). Je m'en suis tenu aux occurrences où se trouve explicitement évoquée la notion de prédestination ou d'appel (respectivement 3 et 1 : soit d'une part Fid. V, 6, 83 : O. Faller, CSEL 78 [Vindobonae 1962], p. 246-247; Iac. I, 6, 26 : SC 534, p. 384; Hex. VI, 8, 46 : CSEL 32/1, p. 237; d'autre part Ep. 16 [M 76], 4.5 : O. Faller, CSEL 82/1 [Vindobonae 1968], p. 115.116; je laisse de côté Sacr. VI, 2, 8 : O. Faller, CSEL 73 [Vindobonae 1955], p. 74, vu le soupçon, justifié, qui pèse sur l'authenticité de cette œuvre). L'enquête fait apparaître, semble-t-il, une étrange contradiction. On opposera en effet Fid. V, 6, 83 ([…] *ut ostenderet patrem quoque non petitionibus deferre solere* […] *Vnde et apostolus ait : 'Quos praesciuit et praedestinauit'. Non enim ante praedestinauit quam praesciret, sed quorum merita praesciuit, eorum praemia praedestinauit.* / « […] pour montrer que le Père non plus n'a pas l'habitude de déférer aux réclamations, mais aux mérites […] C'est pourquoi l'Apôtre dit : ‹Ceux qu'il a connus d'avance et prédestinés›. Car il n'a pas prédestiné avant de connaître, et ceux dont il a connu d'avance les mérites, il a prédestiné leurs récompenses»; trad. PM) et Iac. I, 6, 26 (*Nihil est* […] *quod negari posse uereamur, nihil est in quo de munificentiae diuinae diffidere perseuerantia debeamus, cuius fuit in tantum diuturna et iugis ubertas, ut primo praedestinaret, deinde uocaret 'et quos uocaret hos et iustificaret et quos iustificaret hos et clarificaret'.* / « Nous n'avons […] pas à craindre qu'il puisse rien nous refuser, nous n'avons aucune raison de mettre en doute la persévérance de la générosité divine, dont l'abondance, constante et intarissable, est telle qu'elle nous a d'abord prédestinés, puis appelés, et que ceux qu'elle appelait, elle les a aussi justifiés, et ceux qu'elle justifiait, elle les a aussi glorifiés»; éd. SC citée, p. 385, l. 1-5; trad. ibid., retouchée). Mais je me garderai de presser la contradiction : est-il légitime d'étendre sans autre précaution aux grâces dont tous les hommes indistinctement sont les bénéficiaires ce qui est dit des privilèges préparés pour les Apôtres (contexte de Fid. *l.c.*, qui commente la requête de la mère des fils de Zébédée selon Mt 20, 20-23)? D'autant plus que la formulation du présent texte semble heurter également la *sententia* de Fug. 6, 36 rapportée plus haut, texte correspondant à la n. 14.

Conclusion

Les analyses qui précèdent permettent de mesurer que la doctrine ambrosienne du péché originel et de la grâce ne sauraient se ramener, telle quelle, à aucun enseignement développé par les théologiens subséquents. À cet égard, et pour nous en tenir, sommairement, à des aspects globaux, trois réflexions, dont la disparate apparente donne de vérifier le caractère *irréductible* de la position de notre auteur :

(1) La pensée d'Ambroise sur l'universalité du péché et sa spiritualité heurtent de front l'idée d'*impeccance*. Augustin a raison de le souligner contre Pélage[28].

(2) Ce qui peut perdurer de capacité en l'homme déchu est pour Ambroise comme une grâce ; et c'est une grâce du Christ : à ses yeux, les deux économies successives du salut se déroulent en Christ – aussi bien chez lui non plus le vocable *natura* ne doit prêter à confusion. Pour autant, il n'est pas légitime d'aller trop loin dans une comparaison entre ces intuitions (dont la première d'ailleurs, et qui serait en l'espèce la plus décisive, reste, on l'a dit, problématique), et ce que l'on entrevoit de la permanence de la grâce primitive en tout homme selon les prétendus « semi-pélagiens », Jean Cassien et Fauste de Riez[29].

(3) Ambroise ne semble pas toujours conséquent, au moins *in terminis* (ainsi sur l'initiative humaine dans la confession de foi justifiante et la com-

---

[28] Voir De gratia Christi et de peccato originali libri duo I, 43, 47 et 48, 53. Sur « l'utilisation de l'œuvre ambrosienne en 'De gratia Christi et de peccato originali' (contre les interprétations avancées par Pélage), consulter, portant ce titre A. de Veer, NC 6, BA 22 (Paris 1975), p. 694–697.

[29] Sur cette doctrine chez Jean Cassien, voir J. Delmulle, Prosper d'Aquitaine contre Jean Cassien. Le Contra collatorem, l'appel à Rome du parti augustinien dans la querelle post-pélagienne, Textes et Études du Moyen Âge 91 (Barcelone – Rome 2018) ; chez Fauste de Riez, voir P. Mattei, Le fantôme semi-pélagien. Lecture du traité De gratia de Fauste de Riez, *Augustiniana* 60 (2010) 87–117 ; P. Mattei, Genèse 1, 26–27 dans le De gratia de Fauste de Riez, in : T. Hainthaler, F. Mali, G. Emmenegger, A. Morozov (éds.), Imago Dei (Innsbruck – Vienne 2021) 222–250 (conférence donnée au Colloque homonyme de Lviv, 12–14 septembre 2019). Dans ces deux articles (respect. p. 112–113 ; p. 235) j'ai avancé que Dieu, selon l'évêque de Riez, guette avec sollicitude chez l'homme le moindre réveil de la grâce primitive rémanente pour s'empresser d'impartir la seule grâce qui, en l'état actuel, pourvoit véritablement au salut, à savoir celle de Jésus-Christ : une telle articulation, nous l'avons vu, si elle est présente chez Ambroise, n'est jamais aussi nettement exprimée par lui.

mission d'un acte bon[30]), et il ne fait pas de la prédestination un objet d'enquête approfondi. Cela, cette fois, quoi qu'affirme Augustin, et malgré tel ou tel rapprochement possible, probable, ou indubitable[31].

Touchant la situation d'Ambroise par rapport d'un côté aux semi-pélagiens, de l'autre à Augustin, tout se passe en fait comme si le Milanais conservait, fût-ce d'une manière souvent voilée, des traits hérités d'une tradition demeurée prépondérante dans la patristique grecque et qui met plutôt l'accent sur la force rémanente de l'humanité *post lapsum*, et, dans le même temps, non sans incertitudes, s'ouvrait davantage à une théologie de la grâce victorieuse qui, encore que nullement nouvelle elle non plus (saint Cyprien!), prendrait le dessus dans l'Occident latin.

Bien entendu, il est logique de comprendre ces «dérobades» ambrosiennes dans l'histoire : on ne saurait demander au Milanais d'anticiper sur des débats qui n'éclateraient qu'après lui. Néanmoins, il convient aussi de les interpré-

---

[30] L'initiative dans la confession de foi justifiante peut s'expliquer, chez le païen, au moins en certains cas, par la mise en œuvre d'un vestige de la grâce primitive : je ne reviens pas sur la plausibilité d'une telle explication et, malgré ses lacunes, l'avantage qu'elle présente de «sauver» Ambroise de la contradiction. Quant à la commission d'un acte bon, l'initiative qu'en prend un baptisé pourrait venir de ce qu'il est muni de la grâce sacramentelle (de même le juste de l'AT, qui est, nous l'avons vu aussi, déjà chrétien *ante litteram*) : hypothèse qui n'est sans doute pas pleinement satisfaisante au regard de la théologie ultérieure (la grâce baptismale est *habituelle* : or il devrait être question de la grâce *actuelle*), mais qui semble valoir également pour Jérôme et qui évite, elle aussi, d'imputer de trop choquantes incohérences au Milanais comme elle épargne pareil grief au Stridonien (voir P. Mattei, Jérôme exégète de Paul dans les questions relatives à la grâce, in : É. Ayroulet, A. Canellis (éds.), L'exégèse de saint Jérôme, Colloque de Saint-Étienne – Lyon, 15–16 octobre 2015 (Saint-Étienne 2018) 283–296, spéc. 291).

[31] Sur l'effort tenté par Augustin pour montrer qu'Ambroise, comme Cyprien, et comme Grégoire de Nazianze, enseigne une dépendance radicale par rapport à la grâce, voir De dono perseuerantiae 19, 49 : PL 45, 1023–1025, où sont exploités les deux textes d'*In Luc* mentionnés plus haut (1, 10; 7, 27). – Il y aurait à réfléchir, plus amplement que je ne l'ai fait, sur la présence dans Ambroise de ce qui serait un thème augustinien majeur : la transmission du péché par voie de génération. Pareillement, sur la prévarication du premier couple comme rupture de l'ordre de subordination Dieu–âme–corps. Sans oublier la question du rapport entre la Loi (de Moïse) et la grâce (de Jésus-Christ) – sur la base des épîtres pauliniennes aux Romains et aux Galates, mais également de Jn 1, 17 (VVLG : [...] *lex per Mosen data est, gratia et veritas per Iesum Christum facta est*), verset qui figure dix fois dans l'œuvre ambrosienne (d'après «Biblindex» – en fait, après contrôle, et sans entrer dans un détail critique hors de saison ici, sept attestations) et qui est cardinal chez Augustin, par exemple dans le *Contra Faustum*. Domaine connexe au précédent : l'opinion d'Ambroise sur les vertus des païens, exprimée, comme on l'a vu, à travers l'image récurrente mais peu thématisée des feuilles et des fruits, serait à mettre en parallèle avec la pensée d'Augustin sur ce motif, telle que, d'une façon autrement plus orchestrée, et tout autre qu'univoque, elle se déploie notamment d'une part dans la *Cité de Dieu*, d'autre part dans la polémique avec Julien d'Éclane.

ter dans les cadres mêmes, doctrinaux et spirituels, qui furent les siens. C'est là qu'il faut revenir au cœur même de la vie et de la pensée de l'évêque : le christocentrisme. Jusque dans ses paradoxes. Tout est grâce de Dieu en Jésus-Christ, à recevoir avec componction, dans l'humilité (même si cette humilité oblige à l'action et ne favorise aucune paresse)[32] ; tout ensemble, il ne saurait s'introduire, si peu que ce soit, concernant ce bienfait, le soupçon que celui qui le reçoit n'a pas à y répondre (sans quoi c'est toute l'entreprise de la prédication ambrosienne en son versant moral qui deviendrait inintelligible), et il est exclu que la charité divine fasse acception de personne ou mette des bornes à sa volonté salvatrice[33]. En définitive (et c'est peut-être là un dernier mot étrange, s'il est vrai que la présente communication prend sa place dans des journées d'étude sur le «péché d'origine» – mais ce dernier mot en soi n'a rien pour surprendre, et je ne prétends pas, en le prononçant, découvrir l'Amérique!), ce qui importe à Ambroise, ce n'est pas la faute, c'est le relèvement, auquel Dieu ne se lasse pas de travailler et auquel l'homme est appelé à consentir. *Felix culpa*!

---

[32] Le Verbe incarné étant le modèle, à suivre, de cette humilité, selon un motif récurrent dans *In Psalm.* 118, et qu'il conviendrait d'approfondir. Sur l'humilité selon Ambroise, et sa postérité chez Augustin, voir V. Grossi, Nota sulla presenza dell'*humilitas* ambrosiana in Agostino d'Ippona, in : C. Bernard-Valette, J. Delmulle, C. Gerzaguet (éds.), Nihil ueritas erubescit. Mélanges offerts à Paul Mattei par ses élèves, collègues et amis, Instrumenta Patristica et Mediaeualia 74 (Turnhout 2017) 203–214.

[33] La charité divine est telle, au demeurant, qu'elle va jusqu'à transfigurer la signification de la mort physique. La mort, pour Adam et sa race, est, on l'a dit, la suite de la faute. Mais Dieu en fait un secours et un remède – une libération de la chair de péché : thème qui court à travers tout le *De bono mortis*. Thème aussi que le Milanais n'a pas inventé : en voir par exemple une esquisse dans Novatien, *Trin.* 1, 12 (cf. P. Mattei, Anthropologie de Novatien [art. cité *supra*, n. 6], 252).

Lenka Karfíková, Prague and Olomouc (Czech Republic)

Hereditary Sin? Augustine and Origen

Abstract:
Augustine's construction of hereditary sin as referable guilt which is transmitted by libidinous procreation and which in itself, without any contribution of individual human beings, merits eternal damnation, was systematically formulated for the first time in his first anti-Pelagian writing De peccatorum meritis *(411/12). In my paper, Augustine's ideas as expressed in this writing and elsewhere, are compared with Origen whose "Commentary on Romans" seems to have been used in Augustine's construction of hereditary sin. However, there are important differences between both authors. What is transmitted in the human race, according to Origen, is not sin as referable guilt but the mortal body born from libidinous procreation and affected by sin. As Augustine left Origen's idea of the soul, which committed sin before its incarnation, he is unable to explain how the misery of sin, transmitted by the body, can affect the soul. What is more, his conviction that all people are affected by inherited sin as referable guilt from their very birth casts doubt upon God's righteousness.*

In his insightful essay *"Original Sin": A Study in Meaning*, Paul Ricœur analyses the intersubjective aspect of human guilt, i.e. sin not only as an individual act based on the individual will but, at the same time, as a state from which human beings need to be liberated.[1] Although Ricœur does not hesitate to "deconstruct the concept" (*défaire le concept*) of hereditary sin, he tries to hold its symbolic message as a "rational symbol" (*symbol rationnel*), i.e. as a stimulus of thinking and interpretation.[2]

Ricœur concentrates his main attention on Augustine, who, in his anti-Manichean polemics, emphasised the voluntary character of sin but, at the same time, against the Pelagians insisted on sin as a state which motivates voluntary actions and which was not brought about by the will of each human

---
[1] P. Ricœur, Le „péché originel": Étude de signification, in: idem, Conflit des interprétations: Essais d'herméneutique (Paris 1969) 265–282. English transl. by P. McCormick in: P. Ricœur, The Conflict of Interpretations: Essays in Hermeneutics (Evanston 1974) 269–286.
[2] P. Ricœur, Le „péché originel", 266.

being individually.[3] This emphasis on solidarity in sin is something very important in Ricœur's interpretation: "I do not hesitate to say", as he puts it, "that Pelagius can be right a thousand times against the pseudo-concept of original sin. Nevertheless, Saint Augustine transmits with this dogmatic mythology something essential that Pelagius completely misunderstood."[4]

As we can see in this quote, Augustine is also responsible for the effort, unlucky in Ricœur's eyes, to rationalise the symbol of hereditary sin into a doctrine.[5] Therefore, in dealing with hereditary sin, I choose to concentrate on Augustine and his idea of sin transmitted in the human race. Taking into account the ecumenical debate of this conference, I will equally treat Augustine's relation to Origen in this issue.

Hereditary sin in Augustine's *De peccatorum meritis*

Augustine's construction of hereditary sin as referable guilt which is transmitted by libidinous procreation and which in itself, without any contribution of individual human beings, merits eternal damnation, was systematically formulated for the first time in his first anti-Pelagian writing *De peccatorum meritis et remissione et de baptismo parvulorum* from 411–412, addressed to Flavius Marcellinus and refuting Caelestius' doctrines.[6]

Against the idea of his opponents, according to which sin and, as its consequence, death diffuse by moral "imitation" (*imitatione*) of individual human beings,[7] Augustine defends the archaic conviction concerning the biological and moral solidarity of the human race in sin and death. As the biblical evidence, he claims the verses of the apostle Paul Rom 5:12: "by one man sin

---

[3] P. Ricœur, Le „péché originel", 270–277. Another aspect, namely the understanding of evil and sin as nothingness or a tendency to nothingness, is found in both authors by *J. Chelius Stark*, The Problem of Evil: Augustine and Ricœur, AugSt 13 (1982) 111–121.

[4] P. Ricœur, Le „péché originel", 277: "Je n'hésite pas à dire que Pélage peut avoir mille fois raison contre le pseudo-concept de péché originel, saint Augustin fait passer à travers cette mythologie dogmatique quelque chose d'essentiel que Pélage a entièrement méconnu." English transl. P. McCormick, "Original Sin", 281.

[5] P. Ricœur, Le „péché originel", 273f.; 277; 281.

[6] On this work, cf. *B. Delaroche*, Saint Augustin, lecteur et interprète de saint Paul dans le De peccatorum meritis et remissione (hiver 411–412) (Paris 1996). My analysis, in the present paper, is based on my book: *L. Karfíková*, Grace and the Will according to Augustine (Leiden 2012) 172–181.

[7] Aug., Pecc. mer. I, 9, 9: C. F. Vrba – J. Zycha, CSEL 60 (Wien 1913), p. 10,15f.

entered into the world, and death by sin; in him (*in quo*) all have sinned"[8] and 1Cor 15:22: "in Adam all die".[9]

In its Vulgate version quoted by Augustine, the former of these verses, "in him (*in quo*) all have sinned", does not interpret the Greek original ἐφ' ᾧ πάντες ἥμαρτον ("because all sinned") fully adequately, as Augustine's "Pelagian" opponent Julian of Aeclanum rightly emphasised.[10] Augustine takes two interpretations of this verse into account, both of them confirming his idea: *In quo* refers either to sin which, through the first man, entered into the world, i.e. "all sinned by this sin (*in quo*)", or, to the first man, "in whom (*in quo*) all sinned". In both cases, the idea remains the same, according to Augustine, as all descendants of Adam committed this sin together with their forefather.[11]

As Augustine puts it, all human individuals were, at the beginning, "one human being"; they were included in Adam in the moment of his transgression, and his sin is thus their own sin as well.[12] Therefore, the other way

---

[8] *Aug.*, Pecc. mer. I, 9, 10 – 10, 11: CSEL 60, p. 12.

[9] *Aug.*, Pecc. mer. I, 8, 8: CSEL 60, p. 9; II, 30, 49: CSEL 60, p. 120; III, 11, 19: CSEL 60, p. 145.

[10] Augustine quotes Julian's argumentation in *Aug.*, C. Iul. imp. II, 174: M. Zelzer (post E. Kalinka), CSEL 85/1 (Wien 1974), p. 294. The sin which enters into the world in Adam (Rom 5:12) is a bad example (*exemplum*) and an unfortunate influence, in Julian's eyes (*Aug.*, C. Iul. imp. II, 47: CSEL 85/1, p. 195f.). On Julian's interpretation of Rom 5:12 cf. *J. Lössl*, Julian von Aeclanum. Studien zu seinem Leben, seinem Werk, seiner Lehre und ihrer Überlieferung (Leiden 2001) 213f.; on his theology further *F. Outrata*, Julian von Aeclanum, in: L. Karfíková et al. (eds.), Handbuch der Dogmengeschichte, III/5a(1): Gnadenlehre in Schrift und Patristik (Freiburg i.B. 2016) 606–622.

[11] *Aug.*, Pecc. mer. I, 10, 11: CSEL 60, p. 12,9.11-17. However, as many interpreters emphasise, Augustine did not develop his doctrine of inherited sin from the false exegesis of one verse alone, but came to it in a theological deduction based on the earlier tradition of the church. Cf. e.g. *S. Lyonnet*, Rom. V,12 chez saint Augustin. Note sur l'élaboration de la doctrine Augustinienne du péché originel, in: *L'homme devant Dieu. Mélanges offerts au Père de Lubac*, vol. I (Paris 1963) 327–339; *idem*, À propos de Romains 5,12 dans l'œuvre de S. Augustin. Note complémentaire, Biblica 45 (1964) 541–542; *idem*, Augustin et Rm 5,12 avant la controverse pélagienne. À propos d'un texte de saint Augustin sur le baptême des enfants, NRTh 89 (1967) 842–850. See also *B. Delaroche*, Saint Augustin, 142–145; 147–149; 212–217; 297f.; 311–314; 317; 321–323; *G. Di Palma*, Ancora sull'interpretazione agostiniana di Rom 5,12: „et ita in omnes homines pertransiit, in quo omnes peccaverunt", Augustinianum 44 (2004) 113–134.

[12] The inclusion of all human beings in the forefather of the race and the transmission of his guilt (*reatus*) to all individuals descended from him is already emphasised by Augustine in *Aug.*, Ep. 98, 1: A. Goldbacher, CSEL 34/2 (Prag etc. 1898), p. 521,5–7.10-12: […] *sed ideo ex Adam traxit, quod sacramenti illius gratia solveretur, quia nondum erat anima separatim vivens, id est altera anima […]. Traxit ergo reatum, quia unus erat cum illo et in illo, a quo traxit, quando, quod traxit admissum est.* This letter to Bonifatius can be dated to between 408 or 411 (cf. *B. Delaroche*, Saint Augustin, 353–356) and 413 (cf. *V. Grossi*, La liturgia battesimale in S.

round, sin and death can be said to transmigrate to Adam's descendants by the very propagation (*propagatione*)[13] in which biological life is transmitted. Both these ideas, i.e. the inclusion of all humanity in the ancestor and the biological transmission of sin and death, are complementary in Augustine's eyes.[14]

Through the principle of "imitation", the individual members of Adam's race certainly add their own voluntary sins to the hereditary one;[15] nevertheless, these individual sins are not hinted at in Paul's statement. Otherwise, he would have had to say that sin entered into the world through the devil, whom all rebels against God's will imitate, not through the first man from whom they biologically descend.[16]

Sexual propagation is thus the place where hereditary sin is transmitted, according to Augustine. In its libidinous character, as the sexual organs do not obey the control of the will, it is even the very medium of its transmission:

> The fact, then, that the ardor of concupiscence stirs disobediently in the members of the body of this death, that it tries to cast down and draw the whole mind to itself, that it does not arise when the mind wants and does not quiet down when the mind wants, is due to the evil of sin with which every human being is born.[17]

Everything born in this way as a fruit of "evil concupiscence" (*concupiscentiae malum*) or libido (*libido*), is but the "body of sin" (*corpus peccati*).[18] Christ alone, being born from his virginal mother without any intervention of the libido[19] and whose death was caused not by sin but obedience,[20] is able to save human beings from this "body of death" and deliver the remedy for the disease of concupiscence and mortality as its consequence.[21]

Agostino. Studio sulla catechesi del peccato originale negli anni 393–412 (Roma 1993) 103).
[13] *Aug.*, Pecc. mer. I, 9, 9: CSEL 60, p. 11.
[14] *Aug.*, C. Iul. imp. I, 48: M. Zelzer, CSEL 85/2 (Wien 2004), p. 38,57–59: [...] *in lumbis Adam fuisse omnes, qui ex illo fuerant per concupiscentiam carnis orituri.* See also IV, 104: CSEL 85/2, p. 108–111.
[15] *Aug.*, Pecc. mer. I, 9, 10: CSEL 60, p. 11.
[16] *Aug.*, Pecc. mer. I, 9, 9: CSEL 60, p. 10; I, 13, 17: CSEL 60, p. 17.
[17] *Aug.*, Pecc. mer. I, 29, 57: CSEL 60, p. 56,4–8: *Quod igitur in membris corporis mortis huius inoboedienter movetur totumque animum in se deiectum conatur adtrahere et neque cum mens voluerit exsurgit neque cum mens voluerit conquiescit, hoc est malum peccati, cum quo nascitur omnis homo.* English transl. R. J. Teske, Answer to the Pelagians (New York 1997) 66f.
[18] *Aug.*, Pecc. mer. I, 29, 57: CSEL 60, p. 56.
[19] *Aug.*, Pecc. mer. I, 29, 57: CSEL 60, p. 57,2–5: *Solus sine peccato natus est, quem sine virili complexu non concupiscentia carnis, sed oboedientia mentis virgo concepit; sola nostro vulneri medicinam parere potuit, quae non ex peccati vulnere germen piae prolis emisit.*
[20] *Aug.*, Pecc. mer. II, 31, 51: CSEL 60, p. 122.
[21] *Aug.*, Pecc. mer. I, 28, 56: CSEL 60, p. 55,20–23: [...] *sic omnes filios mulieris, quae serpenti*

Who from the human race is given the grace of being justified is an incomprehensible decision of God, independent of human faith and acts but causing them, according to Augustine. Human beings, corrupted and guilty from their very birth, are only able to merit condemnation by their own acts. Augustine cannot say why, of two human beings, God wishes to convert one while leaving the other in his or her inherited ignorance and weakness of the will and why God predestined the one to condemnation (*damnandi praedestinati*) because of his or her pride, while showing mercy to the other in spite of it.[22] Equally, he cannot say why, of two babies, one is brought to baptism and thus saved, while the other, being unbaptised, falls into condemnation. At any rate, God is not unjust, Augustine assures us.[23]

Infant baptism, which saves newborn babies from condemnation in the event of their early death,[24] serves as important evidence for Augustine's theological construction. On the one hand, it attests the unmerited nature of grace, which it is impossible to gain by human efforts;[25] on the other hand, it proves that babies, who do not have any individual sins, are born with the "sin of their origin" (*peccatum originale*).[26] The baptism, as Augustine puts it, is accorded because of the remission of sin; thus, it would be useless for babies to be baptised if they were not laden with sin and condemnation from their very birth:

> Nothing else is accomplished by the baptism of little ones but that they are incorporated into the Church, that is, that they are joined to the body and members of Christ. Hence, it clearly follows that they would be subject to condemnation (*damnatio*) if baptism were not conferred upon them. But they could not be condemned if they had no sin whatsoever. Since at their age they could not contract any sin in their personal life, we are left to understand or, if we cannot yet understand it, at least to believe that little ones bring with them original sin (*trahere [...] originale peccatum*).[27]

---

credidit (cf. Gen 3:1–6), *ut libidine corrumperetur, non liberari a corpore mortis huius nisi per filium virginis, quae angelo credidit, ut sine libidine fetaretur* (cf. Luke 1:26–38).

[22] Aug., Pecc. mer. II, 17, 26: CSEL 60, p. 99,7–9: *[...] sive damnandi praedestinati sunt propter iniquitatem superbiae sive contra ipsam suam superbiam iudicandi et erudiendi, si filii sunt misericordiae*. Similarly, Aug., Pecc. mer. II, 18, 32: CSEL 60, p. 103,6–11.

[23] Aug., Pecc. mer. I, 21, 29–30: CSEL 60, p. 27–29.

[24] Aug., Pecc. mer. I, 16, 21: CSEL 60, p. 20,20–22: *Potest proinde recte dici parvulos sine baptismo de corpore exeuntes in damnatione omnium mitissima futuros. Multum autem fallit et fallitur, qui eos in damnatione praedicat non futuros.*

[25] Aug., Pecc. mer. I, 21, 29: CSEL 60, p. 28,13–17.

[26] Aug., Pecc. mer. I, 34, 64: CSEL 60, p. 64f.

[27] Aug., Pecc. mer. III, 4, 7: CSEL 60, p. 133,24–134,3: *Unde fit consequens, ut, quoniam*

For his idea of infant baptism which removes the sin of origin, Augustine claims the testimony of the African martyr Cyprian, who spoke about the "contagion of the ancient death" (*contagium mortis antiquae*), which transmigrates to babies by their biological birth, "not as their own sins but alien ones (*aliena peccata*)",[28] and equally the biblical scholar Jerome.[29]

Augustine could not accept the Pelagian explanation which said that babies are baptised to become sanctified (*ut sanctificentur in Christo*), not to be absolved from sins which they cannot have committed.[30] Against this very rational argumentation, Augustine develops his ideas of the inherited burden of Adam's sons affected by the sin of their ancestor from their very birth. Thanks to the grace of the divine Saviour, bestowed in baptism, this sin loses its character of imputable guilt (*reatus*) and thus cannot bring eternal condemnation; nevertheless, it remains in its consequences, especially concupiscence[31] and mortality.[32]

Even baptised people succumb to physical death, although, in its nature of merited punishment, death has been overcome and one day, in the resurrec-

---

nihil agitur aliud, cum parvuli baptizantur, nisi ut incorporentur ecclesiae, id est Christi corpori membrisque socientur, manifestum sit eos ad damnationem, nisi hoc eis conlatum fuerit, pertinere. Non autem damnari possent, si peccatum utique non haberent. Hoc quia illa aetas nullum in vita propria contrahere potuit, restat intellegere vel, si hoc nondum possumus, saltim credere trahere parvulos originale peccatum. English transl. R. J. Teske, Answer to the Pelagians, 124. Similarly, Aug., Pecc. mer. I, 20, 28: CSEL 60, p. 27,16–21: [...] *profecto illi, quibus sacramentum defuerit, in eis habendi sunt qui non credunt filio; atque ideo si huius inanes gratiae corpore exierint, sequetur eos quod dictum est: "Non videbunt vitam, sed ira dei manet super eos" (John 3:36). Et unde hoc, quando eos clarum est peccata propria non habere, si nec originali peccato teneantur obnoxii?* Aug., Pecc. mer. I, 19, 24: CSEL 60, p. 24,18–20: *Et ideo quia suae vitae propriae peccatis nullis adhuc tenentur obnoxii, originalis in eis aegritudo sanatur in eius gratia, qui salvos facit per lavacrum regenerationis.*

[28] Aug., Pecc. mer. III, 5, 10: CSEL 60, p. 137,2–7: [...] *recens natus nihil peccavit, nisi quod secundum Adam carnaliter natus contagium mortis antiquae prima nativitate contraxit! Qui ad remissam peccatorum accipiendam hoc ipso facilius accedit, quod illi remittuntur non propria, sed aliena peccata.* Cf. Cypr., Ep. 64, 5: G. F. Diercks, CCL 3C (Turnhout 1996), p. 720,20–721,2. On this idea, perhaps of African origin, cf. G. Bonner, Les origines africaines de la doctrine augustinienne sur la chute et le péché originel, in: I. Oroz-Reta (ed.), Augustinus (Madrid 1967) 97–116; P. F. Beatrice, Tradux peccati: Alle fonti della dottrina agostiniana del peccato originale (Milano 1978).

[29] Aug., Pecc. mer. III, 6, 12 – 7, 13: CSEL 60, p. 138–140. Cf. Hier., In Ion. 3, 5: M. Adriaen, CCL 76 (Turnhout 1969), p. 406; Adv. Iovin. II: PL 23, 284a–b.

[30] Aug., Pecc. mer. III, 6, 12: CSEL 60, p. 139.

[31] Aug., Pecc. mer. II, 28, 46: CSEL 60, p. 117,20f.: [...] *manentis concupiscentiae reatum praeterire post peccatorum remissionem.*

[32] Aug., Pecc. mer. III, 13, 23: CSEL 60, p. 150.

Hereditary Sin? Augustine and Origen 275

tion of the body, it will be overcome fully.[33] Similarly, even baptised people succumb to concupiscence and have to struggle against it until the end of their terrestrial life.[34] With the force of their concupiscence, not with the power of their new birth, they beget their children, who are thus affected by concupiscence as well.[35]

Thus, the body seems to be the very domain of inherited sin in Augustine's eyes (*caro peccati, corpus mortis,* cf. Rom 6:6; 7:24). Therefore, the divine Physician of this deadly disease became incarnate, "similar to the sinful flesh" (Rom 8:3), in order to overcome sin and death by his bodily resurrection.[36] However, Augustine cannot explain how the soul is involved in this misery, as he cannot answer the difficult question of the origin of individual souls, which is not treated in the Bible.[37] Is God to be supposed to create all individual souls anew, as Augustine's opponents have it, or are the souls propagated *ex traduce,* i.e. from the souls of the biological parents? Augustine does not even exclude a third alternative, according to which the soul is not created "in the body" (*in corpore*), but "because of the body" (*propter corpus*) and sent to it (*mitti*).[38] Nevertheless, he rejects very clearly the "improbable fictions" (*fabulas improbabiles*) of the heavenly sin of the soul, i.e. of its transgression preceding its incarnation.[39]

Although traducianism seems to fit logically into his idea of inherited guilt,

---

[33] Aug., Pecc. mer. III, 11, 20: CSEL 60, p. 146f.
[34] Aug., Pecc. mer. II, 4, 4: CSEL 60, p. 73f.
[35] Aug., Pecc. mer. III, 8, 16 – 9, 17: CSEL 60, p. 142–144; III, 12, 21: CSEL 60, p. 149,16f.
[36] Aug., Pecc. mer. III, 12, 21: CSEL 60, p. 148,13–17: *Quemadmodum ab origine trahitur mors in corpore mortis huius* (cf. Rom 7:24), *sic ab origine tractum est et peccatum in hac carne peccati; propter quod sanandum et propagine adtractum et voluntate auctum atque ipsam carnem resuscitandam medicus venit in similitudine carnis peccati* (cf. Rom 8:3). See also Aug., Pecc. mer. I, 28, 56: CSEL 60, p. 55.
[37] Aug., De pecc. mer. II, 36, 59: CSEL 60, p. 127f.
[38] Aug., De pecc. mer. III, 9, 17: CSEL 60, p. 143. See also Aug., De pecc. mer. I, 38, 69: CSEL 60, p. 70,4f.: [...] *sive et ipsa ex parentibus tracta sit sive ibidem creata sive desuper inspirata.* A similar list of alternatives is also to be found in Origen, De princ., Praef. 5: H. Crouzel – M. Simonetti, SC 252 (Paris 1978), p. 84: *De anima vero utrum ex seminis traduce ducatur, ita ut ratio ipsius vel substantia inserta ipsis corporalibus seminibus habeatur, an vero aliud habeat initium, et hoc ipsum initium si genitum est aut non genitum, vel certe si extrinsecus corpori inditur, necne: non satis manifesta praedicatione distinguitur.* See also Orig. Comm. Cant. II, 5, 22–23: L. Brésard et al., SC 375 (Paris 1991), p. 366–368.
[39] Aug., De pecc. mer. I, 22, 31: CSEL 60, p. 31,6f.; I, 22, 31: CSEL 60, p. 29,17–20: *An forte illud iam explosum repudiatumque sentiendum est, quod animae prius in caelesti habitatione peccantes gradatim atque paulatim ad suorum meritorum corpora veniant, ac pro ante gesta vita magis minusve corporeis pestibus adfligantur?*

Augustine never opted for this solution definitively.[40] As he assures us, God cannot be the source of any guilt, even if he is supposed to create the individual souls anew. The guilt is thus either transmitted from parents' souls, if the soul is propagated from them, or it is burdened with guilt in its very "mingling with the body" in the mother's womb, where the soul, as newly created, has been sent.[41]

As we can see, Augustine's construction has a serious gap, as it is unable to explain how the soul can become contaminated with sin, which is transmitted in the body. Nevertheless, Augustine repeats his speculation many times in his anti-Pelagian polemics[42] and he even achieves Church condemnation for his opponents.[43]

In the present paper, I do not intend to demur at Augustine's confusing theological ideas, scarcely defended by anyone in their integrity, but to point, in the second part of my presentation, to Augustine's relation to Origen in this issue.

Augustine's critical inspiration by Origen

A certain similarity between Augustine's idea of the sin transmitted by procreation and Origen's conviction about the stain connected with physical birth,

---

[40] On this issue, see my book: L. Karfíková, Grace, 214–224.
[41] Aug., Pecc. mer. II, 36, 59: CSEL 60, p. 127,8–11.15–23: *De anima vero, utrum et ipsa eodem modo propagata reatu, qui ei dimittatur, obstricta sit – neque enim possumus dicere solam carnem parvuli, non etiam animam indigere salvatoris et redemptoris auxilio* [...] –, *an etiam non propagata eo ipso, quo carni peccati aggravanda misceatur, iam ipsius peccati remissione et sua redemptione opus habeat, deo per summam praescientiam iudicante, qui parvulorum ab isto reatu non mereantur absolvi, etiam qui nondum nati nihil habeant propria sua vita egerunt vel boni vel mali* (cf. Rom 9:11), *et quomodo deus, etiamsi non de traduce animas creat, non sit tamen auctor reatus eiusdem, propter quem redemptio sacramenti necessaria est animae parvuli, magna quaestio est* [...].
[42] Aug. Gr. et pecc. or. II, 30, 35 – 31, 36: F. Vrba – J. Zycha, CSEL 42 (Wien 1902), p. 194f.; II, 37, 42 – 38, 43: CSEL 42, p. 200f.; Nupt. concup. I, 23, 25 – 25, 28: CSEL 42, p. 237–241; I , 32, 37: CSEL 42, p. 248f.; II, 5, 14–15: CSEL 42, p. 265–268; II, 26, 42: CSEL 42, p. 294–296; II, 27, 46: CSEL 42, p. 299–302; C. Iul. III, 15, 29: N. Cipriani, NBA 18/1 (Roma 1985), p. 612–614; III, 21, 46: NBA 18/1, p. 632; VI, 19, 60: NBA 18/1, p. 944–946; VI, 24, 79: NBA 18/1, p. 972; C. Iul. imp. I, 48: CSEL 85/1, p. 40,108f.; II, 7: CSEL 85/1, p. 167f.; II, 42: CSEL 85/1, p. 193; II, 177: CSEL 85/1, p. 296f.; III, 4: CSEL 85/1, p. 353; III, 25: CSEL 85/1, p. 366; V, 12: CSEL 85/2, p. 183.
[43] On this conflict, cf. O. Wermelinger, Rom und Pelagius (Stuttgart 1975). I tried to summarise it in my book: L. Karfíková, Grace, 159–171. The idea of the sin transmitted by procreation is still present in Tridentinum; cf. Decretum super peccato originali 3: S. Ehses, Concilium Tridentinum, V/2 (Freiburg i.B. 1911), p. 197; see also Decretum de iustificatione 3: S. Ehses, Concilium Tridentinum, p. 510.

as formulated in his exegetical writings, was already noted by Adolf von Harnack a hundred years ago,[44] although the German scholar realised very well that Origen did not have hereditary sin (*Erbsünde*) in his mind.[45] As Caroline Hammond Bammel puts it in her careful analysis of this question, Augustine, in his first anti-Pelagian writing, *De peccatorum meritis*, drew from Origen's *Commentary on Romans*, which had been (recently?) at his disposal in Rufinus' Latin translation. This fact can explain not only Augustine's frequent references to this biblical book but also some of his theological ideas, e.g. his emphasis on the "body of sin" (cf. Rom 6:6 and 8:3), understood as the body affected by concupiscence transmitted by procreation, from which Christ alone, having being born from a virgin, is exempt.[46]

At the same time, Augustine opposes Origen on the issue of inherited guilt, especially his idea, expressed in *De principiis* and concerning the original unity of rational beings, who were differentiated into angels, souls and demons as a result of the weakening of their will, and obtained bodies according to their moral level.[47] As we can remember, this polemic appeared in *De peccatorum meritis*, where Augustine rejected the "improbable fictions" about the heavenly sin of the soul.[48] Besides some anonymous critical remarks concerning the idea of souls having sinned before their incarnation,[49] Augustine explicitly

---

[44] A. von *Harnack*, Der kirchengeschichtliche Ertrag der exegetischen Arbeiten des Origenes, I (Leipzig 1918) 60.
[45] A. von *Harnack*, Der kirchengeschichtliche Ertrag, II (Leipzig 1919) 123f.
[46] *Orig.*, Comm. Rom. V, 1: C. P. Hammond Bammel, SC 539 (Paris 2010), p. 348-402; V, 9, 7-14: SC 539, p. 492-500; VI, 12, 4: C. P. Hammond Bammel, SC 543 (Paris 2011), p. 206. See *C. P. Bammel*, Rufinus' Translation of Origen's Commentary on Romans and the Pelagian Controversy, in: Storia ed esegesi in Rufino di Concordia (Atti del secondo Convegno internazionale di studi su "Esegesi e storia in Rufino di Concordia") (Udine 1992) 131-142, here 135-137; *eadem*, Augustine, Origen and the Exegesis of St. Paul, Augustinianum 32 (1992) 341-368, here 359. Augustine is even supposed to have had a certain knowledge of Origen's *Commentary* (e.g. his interpretation of Rom 8:3) before 411 by *D. Keech*, The Anti-Pelagian Christology of Augustine of Hippo, 396-430 (Oxford 2012). However, this hypothesis seems rather unsure.
[47] *Orig.*, De princ. II, 9, 7: SC 252, p. 368-370; IV, 4, 8: H. Crouzel – M. Simonetti, SC 268 (Paris 1980), p. 422,320-326: [...] *mutabilis et convertibilis erat natura rationabilis, ita ut pro meritis etiam diverso corporis uteretur indumento illius vel illius qualitatis, necessario sicut diversitates praenoscebat deus futuras vel animarum vel virtutum spiritalium, ita etiam naturam corpoream faceret, quae permutatione qualitatum in omnia, quae res posceret, conditoris arbitrio mutaretur.* On the development of Augustine's attitude to the doctrine of Origen, cf. *G. Gasparro*, Agostino di fronte alla „eterodossia" di Origene: Un aspetto della questione origeniana in Occidente, in: B. Bruning et al. (eds.), Collectanea Augustiniana: Mélanges T. J. van Bavel (Leuven 1990) 220-243.
[48] *Aug.*, De pecc. mer. I, 22, 31: CSEL 60, p. 30f.; cf. above, n. 39.
[49] See e.g. *Aug.*, Gr. et pecc. or. II, 31, 36: CSEL 42, p. 195; Ser. 165, 6: S. Boodts, CCL

rebukes Origen because of it, in the eleventh book of *De civitate dei*:

> [These philosophers] also claim that souls [...] have sinned by withdrawing from the Creator and, according to the gravity of their sins, have been imprisoned in bodies ranging, by degrees, from heaven down to earth [...]. Origen has been rightly reproved for holding and expressing such views in his work, which he calls περὶ ἀρχῶν, that is, *Of Origins*.[50]

Equally, the anonymous anti-Origenian remark in Augustine's letter 166 to Jerome from 415 is very interesting in our context,[51] as Augustine asks his correspondent where the soul took on its guilt which affects it from the very birth. He writes here, among other things:

> But that souls sin in another previous life and are therefore thrust down into fleshly prisons I do not believe, I do not agree to, I do not accept [...]. Because [...] there is a great difference between sinning in Adam, as the Apostle says: "In whom all sinned" (Rom 5:12), and sinning out of Adam somewhere or other, and for that reason being thrust down in Adam, that is, into the flesh which is derived from Adam, as into a prison.[52]

According to Augustine's biblical argument, to sin "in Adam" (Rom 5:12), i.e. as a part of the human race included in its forefather, is something completely different than to be included "into Adam" as a punishment for the preceding individual sin of the soul.

Augustine's complicated relationship to Origen concerning inherited sin certainly raises the question of what Origen's own attitude to this issue was.

41Bb (Turnhout 2016), p. 301f.

[50] *Aug.*, Civ. XI, 23: B. Dombart – A. Kalb, CCL 48 (Turnhout 1955), p. 341,8–11.13–15: [...] *sed animas dicunt [...] peccasse a Conditore recedendo et diversis progressibus pro diversitate peccatorum a caelis usque ad terras diversa corpora quasi vincula meruisse [...]. Hinc Origenes iure culpatur. In libris enim quos appellat περὶ ἀρχῶν, id est de principiis, hoc sensit, hoc scripsit.* English transl. G. G. Walsh – G. Monahanthe, The City of God, Books VIII–XVI (Washington, D.C. 1952) 222. Civ. XI can probably be dated to 417; cf. A.-M. La Bonnardière, Recherches de chronologie augustinienne (Paris 1965) 70.

[51] *Aug.*, Ep. 169, 4, 13: A. Goldbacher, CSEL 44 (Wien 1904), p. 620. Cf. A. Goldbacher, CSEL 58 (Wien 1923), p. 44.

[52] *Aug.*, Ep. 166, 9, 27: CSEL 44, p. 583: *Sed in alia superiore vita peccare animas et inde praecipitari in carceres carneos non credo, non adquiesco, non consentio* [...] *longe aliud est in Adam peccasse, unde dicit apostolus: "In quo omnes peccaverunt", et aliud est extra Adam nescio ubi peccasse et ideo in Adam, id est in carnem, quae ex Adam propagata est, tamquam in carcerem trudi.* English transl. W. Parsons, Letters, vol. 4 (Washington, D.C. 1955) 30f.

Origen on humanity included in Adam

Origen's exposition in *De principiis*, already mentioned above, seems to exclude the idea of the guilt transmitted in Adam's race, as each soul answers individually for its own falling away from God.[53] As biblical evidence of this idea, Origen claims the very different lot of the twins Esau and Jacob, one of whom was hated and the other beloved by God in the very womb of their mother (cf. Rom 9:11). This would certainly be unjust, had it not responded to the behaviour of both brothers before their incarnation.[54]

On the other hand, in his Commentary on Romans, Origen mentions the "dirt of sin" (*sordes peccati*), sticking to babies in their birth,[55] or the "contagion" (*contagio*)[56] and "impurity of sin" (*pollutio peccati*) transmitted by the "motion of concupiscence" (*ex concupiscentiae motu*) during propagation.[57] Can this idea be connected with Origen's doctrine from his early treatise *De principiis*, or are we to suppose a development of the Alexandrian scholar from the teaching of the pre-existence of souls to a more biblical anthropology (or, at least, to a more cautious formulation of his thoughts)?[58] Or should we sus-

---

[53] Origen's idea of the pre-existence of the soul can only be connected with the biblical narratives in Gen 1–3 with difficulty; cf. G. *Sfameni Gasparro*, Doppia creazione e peccato di Adamo nel "Peri Archon": Fondamenti biblici e presupposti platonici dell'esegesi origeniana, in: H. Crouzel – A. Quacquarelli (eds.), Origeniana Secunda: Second colloque international des études origéniennes, Bari, 20–23 septembre 1977 (Roma 1980) 57–67; P. *Pisi*, Peccato di Adamo e caduta dei noes nell'esegesi origeniana, in: L. Lies (ed.), Origeniana Quarta: Die Referate des 4. Internationalen Origeneskongresses, Innsbruck, 2.-6. September 1985 (Innsbruck 1987) 322–335; C. P. *Bammel*, Adam in Origen, in: R. Williams (ed.), The Making of Orthodoxy: Essays in Honour of Henry Chadwick (Cambridge 1989) 62–93.

[54] *Orig.*, De princ. I, 7, 4: SC 252, p. 214–216; II, 9, 7: SC 252, p. 366–370; *Comm. Ioh.* II, 31, 192: C. Blanc, SC 120bis (Paris ²1996), p. 340. I treated Origen's interpretation of this verse in my paper: L. *Karfíková*, Is Romans 9:11 proof for or against the pre-existence of the soul? Origen and Augustine in comparison, in: B. Bitton-Ashkelony et alii (eds.), Origeniana Duodecima. Origen's Legacy in the Holy Land—A Tale of Three Cities: Jerusalem, Caesarea and Bethlehem, Proceedings of the 12th International Origen Congress, Jerusalem, 25–29 June, 2017 (Leuven etc. 2019) 627–641, here 627–630.

[55] *Orig.*, Comm. Rom. V, 9, 13: SC 539, p. 498,4.

[56] *Orig.*, Comm. Rom. VI, 12, 4: C. P. Hammond Bammel, SC 543 (Paris 2011), p. 206,7.

[57] *Orig.*, Comm. Rom. VI, 12, 4: SC 543, p. 206,10f.: [...] *pollutionem* [...] *peccati quae ex concupiscentiae motu conceptis traditur.*

[58] Cf. A. *Castagno Monaci*, L'idea della preesistenza delle anime e l'esegesi di Rm 9,9–21, in: H. Crouzel – A. Quacquarelli (eds.), Origeniana Secunda: Second colloque international des études origéniennes, Bari, 20–23 septembre 1977 (Roma 1980) 69–78, here 76. A certain development in Origen's idea of pre-existence has been supposed by Ch. *Bigg*, The Christian Platonists of Alexandria: Eight lectures preached before the University of Oxford in the year 1886 (New York 1886, reprinted 1970) 202–206; N. P. *Williams*, The Ideas of the Fall and of Original Sin: A Historical and Critical Study (London 1927) 208–231; R. *Cadiou*,

pect Rufinus, who, by his own admission, shortened Origen's *Commentary on Romans* by half and modified it in important ways,[59] of changing the sense of Origen's exposition?[60]

In answering this difficult question, we can base our reaction on the Greek passage from Origen's late polemic *Contra Celsum*, where he quotes the words of the apostle Paul that "in Adam all die" (1Cor 15:22), in order to explain the common lot of all human beings:

> Adam means *anthropos* (man) in the Greek language, and in what appears to be concerned with Adam Moses is speaking of the nature of man (περὶ τῆς τοῦ ἀνθρώπου φύσεως). For, as the Bible says, "in Adam all die" (1Cor 15:22), and they were condemned in "the likeness of Adam's transgression" (Rom 5:14). Here the divine Word says this not so much about an individual as of the whole race. Moreover, in the sequence of sayings which seem to refer to one individual, the curse (ἡ ἀρά) of Adam is shared by all men.[61]

Le développement d'une théologie. Pression et aspiration, RechSC 23 (1933) 411–429, here 414f.; *M. Harl*, La préexistence des âmes dans l'œuvre d'Origène, in: L. Lies (ed.), Origeniana Quarta: Die Referate des 4. Internationalen Origeneskongresses, Innsbruck, 2.-6. September 1985 (Innsbruck – Wien 1987) 238–258; reprinted in: *M. Harl*, Le déchiffrement du sens. Études sur l'herméneutique chrétienne d'Origène à Grégoire de Nysse (Paris 1993) 247–268, here 261f.

[59] *Orig.*, Comm. Rom., Praef. Ruf.: C. P. Hammond Bammel, SC 532 (Paris 2009), p. 136; Comm. Rom., Epil. Ruf. 2: C. P. Hammond Bammel, SC 555 (Paris 2012), p. 452.

[60] *C. P. Hammond Bammel* (Rufinus' Translation, 142) surmises that Rufinus might have suppressed some problematic points in Origen's doctrine, e.g. the pre-existence of souls. Otherwise, the author, having analysed especially the commentary on Rom 7, supposes that Rufinus has not changed the meaning of the text significantly; cf. *C. P. Hammond Bammel*, Philocalia IX, Jerome, Epistle 121, and Origen's Exposition of Romans VII, JThS 32 (1981) 79–81; *eadem*, Der Römerbrieftext des Rufin und seine Origenes-Übersetzung (Freiburg i.Br. 1985) 92.

[61] *Orig.*, C. Cels. IV, 40: M. Borret, SC 136 (Paris 1968), p. 288,11-19: […] καθ' Ἑλλάδα φωνὴν ὁ Ἀδὰμ ἄνθρωπός ἐστι, καὶ ἐν τοῖς δοκοῦσι περὶ τοῦ Ἀδὰμ εἶναι φυσιολογεῖ Μωϋσῆς τὰ περὶ τῆς τοῦ ἀνθρώπου φύσεως. Καὶ "γὰρ ἐν τῷ Ἀδάμ", ὥς φησιν ὁ λόγος, "πάντες ἀποθνῄσκουσι", καὶ κατεδικάσθησαν ἐν "τῷ ὁμοιώματι τῆς παραβάσεως Ἀδάμ", οὐχ οὕτως περὶ ἑνός τινος ὡς περὶ ὅλου τοῦ γένους ταῦτα φάσκοντος τοῦ θείου λόγου. Καὶ γὰρ ἐν τῇ τῶν λεγομένων ὡς περὶ ἑνὸς ἀκολουθίᾳ ἡ ἀρὰ τοῦ Ἀδὰμ κοινὴ πάντων ἐστί. English transl. H. Chadwick, Contra Celsum (Cambridge 1953) 216. On Origen's interpretation of Adam as humanity in general, see *G. Bürke*, Des Origenes Lehre vom Urstand des Menschen, ZKTh 72 (1950) 1–39, here 34f.; *C. P. Bammel*, Adam in Origen; *P. W. Martens*, Origen's Doctrine of Pre-Existence and the Opening Chapters of Genesis, ZACh 16 (2012) 516–549, here 534; *M. Przyszychowska*, We Were All in Adam: The Unity of Mankind in Adam in the Teaching of the Church Fathers (Warsaw – Berlin 2018) 59–78.

Hereditary Sin? Augustine and Origen 281

If we compare this exposition with Augustine's ideas, we can see that unlike Augustine, Origen does not speak about all human beings who "have sinned" in Adam but who "die" in him.[62] As already mentioned, Augustine's statement is based on an erroneous reading of Rom 5:12, which, however, was not isolated in Western Christianity,[63] although e.g. Pelagius, equally inspired by Origen, did not share it.[64]

How Origen himself understood this verse can only be surmised. In his writings surviving in Greek, we can find Rom 5:12 quoted e.g. in the Commentary on John, where Origen emphasises that through Adam's sin death entered into the world, without answering our query explicitly.[65] The diffusion of sin seems rather to be a question of a similar behaviour, as Origen mentions it in the passage cited above (and elsewhere), quoting the apostle: the "likeness of Adam's transgression" (Rom 5:14: τῷ ὁμοιώματι τῆς παραβάσεως Ἀδάμ).[66]

The inclusion of the "nature of man" (τῆς τοῦ ἀνθρώπου φύσεως) in Adam, and the "curse" (ἡ ἀρά) common to all the members of his race, in the quoted passage,[67] very probably concerns the lot of mortality, not the sharing of sin. Origen does not suppose this idea to be an alternative to the pre-existence of the soul, as the continuation of his polemics against Celsus makes clear:

> And the statement that the man who was cast out of the garden with the woman was clothed with "tunics of skins" (Gen 3:21) which God made for those who had sinned on account of the transgression of mankind, has a certain secret and mysterious meaning, superior to the Platonic doctrine of the descent of the soul which loses its wings and is carried hither "until it finds something firm as its resting-place" (Phaedrus 248c2–3).[68]

---

[62] Similarly, *Orig. Comm. Ioh.* XX, 25, 224: C. Blanc, SC 290 (Paris 1982), p. 268.

[63] Cf. *Ambst.*, Comm. Rom. 5, 12: H. J. Vogels, CSEL 81/1 (Wien 1966), p. 164f.; on this commentary dated to 363–384, see V. Hušek, Ambrosiaster, in: L. Karfíková et al. (eds.), Gnadenlehre, 484–486.

[64] As Pelagius explains, sin entered into the world "as an example or form" (*exemplo vel forma*) bringing death to everyone who imitates it. However, it is only hyperbolically that it can be said that this unhappy situation concerns "all", as Abraham and Isaac (and Jacob) seem to live (cf. Luke 20:37f.); see *Pelag.*, Expos. Rom. 5, 12: A. Souter (Cambridge 1926), p. 45. On Rom 5:12 in Pelagius' interpretation, cf. V. Hušek, Pelagius, in: L. Karfíková et al. (eds.), Gnadenlehre, 520–522. On Pelagius' inspiration by Origen, cf. A. J. Smith, The Commentary of Pelagius on Romans Compared with That of Origenes-Rufinus, JThS 20 (1919) 127–177; C. P. Bammel, Rufinus' Translation.

[65] *Orig.*, Comm. Ioh. XX, 39, 364: SC 290, p. 334.

[66] *Orig.*, Comm. Ioh. XX, 39, 364–365: SC 290, p. 334,18f.

[67] *Orig.*, C. Cels. IV, 40: SC 136, p. 288,13f. and 19.

[68] *Orig.*, C. Cels. IV, 40: SC 136, p. 288,20–290,26: Καὶ ὁ ἐκβαλλόμενος δὲ ἐκ τοῦ παραδείσου ἄνθρωπος μετὰ τῆς γυναικός, τοὺς "δερματίνους" ἠμφιεσμένος "χιτῶνας", οὓς διὰ τὴν

In the same vein, Origen, in the *Commentary on Romans*, speaks about the human race being included in "Adam's loins" (*in lumbis Adae*) and, together with him, expelled from paradise.[69] This idea seems to come close to Augustine,[70] although Origen does not speak about a common sin but, again, a common "curse" (*condamnatio*), i.e. shared mortality, not hereditary guilt.[71] The transmission of sin could perhaps be hinted at by the "likeness of transgression" (*similitudo praevaricationis*), which does not have its origin in Adam's "seed" alone (*ex semine eius*) but is equally "adopted by education" (*ex institutione suscepta*).[72] However, the emphasis of this text seems to be rather on the education than the seed, and the "likeness of transgression" does not necessarily point to the referable guilt (as Augustine has it) but rather to a *tendency* of transgressing.

The fact that even a newborn baby is burdened with sin, as Origen indicates it elsewhere in the Commentary on Romans,[73] need not necessarily have the Augustinian meaning but may rather hint at the sin preceding the incarnation of the soul (which Origen might have cautiously not mentioned or Rufinus suppressed in his translation). In the same vein, Origen, in the polemic *Contra Celsum*, reminds his Platonising opponent that the "coming-to-be" or "birth" (γένεσις) is necessarily connected to error (πλάνη). In the same context, he

---

παράβασιν τῶν ἀνθρώπων ἐποίησε τοῖς ἁμαρτήσασιν ὁ θεός, ἀπόρρητόν τινα καὶ μυστικὸν ἔχει λόγον, ὑπὲρ τὴν κατὰ Πλάτωνα κάθοδον τῆς ψυχῆς, πτερορρυούσης καὶ δεῦρο φερομένης, "ἕως ἂν στερεοῦ τινος λάβηται". English transl. *H. Chadwick*, Contra Celsum, 216f. (modified). Cf. *Plato*, Phdr. 248c2–3: ἡ δὲ πτερορρυήσασα φέρεται ἕως ἂν στερεοῦ τινος ἀντιλάβηται, οὗ κατοικισθεῖσα, σῶμα γήϊνον.

[69] *Orig.*, Comm. Rom. V, 1, 12: SC 539, p. 364,7–366,12: [...] *omnes homines qui in hoc mundo nascuntur et nati sunt in lumbis erant Adae cum adhuc esset in paradiso et omnes homines cum ipso vel in ipso expulsi sunt de paradiso cum ipse inde depulsus est; et per ipsum mors quae ei ex praevaricatione venerat consequenter et in eos pertransiit qui in lumbis eius habebantur.* Similarly, in *Orig.*, Hom. Ez. 1, 3: M. Borret, SC 352 (Paris 1989), p. 48, Origen mentions Levi "in the loins" of Abraham and he also adds a remark on the punishment purifying from propagation and libido (*generationis enim et libidinis opera gehennae suppliciis corripiuntur*).

[70] *Aug.*, Pecc. mer. I, 10, 11: CSEL 60, p. 12; C. Iul. imp. I, 48: CSEL 85/1, p. 38,57–59 (quoted above, n. 14).

[71] *Orig.*, Comm. Rom. V, 4, 3: SC 539, p. 432,5 and 9f.: [...] *condemnatio quae in omnes homines sine dubio pervenit.* [...] *unusquisque de paradiso trusus videtur et excepisse condemnationem*.

[72] *Orig.*, Comm. Rom. V, 1, 33: SC 539, p. 392,16–19: [...] *omnes qui ex Adam praevaricatore nati sunt indicari videantur et habere in semet ipsis similitudinem praevaricationis eius non solum ex semine eius sed et ex institutione susceptam*.

[73] *Orig.*, Comm. Rom. V, 9, 10–13: SC 539, p. 494–498.

reminds us of the Jewish practice of sacrificing for newborn babies, who need purifying from sin.[74]

Finally, his remark concerning the "body of sin" (*corpus peccati*), which affects all human individuals except Christ, who was conceived without any "motion of concupiscence" (*ex concupiscentiae motu*),[75] points, equally, to the quality of the transmitted body. This idea might have expressed, in Origen's eyes, the connection of mortality, as a punishment for sin, with the way in which human beings are physically conceived. Libidinous procreation and death are two sides of the same coin, i.e. γένεσις, the coming-to-be as Origen discusses it with Celsus.

None of the above-mentioned passages substantiates the suspicion that Origen understood the solidarity of the human race with its forefather as the transmission of referable guilt. What is actually transmitted in the human race is the mortal body born from libidinous procreation and affected by sin, which is the common "curse" of Adam's race.

Augustine's question of how the soul can become infected by the sin transmitted by the body seems rather distant to Origen, as the soul, according to his understanding, sinned even before its incarnation (except those souls which descend into the body, not because of their weakness but because of their being called to a service, such as Christ's soul and the souls of stars).[76] The mortal body, which the soul receives as its terrestrial dwelling, is adapted to its moral state and, therefore, it is affected by sin from the very beginning of human bodily existence. This idea seems to correspond to Origen's doctrine of the

---

[74] Orig., C. Cels. VII, 50: M. Borret, SC 150 (Paris 1969), p. 130,1-6: Ὁ μὲν οὖν οὐκ ἐσαφήνισε, πῶς μετὰ γενέσεώς ἐστι πλάνη, οὐδὲ παρέστησεν ὅ τι περ ἐβούλετο, ἵνα κατανοήσωμεν συγκρίνοντες τὰ αὐτοῦ τοῖς ἡμετέροις· οἱ δὲ προφῆται, αἰνιττόμενοι ὅ τι περὶ τῶν γενέσεως πραγμάτων σοφόν, θυσίαν "περὶ ἁμαρτίας" λέγουσιν ἀναφέρεσθαι καὶ περὶ τῶν ἄρτι γεγενημένων ὡς οὐ καθαρῶν ἀπὸ ἁμαρτίας. On the "dirt" (*sordes*) of newborn babies, which was purified by the prescribed sacrifice, see also Orig., Hom. Lev. 8, 3: GCS 29, p. 396-398; 12, 4: GCS 29, p. 460; Hom. Luc. 14, 3: H. Crouzel et al., SC 87 (Paris 1962), p. 220. In this last passage, Origen differentiates between "dirt" and "sin", connecting "dirt" with the entrance of the soul into the body: *Omnis anima, quae humano corpore fuerit induta, habet sordes suas* (Hom. Luc. 14, 4: SC 87, p. 220).

[75] Orig., Comm. Rom. VI, 12, 4: SC 543, p. 206,11.

[76] Cf. Orig., De princ. II, 6, 3-5: SC 252, p. 320 on the soul of Christ; De princ. III,5,4: SC 268, p. 226 on the souls of stars. I treated these questions in more detail in my papers: L. Karfíková, Christus Gott und Mensch nach Origenes, in: Th. Hainthaler et al. (eds.), Jesus der Christus im Glauben der einen Kirche: Christologie - Kirchen des Ostens - Ökumenische Dialoge (Freiburg i.B. 2019) 146-164, here 154-157; *eadem*, Souls of Stars and Ideas of Individuals: Origenian Material in Augustine's Ep. 14?, StPatr 118 (2021) 41-55.

body, which, in its quality, is adapted to the soul as its inhabitant.[77] It has nothing in common, as I understand it, with Augustine's idea of the referable sin transmitted by procreation.

It would certainly be naïve to suppose human sins to be completely autonomous acts caused exclusively by the individual will, as Augustine rebukes the Pelagians for affirming. On the other hand, it is equally unacceptable, in my eyes, to conceive the common burden of the human race as guilt imputable to everyone from his or her very birth. Origen's position, as reconstructed above, offers a reasonable way between these extremes. Each soul answers for its own wrongdoings and it is for them alone that it can be justly punished. At the same time, human beings, born one from the other, carry the common burden of the inherited tendency to sin and of mortality.

The price which Origen had to pay for this moderate position was the Platonic idea of the pre-existing soul and the guilt preceding its incarnation. Without this speculative presupposition, it seems rather difficult to understand all events and developments in human world as just. If Origen wished to behold a righteous creator who offers the same chance to all rational beings, he could not do otherwise than keep this metaphysical precondition. Therefore, it does not seem very probable that he would abandon it in his old age. Augustine, on the other hand, did leave it[78] and opted for speculation about the transmitted sin (not being able to explain its transmission from the body to the soul) and the creator, who (for reasons that Augustine cannot explain either) predestined, before their very birth, only some people to eternal salvation while leaving others to condemnation.[79]

What I find entirely unacceptable in Augustine's theory of inherited sin is not only the transmission of sin by physical procreation (which, in its consequences, makes human sexuality feel guilty), but, above all, the idea of inher-

---

[77] Cf. *Orig.*, De princ. III, 6, 4–5: SC 268, 244–246. I dealt with this issue in more detail in my paper: L. Karfíková, The Resurrection of the Body in Origen's De principiis, in: F. Mali – A. Morozov (eds.), Résurrection charnelle: entre orthodoxie et hérésie (in print).

[78] In his early writings, Augustine seems to have presupposed the pre-existence of the soul; cf. *Aug.*, Ep. 7, 1, 2: A. Goldbacher, CSEL 34/1 (Prag etc. 1895), p. 14. See R. J. O'Connell, Pre-existence in Augustine's Seventh Letter, REAug 15 (1969) 67–73; idem, Pre-existence in the Early Augustine, REAug 26 (1980) 176–188; vs. G. O'Daly, Did St. Augustine Ever Believe in the Soul's Pre-existence?, in: idem, Platonism Pagan and Christian: Studies in Plotinus and Augustine (Aldershot 2001) N° IV. I tried to follow the development of Augustine's ideas on this issue in my paper: L. Karfíková, Augustine on Recollection between Plato and Plotinus, StPatr 75 (2017) 81–102.

[79] I struggled with this doctrine in my book: L. Karfíková, Grace.

ited, i.e. collectively referable guilt, which casts doubt upon God's righteousness.

Vittorino Grossi, Roma (Italia)

Per una rilettura del peccato originale in Agostino d'Ippona Modalità attuali della ricerca

Abstract:
In this note regarding a new reading of the texts by Augustine on original sin, we suggest two guidelines: 1. we are presenting an analysis of Genesis 3, from the three Commentaries on Genesis by Augustine; this analysis will be preceded by notes on the subject that are present in De peccatorum meritis et de baptismo parvulorum, *which is considered the watershed work on this issue; 2. we are summarizing the exegesis and the theology of Rom 5:12 in the works of Augustine, before and after 411. The conclusion displays the key in which Augustine's texts on original sin are to be read, and it also points the current paths of research.*

Nella nota presente diamo prima brevi indicazioni sul peccato originale in Agostino dal *De peccatorum meritis et de baptismo parvulorum* che, nel 411–412, mise a tema tale problematica e dall'analisi dei tre *Commentari* agostiniani alla Genesi (cap. 3), sintetizzando la sua esegesi e teologia di Rom 5, 12. Quindi, a conclusione, indichiamo i nuovi approcci al problema da parte degli agostinologi che, nella lettura dei testi agostiniani, va oltre la polemica dell'Ipponate con i manichei e i pelagiani e le letture fattane poi da Giuliano di Eclano e nel tempo della Riforma.

I. Il '*De peccatorum meritis*'

Nell'elaborazione agostiniana del peccato originale il *De peccatorum meritis*[1] può essere considerata l'opera spartiacque del problema. Datata l'anno 411–412, come prima opera antipelagiana, sintetizza la tesi pelagiana sul peccato dei progenitori e il suo rapporto con i discendenti. In tale opera, soprattutto

---

[1] *Aug.*, Pecc. meritis: K. F. Vrba – J. Zycha, CSEL 60 (Vindobonae 1986), p. 3–151; tr. it.: I. Volpi, NBA XVII/1 (Roma 1981).

Per una rilettura del peccato originale in Agostino d'Ippona 287

nel libro I, si ha già come normale la dicitura «*originale peccatum*»[2], nel libro II è presente solo una volta[3], ritorna spesso nel libro III[4].

I pelagiani, informa Agostino, davano una nuova versione di Rom 5, 12 (*Per unum hominem peccatum intravit in mundum et per peccatum mors*), limitando la morte al corpo e non all'anima che inoltre, peccando, avrebbe trasmesso il suo peccato non per generazione ma con l'esempio. In tale ottica essi, nel battesimo conferito ai bambini, lo negavano per il perdono di un peccato, che per Agostino poteva essere solo quello originale[5].

Agostino sin dall'inizio di tale polemica fece presente che la sua comprensione del peccato originale era stata sempre la stessa, quindi, non aveva mai cambiato opinione, come anche pensavano Cipriano[6] e Girolamo. Quest'ultimo, infatti, nel *Commentario al profeta Giona*, aveva scritto che in Adamo si è tutti peccatori[7]. Nel libro III del *De peccatorum meritis*, Agostino informa

---

[2] Cfr. Aug., Pecc. meritis 1, 9, 9; 1, 11, 13: *qui nondum sua et propria voluntate sicut ille peccaverunt, sed ab illo 'peccatum originale' traxerant, qui est forma futuri, quia in illo constituta est forma condemnationis futuris posteris, qui eius propagine crearentur, ut ex uno omnes in condemnationem nascerentur, ex qua non liberat nisi gratia Salvatoris.* Vedi anche: ibid. 1, 11, 14; 1, 12, 15; 1, 13, 16; 1, 15, 20; 1, 21, 30; 1, 23, 33; 1, 26, 39; 1, 28, 55; 1, 34, 64; 1, 15.

[3] Aug., Pecc. meritis 2, 25, 41: *eos* [i bambini] *dicant non habere ullum vel proprium vel originale peccatum.*

[4] Aug., Pecc. meritis 3, 1, 1: [...] *cum ad illum venisset locum, ubi dicit Apostolus* per unum hominem peccatum intrasse in mundum et per peccatum mortem atque ita in omnes homines pertransisse, *quamdam eorum argumentationem qui negant parvulos peccatum originale gestare, quam, fateor, in illis tam longis voluminibus meis non refelli, quia in mentem mihi omnino non venerat quemquam posse talia cogitare vel dicere.* Vedi anche: ibid. 3, 2, 3; 3, 2, 4; 3, 4, 7.

[5] Aug., Pecc. meritis 1, 9, 9: *Hoc autem apostolicum testimonium, in quo ait:* Per unum hominem peccatum intravit in mundum et per peccatum mors, *conari eos quidem in aliam novam detorquere opinionem tuis litteris intimasti, sed quidnam illud sit quod in his verbis opinentur tacuisti. Quantum autem ex aliis comperi, hoc ibi sentiunt, 'quod et mors ista, quae illic commemorata est, non sit corporis, quam nolunt Adam peccando meruisse, sed animae, quae in ipso peccato fit, et ipsum peccatum non propagatione in alios homines ex primo homine, sed imitatione transisse'. Hinc enim etiam in parvulis nolunt credere per baptismum solvi originale peccatum, quod in nascentibus nullum esse omnino contendunt.*

[6] Aug., Pecc. meritis 3, 5, 10: *Aliud est enim peccato a se commisso gravari, aliud alieni quamlibet magni contagione respergi. Propter quod parvuli ad remissionem peccatorum, sicut ait Poenus, poena vestra, Cyprianus, hoc ipso facilius accedunt, quod eis remittuntur non propria, sed aliena peccata* (Cyprianus, Ep. 64 ad Fidum); ibid. 4, 113: *dicta vel Ambrosii, vel Cypriani, vel aliorum catholicorum, quae contra vos ponimus, si vera esse concesseris, peccatum originale firmabis.*

[7] Aug., Pecc. meritis 3, 6, 12: *Quando enim primitus hoc disputari coeperit nescio; illud tamen scio quod etiam sanctus Hieronymus* [...] *ubi commemorantur etiam parvuli ieiunio castigati:* Maior, inquit, aetas incipit, usque ad minorem pervenit. Nullus enim absque peccato nec si unius quidem diei fuerit vita eius et numerabiles anni vitae illius. Si enim stellae non sunt mundae in conspectu Dei, quanto magis vermis et putredo et hi qui peccato offendentis Adam tenentur obnoxii (Hier., In Ionam 3: PL 25, 1195); *Aug.,* Pecc. meritis 3, 7, 13: *verum etiam ad quaedam eius vana*

ancora il tribuno Marcellino come aveva sentito dire che a Cartagine alcuni dicevano di battezzare i bambini per la loro santificazione e non per rimettere un peccato[8].

II. Gen 3 nei 'Commentari' agostiniani alla Genesi

Agostino, in sequenza cronologica, scrisse tre *Commentari* alla Genesi: nel 389 da laico il *De genesi contra Manichaeos*[9]; nel 393 da presbitero il *De genesi ad litteram imperfectus liber*[10]; dopo il 401 da vescovo in 12 libri scrisse il *De genesi ad litteram*[11], da ascrivere riteniamo per la composizione dei libri 7-12 non oltre il 410.

Quanto al primo *Commentario*, Agostino lo scrisse perché i manichei criticavano l'Antico Testamento[12]; per la nostra ricerca interessa il commento a Gn 1, 28 (*Li creò maschio e femmina e Dio li benedisse*) trattandosi ivi del peccato dei progenitori[13].

---

refutanda hoc tamquam certissimum de hominis originali peccato, unde utique nec ipsum dubitare credebat, inter multa sua documenta deprompsit (cita *Hier.*, Contra Iovinianum 2: PL 23, 285s); *Aug.*, Pecc. meritis. 3, 7, 14: *in sanctis canonicis libris viget huius sententiae clarissima et plenissima auctoritas*. Clamat Apostolus: Per unum hominem peccatum intravit in mundum et per peccatum mors et ita in omnes homines pertransiit, in quo omnes peccaverunt.

[8] *Aug.*, Pecc. meritis 3, 6, 12: *Unde nobis hoc negotium repente emerserit nescio. Nam ante parvum tempus a quibusdam transitorie colloquentibus cursim mihi aures perstrictae sunt, cum illic apud Carthaginem essemus,* non ideo parvulos baptizari, ut remissionem accipiant peccatorum, sed ut sanctificentur in Christo; vedi anche, *Aug.*, De Gestis Pelagii 22, 46: K. F. Vrba - J. Zycha, CSEL 42 (Vindobonae 1902), p. 100-101. Tra le altre informazioni Agostino aveva anche raccolto la notizia che Pelagio portava la questione sull'origine dell'anima (*Aug.*, Pecc. meritis 3, 10, 18).

[9] *Aug.*, Gn. c. Man.: PL 34, 173-220; tr. it.: L. Carrozzi, NBA 9/1 (Roma 1988).

[10] *Aug.*, Gn. litt. Imp.: J. Zycha, CSEL 28/1 (Vindobonae 1894), p. 457-503.

[11] *Aug.*, Gn. litt.: J. Zycha, CSEL 28/1 (Vindobonae 1894), p. 1-435; tr. it.: L. Carrozzi, NBA 9/2 (Roma 1989).

[12] *Aug.*, Gn. c. Man. 1, 1, 2: «I manichei, dunque, sono soliti criticare le Scritture dell'Antico Testamento anche senza conoscerle e con le loro critiche prendere in giro e ingannare i nostri fedeli deboli e semplici». Annota nel *Aug.*, Gn. litt. 8, 2, 11: «Io stesso, poco dopo la mia conversione, scrissi due libri contro i manichei i quali sono in errore non perché intendono questi libri dell'Antico Testamento in senso diverso da quello dovuto, ma perché li rigettano del tutto e, nel rifiutarli, ne fanno oggetto di bestemmie sacrileghe. Allora io desideravo confutare subito le loro aberrazioni o stimolarli a cercare nelle Sacre Scritture, da essi aborrite, la fede insegnata da Cristo e consegnata nei Vangeli. In quel tempo però non mi si presentava alla mente in qual modo tutti quei fatti potessero intendersi in senso proprio, anzi mi pareva che non fosse possibile o lo fosse solo a stento e difficilmente».

[13] *Aug.*, Gn. c. Man. 1, 19, 30: «la procreazione spirituale di gioie intelligibili e immortali riempiva la terra, cioè dava vita al corpo e lo dominava, lo teneva talmente sottomesso che l'uomo non aveva a soffrire da parte di esso alcuna opposizione e alcuna molestia. Si deve cre-

Quanto al cap. 3 della Genesi Agostino, dopo di aver premesso che esso va letto in un senso conforme alla fede[14], passa all'interpretazione del primo peccato dell'umanità, commesso dall'anima per superbia[15] volendo diventare simile a Dio[16]. Con tale disordine portato nell'*ordo amoris* della creatura umana[17] la donna, il serpente e l'uomo sperimentarono il castigo del peccato. Il che, sottolinea Agostino, avvenne anche per i discendenti di Adamo[18], peccato indicato ora con il termine 'morte'[19].

Nel II *Commentario*, il *De Genesi ad litteram imperfectus liber* (a. 393), Agostino solo precisa il significato di peccato (libero consenso della volontà benché illegittimo) e di male quale carenza di bene.

Nel III *Commentario*, il *De Genesi ad litteram*, abbiamo l'esegesi agostiniana completa del cap. 3 della Genesi[20].

---

dere così per il fatto che non erano ancora nati i figli di questo mondo prima che i progenitori peccassero».

[14] *Aug., Gn. c. Man.* 2, 2, 3: «Tutto questo racconto della Scrittura dev'essere dunque esaminato anzitutto in senso conforme alla storia e in secondo luogo in senso profetico. Secondo la storia vengono narrati dei fatti compiuti, secondo la profezia invece vengono preannunciate delle realtà future [...] intendere le affermazioni della Scrittura in un senso conforme alla fede e in un modo degno di Dio, credendole presentate sotto forma simbolica ed enigmatica».

[15] *Aug., Gn. c. Man.* 2, 5, 6–7: «Quando però l'anima veniva irrigata da questa sorgente, non aveva ancora gettato via l'intimo del proprio cuore a causa della superbia. Poiché *l'inizio della superbia dell'uomo è allontanarsi da Dio* (Sir. 10, 14). [...] Con queste poche frasi ci viene dunque indicata tutta la creazione prima del peccato commesso dall'anima». Entro tale contesto Agostino, relazionando l'anima al peccato, inizia a porsi anche il problema dell'origine dell'anima che si trascinerà sino alla fine della vita.

[16] *Aug., Gn. c. Man.* 2, 17, 25: «Poiché l'uomo peccò volendo essere uguale a Dio, cioè libero dal suo dominio come è libero da ogni dominio Lui stesso, essendo il Signore di tutti».

[17] *Aug., Gn. c. Man.* 2, 9, 12: «Le viene dunque ingiunto di mangiare d'ogni albero del paradiso, ma di astenersi dall'albero in cui è il discernimento del bene e del male, cioè di non goderne mangiandone, per così dire, inmodo da non violare e corrompere l'ordinata integrità della propria natura (*ut ipsam ordinatam integritatem naturae suae, quasi manducando violet atque corrumpat*)».

[18] *Aug., Gn. c. Man.* 2, 21, 32: «D'altra parte tutti noi che siamo nati da Adamo siamo stati destinati dalla natura a pagarle il debito di subire la morte minacciata da Dio quando diede il precetto di non mangiare il frutto dell'albero. La morte era dunque simboleggiata nelle tuniche di pelle [...]. I progenitori poi restarono nel paradiso [...] finché non si giunse alle tuniche di pelle, cioè alla condizione mortale di questa vita».

[19] *Aug., Gn. c. Man.* 2, 21, 31: «la vita vissuta nei peccati di solito è chiamata "morte" nelle Scritture, allo stesso modo che, secondo quanto dice l'Apostolo, la vedova che vive nel piacere è morta [...]. Invece di peccato lo scrittore sacro usa la parola morto».

[20] Sulla datazione dell'opera sono importanti alcuni dati presenti nella stessa opera: nel libro II (9, 22) Agostino cita *Confessioni* 13, 15 del 401–402 (il secondo libro, quindi, fu scritto dopo il 401); nel libro IX (7, 12) cita *De bono coniugali* (opera del 401) come scritto di recente; nel libro XI (15, 20) rivela che scriverà il *De civitate Dei* iniziata il 413. Il *De genesi ad litteram*, quindi, venne scritta prima del 413 e prima del 411, forse non oltre il 409 dato che nell'*Ep.*

Agostino, invocato il testo di Paolo Rom 5, 12, per sottolineare che tutti si nasce nel peccato, rigetta la teoria platonica della preesistenza delle anime che, cadendo nella materia, contraggano il peccato[21]. Si pone poi espressamente la questione del peccato originale nei discendenti, ma la rimanda per considerarla «a suo tempo»[22], dovendo per il momento dedicare la sua attenzione alla questione dell'anima cui dedica il libro VII e in sintesi il libro X.

Al cap. 3 della Genesi Agostino dedica i libri VIII–X. Nei libri IX e X, evidenziando prima il legame di unità di Adamo e di Eva col genere umano[23], quindi dopo il peccato il legame nei progenitori e nei discendenti con la presenza della concupiscenza e della mortalità[24]. Su tale argomento lui chiama

---

143, 4 (a Marcellino, datata il 411–412) dice di avere presso di sé il *De genesi ad litteram* per rivederla. Infatti, informa l'amico, non ancora dà al pubblico due suoi scritti (*De genesi ad litteram* e *De trinitate*) perché li sta rivedendo. Nella lettera ad Evodio (*Ep.* 159, 2; a. 414–415), Agostino dice che l'opera non è ancora messa a disposizione dei lettori. Nell'*Ep.* 162, 2 (ancora ad Evodio del 414–415) ribatte: «Molti di quei (quesiti), che ora mi hai proposti, sono stati risolti nei miei libri ancora non pubblicati *Intorno alla Trinità* e *Intorno alla Genesi*»; nell'*Ep.* 169, 1, 1 (del 415) *infine* dice di avere aggiunto al *De civitate*, ai tre già scritti, altri due libri iniziati nel 413.

[21] Aug., Gn. litt. 6, 9, 15: «Tuttavia non senza ragione sta scritto che neppure un bambino avente un sol giorno di vita sulla terra è esente dal peccato, e quanto è detto nel Salmo: *Io sono stato concepito nella colpa e nel peccato mi ha nutrito mia madre nel suo seno* (Iob 14, 4), e [San Paolo dice] che tutti muoiono in Adamo poiché in lui hanno peccato tutti (Rom 5, 12) [...]. L'opinione poi secondo la quale alcuni pensano che le anime hanno commesso peccati più o meno gravi in un altro mondo e sono state precipitate in corpi diversi secondo la gravità dei peccati, non è conforme all'asserzione dell'Apostolo, poiché questi dice assai chiaramente che quelli non ancora nati non hanno fatto nulla di bene o di male».

[22] Aug., Gn. litt. 6, 9, 16: «C'è pure un'altra questione da trattare a suo tempo: in qual misura cioè l'intera massa del genere umano fu contaminata dal peccato dei progenitori, che furono i due soli a commetterlo (*Ac per hoc alia quaestio est suo loco retractanda, quid de peccato primorum parentum, qui duo soli fuerunt, generis humani contraxerit universa consparsio*)».

[23] Aug., Gn. litt. 9, 9, 15: «[...] persone provenienti da un unico capostipite, per stabilire una più stretta relazione di parentela e mettere in maggior risalto possibile il legame dell'unità».

[24] Aug., Gn. litt. 9, 10, 16: «*Il giorno in cui ne mangerete, morrete sicuramente* (Gen 2, 17). Per conseguenza quel giorno produsse in loro la condizione [di dissidio] che l'Apostolo esprime in questi termini: *Nel mio intimo io sono d'accordo con la legge di Dio, ma nelle mie membra vedo un'altra legge che contrasta fieramente la legge della mia ragione e mi rende schiavo della legge del peccato che è nelle mie membra. Me sventurato! Chi mi libererà dal corpo che porta questa morte? La grazia di Dio per mezzo di Gesù Cristo nostro Signore* (Rom 7, 22–25)»; vedi anche: ibid. 9, 10, 17. Agostino riprende l'argomento nel libro 11, 1, 3. Per la concupiscenza, vedi: ibid. 10, 12, 20: «la causa della stessa concupiscenza carnale non risiede solo nell'anima, bensì risiede molto meno solo nella carne. Essa, infatti, deriva dall'una e dall'altra: dall'anima poiché senza di essa non si percepisce alcun godimento, dalla carne poi per il fatto che senza di essa non si può sentire alcun piacere carnale»; vedi anche: ibid. 10, 12, 21: «in questo corpo votato alla morte sussiste una violenta seduzione della carne proveniente dal castigo del peccato in cui siamo concepiti e a causa del quale tutti sono figli della collera». Qui Agostino

in causa alcuni interlocutori non nominati (i pelagiani) che in un nascituro negavano la presenza di un peccato e pertanto non vedevano la necessità di battezzarlo[25].

Agostino in conclusione, nel contesto delle questioni circa l'origine dell'anima, legge Gn 3 alla luce di Rom 5, 12, nella cui ottica da Adamo si riceve l'anima e il corpo anche se è solo l'anima a peccare[26]. Inoltre, nel medesimo contesto lui inserisce, e per la prima volta nei suoi scritti, la comprensione del battesimo dei bambini perché eredi del peccato di Adamo[27]. Per lui tale usanza

---

distingue tra la concupiscenza (castigo del peccato) e il peccato in cui si nasce.

[25] *Aug.*, Gn. litt. 10, 13, 22: «Secondo questa interpretazione noi non diciamo né che la carne ha desideri sensuali senza l'anima – opinione del tutto assurda – né siamo d'accordo con i manichei i quali, vedendo che la carne non può aver desideri sensuali senza l'anima, hanno pensato che la carne avrebbe un'altra anima sua propria derivante da un'altra natura contraria a Dio e per causa della quale essa avrebbe desideri contrari a quelli dello spirito. Noi non siamo nemmeno costretti ad affermare che a qualche anima non è necessaria la grazia di Cristo allorché qualcuno ci obietta: "Che colpa ha commesso l'anima d'un bimbo per cui gli sarebbe funesto il morire senza aver ricevuto il sacramento del Battesimo cristiano, se non ha commesso alcun peccato personale e non deriva dalla prima anima che peccò in Adamo?"».

[26] *Aug.*, Gn. litt. 10, 11, 18: «Ecco che dice la Scrittura: *Per causa d'un sol uomo il peccato è entrato nel mondo e attraverso il peccato la morte, e così è passata in tutti gli uomini, perché tutti hanno peccato in lui* (Rom 5, 12), e poco dopo: *Come per la colpa di un solo uomo furono condannati tutti gli uomini, così per la giustizia d'un sol Uomo tutti gli uomini sono giunti alla giustificazione della vita. Come infatti a causa della disubbidienza d'un sol uomo tutti sono diventati peccatori, così anche per l'ubbidienza d'un sol Uomo la maggior parte* [degli uomini] *saranno fatti giusti* (Rom 5, 18–19). Coloro che sostengono l'opinione della propagazione delle anime tramite la generazione in base a queste parole dell'Apostolo tentano di provarla a questo modo. Se il peccato o il peccatore si possono intendere solo in relazione al corpo, dalle citate parole dell'Apostolo siamo costretti a credere che l'anima deriva dai genitori; se invece, pur cedendo alla seduzione della carne, è tuttavia solamente l'anima a peccare, in qual senso devono intendersi le parole: *nel quale tutti hanno peccato*, se da Adamo non è trasmessa anche l'anima con il corpo? Oppure in qual modo *a causa della disubbidienza* di Adamo *gli uomini sono stati resi peccatori*, se erano in lui solo in quanto al corpo e non anche all'anima?».

[27] *Aug.*, Gn. litt. 10, 11, 19: «Dobbiamo badare infatti a non cadere nell'errore di far sembrare Dio autore del peccato se infonde l'anima al corpo, per mezzo del quale è inevitabile ch'essa commetta il peccato o che possa esserci un'anima – all'infuori di quella di Cristo – che, per essere liberata dal peccato, non abbia bisogno della grazia di Cristo perché non avrebbe peccato in Adamo, se la Scrittura dice che tutti hanno peccato in lui soltanto in rapporto al corpo e non anche all'anima (*quia – Christus – non peccavit in Adam, si omnes in eo peccasse secundum carnem tantum quae de illo creata est, non etiam secundum animam*). Questa tesi è talmente contraria alla fede della Chiesa che i genitori si affrettano a condurre con sé i loro bambini più piccoli e più grandicelli a ricevere la grazia del santo battesimo. Se in essi viene sciolto il vincolo del peccato che è solo della carne e non anche dell'anima, a buon diritto ci si potrebbe chiedere qual danno potrebbe loro derivare, se alla loro età morissero senza battesimo».

della Chiesa non può avere altre spiegazioni se non il peccato in Adamo[28]. Lui, tuttavia, riporta l'obiezione (dei pelagiani) circa la natura dell'anima creata buona, che non potrebbe veicolare un peccato personalmente non suo[29].

III. Rom 5, 12 nell'esegesi e teologia di Agostino prima e dopo il 411

Il testo di Rom 5, 12 presenta in Agostino una questione testuale, esegetica e teologica.

1. La questione testuale ed esegetica

Il versetto di Rom 5, 12 è citato in Agostino per intero la prima volta nel *Contra Faustum* (a. 397/98)[30] e con un testo differente da quello della Vulgata. Da

---

[28] *Aug.*, Gn. litt. 10, 11, 19: «[...] la Chiesa universale conserva costantemente quest'usanza d'accorrere con i [bambini] viventi e di soccorrerli per evitare che, una volta morti, non possa farsi più nulla per la loro salvezza; non vediamo quindi come possa spiegarsi diversamente quest'usanza se non ritenendo che ogni bimbo non è altro che Adamo quanto al corpo e quanto all'anima e perciò gli è necessaria la grazia di Cristo».

[29] *Aug.*, Gn. litt. 10, 15, 26: «Al contrario quel dato contagio trasmesso da una carne di peccato non può essere imputato in alcun modo all'anima [del bambino] se non fu creata dalla prima anima peccatrice [di Adamo]. Poiché ciò accade non a causa d'alcun peccato ma a causa della natura per cui l'anima è fatta a questo modo e per dono di Dio è data al corpo».

[30] *Aug.*, C. Faust. 24, 2: J. Zycha, CSEL 25/1 (Vindobonae 1891), p. 723: *Per unum hominem peccatum intravit in mundum, et per peccatum mors; et ita in omnes homines pertransivit, in quo omnes peccaverunt*. L'interpretazione di Rom 5, 12 all'interno anche di altri testi biblici nell'ottica della trasmissione del peccato di Adamo e dell'unica redenzione di Cristo, si ha in *Aug.*, Pecc. meritis 3, 4, 8–9, dove l'*Adam è forma futuri* (Rom 5, 14); vedi: ibid. 3, 7, 14: *Clamat Apostolus: Per unum hominem peccatum intravit in mundum et per peccatum mors et ita in omnes homines pertransiit, in quo omnes peccaverunt. Unde nec illud liquide dici potest, quod peccatum Adae etiam non peccantibus nocuit, cum Scriptura dicat: In quo omnes peccaverunt. Nec sic dicuntur ista aliena peccata, tamquam omnino ad parvulos non pertineant – si quidem in Adam omnes tunc peccaverunt, quando in eius natura illa insita vi, qua eos gignere poterat, adhuc omnes ille unus fuerunt*. Nel *Contra duas epistolas pelagianorum* (4, 4, 6), contro quelli che dicevano che col peccato di Adamo si era trasmessa la morte e non il suo peccato, Agostino richiama in proposito l'interpretazione di Ilario: *Quodsi propterea non potest illis verbis Apostoli peccatum intellegi, in quo omnes peccaverunt, quia in graeco, unde translata est epistula, peccatum feminino genere positum est, restat, ut in illo primo homine peccasse omnes intellegantur, quia in illo fuerunt omnes quando ille peccavit, unde peccatum nascendo trahitur, quod nisi renascendo non solvitur. Nam sic et sanctus Hilarius intellexit quod scriptum est: In quo omnes peccaverunt; ait enim: In quo, id est Adam, omnes peccaverunt. Deinde addidit: Manifestum in Adam omnes peccasse quasi in massa; ipse enim per peccatum corruptus, omnes quos genuit nati sunt sub peccato. Haec scribens Hilarius sine ambiguitate commonuit, quomodo intellegendum esset: In quo omnes peccaverunt* (*Aug.*, Contra duas epistolas pelagianorum 4, 4, 7). Per studi sulla lettura di Agostino di Rom 5, 12, vedi, tra gli altri, S. Lyonnet, Rom 5, 12 chez saint Augustin. Note sur l'élaboration de la doctrine augustinienne du péché originel, in: L'homme devant

Agostino, infatti, l'«*in quo omnes peccaverunt*» è riferito al peccato di Adamo per il quale la morte è entrata nell'uomo, mentre nella versione della Vulgata esso è riferito alla morte. L'Ipponate non accetta la versione della Vulgata perché «*mors*» in latino è di genere femminile. Una seconda variante di lettura è data dal testo greco ἐφ' ᾧ (*eo quod omnes peccaverunt*), in cui il peccato è riferito alla morte nel significato di peccato personale.

Nel libro XI del *De genesi ad litteram* il testo di Rom 5, 12 è presente due volte. Agostino, relazionando Rom 5, 12 a 1 Cor 15, 22, riferisce come di solito l'*'in quo'* direttamente ad Adamo[31], una lettura che si conserva costante nei suoi scritti dal *De peccatorum meritis* in poi (a. 411–412).

2. La questione teologica

Nel *De peccatorum meritis* (a. 411–412) Agostino legge Rom 5, 12 in merito al peccato di Adamo nei discendenti come pensiero dell'apostolo Paolo[32], facendone anche l'applicazione al battesimo dei bambini per il perdono del loro peccato originale[33]. Pure i pelagiani ponevano in Adamo il capostipite del peccato nell'umanità, ma come il primo cattivo esempio, spie-

---

Dieu. Mélanges offerts au Père Henri de Lubac, vol. I, Théologie 56 (Paris 1963) 327–339; S. Lyonnet, Augustin et Rom 5, 12 avant la controverse pélagienne, NRTh 89 (1967) 842–849; G. Di Palma, Ancora sull'interpretazione agostiniana di Rom 5,12: 'et ita in omnes homines pertransiit, in quo omnes peccaverunt', Aug 44 (2004) 113–134.

[31] Aug., Gn. litt. 11, 18: Per unum hominem peccatum in hunc mundum intravit, et per peccatum mors, et ita in omnes homines pertransiit, in quo omnes peccaverunt; e in 11, 16, 29: Sicut in Adam omnes moriuntur, sic et in Christo omnes vivificabuntur (1 Cor 15, 22) [...] *eosdemque multos peccatores, non quibusdam exceptis, sed omnes intellegi volens, superius ait de Adam:* In quo omnes peccaverunt (Rom 5, 12): *unde utique infantum animas non posse secerni, et eo quod dictum est,* omnes, *et eo quod eis per Baptismum subvenitur, non absurde credunt, qui animas ex unius traduce sapiunt.*

[32] Aug., Pecc. meritis 1, 9, 9, testo citato sopra, nota 5.

[33] Aug., Pecc. meritis 1, 34, 64: «Ti rendi conto ormai delle differenti opinioni sorte in mezzo a quelli contro i quali in quest'opera ho già discusso a lungo e con molti argomenti e di uno dei quali ho letto anche un libro che contiene gli errori da me confutati, come ho potuto. Ti avvedi dunque, come avevo cominciato a dire, quanto ci corra tra l'affermazione degli uni che i fanciulli sono assolutamente puri e liberi da qualsiasi peccato, sia originale sia proprio, e l'affermazione degli altri convinti che i bambini appena nati hanno contratto peccati propri, dai quali li credono bisognosi d'esser purificati mediante il battesimo. Perciò questi ultimi, guardando alle Scritture e all'autorità di tutta la Chiesa e al rito dello stesso sacramento, hanno ben visto che per mezzo del battesimo si fa nei fanciulli remissione di peccati, ma che sia il peccato originale quel qualsiasi peccato che è presente nei bambini non lo vogliono dire o non lo possono vedere [...] gli uni e gli altri concederanno a noi che non resta nessun peccato da cancellare nei bambini per mezzo del battesimo all'infuori del peccato originale».

gandone la diffusione nei discendenti per imitazione e non per propagazione generativa[34].

Agostino, nella polemica pelagiana, riferisce Rom 5, 12 al battesimo dei bambini per la remissione del peccato originale, come fede della Chiesa universale nella redenzione di Cristo[35], quindi al di là dei problemi filologici del testo. I pelagiani, dal canto loro, spiegavano il significato del battesimo dei bambini come rinascita della vita in Cristo, per renderli coeredi del regno dei cieli[36].

Nell'ammissione del peccato di Adamo nei discendenti c'era comunque da spiegare la *tradux peccati* e cioè la peccaminosità dell'anima che i pelagiani negavano sulla base della tesi del creazionismo dell'anima. Agostino sentì la difficoltà dell'obiezione e la prese in considerazione ogni qualvolta gli si presentava la questione dell'origine dell'anima. Lui la esaminò già nel libro III del *De peccatorum meritis*, avendo tuttavia coscienza che la relazione tra il peccato originale e l'origine dell'anima rimane comunque per tutti, Pelagio compreso, «una questione oscura»[37].

Nell'*Ep.* 166, 3, 6 dell'anno 415 si pone ancora la domanda di come il peccato originale si possa spiegare col creazionismo; tuttavia, non si sente ancora di sposare tale soluzione[38]. Lui, nell'*Ep.* 166, esposte le varie opinioni sull'anima

---

[34] Aug., Pecc. meritis 1, 9, 10: *Imitantur quidem Adam, quotquot per inoboedientiam transgrediuntur mandatum Dei; sed aliud est quod exemplum est voluntate peccantibus, aliud quod origo est cum peccato nascentibus* [...]. *Per unum, inquit, hominem peccatum intravit in mundum et per peccatum mors: hoc propagationis est, non imitationis*; vedi anche: ibid. 1, 10, 11.

[35] Aug., De gratia Christi et de peccato originali 2, 29, 34: «Chiunque pertanto sostiene che la natura umana in qualsiasi epoca non ha bisogno del secondo Adamo come medico, perché non è stata viziata nel primo Adamo, risulta con evidenza di prove nemico della grazia di Dio [...]. Nessuno, pertanto, è stato liberato o è liberato o sarà liberato dalle mani del perditore se non in forza della grazia del Redentore».

[36] Aug., Pecc. meritis 1, 18, 23: *Sed illi movent et aliquid consideratione ac discussione dignum videntur afferre, qui dicunt parvulos recenti vita editos visceribus matrum, non propter remittendum peccatum percipere baptismum, sed ut spiritalem procreationem habentes creentur in Christo et ipsius regni caelorum participes fiant, eodem modo filii et heredes Dei, coheredes autem Christi*.

[37] Aug., Pecc. meritis 3, 10, 18.

[38] Aug., Ep. 166, 4, 8: «tu [Girolamo] pensi certamente che Dio crei anche adesso di volta in volta un'anima per ogni persona che nasce [...]. Ebbene, io desidero far mia la tua teoria, ma ti dico francamente che non è ancora la mia. Come può il 'creazionismo' spiegare il peccato originale?». Nell'*Ep.* 190 a Ottato del 418 lui richiama la lettera di Girolamo, *Aug., Ep.* 190, 6, 20: «Nella sua medesima breve lettera [Girolamo] faceva tuttavia capire che propendeva più verso il creazionismo che non verso il generazionismo. Nello stesso tempo ricordava pure che è l'opinione più comune nella Chiesa d'Occidente – egli invece si trova in Oriente – è che le anime vengano trasfuse nei figli attraverso la riproduzione generativa»; *Aug., Ep.* 190, 6, 21: «Sono dunque in attesa che mi risponda quel dotto o che io stesso, a Dio piacendo, riesca a capire in qualche modo per quale motivo le anime, se non derivano da quella

e la sua origine (nn. 5-7), chiede di muoversi nella questione partendo da due dati irrinunciabili: ogni anima umana nasce nella colpa e necessita della grazia di Cristo per esserne liberata[39]. Nel 418 Agostino ritornò sul problema nelle lettere 190 e 195 ma senza apportarvi novità di riflessione[40]. Nel 420 poi, scrivendo il *De natura et origine animae*, confessa ancora di non saper risolvere la questione di come l'anima venga infettata del peccato di Adamo[41].

Nella successiva polemica col vescovo di Eclano, oltre alla discussione testuale di Rom 5, 12[42] e all'abituale accusa ad Agostino di manicheismo, da

peccatrice di Adamo, si macchiano del peccato originale che non può non essere in tutti i bambini senza che ve le costringa Dio se sono innocenti, poiché non è autore del peccato, né alcun'altra sostanza del male, poiché questa non esiste: in tale attesa non oserò proclamare nulla di simile».

[39] Aug., Ep. 166, 2, 5: «se l'anima è caduta in peccato, non è stato per alcuna colpa o necessità di Dio o per alcuna necessità della propria natura, ma per volontà sua personale e non può liberarsi di questo corpo di morte né di sua propria volontà, come se per farlo avesse in se stessa una forza sufficiente, né per la morte del proprio corpo, ma solo in virtù della grazia di Dio per mezzo di Gesù Cristo nostro Signore; inoltre in tutto il genere umano non esiste assolutamente nessun'anima che per esserne liberata non abbia bisogno del Mediatore tra Dio e gli uomini, cioè dell'uomo Cristo Gesù [...]. Questi sono i capisaldi che io credo in modo assolutamente fermo a proposito dell'anima»; vedi anche: Aug., C. Iul. o. imp. 6, 36.

[40] Aug., Ep. 190, 1, 3: «Ecco la verità su cui soprattutto si basa la fede cristiana: *Per mezzo d'un uomo* (è venuta) *la morte e per mezzo d'un Uomo v'è la risurrezione dei morti; come infatti tutti muoiono in Adamo, così tutti saranno vivificati nel Cristo* e inoltre: *A causa d'un solo uomo il peccato entrò nel mondo e per causa del peccato la morte e in tal modo si estese a tutti gli uomini, poiché in lui* (Adamo) *tutti peccarono* [...] anche se ci è ignota l'origine dell'anima, purché ci sia ben nota la sua redenzione, non c'è alcun pericolo, perché noi non crediamo in Cristo per nascere ma per rinascere, quale che sia il modo in cui siamo nati»; Aug., Ep. 190, 4, 15: Il punto fermo è che «tutte le anime, non escluse quelle dei bambini, le quali vengono battezzate dalla Chiesa per procurare loro non già una falsa ma una autentica remissione dei peccati, contraggono il peccato originale commesso di propria volontà dal primo uomo e trasmesso in tutti i posteri con la generazione e cancellabile solo con la rigenerazione»; Aug., Ep. 190, 5, 16: «Resta, tuttavia, sempre il problema se Dio crea le altre anime derivandole dall'unica prima anima come ogni corpo umano dall'unico primo corpo o se invece i nuovi corpi li crea bensì derivandoli da un solo corpo, ma le nuove anime le trae dal nulla».

[41] Aug., Nat. et orig. an. 4, 8, 8: «Noi vediamo che l'anima è liberata dal peccato mediante la grazia, ma non vediamo in che modo abbia meritato di rimanere impaniata nel peccato»; 4, 13, 16: «(Vincenzo Vittore) dirà che i bambini non contraggono il peccato originale, né hanno alcunché che li faccia condannare, se escono da questa vita senza aver ricevuto il sacramento della rigenerazione, incorrerà nell'eresia pelagiana, senza dubbio condannabile, ed egli stesso sarà da condannare. Perché questo non gli capiti, quanto *sarebbe meglio che si attenesse alla mia esitazione sull'origine dell'anima* [...] (4, 14, 21) pur nella certezza che è Dio a farla, dobbiamo chiederci ulteriormente da che cosa la faccia: se attraverso la propaggine come il corpo o se ispirandola come fece la prima».

[42] Giuliano faceva sempre rilevare ad Agostino che in Paolo si trasmette la morte e non il peccato, vedi: Aug., C. Iul. o. imp. 2, 63: Sed ideo «per unum hominem» dixit, a quo generatio utique hominum coepit ut per generationem doceret ipse per omnes originale peccatum. In hoc

parte di Giuliano, si aggiunsero ancora tre accuse connesse al peccato originale e cioè: Dio sarebbe ingiusto nel punire un innocente (il bambino è incapace di peccare), e sarebbero peccato anche il matrimonio e la stessa creazione dell'uomo e della donna.

Agostino gli rispose che, al di là di altre letture del testo, l'«*in quo*» può riferirsi solo ad Adamo da cui consegue la morte, altrimenti si dovrebbe ammettere una pena senza la sua causa[43]. Lui, pertanto, si limita a distinguere il peccato originale dalla pena per il peccato personale di Adamo, da cui nell'umanità ha avuto origine la trasmissione del peccato originale[44].

Quanto alla seconda accusa (il matrimonio come peccato) Agostino parla di un peccato «naturale» nel significato che è trasmesso dalla natura umana ferita (il peccato originale), il che per Giuliano era contrario ad ogni sana considerazione[45]. Alla terza accusa che l'amore coniugale fosse poi peccato nella

---

ergo mentitur, quod affirmat beatum Paulum pronuntiasse, quia per unum hominem peccatum intraverit in mundum, atque ita in omnes homines pertransierit; hoc, inquam, in Magistri Gentium sermonibus non tenetur; ille quippe non dixit peccatum transisse, sed mortem.

[43] *Aug.*, C. Iul. o. imp. 2, 63: *In eo quidem loco, ubi dictum est*: Per unum hominem peccatum intravit in mundum, et per peccatum mors; et ita in omnes homines pertransiit; *utrum peccatum, an mors, an utrumque per omnes homines pertransisse dictum sit, videtur ambiguum; sed quid horum sit, res ipsa tam aperta demonstrat. Nam si peccatum non pertransisset, non omnis homo cum lege peccati, quae in membris est, nasceretur; si mors non pertransisset, non omnes homines, quantum ad istam conditionem mortalium pertinet, morerentur. Quod autem dicit Apostolus:* In quo omnes peccaverunt; in quo, *non intellegitur nisi in Adam, in quo eos dicit et mori; quia non erat iustum, sine crimine transire supplicium* [...]. *Transiit ergo cum morte peccatum; quid est quod nunc dicis, non peccatum transisse, sed mortem?*

[44] *Aug.*, C. Iul. o. imp. 1, 47: «il peccato originale è tale peccato da essere per se stesso anche pena del peccato. Il qual peccato originale è già presente, sì, nei bambini quando nascono, ma comincia ad apparire in essi quando crescono e diventa necessaria a loro la sapienza, perché sono insipienti, e la continenza, perché bramano i mali. Tuttavia l'origine anche del peccato originale discende dalla volontà di colui che ha peccato. (E cita di Ambrogio) *"Esisteva infatti Adamo e in lui esistevamo noi tutti; perì Adamo ed in lui sono periti tutti"* (Ambrosius, In Lucam 7, 234)».

[45] *Aug.*, C. Iul. o. imp. 1, 48: «è qui tutta la causa della nostra discussione. Rimossi dunque tutti i sipari, porta finalmente alla piena luce la ragione per cui inseguì l'esistenza del peccato naturale (*doceas naturale esse peccatum*)», vedi anche: ibid. 2, 193: Iul. *Quae divisio naturali peccato non potest convenire, quod si esset, omnes prorsus aequaliter colligaret; nemo ergo esset, cui malum hoc non inesset, et nullus inveniretur, de quo vere posset dici, quia in similitudine peccati illius non deliquisset, in cuius omnes veritate peccassent.* Aug. *Quod renitendo clamas, hoc verum est et contra vos est: omnes prorsus originale peccatum aequaliter colligavit; nemo esset, cui malum hoc non inesset, nisi per Christum gratia divina prodesset. In eos enim, qui non peccaverunt, id est qui sua peccata propria non fecerunt, ut mors regnaret, similitudo meruit praevaricationis Adae, qui est forma futuri, id est Christi; sicut enim primo homine, qui nascuntur, ita secundo homine, qui renascuntur, induuntur.*

stessa creazione dell'uomo e della donna[46], Agostino spiega come la *concupiscentia carnis* nei coniugi non sia peccato ma solo *vitium substantiae bonae*. Era quindi da distinguere la *vis naturalis* della creazione che è un bene, dal *vitium* peccato annidatosi nella natura umana con l'eredità di Adamo.

IV. Conclusione

Una rilettura di Agostino sul peccato originale dall'analisi dei suoi tre *Commentari* alla Genesi, può offrire tre osservazioni conclusive, che riassumano e che meglio inquadrano il suo pensiero: la prima, sul vocabolario agostiniano del peccato originale prima del 411; la seconda, sulla riflessione teologica del peccato originale in relazione ad Agostino dal Concilio di Trento ad oggi; la terza sulle nuove modalità di ricerca da parte degli studiosi.

1. Prima conclusione

Prima del 411 il peccato dei progenitori viene veicolato da Agostino quale *peccatum naturae*[47], che si manifesta nell'esperienza della morte e della

---

[46] *Aug.*, C. Iul. o. imp. 2, 24 (accusa Giuliano): «anche noi concordiamo pacificamente che il peccato è opera della cattiva volontà o è opera del diavolo. Ma per quale via questo peccato viene a trovarsi in un bambino? Attraverso la volontà? Ma in lui non c'è stata nessuna volontà. Attraverso la forma del corpo? Ma essa l'ha data Dio. Attraverso l'ingresso dell'anima? Ma non deve nulla al seme corporale l'anima che viene creata nuova da Dio. Attraverso le nozze? Ma le nozze appartengono all'attività dei genitori e tu avevi premesso che essi non hanno peccato in questo loro atto. Se non l'avevi concesso con sincerità, come indica lo sviluppo del tuo discorso, allora sono da esecrarsi le nozze che hanno causato il male. Le nozze però non hanno una propria sostanza, ma stanno a indicare con il loro nome l'attività delle persone: sono quindi giustamente da condannare i genitori che con la loro unione hanno causato il peccato. Perciò non si può più dubitare: i coniugi sono destinati all'eterno supplizio, perché la loro opera ha portato il diavolo ad esercitare il suo dominio sugli uomini. [...]». Risponde Agostino, ibid. 2, 24 e 25 che lui gli ha già risposto in merito nel *Contra Iulianum* 3, 54 e 57 e nel *De nuptiis et concupiscentia* 2, 44-49. Aveva poi già scritto nel *De gratia Christi et de peccato originali* 2, 33, 38: «Nella nostra questione attuale [...] occorre guardare non a ciò che di buono c'è nella procreazione naturale, ma a ciò che di male c'è nel peccato dal quale è certo che sia stata viziata la natura. Ora, si propagano ambedue insieme: e la natura e il vizio della natura [...], il vizio della natura addita Dio come punitore della disobbedienza, e infine lo stesso e medesimo Cristo per creare il bene della natura ha fatto l'uomo e per sanare il vizio della natura si è fatto uomo».

[47] Per il «*peccatum naturae*», vedi: *Aug.*, De vera religione 3, 5; ibid. 28, 51: *Ita de peccato nostro, quod in homine peccatore ipsa natura nostra commisit*; ibid. 46, 88: *Vocamur autem ad perfectam naturam humanam, qualem ante peccatum nostrum Deus fecit*; Exp. q. p. ex Ap. ad Rom. 22, 29, 1: *Quod autem ait: Sed regnavit mors ab Adam usque ad Moysen et in his, qui non peccaverunt in similitudinem praevaricationis Adae, duobus modis distinguitur; aut: In similitudinem praevaricationis Adae regnavit mors, quia et qui non peccaverunt, ex origine mortalitatis*

concupiscenza e, abitualmente, da lui indicato col termine «*mors*».
Dopo il 411 la sua riflessione si articola nella comprensione di Rom 5, 12.
Nell'*Ep.* 166 (a. 416), Agostino cerca di capire il testo paolino di Rom 5, 12
all'interno dei due capostipiti dell'umanità, Adamo e Cristo. Lui scrive:

> Nessuno incorre nella morte se non per causa di Adamo (e quindi anche i bambini)
> e nessuno arriva alla vita eterna se non per mezzo di Cristo. Questo vogliono si-
> gnificare quei due *tutti*: come *tutti* hanno relazione con Adamo per via della prima
> generazione cioè la carnale, così *tutti* gli uomini che giungono a Cristo vi arrivano
> attraverso la seconda generazione, cioè quella spirituale[48].

Per il vescovo d'Ippona, inoltre, l'irrisolvibile problema dell'infettarsi
dell'anima non deve pregiudicare il conferimento del battesimo dei bambini,
perché esso è un rito della Chiesa amministrato per il perdono dei peccati[49].

L'insistere del vescovo d'Ippona sul battesimo dei bambini, quale rito della
Chiesa, si comprende dall'allora intelligenza patristica delle sacre Scritture e
delle tradizioni della Chiesa. Le sacre Scritture erano i *Kerigmata* (l'annuncio
evangelico); le tradizioni ecclesiastiche i *Dogmata*, ambedue di rilevanza di
fede: nelle Scritture divine e nella Chiesa cattolica. Il rito del battesimo dei
bambini rientrava tra i «dogmata». Un «dogma» , quale risultato dell'azione
della Chiesa, ad esempio il Simbolo e i riti dell'iniziazione, era l'ambito della
tradizione degli apostoli (*traditio apostolorum*), in pratica l'iniziazione cristia-

---

Adam mortui sunt, aut certe: Regnavit mors et in his, qui non in similitudinem praevaricationis Adae peccaverunt, *sed ante legem peccaverunt, ut illi peccasse intellegantur in similitudinem praevaricationis Adae, qui legem acceperunt, quia et Adam accepta praecepti lege peccavit.*

[48] Aug., Ep. 166, 7, 21. Nella stessa linea scrisse il *De natura et origine animae* (a. 420; K. F. Vrba – J. Zycha, CSEL 60 [Vindobonae 1913]).

[49] Cfr. ad esempio, *Aug.*, C. Iul. o. imp. 4, 136: *Catholica potius fides peccatum esse originale non dubitat; quam fidem non pueruli, sed graves atque constantes viri, docti in Ecclesia, et docentes Ecclesiam, usque ad diem sui obitus defenderunt.* [...] *Quamvis nemo ita esse debeat gravis corde, ut decipiatur ratione Pelagii, quam velut exponens Apostolum protulit, et ait:* Corpus mortuum propter peccatum, ideo dictum, quia corpus moritur peccatis, quando avertitur a peccatis; ibid. 6, 7: *relicta auctoritate divina, humana vanitate iactaris, et argumentationibus cordis tui Sanctarum Scripturarum veritati adversaris et obstrepis. Nam utique si christiano atque catholico animo attenderes quod ait Apostolus:* Corpus quidem mortuum est propter peccatum; Praed. sanctorum 12, 24: *Ad quod tempus corporis pertinet etiam quod pelagiani negant, sed Christi Ecclesia confitetur, originale peccatum: quo sive soluto per Dei gratiam, sive per Dei iudicium non soluto, cum moriuntur infantes, aut merito regenerationis transeunt ex malis ad bona, aut merito originis transeunt ex malis ad mala. Hoc catholica fides novit.*

na e la *pietas* cristiana[50]. In epoca patristica, quindi, il Kerigma convogliava direttamente un riferimento alle sacre Scritture, mentre il dogma indicava la '*traditio apostolorum*', vale a dire l'azione della Chiesa nella sua operatività, dai Sinodi ai riti. Un «dogma», pertanto, non era inteso quale spesso si ha nel significato moderno, di una verità che non si può capire e, quindi, è solo da credere, ma nell'essere un'azione posta dalla Chiesa che non può essere mai falsa. In tale contesto, ad esempio, scriveva Agostino a Ottato vescovo di Milevi nel 418 richiamando una lettera di papa Zosimo:

> «Per mezzo della sua morte (di Gesù) viene distrutto il decreto della condanna a morte procurata e trasmessa ad ogni anima da Adamo mediante la discendenza carnale, decreto da cui sono colpiti assolutamente tutti coloro che nascono finché non ne siano liberati mediante il battesimo». In queste parole della Sede Apostolica è contenuta l'espressione della fede della Chiesa Cattolica, tanto antica e salda, tanto sicura e chiara che un cristiano commetterebbe un'empietà, se avesse qualche dubbio al riguardo[51].

2. La riflessione teologica sul peccato originale dal Concilio di Trento ad oggi

I primi lavori dei Padri del Tridentino approdarono al *Decretum de peccato originali* (1546), coinvolgendovi il pensiero di Agostino[52]. Il Tridentino, tut-

---

[50] Per un'indicazione manifesta, vedi: *Basilius*, De spiritu sancto 27, 66: PG 32, 187; tr. it. G. *Azzali Bernardelli*, Basilio. Lo Spirito Santo, Testi pastristici 106 (Roma 1993), p. 161-162: «Altro è il dogma, altro il kerygma, l'uno col silenzio, l'altro con la proclamazione». Nella Chiesa – egli spiega – vi sono «dogmi» e proclamazioni («*Kerigmata*»). Queste ultime si hanno dall'insegnamento scritto; gli altri (dogmi) dalla tradizione degli apostoli conservata «en mysterio» cioè per i già aspiranti al cristianesimo e per i cristiani, vedi: V. *Grossi*, Linee di ecclesiologia patristica. Il formarsi della coscienza di Chiesa nei primi sette secoli (Roma 2014) 164-174 (cap. «Chiesa e Dogma»).

[51] *Aug.*, Ep. 190, 6, 23; vedi anche la risposta di Girolamo ad Elvidio sulla verginità della Madonna (*Contro Elvidio*), vedi in: *Hier.*, Aduersus Helvidium de Mariae uirginitate perpetua 2: PL 23, 185; tr. it.: M. I. *Danieli*, Girolamo. La perenne verginità di Maria, Testi patristici 70 (Roma 1988), p. 30-31: «Elvidio ha potuto sì leggere quello che è stato scritto, ma non ha potuto conoscere quello che è stato convalidato dalla pietà»; ibid. 19: PL 23, 203; tr. it.: M. I. *Danieli*, p. 63: «Come noi non neghiamo le cose che sono state scritte, così non rifiutiamo quelle che non sono state scritte. Crediamo che Dio sia nato da una vergine perché lo abbiamo letto; non crediamo che Maria abbia contratto nozze dopo il parto, perché non l'abbiamo letto».

[52] V. *Grossi*, L'auctoritas di Agostino nella dottrina del "peccatum originis" da Cartagine (418) a Trento (1546), Augustinianum 31 (1991) 329-360; V. *Grossi*, Agostino d'Ippona e il Concilio di Trento, in: G. Alberigo – I. Rogger (eds.), Il Concilio di Trento nella prospettiva del Terzo Millennio (Brescia 1997) 313-341.

tavia, non recepì il peccato originale a livello di fisicità (la *rixa concupiscentiae* di Agostino), né i dettami della scuola teologica dell'Ordine di s. Agostino, che pensava la concupiscenza come qualcosa che dispiace a Dio[53], né l'antropologia luterana dell'*homo peccator* che, assoggettato alla concupiscenza, non ha possibilità di redenzione. Lo recepì invece a livello di privazione della grazia in relazione alle possibilità del libero arbitrio nell'uomo postlapasario. In tal modo il Tridentino aprì un capitolo nuovo di riflessione nella storia della comprensione del peccato originale e, di conseguenza, anche nel modo di leggere le affermazioni di Agostino sul peccato originale. Il Tridentino, infatti, spostò la riflessione sul peccato originale dalla concupiscenza al libero arbitrio. E, contro la concezione dei riformatori protestanti di un libero arbitrio totalmente corrotto[54], nella linea del Concilium Aurasicanum II (a. 529)[55] affermò un libero arbitrio che, pur «*attenuatum et inclinatum*» dal peccato dei progenitori, non è affatto distrutto[56]. L'equilibrio tridentino sul peccato originale, opera soprattutto di Girolamo Seripando[57], espresso nella mozione finale del *Decreto* (17 giugno 1546), si appoggiò sulla lettura agostiniana di Rom 5, 12, pur senza codificarla.

3. Modalità attuali della ricerca

La riflessione del peccato originale, in relazione alle possibilità del libero arbitrio, nei tempi moderni è stata ripresa nel documento luterano-cattolico sulla *Dichiarazione congiunta sulla dottrina della giustificazione* (31 ottobre 1999)[58],

---

[53] V. Grossi, Girolamo Seripando e la scuola agostiniana del Cinquecento, in: A. Cestaro (ed.), Girolamo Seripando e la Chiesa del suo tempo, Storia e Letteratura (Roma 1997) 51–79.
[54] M. Lutero, De servo arbitrio.
[55] Nel Concilium Aurasicanum venne affermata più volte la possibilità del libero arbitrio non totalmente distrutta dal peccato di Adamo ([33]DS, Herder 1965, can. 1 DS 371; can. 8 DS 378; can. 13 DS 383; Conclusio a Caesario episc. Arelat. DS 396: *per peccatum primi hominis ita inclinatum et attenuatum fuerit liberum arbitrium*).
[56] Concilium Tridentinum, Decretum de iustificatione, c. 1: Enchiridium Symbolorum, Herder 1965, [33]DS 1521: *in eis liberum arbitrium minime extinctum esset, viribus licet attenuatum et inclinatum*.
[57] Vedi H. Jedin, Girolamo Seripando. Sein Leben und Denken im Geisteskampf des 16. Jahrhunderts, I–II (Würzburg 1937); ed. italiana: G. Colombi – A. M. Vitale (eds.), Girolamo Seripando. La sua vita e il suo pensiero nel fermento spirituale del XVI secolo, 2 voll. (Brescia 2016).
[58] Il Documento del Pontificio Consiglio per la promozione dell'unità dei cristiani – Federazione luterana mondiale (Augsburg 31 ottobre 1999) è stato pubblicato in italiano come supplemento dall'Osservatore Romano 260 (1999) – venerdì 12 novembre. Una delle prime valutazioni la diede M. Fédou, L'accord luthéro-catholique sur la justification, Nouvelle Revue Théologique 122 (2000) 37–50.

quale centralità della rivelazione cristiana conservando a Dio il primato della sua misericordia di salvezza[59]. Oltre a questa indicazione del magistero[60], gli agostinologi fanno oggi il punto su come approcciare i testi agostiniani sul peccato originale.

La ricerca attuale, anzitutto, non considera la questione «*originis peccatum*» negli scritti del vescovo d'Ippona come una questione estrapolata a sé stante: essa va contestuata relazionandola:

1. all'interno del problema del male di estrazione manichea, perché i manichei leggevano l'incarnazione del Verbo come un imbrattare la natura divina, data la sua unione ad un corpo che di per sé è «*male*»[61].

2. in relazione alla kenosi del Verbo, che libera l'uomo dal peccato[62]. La «*gratia Christi*», infatti, in Agostino è la correlazione principale nel trattare il peccato originale.

3. in correlazione con l'«*imago Dei*» impressa nell'anima dell'uomo, benché in tale contesto per Agostino si ebbe l'assillante problema dell'origine dell'anima con il suo infettarsi e la modalità della sua liberazione[63]. Lui, infatti, già nel *De libero arbitrio* (3, 20, 56) aveva chiarito la domanda su cui riflettere ponendosi le quattro possibilità circa l'origine dell'anima, avendo tuttavia già come certezza il legame di ogni nascituro in Adamo peccante[64]. Il peccato dei progenitori, d'altra parte, offu-

---

[59] V. Grossi, La dottrina tridentina della giustificazione: Verso nuove letture?, Lateranum 66 (2000) 481-507.

[60] Vedi anche il discorso sul peccato originale di *Paulus VI*, His qui interfuerunt Coeti v. d. «Simposio» a theologis doctisque viris habito de originali peccato (11 luglio 1966), Acta Apostolicae Sedis 58 (1966) 649-655.

[61] *Aug.*, Conf. 5, 10, 20 e 7, 21, 27. Per Agostino l'uomo è creato buono in tutto il suo essere e il peccato, che trascina l'anima lontano da Dio (*Aug.*, Natura et gratia 11, 12; 16, 17), è frutto della volontà (vedi, ad esempio, *Aug.*, De duabus animabus 11, 15; Retractationes 1, 9, 3).

[62] *Aug.*, In Ioannis evangelium 3, 12: *Quia natus cum traduce peccati et mortis. De Adam natus, traxit secum quod ibi conceptum est. Cecidit primus homo; et omnes qui de illo nati sunt, de illo traxerunt concupiscentiam carnis. Oportebat ut nasceretur alius homo qui nullam traxit concupiscentiam.*

[63] Qui si pone anche lo studio del possibile rapporto tra Agostino e Porfirio. Quest'ultimo, per ritornare a Dio, considerava lo pneuma (lo spirito) il veicolo dell'anima (l'anima pneumatica, la seconda anima) (*Porfirio*, Lettera a Marcella, cc. 13 e 15).

[64] *Aug.*, De libero arbitrio 3, 20, 56: *Deinde, si una anima facta est, ex qua omnium hominum animae trahuntur nascentium, quis potest dicere non se peccasse, cum primus ille peccavit? Si autem singillatim fiunt in unoquoque nascentium, non est perversum, imo convenientissimum et ordinatissimum apparet, ut malum meritum prioris, natura sequentis sit*; le quattro ipotesi sull'origine dell'anima (ibid. 3, 20, 55-58), che criticherà nel 415, vedi *E. Dubreucq*, Chair, Corps et âme. Les formulations de la question de l'âme chez S. Augustin, RecSR 83 (1993) 365-366.

scando nell'uomo l'immagine di Dio, indebolì il suo slancio originario verso Dio che, tuttavia, nella condizione postlapsaria si può ricuperare con la grazia del Redentore[65].

Gli studiosi di Agostino, pertanto, non isolando la sua riflessione sul peccato originale, la considerano in relazione ad altre componenti, quali il male, la «*gratia Christi*», l'immagine di Dio, e anche oltre lo stesso contesto polemico manicheo e pelagiano. La ricerca attuale, perciò, nel rileggere in Agostino la questione del peccato originale non la esemplifica considerandola ancora un «teologumeno», inventato e accreditato dall'autorità di Agostino[66].

Il vescovo d'Ippona, concludendo, nata in Africa la questione circa il significato del battesimo dei bambini, ne attestò la tradizione in uso rilevandone: negli scritti prima del 411 l'*inordinata integritas* nell'ambito dell'*ordo amoris*; negli scritti dal 411 in poi primariamente l'aspetto soteriologico di Cristo accanto a quello di vita nuova in Lui.

---

[65] Se Origene spiegava il distacco della volontà da Dio come perdita vitale del *noûs* sino a divenire anima (psiché) cioè freddo (*Orig.*, De princ. Praef. 5: H. Crouzel – M. Simonetti, SC 252 [Paris 1978], p. 68), Agostino privilegia il termine «anima» anche come equivalente di spirito (*Aug.*, De beata vita 1, 4; De moribus ecclesiae catholicae 5, 7-8), vedi *I. Bochet*, Le statut de l'image dans la pensée augustinienne, Archive de Philosophie 72 (2009) 260–261; *J. Lagouanère*, Le Corps chez saint Augustin. La Pesanteur et la Grâce, in: Ph. Guisard – Chr. Laizé (eds.), Le Corps (Paris 2015) 662–680.
[66] Vedi *J. Gross*, Entstehungsgeschichte des Erbsündendogmas. I. Von der Bibel bis Augustinus (München – Basel 1960) 375.

Vít Hušek, Olomouc (Czech Republic)

Inherited Sin in Ambrosiaster and Pelagius

Abstract:
Ambrosiaster and Pelagius describe in a very similar way how sin is transmitted from Adam to his posterity through a bad example and how repeated sin creates a hard-to-change habit. They both emphasize a personal responsibility for voluntary appropriation and imitation of sinning. Their views, however, on inherited sin differ. Ambrosiaster describes a hereditary corruption transmitted from Adam to all his posterity but is reluctant to admit that someone could be punished without personal guilt. Pelagius rejects the idea of inherited sin and only focuses on the voluntarily accepted consequences of Adam's sin.

Ambrosiaster and Pelagius had a great deal in common. They both were priests, both lived in Rome (or near) at the turn of the fifth century, both wrote commentaries on the Pauline epistles and both took part in contemporary debates about the transmission of sin.

I. Ambrosiaster

In Ambrosiaster's view, the central message of Rom 5:12-21 is to demonstrate God's providence and the arrangement of the grace of God that was given in Christ. An appropriate human response is to give thanks to God for the gift of salvation and render honor to Jesus Christ:

> to glory through Jesus Christ in God, who saw fit that with his Son as arbitrator we (who were ungodly and enemies) should be called friends, so that we rejoice in all the benefits that we have received through Christ[1].

---

[1] *Ambrosiaster*, Comm. Rom. 5,11,β.γ: H. J. Vogels, CSEL 81/1 (Vindobonae 1966), p. 161-163: 'gloriandum per Iesum Christum in deo, qui dignatus est filio suo arbitro ex impiis et inimicis dici nos suos amicos, ut omnia beneficia per Christum consecutos nos gaudeamus […]'. Transl. *Th. de Bruyn*, Ambrosiaster's Commentary on the Pauline Epistles: Romans (Atlanta 2017), p. 95. Cf. also *Ambrosiaster*, Comm. Rom. 5,12,1,β.γ: CSEL 81/1, p. 162-163. Cf. *J. B. Valero*, Pecar en Adán según Ambrosiaster, EE 65 (1990) 147-191, esp. 149-151.

Ambrosiaster's interpretation of Romans 5 is based on a parallel between "one Adam" and "one Christ". The origin of sin in Adam is opposed to God's providence that restored "through one person what through one person had fallen and been dragged into death"[2].

Ambrosiaster is convinced that all people participate in some way in the sin of Adam (and Eve)[3]. His Latin version of Rom 5:12 does not repeat the word θάνατος ("death") and the phrase ἐφ' ᾧ ("because", "for") is translated *in quo* (in whom)[4]. Ambrosiaster is often referred to as the one who coined the phrase *in quo*. It is more likely, however, that the phrase *in quo* was already present in the Latin manuscripts used in Rome in Ambrosiaster's time. After all, it is not the only case where Ambrosiaster has a preference for the Latin manuscripts over the Greek ones[5].

Ambrosiaster's commentary further develops the idea of our participation in Adam's sin: "*In whom* – that is, in Adam – *all sinned*"[6]; "Adam [...] sinned in everyone"[7]; "all sinned in Adam as in a lump" (*quasi in massa*)[8]. Ambrosi-

---

[2] *Ambrosiaster*, Comm. Rom. 5,12,1,γ: CSEL 81/1, p. 163: 'Ut ipsa primordia peccati manifestaret, ab Adam coepit, qui primum peccavit, ut providentiam unius dei per unum reformasse doceret, quod per unum lapsum fuerat et tractum in mortem'. Transl. *Th. de Bruyn*, Ambrosiaster's Commentary, p. 96.

[3] For Adam and Eve, cf. *Ambrosiaster*, Comm. Rom. 5,12,1,γ: CSEL 81/1, p. 163: 'ut quia unus Adam – id est Eva, quia et mulier Adam est – peccavit in omnibus [...]'. Transl. *Th. de Bruyn*, Ambrosiaster's Commentary, p. 96 and n. 44.

[4] Ambrosiaster, Comm. Rom. 5,12: CSEL 81/1, p. 162–163: '*Propterea sicut per unum hominem peccatum in hunc mundum intravit et per peccatum mors et sic in omnes homines pertransiit in quo omnes peccaverunt*'. Transl. *Th. de Bruyn*, Ambrosiaster's Commentary, p. 95, my emphasis: 'Therefore, just as sin came into this world through one person and death through sin, and so *it* passed on to all people, *in whom* all sinned'. Cf. Rom 5:12 (NA26): Διὰ τοῦτο ὥσπερ δι' ἑνὸς ἀνθρώπου ἡ ἁμαρτία εἰς τὸν κόσμον εἰσῆλθεν καὶ διὰ τῆς ἁμαρτίας ὁ θάνατος, καὶ οὕτως εἰς πάντας ἀνθρώπους ὁ θάνατος διῆλθεν, ἐφ' ᾧ πάντες ἥμαρτον. Rom 5:12 (NRSVCE, my emphasis): 'Therefore, just as sin came into the world through one man, and death came through sin, and so *death* spread to all *because* all have sinned'.

[5] A. Gaudel, Péché originel, in: DThC 12/1 (Paris 1933) 275–606, here 368; *J. B. Valero*, Pecar en Adán, 182; *V. Hušek*, The True Text: Ambrose, Jerome and Ambrosiaster on the Variety of Biblical Versions, in: J. Dušek, J. Roskovec (eds.), Process of Authority. The Dynamics in Transmission and Reception of Canonical Texts (Berlin 2016) 319–336, here 328–333.

[6] *Ambrosiaster*, Comm. Rom. 5,12,2a,β.γ: CSEL 81/1, p. 164–165: '*In quo* – id est in Adam – *omnes peccaverunt*'. Transl. *Th. de Bruyn*, Ambrosiaster's Commentary, p. 96.

[7] *Ambrosiaster*, Comm. Rom. 5,12,1,γ: CSEL 81/1, p. 163: '[U]nus Adam (...) peccavit in omnibus'. Transl. *Th. de Bruyn*, Ambrosiaster's Commentary, p. 96.

[8] *Ambrosiaster*, Comm. Rom. 5,12,3,γ: CSEL 81/1, p. 165: 'Manifestum est itaque omnes in Adam peccasse quasi in massa'. Transl. *Th. de Bruyn*, Ambrosiaster's Commentary, p. 97. Cf. *Ambrosiaster*, Comm. Rom. 9,21,1: CSEL 81/1, p. 327–329. Cf. *P. F. Beatrice*, Tradux peccati. Alle fonti della dottrina agostiniana del peccato originale (Milano 1978) 166–167. According to Gross, these statements are an echo of the "generic realism" of Irenaeus or Gregory of Nyssa,

aster also states that Adam's sin is transmitted to all his descendants: all human beings are "born under sin", "all sinners, therefore, derive from him"[9]. With these formulations, Ambrosiaster wants to express that we all sinned in Adam by virtue of our belonging to the human *genus*; Adam's sin is a sin of the human race; the relationship between Adam and his descendants is "real and universal"[10]. The solidarity of all people in Adam the sinner corresponds, however, to the solidarity of all people in Christ the Savior.

1. Adam's sin and its consequences

What exactly and how is being transmitted from Adam? The first consequence of Adam's sin is death. All Adam's posterity obtained death "by title of inheritance" (*hereditatis titulo*)[11]. There are, however, two types of death. The first, bodily death (separation of body and soul) affects all people; it is a direct consequence of Adam's sin (a result of our sinning "in Adam"). The second, spiritual death is a punishment for one's own sins committed by the opportunity of Adam's sin (*eius occasione*); it relates to Adam's sin only indirectly[12] and affects those who followed Adam's negative example and "sinned after the manner of Adam's transgression", i.e. by idolatry (a result of our sinning "like Adam")[13]. Perhaps Ambrosiaster is trying to avoid the objection as to how Adam's descendants may bear the consequences of a sin voluntarily committed by Adam alone, but not by his descendants[14].

---

see *J. Gross*, Geschichte des Erbsündendogmas: ein Beitrag zur Geschichte des Problems vom Ursprung des Übels. Bd. I (München 1960) 233. See also *M. Przyszychowska*, We Were All in Adam. The Unity of Mankind in Adam in the Teaching of the Church Fathers (Warsaw 2018) 114–118.

[9] Cf. *Ambrosiaster*, Comm. Rom. 5,12,3,γ: CSEL 81/1, p. 165: 'Ipse enim per peccatum corruptus quos genuit, omnes nati sunt sub peccato. Ex eo igitur cuncti peccatores, quia ex ipso sumus omnes'. Transl. *Th. de Bruyn*, Ambrosiaster's Commentary, p. 97.

[10] *J. B. Valero*, Pecar en Adán, 152–153.

[11] *Ambrosiaster*, Comm. Rom. 8,12: CSEL 81/1, p. 268–269. Transl. *Th. de Bruyn*, Ambrosiaster's Commentary, p. 153.

[12] Cf. *Ambrosiaster*, Comm. Rom. 5,12,4,β.γ: CSEL 81/1, p. 164–165: 'Est et alia mors, quae secunda dicitur in gehenna, quam non peccato Adae patimur, sed eius occasione propriis peccatis adquiritur'. Transl. *Th. de Bruyn*, Ambrosiaster's Commentary, p. 97. *Ambrosiaster*, Comm. Rom. 5,15,1: CSEL 81/1, p. 178–181. Cf. *Th. de Bruyn*, Ambrosiaster's Commentary, xci–xciii.

[13] The distinction between the first and second death is also discussed in *Ambrosiaster*, Comm. Rom. 5,14: CSEL 81/1, p. 168–179, with significant differences between the recension α, β, and γ. See *V. Hušek*, The True Text, 331.

[14] Cf. *J. B. Valero*, Pecar en Adán, 175–176; *A. Pollastri*, Ambrosiaster, commento alla Lettera ai Romani: aspetti cristologici (L'Aquila 1976) 121–122, n. 345–347.

As a second consequence of Adam's sin, all human souls are held by the Devil and suffer in the underworld. The reign of the Devil is based on a "written bond with its decrees", a "list of charges" or a "promissory note"[15]. While the redemption is related to the power of the Devil and the liberation of the souls of the deceased from his power, the remission of sins is related to God and surprisingly unrelated to Christ's death[16].

The third consequence is the corruption of the body. Human beings are composed of soul and body and there was a harmony between soul and body in the beginning[17]. In Ambrosiaster's view, Adam sinned primarily in his soul while his body was affected by sin only subsequently. Although the body was created good, it became corruptible through Adam's sin[18]. The corruption of the body is passed from parents to their children. The corruption of the soul, on the contrary, cannot be transmitted in this way because the human soul is not generated from the souls of the parents. Ambrosiaster is convinced that every human soul is created directly by God[19]. For this reason, a sin of the soul cannot be transmitted from Adam to his descendants.

2. Corruption of the body and the seduction of the Devil

Even a corrupted body is not completely bad, although it is not the good that dwells within it, but the sin (cf. Rom 7:18). Ambrosiaster strictly rejects the

---

[15] *Ambrosiaster*, Comm. Rom. 5,12,4: CSEL 81/1, p. 165–167: 'cirografum in decretis' (Transl. Th. de Bruyn, Ambrosiaster's Commentary, p. 98: 'written bond with its decrees'); *Ambrosiaster*, Comm. Rom. 7,4,3: CSEL 81/1, p. 215: 'cirografum quod peccato Adae decretum erat' (Transl. Th. de Bruyn, Ambrosiaster's Commentary, p. 125: 'the written bond that had been decreed on account of Adam's sin'); *Ambrosiaster*, Comm. 1Cor. 15,57: H. J. Vogels, CSEL 81/2 (Vindobonae 1968), p. 187: 'cirografum, id est sententia, qua tenebatur genus humanum [...]'; *Ambrosiaster*, Comm. 2Cor. 13,4,1: CSEL 81/2, p. 310: 'cirografum Adae'; *Ambrosiaster*, Comm. Col. 2,13: H. J. Vogels, CSEL 81/3 (Vindobonae 1969), p. 184: '*delete cirografo, quod adversum nos erat in decretis*'; *Ambrosiaster*, Comm. Col. 2,15,α: CSEL 81/3, p. 185: 'cirografum quod erat decretum adversus nos peccato Adae'; *Ambrosiaster*, Comm. Col. 2,15,γ: CSEL 81/3, p. 186: 'cirografum quod erat adversarium nobis'.

[16] I discussed this aspect at the colloquy in Esztergom in 2012. Ambrosiaster's original contribution is an independent relationship between the remission of sins and redemption. See V. Hušek, Duplex gratia: Ambrosiaster and the Two Aspects of his Soteriology, in: Th. Hainthaler et al. (eds.), Für uns und für unser Heil. Soteriologie in Ost und West (Innsbruck – Wien 2014) 151–159.

[17] Cf. *Ambrosiaster*, Comm. Rom. 7,24–25,5: CSEL 81/1, p. 247.

[18] Cf. *Ambrosiaster*, Comm. Rom. 1,24,3: CSEL 81/1, p. 49; Comm. Rom. 7,18,1: CSEL 81/1, p. 237. Cf. A. Pollastri, Ambrosiaster, 107–108, n. 299.

[19] *Ambrosiaster*, Quaest. 23: A. Souter, CSEL 50 (Vindobonae 1908), p. 49–51, entitled: "An ex traduce sint animae sicut corpora". Surprisingly, transmission of sin is not discussed in this context.

idea that "the flesh is evil" (as suggested by some of his contemporaries)[20]. He describes the corruption of body as "the sign of the law of the Devil" (*signum legis diaboli*) or "the sign of the Devil" (*signum diaboli*) which is a consequence of the judgment handed down over Adam[21]. This allows the Devil to access the body "as if to his own law" and tempt human beings "with evil suggestions" not to do "what the law ordains"[22]. People strive to fulfill what the law commands and their effort demonstrates the compliance of the requirements of the law with human nature[23]. But "the ability and the strength to fulfill it is missing" because "someone else is the master of its ability"[24]. This is why people sin again and again, and "the habit of sinning" (*consuetudo peccandi*) puts a strain on them, making it easier to succumb to a sin than to fulfill the law; although they want to do good, the sinful habit overwhelms them[25]. Yet one is not relieved of responsibility because the primary cause of this condition is one's negligence; sin reigns only over those who have accepted its slavery[26].

Sin does not dwell in the soul but "in the flesh" because "all flesh is sinful through transmission" (*per traducem*)[27]. Sin dwells in the flesh "as if at the doorway of the soul" (*quasi ad ianuas animae*) and cannot enter unless as a result of the free choice of the will[28]. No one can make excuses for "sinning against one's will". Whenever "I do what I do not want" (Rom 7:20), it is a result of our previous "failing and indolence" (*ipsius enim vitio et desidia haec*

---

[20] *Ambrosiaster*, Comm. Rom. 7,18,1,β.γ: CSEL 81/1, p. 236–237.
[21] *Ambrosiaster*, Comm. Rom. 7,18,1,α; 7,18,1,β.γ: CSEL 81/1, p. 236–239. Transl. *Th. de Bruyn*, Ambrosiaster's Commentary, p. 136.
[22] *Ambrosiaster*, Comm. Rom. 7,18,2: CSEL 81/1, p. 236–239. Transl. *Th. de Bruyn*, Ambrosiaster's Commentary, p. 136.
[23] *Ambrosiaster*, Comm. Rom. 7,18,3: CSEL 81/1, p. 238–239.
[24] *Ambrosiaster*, Comm. Rom. 7,18,4,γ: CSEL 81/1, p. 239: 'Et placet ergo quod a lege iubetur et voluntas est faciendi, sed ut inpleatur potestas et virtus deest, quia sic pressus est dominatione peccati, ut non possit ire quo vult, neque valeat aut audeat contradicere, quia potestatis eius alter est dominus'. Transl. *Th. de Bruyn*, Ambrosiaster's Commentary, p. 136.
[25] *Ambrosiaster*, Comm. Rom. 7,18,4,γ: CSEL 81/1, p. 239. Transl. *Th. de Bruyn*, Ambrosiaster's Commentary, p. 136.
[26] Cf. A. Gaudel, Péché originel, 369.
[27] *Ambrosiaster*, Comm. Rom. 7,22,γ: CSEL 81/1, p. 241: '[N]on in animo habitat peccatum, sed in carne, quia est ex origine carnis peccati, et per traducem omnis caro fit peccati'. Transl. *Th. de Bruyn*, Ambrosiaster's Commentary, p. 137. See J. Jäntsch, Führt der Ambrosiaster zu Augustinus oder Pelagius?, Scholastik 9 (1934) 92-99, here 98, n. 28-30; A. *Pollastri*, Ambrosiaster, 113, n. 320.
[28] *Ambrosiaster*, Comm. Rom. 7,22,γ: CSEL 81/1, p. 241: 'Igitur in carne habitat peccatum quasi ad ianuas animae, ut non illam permittat ire quo vult'. Transl. *Th. de Bruyn*, Ambrosiaster's Commentary, p. 137–138.

coepta sunt) and our "own consent" (*per adsentum*) to subject to sin[29]. There are two laws fighting each other (cf. Rom 7:23). The law of the mind resides in the soul but the soul was "overwhelmed by the violence of sin, and indeed by its own heedlessness" (*pressa est violentia peccati, neglegentia quidem sua*) when it "delighted in faults" and "subjected itself to sin", so that now it is "held prisoner by its very habit"[30].

The deliverance from the sinful habit is possible through the grace of God in baptism. All sins are forgiven in baptism. The words of the apostle, "I myself serve the law of God with the mind but the law of sin with the flesh" (Rom 7:25), also apply to the situation of those who received baptism. All their sins were forgiven but the Devil still "floods the soul with evil suggestions by way of the flesh which is still subject to him"[31]. Ambrosiaster explains:

> The apostle said that he serves the law of God with the mind, because the soul is dedicated to God and, once it has regained its power, is able to fight against sin, which operates through the flesh[32].

Even after baptism, Christians are exposed to the temptation of the Devil through the body, but their mind serves God and is able to resist sin.

3. *Hereditas praevaricationis*

The apostle's cry, *infelix ego homo* (Rom 7:24–25, "What a wretched person I am! Who will set me free from the body of this death?"), is explained by Ambrosiaster: "because he was born under sin"[33]. The situation of humankind

---

[29] Cf. *Ambrosiaster*, Comm. Rom. 7,20,β.γ: CSEL 81/1, p. 238–241: 'Ipsius enim vitio et desidia haec coepta sunt; quia enim mancipavit se per adsensum peccato, iure illius dominatur'. Transl. *Th. de Bruyn*, Ambrosiaster's Commentary, p. 137.

[30] Cf. *Ambrosiaster*, Comm. Rom. 7,23,1,γ: CSEL 81/1, p. 243. Transl. *Th. de Bruyn*, Ambrosiaster's Commentary, p. 138. See also *Ambrosiaster*, Comm. Gal. 5,17,1-2: CSEL 81/3, p. 59-60.

[31] *Ambrosiaster*, Comm. Rom. 7,24–25,5,β.γ: CSEL 81/1, p. 247: 'Liberatus ergo de corpore mortis gratia dei per Christum mente vel animo servio legi dei, carne autem legi peccati, id est diaboli, qui per subiectam sibi carnem suggestiones malas ingerit animae'. Transl. *Th. de Bruyn*, Ambrosiaster's Commentary, p. 140.

[32] *Ambrosiaster*, Comm. Rom. 7,24–25,5,β.γ: CSEL 81/1, p. 247: 'Legi dei mente servire se dixit, quia animus devotus est deo et recuperata sui potestate repugnare potest peccato, quod per carnem operatur'. Transl. *Th. de Bruyn*, Ambrosiaster's Commentary, p. 140–141.

[33] *Ambrosiaster*, Comm. Rom. 7,24–25,1a,β.γ: CSEL 81/1, p. 245: 'Infelicem hominem dicit, quia nascitur sub peccato'. Transl. *Th. de Bruyn*, Ambrosiaster's Commentary, p. 139.

seems wretched, after falling heir to the "inheritance of transgression"[34]. This inheritance consists primarily in the submission to sin, in the sense of corruption of the body and sinful suggestions of the Devil as described above[35]. In Ambrosiaster's words:

> For what does it mean to be subject to sin, but to have a body that is corrupted through the weakness of the soul, by which sin insinuates itself and drives a person like a prisoner to transgressions, so that he does its [*sc.* sin's] will?[36]

To be "sold under sin" (Rom 7:14) means "to derive one's origin from Adam, who was the first to sin, and to become subject to sin by one's own transgression"[37]. Adam is "the father of all sinners"[38], his sin is in some way present in the personal sins of all people[39]. We can say that the sin of Adam in which we all sinned is a "generic sin" in the sense that Adam's transgression is the root of all personal sins[40]. The transmission of Adam's sin is limited, however, to weakness of the body leading to physical death, Adam's bad example and opportunity to sin, but the decisive step into the slavery of sin is one's own transgression.

The transmission of sin and the specific role of Adam and Eve is also discussed in Ambrosiaster's *quaestio* "On the sin of Adam and Eve"[41]. Here the author opposes radical ascetic views and defends the goodness of God's creation including the act of procreation, disproves the view that the sin of Adam and Eve implies any denigration of human sexuality (in apparent opposition

---

[34] *Ambrosiaster*, Comm. Rom. 7,24–25,1: CSEL 81/1, p. 245: 'Numquid non vere infelix est homo, qui in hanc hereditatem praevaricationis successit [...]'. Transl. *Th. de Bruyn*, Ambrosiaster's Commentary, p. 139.
[35] A. *Gaudel*, Péché originel, 369; A. *Pollastri*, Ambrosiaster, 111.
[36] *Ambrosiaster*, Comm. Rom. 7,14,4,β.γ: CSEL 81/1, p. 235: 'Quid est enim subiectum esse peccato, nisi corpus habere vitio animae corruptum, cui se inserat peccatum et inpellat hominem quasi captivum delictis, ut faciat voluntatem eius?' Transl. *Th. de Bruyn*, Ambrosiaster's Commentary, p. 134. Cf. *Ambrosiaster*, Quaest. 112,8: CSEL 50, p. 290. Cf. A. *Pollastri*, Ambrosiaster, 111–113.
[37] *Ambrosiaster*, Comm. Rom. 7,14,2,β.γ: CSEL 81/1, p. 232–233: 'Hoc est venditum esse sub peccato, ex Adam, qui prior peccavit, originem trahere et proprio delicto subiectum fieri peccato'. Cf. *Ambrosiaster*, Comm. Rom. 7,14,3: CSEL 81/1, p. 233–235.
[38] *Ambrosiaster*, Comm. Col. 1,13: CSEL 81/3, p. 170: '[...] qui est pater omnium peccantium [...]'. Transl. *G. Bray*, Ambrosiaster: Commentaries on Galatians – Philemon (Downers Grove 2009), p. 82.
[39] *Ambrosiaster*, Comm. Rom. 5,13: CSEL 81/1, p. 166–169.
[40] Cf. *J. B. Valero*, Pecar en Adán, 153.
[41] *Ambrosiaster*, Quaest. 127: CSEL 50, p. 399–416. For a detailed analysis, see *D. G. Hunter*, On the Sin of Adam and Eve: A Little-known Defense of Marriage and Childbearing by Ambrosiaster, HTR 82 (1989) 283–299.

to Jerome's Epistle 22), and discusses the practice of clerical celibacy in relation to sexual relations of married Christians. Ambrosiaster strictly denies any connection between the sin of Adam and Eve and their sexuality. In his view, the original sin consists in the transgression of God's command which is the sin of the soul. As a consequence of this transgression, however, the body is "subjugated" to sin and people are "born under sin", "subject to corruption and mortal"[42]. The human body is "stained" (*maculatum*) by sin but without any reference to concupiscence[43].

Does it mean that people are born either sons of God or sons of the Devil, depending solely on God's decision? Absolutely not. Everyone is born with the ability to learn the truth (*capax est ediscere veritatem*). Only he is the son of the Devil, who instills evil things and directs his attention to them. It is by deeds and confession (*operibus et professione*) that one becomes the son of the Devil. Everyone has a possibility to learn either good or evil, and subsequently will we be remunerated or punished[44]. As already mentioned, Ambrosiaster opposes traducianism and is convinced that human souls are not derived from the souls of their parents. Therefore, what parents pass to their children is mediated by the body while the human soul is immune to hereditary corruption. Ambrosiaster states that "all flesh is sinful through transmission" but "sin is not allowed to dwell in the soul on account of the free choice of the will"[45].

4. *Inpossibilitas non peccandi*

Despite sincere efforts to live a virtuous life, Christians constantly experience their weakness and repeatedly sin. The question arises as to whether sins committed after baptism can be forgiven and whether it is at all possible for man to avoid sin[46].

---

[42] *Ambrosiaster*, Quaest. 127,24: CSEL 50, p. 409. Cf. D. G. Hunter, On the sin, 291.

[43] *Ambrosiaster*, Quaest. 127,23: CSEL 50, p. 408–409.

[44] *Ambrosiaster*, Quaest. 80: CSEL 50, p. 135–136, entitled: "Certe aut filius dei quis est aut diaboli: semper ergo filius est, sed aliquando dei, aliquando diaboli, quid ergo nascimur requirendum est".

[45] *Ambrosiaster*, Comm. Rom. 7,22,γ: CSEL 81/1, p. 241: 'Hic est interior homo, quia non in animo habitat peccatum, sed in carne, quia est ex origine carnis peccati, et per traducem omnis caro fit peccati. In animo autem non permittitur habitare propter arbitrium liberum voluntatis'. Transl. Th. de Bruyn, Ambrosiaster's Commentary, p. 137. Cf. A. Pollastri, Ambrosiaster, 112.

[46] Ambrosiaster addresses these issues in relation to several passages of Romans, Colossians, Psalms 1, 23/24 and 50/51 (Quaest. 110–112) and against Novatian (Quaest. 102).

Inherited Sin in Ambrosiaster and Pelagius 311

At baptism, all sins are forgiven. Sins committed after baptism can also be forgiven but only after adequate repentance, "no longer free" (*non iam gratis*)[47]. It is not an extraordinary situation that a person sins after baptism, but rather a common part of human experience. In this context, Ambrosiaster states: "It is impossible for man that he does not sin"[48]. He refers to 1 John where the assumption that we have no sin is called self-deception (1 John 1:8) and anyone who does sin is assured of an advocate with the Father (1 John 2:1)[49]. Ambrosiaster has a deep understanding of the complexity of the human situation. Of course, it is not allowed to sin; but is it possible without exception? God knows how fragile the human race is and is always ready to offer his salutary remedy[50].

Psalm 1 describes the blessed man who does not *walk* in the counsel of the wicked, does not *stand* in the way of sinners and does not *sit* in the chair of pestilence[51]. Ambrosiaster interprets this triad as a typology of sins and their corresponding punishments. He states that it is impossible to avoid sin in general but it is certainly possible to avoid the most serious kind of sin, *impietas*, consisting in rebellion against God and idolatry[52]. Other kinds of sin are less serious and one "often sins suddenly without intending to"[53].

The verse of Psalm 50/51,5 ("Indeed, I was conceived in iniquities, and in sins did my mother conceive me") describes the weakness of the human race which is attested to (among other things) by the fact that "it is easy for a man to sin"[54]. This situation is a consequence of Adam's transgression which affects the entire human race and is passed down from one generation to the

---

[47] *Ambrosiaster*, Quaest. 102,9: CSEL 50, p. 207.
[48] *Ambrosiaster*, Quaest. 102,10: CSEL 50, p. 207: 'Inpossibile est enim homini ut non peccet'.
[49] *Ambrosiaster*, Quaest. 102,10: CSEL 50, p. 207.
[50] *Ambrosiaster*, Quaest. 102,16: CSEL 50, p. 211: 'Quis neget peccari numquam debere, sed si esset possibile? Porro autem sciens deus fragile genus humanum semper remediis salutaribus prosecutus est eos, ut post peccata haberent quo modo se repararent'.
[51] *Ambrosiaster*, Quaest. 110: CSEL 50, p. 268-277. The text of Psalm 1 is quoted in this wording: '*Beatus vir qui non abiit in consilio impiorum et in via peccatorum non stetit et in catedra pestilentiae non sedit*'. See S. Lunn-Rockliffe, Bishops on the Chair of Pestilence. Ambrosiaster's Polemical Exegesis of Ps. 1.1, JECS 19 (2011) 79-99.
[52] *Ambrosiaster*, Quaest. 110,1-4: CSEL 50, p. 269-270; *Ambrosiaster*, Quaest. 111,7: CSEL 50, p. 280.
[53] *Ambrosiaster*, Quaest. 110,4: CSEL 50, p. 270: '[...] dum peccare non cogitat, ex inprouiso incurrit ut peccet'.
[54] *Ambrosiaster*, Quaest. 112,8: CSEL 50, p. 290: 'Nunc hoc adiecto causam et infirmitatem humani generis memorat – quia facile est homini peccare [...]'. Cf. *Ambrosiaster*, Quaest. 1,7: CSEL 50, p. 16; Comm. Rom. 5,14,3,β.γ: CSEL 81/1, p. 170-173: '[...] inpossibile est non peccare'; Comm. Rom. 12,16: CSEL 81/1, p. 409: '[...] acsi non sit peccator, quod inpossibile est'; Comm. Col. 2,13-15,γ: CSEL 81/3, p. 185: '[...] quia inpossibile est esse sine peccato'.

next (*per traducem*), so that every person is born prone to sin (*obnoxii peccato*). Ambrosiaster immediately adds, however, that to be "conceived in sins" means that the human body is subjected to the Devil who can tempt and seduce through it and obstruct a good and virtuous life. People then experience an inner division between good and evil as described in Romans 7[55].

5. Iniquities of parents and the punishments of their children

A question may arise as how to reconcile God's justice with his decision to destroy Sodom and Gomorrah "with all the inhabitants of the cities" (Gen 19:25), i.e. including infants[56]. Does it mean that the sins of the parents are transmitted to their children? Can the punishment of children be sufficiently justified through the guilt of their parents? Ambrosiaster's answer is cautious. The sin of Sodom and Gomorrah is so serious that the punishment has even passed to the children. God's sentence is not based, however, on the foreknowledge of the future crimes of the children but solely on the crimes of the parents. The parents are to blame, not the children. It can also be said that the death of infants was a precautionary measure to their advantage so that they would not fall into the same crimes[57].

The question may also arise as how to reconcile God's justice with his promise about "punishing children for the iniquity of parents, to the third and the fourth generation" (Exod 20:5)?[58] Ambrosiaster explains: surely God will punish children for the sins of their parents but only those who follow their iniquity, who despise God as their parents did. God's threat "to the third and fourth generation" is a warning to grandchildren and great grandchildren not to follow the iniquity of their ancestors, not to contribute to the spread of evil and not to think they are immune to the danger of evil. Ambrosiaster once again advocates the individual responsibility of everyone. It is not possible to make excuses, as the saying goes: "The parents have eaten sour grapes, and the children's teeth are set on edge" (Ezek 18:2). Quite the contrary, "it is only the person who sins that shall die" (Ezek 18:4). And again, "a child shall not suffer for the iniquity of a parent, nor a parent suffer for the iniquity of a child; the righteousness of the righteous shall be his own, and the wickedness

---

[55] *Ambrosiaster*, Quaest. 112,8–9: CSEL 50, p. 290–291.
[56] *Ambrosiaster*, Quaest. 13: CSEL 50, p. 37–39, entitled: "Si iudicium dei iustum est, quare infantes in Sodomis simul cum parentibus cremati sunt?"
[57] *Ambrosiaster*, Quaest. 13,1: CSEL 50, p. 38.
[58] *Ambrosiaster*, Quaest. 14: CSEL 50, p. 39–41, entitled: "Quid est ut deus, qui iustus praedicatur, peccata patrum filiis se reddere promiserit in tertiam et quartam progeniem?"

of the wicked shall be his own" (Ezek 18:20). Nobody is immune to the evil and whoever continues or even increases the iniquity of the parents will be severely punished. On the other hand, God shows his steadfast love to those who love him and keep his commandments not only to the third and fourth but to the thousandth generation (Exod 20:6).

II. Pelagius

According to Pelagius, human beings were created in the image of God and hold the highest position among all creation. They are able to recognize God as Creator and themselves as his servants, God's will about themselves and the goal of human life, to distinguish between good and evil and to act in accordance with God's will. Human freedom includes the natural ability to choose good or evil, to incline one's will to either alternative (*utriusque partis possibilitas*), which is a necessary precondition for moral accountability[59]. The choice of good or evil has an effect on the conscience: joy, certainty and confirmation (in the case of good) or shame, fear, compunction and condemnation (in the case of evil).

1. Adam's sin and its consequences

Pelagius' interpretation of Romans 5 follows the parallel between Adam and Christ. The sin in Adam is opposed to the reconciliation to God through Christ[60]. According to Pelagius, however, the sin that came into the world through Adam is passed on "by example or by pattern" (*exemplo vel forma*)[61], and the death—as a consequence of Adam's sin—is not passed on to everyone but only to those who sin as Adam did: "As long as they sin the same way, they likewise die"[62]. Pelagius also distinguishes between physical and spiritual death but seems to apply the transmission of death to physical death only, as he recalls Abraham, Isaac and Jacob, who are undoubtedly physically dead but do not suffer a spiritual death. Or (which is even more likely) Pelagius

---

[59] I discussed this topic at the colloquy in Lviv in 2019. See V. Hušek, Imago Dei in Pelagius, in: Th. Hainthaler et al. (eds.), Imago Dei (Innsbruck – Wien 2021) 212–221.
[60] *Pelagius*, Comm. Rom. 5,11: A. Souter, Pelagius' Expositions of thirteen epistles of Saint Paul. II. The Text (Cambridge 1926), p. 45.
[61] *Pelagius*, Comm. Rom. 5,12: A. Souter, p. 45. Transl. *Th. de Bruyn*, Pelagius' Commentary on St Paul's Epistles to the Romans (Oxford 1993), p. 92.
[62] *Pelagius*, Comm. Rom. 5,12: A. Souter, p. 45: 'Dum ita peccant, et similiter moriuntur'. Transl. *Th. de Bruyn*, Pelagius' Commentary, p. 92.

understands the universal transmission hyperbolically, as it seems from his comments on *multi* and *omnes*[63].

What, then, does it mean that death reigned "even over those who did not sin after the manner of Adam's transgression" (Rom 5:14)? Pelagius' first interpretation is based on the preceding verse: "sin is not counted against one when the law does not exist" (Rom 5:13). His second interpretation is based on the distinction between two types of sinners: the first, "like Adam, transgressed a commandment", the second violated the law of nature; and they both deserve spiritual death[64].

In other words, the second death is a consequence of one's personal sins. Thus, Adam's sin is a negative example that everyone deliberately decides to follow, or not[65].

2. A bad example and sinful habit

Those who follow the example of Adam's sin, do so of their own will. Pelagius opposes any necessity of sinning. Sin is not a one-time act, however, but mostly is committed again and again. The repetition of sin creates a habit (*consuetudo*)[66], which further aggravates the human situation. The bad habit is so powerful that it seems that man acts almost against his will (*velut invitus*)[67], and as if drunk he does not have full control over his actions[68]. Habitual sin does not cancel the will completely, however, but prevents it from acting, so

---

[63] *Pelagius*, Comm. Rom. 5,12: A. Souter, p. 45. Transl. *Th. de Bruyn*, Pelagius' Commentary, p. 92–93.

[64] *Pelagius*, Comm. Rom. 5,14: A. Souter, p. 46. Transl. *Th. de Bruyn*, Pelagius' Commentary, p. 93.

[65] Cf. *S. Matteoli*, Alle origini della teologia di Pelagio: Tematiche e fonti delle Expositiones XIII Epistularum Pauli (Pisa – Roma 2011) 91–92. See also (91/5) *Pelagius*, Comm. Gal. 5,15: A. Souter, p. 335: 'alter alteri occasio perditionis existit'.

[66] Cf. *A. Souter*, Pelagius' Expositions, I, 97. Cf. also *Pelagius*, Dem. 17: PL 30, 31D; *Pelagius*, Cel. 10: I. Hilberg, M. Kamptner, CSEL 56/1 (Vindobonae ²1996), p. 337. The terms "longus usus peccandi", "longa consuetudo vitiorum" have the same meaning, (*Pelagius*, Dem. 8: PL 30, 23B–C).

[67] See the entire passage *Pelagius*, Comm. Rom. 7,7–24: A. Souter, p. 56–60.

[68] *Pelagius*, Comm. Rom. 7,15: A. Souter, p. 58: 'Venundatus quasi propositus peccato, ut, si consilium eius accepero, ipsius servus efficiar, sponte memet ipse subiciens; et iam quasi inebriatus consuetudine peccatorum, ignoro quid facio'. Transl. *Th. de Bruyn*, Pelagius' Commentary, p. 104.

"the will is here, but not the deed"[69]. Pelagius emphasizes that even in this situation, sin remains something external that does not change human nature and can be removed[70].

A synergy of sinful habit and bad example facilitates the spread of the sin from one generation to another: from childhood, one learns to sin by the example of parents, which is repeatedly confirmed in the habit[71]. When Pelagius describes the situation of humankind enslaved by a sinful habit, he avoids the body-soul contradiction in which Manichaean dualism could be heard. Sin is unthinkable for Pelagius without personal responsibility.

Pelagius also reports on the objections of his contemporaries to the transmission of sin, without taking a clear position on them[72]. In any case, it is unacceptable for Pelagius that the punishment for Adam's sin fall on his posterity and people were held responsible for a sin they did not commit.

Pelagius is not at all optimistic about the situation of humanity in the middle of a widespread sinful habit. He rejects the transmission of sin by procreation but admits that the bad example of ancestors gives the impression that one is already born into sin. He denies that sin could change human nature but admits that the sinful habit leads one to sin "as if naturally" (*quasi naturaliter*)[73]. Even in this state, one remains fully responsible for habitual sin, mainly because he (previously) freely surrendered to it[74].

---

[69] *Pelagius*, Comm. Rom. 7,18B: A. Souter, p. 59: 'Est voluntas, sed non est effectus, quia carnalis consuetudo voluntati resistit'. Transl. *Th. de Bruyn*, Pelagius' Commentary, p. 104. *Pelagius*, Comm. Gal. 5,17b: A. Souter, p. 336: '*Haec enim invicem adversantur (sibi), ut non quaecumque vultis, illa faciatis.* Haec facit ratio, ut voluntatem non sequatur effectus'.
[70] *Pelagius*, Comm. Rom. 7,17: A. Souter, p. 59: 'Habitat quasi hospes et quasi aliut in alio, non quasi unum, ut accidens scilicet, non naturale'. See also *P. Brown*, Pelagius and His Supporters: Aims and Environment, JThS N.S. 19 (1968) 93–114, here 104.
[71] *Pelagius*, Comm. Rom. 7,18; 7,20; 11,24: A. Souter, p. 59; 59; 90; *Pelagius*, Comm. Gal. 3,11; 5,17: A. Souter, p. 319; 336; *Pelagius*, Dem. 8: PL 30, 23B-D.
[72] *Pelagius*, Comm. Rom. 5,15: A. Souter, p. 46–47. See *S. Matteoli*, Alle origini, 80–83 for a detailed discussion of the topic and possible interpretations of the passage.
[73] *Pelagius*, Comm. Eph. 2,3: A. Souter, p. 352: '*Et eramus natura filii irae, sicut et ceteri.* Ita nos paternae traditionis consuetudo possederat, ut omnes ad damnationem nasci videremur'. *Pelagius*, Comm. Rom. 7,23; 11,24: A. Souter, p. 60; 90.
[74] *Pelagius*, Comm. Rom. 7,17.18b: A. Souter, p. 58–59: 'Ante consuetudinem ergo ego ipse libens faciebam. (…) Est voluntas, sed non est affectus, quia carnalis consuetudo voluntati resistit'.

3. The example of Christ and the grace of forgiveness

Adam is "an antithetical type" of Christ (*forma a contrario*): "Adam is the source of sin (…) Christ is the source of righteousness"[75]. In Pelagius' view, "the example of Adam's disobedience" is opposed to justification through "Christ's obedience"[76]. The effect of Christ's action far exceeds, however, the effect of Adam's action (cf. Rom 5:15–19). In Pelagius' words, "Adam became only the model for transgression, but Christ [both] forgave sins freely and gave an example of righteousness"[77].

In fact, there are three aspects of Christ's saving action: the gratuitous forgiveness of past sins, Christ's teaching and his example to be followed by free choice[78]. Pelagius does not emphasize one aspect compared to the others but stresses the unity of Christ's action in all of them[79]. Thus, the effect of divine grace is not limited to the forgiveness of past sins but also relates to everyone's personal commitment to imitate Christ. Those who accept forgiveness in Christ and follow his example, finally receive eternal glory[80].

The forgiveness of sins is closely linked with faith and baptism. The sacrament of justification by faith alone is baptism where our past sins are forgiven, we are even freed from sinful habit and no longer experience the inner conflict (described in Romans 7)[81]. Pouring water on the body must be accompanied by a personal decision, i.e. a voluntary decision to follow God's commandments[82].

It should be mentioned in this context that Pelagius' attitude towards infant baptism remains unclear. On the one hand, infants are incapable of personal decision because they do not make use of their reason and will. On the other hand, Pelagius never questioned (as far as we know) the infant baptism prac-

---

[75] *Pelagius*, Comm. Rom. 5,14: A. Souter, p. 46. Transl. *Th. de Bruyn*, Pelagius' Commentary, p. 93.
[76] *Pelagius*, Comm. Rom. 5,19: A. Souter, p. 48. Transl. *Th. de Bruyn*, Pelagius' Commentary, p. 95.
[77] *Pelagius*, Comm. Rom. 5,16: A. Souter, p. 47. Transl. *Th. de Bruyn*, Pelagius' Commentary, p. 95. See *Th. de Bruyn*, Pelagius' Commentary, 33–34 and 95 n. 38 for a possible interpolation of Pelagius' text emphasizing the role of the example.
[78] *Pelagius*, Comm. 1Thess. 1,10: A. Souter, p. 420: 'Dimittendo peccata et doctrina sua et exemplo ab ira nos iudicii liberavit, quia iam in spe[m] libertatem habemus'.
[79] *Pelagius*, Comm. 2Cor. 5,18: A. Souter, p. 261.
[80] *Pelagius*, Comm. Rom. 5,15–21: A. Souter, p. 46–48. Transl. *Th. de Bruyn*, Pelagius' Commentary, p. 94–96. Cf. *S. Matteoli*, Alle origini, 97; *Th. de Bruyn*, Pelagius' Commentary, 41.
[81] *V. Hušek*, Imago Dei, 218.
[82] *Pelagius*, De lege divina 2: PL 30, 107A–C.

tice of his time and recommended its administration with the same words (*isdem sacramenti verbis*) as in adult baptism[83]. Likewise, the question of infants who died without baptism is unclear[84]. Another unclear issue is the consequences of Adam's fall, which are passed down from generation to generation unrelated to free choice. Pelagius seems to focus on Adam's example and its imitation but does not say more about ignorance, weakness of the body and spirit, mortality and concupiscence[85].

Conclusion

Ambrosiaster and Pelagius describe the transmission of sin through bad example and its imitation. Adam was the first to set an example of sinning, then sin passed on from one generation to another by imitation.

The views of Ambrosiaster and Pelagius differ on the issue of the transmission of Adam's sin and our participation in it. Ambrosiaster seems to hesitate between two positions. On the one hand, he is convinced that there is a hereditary corruption transmitted from Adam to all his posterity (which must be passed through the body because the soul is not derived from the souls of the parents). On the other hand, he is convinced that just punishment can only result from personal guilt, and therefore he refutes the condemnation of all people based on the participation in and co-responsibility for Adam's sin. As a consequence of the efforts to defend both positions, Ambrosiaster's views on inherited sin may seem inconsistent[86].

Pelagius focuses on the bad example of Adam's sin and its volitional appropriation. He opposes fatalism that results from a traducianist understanding of inherited sin. Adam's sin passed on to his descendants and affected most of humanity, but the soul and body are not the means of this transmission[87]. The saving action of Christ includes his teaching, the forgiveness of sins and his example of righteousness to be followed[88].

---

[83] *Pelagius*, Libellus fidei 7 [17], in *Augustine*, De gratia Christi et de pecccato originali 2,21,24: H. Chirat et al., La crise pélagienne II, BA 22 (Paris 1975), p. 200.
[84] L. Karfíková, Grace and the Will According to Augustine (Leiden 2012) 205.
[85] Th. de Bruyn, Pelagius' Commentary, 23.
[86] J. B. Valero, Pecar en Adán, 182–185; A. Pollastri, Ambrosiaster, 112, S. Matteoli, Alle origini, 98.
[87] Cf. J. B. Valero, Pecar en Adán, 187; Th. de Bruyn, Pelagius' Commentary, 40–41.
[88] This article is a result of research funded by Palacký University Olomouc as the project "Continuity—Discontinuity—Progression" (IGA_CMTF_2021_009).

Dominique Gonnet, Lyon (France)

Césaire d'Arles, le Concile d'Orange II et le péché originel

Abstract :
Nous avons conservé de Césaire d'Arles un grand nombre d'homélies. Cependant, il n'a pas été seulement prédicateur, il a aussi préparé et présidé des conciles locaux (4) avec le soutien des papes successifs. Un de ces conciles a eu un grand retentissement, celui d'Orange II, où la thèse de la prédestination au mal a été condamnée. Or, il semble que la manière de parler du péché originel diffère entre d'une part les canons et documents de ce concile, et d'autre part, sa prédication. C'est ce point-là que j'ai voulu approfondir : peut-on dire que la rigueur de l'enseignement conciliaire est tempérée par le souci pastoral de la prédication ? Finalement, derrière les conseils d'Augustin aux prédicateurs pour qu'ils ne découragent pas leurs ouailles, ne peut-on pas dire en paraphrasant la formule : Lex praedicandi, lex credendi ? Le mode allégorique sous lequel Césaire interprète les Écritures en les référant très souvent au péché originel et à Adam pour les tourner vers le salut du Christ n'est-il pas là pour rappeler la priorité du salut, du pardon et de la miséricorde de Dieu sur la condamnation ? Ce que confirme l'utilisation uniquement positive de la prédestination et de la grâce que tout homme peut recevoir.

Dans le livre intitulé : *Le Don de la persévérance* (*De dono perseuerantiae*), Augustin consacre un chapitre entier sur « la manière de prêcher au peuple la prédestination »[1]. C'est effectivement une question aussi difficile que celle du péché originel et lié à lui dans le contexte occidental. L'idée de prédestination peut conduire à douter totalement de la miséricorde de Dieu si elle est mal comprise. Augustin souligne combien il faut être prudent dans la prédication. Comment la doctrine du péché originel comme celle de la prédestination ne risque-t-elle pas d'être contraire au message de salut pour tous que porte le Christ, le Nouvel Adam ? Saint Paul ne l'introduit qu'en associant immédiatement l'Ancien Adam pécheur au Nouvel Adam sauveur[2]. L'exposé portera sur la différence entre la manière de parler du péché originel dans les ca-

---

[1] Aug., De dono perseuerantiae 22, 57–62 : J. Pintard, BAug 24 (Paris 1962), p. 741–751.
[2] Rm 5, 18 : « Bref, comme par la faute d'un seul ce fut pour tous les hommes la condamnation, ainsi par l'œuvre de justice d'un seul, c'est pour tous les hommes la justification qui donne la vie ».

nons du Concile d'Orange, suscité par Césaire d'Arles, et sa prédication, en l'occurrence ses homélies.

Césaire est né vers 470 à Chalon-sur-Saône. Il fut évêque d'Arles de 502 jusqu'à sa mort en 542. Nommé vicaire du Pape pour la Gaule et l'Espagne en 514, il convoque et préside plusieurs conciles, dont le second concile d'Orange en 529, qui condamne le semi-pélagianisme et donne une formulation théologique de la grâce qui tempère celle d'Augustin, de Fauste de Riez et d'autres encore. J'ai choisi de comparer les documents de ce concile avec les *Sermons* de Césaire. Pour cela, je m'appuie sur les occurrences de l'expression : « péché originel », mais aussi de celles d'« Adam » dans les deux corpus. Ce que je voudrais montrer, c'est comment dans la prédication, le thème de la faute d'Adam est essentiellement associé au salut par le Christ dans la droite ligne de l'enseignement de saint Paul dans Romains 5, 12–21.

Après avoir présenté les éléments concernant le péché originel dans le Concile d'Orange, je regarderai l'enseignement de Césaire dans ses discours : l'extension du péché originel, ses conséquences morales, son lien systématique avec le salut, non seulement des baptisés, mais de toute l'humanité, et les questions que sa présentation chez Césaire pose.

I. Le deuxième concile d'Orange (529)

Il semble bien que la réunion du deuxième concile d'Orange soit due à l'initiative de Césaire qui voulait faire prévaloir la doctrine de saint Augustin contre le semi-pélagianisme[3]. C'est à l'occasion de la dédicace d'une nouvelle église que quatorze évêques sont réunis. Il y a un échange sur les problèmes du moment, à savoir les questions de la grâce et du libre-arbitre. Césaire a sans doute préparé longtemps avant le concile le choix des textes qui vont servir de canons par des échanges avec le siège apostolique à Rome. Dans une situation semblable, les délibérations étaient réduites à un minimum qui ne tendait à rien. En 524, par exemple, les évêques sont réunis pour la dédicace de Notre-Dame d'Arles. Après la cérémonie, Césaire fait apporter un parchemin qui contient un règlement canonique en quatre articles, et le donne à signer aux dix-huit évêques présents ou représentés. C'est ce qu'il appelle « une définition des saints frères [les évêques] ou, si vous voulez, la mienne »[4] !

---

[3] G. Fritz, Art. Orange (2ᵉ concile d'), in : DTC 11-1 (Paris 1931) 1089.
[4] *Concil. Arelat. IV*, Subscriptiones : J. Gaudemet, B. Basdevant, SC 353 (Paris 1989), p. 142: *difinitionem hanc sanctorum fratrum uel meam*. Trad. française : P. Lejay, Le rôle théologique de Césaire d'Arles (Paris 1906), p. 94.

Il s'agit essentiellement pour les évêques présents à Orange de signer ces documents contre les évêques du « nord de l'Isère ». Ces derniers se sont réunis à Valence, à une centaine de kilomètres au nord d'Orange, toujours dans la vallée du Rhône. Ils sont semi-pélagiens et donnent une trop grande place au libre-arbitre d'après le pape Boniface II. Selon le pape :

> Ils prétendent que seule la foi par laquelle nous croyons au Christ relève de la nature, non de la grâce ; que pour les hommes, depuis Adam, elle est demeurée au pouvoir du libre-arbitre, et non qu'elle est accordée maintenant à chacun par une largesse de la miséricorde divine[5].

Les documents rassemblés par Césaire autour du Concile d'Orange comprennent[6] :

- Vingt-cinq *Canons* dont les 7 premiers commencent par : « Si quelqu'un affirme [...] » et les dix-sept *Canons-sentences* qui sont des extraits de textes d'Augustin déjà sélectionnés par Prosper d'Aquitaine, et déjà validés par le Pape Boniface II ;

- Une *Définition de foi* ;

- Les *Souscriptions des évêques* ;

- Un *Rescrit* sous forme d'une longue lettre du pape Boniface II à Césaire confirmant toutes les décisions du concile local, écrite deux ans après le Concile, en 531 ;

- Une « préface de Césaire d'Arles ajoutée à la confirmation pontificale [du même pape] et aux actes du concile » soulignant la prééminence du siège apostolique pour l'approbation des *Canons* du Concile.

---

[5] *Boniface II*, Ep. ad Caesarium 1: SC 353 (Paris 1989), p. 176–179.
[6] Ils sont édités et traduits dans : J. Gaudemet, B. Basdevant, Les Canons des conciles mérovingiens, T. I, SC 353 (Paris 1989), p. 154–185.

Quant au contenu des *Canons*, l'accent est mis sur l'absolue prépondérance de la foi sur la volonté de l'homme, mais avec quelques nuances. Ce qui nous importe ici, c'est la place de la « faute de la prévarication d'Adam » par laquelle « l'homme tout entier, c'est-à-dire quant au corps et quant à l'âme, est changé en pire »[7]. Cette expression désigne donc le péché d'Adam dans les *Canons* du Concile. On peut traduire le mot « prévarication » par « transgression » de la loi divine, mais si l'on remonte à son sens classique, on s'aperçoit qu'il s'agit d'« intelligence avec l'ennemi », ce sens est confirmé par la troisième citation biblique de ce *Canon*[8] : « Être vaincu par quelqu'un, c'est devenir son esclave ». « La liberté de l'âme » n'est pas « intacte », tel est le sens de ce *Canon*.

Le premier *Canon* ne parle pas d'hérédité, mais dans le *Canon* 2, le mot « descendance » apparaît. C'est la « descendance » d'Adam qui hérite du péché qui « par un seul homme est entré dans le monde, tous ayant péché en lui ». La précision de saint Paul : « tous ayant péché en lui »[9] introduit déjà l'idée qu'Adam représente toute l'humanité. Le reste des *Canons* concernent la grâce.

Il n'est plus question ensuite d'Adam et de sa « prévarication ». Dans le 21ᵉ *Canon-sentence* qui cite le *De gratia et libero arbitrio* d'Augustin[10], il est dit que « Le Christ [...] est mort [...] pour que la nature, perdue par Adam, fût restaurée par le Christ, qui a dit qu'il était venu ‹ pour chercher et sauver ce qui était perdu › »[11]. Il est à noter que le texte choisi par le Concile d'Orange met en relation la perte de la nature en Adam avec sa restauration par le Christ. Or c'est ce thème qui va constamment dominer toute la prédication de Césaire. Nous allons voir comment.

La *Définition de foi* a été rendue publique et archivée par Césaire comme il le dit à la fin, parce qu'elle est destinée aux hommes d'Église (*religiosi*) comme aux laïcs[12]. Il n'y est pas question du péché originel, et pourtant tout porte sur les conséquences de la faute d'Adam sur le libre-arbitre de l'homme. C'est dans cette *Définition de foi* que le Concile mentionne plusieurs hommes justes

---

[7] *Concil. Arausic. II*, De gratia et libero arbitrio 1 : SC 353 (Paris 1989), p. 155.
[8] *Concil. Arausic. II*, De gratia et libero arbitrio 2 : SC 353 (Paris 1989), p. 156 citant 2 P 2, 19.
[9] Rm 5, 12 ; cf. *Aug.*, Contra duas epistolas pelagianorum 4, 4, 6 : F.-J. Thonnard, BAug 23 (Paris 1974), p. 561–563 : Augustin réfute la thèse pélagienne de l'unique transmission de la peine – à savoir la mort – et pas du péché.
[10] *Concil. Arausic. II*, De natura et gratia 21 : SC 353 (Paris 1989), p. 167 ; Cf. *Aug.*, De gratia et libero arbitrio 13, 25 : J. Pintard, BAug 24 (Paris 1962), p. 149.
[11] *Concil. Arausic. II*, De natura et gratia 21 : SC 353 (Paris 1989), p. 167 citant Lc 19, 10.
[12] Cf. *Concil. Arausic. II*, Definitio fidei : SC 353 (Paris 1989), p. 173 (juste avant les souscriptions).

pour l'Ancien Testament : « Abel, Noé, Abraham, Isaac, Jacob, et toute la multitude des saints anciens »[13] et pour le Nouveau Testament : le bon larron, Corneille et Zachée en disant que, pour les uns et les autres, leur « admirable foi que chante à leur louange l'apôtre Paul n'a pas été accordée par la bonté de la nature donnée primitivement à Adam, mais par la grâce de Dieu »[14]. Adam a donc perdu cette « bonté de la nature ».

En outre, dans les conclusions de Césaire à ce Concile, il y a un anathème contre ceux qui croient à une prédestination au mal. Mais nous reviendrons sur celui-ci en le comparant aux passages des *Sermons* qui peuvent lui ressembler.

II. Les *Sermons*[15] de Césaire et leurs références à Adam et au péché originel

Je m'appuie donc sur les occurrences du péché originel et de celles d'Adam chez Césaire : en effet, on ne peut guère séparer les deux, car Adam existe essentiellement par sa faute, et Ève avec lui. L'arrière-fond reste le péché originel.

Césaire a d'ailleurs mis dans son recueil le *Sermon* 151 d'Augustin auquel il a donné pour titre : *Sermon de Saint Augustin sur le péché originel*. Comme Césaire le reprend intégralement avec quelques petites modifications qui n'en changent pas le sens[16], on peut considérer qu'il en adopte les conclusions en particulier sur le lien entre péché originel et concupiscence, d'autant qu'il développe avec plusieurs exemples la dernière phrase du *Sermon* d'Augustin : « C'est de la partie du corps qu'Adam et Ève couvrirent que la rébellion se fit sentir. C'est de là que vient le péché originel »[17]. Le lien du péché originel avec un aspect de la concupiscence, à savoir la sexualité, présentée par Augustin

---

[13] *Concil. Arausic. II*, Definitio fidei : SC 353 (Paris 1989), p. 171.
[14] *Concil. Arausic. II*, Definitio fidei : SC 353 (Paris 1989), p. 173.
[15] Les *Sermons* de Césaire ont été intégralement traduits en anglais par : M. M. Mueller, FaCh 31, 47 et 66 (Washington, D.C. 1956, 1964, 1973). Les *Sermons* 1 à 105 sont publiés et traduits par : M.-J. Delage, SC 175, 243, 330 (Paris 1971, 1978, 1986) et J. Courreau, SC 447 (Paris 2000). Les suivants, déjà traduits par J. Courreau, sont en cours de révision par Marie Pauliat et pas encore publiés. Les références aux *Sermons* 106 et suivants ne concernent donc que le texte latin. Je remercie ici Marie Pauliat pour les *Sermons* 106–143 qu'elle a déjà révisés ainsi que l'Abbaye de Ligugé pour la communication des archives de J. Courreau.
[16] Cf. *G. Morin*, Un nouveau recueil inédit d'homélies de S. Césaire d'Arles, RBen 16 (1899) 243-244, note quelques différences : des expressions de Césaire – *cum Dei adiutorio* […] –, et un ajout à la fin dans un langage plus direct sur la sexualité.
[17] *Aug.*, Serm. 151 : G. Partoens, CCL 41Ba (Turnhout 2008), p. 23 ; *Caes. Arel.*, Serm. 177, 1 : G. Morin, CCL 104 (Turnhout 1953), p. 717 : *Quod texerunt, ibi senserunt. Ecce unde trahitur originale peccatum.*

comme l'origine du péché originel, n'est donc pas absent chez Césaire, mais il est pour ce dernier une cause parmi d'autres.

1. Le Péché originel assimilé au péché de tous les hommes

Il y a une tendance chez Césaire à élargir la notion de péché originel et à l'associer aux autres péchés au point de penser qu'il ne se distingue pas du péché de l'humanité. En outre, l'expression « Adam ou le genre humain en son entier » revient à plusieurs reprises. Il y a donc là comme un dépassement de cette centration autour du personnage d'Adam, et il est peut-être ainsi plus proche des Pères grecs.

a. L'emploi du pluriel : « les péchés originels »

Un premier point est l'utilisation par Césaire de l'expression « péchés originels » au pluriel, par exemple quand « les Égyptiens symboliques » de la sortie d'Égypte sont identifiés aux « péchés originels » et aux « fautes (*crimina*) actuelles »[18]. En quelque sorte, un pluriel appelle l'autre : celui des fautes actuelles appelle celui des péchés originels. L'interprétation allégorique de la traversée de la mer Rouge en est une autre occasion, car Césaire « définit le baptême comme une destruction des péchés ‹tant originels qu'actuels› »[19]. De même à propos des nations qui occupaient la terre promise :

Par la grâce de l'Évangile, les nations cruelles et féroces, c'est-à-dire les péchés originels et les fautes actuelles, se sont vus chassés de la Terre promise, c'est-à-dire du cœur des chrétiens[20].

Cette association entre des « péchés originels » employés au pluriel avec les « fautes actuelles » rappellent qu'elles ont une origine commune. Césaire emploie l'expression ailleurs, à chaque fois en relation avec une figure plurielle : les Égyptiens, les nations et aussi les premiers-nés de la dixième plaie d'Égypte condamnés à mourir et qui représentent « aussi bien les esprits du mal que les péchés originels »[21]. Ce pluriel, « les péchés originels », semble donc une manière d'en élargir le sens à tous ceux qui peuvent être commis dans l'humanité et d'en montrer l'unité. Peut-être faut-il y voir aussi celui de Caïn : « Dès le commencement du monde, c'est par envie qu'Abel le juste fut tué par Caïn, le frère injuste »[22].

---

[18] *Caes. Arel.*, Serm. 97, 1 : SC 447 (Paris 2000), p. 293.
[19] J. Courreau, Annotation, in : J. Courreau, SC 447 (Paris 2000) 293, n. 2.
[20] *Caes. Arel.*, Serm. 114, 3 : G. Morin, CCL 103 (Turnhout 1953), p. 475.
[21] *Caes. Arel.*, Serm. 99, 3 : SC 447 (Paris 2000), p. 321.
[22] *Caes. Arel.*, Serm. 90, 1 : SC 447 (Paris 2000), p. 209.

b. Adam ou le genre humain : Le bois fait flotter le fer de la hache
Césaire en vient même à identifier Adam avec le genre humain lorsqu'il commente l'un des miracles du prophète Élisée. Le fer d'une hache est tombé au fond de l'eau. Le prophète y jette un manche de bois. Il récupère ainsi la hache. Césaire écrit : «La hache qui chuta signifia, semble-t-il, Adam ou le genre humain en son entier»[23]. Le bois de la hache est le symbole du bois de la Croix, le fer de la hache est celui du «péché de l'humanité». En effet, «le genre humain s'arracha lui aussi, par orgueil, de la main du Dieu tout-puissant, chuta et s'engloutit dans le fleuve de la luxure ou dans le gouffre de tous les péchés»[24].

c. Le «crime des hommes» et le péché originel acquittés par le Christ
Il en est de même dans cet autre *Sermon* : «Ce qu'Adam devait à Dieu, le Christ l'a acquitté entièrement en assumant la mort; certainement il s'est offert en sacrifice pour le crime des hommes et leur descendance»[25]. Là encore Césaire élargit à toute l'humanité le crime d'Adam.

À travers ces différentes expressions : «péchés originels» associés à «péchés actuels», «péché de l'humanité», «crime des hommes et de leur descendance», nous pouvons reconnaître l'élargissement au péché dans un sens général, ce que certains théologiens appellent le «péché immémorial» ou le «péché ancestral». Il y a une conscience chez Césaire que ce péché dépasse largement celui d'Adam.

2. Il faut tout faire pour éviter d'être comme Adam!

Le premier enseignement du péché d'Adam, c'est l'invitation à entrer dans le combat de la liberté. Finalement, chacun a son libre arbitre et peut en user mieux qu'Adam, tout en sachant que chacun est affaibli et entravé par le péché originel.

a. Adam et Ève avaient bien leur libre arbitre
Il aurait pu en être autrement :

> Telle avait été formée la volonté de tous les deux [Adam et Ève], tel avait été créé le libre arbitre, que si un refus avait été opposé au serpent, le serpent, embarrassé dans son mensonge, se retirerait et que l'homme demeurerait, affermi dans le Seigneur créateur[26].

---

[23] *Caes. Arel.*, Serm. 130, 1 : CCL 103 (Turnhout 1953), p. 535.
[24] Ibid.
[25] *Caes. Arel.*, Serm. 11, 5 : SC 175 (Paris 1971), p. 397.
[26] *Caes. Arel.*, Serm. 59, 4 : SC 330 (Paris 1986), p. 49–51.

Mais il en reste des conditionnements : la nature de l'homme faite de poussière et « l'enfer » du monde :

b. Adam est terre, et le démon mange la terre
Quand Adam pécha, il lui fut dit qu'il était poussière, cette poussière que mange le serpent et qui représente « les personnes à l'esprit tourné vers la terre par la sensualité, l'orgueil, qui aiment la terre et place toute leur espérance en elle »[27].

c. Les deux enfers
Également l'envoi dans le monde ne favorise pas l'exercice du libre-arbitre : « Notre père Adam fût placé dans un paradis de délices ; mais, méprisant les ordres de Dieu par la persuasion du diable, il fut précipité dans les misères de ce monde »[28].

C'est le premier enfer, mais il y en a un plus profond…

d. Agir maintenant car il n'y a plus d'aide après la mort
Il s'agit pourtant de se décider maintenant. Lazare est au ciel, le mauvais riche en enfer sans aucune aide, mais cela rappelle que « tous les saints et justes peuvent venir en aide aux pécheurs par leur intercession, tant que ces pécheurs sont en cette vie, et demandent leur aide »[29].

e. Sensualité et péchés rasées comme les cheveux de Samson par Dalila
Armons-nous contre le rasoir ennemi, celui qui a rasé la tête d'Adam et d'Ève et qui peut raser la nôtre :

> Avec l'aide de Dieu, prenons garde que le rasoir ennemi, qui, en Adam et Ève trompés par ruse, rasa la tête du genre humain, n'atteigne aussi notre tête […]. Mais prions plutôt le Seigneur pour que nos péchés, qui tiennent notre âme nouée plus que le sont les cheveux de notre tête, ne soient pas coupés à moitié, mais retranchés à la racine, comme par la lame d'un rasoir[30].

f. Les bébés pleurent de la souffrance héritée d'Adam
Cette souffrance de la nature humaine que les bébés manifestent déjà par leurs pleurs est à la mesure de la « félicité » à laquelle nous sommes destinés. Les enfants pleurent spontanément et annoncent ainsi leurs malheurs futurs car

---
[27] *Caes. Arel.*, Serm. 136, 7 : CCL 103 (Turnhout 1953), p. 564.
[28] *Caes. Arel.*, Serm. 150, 1 : CCL 104 (Turnhout 1953), p. 613.
[29] *Caes. Arel.*, Serm. 165, 3 : CCL 104 (Turnhout 1953), p. 677.
[30] *Caes. Arel.*, Serm. 120, 1 : CCL 103 (Turnhout 1953), p. 501.

la souffrance est une loi commune à tous les hommes, par suite du péché d'Adam. Nous naissons pour souffrir. Mais à côté de cette origine qui nous voue au malheur, la Providence de Dieu a mis la régénération qui doit nous en délivrer. Notre origine nous condamne à la douleur ; notre régénération nous destine à la félicité[31].

L'enseignement sur ce que l'on doit faire dans notre condition de fils d'Adam et Ève ne manque pas. Mais ce qui domine comme nous venons de le voir à propos de la félicité, c'est bien la perspective du salut qui n'est pas isolé du péché originel auquel Adam est associé.

3. Le Péché originel associé systématiquement au salut dans les *Sermons*

Les *Sermons* de Césaire ne manquent pas d'associer le péché originel au salut, comme si c'était un problème grave pour les auditeurs des *Sermons* désespérant d'en rester à l'enseignement sur le péché originel. Césaire multiplie les mises en parallèle des figures de l'Ancien Testament, où le péché originel symbolisé est opposé au salut des baptisés. C'était le cas dans les exemples que nous avons déjà vus, à savoir les Égyptiens avec leurs premiers-nés et leur armée ou les nations qui occupent la Terre promise, opposés à la victoire du peuple hébreu. Pour l'instant, nous ne parlons pas des non-baptisés, mais nous y reviendrons. Nous pouvons poursuivre cette comparaison avec les exemples suivants.

a. Même lieu pour le tombeau d'Adam et la Croix

Césaire s'en remet à l'enseignement que Jérôme a reçu « d'anciens et vénérables juifs, à savoir qu'à l'endroit où fut offert Isaac, là fut crucifié plus tard notre Seigneur le Christ »[32]. Césaire se réfère à :

> des anciens [en l'occurrence Origène[33]] qui ont même rapporté que le premier Adam, lui aussi, avait été enseveli jadis à l'endroit même où fut plantée la croix et que l'endroit fut dit « du Calvaire » parce que la première tête du genre humain, selon la tradition, aurait été ensevelie à cet endroit[34].

---

[31] Cf. *Caes. Arel.*, Serm. 181, 3 : CCL 104 (Turnhout 1953), p. 736.
[32] *Caes. Arel.*, Serm. 84, 5 : SC 447 (Paris 2000), p. 137.
[33] *Orig.*, Serm. in Matth. 126 : E. Klostermann, E. Benz, U. Treu, Origenes Werke XI, GCS 38 (Berlin ²1976), p. 265.
[34] *Caes. Arel.*, Serm. 84, 5 : SC 447 (Paris 2000), p. 137.

b. La terre des Cananéens redevenue terre promise

La terre promise primitive était «la demeure des vertus», mais les Cananéens l'ont occupée quand Adam a péché, elle est devenue «un repaire de brigands» et «les vices régnaient en nous. Maintenant donc que Jésus notre Seigneur vient à notre secours, hâtons-nous de chasser de chez nous les nations ennemies»[35]. Il est donc question du salut du Christ qui nous soutient dans le combat, loin de nous y abandonner. Or les expressions : *cum Dei auxilio* (avec le secours de Dieu), *Deo auxiliante* (avec le secours de Dieu), *cum Dei adiutorio* (avec l'aide de Dieu) sont très caractéristiques de Césaire.

c. La source amère rendue potable par Élisée

Élisée représente le Sauveur. La source amère[36], c'est Adam d'où le genre humain est sorti. Avant la venue du vrai Élisée, le genre humain par le péché du premier homme gisait dans la stérilité ou l'amertume. Le vase neuf représente le mystère de l'Incarnation du Seigneur. Puisque le sel est le symbole de la sagesse[37], et que le Christ n'est pas seulement Force de Dieu, mais Sagesse de Dieu, le vase neuf de la divine Sagesse[38] est rempli de sel quand le Verbe s'est fait chair. Les eaux amères sont devenues douces et fécondes[39].

d. Le bâton sur le visage de l'enfant[40]

Le bâton de Guéhazi ne ressuscite pas le jeune garçon. Il figure le bâton de Moïse qui fit des prodiges, mais sans le Christ, il ne peut délivrer ni du péché originel, ni du péché actuel, nous dit Césaire. «La loi n'amène rien à la perfection»[41]. Le bâton sans Élisée, la Croix sans le Christ ne pouvaient rien faire.

e. «La chair *de Naaman* est devenue comme celle d'un petit enfant»[42]

Césaire poursuit en disant que :

> Tous ceux qui sont baptisés, qu'ils soient jeunes ou vieux, sont tous cependant appelés «enfants»; ceux qui en Adam et Ève sont nés vieux, par le Christ et l'Église renaissent neufs. La première génération conduit l'homme à la mort, la seconde génération le conduit à la vie : la première engendre des enfants de colère, la seconde

---

[35] *Caes. Arel.*, Serm. 116, 5 : CCL 103 (Turnhout 1953), p. 485.
[36] Cf. 2 R 2, 19.
[37] Cf. Col 4, 6.
[38] Cf. 1 Co 1, 30.
[39] Cf. *Caes. Arel.*, Serm. 126, 2 : CCL 103 (Turnhout 1953), p. 521–522.
[40] Cf. *Caes. Arel.*, Serm. 128, 7 : CCL 103 (Turnhout 1953), p. 530.
[41] He 7, 19 cité par *Caes. Arel.*, Serm. 128, 7 : «La loi ne conduit rien à la perfection».
[42] *Caes. Arel.*, Serm. 129, 5 : CCL 103 (Turnhout 1953), p. 533.

régénère des vases de miséricorde, comme le dit l'Apôtre : « Tous meurent en Adam, tous sont vivifiés dans le Christ »[43].

Cette interprétation typologique représente au plus fort le lien entre le péché qui conduit à la mort et le salut du Christ qui sauve. Dans un autre *Sermon*, « Adam était vieux et il est devenu nouveau »[44] dans le Christ.

f. L'homme blessé par le diable et sauvé par le Bon Samaritain
La parabole du Bon Samaritain est une parabole du péché et du salut de l'homme : l'homme, c'est Adam qui vient de Jérusalem dont l'étymologie évoque la paix du Paradis et descend à Jéricho dont l'étymologie évoque la lune changeante, naissante et mourante du Monde. Quand il est descendu, c'est qu'il est tombé dans le péché, et les voleurs sont le diable et ses anges. Le bon samaritain, dont l'étymologie évoque un gardien, figure le Christ, le gardien d'Israël, qui soigne avec l'huile et le vin, symboles de la grâce qui libère des péchés. L'hôtelier, c'est saint Paul qui a « le souci de toutes les Églises »[45]. Les deux deniers sont Passion et Résurrection, ou encore les deux commandements de l'amour de Dieu et du prochain[46].

g. Le Père rend l'immortalité par la tunique dont il revêt le Fils prodigue
Dans la parabole du Fils prodigue, comme dans la parabole du Bon Samaritain, tout est interprété dans le sens du salut du Christ. La tunique du Fils prodigue, c'est l'immortalité :

> Le père dit : « Donnez-lui sa première tunique », il lui rendit l'immortalité qu'Adam avait perdu en péchant [...]. L'anneau est le Saint Esprit. Le veau gras est la passion du Christ. Le chœur harmonieux est l'unique volonté du peuple chrétien[47].

h. Les vases de Cana
Le premier vase de Cana est l'âge d'Adam, qui est identifié à l'enfance de l'humanité, ce qui peut nous rappeler la façon dont Irénée parle d'Ève et de lui. Dans la *Démonstration de la prédication apostolique*, ils sont présentés comme des enfants qui désobéissent pour la première fois, entamant ainsi une étape décisive vers l'âge adulte. Irénée écrit : « Il y avait en Adam et Ève un esprit

---

[43] *Caes. Arel.*, Serm. 129, 5 : CCL 103 (Turnhout 1953), p. 533, citant 1 Co 15, 22.
[44] *Caes. Arel.*, Serm. 180, 3 : CCL 104 (Turnhout 1953), p. 732.
[45] 2 Co 11, 28.
[46] Cf. *Caes. Arel.*, Serm. 161, 1 : CCL 104 (Turnhout 1953), p. 660–662.
[47] *Caes. Arel.*, Serm. 163, 2 : CCL 104 (Turnhout 1953), p. 670 (citant Lc 15, 22), et *Caes. Arel.*, Serm. 163, 4 : CCL 104 (Turnhout 1953), p. 672.

ingénu et enfantin »⁴⁸. Mais en plus de la référence aux âges de l'humanité, antérieurement même à la faute d'Adam, à la création déjà, la passion et la naissance de l'Église sont déjà signifiés. Le premier vase fut rempli au temps d'Adam, quand «Dieu, lui ayant envoyé un sommeil profond, tira une de ses côtes, dont il fit la femme »⁴⁹. C'est une image de la passion du Sauveur :

> Le Christ dormit sur la croix, et de son flanc sortit l'Église [...]. Dieu n'aurait pas pu façonner Ève de la même source d'où il avait fait Adam. Mais déjà dans ce vieil Adam, dont une côte avait été façonnée pour devenir Ève, était signifié le nouvel Adam, dont le flanc devait enfanter l'Église⁵⁰.

i. L'Aveugle de naissance a-t-il le péché originel ?

Césaire est embarrassé par la parole de Jésus à propos de l'aveugle-né quand Jésus dit : « Ni lui ni ses parents n'ont péché »⁵¹.

Pourtant, à cause du « péché originel, même les petits enfants doivent être baptisés »⁵². Malgré lui, nous ne naissons pas aveugles. Alors pourquoi la guérison de l'aveugle-né ? pour que nous soyons « illuminés de cœur » :

> Cet aveugle a été préparé comme un collyre pour le genre humain. C'est pourquoi il a été illuminé corporellement pour que par la considération de ce miracle, nous soyons illuminés de cœur [...]. Nous, donc, frères très chers, qui avions perdu en Adam les yeux du cœur, et les avons reçus dans le Christ, rendons pleinement grâce, à celui qui, sans aucun mérite antécédent, a daigné nous illuminer⁵³.

On sent là à la fois la tendance de Césaire à justifier le péché originel et la manière de faire voir le salut à partir des signes et miracles de l'Évangile !

j. En antithèse, la responsabilité totale du diable dans le péché originel

Alors que face au péché originel, Césaire met en parallèle systématiquement le salut donné par le Christ, la perspective de relativiser la faute d'Adam en donnant toute la responsabilité au diable, assassin de l'âme et du corps d'Adam, est nette dans cette description de l'attaque du diable contre Adam. D'abord l'horreur du diable :

---

⁴⁸ Iren. Lugd., Ostensio apostolicae praedicationis 14 : A. Rousseau, SC 406 (Paris 1995), p. 103.
⁴⁹ Gn 2, 21–22.
⁵⁰ Caes. Arel., Serm. 169, 2 : CCL 104 (Turnhout 1953), p. 692.
⁵¹ Jn 9, 3.
⁵² Caes. Arel., Serm. 172, 1 : CCL 104 (Turnhout 1953), p. 702.
⁵³ Caes. Arel., Serm. 172, 1, 4 : CCL 104 (Turnhout 1953), p. 702–704.

> Adversaire du genre humain, inventeur de la mort, qui a institué l'orgueil, racine de la malice, tête des crimes, prince de tous les vices, qui persuade de toutes les honteuses voluptés [...] jaloux et envieux de ce que l'homme eût reçu ce que lui-même, alors qu'il était un ange, avait perdu par orgueil, frappé de l'intérieur par le venin de la malignité, insatiable pour nous tuer, il ruine nos premiers parents, les dépouille et leur enlève ces dons et tant de biens : [...] la foi, la pudeur, la continence, la charité, l'immortalité[54],

à savoir toutes les qualités de l'homme avant la chute. La responsabilité de l'homme n'est même pas en cause dans cette agression du diable contre lui. Il s'agit de se libérer des « linges sales » que le diable nous a laissés.

k. L'Église à la fois noire et belle

Enfin, cette association du péché et du salut est intrinsèque à la vie de l'Église, manifestant en quelque sorte à quel point ils sont inséparables dans l'Église pécheresse et sauvée : « L'Église dit : ‹Je suis noire et belle› [...]. Noire, elle l'est par nature, belle par grâce; noire, elle l'est par le péché originel, belle par le sacrement de baptême »[55].

Ce choix de textes donne l'idée d'une prédication que l'on peut considérer comme loin de suivre les positions les plus extrêmes d'Augustin. Mal interprété, Augustin peut mettre l'accent sur une certaine fatalité associé au péché originel, et à une interprétation très restrictive de la prédestination tel que saint Paul en parle. Nous sommes certes en face de notre libre-arbitre, mais d'une certaine façon pas plus qu'Adam qui n'a pas été plus protégé de la faute que nous.

4. Un salut universel à la mesure du péché originel et de ses conséquences

Un certain nombre de textes manifestent une ouverture à l'idée d'un salut beaucoup plus large que ce que nous pouvons imaginer après ces réflexions de Césaire sur le péché originel, incluant les non-baptisés.

a. Exilés dans le monde, les hommes reçoivent les messagers de Dieu comme des lettres

D'abord, il y a ce passage qui fait penser à la manière dont saint Irénée envisage l'action de Dieu en vue du salut de tout homme. Césaire écrit que les hommes exilés dans le monde par la faute d'Adam reçoivent les messagers de Dieu comme des lettres :

---

[54] *Caes. Arel.*, Serm. 178, 2 : CCL 104 (Turnhout 1953), p. 722.
[55] *Caes. Arel.*, Serm. 95, 2 : SC 447 (Paris 2000), p. 271 citant Ct 1, 5.

Notre patrie, c'est le paradis : nos parents, ce sont les patriarches, les prophètes, les apôtres et les martyrs ; nos concitoyens, les anges ; notre roi, le Christ. Quand Adam a péché, nous avons alors été pour ainsi dire jetés, en lui, dans l'exil de ce monde ; mais, parce que notre roi est pieux et miséricordieux plus qu'on ne peut le penser et le dire, il a daigné nous envoyer par l'intermédiaire des patriarches et des prophètes, les saintes Écritures, comme des lettres d'invitation, par lesquelles il nous invitait dans notre éternelle et première patrie[56].

b. Amour du Christ pour tous les hommes
Cet autre passage met en valeur l'enseignement de saint Paul sur la volonté de salut universel du Christ :

Le Christ, notre Seigneur, a trouvé tous les hommes non seulement mauvais, mais même morts à cause du péché originel ; et cependant, alors que nous étions tels, « il nous a aimés et s'est livré lui-même pour nous » ; et en agissant ainsi, il a aimé même ceux qui ne l'aimaient pas, comme l'apôtre Paul le dit aussi : « Le Christ est mort pour des impies ». Et dans sa miséricorde ineffable, il a donné cet exemple au genre humain : « Instruisez-vous auprès de moi, car je suis doux et humble de cœur »[57].

« Il a aimé même ceux qui ne l'aimaient pas », « le genre humain » : ces expressions manifestent le salut universel.

c. Ton prochain est tout homme
À propos de la phrase : « repoussant le mensonge, dites la vérité, chacun à son prochain »[58], Césaire cite Augustin qui refuse de :

dire la vérité avec un chrétien et le mensonge avec un païen [...]. Ton prochain c'est tout homme : ton prochain est celui qui, comme toi, est né d'Adam et Ève [...]. Tu ne sais pas ce qu'il est aux yeux de Dieu ; tu ignores comment Dieu le voit dans sa prescience. Parfois celui que tu railles parce qu'il adore des pierres se convertit et adore Dieu avec plus de piété peut-être que toi, qui naguère le raillait. Nous avons donc des prochains cachés parmi ceux qui ne sont pas encore dans l'Église ; et il y a, cachés dans l'Église, des hommes qui sont loin de nous[59].

---

[56] *Caes. Arel.*, Serm. 7, 2 : SC 175 (Paris 1971), p. 341.
[57] *Caes. Arel.*, Serm. 37, 3 : SC 243 (Paris 1978), p. 233, citant dans l'ordre : Eph 5, 2 ; Rm 5, 6 ; Mt 11, 29.
[58] Eph 4, 25.
[59] *Caes. Arel.*, Serm. 180, 1 : CCL 104 (Turnhout 1953), p. 730 citant *Aug.*, Enarrationes in Psalmos 25, 2, 2 : M. Dulaey, BAug 57/B (Paris 2009), p. 267 ; et note complémentaire : ibid., p. 332–333 : « Voir en chacun son prochain ».

5. Quelle est la pensée de Césaire sur le péché originel ?

Césaire montre la cohérence de ses *Sermons* avec sa *Définition de foi* du Concile d'Orange lorsqu'il condamne sous forme d'anathème toute affirmation de la prédestination au mal. Il écrit :

> Non seulement nous ne croyons pas que certains soient prédestinés au mal par la puissance divine, mais même, s'il se trouvait des gens disposés à croire à pareille malédiction, nous leur jetons avec toute réprobation l'anathème[60].

Est-ce que cela ne veut pas dire clairement que tout non-baptisé n'est pas nécessairement condamné ? En outre, il n'emploie le mot « prédestination » ou « prédestiné » que dans un sens positif dans son œuvre[61]. Mais il reste que dans son *Petit traité de la grâce*, en s'adressant à « ceux qui disent : Pourquoi Dieu donnerait-il la grâce aux uns et pas aux autres ? »[62], il maintient qu'il faut s'incliner devant les décisions de Dieu et admettre la logique d'un péché originel qui ne peut être effacé que par le baptême et qui demeure une source de condamnation pour « les petits enfants, les hérétiques, les juifs et les païens qui n'ont ni la volonté, ni les moyens de pouvoir désirer le baptême »[63].

Cette terrible affirmation ne se retrouve pas dans le *Sermon* 211 sur les dons spirituels où il dit :

> Si l'Esprit ne répartit ses dons qu'entre ceux qu'il veut, il n'y a donc pas de faute pour qui ne reçoit pas de don, car le partage des grâces ne dépend pas du désir de celui qui reçoit, mais de la volonté de celui qui fait la répartition[64].

Il exempt ainsi d'une condamnation tous ceux qu'il a mentionnés dans son *Petit traité de la grâce*. Il semblerait donc qu'il y ait trois positions chez Césaire : celle du *Petit traité*, la plus extrême, celle du Concile d'Orange et celle des *Sermons*. On ne peut qu'être interrogé par cette diversité, qui fait que l'on ne connaît pas vraiment sa pensée profonde. Mais il y a peut-être une hypothèse pour le savoir, et c'est ce que je voudrais exposer en conclusion.

---

[60] *Concil. Arausic. II.*, Definitio fidei : SC 353 (Paris 1989), p. 173.
[61] Cf. *Caes. Arel.*, Serm. 87, 5 : CCL 103 (Turnhout 1953), p. 359 ; *Caes. Arel.*, Serm. 104, 6 : CCL 103 (Turnhout 1953), p. 433 ; *Caes. Arel.*, Serm. 117, 1 : CCL 103 (Turnhout 1953), p. 487 ; *Caes. Arel.*, Serm. 157, 2 : CCL 104 (Turnhout 1953), p. 642.
[62] *Caes. Arel.*, Opusculum de gratia Tit. : G. Morin, Opera varia 2 (Maredsous 1942), p. 159.
[63] Ibid., p. 162.
[64] *Caes. Arel.*, Serm. 211, 2 : CCL 104 (Turnhout 1953), p. 841.

Conclusion : *lex praedicandi, lex credendi* ?

Nous constatons dans les *Homélies* la prédominance d'un langage qui rappelle le péché originel mais l'associe au salut reçu par le Christ. Faut-il entendre ici que face au langage dogmatique du Concile d'Orange et du *Petit traité sur la grâce* – deux textes destinés à arrêter les excès pélagiens sur un ton sévère –, Césaire dans ses *Homélies* suit les conseils que formule Augustin dans *Le don de la persévérance* (*De dono perseverantiae*)? Que dit Augustin ? Il s'agit de ne pas enfermer les personnes dans l'idée que quoi qu'elles fassent, elles sont déterminées par la connaissance de leur destin par Dieu ; il faut donc surtout ne pas dire : « Que vous courriez, ou que vous dormiez, vous serez toujours ce qu'a prévu de vous celui qui ne peut pas se tromper ». Il faut dire : « Courez de manière à remporter le prix »[65]. De même il faut dire : « Si quelques-uns parmi vous ne sont pas encore appelés, prions pour eux afin qu'ils le soient »[66] plutôt qu'ils doutent du don de la grâce.

Mais faut-il penser qu'il y a autant de calcul chez Césaire ? Il parle à son peuple, et utilise tous les moyens de persuasion pour les maintenir fidèles dans leur foi. En rappelant à l'occasion des récits, paraboles, miracles de l'Ancien et du Nouveau Testament, le continuel passage d'un manque à une abondance, d'un mal à un bien, du péché originel à la Rédemption, il maintient éveillée en eux cette flamme, tout à fait dans l'esprit de saint Paul pour qui « là où le péché a abondé, la grâce a surabondé »[67]. En somme, cette loi pastorale qui préside à la vraie prédication, n'est-elle pas profondément celle de la foi authentique ? En imitant l'adage, résumé d'une thèse attribuée à Prosper d'Aquitaine[68] : *Lex orandi lex credendi*, « La loi de la prière, c'est la loi de la foi » – elle la corrobore, elle l'authentifie –, ne peut-on pas dire : *Lex praedicandi, lex credendi*, « La loi de la prédication, c'est la loi de la foi », c'est-à-dire qu'une authentique prédication, tout orientée vers la foi, ne peut que représenter la justesse de ce qu'il faut croire et la surabondance de la grâce par rapport au péché qui concerne tout homme et toute femme venant dans ce monde.

---

[65] *Aug.*, De dono perseuerantiae 22, 57 : BAug 24 (Paris 1962), p. 741, citant 1 Co 9, 24.
[66] *Aug.*, De dono perseuerantiae 22, 60 : BAug 24 (Paris 1962), p. 745.
[67] Rm 5, 20.
[68] Cf. *Prosper Aquitanus*, Capitula, seu Auctoritates de gratia 8 : PL 51, 209–210 ; cité et commenté par P. De Clerck, Existe-t-il une loi de la liturgie ?, RThL 38 (2007) 190, n. 1.

Hilary Mooney, Weingarten (Germany)

Leaving paradise: Eriugena's theology of 'inherited sin'

Abstract:
Eriugena mentions 'peccatum originale' in his writings. He embeds his treatment of original sin within a comprehensive investigation of how humans are involved both with sin and with the hope of redemption. This paper looks at his analysis of the current human situation. It asks whether the author considers the state of this world primarily as a punishment for sin or whether he considers the world primarily as a suitable stage for a grace-embued return of humans to God. Eriugena's Christocentric vision for the return of humanity to God is outlined.

Introduction
The human condition and the heuristic construction of 'inherited sin'

Humans have long reflected on the widespread existence of suffering in this world. Innocent children are born into poverty and deprivation. Good people and pillars of the community are struck down with incurable diseases. The limitation of hope, which the inevitability of death seems to imply, is also the object of human concern. Humans live in fear of death. Moreover, the paradoxical phenomenon of wanting to do good but being thwarted in the attempt by one's own weakness is a constant in human inner experience. An ongoing, never-ending search for the meaning of this uncomfortable existence, which, at times, seems absurd and pointless, has long occupied humanity. Shakespeare lets Hamlet opine on the "heartache and the thousand natural shocks/[t]hat flesh is heir to."[1]

The judaeo-christian scriptures bear witness to generations of believers who have brought these deep layers of human experience before their God. The solace, which the biblical authors have experienced in their faith encounter with God, is communicated. The narratives with which the biblical revelation addresses the many urgent issues provide impulses for further generations of believers. Myriad generations of Christian theologians have correlated their

---
[1] W. *Shakespeare*, The Tragedy of Hamlet, Prince of Denmark, Act 3, scene 1, 62–63: T. J. B. Spencer, Penguin Classics (London 1996), p. 66.

own significant human experiences with the experiences of believers articulated in the books of the bible. The theologians untangle, sort, and lay out the threads within biblical writings which themselves reflect the perennial fabric of human life. An appreciation of creation, but also, experiences of deep need and of outreach to God have their place.

This paper shows how Johannes Scottus Eriugena interprets the biblical narratives concerning the human condition, drawing as he does on the wisdom of scripture, on explanations of past theologians and of the philosophical community of which he is part. Writing as he does as a believing Christian he adopts in this process the biblical heuristic notion of 'inherited sin.' Itself a tradition, in this sense, an inherited assertion, it is the pattern which helps him make sense of the mysteries of the human situation.

A passage in his *Homily on the Prologue to John's Gospel* Eriugena offers an example of how he brings perennial human experience and an interpretation of the biblical passages on inherited sin into contact with each other.

> Whence do human beings come into this world? Into what world do they come? And if those are meant who come into this world from the hidden folds of nature through generation in times and places, then what sort of illumination is possible for them in this life where we are born but to die, grow but to decay, coagulate but to be dissolved again, falling from the restfulness of silent nature into the restlessness of bustling misery? Tell me, please, what kind of spiritual and true light there is for those procreated in a transitory and false life? [...] Is it not justly called the region of the shadow of death, the valley of tears, the abyss of ignorance, the earthly habitation that weighs down the human soul and expels the true beholding of the Light from the inner eyes?[2]

In this passage the basic questions of life are addressed—the question 'from whence' (*unde*) do we come?; the search for the meaningful of existence, in this sense, for 'illumination' (*illuminatio*); the uncomfortable limitation of a 'transitory' lifespan 'born but to die'; the perceived suffering within this world,

---

[2] Eriugena, Homilia super 'in principio erat verbum' 17, 3–16: É. Jeauneau, CCM 166 (Turnhout 2008), p. 31–32: *Et unde uenit in mundum? Et in quem mundum uenit? Si de his qui de occultis naturae sinibus in hunc mundum per generationem locis temporibusque ueniunt acceperis, qualis illuminatio est in hac uita nascentibus ut moriantur, crescentibus ut corrumpantur, compositis ut soluantur, de quietudine silentis naturae in inquietudinem tumultuantis miseriae cadentibus? Dic, quaeso, qualis lux est spiritualis et uera procreatis in uita transitoria et falsa?* [...] *Nunquid regio umbrae mortis et lacrimarum uallis, et ignorantiae profundum, et terrena habitatio humanum animum aggrauans et ex ueri luminis contuitu interiores oculos elimitans non immerito dicitur?* English trans. Ch. Bamford, The Voice of the Eagle. The Heart of Celtic Christianity. John Scotus Eriugena's Homily on the Prologue of the Gospel of St. John (Hudson – New York ²2000), p. 100.

'the valley of tears' (*lacrimarum uallis*). These provide the starting point for Eriugena's theological reflection. It is within this context of reflecting on the many-fold trials and perils of concrete human living, that Eriugena approaches the question of the 'rationale' of the current state of humanity: why does this situation exist? for what purpose does it exist?

In the same passage he asks: "Is not precisely this world a fit dwelling (*conueniens habitatio est*) for those alienated from the true Light?"[3]

As many authors before him, biblical and patristic, the question of 'original sin' (*peccatum originale*)[4] arises for Eriugena within a consideration of the limitations of human living in this world. Both interior weakness and suffering due to external causes are considered. The hypothesis which he considers worthy of investigation is that this *conditio humana* is somehow 'fitting'. Fitting as punishment? fitting as challenge and invitation to develop? and, as a related question, how is this human situation oriented to an elevating alignment with the fate of Christ?—these are strands of investigation which the author fingers in the writings of his sources, intellectually unravels and reincorperates within the web of his own writings. This paper will draw attention to the threads of reasoning woven into some of his writings.

Interpreting the Genesis narrative

Biblical passages which have given rise to a theology of inherited sin include Genesis chapter two and, especially, chapter three[5]. Which approaches to the 'succession' of perfection, deterioration and restoration of human nature do we find in Eriugena's treatment of the Genesis narrative of the fall and its con-

---

[3] *Eriugena*, Homilia 17, 11–12: É. Jeauneau, CCM 166, p. 32: *Nunquid mundus iste alienatis a uero lumine conueniens habitatio est?* English trans. Ch. Bamford, The Voice of the Eagle, p. 100.
[4] A sustained use of the expression is to be found here: *Eriugena*, Commentarius in Euangelium Iohannis 1, 31: É. Jeauneau, CCM 166 (Turnhout 2008), p. 71–72; for example, Comm. Ioh. 1, 31, 55: É. Jeauneau, CCM 166, p. 71: *Hoc igitur generale peccatum originale dicitur*. See too *Eriugena*, De diuina praedestinatione liber 13, 4, 86–93: G. Madec, CCM 50 (Turnhout 1978), p. 81.
[5] See M. Theobald, Art. Erbsünde, Erbsündenlehre: I Der Befund der Schrift, in: LThK 3 (Freiburg 1995) 743–744, here 743: "Zentraler Schriftbeleg für die klass. Lehre v. d. E. ist Röm 5, 12, wobei sich an diesen Vers die Erwartung knüpft, mit ihm den atl. Grundtext Gen 2f. authentisch aufschließen zu können."

Leaving paradise: Eriugena's theology of 'inherited sin' 337

sequences? His work *Periphyseon* is an important source⁶. Writing on Genesis chapter three, Eriugena remarks:

> In this connection we ought to study well the text of the Divine words, which, because of the sluggishness of our wits and the carnal senses which subject us, corrupted by our original sin, to this spatio-temporal existence, has set out—as though taking place in space and time, but in a marvellous order full of mystic meaning—things which occurred simultaneously and which are not divided by any intervals of time.⁷

By means of this abstraction from the notion of time, Eriugena establishes the hermeneutical context within which he interprets the story of Paradise. Central for Eriugena is that 'Paradise' "is a mere figure of speech by which Holy Scripture signifies the human nature that was made in the image of God."⁸ He recapitulates:

> We have said: That the plantation of God, namely, Paradise, in Eden, that is to say, in the joy of the eternal and blessed happiness, is human nature made in the image of God.⁹

He writes:

---

⁶ Édouard Jeauneau has edited *Periphyseon* for Corpus Christianorum Continuatio Mediaeualis. This edition both shows the various stages in the emergence of *Periphyseon* as a text, and provides a standard critical edition of the text: *Eriugena, Periphyseon, Liber Primus; Liber Secundus; Liber Tertius; Liber Quartus; Liber Quintus, Editionem nouam a supposititiis quidem additamentis purgatam, ditatam uero apppendice in qua uicissitudines operis synoptice exhibentur*, CCM 161-165, É. Jeauneau (ed.) (Turnhout 1996; 1997; 1999; 2000; 2003).

⁷ Eriugena, Periphyseon IV, 4631-4637: É. Jeauneau, CCM 164, p. 151: *Vbi pulchre diuinorum uerborum textum animaduertere debemus. Ea siquidem, quae simul facta sunt absque temporalium morularum interstitiis, propter nostram tarditatem carnalesque sensus, quibus originali peccato corrupti locis temporibusque succumbimus, ordine quodam mirabili, mysticorum sensuum plenissimo, ueluti locis temporibusque peracta contexuit.* English trans. J. J. O'Meara - I. P. Sheldon-Williams, Periphyseon (De Diuisione Naturae), SLH XIII (Dublin 1995), p. 247.

⁸ Eriugena, Periphyseon IV, 3422-3425: É. Jeauneau, CCM 164, p. 114: *Quisquis diligenter praefati theologi uerba perspexerit, nil aliud, ut opinor, in eis reperiet suaderi quam humanam naturam ad imaginem dei factam paradisi uocabulo, figuratae locutionis modo, a diuina scriptura significari.* English trans. J. J. O'Meara - I. P. Sheldon-Williams, Periphyseon, p. 189.

⁹ Eriugena, Periphyseon IV, 3777-3779: É. Jeauneau, CCM 164, p. 125: *Plantationem dei (hoc est paradisum) in Edem (hoc est in deliciis aeternae ac beatae felicitatis) humanam naturam esse diximus ad imaginem dei factam.* English trans. J. J. O'Meara - I. P. Sheldon-Williams, Periphyseon, p. 207.

Anyone who examines closely the meaning of such discussions may see for himself that Paradise is not a localised or particular piece of woodland on earth, but a spiritual garden sown with the seeds of the virtues and planted in human nature, or, to be more explicit, is nothing else but the human substance itself created in the image of God.[10]

The affirmation of the a-temporality of what is said to occur and the interpretation of Paradise as human nature created in the image of God both colour his interpretation of further details of the narrative. Eriugena writes:

So the trance of Adam, and the sleep that followed it, and the removal of his rib, and the division of the one nature into two sexes, and the mystical recognition of his wife, and all the other events which prefigure Christ and the Church; as well as their recognition of their nakedness, that is, of the purity of their nature (which did not at first cause them to blush because they were clothed in the raiment of the virtues which is unspotted by the delights of the irrational emotions), which in sinning they lost, and in losing became conscious of the deceptive and crafty persuasion of the serpent, the conversation between the woman and the serpent, her seduction by him, the illicit plucking of the fruit of the Forbidden Tree, and the fatal tasting of it; the willing consent and the fall of the man, not because he didn't know that it was a sin, but because he thought it but a light one to consent to his only wife [...] the opening of their eyes by which they saw their nakedness, the sewing of the girdles from fig-leaves, the hearing of the voice of the Lord walking in Paradise, the flight of both of them, Adam and his wife, from the face of the Lord God, their hiding of themselves in the tree, and all the other events up to the expulsion of man from Paradise: all these things Holy Scripture records by anticipation and out of their prior consequence as having taken place in Paradise, whereas they are the consequences of sin.[11]

---

[10] Eriugena, Periphyseon IV, 4323–4328: É. Jeauneau, CCM 164, p. 142: *Talium sermonum uirtutem quisquis acute perspexerit, inueniet paradisum non localem terrenumue quendam locum esse nemorosum, sed spiritualem, germinibus uirtutum consitum et in humana natura plantatum et, ut apertius dicatur, non aliud praeter ipsam humanam substantiam ad imaginem dei factam.* English trans. J. J. O'Meara – I. P. Sheldon-Williams, Periphyseon, p. 233 (Here and elsewhere the exclusive use of the masculine for human persons is the decision of the original translators—HM).

[11] Eriugena, Periphyseon IV, 4157–4178: É. Jeauneau, CCM 164, p. 137: *Sopor itaque Adam, sequensque eum dormitus, et ablatio costae, et diuisio simplicis naturae in duplicem sexum, et mystica uxoris agnitio, caeteraque quae in figura Christi et ecclesiae praefigurata sunt, cognitio quoque nuditatis, hoc est naturae sinceritatis (atque ideo non de ipsa erubescebant, quoniam uirtutum tegmina induebantur, delectationibus uero irrationabilium motuum omnino absoluta), quam peccando perdiderant et perdendo recognouerant, fallax item suasio serpentis et subdola, mulierisque cum serpente disputatio atque seductio, ac de fructu uetiti ligni illicita assumptio loetiferque gustus, uiri quoque consensus et casus, non ignorantis, sed leue peccatum existimantis unicae suae uxori con-*

The last sentence is significant. Eriugena here presents a narrative of the Fall and its consequences and comments:

> all these things Holy Scripture records by anticipation and out of their proper sequence as having taken place in Paradise, whereas they are the consequences of sin (*[h]aec omnia in paradiso per anticipationem praepostere facta esse diuina narrat scriptura, dum sint peccatum consecuta*).[12]

The narrative of Eden is thus once more presented as an 'event' which 'occurs' outside of time. Nevertheless, causality is affirmed and consequences are said to result.

Elsewhere he writes:

> And if you ask why God should create in man before he sinned the characteristics which were made because of sin, remember that in God nothing is before and nothing after, because for him there is nothing past, nor future, nor between past and future, for to Him all things are at once present. [...] to God the foreknowledge of sin and the consequence of sin itself were contemperaneous.[13]

The timelessness of the narrative, the identification of paradise with human nature, and his understanding of how consequences and divine foreknowledge interplay, dictate how Eriugena understands 'the fall'. He writes:

> [...] if Paradise is human nature as it is made in the image of God and established on an equality with the blessed state of angels, then as soon as it willed to run away from its Creator, in that very moment it fell from the dignity of its nature.[14]

---

sentire [...] *apertio item oculorum qua suam nuditatem cognouerant, perizomatumque de foliis fici consutio, uocis item deambulantis domini dei in paradiso auditus, amborumque (Adam uidelicet et uxoris eius) a facie domini dei fuga et in medio ligni absconsio, et caetera usque ad expulsionem hominis de paradiso: Haec omnia in paradiso per anticipationem praepostere facta esse diuina narrat scriptura, dum sint peccatum consecuta.* English trans. J. J. O'Meara – I. P. Sheldon-Williams, Periphyseon, p. 225.

[12] See footnote 11.

[13] Eriugena, Periphyseon IV, 2808–2816: É. Jeauneau, CCM 164, p. 94: *Et si te mouet quare deus in homine fecerit, priusquam peccaret, quae propter peccatum facta sunt, animaduerte quod deo nihil est ante, nihil post, cui nihil praeteritum, nihil futurum, nihil medium inter praeteritum et futurum, quoniam ipsi omnia simul sunt.* [...] *Deo autem simul erant et peccati praescientia eiusque consequentia.* English trans. J. J. O'Meara – I. P. Sheldon-Williams, Periphyseon, p. 157.

[14] Eriugena, Periphyseon IV, 4179–4182: É. Jeauneau, CCM 164, p. 137: *Si* [...] *paradisus est humana natura ad imaginem dei condita, et in angelicae beatitudinis aequalitate constituta, mox profecto ut creatorem suum deserere uoluit, ex dignitate suae naturae lapsa est.* English trans. J. J. O'Meara – I. P. Sheldon-Williams, Periphyseon, p. 225.

The sinning in Paradise is mentioned and it is considered a reality with ongoing effects on the human condition in general and on human cognitive faculties in particular. However, the biblical narrative of the fall from original perfection, of before and after the fall, is declared to be full of mystical meaning and is not considered a chronological reportage of something which happened in the interaction of two humans. The Bible, according to Eriugena, is telling us something about humanity not something which happened exclusively to one human couple. Thus, again in the fourth book of *Periphyseon* Eriugena explains that the biblical text, 'God created mankind' (*fecit Deus hominem*) does not only apply to a limited number of individuals but applies to the whole of humanity (*infinita significatione omnem humanitatem ostendit*)[15].

Eriugena's interpretation involves three points of argument—the span of time is considered to be collapsed and concentrated into a single point, the possibility of God 'proactively' taking human weakness into account is defended, and the whole of humanity is proposed as the object of consideration. He also makes clear that the current human condition results from sin and deservingly so ('*[m]erito*').[16]

The prospective of a good, God-granted solution, is however, according to Eriugena and his source, Gregory of Nyssa, present from the outset. In the particular matter of the postlapsarian form of human propagation Eriugena, quoting Gregory, writes on God's strategy:

> [...] since He foresaw by His contemplative power that man's will would not go straight for the good and would therefore fall away from the angelic way of life, He formed in our nature a plan of propagation suitable to those who have been snared into sin [...] and implanted in man the irrational method of propagation from one another of the beasts of the field in place of the glorious fecundity of the angels.[17]

---

[15] *Eriugena*, Periphyseon IV, 2301–2303: É. Jeauneau, CCM 164, p. 79.

[16] *Eriugena*, Periphyseon IV, 3209–3211: É. Jeauneau, CCM 164, p. 108: *Merito ergo quod propter peccatum adiectum est, extra paradisum ac ueluti in inferiori loco factum fuisse de terra plasmationis narratur.*

[17] *Eriugena*, Periphyseon IV, 2371–2378: É. Jeauneau, CCM 164, p. 81: *Quoniam uero praeuidit contemplatoria uirtute non recte euntem ad bonum uoluntatem, atque ideo ex angelica uita recedentem, [...] propterea conuenientem in peccatum annullatis incrementi excogitationem in natura conformauit, pro angelica magnificentia pecudalem et irrationalem ex se inuicem successionis modum humanitati inserens.* English trans. J. J. O'Meara – I. P. Sheldon-Williams, Periphyseon, p. 135–137. In Periphyseon IV, 2333–2384: É. Jeauneau, CCM 164, p. 80–81 Eriugena quotes his own Latin translation of *Gregory of Nyssa*, De hominis opificio 17. Eriugena calls this work 'De imagine.' See *Eriugena*, De imagine 18 (17), 30–78: Ch. Tommasi – G. Mandolino, CCM 167 (Turnhout 2020), p. 119–120. See, too, M. Cappuyns, Le 'De Imagine' de Grégoire de Nysse traduit par Jean Scot Érigène, Recherches de théologie ancienne et médiévale 32 (1965) 205–262, here 237 (chapter 17, according to Eriugena chapter 18, 27–33).

Significant is that the 'new' situation is not presented as a punitive scheme but as a thoughtfully devised, suitable plan (*conuenientem* [...] *excogitationem*). The redemptive way back opens up in the very moment of leaving Eden. The road opening up is not only suitable for insuring that the number of humans increases, it is suitable for leading these humans back to God.

What, then, is the rationale of human nature as communicated through the Genesis-based story of the fall and its consequences? In search of an answer, it is important to consider also Eriugenas eschatology as presented in the fifth book of *Periphyseon*.

Here he writes extensively on the eschatological return of humanity to God. As in so many Christian thinkers, Eriugena's protology and his eschatology are closely intertwined. He insists that the present state of affairs should be considered an invitation to return to the Creator rather than a random punishment for sin.

> And if anyone should argue that the transformations through birth and dissolution of sensible bodies within themselves are the results of the sin of human nature, and therefore may rightly be termed destructions, let him remember that in the spatial and temporal changes of nature consist the beauty and the order of the whole visible creature, and that mutability and variety have no cause but the dispositions of the Divine Providence, and that they rather contribute to the perfecting of human nature and to its recall to its Creator (*ad creatorem suum reuocationem*) than to the punishment of sin.[18]

The human situation is, according to Eriungena, best interpreted, not as a punishment but as an appell to return to the God.

In line with many of the church fathers whose writings inspire him, Eriugena offers, in his interpretation of the Genesis narrative, a highly spiritual interpretation of the 'event' of the fall and its significance for all generations of humanity. What he offers us is a reflection on the human situation in its weakness, in its experiences of limitation and of mortality; experiences which apply to all generations of humans. He is analysing a human condition common to

---

[18] *Eriugena*, Periphyseon V, 4477–4486: É. Jeauneau, CCM 165, p. 138: *Et si quis dixerit sensibilium corporum in semet ipsis transfusiones per generationem et solutionem propter peccatum humanae naturae fieri, ac per hoc ueraciter corruptiones posse uocari, uideat totius uisibilis creaturae ordinem et pulchritudinem non nisi in uicissitudinibus rerum per loca et tempora constare, illasque uicissitudines ac uarietates non aliunde nisi diuina prouidentia et administratione causas ducere, et plus ad humanae naturae eruditionem et ad creatorem suum reuocationem factas fuisse, quam ad peccati ultionem.* English trans. J. J. O'Meara – I. P. Sheldon-Williams, Periphyseon. The Division of Nature, Cahiers d'études médiévales, cahier spécial 3 (Dumbarton Oaks – Washington 1987), p. 639-640.

all generations. Again and again he insists on the timelessness of the Genesis story. And in his own writings protological and eschatological reflection are rarely far apart. His eschatology offers the hope that the very consequences of sin, this human condition as we experience it, is in itself not a random punishment but a situation which—the invitation of God presumed—suitably facilitates our return. Leaving paradise—the 'first' steps out of the garden of Paradise, represent 'already' the 'beginning' of a return to paradise.

The theological challenge posed by Pauline thought

The Christian theory of inherited sin is also heavily reliant on certain New Testament texts. First and foremost, a verse from Paul's Letter to the Romans has attracted much theological attention.

> Therefore, just as sin came into the world through one man, and death came through sin, and so death spread to all because all have sinned.[19]

An initial observation: interestingly, Eriugena devotes much more attention to a Pauline theology of redemption, appealing to the various ways of being in Christ, than to a Pauline theology of the effects of the fall. The remedy receives proportionally much more attention than the fallen state or speculation on the cause of our fallen state. Romans 5:12 does, however, receive some limited attention within the corpus of Eriugena's writings.[20]

---

[19] Rom 5:12: New Revised Standard Version Catholic Edition, Anglicized Text (New York 2007). Eriugena was familiar with the Latin translation *"in quo omnes peccauerunt"* and cites it three times in *Periphyseon*. In book four the text is simply quoted: *Eriugena*, Periphyseon IV, 2393: É. Jeauneau, CCM 164, p. 81. In the Augustinian context of *Periphyseon* (*Eriugena*, Periphyseon V, 5285: É. Jeauneau, CCM 165, p. 162) Eriugena speaks of all sinning in the first human (primus homo). Eriugena had a working knowledge of Greek and was not completely reliant on the contemporary Latin translations and patristic interpretations. He was also a creative thinker. In *Eriugena*, Periphyseon V, 3776–3778: É. Jeauneau, CCM 165, p. 118 he prefers to speak of all sinning in the primordial sin "Pride is said to be the beginning, not the cause of sin, because it is the first step and flood of the first sin (primordialis peccati), in which all have sinned." English trans. *J. J. O'Meara – I. P. Sheldon-Williams*, Periphyseon. The Division of Nature, p. 622.

[20] It is, for example *Eriugena*, De diuina praedestinatione liber: G. Madec, CCM 50 (Turnhout 1978). English trans. *M. Brennan*, Eriugena, Treatise on Divine Predestination, Notre Dame Texts in Medieval Culture, vol. 5, (Indiana 1999). See, for example (within the context of a discussion of original sin) *Eriugena*, De diu. praed., 16, 3, 72–83: G. Madec, CCM 50, p. 96.

Relying on Pauline and Johannine texts alike, the New Testament discussion of inherited sin is traditionally connected not only with the effects of the 'expulsion' from Paradise such as encounter with suffering, the obligation to toil for survival, the painful experience on the inevitability of death but considers too the human experience of moral weakness and alienation from God. Eriugena, in turn, addresses these matters.

Eriugena's *De praedestinatione* is an important source for his thought and must be considered next. *De praedestinatione* is considered an early work (850 or 851). Scholarly consensus is that it was completed before both Eriugena's major literary work, *Periphyseon* and his biblical commentaries on the Gospel of John. *De praedestinatione* is a position paper, requested of Eriugena by Hincmar, Archbishop of Rheims. The occasion was provided by the writings of the scholar Gottschalk who, relying on certain Augustinian texts (for example, the anti-Pelagian texts), played down the role of human freedom in co-operating with divine grace and suggested that God predestines all humans, some positively to eternal happiness, and some negatively to eternal damnation. Gottschalk had spoken of a *"gemina praedestinatio."* Eriugena (using other texts from Augustine) argued that a twofold (*gemina*) predestination in Gottschalk's sense of this expression, insofar as it includes a *positive* divine predestination of some individuals to hell, would—firstly—fail to do justice both to the divine simplicity and—secondly—would fail to recognise evil as a privation. Various aspects of the 'prelapsarian' and 'postlapsarian' human situations are outlined and human freedom and the nature of evil are considered[21]. The differences between Gottschalk and Eriugena on these matters and Eriugena's debt to the early writing of Augustine (*De uera religione; de libero arbitrio*) in his argumentation has been outlined in existing academic studies.[22]

The issue of God's causality with regard to sin and the consequences of sin is relevant to the topic of this paper. Eriugena presents the current situation of humans as an experience of weakness in the face of temptation. Notwithstanding the fact that reason dictates a course of action other than that desired by our corporeal senses, humans often give in to the demands of the senses. Referring to Romans 7:25 he writes:

---

[21] Formal issues are also at stake such as the question how one should read controversial passages in scripture and the theological tradition. It is no surprise then, that Eriugena in his position paper openly addresses the matter of biblical hermeneutics. *Eriugena*, De diu. praed. 11, 2, 49–50: G. Madec, CCM 50, p. 68.

[22] See for example, G. *Madec*, Jean Scot et ses auteurs : Annotations érigéniennes, Collection des études augustiniennes. Série Moyen Âge et Temps modernes 19 (Paris 1988).

For the corporeal senses did not obey the precepts of mind according to the laws of nature. And this divorce has been clearly and beautifully alluded to by the Apostle: 'In my mind I serve the law of God, but in my flesh the law of sin.' By flesh he means the carnal sense which disobediently resists the rational motions of the mind even in those who are perfect.[23]

Thus, not only the suffering in this world is the object of reflection in *De praedestinatione* but also the human experience of temptation, weakness and sinning. Eriugena outlines our weakness and inability to follow through on our good intentions using scripture as a basis for his position.

Hence the Lord in the gospel said to his disciples: 'Without me you can do nothing;' he did not say: 'you can will nothing;' and the apostle: 'it is for me to will but not to accomlish.'[24]

Significantly, the image with which he illustrates this is that of being in a dark room, having the capacity of sight, but not being able to see. He considers a subjective aspect of the effect of original sin—the 'closed eye' of a weak will, and an 'environmental' one—the dense darkness within which the eye finds itself and, eventually, the light which comes from outside.[25] He draws the comparison:

So the will of man, for as long as it is covered by the shadow of original sin (*originalis peccati*) and its characteristics, is hindered by its darkness. But when the light of divine mercy shines in, it dissipates not only the night of all sins and their guilt, but also by its healing it opens up the eye of a weak will, and, purifying it by good works, makes it fit to contemplate the light.[26]

---

[23] Eriugena, Periphyseon IV, 4973-4979: É. Jeauneau, CCM 164, p. 161: *Non enim obtemperat sensus corporeus iussionibus animi iuxta leges naturae. Quod diuortium Apostolus aperte pulchreque expressit dicens: 'Mente seruio legi dei, carne autem legi peccati', carnem uidelicet carnalem sensum appellans, qui rationabilibus animi motibus, etiam in his qui perfecti sunt, inoboediens resistit.* English trans. J. J. O'Meara – I. P. Sheldon-Williams, Periphyseon, p. 265. See too, Eriugena, Periphyseon IV, 471-472: É. Jeauneau, CCM 164, p. 18.

[24] Eriugena, De diu. praed. 4, 8, 218-220: G. Madec, CCM 50, p. 33: *Hinc dominus in euangelio suis ait discipulis: Sine me nihil potestis facere; non dixit: nihil potestis uelle; et apostolus: Velle adiacet mihi, perficere autem non.* English trans. M. Brennan, Eriugena, p. 31.

[25] See Eriugena, De diu. praed. 4, 8, 227-231: G. Madec, CCM 50, p. 34: *Sicut enim homo in densissimis tenebris positus, habens sensum uidendi quidem, nihil uidet, quia nihil potest uidere, antequam extrinsecus ueniat lux quam etiam adhuc clausis oculis sentit, apertis uero et eam et in ea cuncta circumposita conspicit;* [...].

[26] Eriugena, De diu. praed. 4, 8, 231-237: G. Madec, CCM 50, p. 34: *[S]ic uoluntas hominis, quandiu originalis peccati propriorumque umbra tegitur, ipsius caligine impeditur. Dum autem lux diuinae misericordiae illuxerit, non solum noctem peccatorum omnium eorumque reatum destruit, sed etiam obtutum infirmae uoluntatis sanando aperit et ad se contemplandum bonis operibus purgando idoneam facit.* English trans. M. Brennan, Eriugena, p. 31.

We turn to a passage within *De praedestinatione* which represents a significant exposition of Rom 5:12. In chapter sixteen of his treatise, Eriugena is presenting an argument which he has found within Augustine, *De Genesi ad litteram*, namely, that God does not directly punish a substance which God has created. Eriugena quotes Augustine's position extensively including the remark "it is contrary to justice itself that God would condemn in anyone, for nothing previously merited, what he himself had created in them."[27] Eriugena then affirms this position as his own when he asks "why wonder if that same divine justice prevents the human substance being punished even in the most wicked men?"[28] Significant is Eriugena's adoption of the position that evil is 'no thing.' He too considers it to be a privation and he holds that one therefore may not conceive of God in a causal relationship to evil. This point—coloured as it is in his writings by a strong influence of Augustine and Prudence—is again and again repeated throughout chapters fifteen and sixteen. Eriugena is convinced that God does not punish the things God made, nor does God take from the gifts of nature back from them.[29] This is important with respect to the relationship between humans and their God. Neither with regard to this life nor the next, God does not will that humans are alienated from God.

Within this framework he comments extensively on Romans 5:12. His thought centres on the distinction between substance and individual sinning will. Here a further passage from chapter sixteen is reproduced:

> Since, therefore, God created in the first man the univeral nature of all men, for as yet, as Augustine says, that one man was everyone, that which in him was naturally created could by no means transgress the natural law of the creator. That in him, therefore, did not sin which God created in him; yet in him all men sinned, and hence in him all die and consequently all are punished. Accordingly, it is quite correctly believed that as God wished to create in him the universal substance of the human race, so also he created the individual will of all men. For if in one man there was created, as the totality, both the corporal and spiritual human nature common to all men, there was necessarily in him the individual will of each one. In him, therefore, it was not the generality of nature that sinned but the individual will of each one ([n]on itaque in eo peccauit naturae generalitas, sed uniuscuiusque indiuidua uoluntas), because if that nature offended, since it is one, the whole would certainly perish. But it did not perish, since the remedy for the wound, that is the

---

[27] Augustine, De Genesi ad litteram XI, 21, 28 - 22, 29 is quoted by *Eriugena*, De diu. praed. 16, 2: G. Madec, CCM 50, p. 94-95. English trans. M. Brennan, Eriugena, p. 102.

[28] *Eriugena*, De diu. praed. 16, 2, 53-55: G. Madec, CCM 50, p. 95. English trans. M. Brennan, Eriugena, p. 102.

[29] *Eriugena*, De diu. praed. 15, 10, 214-215: G. Madec, CCM 50, p. 93 with reference to Prudence. English trans. M. Brennan, Eriugena, p. 99.

substance of a redeemer, remained in it incorrupt, apart from the fact that all sinned simultaneously in one man. For it was not he that sinned in all, but all in him. For just as he had his own personal will, so also he had his personal sin; and as in him each one had become master of the indivisible individuality of his own will, so in him each one of his own accord was able to commit his personal offence. For in no one is the sin of another justly punished (*In nullo quippe uindicatur iuste alterius peccatum*). Accordingly, in no one is nature punished, because it is from God and does not sin. But the motion of the will wantonly misusing that good of nature is deservedly punished, because it trangresses the law of nature, which beyond doubt it would not transgress if it were substantially created by God.[30]

In the past quotation an important tenet of Eriugena's argumentation with regard to the issue of inherited sin is expressed: "in no one is the sin of another justly punished." Eriugena adopts the position that punishment is not transferable. From a systematic point of view, however, this does not imply that the sin of the other(s) is irrelevant to human lived experience. The sin of others, past and contemporary, may be relevant to the human experience of temptation and distraction from the better way of behaving. Each generation is born into a societal, cultural and economic world which has been warped by the sins of previous humans. Society as we find it is, in this sense, indeed a consequence of all men sinning. The pattern repeats itself—each human is born into a sin-warped society. This inherited world is, however, not (to return to the explicit argumentation of Eriugena) a random, extrinsic punishment bestowed by the hand of God on humans.

---

[30] *Eriugena*, De diu. praed. 16, 3, 68–96: G. Madec, CCM 50, p. 95–96: *Cum itaque omnium hominum uniuersam naturam in primo homine deus condiderit, adhuc enim, ut ait Aug<ustinus>, ille unus omnes fuit, quod in ipso naturaliter creatum est nullo modo potuit naturalem legem creatoris transire. Non igitur in illo peccauit quod in illo deus creauit; in quo tamen omnes peccauerunt, ac per hoc in ipso omnes moriuntur, et consequenter omnes puniuntur. Proinde rectissime creditur, quemadmodum in illo deus generalem humani generis creare uoluit substantiam, ita et omnium hominum propriam substituit uoluntatem. Si enim in uno communis omnium et corporalis et spiritualis naturae humanae plenitudo sit constituta, necessario ei inerat singulorum uoluntas propria. Non itaque in eo peccauit naturae generalitas, sed uniuscuiusque indiuidua uoluntas. Siquidem, si ea natura delinqueret, cum una sit, tota profecto periret. Sed non periit, quando medicamentum uulneris, hoc est substantia redemptoris, in ea remansit incorruptum, praeter quod omnes peccauerunt simul in uno homine. Non enim ille peccauit in omnibus, sed omnes in illo. Sicut enim ille habebat propriam uoluntatem, ita et proprium peccatum; et quemadmodum in illo unusquisque uoluntatis suae indiuiduum possederat numerum, ita in illo per se ipsum singulus quisque potuit proprium committere delictum. In nullo quippe uindicatur iuste alterius peccatum. Proinde in nullo natura punitur, quia ex deo est et non peccat. Motus autem uoluntarius, libidinose utens naturae bono, merito punitur, quia naturae legem transgreditur, quam procul dubio non transgrederetur, si substantialiter a deo crearetur.* English trans. M. Brennan, Eriugena, p. 103–104.

In addition to the observation that sin is 'owned' by the individual sinner and any 'punishment' affects them directly, how, then, is this individual 'punishment' to be understood? Avital Wohlmann interprets Eriugena's position as follows: "The only punishment is immanent to sin itself, confining sinners in the prison of their own conscience."[31] Eriugena, agreeing with Augustine on this matter, writes:

> [...] there is no sin that does not punish the sinner. For in every sinner the original emergence of the sin and the punishment of it are simultaneous (*simul incipiunt oriri et peccatum et poena eius*); because there is no sin which does not punish itself (*quia nullum peccatum est quod non se ipsum puniat*), secretly in this life, but openly in the other life which is to come.[32]

Even in the case of individual sin, the resulting human alienation from God may not be considered a random, extrinsic punishment for sin. The position implied in Eriugena's writings seems to be that any loss of a specific relationship to God may be understood as the consequence of sin. The term 'punishment' (*poena*) applies only in this sense. Furthermore, the same understanding of the sin / loss nexus visible in the quotation from Eriugena above, seems to be applicable, not only to individual sin, but also to the communal situation in the case of being born into a sin-imbued world. The state in which humans find themselves 'after the fall' is that of inhabiting a world out of a relationship of distance to God and one's fellow humans. This communal situation, too, is better understood as the consequence of sin, rather than a random punishment for the sins of our predecessors, imposed extrinsically by a third party (God).

So far, this paper has addressed various aspects of Eriugena's thought. The issue of whether the current human situation may be better interpreted as a random punishment for sin dictated by a third party or as the consequence of sin has been reviewed. The environmental hardships of the human situation were seen as a way back to God. The concept of 'punishment' for individual sin is interpreted as the self-generated inner experience of alienation. Communally viewed, the sins of earlier generations lead to the societal consequence of being born into a human race of sinners for subsequent generations.

---

[31] A. Wohlmann, Introduction to the English Translation, in: M. Brennan (trans.), John Scottus Eriugena. Treatise on Divine Predestination (Notre Dame, Indiana 1998) XXV.
[32] *Eriugena*, De diu. praed. 16, 6, 233–239: G. Madec, CCM 50, p. 101: *Nullum autem peccatum est quod peccantem non puniat. In omni enim peccatore simul incipiunt oriri et peccatum et poena eius, quia nullum peccatum est quod non se ipsum puniat, occulte tamen in hac uita, aperte uero in altera quae est futura.* English trans. M. Brennan, Eriugena, p. 107.

Temptation, dilemma situations, the lure of bad example—all tumble on from generation to generation.

Comments on the Gospel of John

Remaining within the context of the New Testament, we turn next to Eriugena's commentaries on Johannine writings.[33] Jeauneau considers Eriugena's Commentary on John's Gospel to be a late work.[34] In the *Commentary* Eriugena writes on the meaning of the expression '*peccatum originale.*' Speaking of the sin which the lamb of God takes away (Jn 1:29) he comments that this sin is called original sin, namely, sin which is common to the whole world, that is the whole human nature: "*PECCATUM MUNDI dicitur originale peccatum, quod commune est totius mundi, hoc est totius humanae naturae.*"[35] We note that here communality, not the how or why of its origin or its manner of transmission, is emphasized.

A little later, he writes that the general sin (*generale peccatum*), that by which the whole human race all at once disobeyed the command of God in paradise, (*quo simul totum genus humanum praeuaricatum est mandatum dei in paradiso*) is rightly (*[n]ec immerito*) called original because it is the sin of the common origin of all (*quoniam peccatum communis omnium originis est*).[36] The expressions general sin and original sin are thus used interchangeably.[37]

---

[33] In addition to his *Homily on the Prologue to John's Gospel* there exists a commentary on John's Gospel which is extant in fragmentary form. Only the comments on John 1, 11–29; 3, 1–4, 28a; 6, 5–14 have survived; see É. Jeauneau, Introduction, in: É. Jeauneau, Jean Scot. Commentaire sur l'Évangile de Jean. Introduction, Texte critique, Traduction, Notes et Index, SC 180 (Paris 1972) 11–87, esp. 13.

[34] É. Jeauneau, Introduction, p. 20: "Peut-on, au moins approximativement, fixer la date de sa composition? Selon toute probabilité, il faut la situer vers la fin de la vie de l'auteur." The date of his death may only be estimated. Michael Herren has dated Eriugena's poem *Aulae sidereae* to 870 and suggested that it is the last sign of literary activity for which a date may be argued with relative certainty, see M. W. Herren, Iohannis Scotti Erivgenae Carmina, SLH 12 (Dublin 1993) 4 (footnote 19).

[35] Eriugena, Comm. Ioh. I, XXXI, 31–32: É. Jeauneau, CCM 166, p. 70.

[36] Eriugena, Comm. Ioh. I, XXXI, 49–56: É. Jeauneau, CCM 166, p. 71: *Diuisio quippe naturae in duplicem sexum, [...] poena generalis peccati est, quo simul totum genus humanum praeuaricatum est mandatum dei in paradiso. Hoc igitur generale peccatum originale dicitur. Nec immerito, quoniam peccatum communis omnium originis est.*

[37] Eriugena, Comm. Ioh. I, XXXI, 55: É. Jeauneau, CCM 166, p. 71: *Hoc igitur generale peccatum originale dicitur.*

In a soteriological context, Christ is presented as a mystical lamb, who is prefigured in the paschal lamb. In a passage heavily reliant on Maximus' thoughts in *Ambigua to John*, Eriugena observes, that a paschal lamb is said to have been immolated in each household within Israel.[38] Working with this image of relatively individualised, family-based religious ritual Eriugena proceeds to analyse the individual relationship of each believer to Christ. He reflects on the subjective side of redemption and speaks of an act of spiritual immolating on the part of each believer which is enacted when he or she believes and intellectually grasps the mysteries of Christ's incarnation, death and resurrection. This 'spiritual immolating' (*spiritualiter eum immolamus*) is combined with an 'intellectual consuming' (*intellectualiter [...] comedimus*) of this mystical Lamb's flesh.[39] The position proposed by Maximus and adopted by Eriugena is that we individually destroy that which separates us from Christ, thus making room for 'containing' Christ through faith and understanding and, that we bring this ourselves in this Christ-aligned condition before God. This is developed in chapter thirty-two of Eriugena's *Commentary*.[40]

The themes of spiritual alignment with the crucified Christ, being crucified with him (*concrucifixus*) and crucifying him are presented.

> *Itaque unusquisque credentium Christo, secundum propriam uirtutem et subiectum sibi uirtutis habitum et qualitatem, et crucifigitur et crucifigit sibimet Christum, Christo uidelicet concrucifixus.*[41]

Eriugena explains how sinful aspects of our nature are crucified. Just as Maximus had done, Eriugena outlines a series of levels of this crucifixion of weakness and of vice. For example, he writes:

---

[38] See Eriugena, Comm. Ioh. I, XXXI, 67–70: É. Jeauneau, CCM 166, p. 71: *Hic est unicus et singularis agnus mysticus, in cuius figura israheliticus populus singulos agnos per singulas domus paschali tempore immolabat.*

[39] Eriugena, Comm. Ioh. I, XXXI, 70–74: É. Jeauneau, CCM 166, p. 71–72: *Nam et nos, qui post peractam eius incarnationem et passionem et resurrectionem in eum credimus eiusque mysteria, quantum nobis conceditur, intelligimus, et spiritualiter eum immolamus et intellectualiter, mente non dente, comedimus.* See footnote 12 in Eriugena, Comm. Ioh. XXXI, 73–77: É. Jeauneau, SC 180, p. 178 where Jeauneau notes the dependency on Augustine and cites many references.

[40] Édouard Jeauneau has pointed out that Eriugena offers us here an extended paraphrase of passages from the *Ambiguum* 47 of Maximus Confessor. See his appendix II: Eriugena, Comm. Ioh: É. Jeauneau, SC 180, p. 383–395 (appendix II).

[41] Eriugena, Comm. Ioh. I, XXXII, 1–4: É. Jeauneau, CCM 166, p. 72.

> Vnus quidem soli peccato crucifigitur, dum ab omnibus operationibus ipsius in carne et per carnem suam quietus, ueluti quadam morte obrutus efficitur; et illud (peccatum dico) clauis timoris domini confixum mortificat, dum omnes ipsius impetus, ne quid in sua carne operari ualeant, refrenat. Alius passionibus, hoc est infirmis animae actionibus [...] crucifigitur, dum per potentias restauratae animae sanatur.[42]

Through the process of destroying our vices, each believer's faith in Christ is increasingly enhanced by a knowledge of the (corresponding) mysteries.

> Vnisquisque enim fidelium, qualem in animo habuerit habitudinen per incrementa uirtutum, talem de Christo habebit fidem per augmenta intelligentiarum.[43]

Jeauneau comments: "La mort et la crucifixion mystiques sont transposées par l'Érigène sur le plan de la connaissance."[44]

Christ, according to the original text from the hand of Maximus which is inspiring Eriugena, becomes our sacrifice. We offer him to God; in this sense, we sacrifice him. Maximus had written

> that each of us in his own rank—as if in a kind of house, built on the level of virtue that is appropriate to him—sacrifices the Divine Lamb.[45]

Eriugena is most probably thinking of this passage when he writes of our crucifying Christ. Yet he develops the idea which he has inherited from Maximus. Eriugena transposes not only the ideas of our self-crucifixion onto a cognitive level, he also transposes the idea of our crucifying Christ onto a cognitive level. According to Eriugena the Christian destroys false or imperfect notions about Christ—crucifying Christ in this sense—before replacing these notions with higher insights into who Christ is.

> Et quotiens prioris uitae modis et inferioris moritur, et in altiores gradus subuehitur, totiens opiniones de Christo, quamuis simplices, tamen in ipso et cum ipso morientur et in sublimiores de eo theophanias fide atque intelligentia prouehentur. Itaque in suis fidelibus Christus cotidie moritur et ab eis crucifigitur, dum carnales de eo cogitationes, seu spirituales adhuc tamen imperfectas, interimunt, semper in altum ascendentes, donec ad ueram eius notitiam perueniant. Infinitus enim infinite, etiam in purgatissimis mentibus, formatur.[46]

---

[42] *Eriugena*, Comm. Ioh. I, XXXII, 4–13: É. Jeauneau, CCM 166, p. 72.
[43] *Eriugena*, Comm. Ioh. I, XXXII, 30–32: É. Jeauneau, CCM 166, p. 73.
[44] *Eriugena*, Comm. Ioh. I, XXXII, 38: É. Jeauneau, SC 180, p. 182 (footnote 7).
[45] *Maximus Confessor*, Ambigua ad Iohannem 47, 2: N. Constas, On the Difficulties in the Church Fathers. The Ambigua, vol. II (Cambridge – Massachusetts 2014), p. 210–211 (text and trans.): τὸν θεῖον ἀμνὸν ἕκαστος ἡμῶν, ὡς ἐν οἰκίᾳ τινί, τῷ ἰδίῳ τάγματι (1 Cor 15:23) τῆς κατ' ἀρετὴν ἁρμοζούσης αὐτῷ καταστάσεως θύει τε τὸν ἀμνόν.
[46] *Eriugena*, Comm. Ioh. I, XXXII, 32–41: É. Jeauneau, CCM 166, p. 73.

The manner in which Eriugena understands and presents the pivotal point in the destiny of humanity is highly significant. The turning point which Christianity generally calls salvation or justification is presented, not in terms of a random punishing of humans and a vicarious suffering on the part of Christ in humanity's stead, rather, the turning point is presented as a faith event and as a spiritual act of conscious alignment with Christ.[47] The focus is clearly on the subjective side of salvation. The Christian is aligned to Christ in his or her profession of faith in the dying and rising of Christ. She/he contemplates this mystery and attains as much understanding of it as grace permits. This effects the eradication of sin within a believer. Just as sin brings about a situation of alienation from God; alignment with Christ in faith, understanding and sacrament reorientates human focus and the human takes on the perspective of Christ.

'Taking away sin' is for Eriugena a metaphor for the restoration of a right relationship to God. We can observe this in his explanation of what taking sin away really is. It is not to be understood as a physical removal or displacement either in time or space. In the *Commentary* he writes:

> Tollit, ait, non de loco ad locum, uel de tempore in tempus, sed omnino tollit, ne omnino sit, et per suae sanctissimae carnis interemptionem omnino totum mundi peccatum interemit.[48]

Despite occasionally using the metaphor of healing, Eriugena is not thinking about a form of physical transformation.[49] What is realised, according to the thought of Eriugena, is an interior alignment with the pattern of Christ's life. Eriugena's use, not only of *imitatores Dei*, but also of *cooperatores Dei* in his *Expositiones in hierarchiam caelestem* reinforces this point. His position is that the restoration of the image and likeness to God is to be understood most correctly, not in external or 'quasi-magical,' physical terms, but in behavioural and conscious terms.

---

[47] Baptism is the liturgical realisation of the restorative moment. See *Eriugena*, Comm. Ioh. III, V, 68–72: É. Jeauneau, CCM 166, p. 88: *Nemo ex spiritu nascitur per baptismum nisi in morte Christi, sicut ait Apostolus: 'Consepulti sumus cum Christo per baptismum in mortem ut quemadmodum Christus surrexit a mortuis in gloriam patris, ita et nos in nouitate uitae ambulemus.'*

[48] *Eriugena*, Comm. Ioh. I, XXXI, 27–30: É. Jeauneau, CCM 166, p. 70.

[49] The implication of the metaphor is that original sin is like a wound: *Eriugena*, Comm. Ioh. I, XXXI, 58–63: É. Jeauneau, CCM 166, p. 71: *Solus siquidem, ad medicamentum uulneris, redemptor noster in illa massa totius humani generis absque peccato relictus est, ut per illum solum semper saluum totius naturae uulnus curaretur ac, per hoc, ad pristinum statum salutis, totum quod uulneratum est restitueretur.*

> *Est, inquit, perfectio et finis uniuscuiusque ierarchiam participantium; et ipsa quidem perfectio est in diuinam similitudinem ascendere, quantum unicuique iuxta suam proportionem conceditur, hoc est in quantum diuini luminis particeps efficitur et, quod est omnium uirtutum diuinius, sicut ait Apostolus, 'imitatores Dei, cooperatores autem Christi' esse.*[50]

Conclusion

Is this world an appropriate place for persons who toil against the adversities of this world, who experience a residual freedom but who experience daily the lure of sin and the seemingly inevitability of, sooner or later, concurring with sinful structures? This paper concludes that Eriugena is slow to understand the state of this world as a random destructive punishing on God's part of an original human sin. Rather, Eriugena regards this world as a privileged road back to communion with God. Thus the step with which humanity leaves paradise is also the first step in the return. Moreover, Eriugena interprets the *convenientia* in terms of a desired spiritual alignment with the incarnated Lord: this world is a fitting place to stretch out towards Christ Jesus, to be aligned with the pattern of his life, to seek to know him. Furthermore, this grace-enhanced alignment is presented by Eriugena as being more than a mere remedy for transgressions, be they in the 'past' or in the present. It is a step towards the gift of friendship with God.

---

[50] See *Eriugena*, Expositiones in hierarchiam caelestem III, 182–204: J. Barbet, CCM 31 (Turnhout 1975), p. 60–61, here 182–188.

Greek Tradition

Viacheslav V. Lytvynenko, Prague (Czech Republic)

The Imagery of Movement in the Descriptions of Sin and Christian Life in the *Vita Antonii*[1]

Abstract:
This study explores the imagery of movement in the descriptions of sin and Christian life in the Vita Antonii. *It suggests that movement is an important category for seeing the links between Athanasius' early treatises—*Contra Gentes *and* De Incarnatione Verbi*—and his* Vita Antonii. *More specifically, it considers the way Athanasius describes original humanity and sin in his early works and the way he develops these themes in his reflections about Christian life as a fight with sin and the Devil. The main focus of this study is on Antony as the most palpable representative of Athanasian theology and on the way the ascetic applies this theology in action.*

We will search in vain for a systematic treatment of sin in Athanasius, and yet as Fairbairn notes, his "understanding of sin significantly shapes his better-known thought on the status of the Son with respect to the Father"[2]. The researcher shows that "Athanasius' discussions of sin explicitly tie together the great movements of Christian redemptive history—creation, fall, and redemption", and he argues that "the specific way in which he ties these together constitutes his major contribution to the Christian doctrine of sin". If Athanasius' understanding of sin significantly shapes these central doctrines of theology, to what extent does it also color his description of more practical matters related to Christian life and spirituality?

By all means, the one writing where Athanasius is presented as the author who specifically discusses sin from the practical standpoint is the *Quaestiones ad Antiochum Ducem* (henceforth *QAD*)[3]. It asks and answers such questions as "Are the sins of the fathers even now visited on the children of the third and

---

[1] This study represents research funded by the Charles University Research Centre program No. 204053.
[2] D. *Fairbairn*, Athanasius, in: K. Johnson, D. Lauber (eds.), T&T Clark Companion to the Doctrine of Sin (London 2016) 165.
[3] Here I use the following edition: У. Федер (ed.), Псевдо-Атанасий Александрийски. Въпроси и отговори към княз Антиох. Текст. Том 2 (Шумен 2016) [*W. Veder* (ed.), Pseudo-Athanasius. Questions and Answers to Antiochus the Duke. Text. Vol. 2 (Shumen 2016)].

the fourth generation?"⁴; "Can one be forgiven through repentance if one had rejected Christ and blasphemed the Holy Spirit?"⁵; "What sin makes the prayer of man unacceptable to God?"⁶; "What sin makes repentance before God impossible?"⁷; "What sin is the most grievous one?"⁸; "Is practicing charity able to do away with every sin of man or not?"⁹, and many others. But even though the issue of sin and Christian life is addressed here more explicitly than anywhere else in Athanasius, we know that *QAD* is a pseudo-Athanasian work, and its origin has to do with very different concerns and time period¹⁰.

Of the genuine works of Athanasius, it is the *Vita Antonii* (henceforth *VA*)¹¹ where the issues of the Christian life are expressed most strikingly, and where the central scenes of the narrative are the stories of battle with sin. In this study, I will look into the question of what exactly causes sin and how Antony was able to overcome it. In dealing with this question, I will pay special attention to the imagery of movement in the descriptions of sin and Christian life and suggest that this perspective is particularly helpful for seeing the links between Athanasius' early thought and the points he makes in the *VA*¹². My arguments are based on the accepted view that the main hero of the *Vita Antonii* is a spokesman of Athanasian theology who goes about defending the

---

[4] *Pseudo-Athan.*, QAD 67: W. Veder, Questions and Answers (Shumen 2016), p. 114: Ἆρα καὶ μέχρι νῦν ἐπάγονται ἁμαρτίαι πατέρων ἐπὶ τέκνα περὶ τρίτην καὶ τετάρτην γενεάν;

[5] *Pseudo-Athan.*, QAD 73: W. Veder, Questions and Answers (Shumen 2016), p. 142: Ἔχει ἄφεσιν διὰ μετανοίας ὁ τὸν Χριστὸν ἀρνησάμενος καὶ βλασφημῶν εἰς τὸ Πνεῦμα τὸ ἅγιον;

[6] *Pseudo-Athan.*, QAD 74: W. Veder, Questions and Answers (Shumen 2016), p. 145: Ποία ἁμαρτία ποιεῖ τὴν προσευχὴν τοῦ ἀνθρώπου ἀπρόσδεκτον παρὰ Θεῷ;

[7] *Pseudo-Athan.*, QAD 75: W. Veder, Questions and Answers (Shumen 2016), p. 146: Ποία ἁμαρτία οὐ δύναται μετανοῆσαι τῷ Θεῷ;

[8] *Pseudo-Athan.*, QAD 76: W. Veder, Questions and Answers (Shumen 2016), p. 147: Ποία ἁμαρτία ἐστὶ βαρυτέρα;

[9] *Pseudo-Athan.*, QAD 88: W. Veder, Questions and Answers (Shumen 2016), p. 163: Ἰσχύει ἐλεημοσύνη πᾶσαν ἁμαρτίαν ἀνθρώπου ἐξαλεῖψαι ἢ οὔ;

[10] C. Macé, Les Quaestiones ad Antiochum ducem d'un Pseudo-Athanase (CPG 2257). Un état de la question, in: M. Bussières (ed.), La littérature des questions et réponses dans l'Antiquité profane et chrétienne: de l'enseignement à l'exégèse, vol. 64 (Turnhout 2012) 121–150.

[11] Here I use the following edition: G. *Bartelink*, Athanase d'Alexandrie. Vie d'Antoine: Introduction, texte critique, traduction, notes et index, SC 400 (Paris 1994). Eng. trans. comes from R. *Gregg*, Athanasius. The Life of Antony and the Letter to Marcellinus, CWS (New Jersey 1980).

[12] The early treatises are commonly dated between A.D. 318 and 328, while the *VA* is dated between A.D. 356 and 362. On the dating of the former, see J. *Ernest*, The Bible in Athanasius of Alexandria, vol. 2 (Leiden 2004) 423–424; on the dating of the latter, see B. *Brennan*, Dating Athanasius' Vita Antonii, Vigilae Christianae 30 (1976) 52–54.

deity of Christ against the pagan philosophers and the Arian heretics[13]. Taking things a step further, I will seek to show that Antony's whole life—and especially his fight with sin and the Devil—is a major way in which he is made to speak for Athanasius.

While Antony avoids much technical speculation about the origin and consequences of sin, he spends a lot of time discussing the practical aspects of dealing with sin and focuses on the fact that it is caused by the Devil and leads to destruction. To be sure, the "Savior condemned sin in the flesh"[14]; "the enemy is fallen and his powers have diminished"[15]; and the "demons lack the power to do anything"[16], which means that "we must not fear them"[17]. Nevertheless, the Devil, who is described as the "lover of sin" (φιλαμαρτήμων)[18], continues to prowl like a lion, seeking an opportunity to attack[19]. He and his demons are believed to be "in the air around us"[20], and "they intend malice and are ready to do harm"[21] for the single purpose of bringing believers under their control and destroying them[22]. It is no surprise, then, that most of Antony's exhortations are concentrated on exposing the various ways in which the demons try to tempt believers into sin and how they can be combated[23].

The emphasis on the practical ways of dealing with sin in the VA is also reflected in the terminology. We do not find any place in the text where "sin" is used in the plural, whereas the words that depict various manifestations of

---

[13] R. Gregg, D. Groh, Early Arianism: A View of Salvation (Philadelphia 1981) 131-159.
[14] Athan., VA 7.3-4: G. Bartelink, SC 400 (Paris 1994), p. 150: ἁμαρτίαν κατακρίναντος ἐν τῇ σαρκί. Eng. trans. in: R. Gregg, Life of Antony (New Jersey 1980), p. 35.
[15] Athan., VA 28.4: G. Bartelink, SC 400 (Paris 1994), p. 212: πέπτωκεν ὁ ἐχθρός, καὶ ἠσθένησαν αἱ δυνάμεις αὐτοῦ. Eng. trans. in: R. Gregg, Life of Antony (New Jersey 1980), p. 52.
[16] Athan., VA 28.50-51: G. Bartelink, SC 400 (Paris 1994), p. 216: Οἱ δὲ μηδὲν δυνάμενοι, οἷοί εἰσιν οἱ δαίμονες. Eng. trans. in: R. Gregg, Life of Antony (New Jersey 1980), p. 53.
[17] Athan., VA 27.14-15: G. Bartelink, SC 400 (Paris 1994), p. 210: Οὐ δεῖ φοβεῖσθαι αὐτούς. Eng. trans. in: R. Gregg, Life of Antony (New Jersey 1980), p. 52.
[18] Athan., VA 7.14-15: G. Bartelink, SC 400 (Paris 1994), p. 150. Eng. trans. in: R. Gregg, Life of Antony (New Jersey 1980), p. 36.
[19] Athan., VA 7.8-10: G. Bartelink, SC 400 (Paris 1994), p. 150. Eng. trans. in: R. Gregg, Life of Antony (New Jersey 1980), p. 35 (an allusion to 1 Peter 5:8).
[20] Athan., VA 21.14: G. Bartelink, SC 400 (Paris 1994), p. 194: ἐν τῷ καθ' ἡμᾶς ἀέρι. Eng. trans. in: R. Gregg, Life of Antony (New Jersey 1980), p. 47.
[21] Athan., VA 28.16-17: G. Bartelink, SC 400 (Paris 1994), p. 212: εἰσὶ δὲ κακοθελεῖς καὶ πρὸς τὸ βλάπτειν ἕτοιμοι. Eng. trans. in: R. Gregg, Life of Antony (New Jersey 1980), p. 52.
[22] Athan., VA 31.4-6: G. Bartelink, SC 400 (Paris 1994), p. 220. Eng. trans. in: R. Gregg, Life of Antony (New Jersey 1980), p. 55.
[23] Athan., VA 21-22: G. Bartelink, SC 400 (Paris 1994), p. 192-196. Eng. trans. in: R. Gregg, Life of Antony (New Jersey 1980), p. 47-48.

sin are abounding: fornication, corruption, anger, wickedness, treachery, evil thoughts, malice, cunning, filthy pleasure, fraud, disorder, craving for evil, to name just a few[24]. These are often contrasted with numerous sets of virtues that Christians are to develop as they strive to overcome sin: prudence, justice, temperance, courage, understanding, love, concern for the poor, faith in Christ, freedom from anger, hospitality, and the like[25]. In the entire text, the word "sin" is used only seven times: once in ch. 7, twice in ch. 22, and four times in ch. 55. To this we may add four occurrences of the term "sinner(s)" in chs. 13, 26, 27, and 28, as well as six instances of the verb "to sin": twice in ch. 19 and four times in ch. 55. This relatively infrequent use of the term "sin" and its cognates in comparison with the many more words for the manifestation of sin clearly suggests that the intent of the VA is not on the abstract concept of sin but on the practical ways of dealing with it.

Of course, Athanasius' emphasis on the practical aspect of sin significantly determines what he has to say about it in the VA and also raises a question as to how it relates to his theological descriptions of sin elsewhere. Here, I would like to suggest that the points about sin in the VA directly flow from his theological notion of sin that we find in his early treatises *Contra Gentes* and *De Incarnatione Verbi* (henceforth *CG* and *De Inc.*). In these two works, the theological conceptualization of the fall and sin surfaces most clearly, and at the most basic level, it can be described as a change of orientation, or movement in the wrong direction. In *CG*, Athanasius begins by describing the primordial state of humanity (ch. 2) and then talks about the fallen situation (chs. 3–5) and the effects of sin (chs. 6–29). In *De Inc.*, he briefly reiterates the same themes in the beginning (chs. 3–6, 11), and spends the rest of his time explaining how the incarnation of Christ dealt with sin.

More specifically, Athanasius teaches that before the fall humanity "lived a happy and truly blessed life"[26] in paradise and describes that life in ontological and relational terms: "remaining in incorruptibility"[27] and "rejoicing and

---

[24] Athan., VA 9.13, 21.2, 21.13, 22.16, 23.5, 23.9–10, 28.37, 36.4, 36.7: G. Bartelink, SC 400 (Paris 1994), p. 160, 192, 196, 198, 214, 232, 234. Eng. trans. in: R. Gregg, Life of Antony (New Jersey 1980), p. 38, 44, 47, 48, 53, 58.

[25] Athan., VA 17.25–27: G. Bartelink, SC 400 (Paris 1994), p. 182. Eng. trans. in: R. Gregg, Life of Antony (New Jersey 1980), p. 44. Cf. Athan., VA 30.6–10, 36.10–13: G. Bartelink, SC 400 (Paris 1994), p. 218, 234. Eng. trans. in: R. Gregg, Life of Antony (New Jersey 1980), p. 54, 58.

[26] Athan., De Inc. 1.20: R. Thomson, OECT (Oxford 1971), p. 161–162: ζῶσι τὸν εὐδαίμονα καὶ μακάριον ὄντως βίον. Here and elsewhere, Eng. trans. comes from the same edition.

[27] Athan., De Inc. 4.12: R. Thomson, OECT (Oxford 1971), p. 142–143: Μένειν [...] ἐν ἀφθαρσίᾳ.

conversing with God"[28]. Accordingly, the task of the first people was "to remain (διαμένειν) in felicity and live the true life in paradise"[29], meaning that their original state was "neither one of static, natural immortality (as the forms possessed in Plato's cosmology), nor one of human achievement of immortality, but one of an immortality given by grace in which humanity was called to remain through obedience"[30]. Portraying humanity as "being by nature mobile (εὐκίνητος)"[31] and "able to incline to the good or turn away from the good"[32], Athanasius explains their fall as a movement in the wrong direction:

> Yet the soul abandoned the contemplation of the good and virtuous activity, and was from then on deceived and moved in the opposite direction (κινεῖται εἰς τὰ ἐναντία). Then, seeing its abilities [...] and misusing them, it realized that it could also move (κινεῖν) its bodily members in the opposite direction; and therefore, it turned aside (ἀποστρέφει) its eyes to desires instead of the contemplation of creation, showing it had that power. And it thought that provided it was in motion (κινουμένη) it would preserve its own integrity and would not be at fault in exercising its capabilities, not realizing that it had been created not simply for movement (κινεῖσθαι), but for movement (κινεῖσθαι) towards the right objective[33].

In this context, Athanasius compares the fallen soul with a charioteer who disregards the goal to which he or she should drive, and by turning away from it, the charioteer rushes into people. In a similar way, the human soul "no longer moves (κινεῖται) on the path of virtue, nor with a view to seeing God"[34], and by failing to do so, it rushes itself into all kinds of evil: murder, disobedience,

---

[28] *Athan.*, CG 2.14: R. Thomson, OECT (Oxford 1971), p. 6–7: Ἀγάλληται καὶ συνομιλῇ τῷ Θείῳ.

[29] *Athan.*, De Inc. 3.23–24: R. Thomson, OECT (Oxford 1971), p. 140–141: Διαμένειν ἐν μακαριότητι δυνηθῶσι, ζῶντες τὸν ἀληθινὸν καὶ ὄντως τῶν ἁγίων ἐν παραδείσῳ βίον.

[30] D. *Fairbairn*, Athanasius, in: K. Johnson, D. Lauber (eds.), T&T Clark Companion to the Doctrine of Sin (London 2016) 167.

[31] *Athan.*, CG 4.15: R. Thomson, OECT (Oxford 1971), p. 10–11: τὴν φύσιν οὖσα [...] εὐκίνητος.

[32] *Athan.*, CG 4.12–13: R. Thomson, OECT (Oxford 1971), p. 10–11: πρὸς τὰ καλὰ νεύειν, οὕτω καὶ τὰ καλὰ ἀποστρέφεσθαι.

[33] *Athan.*, CG 4.25–33: R. Thomson, OECT (Oxford 1971), p. 12–13: ἡ ψυχὴ ἀποστᾶσα τῆς πρὸς τὰ καλὰ θεωρίας, καὶ τῆς ἐν αὐτοῖς κινήσεως, λοιπὸν πλανωμένη κινεῖται εἰς τὰ ἐναντία. Εἶτα τὸ δυνατὸν ἑαυτῆς [...] ὁρῶσα, καὶ τούτῳ καταχρωμένη, ἐνενόησεν ὅτι καὶ εἰς τὰ ἐναντία δύναται κινεῖν τὰ τοῦ σώματος μέλη· καὶ διὰ τοῦτο ἀντὶ τοῦ τὴν κτίσιν ὁρᾶν, εἰς ἐπιθυμίας τὸν ὀφθαλμὸν ἀποστρέφει, δεικνύουσα ὅτι καὶ τοῦτο δύναται· καὶ νομίζουσα ὅτι, ἅπαξ κινουμένη, σώζει τὴν ἑαυτῆς ἀξίαν, καὶ οὐχ ἁμαρτάνει ποιοῦσα ὃ δύναται· οὐκ εἰδυῖα ὅτι οὐχ ἁπλῶς κινεῖσθαι, ἀλλ' εἰς ἃ δεῖ κινεῖσθαι γέγονε.

[34] *Athan.*, CG 4.9–10: R. Thomson, OECT (Oxford 1971), p. 10–11: κινεῖται οὖν οὐκ ἔτι μὲν κατὰ ἀρετήν, οὐδὲ ὥστε τὸν Θεὸν ὁρᾶν.

adultery, blasphemies, abuse, perjury, stealing, assaulting fellow men, shedding blood, drunkenness, and gluttony[35]. Athanasius insists that "all these things are evil and sins of the soul, but they have no other cause save the turning away (ἀποστροφή) from better things"[36]. Most importantly, the fall became the cause of the broken relationship with God and the subsequent loss of immortality:

> But men, turning away (ἀποστραφέντες) from things eternal and by the counsel of the devil turning (ἐπιστραφέντες) towards things corruptible, were themselves the cause of the corruption in death. They are, as I said, corruptible by nature, but by the grace of the participation of the Word they could have escaped from the consequences of their nature if they had remained (μεμενήκεισαν) virtuous. For on account of the Word who was in them, even natural corruption would not have touched them [...]. Since this happened, men died, and corruption thenceforth took a strong hold on them[37].

Describing sin as the change of orientation "from things eternal" towards "things corruptible", Athanasius explains that it broke the original link between humanity and God and threw people into corruption. Elsewhere, he also makes it clear that fallen humanity suffered the condemnation of sin[38] and enslavement to the Devil[39] as two other fundamental consequences of the

---

[35] Athan., CG 5.4–10: R. Thomson, OECT (Oxford 1971), p. 12–13.
[36] Athan., CG 5.10–11: R. Thomson, OECT (Oxford 1971), p. 12–13: ἅπερ πάντα κακία καὶ ἁμαρτία ψυχῆς ἐστιν. Αἰτία δὲ τούτων οὐδεμία, ἀλλ' ἡ τῶν κρειττόνων ἀποστροφή.
[37] Athan., De Inc. 5.2–12: R. Thomson, OECT (Oxford 1971), p. 144–145: Οἱ δὲ ἄνθρωποι, ἀποστραφέντες τὰ αἰώνια, καὶ συμβουλίᾳ τοῦ διαβόλου εἰς τὰ τῆς φθορᾶς ἐπιστραφέντες, ἑαυτοῖς αἴτιοι τῆς ἐν τῷ θανάτῳ φθορᾶς γεγόνασιν, ὄντες μὲν ὡς προεῖπον κατὰ φύσιν φθαρτοί, χάριτι δὲ τῆς τοῦ Λόγου μετουσίας τοῦ κατὰ φύσιν ἐκφυγόντες, εἰ μεμενήκεισαν καλοί. Διὰ γὰρ τὸν συνόντα τούτοις Λόγον, καὶ ἡ κατὰ φύσιν φθορὰ τούτων οὐκ ἤγγιζε [...]. τούτου δὲ γενομένου οἱ μὲν ἄνθρωποι ἀπέθνησκον, ἡ δὲ φθορὰ λοιπὸν κατ' αὐτῶν ἤκμαζε.
[38] The legal aspect of sin in the early treatises goes closely together with the legal aspect of salvation, which includes such things as "forgiveness of sins" (τῆς τῶν ἁμαρτιῶν ἀφέσεως) in Athan., De Inc. 14.8: R. Thomson, OECT (Oxford 1971), p. 166–167 and Christ's "death as a ransom for the salvation of all" (ὑπὲρ τῆς πάντων σωτηρίας ἀντίψυχον τὸ ἑαυτοῦ σῶμα εἰς θάνατον παραδούς) in Athan., De Inc. 37.48–49: R. Thomson, OECT (Oxford 1971), p. 226–227, which can also be depicted as the fact that Christ "on behalf of all men offered the sacrifice [...] in order to make them guiltless and free from the first transgression" (ὑπὲρ πάντων τὴν θυσίαν ἀνέφερεν [...] ἵνα τοὺς μὲν πάντας ἀνυπευθύνους καὶ ἐλευθέρους τῆς ἀρχαίας παραβάσεως ποιήσῃ) in Athan., De Inc. 20.14–17: R. Thomson, OECT (Oxford 1971), p. 182–183. See also Athan., De Inc. 5.14, 10.43–47, 21.3: R. Thomson, OECT (Oxford 1971), p. 144–145, 158–159, 184–185.
[39] This aspect of sin in the early treatises goes closely together with the way Christ freed humanity from the slavery of the Devil: e.g., Athan., De Inc. 10.32, 20.38–41, 25.24: R. Thomson, OECT (Oxford 1971), p. 156–157, 184–185, 194–195.

fall. Athanasius never deals with the concept of original sin nor discusses Romans 5:12 in his early treatises. In fact, the only place where he does address this topic—rather generally—is *Contra Arianos* 1.51. In that passage he insists that the fall altered Adam and through him death[40] and sin reached "unto all men"[41]. The fall allowed the Devil to enslave sinful humanity, and the second Adam had to be unalterable in order to "condemn sin in it [the flesh]"[42] and make "the Serpent powerless in his assault against all"[43].

With this background, we can now ask how these aspects of sin are reflected in the *VA*. In what follows, we will consider the places where Athanasius uses the terminology of movement and direction to describe sin and the way Antony wrestled with it. Such places are not numerous, but I suggest that looking at the ideas of sin and Christian life from this perspective is particularly helpful for detecting the typically Athanasian points.

To begin with, while movement as such is a natural thing exercised by all created living beings[44], it can be sinful if it is directed in the wrong way. Thus, whereas the Christian life is directed *upward* to God[45] and *forward* to the godly goals[46], the movement of demons is rather chaotic and turbulent, leading to all kinds of evil and sinful things:

> The assault and appearance of the evil ones [...] is something troubling, with crashing and noise and shouting—the sort of movement (κινήματα) one might expect from tough youths and robbers. From this come immediately terror of soul, confusion and disorder of thoughts, dejection, enmity toward ascetics, listlessness, grief, memory of relatives, and fear of death; and finally, there is craving for evil, contempt for virtue, and instability of character[47].

---

[40] *Athan.*, CA 1.51: K. Metzler, K. Savvidis, AW 1/1/2 (Berlin 1998), p. 161: εἰς πάντας τοὺς ἀνθρώπους.

[41] *Athan.*, CA 1.51: K. Metzler, K. Savvidis, AW 1/1/2 (Berlin 1998), p. 161: "the first man Adam changed, and through sin death came into the world" (ὁ πρῶτος ἄνθρωπος Ἀδὰμ ἐτράπη καὶ διὰ τῆς ἁμαρτίας θάνατος εἰσῆλθεν εἰς τὸν κόσμον).

[42] *Athan.*, CA 1.51: K. Metzler, K. Savvidis, AW 1/1/2 (Berlin 1998), p. 161: τὴν μὲν ἁμαρτίαν ἐν αὐτῇ κατακρίνῃ.

[43] *Athan.*, CA 1.51: K. Metzler, K. Savvidis, AW 1/1/2 (Berlin 1998), p. 161: πρὸς πάντας ὁ ὄφις ἀσθενὴς τοῖς ἐπιχειρήμασι γένηται.

[44] Thus, each of the animals (lions, bears, leopards, bulls, serpents, asps, scorpions, and wolves) moves according to its nature in *Athan.*, VA 9.21-24: G. Bartelink, SC 400 (Paris 1994), p. 160: ἕκαστον μὲν τούτων ἐκινεῖτο κατὰ τὸ ἴδιον σχῆμα. Eng. trans. in: *R. Gregg*, Life of Antony (New Jersey 1980), p. 38.

[45] *Athan.*, VA 22.7-9: G. Bartelink, SC 400 (Paris 1994), p. 196. Eng. trans. in: *R. Gregg*, Life of Antony (New Jersey 1980), p. 47.

[46] *Athan.*, VA 7.45-47: G. Bartelink, SC 400 (Paris 1994), p. 154. Eng. trans. in: *R. Gregg*, Life of Antony (New Jersey 1980), p. 37.

[47] *Athan.*, VA 36.1-8: G. Bartelink, SC 400 (Paris 1994), p. 233-234: Ἡ δὲ τῶν φαύλων ἐπι-

Originally, the "demons were made good, but after falling from (ἐκπεσόντες) the heavenly wisdom and now wandering (καλινδούμενοι) around the earth"[48], they act against Christians. Therefore, Antony warns his disciples that "the treacheries and moves (κινήματα) in the [demons'] plot are numerous"[49] and that "they move (κινοῦσιν) all things in their desire to frustrate our journey (ἀνόδου) into heavens, so that we might not ascend (ἀνέλθωμεν) to the place from which they themselves fell (ἐξέπεσον)"[50].

At times, though, the demons mask their evil movements to make them look good and innocent. They can pretend to read the words of Scripture, or sing the Christian songs, or fake the speech of holy people[51]. In doing so, their sole purpose is to "deceive, and then drag (ἑλκύσωσι) their victims wherever they wish"[52], prompting them to "such practices and thoughts that are subversive of the way that leads to virtue"[53]. For that reason, one of the significant marks of the spiritual victories of Antony is the ability to recognize the different movements of the demons: "This too was great in Antony's asceticism—that possessing the gift of discerning spirits [...] he recognized their movements (τὰ κινήματα) and he knew that for which each one of them had a desire and appetite"[54].

δρομὴ καὶ φαντασία τεταραγμένη, μετὰ κτύπου καὶ ἤχου καὶ κραυγῆς, οἵα ἂν γένοιτο νεωτέρων ἀπαιδεύτων καὶ λῃστῶν κινήματα. Ἐξ ὧν εὐθὺς γίνεται δειλία ψυχῆς, τάραχος καὶ ἀταξία λογισμῶν, κατήφεια, μῖσος πρὸς τοὺς ἀσκητάς, ἀκηδία, λύπη, μνήμη τῶν οἰκείων καὶ φόβος θανάτου· καὶ λοιπὸν ἐπιθυμία κακῶν, ὀλιγωρία πρὸς τὴν ἀρετὴν καὶ τοῦ ἤθους ἀκαταστασία. Eng. trans. in: R. Gregg, Life of Antony (New Jersey 1980), p. 58. Cf. Athan., VA 26.18–23: G. Bartelink, SC 400 (Paris 1994), p. 208. Eng. trans. in: R. Gregg, Life of Antony (New Jersey 1980), p. 51.

[48] Athan., VA 22.3–5: G. Bartelink, SC 400 (Paris 1994), p. 194–196: καλοὶ μὲν γεγόνασι καὶ αὐτοί, ἐκπεσόντες δὲ ἀπὸ οὐρανίου φρονήσεως, καὶ λοιπὸν περὶ τὴν γῆν καλινδούμενοι. Eng. trans. in: R. Gregg, Life of Antony (New Jersey 1980), p. 47 (slightly modified).

[49] Athan., VA 22.15–16: G. Bartelink, SC 400 (Paris 1994), p. 196: Πολλὰ γὰρ αὐτῶν ἐστι τὰ πανουργεύματα καὶ τὰ τῆς ἐπιβουλῆς κινήματα. Eng. trans. in: R. Gregg, Life of Antony (New Jersey 1980), p. 48 (slightly modified).

[50] Athan., VA 22.7–9: G. Bartelink, SC 400 (Paris 1994), p. 196: Πάντα κινοῦσιν, θέλοντες ἐμποδίζειν ἡμᾶς τῆς εἰς οὐρανοὺς ἀνόδου, ἵνα μὴ ὅθεν ἐξέπεσον αὐτοὶ ἀνέλθωμεν ἡμεῖς. Eng. trans. in: R. Gregg, Life of Antony (New Jersey 1980), p. 47 (slightly modified).

[51] Athan., VA 25.1–13: G. Bartelink, SC 400 (Paris 1994), p. 206. Eng. trans. in: R. Gregg, Life of Antony (New Jersey 1980), p. 50.

[52] Athan., VA 25.11–13: G. Bartelink, SC 400 (Paris 1994), p. 206: Πλανήσωσι καὶ λοιπὸν ἔνθα θέλουσιν ἑλκύσωσι τοὺς ἀπατηθέντας παρ' αὐτῶν. Eng. trans. in: R. Gregg, Life of Antony (New Jersey 1980), p. 50 (slightly modified).

[53] Athan., VA 26.3–5: G. Bartelink, SC 400 (Paris 1994), p. 208: Τὰ [...] τοιαῦτα ἐπιτηδεύματα καὶ ἐνθυμήματα ἀνατρεπτικὰ τῆς εἰς ἀρετὴν φερούσης ἐστὶν ὁδοῦ. Eng. trans. in: R. Gregg, Life of Antony (New Jersey 1980), p. 51.

[54] Athan., VA 88.1–5: G. Bartelink, SC 400 (Paris 1994), p. 360: Καὶ γὰρ καὶ τοῦτο ἦν μέγα τῆς

Apart from speaking of sin in terms of promptings of the Devil, Antony also construes it as a wrong movement of the soul. In what is arguably the most explicit episode where Antony reflects about the issue of sin on the technical level, he describes virtue and sin as two opposing trajectories:

> As far as the soul is concerned, being straight consists in its intellectual part being according to nature, as it was created. But when it turns from its course and is twisted away from what it naturally is (ὅταν κλίνῃ καὶ ἐν διαστροφῇ τοῦ κατὰ φύσιν γένηται), then we speak of the vice of the soul. So the task is not difficult, for if we remain (μείνωμεν) as we were made, we are in virtue, but if we turn our thoughts toward contemptible things, we are condemned as evil[55].

This is remarkably reminiscent of what we earlier found in the *CG*, where the task of the first people was described as remaining in the original state in which they were created and where sin was understood as a movement in the wrong direction. Thus, at the most basic level sin is believed to be a change of orientation, and the one area where Athanasius develops it in the *VA* is in the way Christians can fight sin in their daily lives. This is most clearly articulated in two specific passages where Antony gives some practical advice to his disciples on how not to fall into sin. In the first one, he suggests to record one's actions and the movements of one's soul:

> Let each one of us note and record our actions and the movements of our souls (τὰ κινήματα τῆς ψυχῆς) as though we were going to give an account to each other. And you can be sure that, being particularly ashamed to have them made known, we would stop sinning and even meditating on something evil. For who wants to be seen sinning? Or who, after sinning, would not prefer to lie, wanting it to remain unknown? So then, just as we would not practice fornication if we were observing each other directly, so also we will doubtless keep ourselves from impure thoughts, ashamed as if reporting them to each other. Let this record replace the eyes of our fellow ascetics, so that, blushing as much to write as to be seen, we might never be absorbed by evil things. Patterning (τυποῦντες) ourselves in this way, we shall be

---

ἀσκήσεως Ἀντωνίου ὅτι […] χάρισμα διακρίσεως πνευμάτων ἔχων, ἐγίνωσκεν αὐτῶν τὰ κινήματα καὶ πρὸς ὅ τις αὐτῶν ἔχει τὴν ὁρμὴν καὶ τὴν σπουδὴν τοῦ ἐπιβουλεύειν. Eng. trans. in: R. Gregg, Life of Antony (New Jersey 1980), p. 94.

[55] Athan., VA 20.25-31: G. Bartelink, SC 400 (Paris 1994), p. 190: Τὸ γὰρ εὐθεῖαν εἶναι τὴν ψυχήν, τοῦτό ἐστι τὸ κατὰ φύσιν νοερὸν αὐτῆς ὡς ἐκτίσθη. Πάλιν δὲ ὅταν κλίνῃ καὶ ἐν διαστροφῇ τοῦ κατὰ φύσιν γένηται, τότε κακία ψυχῆς λέγεται. Οὐκοῦν οὐκ ἔστι δυσχερὲς τὸ πρᾶγμα. Ἐὰν γὰρ μείνωμεν ὡς γεγόναμεν, ἐν τῇ ἀρετῇ ἐσμεν· ἐὰν δὲ λογιζώμεθα τὰ φαῦλα, ὡς κακοὶ κρινόμεθα. Eng. trans. in: R. Gregg, Life of Antony (New Jersey 1980), p. 46.

able to enslave the body, as well as please the Lord and trample on the deceptions of the enemy[56].

The main point which Antony makes here is that sin can be stopped by exercising the acts of personal accountability, and the particular method which he suggests is to keep a record of "our actions and the movements of our souls (τὰ κινήματα τῆς ψυχῆς)". This idea fits a similar insistence where Antony urges that "the ascetic must always acquire knowledge of his own life as from a mirror"[57]. The end purpose of such a self-reflection is the ability to discern the tactics of the Devil and keep the body under control.

In the second passage where Antony teaches about the ways of keeping oneself from sin, he elaborates on the words of Paul from 1 Cor 15:31—"I die daily"—as a life principle that can stop a "declining soul" (τὴν ψυχὴν κλίνουσαν) from falling into sin:

> It is good to carefully consider the Apostle's statement: "I die daily". For if we so live as people dying daily we will not commit sin. The point of the saying is this: As we rise daily, let us suppose that we shall not survive till evening, and again, as we prepare for sleep, let us consider that we shall not awaken. By its very nature our life is uncertain, and is meted out daily by providence. If we think this way, and in this way live—daily—we will not sin, nor will we crave anything, nor bear a grudge against anyone, nor will we lay up treasures on earth, but as people who anticipate dying each day we shall be free of possessions, and we shall forgive all things to all people. The desire for a woman, or another sordid pleasure, we shall not merely control—rather, we shall turn from (ἀποστραφησόμεθα) it as something transitory, forever doing battle and looking toward the day of judgment. For the larger fear and dread of the torments always destroys pleasures' smooth allure, and rouses the declining soul (τὴν ψυχὴν κλίνουσαν)[58].

---

[56] Athan., VA 55.37-53: G. Bartelink, SC 400 (Paris 1994), p. 285–286: Ἕκαστος τὰς πράξεις καὶ τὰ κινήματα τῆς ψυχῆς, ὡς μέλλοντες ἀλλήλοις ἀπαγγέλλειν, σημειώμεθα καὶ γράφωμεν. Καὶ θαρρεῖτε ὅτι, πάντως αἰσχυνόμενοι γνωσθῆναι, παυσόμεθα τοῦ ἁμαρτάνειν καὶ ὅλως τοῦ ἐνθυμεῖσθαί τι φαῦλον. Τίς γὰρ ἁμαρτάνων θέλει βλέπεσθαι; Τίς ἁμαρτήσας, οὐ μᾶλλον ψεύδεται, λανθάνειν θέλων; Ὥσπερ οὖν βλέποντες ἀλλήλους οὐκ ἂν πορνεύσαιμεν, οὕτως, ἐὰν ὡς ἀπαγγέλλοντες ἀλλήλοις τοὺς λογισμοὺς γράφωμεν, πολὺ τηρήσομεν ἑαυτοὺς ἀπὸ λογισμῶν ῥυπαρῶν, αἰσχυνόμενοι γνωσθῆναι. Ἔστω οὖν ἡμῖν τὸ γράμμα ἀντὶ ὀφθαλμῶν τῶν συνασκητῶν, ἵνα, ἐρυθριῶντες γράψαι ὡς τὸ βλέπεσθαι, μηδ' ὅλως ἐνθυμηθῶμεν τὰ φαῦλα· οὕτω δὲ τυποῦντες ἑαυτούς, δυνησόμεθα δουλαγωγεῖν τὸ σῶμα καὶ ἀρέσκειν μὲν τῷ Κυρίῳ, πατεῖν δὲ τὰς τοῦ ἐχθροῦ μεθοδείας. Eng. trans. in: R. Gregg, Life of Antony (New Jersey 1980), p. 73 (slightly modified).

[57] Athan., VA 7.55-57: G. Bartelink, SC 400 (Paris 1994), p. 156: Δεῖ τὸν ἀσκητὴν […] ὡς ἐν ἐσόπτρῳ τὸν ἑαυτοῦ βίον ἀεί. Eng. trans. in: R. Gregg, Life of Antony (New Jersey 1980), p. 37 (slightly modified).

[58] Athan., VA 19.5-22: G. Bartelink, SC 400 (Paris 1994), p. 186: καλὸν τὸ τοῦ ἀποστόλου

By remembering that life is uncertain and death may come any time, a believer is encouraged to turn away (ἀποστραφησόμεθα) from the things of transitory nature and thus stop sinning. To put it differently, the sinful actions of the body can be prevented by having the mind oriented in the right way. This connection between the body and the mind/soul is so important for Athanasius that he uses it to portray Antony himself, when he says that "from the soul's joy his face was cheerful as well, and from the movement of the body (τῶν τοῦ σώματος κινημάτων) it was possible to sense and perceive the stable condition of the soul (τὴν τῆς ψυχῆς κατάστασιν)"[59]. In the end, Athanasius depicts Antony as the one who "maintained equilibrium, like one guided by reason and steadfast in that which accords with nature"[60] and as the one who "remained immovable (ἀκίνητος) in [his] thinking"[61] when being tempted by the demons.

This state of equilibrium and immovability is doubtless a reflection of the Logos, and both of these categories evoke similar ideas elsewhere in Athanasius. As Harmless notes, "for Athanasius, becoming like Christ the Logos included taking on the calm unchanging passionlessness of God"[62], and one of the illuminating passages that unpacks it is *CA* 3.34:

> The Logos is by nature free of passion. But because of the flesh which Christ put on, certain things [like being born, hungering, thirsting, weeping, and sleeping] are ascribed to him, since they are proper to the flesh, and the body itself is proper

---

ῥητὸν μελετᾶν, τὸ "Καθ' ἡμέραν ἀποθνῆσκω". Ἂν γὰρ καὶ ἡμεῖς, ὡς ἀποθνῄσκοντες καθ' ἡμέραν, οὕτω ζῶμεν, οὐχ ἁμαρτήσομεν. Ἔστι δὲ τὸ λεγόμενον τοιοῦτον ἵνα, ἐγειρόμενοι καθ' ἡμέραν, νομίζωμεν μὴ μένειν ἕως ἑσπέρας, καὶ πάλιν μέλλοντες κοιμᾶσθαι, νομίζωμεν μὴ ἐγείρεσθαι, ἀδήλου φύσει καὶ τῆς ζωῆς ἡμῶν οὔσης καὶ μετρουμένης καθ' ἡμέραν παρὰ τῆς προνοίας. Οὕτω δὲ διακείμενοι καὶ καθ' ἡμέραν οὕτω ζῶντες, οὔτε ἁμαρτήσομεν οὔτε τινὸς ἐπιθυμίαν ἕξομεν οὔτε μηνιοῦμέν τινι οὔτε θησαυρίσομεν ἐπὶ τῆς γῆς, ἀλλ' ὡς καθ' ἡμέραν προσδοκῶντες ἀποθνῄσκειν, ἀκτήμονες ἐσόμεθα καὶ πᾶσι πάντα συγχωρήσομεν. Ἐπιθυμίαν δὲ γυναικὸς ἢ ἄλλης ῥυπαρᾶς ἡδονῆς οὐδ' ὅλως κρατήσομεν, ἀλλ' ὡς παρερχομένην ἀποστραφησόμεθα, ἀγωνιῶντες ἀεὶ καὶ προβλέποντες τὴν ἡμέραν τῆς κρίσεως. Ἀεὶ γὰρ ὁ μείζων φόβος καὶ ὁ ἀγὼν τῶν βασάνων διαλύει τὸ λεῖον τῆς ἡδονῆς, καὶ τὴν ψυχὴν κλίνουσαν ἀνίστησιν. Eng. trans. in: *R. Gregg*, Life of Antony (New Jersey 1980), p. 45–46.

[59] *Athan.*, VA 67.20-23: G. Bartelink, SC 400 (Paris 1994), p. 312: ὡς ἀπὸ τῆς χαρᾶς τῆς ψυχῆς ἱλαρὸν ἔχειν καὶ τὸ πρόσωπον, καὶ ἀπὸ τῶν τοῦ σώματος κινημάτων αἰσθέσθαι καὶ νοεῖν τὴν τῆς ψυχῆς κατάστασιν. Eng. trans. in: *R. Gregg*, Life of Antony (New Jersey 1980), p. 81.

[60] *Athan.*, VA 14.18–19: G. Bartelink, SC 400 (Paris 1994), p. 174: ὅλος ἦν ἴσος, ὡς ὑπὸ τοῦ λόγου κυβερνώμενος καὶ ἐν τῷ κατὰ φύσιν ἑστώς. Eng. trans. in: *R. Gregg*, Life of Antony (New Jersey 1980), p. 42.

[61] *Athan.*, VA 39.24: G. Bartelink, SC 400 (Paris 1994), p. 242: ηὐχόμην ἀκίνητος μένειν τῷ φρονήματι. Eng. trans. in: *R. Gregg*, Life of Antony (New Jersey 1980), p. 61 (trans. mine).

[62] *W. Harmless*, Desert Fathers. An Introduction to the Literature of Early Monasticism (Oxford 2004) 90–91.

to the Savior. And he himself, being passionless by nature, remains as he is, not harmed by these affections. But human beings themselves—because their passions are changed into passionlessness and done away with in the Impassible [Christ]—become passionless and free of these experiences for eternity"[63].

By becoming a partaker of the divine Savior who is impassible by nature, Antony himself became passionless by grace.

Likewise, the immovability that characterizes Antony is another reflection of the Logos, who is unchangeable by nature as God and who remained that way even after the incarnation: "the Word of God was not changed, but remaining the same he assumed a human body for the salvation and benefit of mankind"[64]. By participating in the unchangeability of Christ[65], Antony has become the perfect exemplar of deification—the "mystagogue" (μεμυσταγωγημένος) and "God-bearer" (θεοφορούμενος)[66]. The broken relationships which sin was once causing between God and humanity and which are vividly described in the *CG* and *De Inc.* are now shown to be fully restored in the life of Antony. He is completely immersed in fellowship with God, and his orientation toward him is a continuous reality that secures his victories over sin.

It remains to say that while Antony's achievements and feats are indeed impressive[67], Athanasius does not stop emphasizing that it was Christ who solved the problem of sin and overcame the demons in the first place. As I have shown in my other study[68], Athanasius makes this point by drawing a deliberate contrast between the actions of Antony and those of Christ in ten specific passages

---

[63] Athan., CA 3.34: K. Metzler, K. Savvidis, AW 1/1/3 (Berlin 2000), p. 345–346: ὡς τὴν φύσιν αὐτὸς ὁ λόγος ἀπαθής ἐστι καὶ ὅμως δι' ἣν ἐνεδύσατο σάρκα λέγεται περὶ αὐτοῦ ταῦτα, ἐπειδὴ τῆς μὲν σαρκὸς ἴδια ταῦτα, τοῦ δὲ σωτῆρος ἴδιον αὐτὸ τὸ σῶμα. καὶ αὐτὸς μὲν ἀπαθὴς τὴν φύσιν, ὡς ἔστι, διαμένει μὴ βλαπτόμενος ἀπὸ τούτων, ἀλλὰ μᾶλλον ἐξαφανίζων καὶ ἀπολλύων αὐτά· οἱ δὲ ἄνθρωποι ὡς εἰς τὸν ἀπαθῆ μεταβάντων αὐτῶν τῶν παθῶν καὶ ἀπηλειμμένων ἀπαθεῖς καὶ ἐλεύθεροι τούτων λοιπὸν καὶ εἰς τοὺς αἰῶνας γίνονται. Eng. trans. in: *W. Harmless*, Desert Fathers (Oxford 2004), p. 91.
[64] Athan., VA 74.13–15: G. Bartelink, SC 400 (Paris 1994), p. 324: Ὁ τοῦ θεοῦ Λόγος οὐκ ἐπλανήθη, ἀλλ' ὁ αὐτὸς ὤν, ἐπὶ σωτηρίᾳ καὶ εὐεργεσίᾳ τῶν ἀνθρώπων ἀνείληφε σῶμα ἀνθρώπινον. Eng. trans. in: *R. Gregg*, Life of Antony (New Jersey 1980), p. 85.
[65] Athan., VA 74.16–17: G. Bartelink, SC 400 (Paris 1994), p. 324: ἵνα, τῇ ἀνθρωπίνῃ γενέσει κοινωνήσας, ποιήσῃ τοὺς ἀνθρώπους κοινωνῆσαι θείας καὶ νοερᾶς φύσεως. Eng. trans. in: *R. Gregg*, Life of Antony (New Jersey 1980), p. 85.
[66] Athan., VA 14.7: G. Bartelink, SC 400 (Paris 1994), p. 172. Eng. trans. in: *R. Gregg*, Life of Antony (New Jersey 1980), p. 42.
[67] Athan., VA 5.13–17; 6.20–21: G. Bartelink, SC 400 (Paris 1994), p. 142, 148. Eng. trans. in: *R. Gregg*, Life of Antony (New Jersey 1980), p. 34–35.
[68] *V. Lytvynenko*, The Doctrine of God and Deification in Athanasius of Alexandria: Relations and Qualities. Ph.D. Diss. (Prague 2014) 308–310.

in the *Vita Antonii*. Accordingly, in fighting the demons, Antony may say that "I was not the one who stopped them and nullified their actions—it was the Lord"[69]; in performing the miracles, he may make a qualification that "the performance of signs does not belong to us—this is the Savior's work"[70]; and in healing the sick, he may warn that "this good deed is not mine [...] rather, the healing is from the Savior who works his mercy everywhere for those who call on him"[71]. By describing Antony this way, Athanasius makes him act as the defender of Christ's divinity, demonstrating in practice the truthfulness of his theological claims.

Based on these observations, we may conclude that movement is the most basic category which Athanasius uses to discuss sin and Christian life in the *Vita Antonii*. By looking into the imagery of movement we are able to see familiar links with his early treatises *Contra Gentes* and *De Incarnatione Verbi*. More specifically, we find that the task of the first people to remain in the state of original creation and the description of sin as a movement in the wrong direction connects with the same points in the *VA*. Furthermore, this understanding of humanity and sin colors Athanasius' practical reflections about Christian life as a fight with sin and the Devil. One can guard oneself from sin by paying attention to the movements of one's soul and by orienting one's mind in the right direction. Antony's own life is the ideal example of how one can live the life originally designed by the Creator, and above all a witness of how Christ overcomes sin and the Devil in the lives of the faithful.

---

[69] *Athan.*, VA 40.19-21: G. Bartelink, SC 400 (Paris 1994), p. 244: Οὐκ ἐγὼ δὲ ἤμην ὁ παύων ἐκείνους καὶ καταργῶν, ἀλλ' ὁ Κύριος ἦν. Eng. trans. in: R. Gregg, Life of Antony (New Jersey 1980), p. 61.

[70] *Athan.*, VA 38.6-7: G. Bartelink, SC 400 (Paris 1994), p. 238: τὸ γὰρ ποιεῖν σημεῖα οὐχ ἡμῶν, τοῦ δὲ Σωτῆρός ἐστι τὸ ἔργον. Eng. trans. in: R. Gregg, Life of Antony (New Jersey 1980), p. 60.

[71] *Athan.*, VA 58.16-21: G. Bartelink, SC 400 (Paris 1994), p. 290: Ὑπάγετε, καὶ εὑρήσετε αὐτήν, εἰ μὴ ἀπέθανεν, τεθεραπευμένην. Οὐ γὰρ ἐμόν ἐστι τοῦτο κατόρθωμα, ἵνα καὶ πρὸς ἐμὲ τὸν οἰκτρὸν ἄνθρωπον ἔλθῃ· ἀλλὰ τοῦ Σωτῆρός ἐστιν ἡ θεραπεία, τοῦ ποιοῦντος ἐν παντὶ τόπῳ τὸ ἔλεος αὐτοῦ τοῖς ἐπικαλουμένοις αὐτόν. Eng. trans. in: R. Gregg, Life of Antony (New Jersey 1980), p. 74.

Marta Przyszychowska, Pego (Spain)

The first sin as a sin of nature according to Gregory of Nyssa[1]

Abstract:
In my paper, I shall show that Gregory of Nyssa considered the first sin to have been a sin of human nature rather than of an individual. I take Gregory's statements that human nature sinned literally and follow a consistent concept of the first sin in all of his writings from supposedly the first De virginitate *to the last* In Canticum Canticorum. *He usually uses the image of nature that committed the sin and put on the garments of skin symbolizing the consequences of the fall. In* De opificio hominis, *he uses a metaphor of double creation to express a similar concept. Those images are parallel and must not be confused. I claim that Gregory could have been influenced by authors from his native Asia Minor such as Irenaeus, Methodius of Olympus, Alexander of Aphrodisias and others, but also by Plotinus whose writings he certainly knew.*

The first sin of man (to avoid the term "original" to not associate Gregory's idea with the Western one) is a theme that appears frequently in Gregory's writings as it is one of the main points of Patristic anthropology in general. What is beyond doubt is that Gregory states very often that all humans participate in the consequences of that first sin[2]. The question is how does this

---

[1] This paper could have not been written without support from Rev. prof. Tomasz Stępień, especially without his profound knowledge of Plotinus. I would like to express my deepest gratitude for the hours of conversations he dedicated to me while I was writing. I also thank the participants of the Colloquy in Vienna whose questions and remarks helped me to understand Gregory better (I hope). Above all, I would like to thank prof. Georgios Martzelos for drawing my attention to In Hexaemeron by Gregory of Nyssa as an important point of reference for his concept of double creation.

[2] *Greg. Nyss.*, Or. dom. I: J. F. Callahan, GNO VII/2 (Leiden – New York – Köln 1992), p. 10; Or. dom. II: J. F. Callahan, GNO VII/2 (Leiden – New York – Köln 1992), p. 26–27; Or. dom. IV: J. F. Callahan, GNO VII/2 (Leiden – New York – Köln 1992), p. 46; Or. dom. V: J. F. Callahan, GNO VII/2 (Leiden – New York – Köln 1992), p. 65–66, Or. cat.: E. Mühlenberg, GNO III/4 (Leiden – New York – Köln 1996), p. 29–30 and 48–49; Tunc et ipse: J. Kenneth Downing, GNO III/2 (Leiden – New York – København – Köln 1987), p. 11–12; Virg. XII, 4: J. P. Cavarnos, GNO VIII/1 (Leiden 1963), p. 302; Inscr. I, 8: J. Mc Donough, GNO V (Leiden 1962), p. 63; Inscr. II, 6: J. Mc Donough, GNO V (Leiden 1962), p. 86; Antirr.: F. Müller, GNO III/1 (Leiden 1958), p. 152; Eccl. II: P. Alexander, GNO V (Leiden 1962), p. 302 and 305; Diem lum.: E. Gebhardt, GNO IX (Leiden 1967), p. 241; Op. hom. 17: PG

participation occur. The basic thought that every individual that appears in nature takes part in the nature that has been changed because of the first sin and its consequences is present in entire Gregory's output from the very first one *De Virginitate* to the one considered to be the last *In Canticum Canticorum*[3]. In my opinion, Gregory must have had in the back of his mind a consistent theory of the first fall that he sometimes expressed more or less clearly depending on the circumstances, different context, different literary genre of the writings, different audience, and different opponents[4]. The common feature of all those statements is that they do not provide an explanation of the issue, but they are rather remarks made in a Trinitarian, soteriological, or Christological context. The writing that presents a supposedly different approach is *De opificio hominis*—the only anthropological treatise of Gregory. I shall try to show that it is not significantly different, but more profound.

Gregory uses two basic images to illustrate his concept of the first sin and its consequences; images that are parallel and must not be confused. The most common in Gregory is the image of nature that committed the sin and put on the garments of skin symbolizing the consequences of the fall[5]. I shall show below that when Gregory speaks about the sin of Adam or a man he means human nature as an indivisible monad rather than the first individual human being. The second image is a metaphor of double creation; here Gre-

---

44, 188–192; Beat. VI: J. F. Callahan, GNO VII/2 (Leiden – New York – Köln 1992), p. 145; Eun. III, 10, 10–11: W. Jaeger, GNO II (Leiden 1960), p. 293; An. et res.: A. Spira, GNO III/3 (Leiden – Boston 2014), p. 113–114; Cant. II: H. Langerbeck, GNO VI (Leiden 1960), p. 51; Cant. XII: H. Langerbeck, GNO VI (Leiden 1960), p. 350–351; Mort.: G. Heil, GNO IX (Leiden 1967), p. 55; Bapt.: H. Polack, GNO X/2 (Leiden – New York – Köln 1996), p. 359.

[3] J. Daniélou, Chronologie des œuvres de Grégoire de Nysse, StPatr 7 (1966) 159–169; G. May, Die Chronologie des Lebens und der Werke des Gregor von Nyssa, in: M. Harl (ed.), Écriture et culture philosophique dans la pensée de Grégoire de Nysse. Actes du Colloque de Chevetogne (22–26 Septembre 1969) (Leiden 1971) 51–66.

[4] In contrast to Johannes Zachhuber [J. Zachhuber, Human Nature in Gregory of Nyssa. Philosophical Background and Theological Significance (Leiden 2000) 178–184] who distinguished three patterns in Gregory's explanation of how a human being, although created at the image of God, is now burdened with passions and mortality: Neoplatonic (as a necessary sequence inherent in the nature of evil itself), Origenian (a connection between the present state and matter), and Apollinarian (universal human nature as a proof that human beings shared in the fall of Adam) that Gregory used independently in different texts.

[5] Greg. Nyss., Mort.: G. Heil, GNO IX (Leiden 1967), p. 53 and 55–56; Cant. II: H. Langerbeck, GNO VI (Leiden 1960), p. 60; Cant. XI: H. Langerbeck, GNO VI (Leiden 1960), p. 327; Or. cat.: E. Mühlenberg, GNO III/4 (Leiden – New York – Köln 1996), p. 30; An. et res.: A. Spira, GNO III/3 (Leiden – Boston 2014), p. 113 -114; Melet.: A. Spira, GNO IX (Leiden 1967), p. 454; Or. dom. V: J. F. Callahan, GNO VII/2 (Leiden – New York – Köln 1992), p. 65; Beat. VIII: J. F. Callahan, GNO VII/2 (Leide – New York – Köln 1992), p. 161.

gory straightforwardly distinguishes the creation of human nature as a monad from the creation of an individual, and instead of the garments of skin (absent in entire *De opificio hominis*) he claims that as a consequence of the sin God (foreseeing the sin that was to be committed) introduced into human nature a distinction between two sexes. The garment of skin and sexes from *De opificio hominis* are clearly the same reality[6]. According to Gregory, the garments of skin are: "sexual intercourse, conception, childbearing, dirt, lactation, nourishment, evacuation, gradual growth to maturity, the prime of life, old age, disease, and death"[7] and in *De opificio hominis* the distinction of sexes is not the change itself. It has been the source or rather the main manifestation of the ontic change that consisted in connection with animal nature. The effects of that change included also "the affections [that] entered man's composition by reason of the animal mode of generation"[8].

I. Gregory's characteristic expressions

Gregory has three ways of speaking about the original sin:

1. Human nature committed the sin

He straightforwardly says that it was human nature that fell down into sin. In the context of the first sin, Gregory uses the following expressions: our nature fell into sin (πεσούσης ἡμῶν εἰς ἁμαρτίαν τῆς φύσεως)[9], human nature lapsed into evil (τὴν ἀνθρωπίνην φύσιν, ἧς πρὸς κακίαν ἀπορρυείσης)[10], human nature has found itself in evil through sin (τὸ ἀνθρώπινον ἐν πονηρίᾳ διὰ τὴν ἁμαρτίαν γενόμενον)[11], our nature (ἡ φύσις ἡμῶν) has failed to preserve the image of God by deliberate assimilation into an evil kinship with

---

[6] I stress that because it is very tempting to mix those two images, cf. E. McClear, The Fall of Man and Original Sin in the Theology of Gregory of Nyssa, ThStud 9 (1948) 181-185. I myself tried to combine those two images until some colleagues at the Gregorian congress in Paris brought to my attention that the garments of skin do not appear at all in *De opificio hominis*, the fact already noticed by J. Daniélou, L'Être et le temps chez Grégoire de Nysse (Leiden 1970) 159.

[7] Greg. Nyss., An. et res.: A. Spira, GNO III/3 (Leiden – Boston 2014), p. 113-114; transl. C. P. Roth, On the Soul and the Resurrection (New York 1993), p. 114.

[8] Greg. Nyss., Op. hom. 18: PG 44, 192; transl. NPNF II, 5, p. 407.

[9] Greg. Nyss., Vit. Moys. II, 45: H. Musurillo, GNO VII/1 (Leiden 1964), p. 45. The expression εἰς ἁμαρτίαν ἔπεσε seems to be quite frequent in the 4th century Christian literature and means simply "committed the sin", although Athanasius, Basil and Didymus the Blind always refer it to individuals.

[10] Greg. Nyss., Eun. III, 3, 51: W. Jaeger, GNO II (Leiden 1960), p. 125-126.

[11] Greg. Nyss., Eun. III, 9, 14: W. Jaeger, GNO II (Leiden 1960), p. 268.

the father of sin[12], through deception human nature has gone astray from the right judgment of the good (τῆς τοῦ καλοῦ κρίσεως ἀπεπλανήθη δι' ἀπάτης ἡ ἀνθρωπίνη φύσις)[13], our nature fell into sin (πεσούσης ἡμῶν εἰς ἁμαρτίαν τῆς φύσεως)[14], human nature (ἡ ἀνθρωπίνη φύσις) has been disobedient[15].

2. A man/the first man/Adam committed the first sin

Usually, when talking about the first sin, Gregory does not mention Adam at all. He says that a man committed the first sin like a man is being saved[16]. Gregory sometimes says that Adam committed the first sin, but he understands Adam not as an individual but as human nature, as unity. It is clear because the same Adam who was lost has been found by Christ[17]. Gregory as well as Irenaeus claims that the same Adam who was cast away from paradise, comes back to God[18]. So, with the name of Adam Gregory does not designate an individual, but he uses that name as a synonym of "man" in general.

Although Gregory sometimes refers to the first woman, she does not seem to him a separate person with her own will, but the first man and the first woman seem to be one being. In *De virginitate*, Gregory distinguishes the consequences of the sin that man and woman suffered, but he calls on everybody to return to the original state of "the first being" as if there were only one human being at the beginning[19]. In chapter 20 of *De opificio hominis*, he says that a woman ate the fruit, but just one chapter before he claims that it was a human being (ὁ ἄνθρωπος) that was leading a spiritual life in Paradise[20]. Sometimes in the context of the first sin he mentions the first human beings

---

[12] Greg. Nyss., Eun. III, 10, 10: W. Jaeger, GNO II (Leiden 1960), p. 293.
[13] Greg. Nyss., Or. dom. III: J. F. Callahan, GNO VII/2 (Leiden – New York – Köln 1992), p. 37–38.
[14] Greg. Nyss., Vit. Moys. II, 45: H. Musurillo, GNO VII/1 (Leiden 1964), p. 45–46.
[15] Greg. Nyss., Cant. II: H. Langerbeck, GNO VI (Leiden 1960), p. 458.
[16] Greg. Nyss., Diem nat.: F. Mann, GNO X/2 (Leiden – New York – Köln 1996), p. 265: "Through a man [δι' ἀνθρώπου] death; through a man salvation. The first fell into sin [εἰς ἁμαρτίαν ἔπεσεν]; the second restored the fallen one"; cf. Mort.: G. Heil, GNO IX (Leiden 1967), p. 55; Or. dom. II: J. F. Callahan, GNO VII/2 (Leiden – New York – Köln 1992), p. 27; Tunc et ipse: J. Kenneth Downing, GNO III/2 (Leiden – New York – København – Köln 1987), p. 11–12; Cant. XII: H. Langerbeck, GNO VI (Leiden 1960), p. 350–351.
[17] Greg. Nyss., Ref. Eun. 175: W. Jaeger, GNO II (Leiden 1960), p. 385–386; Diem lum.: E. Gebhardt, GNO IX (Leiden 1967), p. 241.
[18] Greg. Nyss., Or. dom. I: J. F. Callahan, GNO VII/2 (Leiden – New York – Köln 1992), p. 10.
[19] Greg. Nyss., Virg. XII, 4: J. P. Cavarnos, GNO VIII/1 (Leiden 1963), p. 302; Diem nat.: F. Mann, GNO X/2 (Leiden – New York – Köln 1996), p. 265.
[20] Greg. Nyss., Op. hom. 19–20: PG 44, 196–200.

in plural (οἱ πρῶτοι ἄνθρωποι[21] or οἱ πρωτόπλαστοι[22]), but again they usually (if it is not a simple mention with no further expounding) seem to be one person and even in those passages Gregory interchangeably refers to them in singular (ὁ ἄνθρωπος) or with the pronoun "we".

One text is especially important. Gregory mentions the first man and compares him to one ear of corn, but when he comments on the consequences of his sin, he says that it was our nature that split up into a multitude as if he used those expressions interchangeably:

> The first ear was the first man [ὁ πρῶτος ἄνθρωπος], [Adam][23]. At the entrance of evil our nature [ἡ φύσις] was split up into a multitude like the kernels in the ear[24].

3. The metaphor of double creation

In *De hominis opificio*, Gregory presents his concept of double creation[25] "in the form of exercise" (ἐν γυμνασίας εἴδει)[26]. Nevertheless, the main points of this theory are coherent with Gregory's basic conviction that it was human nature as such that committed the first sin. Besides, Gregory applies the same pattern of double creation worked out in *De opificio hominis* to the creation of the world in the subsequent *Apologia in Hexaemeron* yet not as an exercise, but rather an explanation he was convinced of.

In *De opificio hominis*, Gregory definitely distinguishes two acts of creation. In the first one, God created human nature without gender, and only in the second one an individual human being characterized by a specific sex.

---

[21] *Greg. Nyss.*, Inscr. II, 6: J. Mc Donough, GNO V (Leiden 1962), p. 86; Or. cat.: E. Mühlenberg, GNO III/4 (Leiden – New York – Köln 1996), p. 30; Beat. VI: J. F. Callahan, GNO VII/2 (Leiden – New York – Köln 1992), p. 145; Cant. IX: H. Langerbeck, GNO VI (Leiden 1960), p. 6.

[22] *Greg. Nyss.*, Cant. XIII: H. Langerbeck, GNO VI (Leiden 1960), p. 378; Cant. XV: H. Langerbeck, GNO VI (Leiden 1960), p. 449; Vit. Moys. II, 213: H. Musurillo, GNO VII/1 (Leiden 1964), p. 107; Virg. XIII, 1: J. P. Cavarnos, GNO VIII/1 (Leiden 1963), p. 304; Or. cat.: E. Mühlenberg, GNO III/4 (Leiden – New York – Köln 1996), p. 30; Mart. II: O. Lendle, GNO X/1 (Leiden – New York – København – Köln 1990), p. 163–164; Steph. I: O. Lendle, GNO X/1 (Leiden – New York – København – Köln 1990), p. 76; Op. hom. 17: PG 44, 188.

[23] "Adam" appears in PG, while in GNO edition there is no "Adam".

[24] *Greg. Nyss.*, An. et res.: A. Spira, GNO III/3 (Leiden – Boston 2014), p. 120–121; transl. C. P. Roth, On the Soul and the Resurrection (New York 1993), p. 119.

[25] *Greg. Nyss.*, Op. hom. 16: PG 44, 185; Op. hom. 17: PG 44, 189–192; Op. hom. 22: PG 44, 205.

[26] *Greg. Nyss.*, Op. hom. 16: PG 44, 185.

Image of God, which we behold in the entire human nature [ἐν πάσῃ τῇ ἀνθρωπίνῃ φύσει], had its consummation then; but Adam as yet was not ['Ο δὲ Ἀδὰμ οὔπω ἐγένετο]. [...] Man [ὁ ἄνθρωπος], then, was made in the image of God; that is, the universal nature [ἡ καθόλου φύσις][27].

The cause of the second creation was the first sin that had been foreknown by God before it was committed.

Two things are of crucial significance here. First, in the theory of double creation it is still human nature that commits the sin:

> While looking upon the nature of man in its entirety and fullness [αὐτῷ πληρώματι πᾶσαν τὴν ἀνθρωπίνην φύσιν] [...], He saw beforehand by His all-seeing power that it would not keep its choice in a direct course to what is good [μὴ εὐθυποροῦσαν πρὸς τὸ καλὸν τὴν προαίρεσιν], and it will fall away [ἀποπίπτουσαν] from the angelic life[28].

The inclination of our nature to what was beneath it [ἡ πρὸς τὸ ταπεινὸν τῆς φύσεως ἡμῶν ἐπίκλισις] made such form of generation absolutely necessary for mankind[29].

Inclination (ἐπίκλισις) presumes free choice, which is straightforwardly mentioned in the first quoted passage (ἡ προαίρεσις). So, the fact that human nature fell away (ἀποπίπτουσαν) from the angelic life was caused by an act of choice of human nature, it was not something that just happened because of some physical or any other reasons. It is unimportant whether it happened before or after the individuation, the crucial thing is that the first sin was committed at the higher level than individuals. The concept of second creation made in foreseeing of the sin might have been introduced only in order to "defend" human body from being the direct consequence of the sin (as it happens in the image of the garments of skin).

Many scholars claim that Adam was the only representative of human nature, so when he sinned the entire nature sinned and got separated from God[30]. According to Vives, sin is also a kind of a pleroma, which contains

---

[27] Greg. Nyss., Op. hom. 22: PG 44, 205, transl. NPNF II, 5, p. 411.
[28] Greg. Nyss., Op. hom. 17: PG 44, 189, transl. NPNF II, 5, p. 406 with alterations.
[29] Greg. Nyss., Op. hom. 22: PG 44, 205, transl. NPNF II, 5, p. 411.
[30] E. McClear, The Fall of Man and Original Sin in the Theology of Gregory of Nyssa, 175–212; J. Gaith, La conception de la liberté chez Grégoire de Nysse (Paris 1953) 116; D. L. Balás, Plenitudo Humanitatis: The Unity of Human Nature in the Thought of Gregory of Nyssa, in: D. F. Winslow (ed.), Disciplina nostra: Essays in memory of Robert F. Evans (Cambridge 1979) 124; L. Scheffczyk, Urstand, Fall und Erbsünde: von der Schrift bis Augustinus (Freiburg 1981) 149; J. Zachhuber, Human Nature in Gregory of Nyssa. Philosophical Background and Theological Significance (Leiden 2000) 182–185 (at least in some of Gregory's writings).

sins from the first to the last one. Just like the pleroma of human nature is more than the sum total of individuals, the pleroma of sin is something more than the sum total of sins. The original sin is something like the cause of all current sins[31]. But, as shown above, there are many direct statements of Gregory that it was human nature that sinned. I take them literally. Such a literal interpretation is coherent with his concept of Incarnation, which meant to him that the Son took upon himself the entire human nature understood as an entity/monad[32].

Second, individuation of nature by sexual reproduction comes as a consequence of the (foreseen) sin. But, if not for the fall, human individuals would have come into existence in an angelic way[33]. So, individuation of nature is something intended by God from the very beginning and its goal is that human nature can reach its fullness (πλήρωμα) planned by God at the moment of the first creation. The predefined number of individuals that will come into existence in the history of the world is something necessary, because every creature must be definite, "should have some limit and measure prescribed by the wisdom of its Maker"[34]. So, individuation occurs because of the very fact that human nature is something created, as "it is fitting for God not to regard any of the things made by Him as indefinite (ἀόριστον)"[35].

To show that it is likely that for Gregory it was human nature itself that sinned, I shall point out some possible sources of this concept.

---

[31] J. Vives, El pecado original en San Gregorio de Nisa, Estudios Eclesiásticos 45 (1970) 219.
[32] Gregory uses very suggestive images with reference to the Incarnation: he compares human nature to the sheep Jesus mentioned in the parable (Luke 15, 1-7), lost by the first sin and found by Christ in the Incarnation [Eun. III, 2, 49: W. Jaeger, GNO II (Leiden 1960), p. 68; Eun. III, 10, 11: W. Jaeger, GNO II (Leiden 1960), p. 293; Cant. XII: H. Langerbeck, GNO VI (Leiden 1960), p. 364; Antirr.: F. Müller, GNO III/1 (Leiden 1958), p. 152; Eccl. II: P. Alexander, GNO V (Leiden 1962), p. 304-305]; he says that Christ is the Good Samaritan who put the entire human nature (all people) on his own donkey that symbolizes his body and took care of it [Cant. XIV: H. Langerbeck, GNO VI (Leiden 1960), p. 427-428], he also compares human nature to the dough of which Christ was the first-fruits [Ref. Eun. 83: W. Jaeger, GNO II (Leiden 1960), p. 346, Tunc et ipse: J. Kenneth Downing, GNO III/2 (Leiden - New York - København - Köln 1987), p. 16, Antirr.: F. Müller, GNO III/1 (Leiden 1958), p. 151].
[33] Greg. Nyss., Op. hom. 17: PG 44, 189-192.
[34] Greg. Nyss., Op. hom. 16: PG 44, 185.
[35] Greg. Nyss., Op. hom. 16: PG 44, 185.

II. Gregory's possible sources

1. Writers from Asia Minor

Gregory's way of speaking about the first sin seems to be very close to that of Irenaeus and Methodius of Olympus. All three treat the name Adam as a synonym of "man", all three speak about the real unity of human nature, and all three use the pronoun "we" in reference to the effects of the first sin[36]. For Irenaeus (as well as Methodius and Gregory) the term "Adam" is in most cases a collective noun and stands for man or humanity[37]. Irenaeus conceives a prayer seeking absolution of our sins as a request for forgiveness of the sin committed by Adam with no regard to the fact that the text of the Gospel provides for the plural[38]. The motivation for which Irenaeus omits individual sins and makes us ask for forgiveness of Adam's sin is the parallel between Adam's sin and redemption made by Jesus Christ[39]. Gregory as well as Irenaeus claims that the same Adam who was cast away from paradise, returns to God. He names the creature that was cast away interchangeably with the name of Adam, with the pronoun "we", and with the noun "man"[40]. Adam is at the same time conceived in a general sense—man, and in an individual sense—*this* man. This dual meaning of Adam allows Irenaeus (as well as

---

[36] *Iren. Lugd.*, Adv. haer. III, 23, 1-3: A. Rousseau, L. Doutreleau, SC 211 (Paris 1974), p. 448-450; Adv. haer. III, 23, 6-8: A. Rousseau, L. Doutreleau, SC 211 (Paris 1974), p. 466; Adv. haer. V, 1, 3: A. Rousseau, L. Doutreleau, C. Mercier, SC 153 (Paris 1969), p. 22-24; Adv. haer. V, 14, 2: A. Rousseau, L. Doutreleau, C. Mercier, SC 153 (Paris 1969), p. 186-188; Adv. haer. V, 15, 2-3: A. Rousseau, L. Doutreleau, C. Mercier, SC 153 (Paris 1969), p. 204-206; Adv. haer. V, 16, 3: A. Rousseau, L. Doutreleau, C. Mercier, SC 153 (Paris 1969), p. 218-220; Adv. haer. V, 17, 1: A. Rousseau, L. Doutreleau, C. Mercier, SC 153 (Paris 1969), p. 220-224; Adv. haer. V, 21, 1: A. Rousseau, L. Doutreleau, C. Mercier, SC 153 (Paris 1969), p. 260-262; Adv. haer. V, 23, 2: A. Rousseau, L. Doutreleau, C. Mercier, SC 153 (Paris 1969), p. 290-292; Dem. 11-17: L.-M. Froidevaux, SC 62 (Paris 1959), p. 48-58; Dem. 31-33: L.-M. Froidevaux, SC 62 (Paris 1959), p. 80-86; *Method. Olymp.*, Res. II, 1, 1: N. Bonwetsch, GCS 27 (Leipzig 1917), p. 329-330; Res. II, 2, 1: N. Bonwetsch, GCS 27 (Leipzig 1917), p. 331; Res. II, 2, 4: N. Bonwetsch, GCS 27 (Leipzig 1917), p. 331-332; Res. II, 6, 4: N. Bonwetsch, GCS 27 (Leipzig 1917), p. 340; Symp. III, 4-6: H. Musurillo, SC 95 (Paris 1963), p. 98-102.

[37] J. Vives, Pecado original y progreso evolutivo del hombre en Ireneo, Estudios Eclesiásticos 43 (1968) 564; cf. footnote 6.

[38] *Iren. Lugd.*, Adv. haer. V, 17, 1: A. Rousseau, L. Doutreleau, C. Mercier, SC 153 (Paris 1969), p. 220-224.

[39] A. Orbe, Antropologia de San Ireneo (Madrid 1969) 292-293.

[40] *Greg. Nyss.*, Diem lum.: E. Gebhardt, GNO IX (Leiden 1967), p. 241.

Methodius and Gregory) to pass from the detailed to the general perspective; from a person to human nature[41].

For Irenaeus and Methodius of Olympus the unity of human nature is a basis for participation of every individual in the first sin and its consequences. They both claim that every human being is somehow responsible for the first sin. Gregory uses similar fluidity of the language and stresses that all individuals participate in the consequences of the first sin by very fact that they are humans. The difference is that, first, I do not find in Gregory any trace of individual responsibility for the sin as such and, second, Gregory clearly states that it was human nature that committed the sin—there are no such statements either in Irenaeus or in Methodius. Although we need to remember that we do not have the originals of their writings. The translators into Latin (*Adversus haereses* by Irenaeus) and Old Church Slavonic (*De resurrectione* by Methodius) might have significantly changed the meaning of both writings when reading statements that were too shocking. Contemporary translators reveal the same tendency; for example, Hall usually translates ἡ ἀνθρωπίνη φύσις as "human race" in Gregory.

Looking for the roots of his synonymization of φύσις and οὐσία in Gregory I have found Alexander of Aphrodisias, who apparently treated φύσις and οὐσία as synonyms[42].

The rare expression καθόλου φύσις used by Gregory in *De opificio hominis*[43] appears only in several authors before: Galen[44], Dio Chrysostom[45], Alexander of Aphrodisias[46], Eusebius of Caesarea[47] and Themistius[48] although they do not refer it to nature as a unity/monad.

All of the above mentioned authors (including Irenaeus and Methodius) were from Asia Minor, except for Eusebius of Caesarea who was most probably

---

[41] Y. de Andia, Incorruptibilité et divinisation de l'homme selon Irénée de Lyon (Paris 1986) 118.

[42] *Alexander of Aphrodisias*, De anima: I. Bruns, Commentaria in Aristotelem Graeca, suppl. II/1 (Berlin 1887), p. 5.

[43] *Greg. Nyss.*, Op. hom. 22: PG 44, 205.

[44] *Galen*, De simplicium medicamentorum temperamentis ac facultatibus: C. G. Kühn, Opera omnia, vol. 11 (Leipzig 1826), p. 735.

[45] *Dio Chrysostom*, Orat. XII, 27: J. von Arnim, Quae exstant omnia, vol. 1 (Berlin 1893), p. 162.

[46] *Alexander of Aphrodisias*, In Aristotelis metaphysica commentaria: M. Hayduck (Berlin 1891), p. 267.

[47] *Eusebius of Caesarea*, Praeparatio evangelica III, 3, 19: K. Mras, GCS 43/1 (Berlin 1954), p. 115.

[48] *Themistius*, In Aristotelis libros de anima paraphrasis: R. Heinze, Commentaria in Aristotelem Graeca V/3 (Berlin 1899), p. 3.

from Syria. It seems that there could have been a kind of a philosophical way of speaking typical for Gregory's region.

2. Plotinus

Anyway, I think that Gregory must have been influenced by someone else and my prime suspect here is Plotinus (together with someone else from the Syrian Neoplatonic school, perhaps Iamblichus[49]). It is certain that Gregory must have known Plotinus' writings. It has been already noticed that the understanding of eternity as endless life in Gregory of Nyssa is a transformation of Plotinus' concept[50]. Moreover, Jean Daniélou showed that already in the (possibly his) first writing i.e. *De virginitate* Gregory certainly used Περὶ καλοῦ (*Enneades* I 6) and was influenced by Plotinus' doctrine of evil[51].

It is obvious that Gregory does not follow Plotinus in a systematic way; moreover, he polemicizes with some of his theories (e.g. metempsychosis), but there are some important features of Plotinus' philosophy that can help us understand Gregory better.

The relationship between the hypostasis Soul and individual souls in Plotinus on one hand and between human nature and individual humans in Gregory on the other seems to me parallel. "Plotinus argues that, in addition to all individual souls, including the World Soul, there exists a further soul, the so-called hypostasis Soul, which is not an individual soul. All individual souls, he claims, derive from this hypostasis Soul and are its parts"[52].

---

[49] Federico Fatti established the direct link between Neoplatonism from Asia Minor and the Cappadocian Fathers by showing that Eustathius of Sebastea, the master of Basil the Great, before he converted to Christianity had been Eustathius the Philosopher known from Eunapius of Sardes, F. Fatti, Eustazio di Sebaste, Eustazio filosofo: un'ipotesi sul destinatario di Bas. ep. 1 e sull'identità di Eunap. VS VI, 5, 1-6; 5; 8, 3-9, in: E. López-Tello García, B. S. Zorzi (ed.), Church, Society and Monasticism. Acts of the International Symposium, Rome, May 31-June 3, 2006 (Sankt Ottilien 2009) 443-473.

[50] D. L. Balás, Eternity and time in Gregory of Nyssa' Contra Eunomium, in: H. Dörrie, M. Altenburger, U. Schramm (ed.), Gregor von Nyssa und die Philosophie (Leiden 1976) 147-148; T. Stępień, The Understanding of Time and Eternity in the polemic between Eunomius, Basil the Great and Gregory of Nyssa, in: J. F. Finamore, D. A. Layne (ed.), Platonic Pathways. Selected Papers from the Fourteenth Annual Conference of the International Society for Neoplatonic Studies (The Prometheus Trust 2018) 158-160.

[51] J. Daniélou, Plotin et Grégoire de Nysse sur le mal, in: E. Cerulli (ed.), Plotino e il Neoplatonismo in Oriente e in Occidente: Atti del Convegno Internazionale (Roma, 5-9 ottobre 1970) (Roma 1974) 485-492.

[52] D. Caluori, Plotinus on the World Soul, in: Ch. Helmig (ed.), World Soul – Anima Mundi. On the Origins and Fortunes of a Fundamental Idea (Berlin – Boston 2020) 263; cf. L. P. Gerson, Plotinus (London – New York 1998) 54.

If this is how it is with the whole Soul [i.e. the hypostasis Soul] and the others, the whole [Soul] of which the others are parts, will not be the soul of anything but remain itself by itself[53].

Gregory's definition of nature as an indivisible monad that continually remains one even though it appears in plurality[54] is very close to the abovementioned concept of the hypostasis Soul that always remains one[55], but is at the same time one and many[56]. Alike Plotinus' hypostasis Soul, Gregory's human nature is somehow transcendent and immanent at the same time. Johannes Zachhuber calls it the immanent universal and explains: "The whole is both immanent and indivisible because it is not merely more than the sum total of its parts, it is, in Gregory's logic, something altogether different from them"[57]. In Gregory, the difference or the transcendence of human nature is moreover stressed by its temporal precedence in relation to individuals[58].

According to Armstrong, in Plotinus the process of outgoing is governed by the following principles, which I think in some aspects apply as well to the process of individuation of human nature in Gregory:

> (I) Spiritual being is essentially self-communicative and creative; there can be no limits to its activity; it must actualize all possibilities and bring into being everything that can in any degree be. (II) This process of going out, giving, illuminating, which produces the lower levels of being, leaves the higher unaffected and undiminished.

---

[53] *Plotinus*, Enn. IV 3, 2, 54–56: P. Henry, H.-R. Schwyzer, Plotinus with an English translation by A. H. Armstrong, vol. 4 (Cambridge MA 1984), p. 40, transl. D. Caluori, in: Plotinus on the World Soul, 266: Εἰ δὴ οὕτως ἐπὶ ψυχῆς τῆς τε ὅλης καὶ τῶν ἄλλων, οὐκ ἂν ἡ ὅλη, ἧς τὰ τοιαῦτα μέρη, ἔσται τινός, ἀλλὰ αὐτὴ ἀφ' ἑαυτῆς.

[54] *Greg. Nyss.*, Abl.: F. Müller, GNO III/1 (Leiden 1958), p. 41; transl. NPNF II, 5, p. 332 with alterations: "Nature [ἡ φύσις] is one, at union in itself [πρὸς ἑαυτὴν ἡνωμένη], and an absolutely indivisible monad [ἀδιάτμητος ἀκριβῶς μονάς], not capable of increase by addition or of diminution by subtraction, but it is the same being and continually remaining one [ἓν διαμένουσα] even though it appears in plurality, inseparable continuous, complete, and not divided with the individuals who participate in it."

[55] *Plotinus*, Enn. IV 3, 8, 54–60: P. Henry, H.-R. Schwyzer, Plotinus with an English translation by A. H. Armstrong, vol. 4 (Cambridge MA 1984), p. 60.

[56] *Plotinus*, Enn. IV 8, 3, 11–13: P. Henry, H.-R. Schwyzer, Plotinus with an English translation by A. H. Armstrong, vol. 4 (Cambridge MA 1984), p. 406; Enn. VI, 7, 8, 25–32: P. Henry, H.-R. Schwyzer, Plotinus with an English translation by A. H. Armstrong, vol. 7 (Cambridge MA 1988), p. 110.

[57] J. *Zachhuber*, Once again: Gregory of Nyssa on Universals, JTS NS 56/1 (2005) 83. As opposed to Balás who claimed that human nature is a sum of individuals, D. L. Balás, Plenitudo humanitatis, 123.

[58] M. *Przyszychowska*, The plenitude (πλήρωμα) of human nature according to Gregory of Nyssa, Eos. Commentarii Societatis Philologae Polonorum 104 (2017) 99–101.

(III) The product is always necessarily on a lower level of being than the producer; each stage in the outgoing is lower and weaker than the one before. Plotinus often expresses this progressive inferiority of product to producer in terms of decreasing degrees of unity[59].

In *In Hexaemeron* which is later than *De opificio hominis*, Gregory applies the pattern of double creation to the entire world. Here, he claims that what was created in the first creation exists δυνάμει and the created in the second one ἐνεργείᾳ[60]. Zachhuber[61] noted a parallel relationship between the Mind and its parts, the genera in Plotinus: the Intellect is prior to all actual (ἐνεργείᾳ) individual intellects, contains them in universality and they are, in turn, actually (ἐνεργείᾳ) what they are, and potentially (δυνάμει) the whole[62]. A similar relationship characterizes the Soul and individual souls. As Gerson explains:

> Instances of a Form are the 'same' as the universal, though 'posterior' to the Form. For example, a drawing of a house is, as image, posterior to the real house, though its proportions may be the same as those of the house. [...] Socrates is not an instance of the Form of Humanity, but the bearer of that instance. He is homonymously a man. The humanity in him is a synonymous image of the Form. A reference to the humanity in Socrates is a reference to a synonymous image; a reference to this man in all his particularity is a reference to an homonymous image[63].

There is no fall or sin of the Plotinus' hypostasis Soul, but Plotinus claims straightforwardly that it has its volitive dimension:

> But since there was a restlessly active nature [i.e., soul] which wanted [αὐτῆς βουλομένης] to control itself and be on its own, and chose to seek for more than its present state, this moved, and time moved with it; and so, always moving on to the "next" and the "after," and what is not the same, but one thing after another, we made a long stretch of our journey and constructed time as an image of eternity. For because soul had an unquiet power, which wanted [βουλομένης] to keep on transferring what it saw there to something else, it did not want the whole to be present to it all together[64].

---

[59] A. H. Armstrong, The Plotinian Doctrine of NOUS in Patristic Theology, VigChr 8 (1954) 234.
[60] Greg. Nyss., Hex.: H. R. Drobner, GNO IV/1 (Leiden – Boston 2009), p. 28.
[61] J. Zachhuber, Once again: Gregory of Nyssa on Universals, 97.
[62] Plotinus, Enn. VI 2, 20: P. Henry, H.-R. Schwyzer, Plotinus with an English translation by A. H. Armstrong, vol. 6 (Cambridge MA 1988), p. 164–168.
[63] L. P. Gerson, Plotinus, 90–91.
[64] Plotinus, Enn. III 7, 11, 14–22: P. Henry, H.-R. Schwyzer, Plotinus with an English translation by A. H. Armstrong, vol. 3 (Cambridge MA 1980), p. 338; transl. L. P. Gerson, in: L. P. Gerson, Plotinus, 106.

Individual souls are as if parts of the hypostasis Soul that wants to fulfill its necessary mission of individuation[65]. We find the same ambiguity of will and necessity in Gregory. Human nature has similar natural necessity of individuation that would have been realized independently of whether the first sin was committed or not—without the fall human nature would have generated individuals in the angelic way. But it also has a free will and is able to make its own choices.

I am far from claiming that Gregory copied anybody's theory one for one. Certainly, he created his own concept of human nature and its fall and there is nothing unusual in it. Even in what we use to call philosophical schools no pupil copied ideas of the master, being a student of someone included discussing, thinking and developing own theories. Besides, Gregory of Nyssa undoubtedly read philosophical sources from his Christian point of view which contained first of all the concept of creation and one God in three persons. Nevertheless, I think that looking for his theological and philosophical sources helps to understand his sometimes enigmatic statements.

---

[65] T. Stępień, *Czy dusza ludzka jest indywidualna? Kontrowersje wokół rozumienia duszy w starożytnym neoplatonizmie niechrześcijańskim*, Studia Philosophiae Christianae 48/1 (2012) 94.

Giulio Maspero and Ilaria Vigorelli, Rome (Italy)

Relational Ontology and the Syntactic Dimension of Sin in Gregory of Nyssa

I. Introduction: the Syntactic Approach

The topic of the original sin and its transmission in Gregory of Nyssa is not straightforward.[1] Walther Völker wrote that it is not clear whether or not this Father of the Church, called "the Father of Fathers" at the Second Council of Nicaea,[2] holds a doctrine on the original sin.[3] Lucas Francisco Mateo-Seco stated that the Bishop of Nyssa says nothing about its transmission.[4]

The thesis of the present contribution is that, in order to grasp these elements of Gregory's thought, one must take seriously a double tension that runs through his doctrine and that has sometimes been misclassified by contemporary scholars as incoherent.

In fact, Gregory's thought rests on a double dynamic tension: that between the beginning and the end and that between the social dimension and personal freedom. Some authors tend to read the writings of the bishop of Nyssa platonically, reducing everything to the beginning and the whole, as opposed to the end and the particular. This fails to grasp that this dual tension is irreducible, because it is an expression of the relational ontology of the Cappadocians. Indeed, in order to respond to Eunomius, they had to introduce a new principle

---

[1] See in general on the topic *M. Hauke*, Heilsverlust in Adam. Stationen griechischer Erbsündenlehre: Irenäus – Origenes – Kappadozier (Paderborn 1993) 572–692; *L. F. Mateo-Seco*, Estudios sobre la cristología de San Gregorio di Nisa (Pamplona 1978) 169–228; *E. V. McClear*, The Fall of Man and Original Sin in the Theology of Gregory of Nyssa, Theological Studies 9 (1948) 175–212; *V. Raduca*, Allotriosis. La chute et la restauration de l'homme selon saint Grégoire de Nysse (Fribourg 1985); and *J. Vives*, El pecado original en San Gregorio de Nisa, Estudios eclesiásticos 45 (1970) 203–235.
[2] Epiphanius the Deacon at the II Council of Nicea: G. D. Mansi, Sacrorum conciliorum nova et amplissima collectio, vol. 13 (Florentiae 1767), p. 293E; Ph. Labbé – G. Cossart, Sacrosancta concilia ad Regiam editionem exacta, vol. VII (Paris 1671), p. 477.
[3] Cf. *W. Völker*, Gregor von Nyssa als Mystiker (Wiesbaden 1955) 82.
[4] Cf. *L. F. Mateo-Seco*, Estudios sobre la cristología, 202.

of individuation, unheard of in classical metaphysics. The Persons of the Trinity, in fact, cannot be distinguished on the basis of a substantial difference, but only on the basis of the relation of origin (*schesis*). Because of the creation in the image and likeness and the correspondence between economy and immanence, this relational dimension is partly communicated to creation and to the human being in particular. Thus the relationship between beginning and end cannot be reduced to one of its terms, because it is an ontological relation. Just as there can be no opposition between the social and individual dimensions of the human being, because the identity of every human being is relational and connected to that of every other human being of all times. And this does not apply in a merely moral or physiological sense, but primarily ontological.

A tool that can help to grasp this dimension of Gregory's thought is the distinction between syntax and semantics. It has grammatical origins but takes on a further value, which can be applied to different scientific fields. In fact, if semantics is the science of the meanings that the different signifiers assume, syntax is concerned with the relationships between the signifiers (and therefore, as a consequence, also between the meanings). Semantics studies the value of signs, while syntax studies their relationships. A simple case can be that of a musical note, for example an A, which, written on the staff in the central octave, is a sign that corresponds to a precise frequency of sound, 440 Hz. Semantics, in general, deals with this correspondence. If, on the other hand, we consider a melody, then what counts is not so much the correspondence with the given sound, but the set of relationships between the different notes, so that the pitch can be raised or lowered to perform the music, but the melody itself does not actually change. Music is a language characterised by a very limited semantics, because the notes are few, so that it is all about syntax. Another example to cite could be the flag of a state (semantics) and its national anthem (syntax). Thus it is evident from what has been said that, as in grammar, semantics and syntax are always co-present and mutually related.

This is fundamental for understanding the question of original sin in Gregory of Nyssa. We risk, from the contemporary perspective, to approach it from an exclusively semantic, and not syntactic, key. What does this distinction mean? For us the question of original sin in Gregory can be played out anachronistically on the categories we have developed within the Middle Ages, that is, we can verify which representation among those we already know corresponds to Gregory. An example of this is the entry "Original sin" in *The Brill Dictionary of Gregory of Nyssa*.[5] That article was written by an extremely com-

---

[5] M. Hauke, Original sin, in: L. F. Mateo-Seco – G. Maspero (eds.), The Brill Dictionary on

petent scholar, Manfred Hauke, and is very useful. But its perspective should be complemented with the syntactic one, i.e. by an approach that reads the data of Gregory of Nyssa's thought in the light of the relationship with the theological elements within his thought, his tradition and his time.

An example may be useful: if we ask ourselves what the Greek Fathers thought of the axiom *extra ecclesiam nulla salus*, we may make an interesting discovery, because this approach is totally alien to their thought. In the case of Gregory of Nyssa, for example, we should speak of *extra humanitatem nulla salus*, because the human being, by turning in the opposite direction to the infinite source of life that is God, ceases to be a human being, as Maximus the Confessor explains interpreting the thought of the bishop of Nyssa.[6]

So what does a syntactical approach to the question of original sin mean in this Father of the Church? It means letting the (relational) categories proper to his thought guide our research. And these are extremely peculiar and syntactical, as we will show: apophaticism, the social dimension of human nature, the tunics of skins, *apatheia* and *epektasis*. In fact, these elements find their key to interpretation in the relation (*schesis*), a fundamental element of the metaphysical reshaping carried out by Gregory of Nyssa and the Cappadocians.[7] This means exploring the relational consequences on the human being, created in the image and likeness of the triune God, specifically analysed by Ilaria Vigorelli.[8]

The recourse to these categories proper to Gregory allows a syntactic approach to his doctrine on the original sin, overcoming the limits of a purely semantic approach. The latter is clearly impossible in a theological context marked methodologically by apophaticism, i.e. the affirmation that knowledge of God (and consequently that of the human being and the world) is irreducible to the purely linguistical dimension. The difference with respect to the identification between being and intelligible, as idea or form, in the Platonic-Aristotelian tradition is radical. For the bishop of Nyssa, in fact, concepts risk becoming idols without the syntactic, i.e. relational, dimension.[9] From such a perspective one discovers that the human being is not only defined by

---

Gregory of Nyssa (Leiden 2010) 556–558.
[6] Cf. *Maximus the Confessor*, Quaestiones, interrogationes et responsiones q. 19, I, 13: J. H. Declerck, CCG 10 (Turnhout 1982), p. 17–18.
[7] Cf. G. Maspero, The Trinity, in: M. Edwards (ed.), The Routledge Handbook of Early Christian Philosophy (London – New York 2021) 125–138.
[8] I. Vigorelli, La Relazione: Dio e l'uomo. Schesis e antropologia trinitaria in Gregorio di Nissa (Roma 2020).
[9] *Gregory of Nyssa*, De Vita Moysis II, 165, 4–9: H. Musurillo, GNO VII/1 (Leiden 1964), p. 87,23–88,5.

the beginning, but also by the end,[10] because the return to the beginning, the *apokatastasis*, is a return to a relational and dynamic state, and not an ideal and static one. This is about *isanghelia*, *apatheia* and *epektasis*, elements that converge in the movement of continuous growth in union with God for which the human being was created. It is precisely *epektasis* that is the way to relationally understand backwards original sin and its transmission, since these are precisely the negation of it.

II. The relation Adam-Christ

This leads us to note that, in Gregory's thought, the first Adam is defined by the second, that is, by Christ, not only in gnoseological terms, in the sense that the original sin prevents us from knowing God's true plan, but also in ontological terms, in the sense that, regardless of sin, the human being's full identity is given in Christ, the infinite source of the Father's Life. We were created in Him, therefore we are finite creatures created in a dynamic relational tension with the infinite.

A single text is sufficient to verify how, from the Christological and soteriological perspective, the causal arrow changes its direction:

> Perhaps one who has diligently meditated on the mystery would say with greater reason that the death did not occur because of the birth but, on the contrary, the birth was assumed in view of the death: for He who is for ever did not subject himself to bodily birth out of the need to live but to call us back from death to life.[11]

Freedom and *philanthropia* are the key to Gregory's thought, whose readings too often neglect the Christological and soteriological dimensions. Events are read from the end, from their *skopos*, without this making them determined and alien to freedom. Thus it is impossible to reduce everything platonically to the *arché*, or according to Aristotle's approach to the *telos*, but it is the relationship between the beginning and the end that must be taken into account.

---

[10] Monique Alexandre has shown that this approach was already present in the work of Origen. Cf. *M. Alexandre*, Protologie et eschatologie chez Grégoire de Nysse, in: U. Bianchi (ed.), Arché e Telos. L'antropologia di Origene e di Gregorio di Nissa. Analisi storico-religiosa (Milano 1981) 122–159.

[11] *Gregory of Nyssa*, Or. cat. 32: J. Srawley, The Catechetical Oration of Gregory of Nyssa (Cambridge 1903), p. 115–116: τάχα δ' ἄν τις δι' ἀκριβείας καταμαθὼν τὸ μυστήριον εὐλογώτερον εἴποι μὴ διὰ τὴν γένεσιν συμβεβηκέναι τὸν θάνατον, ἀλλὰ τὸ ἔμπαλιν τοῦ θανάτου χάριν παραληφθῆναι τὴν γένεσιν· οὐ γὰρ τοῦ ζῆσαι δεόμενος ὁ ἀεὶ ὢν τὴν σωματικὴν ὑποδύεται γένεσιν, ἀλλ' ἡμᾶς ἐπὶ τὴν ζωὴν ἐκ τοῦ θανάτου ἀνακαλούμενος. All the translations are by the authors.

A clear example of this relation is Gregory's comment on Rom 5:12, where, as highlighted by Lucas Francisco Mateo-Seco, the bishop of Nyssa follows the line of Irenaeus and Athanasius, replacing the Pauline reference to Adam in terms of 'one man' (δι' ἑνὸς ἀνθρώπου) with the expression 'the first man':[12]

> Since by the disobedience of the *first* man (τοῦ πρώτου ἀνθρώπου) death came in, for this reason by the obedience of the second man it is cast out; because of this the latter becomes obedient unto death, that through obedience the evil which came from disobedience might be healed, and through the resurrection from the dead death might be annihilated, that death which came with disobedience. The annihilation of death, in fact, is the resurrection of the human being from the dead.[13]

As in Gen 1:5, the difference between *one* and *first* is fundamental. In the LXX, in fact, the Hebrew term meaning *one*, and not *first*, is precisely retained (ἡμέρα μία) translating the beginning of creation. The existence of the second day cannot be deduced from that of day one. On the other hand, the Father is the *first* Person of the Trinity, because His identity is related to that of the Son and the Spirit. This implies that the *first* man is defined, in a similar way to the Trinitarian unity, by his relation to the second. The line of thought is: Adam's free disobedience caused death to enter history and this was transmitted to all, until Christ freely assumed it, in such a way that his free obedience restores life. It is a back-and-forth movement in history, between the beginning and the end, between announcement and fulfilment.

Without Christ we cannot truly know the human being according to the divine creation, because we are slaves to death and we have become dark, as the bride in the Canticle says. She explains that no one should attribute the cause of her darkness to the Creator, as its cause is 'the free will of each one' (τὴν ἑκάστου προαίρεσιν). She was not created black, but was later clothed with the dark image (εἴδει):[14]

---

[12] L. F. *Mateo-Seco*, Estudios sobre la cristología, 177–179.
[13] *Gregory of Nyssa*, Antirrheticus adversus Apollinarium: F. Müller, GNO III/1 (Leiden 1958), p. 160,27–161,5: ἐπειδὴ γὰρ διὰ τῆς παρακοῆς τοῦ πρώτου ἀνθρώπου ὁ θάνατος εἰσῆλθε, τούτου χάριν διὰ τῆς ὑπακοῆς τοῦ δευτέρου ἀνθρώπου ἐξοικίζεται. διὰ τοῦτο ὑπήκοος μέχρι θανάτου γίνεται, ἵνα διὰ μὲν τῆς ὑπακοῆς τὸ ἐκ τῆς παρακοῆς θεραπεύσῃ πλημμέλημα, διὰ δὲ τῆς ἐκ νεκρῶν ἀναστάσεως τὸν συνεισελθόντα τῇ παρακοῇ θάνατον ἐξαφανίσῃ. ἀφανισμὸς γάρ ἐστι θανάτου ἡ ἐκ θανάτου τοῦ ἀνθρώπου ἀνάστασις.
[14] *Gregory of Nyssa*, In Canticum canticorum: H. Langerbeck, GNO VI (Leiden 1985), p. 50,5–16.

Temptation, throwing out a fiery heat through deception, expelled the first germ (βλάστην) still imperfect and rootless, and before it had acquired any habit of good, and had taken root deep down through cultivation, drying up immediately, through disobedience made the green and fruitful image (εἶδος) black by means of the heat.[15]

The reference to 'first germ' (βλάστη) is particularly important, because it shows the dynamic dimension of the image, of the form (εἶδος). The original state was not simply static, but was a condition of continuous growth, similar to that of a child, as Irenaeus says.[16]

The original sin introduced death and therefore blackness, eradicating, withering away, this nascent life. In relational terms, it is precisely the connection with the source that was severed by sin.

It should be noted that Gregory of Nyssa's *Homilies on the Song of Songs* have a double *Sitz im Leben*, because they were preached in Nyssa during Lent, following the Jewish tradition of reading this book in preparation for Passover, and were then revised and sent to the community of Olympias. The reference to Lent is important because it reveals that this doctrine is addressed to every Christian, as it is linked to baptism.

This is reinforced by the observation that the Adam-Christ relationship is also paralleled by the relationship between Eve and Mary. The tree of paradise and the tree of the cross typologically correspond to each other:

> Through a man death, and through a man salvation. The first fell into sin, the second lifted up that which had fallen. The woman is defended by the woman. The former opened the way for sin, the latter served the entrance of righteousness. The first followed the serpent's advice, this one offered Him who overcame the serpent and gave birth to the author of light. The first introduced sin by means of a tree; this one, on the contrary, introduced goodness by means of a tree. I refer to the tree of the cross, whose fruit is always luxuriant and comes to be immortal life for those who taste it.[17]

---

[15] *Gregory of Nyssa*, In Canticum canticorum: GNO VI, p. 51,13–19: ὁ δὲ πειρασμὸς τὸν φλογώδη καύσωνα δι' ἀπάτης ἐπιβαλὼν ἁπαλὴν ἔτι καὶ ἄρριζον τὴν πρώτην βλάστην κατέλαβε καί, πρὶν ἕξιν τινὰ τοῦ ἀγαθοῦ κτήσασθαι καὶ διὰ τῆς τῶν λογισμῶν γεωργίας δοῦναι ταῖς ῥίζαις τόπον ἐπὶ τὸ βάθος, εὐθὺς διὰ τῆς παρακοῆς ἀποξηράνας τὸ χλοερόν τε καὶ εὐθαλὲς εἶδος διὰ τῆς καύσεως μέλαν ἐποίησεν.

[16] Cf. *Irenaeus of Lyon*, Epideixis 21.

[17] *Gregory of Nyssa*, Oratio in diem natalem Christi: F. Mann – E. Rhein – G. Heil, GNO X/2 (Leiden 1996), p. 265,3–13: δι' ἀνθρώπου θάνατος, δι' ἀνθρώπου ἡ σωτηρία. ὁ πρῶτος εἰς ἁμαρτίαν ἔπεσεν, ὁ δεύτερος τὸν πεπτωκότα ἀνώρθωσεν. ἀπολελόγηται ὑπὲρ τῆς γυναικὸς ἡ γυνή. ἡ πρώτη τῇ ἁμαρτίᾳ τὴν εἴσοδον ἔδωκεν, αὕτη δὲ τῇ εἰσόδῳ τῆς δικαιοσύνης ὑπηρετήσατο. ἐκείνη τοῦ ὄφεως τὴν συμβουλὴν ἐπεσπάσατο, αὕτη τὸν ἀναιρέτην τοῦ ὄφεως παρεστήσατο. ἐκείνη διὰ τοῦ ξύλου τὴν ἁμαρτίαν εἰσήνεγκεν, αὕτη διὰ τοῦ ξύλου τὸ ἀγαθὸν ἀντεισήνεγκε. ξύλον γὰρ ἦν ὁ σταυρός. ὁ δὲ τοῦ ξύλου τούτου καρπὸς ἀειθαλὴς καὶ ἀμάραντος ζωὴ τοῖς γενομένοις γίνεται.

The restoration of justice is expressed in terms of both plant and human generation, echoing the sense of the βλάστη, because the original state of justice is a dynamic growth, which has been interrupted. This is why it is also difficult to grasp semantically how the transmission of original sin is understood by Gregory. In fact, it is not really a 'transmission', but the absence of transmission of the generative relationship with life. The syntactic perspective is essential, as also demonstrated by Gregory's continuous and profound search for correspondences.

III. Ontology of Freedom

It is essential to recall that in Gregory's ontology the Trinity is the only eternal and infinite nature, metaphysically exceeding human thinking. This is why the transmission of original sin is perceived in the antithesis between what was to be transmitted in the original dynamic of limitless growth, based on the relationship with the divine source, and the lack that is transmitted after the fall:

> But life is opposed to death, power to weakness, blessing to curse, freedom of speech to shame, and all good things to the contrary. That is why mankind now finds itself in the present evils, since that beginning provided the cue for the conclusion we know.[18]

The process we now know is determined by that beginning which introduced the transmission of the lack of life (so also the clash with its finitude), that is, of death, with the transmission of the lack of power and freedom and so on. It is as if a finite dynamic took the place of an infinite one, i.e. as if a static dynamic replaced a real dynamic. Note that freedom emerges here precisely as a relation to the infinite source.

In fact, freedom, which is the exact opposite of slavery to death, is in the human being linked to the desire for immortality, to the tension towards the infinite, which we possess because we were created in the image and likeness of God:

---

[18] *Gregory of Nyssa*, Or. cat. 6: J. Srawley, p. 37: ἀντίκειται δὲ τῇ ζωῇ μὲν ὁ θάνατος, ἡ ἀσθένεια δὲ τῇ δυνάμει, τῇ εὐλογίᾳ δὲ ἡ κατάρα, τῇ παρρησίᾳ δὲ ἡ αἰσχύνη, καὶ πᾶσι τοῖς ἀγαθοῖς τὰ κατὰ τὸ ἐναντίον νοούμενα. διὰ τοῦτο ἐν τοῖς παροῦσι κακοῖς ἐστὶ νῦν τὸ ἀνθρώπινον, τῆς ἀρχῆς ἐκείνης τοῦ τοιούτου τέλους τὰς ἀφορμὰς παρασχούσης.

So also man was created in order to be able to enjoy the goods of God; it was necessary, therefore, that he should have in his nature something connatural (τι συγγενὲς) to Him in whom he participated. For this reason he was adorned with life, with logos, with wisdom, with all the prerogatives that are appropriate to God, so that through each of these properties he might feel the desire to reach that which is related to him (πρὸς τὸ οἰκεῖον τὴν ἐπιθυμίαν ἔχοι). Since, therefore, among the prerogatives of the divine nature there is also eternity, it was absolutely necessary that not even eternity should be lacking in the constitution of our nature, but that it should possess immortality, so that, by the power reposed in it, it might know Him who is superior to it and be desirous of divine eternity (ἐν ἐπιθυμίᾳ τῆς θείας ἀϊδιότητος).[19]

The expression πρὸς τὸ οἰκεῖον is constructed in relational form, since πρὸς τι is the technical formula for relation in the Aristotelian tradition. Now, while the divine character of the soul and the impassibility of the body, as well as the eternity of life, are lost in the transmission of the original sin,[20] freedom is maintained:

For He who created the human being so that this might share in His good things, and who placed within human nature an instinct for all good things, so that at every opportunity its impulse might turn towards that which is similar (πρὸς τὸ ὅμοιον), would not have deprived human beings of the most beautiful and the most precious of goods, that is to say the grace of not being subject to any lord and of having free will (ἀδέσποτον καὶ αὐτεξούσιον). If a necessity were to dominate human life, then the image of God would be false at least in that respect, because it would have become alien and different from the archetype.[21]

---

[19] *Gregory of Nyssa*, Or. cat. 5: J. Srawley, p. 23-24: οὕτως οὖν καὶ τὸν ἄνθρωπον ἐπὶ τῇ τῶν θείων ἀγαθῶν ἀπολαύσει γενόμενον ἔδει τι συγγενὲς ἐν τῇ φύσει πρὸς τὸ μετεχόμενον ἔχειν. διὰ τοῦτο καὶ ζωῇ καὶ λόγῳ καὶ σοφίᾳ καὶ πᾶσι τοῖς θεοπρεπέσιν ἀγαθοῖς κατεκοσμήθη, ὡς ἂν δι' ἑκάστου τούτων πρὸς τὸ οἰκεῖον τὴν ἐπιθυμίαν ἔχοι. ἐπεὶ οὖν ἓν τῶν περὶ τὴν θείαν φύσιν ἀγαθῶν καὶ ἡ ἀϊδιότης ἐστίν, ἔδει πάντως μηδὲ τούτου τὴν κατασκευὴν εἶναι τῆς φύσεως ἡμῶν ἀπόκληρον, ἀλλ' ἔχειν ἐν ἑαυτῇ τὸ ἀθάνατον, ὡς ἂν διὰ τῆς ἐγκειμένης δυνάμεως γνωρίζοι τε τὸ ὑπερκείμενον καὶ ἐν ἐπιθυμίᾳ τῆς θείας ἀϊδιότητος εἴη.
[20] Cf. *Gregory of Nyssa*, Or. cat. 5: J. Srawley, p. 24-25.
[21] *Gregory of Nyssa*, Or. cat. 5: J. Srawley, p. 26: ὁ γὰρ ἐπὶ μετουσίᾳ τῶν ἰδίων ἀγαθῶν ποιήσας τὸν ἄνθρωπον καὶ πάντων αὐτῷ τῶν καλῶν τὰς ἀφορμὰς ἐγκατασκευάσας τῇ φύσει, ὡς ἂν δι' ἑκάστου καταλλήλως πρὸς τὸ ὅμοιον ἡ ὄρεξις φέροιτο, οὐκ ἂν τοῦ καλλίστου τε καὶ τιμιωτάτου τῶν ἀγαθῶν ἀπεστέρησε, λέγω δὴ τῆς κατὰ τὸ ἀδέσποτον καὶ αὐτεξούσιον χάριτος. εἰ γάρ τις ἀνάγκη τῆς ἀνθρωπίνης ἐπεστάτει ζωῆς, διεψεύσθη ἂν ἡ εἰκὼν κατ' ἐκεῖνο τὸ μέρος, ἀλλοτριωθεῖσα τῷ ἀνομοίῳ πρὸς τὸ ἀρχέτυπον.

Once again the relational dimension appears through the expression πρὸς τὸ ὅμοιον which takes up the πρὸς τὸ οἰκεῖον of the previous text. Here we touch a climax in the thought of Gregory of Nyssa, because freedom is both the indestructible trace of being the image of God in the human being, and the origin of evil, when it turns not to what is connatural, but detaches itself from the beautiful (ἀπὸ τοῦ καλοῦ). Evil comes, in fact, 'from within the human being' (τὸ κακὸν ἔνδοθεν), that is, from his turning not towards the infinite, but towards the finite. The key element, therefore, is relationship.[22] It is a matter of syntaxis and not of semantics for sin, being a participation with nothingness, can only be perceived as lack, therefore only in relation, in contact, with the infinite source that is Christ, as shadows are perceived only through light.

On a purely semantic level, however, this dual role of freedom, if not read from the perspective of relationship, may seem inconsistent. Instead, it is only paradoxical, in the literal sense of contrary to *doxa*, to opinion, because opinion can only grasp what is universal, not the personal and therefore relational dimension. *Doxa* grasps necessity, not freedom with the uniqueness that flows from it. In fact, the will has a constitutive ontological dimension since the human being becomes what he chooses,[23] so we are somehow our own parents through our *proairesis*, as Gregory explains with a very powerful metaphor.[24]

The point is fundamental because the will thus establishes a relationship which, if it is directed towards evil, generates a communion with evil itself, that is, with the absence of being and of life. Gregory explains this in his exegesis of Song 1:15.17. He says that in order to purify the gold one introduces it several times into the fire. In the beginning human nature was pure and shining gold, because of its resemblance to pure Good, then mixing with evil (τῇ ἐπιμιξίᾳ τῆς κακίας) caused it to lose this state and made it dark. That is why, as we have seen, the bride from the beginning in the Canticle is called black. And God brings her back to her original beauty, which Gregory reads in the very verses commented upon, where it is said that the Bridegroom attracted the bride back to authentic beauty (τὴν ἐπανάληψιν τῷ προσεγγίσαι πάλιν τῷ ἀληθινῷ κάλλει). The loss of beauty was in fact due to the association with evil (γειτνιάσει τῆς κακίας), which had distanced it from the beauty of the archetype (τοῦ ἀρχετύπου κάλλους).[25]

Thus, in the light of the Bridegroom's gaze, we can understand original sin

---

[22] *Gregory of Nyssa*, Or. cat. 5: J. Srawley, p. 27.
[23] Cf. *Gregory of Nyssa*, In Canticum canticorum: GNO VI, p. 102,3-6.
[24] Cf. *Gregory of Nyssa*, De vita Moysis 2, 3: GNO VII/1, p. 34.
[25] Cf. *Gregory of Nyssa* In Canticum canticorum: GNO VI, p. 100,2-102,3.

and its transmission in Gregory of Nyssa's terms, by contrast and therefore syntactically. Freedom causes a communion with evil, with nothingness:

> Therefore, since our freedom (προαιρέσεως) is constituted in such a way as to be able to dispose ourselves to assume the form (συσχηματίζεσθαι) of what we want, the Word rightly says to the Bride in her new glory: 'You are close to me because you have refused communion with evil (τῆς τοῦ κακοῦ κοινωνίας), and approaching the beauty of the Archetype, you have become beautiful, having taken on my appearance like a mirror'. Indeed, the human being is rightly compared to a mirror because of the possibility of being transformed according to the reflections of his choices (προαιρέσεων).[26]

The expression ἡ τοῦ κακοῦ κοινωνία is typical of Gregory[27] and can be considered one of the most effective synthetic formulations of his doctrine of the transmission of original sin. Human free will can be associated with nothingness, in such a way that the human beings are born in a condition of communion with evil, in society with it, which is a real lack of being. We come to the light turned towards darkness, although we are made for light, as our desire testifies. The relational and syntactic dimension of the bishop of Nyssa's conception is highlighted here.

So the very relationship between the Bridegroom and the bride shows how the dimension of the person and existence is essential to grasp the transmission of the original sin, which is the propagation of an absence, a lack, that is, of something that does *exist*, but *is* not. Evil, in fact, for Gregory, in tune also with the Neo-Platonic tradition, is the absence of good, just as darkness is the absence of light.

IV. *Apatheia–Epektasis*

The primacy of freedom is so strong and radical in Gregory that he states that the devil could only enslave man through deception, driving him to be a murderer and killer of himself (φονέα τε καὶ αὐτόχειρα),[28] since he was:

---

[26] *Gregory of Nyssa*, In Canticum canticorum: GNO VI, p. 103,15–104,4: οὕτω τοίνυν ἐχούσης ἡμῶν τῆς προαιρέσεως, ὡς κατ' ἐξουσίαν ἔχειν ὅπερ ἂν ἐθέλῃ τούτῳ συσχηματίζεσθαι, καλῶς φησι πρὸς τὴν ὡραϊσθεῖσαν ὁ λόγος, ὅτι ἀποστᾶσα μὲν τῆς τοῦ κακοῦ κοινωνίας ἐμοὶ προσήγγισας, πλησιάσασα δὲ τῷ ἀρχετύπῳ κάλλει καὶ αὐτὴ καλὴ γέγονας οἷόν τι κάτοπτρον τῷ ἐμῷ χαρακτῆρι ἐμμορφωθεῖσα· κατόπτρῳ γὰρ ἔοικεν ὡς ἀληθῶς τὸ ἀνθρώπινον κατὰ τὰς τῶν προαιρέσεων ἐμφάσεις μεταμορφούμενον.

[27] See also *Gregory of Nyssa*, In inscriptiones Psalmorum: J. McDonough, GNO V (Leiden 1986), p. 122,26–27.

[28] *Gregory of Nyssa*, Or. cat. 6: J. Srawley, p. 36.

Fortified with the divine blessing (διὰ τῆς θείας εὐλογίας) and constituted in sublime dignity. He had been placed to reign over the earth and everything on it: he was beautiful, for he was the image (ἀπεικόνισμα) of exemplary beauty; impassible (ἀπαθὴς), for he was a copy of the impassible one (τοῦ γὰρ ἀπαθοῦς μίμημα); he was full of confidence (παρρησίας), as befits one who speaks pleasantly face to face with God.[29]

Here *apatheia* is revealed as a central concept. The *chrêsis* that Gregory develops of this first Aristotelian and then Stoic concept is extremely significant. It is not mere absence of passions, but consists in the tension of desire towards the authentic infinite source. The bishop of Nyssa's *apatheia* is, therefore, profoundly dynamic and consists in never ceasing to desire the beautiful and the infinite, in not turning away from the source. And this *apatheia* is at the heart of being created in the image and likeness of God, who is *Apatheia*.

This allows us to grasp in what sense the original state of the human being, before the fall, was that of the angels.[30] In semantic terms, one would immediately deduce a heavenly condition of a static type, because according to the theological categories developed in the Middle Ages, angels contemplate God and are *in patria*. But in Gregory's theological syntax the picture is quite different, as his description of Macrina reveals:

> And it seemed to me that she [Macrina] no longer behaved like human beings, but as if an angel had providentially taken on a human form, an angel who did not have any relationship and affinity with life in the flesh and whose thought in no way was unlikely to remain in impassibility (ἐν ἀπαθείᾳ), insofar as the flesh does not pull it down toward the passions that characterise it. Thus, it seems to me that she showed to everyone that divine and pure love for the invisible Bridegroom, whom she harboured hidden in the depths of her soul, and that she made known to all the disposition (διάθεσιν) that she carried in her heart to cast herself towards the One she desired (ποθούμενον) in order to be with Him free from the constraints of the body as soon as possible. In fact, her haste (δρόμος) was indeed directed as at a lover (ἐραστήν), without any other pleasures of life being able to divert her gaze.[31]

---

[29] Gregory of Nyssa, Or. cat. 6: J. Srawley, p. 36: ἐπειδὴ γὰρ διὰ τῆς θείας εὐλογίας δυναμωθεὶς ὁ ἄνθρωπος ὑψηλὸς μὲν ἦν τῷ ἀξιώματι· βασιλεύειν γὰρ ἐτάχθη τῆς γῆς τε καὶ τῶν ἐπ' αὐτῆς πάντων· καλὸς δὲ τὸ εἶδος· ἀπεικόνισμα γὰρ τοῦ ἀρχετύπου ἐγεγόνει κάλλους· ἀπαθὴς δὲ τὴν φύσιν· τοῦ γὰρ ἀπαθοῦς μίμημα ἦν· ἀνάπλεως δὲ παρρησίας, αὐτῆς κατὰ πρόσωπον τῆς θείας ἐμφανείας κατατρυφῶν.

[30] Gregory of Nyssa, De opificio hominis 17: PG 44, 188D.

[31] Gregory of Nyssa, Vita sanctae Macrinae 22, 26–39: W. Jaeger – J. P. Cavarnos – V. W. Callahan, GNO VIII/1 (Leiden 1986), p. 396,1–4: οὐκέτι μοι ἐδόκει τῶν ἀνθρωπίνων εἶναι, ἀλλ' οἷον ἀγγέλου τινὸς οἰκονομικῶς ἀνθρωπίνην ὑπελθόντος μορφήν, ᾧ μηδεμιᾶς οὔσης πρὸς τὸν ἐν σαρκὶ βίον συγγενείας ἢ οἰκειώσεως οὐδὲν ἀπεικὸς ἐν ἀπαθείᾳ τὴν διάνοιαν μένειν, μὴ καθελκούσης τῆς

The language is evidently Platonic. The *De anima et resurrectione* is known as the Christian *Phaedo*.³² It would perhaps also deserve the name Christian *Symposium*, because the theme is desire. Gregory's question to his sister is whether there will be desire once one is united to God. And here it appears the "impassible passion" (*apathes to pathos*)³³ which is the core of *epektasis*.³⁴

This consists in a *diathesis*, that is, in the condition of being turned from within one's own finite limits towards the infinite source. This is the very existential condition (*katastasis*) of the angels, which Macrina already experiences in her earthly and material life. And this *diathesis* is essentially dynamic:

> In fact, since it was announced that the life after the resurrection will be similar [ὅμοιον] to the condition (καταστάσει) of the angels—and the One who announces it does not lie—, it would be proper that even life in the world would be a preparation for the life we hope for after it, in such a way that those who live in the flesh and in the field of the world do not lead a life according to the flesh nor configure themselves to this world, but practice, in anticipation, the life they long for during their life in this world. Thus the bride inspires in the souls of those who follow her a confirmation, by means of a vow, that their life in this field will be directed at contemplating the Powers, imitating the angelic purity through impassibility (ἀπαθείας). In fact, just as love (ἀγάπης) becomes more and more kindled, that is, is lifted up and, with addition, grows always toward the better, it is said that the good will of God is carried

---

σαρκὸς πρὸς τὰ ἴδια πάθη. διὰ τοῦτό μοι ἐδόκει τὸν θεῖον ἐκεῖνον καὶ καθαρὸν ἔρωτα τοῦ ἀοράτου νυμφίου, ὃν ἐγκεκρυμμένον εἶχεν ἐν τοῖς τῆς ψυχῆς ἀπορρήτοις τρεφόμενον, ἔκδηλον ποιεῖν τότε τοῖς παροῦσι καὶ δημοσιεύειν τὴν ἐν καρδίᾳ διάθεσιν τῷ ἐπείγεσθαι πρὸς τὸν ποθούμενον, ὡς ἂν διὰ τάχους σὺν αὐτῷ γένοιτο τῶν δεσμῶν ἐκλυθεῖσα τοῦ σώματος. τῷ ὄντι γὰρ ὡς πρὸς ἐραστὴν ὁ δρόμος ἐγίνετο, οὐδενὸς ἄλλου τῶν κατὰ τὸν βίον ἡδέων πρὸς ἑαυτὸ τὸν ὀφθαλμὸν ἐπιστρέφοντος.

³² Cf. *C. Apostolopoulos*, Phaedo Christianus: Studien zur Verbindung und Abwägung zwischen dem platonischen Phaidon und dem Dialog Gregors von Nyssa Über die Seele (Frankfurt am Main 1986); *M. Pellegrino*, Il platonismo di S. Gregorio Nisseno nel dialogo "Intorno all'anima e alla risurrezione", Rivista di Filosofia Neoscolastica 30 (1938) 437–474.

³³ Cf. *Gregory of Nyssa*, In Canticum canticorum: GNO VI, p. 23,10. On this topic, see *J. Daniélou*, Platonisme et théologie mystique. Doctrine spirituelle de saint Grégoire de Nysse (Paris 1944) 92–103 and 201–207.

³⁴ On this fundamental topic of Gregory's thought see: *T. Alexopoulos*, Das unendliche Sichausstrecken (Epektasis) zum Guten bei Gregor von Nyssa und Plotin. Eine vergleichende Untersuchung, ZAC 10 (2007) 302–312; *J. Daniélou*, Platonisme et théologie mystique (Paris 1953) 291–307; *E. Ferguson*, Progress in perfection: Gregory of Nyssa's Vita Moysis, StPatr 14 (1976) 307–314; *L. F. Mateo-Seco*, ¿Progreso o inmutabilidad en la visión beatífica? Apuntes de la historia de la Teología, ScrTh 29 (1997) 13–39; *O. Sferlea*, On the Interpretation of the Theory of Perpetual Progress (epektasis). Taking into Account the Testimony of Eastern Monastic Tradition, RHE 109 (2014) 564–587.

out in heaven as on earth because the impassibility of the angels is realised in us as well.[35]

The text is exceptional, because it shows all the syntactic power of Gregory's thought, which does not refer to an ideal dimension, as Platonic semantics did, but shows the relational and real contact with the Divine that takes place in bodily life through human freedom and desire and which, paradoxically, identifies *apatheia* with *epektasis*, that is, with the movement of unlimited growth in participation in the infinite life of God.

This is a rush *from glory to glory*,[36] which arouses the amazement of the angels themselves, who cannot know the triune God with their limited thoughts of creatures, however purely spiritual, but are astonished to see God himself reflected in the Bride. Thus between the human beings and the angels that communion which had been disturbed by original sin is re-established, a communion in movement, in desire, in being directed towards the unlimited source of the gift of being:

> Rendered more divine and transformed by the beautiful change into a higher glory with respect to the glory she [the Bride] had, in such a way as to inspire awe in the choir of angels surrounding the Bridegroom who together address to her the astonished greeting "You have ravished my heart, our sister and bride" (Song 4:9). In fact, having obtained impassibility, this very condition of impassibility, which shines both in her and in the angels, introduces her into kinship and fraternity with the incorporeal beings.[37]

---

[35] *Gregory of Nyssa*, In Canticum canticorum: GNO VI, p. 134,9–135,6: ἐπειδὴ γὰρ τὸν μετὰ τὴν ἀνάστασιν βίον ὅμοιον ἐπήγγελται τῇ ἀγγελικῇ καταστάσει [τῶν ἀνθρώπων] γενήσεσθαι (ἀψευδὴς δὲ ὁ ἐπαγγειλάμενος), ἀκόλουθον ἂν εἴη καὶ τὴν ἐν τῷ κόσμῳ ζωὴν πρὸς τὴν ἐλπιζομένην μετὰ ταῦτα παρασκευάζεσθαι, ὥστε ἐν σαρκὶ ζῶντας καὶ ἐν τῷ ἀγρῷ τοῦ κόσμου διάγοντας μὴ κατὰ σάρκα ζῆν μηδὲ συσχηματίζεσθαι τῷ κόσμῳ τούτῳ, ἀλλὰ προμελετᾶν τὸν ἐλπιζόμενον βίον διὰ τῆς ἐν τῷ κόσμῳ ζωῆς. διὰ τοῦτο τὴν διὰ τοῦ ὅρκου βεβαίωσιν ἐμποιεῖται ταῖς ψυχαῖς τῶν μαθητευομένων ἡ νύμφη, ὥστε τὴν ζωὴν αὐτῶν τὴν ἐν τῷ ἀγρῷ τούτῳ κατορθουμένην πρὸς τὰς δυνάμεις βλέπειν, μιμουμένην διὰ τῆς ἀπαθείας τὴν ἀγγελικὴν καθαρότητα· οὕτω γὰρ ἐγειρομένης τῆς ἀγάπης καὶ ἐξεγειρομένης (ὅπερ ἐστὶν ὑψουμένης τε καὶ ἀεὶ διὰ προσθήκης πρὸς τὸ μεῖζον ἐπαυξομένης) τὸ ἀγαθὸν εἶπε θέλημα τοῦ θεοῦ τελειοῦσθαι ὡς ἐν οὐρανῷ καὶ ἐπὶ γῆς τῆς ἀγγελικῆς καὶ ἐν ἡμῖν ἀπαθείας κατορθουμένης.

[36] Cf. *Gregory of Nyssa*, De perfectione: GNO VIII/1, p. 213,20–214,6. See on this the introduction in J. Daniélou – H. Musurillo, From glory to glory (New York 1979).

[37] *Gregory of Nyssa*, In Canticum canticorum: GNO VI, p. 253,15–254,4: μεταποιηθεῖσα πρὸς τὸ θειότερον καὶ ἀπὸ τῆς δόξης ἐν ᾗ ἦν πρὸς τὴν ἀνωτέραν δόξαν μεταμορφωθεῖσα διὰ τῆς ἀγαθῆς ἀλλοιώσεως, ὡς θαῦμα γενέσθαι τῷ περὶ τὸν νυμφίον τῶν ἀγγέλων χορῷ καὶ πάντας εὐφήμως πρὸς αὐτὴν τὴν θαυμαστικὴν ταύτην προέσθαι φωνὴν ὅτι Ἐκαρδίωσας ἡμᾶς, ἀδελφὴ ἡμῶν νύμφη· ὁ γὰρ τῆς ἀπαθείας χαρακτὴρ ὁμοίως ἐπιλάμπων αὐτῇ τε καὶ τοῖς ἀγγέλοις εἰς τὴν τῶν ἀσωμάτων αὐτὴν ἄγει συγγένειάν τε καὶ ἀδελφότητα τὴν ἐν σαρκὶ τὸ ἀπαθὲς κατορθώσασαν.

In this proposal for a syntactic reading of the transmission of the original sin in Gregory, the identification of *apatheia* and *epektasis* is fundamental, because sin consists precisely in the denial of this dynamic condition. The core of Gregory's approach is that the human being was created for the *koinonia* with the angels in the *epektasis* but through the deceit of the devil man killed himself and ended up in the *koinonia* with evil.

V. Syntactic Unity

This is expressed by Gregory through the beautiful biblical image of the tunic of skins, which translate precisely that communion with evil that is typical of the thought of the bishop of Nyssa:

> Well then, there is a sort of link (σύνδεσίς τις), a union (κοινωνία), between the soul and the body on the one hand, and the passions that arise as a result of sin on the other, and there is a certain analogy (τις ἀναλογία) between the death of the body and the death of the soul. For just as in the flesh we call being separated from the sensible life "death", so also for the soul death is, in our opinion, separation from the true life. Since, therefore, there is just one way for the body and the soul to be in communion, as has been said, to evil (ἡ τοῦ κακοῦ κοινωνία), inasmuch as wickedness comes into action by passing through the one and the other, for this reason, then, death, as dissolution produced by the fact that the tunic of dead skins (τῶν νεκρῶν δερμάτων) has been placed over us, does not touch the soul itself. How, indeed, could that which has not been composed dissolve?[38]

Gregory's reasoning is straightforward: both the soul and the body, through the choice of the will, assume a communion with evil, therefore with death, which for the body is physical while for the soul it is eternal, because the separation concerns the very source of life. The theme of the tunics of hide[39]

---

[38] *Gregory of Nyssa*, Or. cat. 8,68-79: E. Mühlenberg, GNO III/4 (Leiden 1996), p. 30: ἐπειδὴ δὲ σύνδεσίς τις καὶ κοινωνία τῶν κατὰ ἁμαρτίαν παθημάτων γίνεται τῇ τε ψυχῇ καὶ τῷ σώματι, καί τις ἀναλογία τοῦ σωματικοῦ θανάτου πρὸς τὸν ψυχικόν ἐστι θάνατον· ὥσπερ γὰρ ἐν σαρκὶ τὸ τῆς αἰσθητῆς χωρισθῆναι ζωῆς προσαγορεύομεν θάνατον, οὕτως καὶ ἐπὶ τῆς ψυχῆς τὸν τῆς ἀληθοῦς ζωῆς χωρισμὸν θάνατον ὀνομάζομεν· ἐπεὶ οὖν μία τίς ἐστιν ἡ τοῦ κακοῦ κοινωνία, καθὼς προείρηται, ἐν ψυχῇ τε θεωρουμένη καὶ σώματι· δι' ἀμφοτέρων γὰρ πρόεισιν τὸ πονηρὸν εἰς ἐνέργειαν· διὰ τοῦτο ὁ μὲν τῆς διαλύσεως θάνατος ἐκ τῆς τῶν νεκρῶν δερμάτων ἐπιβολῆς τῆς ψυχῆς οὐχ ἅπτεται. πῶς γὰρ ἂν διαλυθείη τὸ μὴ συγκείμενον;

[39] See J. Daniélou, Platonisme et théologie mystique (Paris 1944) 25-31, 55-60; J. Daniélou, L'être et le temps chez Grégoire de Nysse (Leiden 1970) 154-185; E. Moutsoulas, The incarnation of the Word and the theosis of Man, according to the teaching of Gregory of Nyssa (Athens 2000) 49-70; P. F. Beatrice, Le tuniche di pelle, in: U. Bianchi (ed.), La tradizione dell'enkrateia. Atti del Congresso di Milano 1981 (Roma 1986) 433-484.

in Gen 3:21 is taken up and transformed into a fundamental element of the transmission of original sin, because it allows us to exhibit at the same time the radicality of its consequences and the preservation of the core of the image that allows us to turn back to life.

This *chrêsis* clearly distinguishes Gregory from both Philo[40] and the Gnostics,[41] for in their view the tunics of hide denoted the human body. The Bishop of Nyssa, since his first work,[42] follows Clement of Alexandria[43] and Origen,[44] who identified the biblical image with mortality.

James Herbert Srawley pointed out that tunics of hide directly oppose the *apatheia*, taking its place.[45] But this means that after the fall the tunics of hide take the place of the dynamical condition of *epektasis*. Again the syntactic element is fundamental:

> For since, says Moses, the first human beings had done that which was forbidden, and had stripped themselves of that initial bliss, the Lord clothed them with tunics of skin; but this account does not seem to me to mean the usual skins, for the human being had certainly not killed and skinned animals in order to be able to obtain a covering from them. But since every skin removed from the animal is dead, I think that He who cures our wickedness has taken the force that leads to death, which was the prerogative of irrational nature, and has then placed it, as a providential act, on mankind. For the tunic is something foreign, which we put on us and use when our body needs it, but it was not born together with our nature. Therefore, it was by a providential design that the mortal condition was taken from the irrational nature and was placed over our nature, which was created for immortality; it covered its exterior, not its interior; it includes the sensible part of the human being, while it does not touch the image of God. Now the sensible part is dissolved, but not destroyed. And destruction (ἀφανισμός) is the passage into non-being, while dissolution (λύσις) is the disintegration that brings one back to the elements of the world from which a thing was made.[46]

---

[40] Cf. *Philo of Alexandria*, Quaest. Gen. I, 53.
[41] Cf. *Irenaeus of Lyon*, Adv. Haer. I, 5, 5.
[42] Cf. *Gregory of Nyssa*, De virginitate 12 and 13: GNO VIII/1, p. 302–303.
[43] Cf. *Clement of Alexandria*, Stromata, 3, 14.
[44] Cf. *Origen*, Contra Celsum IV, 40: M. Borret, SC 136 (Paris 1968), p. 290 n. 1.
[45] Cf. *J. H. Srawley*, The Catechetical Oration of Gregory of Nyssa (Cambridge 2014) 43 n. 4.
[46] *Gregory of Nyssa*, Or. cat. 8: J. Srawley, p. 42–44: τὸ δὲ τοιοῦτον δόγμα ἱστορικώτερον μὲν καὶ δι' αἰνιγμάτων ὁ Μωσῆς ἡμῖν ἐκτίθεται. πλὴν ἔκδηλον καὶ τὰ αἰνίγματα τὴν διδασκαλίαν ἔχει. ἐπειδὴ γάρ, φησίν, ἐν τοῖς ἀπηγορευμένοις ἐγένοντο οἱ πρῶτοι ἄνθρωποι καὶ τῆς μακαριότητος ἐκείνης ἀπεγυμνώθησαν, δερματίνους ἐπιβάλλει χιτῶνας τοῖς πρωτοπλάστοις ὁ κύριος· οὔ μοι δοκεῖ πρὸς τὰ τοιαῦτα δέρματα τοῦ λόγου τὴν διάνοιαν φέρων· ποίων γὰρ ἀποσφαγέντων τε καὶ δαρέντων ζῴων ἐπινοεῖται αὐτοῖς ἡ περιβολή; ἀλλ', ἐπειδὴ πᾶν δέρμα χωρισθὲν τοῦ ζῴου

The difference between destruction and dissolution is radical, because it means that the tunics of hide constitute on an ontological level a syntactic change that brings man to the painful experience of his limit, of his mortality, thus acting as a medicine, bitter, but a true medicine. This allows God's omnipotence to refound the human being in Christ, through baptism and his Passion and death. In fact, the image is full of sacramental references, which emerge clearly with regard to Christian initiation in *De vita Moysis*.[47] If the original sin is transmitted by the loss of the blessing, the power of the Eucharistic blessing re-establishes the communion of the human nature that Christ assumed with the divinity:

> God, having made himself manifest [i.e. the Logos in the economy], united himself to the transitory human nature so that mankind could be made divine together with Him through communion with the divine nature; for this reason, then, as a result of the economy of grace, the Logos inseminates himself in all believers through the flesh, whose subsistence depends on bread and wine; He unites himself to the body of those who believe, so that man too, by uniting himself to the immortal element, may share in incorruption. And the Logos grants all this, changing into the other species the nature of what is visible, through the power of prayer (τῇ τῆς εὐλογίας δυνάμει).[48]

We could say that in the Eucharist the incarnate Logos lets himself be eaten, lets himself be sown in us, to reintroduce in us that process of growth towards the infinite in which communion with God consists, diametrically opposed to the stasis of the communion with evil. The syntactic dimension is so clear, because salvation goes through the body, through personal and material relationships. Thus it is precisely the syntactic dimension of human unity, a

---

νεκρόν ἐστι, πάντως οἶμαι τὴν πρὸς τὸ νεκροῦσθαι δύναμιν, ἢ τῆς ἀλόγου φύσεως ἐξαίρετος ἦν, ἐκ προμηθείας μετὰ ταῦτα τοῖς ἀνθρώποις ἐπιβεβληκέναι τὸν τὴν κακίαν ἡμῶν ἰατρεύοντα, οὐχ ὡς εἰς ἀεὶ παραμένειν· ὁ γὰρ χιτὼν τῶν ἔξωθεν ἡμῖν ἐπιβαλλομένων ἐστί, πρὸς καιρὸν ἐστι τοῦ χρῆσιν παρέχων τῷ σώματι, οὐ συμπεφυκὼς τῇ φύσει. οὐκοῦν ἐκ τῆς τῶν ἀλόγων φύσεως ἡ νεκρότης οἰκονομικῶς περιετέθη τῇ εἰς ἀθανασίαν κτισθείσῃ φύσει, τὸ ἔξωθεν αὐτῆς περικαλύπτουσα, οὐ τὸ ἔσωθεν, τὸ αἰσθητὸν τοῦ ἀνθρώπου μέρος διαλαμβάνουσα, αὐτῆς δὲ τῆς θείας εἰκόνος οὐ προσαπτομένη. λύεται δὲ τὸ αἰσθητόν, οὐκ ἀφανίζεται. ἀφανισμὸς μὲν γάρ ἐστιν ἡ εἰς τὸ μὴ ὂν μεταχώρησις· λύσις δὲ ἡ εἰς τὰ τοῦ κόσμου στοιχεῖα πάλιν, ἀφ' ὧν τὴν σύστασιν ἔσχε, διάχυσις.

[47] Cf. *Gregory of Nyssa*, De vita Moysis II: GNO VII/1, p. 39–40.
[48] *Gregory of Nyssa*, Or. cat. 37: J. Srawley, p. 151–152: ὁ δὲ φανερωθεὶς θεὸς διὰ τοῦτο κατέμιξεν ἑαυτὸν τῇ ἐπικήρῳ φύσει, ἵνα τῇ τῆς θεότητος κοινωνίᾳ συναποθεωθῇ τὸ ἀνθρώπινον, τούτου χάριν πᾶσι τοῖς πεπιστευκόσι τῇ οἰκονομίᾳ τῆς χάριτος ἑαυτὸν ἐνσπείρει διὰ τῆς σαρκός, ἧς ἡ σύστασις ἐξ οἴνου τε καὶ ἄρτου ἐστί, τοῖς σώμασι τῶν πεπιστευκότων κατακιρνάμενος, ὡς ἂν τῇ πρὸς τὸ ἀθάνατον ἑνώσει καὶ ὁ ἄνθρωπος τῆς ἀφθαρσίας μέτοχος γένοιτο. ταῦτα δὲ δίδωσι τῇ τῆς εὐλογίας δυνάμει πρὸς ἐκεῖνο μεταστοιχειώσας τῶν φαινομένων τὴν φύσιν.

reflection of the ontological syntax of the triune God, that allows both the transmission of original sin and the restoration of salvation in Christ.

Thus Gregory interprets the parable of the lost sheep as referring to the salvation not only of the unity of soul and body of the human being, but also of the whole of human nature.[49] Syntactic unity comes into play here:

> The Lord came to seek and to save that which was lost (cf. Lk 19:10): but it was not only the body that was lost, but the whole human being, who is made up of body and soul joined together; indeed, if the truth be told, the soul was lost before the body. For transgression is a sin of the freedom, not of the body, and the freedom, from which all the misfortune of human nature began, is specific to the soul, as is attested by the words of God, who does not lie, that on the day when they had touched the forbidden things, they would instantly have tested death by eating them (cf. Gen 2:17). And since the human being is made up of two natures, death works in correspondence with the one and the other, inasmuch as he who dies suffers the deprivation of both the one and the other life. The extinguishing of the senses and their dissolution, whereby they return to the elements of their own kind, constitute, in fact, the death of the body. Scripture says, "the soul that sinneth shall die" (Ez 18:20). But sin is the estrangement from God, who is the true and only life.[50]

The text shows a kind of *communicatio idiomatum* between the soul and the body, whereby the life of one passes to the other in the original syntax just as the death of one passes to the other. Note that Gregory could not be further from the Gnostic positions, precisely because of the role attributed to freedom.

To this internal syntax within the human being corresponds an external syntax between human beings, which Gregory expresses in physiological and organic terms. Christ is the firstfruits bringing everything and everyone back to the Father through his own *apatheia*, in which the whole mass participates:

---

[49] *Gregory of Nyssa*, Contra Eunomium III, 10,11 and Refutatio confessionis Eunomii 175.
[50] *Gregory of Nyssa*, Refutatio confessionis Eunomii 173, 9–175, 1: W. Jaeger, GNO II (Leiden 1960), p. 385,16-386,3: ἦλθεν ὁ κύριος ζητῆσαι καὶ σῶσαι τὸ ἀπολωλός, ἀπώλετο δὲ οὐ σῶμα, ἀλλ' ὅλος ὁ ἄνθρωπος ἀπὸ ψυχῆς καὶ σώματος συγκεκραμένος, καὶ εἰ χρὴ τὸν ἀληθέστερον εἰπεῖν λόγον, τοῦ σώματος ἡ ψυχὴ προαπώλετο. ἡ γὰρ παρακοὴ προαιρέσεως, οὐ σώματος ἁμαρτία ἐστίν, ἴδιον δὲ ψυχῆς ἡ προαίρεσις, ἀφ' ἧς πᾶσα ἡ τῆς φύσεως συμφορὰ τὴν ἀρχὴν ἔσχεν, ὡς μαρτυρεῖ τοῖς λόγοις ἡ ἀψευδὴς τοῦ θεοῦ ἀπειλή, ὅτι ἐν ᾗ ἂν ἡμέρᾳ τῶν ἀπηγορευμένων ἅψωνται, ἀνυπερθέτως συναφθήσεται τῇ βρώσει ὁ θάνατος. διπλοῦ δὲ ὄντος τοῦ ἀνθρωπίνου συγκρίματος, καταλλήλως καθ' ἑκάτερον ἐνεργεῖται ὁ θάνατος, τῆς διπλῆς ζωῆς ἐνεργούσης τῷ νεκρουμένῳ τὴν στέρησιν. σώματος μὲν γάρ ἐστι θάνατος ἡ τῶν αἰσθητηρίων σβέσις καὶ ἡ πρὸς τὰ συγγενῆ τῶν στοιχείων διάλυσις· Ψυχὴ δέ, φησίν, ἡ ἁμαρτάνουσα αὐτὴ ἀποθανεῖται. ἁμαρτία δέ ἐστιν ἡ τοῦ θεοῦ ἀλλοτρίωσις, ὅς ἐστιν ἡ ἀληθινή τε καὶ μόνη ζωή.

> Therefore, just as the One who is the first-fruits of the mass (ἡ ἀπαρχὴ τοῦ φυράματος) has united himself with the true God and Father through purity and impassibility (ἀπαθείας), so we also, who are the mass (τὸ φύραμα), will be united through similar paths with the Father of incorruptibility, through the imitation (διὰ τοῦ μιμήσασθαι), as far as possible, of the impassibility (τὸ ἀπαθές) and immutability of the Mediator (τοῦ μεσίτου). For in this way we shall be the crown of the Only-Begotten God, [composed] of precious stones, becoming honour and glory by [our] life.[51]

The equivalence between *apatheia* and *epektasis* allows us to grasp the strength of this text, which at the same time highlights the role of *mimesis*. Here the positive dimension of Gregory's ontological syntax is manifested in the spreading of salvation throughout human nature. But the dynamic is the same as that of the transmission of sin and the suffering associated with it, as Gregory's commentary on Ex 32:26 shows:

> The narrative of this event may provide us with a useful lesson, which is as follows. After all the people had given themselves up to sin in large numbers, and all the people were like one man in their wickedness, the lash fell upon them without distinction. For as he that smiteth with his lashings a man who is caught committing evil strikes with the whip the part that happens to be there, knowing that the suffering of the part then spreads to the whole of the rest of the body, so, in that case, as if the whole body that had joined together to commit evil was punished, the lash that struck one part brought the whole to its senses.[52]

The example, in its physicality, clearly shows the syntactic dimension in its twofold direction, which makes evil pass and makes good pass. The fact that the people and humanity are like a single body returns constantly in Gregory's thought that raises Paul's doctrine to an ontological level through the new metaphysical concept of relationship:

---

[51] *Gregory of Nyssa*, De perfectione Christiana ad Olympium monachum: GNO VIII/1, p. 206,9–16: οὐκοῦν ὥσπερ ἡ ἀπαρχὴ τοῦ φυράματος διὰ καθαρότητός τε καὶ ἀπαθείας ᾠκειώθη τῷ ἀληθινῷ πατρὶ καὶ θεῷ, οὕτω καὶ ἡμεῖς τὸ φύραμα διὰ τῶν ὁμοίων ὁδῶν τῷ πατρὶ τῆς ἀφθαρσίας κολληθησόμεθα διὰ τοῦ μιμήσασθαι, καθὼς ἂν ᾖ δυνατόν, τοῦ μεσίτου τὸ ἀπαθές τε καὶ ἀναλλοίωτον. οὕτω γὰρ ἐσόμεθα τοῦ μονογενοῦς θεοῦ στέφανος ἐκ λίθων τιμίων, τιμὴ καὶ δόξα διὰ τοῦ βίου γενόμενοι.

[52] *Gregory of Nyssa*, De vita Mosis II: GNO VII/1, p. 205,1–10: Ὁ δὲ περὶ τούτου λόγος ταύτην ἂν ἡμῖν παράσχοιτο τὴν ὠφέλειαν. Ἐπειδὴ πανδημεὶ πάντες πρὸς τὸ κακὸν συνεφρόνησαν καὶ ὥσπερ εἷς ἐγένετο τῷ λόγῳ τῆς κακίας τὸ στρατόπεδον ἅπαν, ἀδιάκριτος ἡ κατ' αὐτῶν γίνεται μάστιξ. Ὡς γάρ τινα τῶν ἐπὶ κακίᾳ πεφωραμένων ὁ πληγαῖς αἰκιζόμενος ὅτιπερ ἂν τύχῃ τοῦ σώματος καταξαίνει διὰ τῆς μάστιγος, εἰδὼς ὅτι ἡ ἐπὶ μέρους ὀδύνη πρὸς τὸ πᾶν διεξέρχεται, οὕτως ὡς παντὸς ὁμοίως κολαζομένου τοῦ εἰς τὴν κακίαν συμφυέντος σώματος ἡ ἐπὶ μέρους ἐνεργουμένη μάστιξ τὸ πᾶν ἐσωφρόνισεν.

Relational Ontology and the Syntactic Dimension of Sin

When, therefore, by imitation of the Firstfruits (κατὰ μίμησιν τῆς ἀπαρχῆς) we shall all be freed from evil, then the whole mass of nature (τὸ φύραμα τῆς φύσεως), united inseparably with the Firstfruits and having become one compact body (ἓν κατὰ τὸ συνεχὲς σῶμα), will receive within itself the dominion of good alone.[53]

Here everything goes through relationship because salvation itself is relational. But in the quoted text, *mimesis* also becomes essential, so that the syntactic dimension is never presented as an automatism, but always referred to the freedom of the human being. As we can see, the social and personal dimensions are not opposed, for the same reason that the beginning and the end cannot be set in contrast, but are relationally connected.

Thus, Gregory presents at the same time the original sin with its propagation and salvation. It is the light of the Firstfruits, that is, of Christ, that allows us to see the evil that spreads in the body of humanity. But just as this happens, salvation is already in place:

This, then, is the Firstborn and has brothers, concerning whom He says to Mary: "go to my brothers and say to them: I am ascending to my Father and your Father, my God and your God" (Jn 20:17). For with these words he recapitulates (ἀνακεφαλαιοῦται) the whole purpose of economy for the human being. In fact, by turning away from God, men became slaves of those who by nature are not gods, and from being children of God they became related (προσῳκειώθησαν) to the wicked and false father. For this reason the Mediator between God and men, who assumed the firstfruits (τὴν ἀπαρχὴν) of the whole human nature, sends the announcement to his brethren not from the divine person (ἐκ τοῦ θείου προσώπου), but from ours, saying "I am going to make in myself your Father the true Father, from whom you were separated, and to make in myself your God the true God, from whom you were withdrawn". For through the firstfruits which I have assumed, I bring all mankind into myself to the God and Father. Therefore, since the firstfruits make God the true God and Father the true Father, good is restored in the whole of nature and He becomes Father and God of all men through the firstfruits.[54]

---

[53] *Gregory of Nyssa*, In illud: Tunc et ipse filius: J. K. Downing, GNO III/2 (Leiden 1986), p. 16,13–17: ὅταν οὖν κατὰ μίμησιν τῆς ἀπαρχῆς ἔξω τοῦ κακοῦ πάντες γενώμεθα, τότε ὅλον τὸ φύραμα τῆς φύσεως τῇ ἀπαρχῇ συμμιχθὲν καὶ ἓν κατὰ τὸ συνεχὲς σῶμα γενόμενον τοῦ ἀγαθοῦ μόνου τὴν ἡγεμονίαν ἐφ' ἑαυτοῦ δέξεται.

[54] *Gregory of Nyssa*, Refutatio confessionis Eunomii 82,1–84,4: GNO II, p. 346: οὗτος οὖν ὁ πρωτότοκος καὶ ἀδελφοὺς ἔχει, περὶ ὧν φησι πρὸς τὴν Μαρίαν ὅτι Πορεύθητι καὶ εἰπὲ τοῖς ἀδελφοῖς μου, πορεύομαι πρὸς τὸν πατέρα μου καὶ πατέρα ὑμῶν καὶ θεόν μου καὶ θεὸν ὑμῶν. ὅλον γὰρ τῆς κατὰ ἄν θρωπον οἰκονομίας ἀνακεφαλαιοῦται τὸν σκοπὸν διὰ τῶν εἰρημένων. ἀποστάντες γὰρ τοῦ θεοῦ οἱ ἄνθρωποι ἐδούλευσαν τοῖς φύσει μὴ οὖσι θεοῖς, καὶ ὄντες τέκνα θεοῦ τῷ πονηρῷ τε καὶ ψευδωνύμῳ πατρὶ προσῳκειώθησαν. διὰ τοῦτο ὁ μεσίτης θεοῦ καὶ ἀνθρώπων πάσης τῆς ἀνθρωπίνης φύσεως τὴν ἀπαρχὴν ἀναλαβὼν οὐκ ἐκ τοῦ θείου προσώπου, ἀλλ' ἐκ τοῦ ἡμετέρου

Salvation is relational because true life consists in a relationship with the true Father who is the Father of Christ. On the other hand, original sin consists in becoming slaves of the false father who is the devil and is transmitted as kinship, as communion, in this case in evil, in lack. For this reason, salvation passes from Jesus, the divine Person, to Mary of Magdala, who must announce it to the disciples. Everything is transmitted in communion because salvation itself is communion with the infinite life of God, the only Father to realise human freedom. Therefore original sin is syntactically transmitted as false filiation, overturning the transmission of true life which is the filiation to the Father.

And this salvation flows from the internal syntax of the union of human nature and divine nature in Christ:

> Since God transformed the whole human being into the divine nature through union (ἀνακράσεως) with Himself, at the moment of the economy of the passion [He] did not withdraw from the two parts that with which He had united Himself once and for all (ἅπαξ)—for "the gifts of God are irrevocable" (Rom 11:29)—but the Deity voluntarily separated the soul from the body, showing, however, that He remained in the one and the other.[55]

The syntactic power that saves springs from the very union of the two natures of Christ, because the incarnate Logos does not withdraw from the human being even in death, but continues to keep united in himself the soul and the body that were separated by death. It could be said that from the union of the Son with the whole human being, once and for all, the syntactic omnipotence explodes, leading both body and soul back to the life of the Father, because the divine gift is irrevocable.

We thus come to a long and fundamental text, which closes the path proposed here, because it summarises in an extremely clear way Gregory's conception of the transmission of sin:

πέμπει τοῖς ἀδελφοῖς ἑαυτοῦ τὰ δηλώματα, λέγων ὅτι· πορεύομαι δι' ἐμαυτοῦ ποιῆσαι ὑμῶν πατέρα τὸν ἀληθινὸν πατέρα, οὗ ἐχωρίσθητε, καὶ ποιῆσαι δι' ἐμαυτοῦ θεὸν ὑμῶν τὸν ἀληθινὸν θεόν, οὗ ἀπέστητε· διὰ γὰρ τῆς ἀπαρχῆς, ἣν ἀνέλαβον, προσάγω ἅπαν τῷ θεῷ καὶ πατρὶ ἐν ἐμαυτῷ τὸ ἀνθρώπινον. Τῆς οὖν ἀπαρχῆς θεὸν ἑαυτῆς ποιησαμένης τὸν ὄντα θεὸν καὶ πατέρα τὸν ἀγαθὸν πατέρα, πάσῃ κατορθοῦται τῇ φύσει τὸ ἀγαθὸν καὶ πάντων ἀνθρώπων γίνεται διὰ τῆς ἀπαρχῆς πατὴρ καὶ θεός.

[55] *Gregory of Nyssa*, De tridui inter mortem et resurrectionem domini nostri Jesu: G. Heil et al., GNO IX (Leiden 1967), p. 293,6–12: ὅλον τὸν ἄνθρωπον τοῦ θεοῦ διὰ τῆς πρὸς ἑαυτὸν ἀνακράσεως εἰς τὴν θείαν φύσιν μετασκευάσαντος ἐν τῷ καιρῷ τῆς κατὰ τὸ πάθος οἰκονομίας οὐ θατέρου μέρους τὸ ἅπαξ ἐγκραθὲν ἀνεχώρησεν (ἀμεταμέλητα γὰρ τοῦ θεοῦ τὰ χαρίσματα), ἀλλὰ τὴν μὲν ψυχὴν τοῦ σώματος ἡ θεότης ἑκουσίως διέζευξεν, ἑαυτὴν δὲ ἐν ἀμφοτέροις μένουσαν ἔδειξεν.

If one divides a reed into two sections (for there is nothing to prevent one from explaining the mystery of the economy of the resurrection by a material example) and brings together the ends of the pieces of the reed into one part, necessarily the whole piece of the reed will be brought together by the joining and binding into one part, reuniting with the other part. Just so in Him [Christ] the union of the soul with the body which took place in the resurrection, leads in conjunction (κατὰ τὸ συνεχὲς) the whole human nature, divided by death into soul and body, to the natural union by the hope of the resurrection, uniting the combination of what had been divided. And this is what Paul says: "Christ is risen from the dead, the firstfruits of those who have died" (1 Cor 15:20) and as we all die in Adam, so we shall all receive life in Christ (cf. 1 Cor 15:22). In fact, according to the example of the reed, our nature was separated by sin from the limit represented by Adam, since through death the soul was separated from the body, but through the humanity of Christ it is reunited in one nature. Therefore, we die together with him who died for us, and I do not refer by this to the death that is necessary and common to our nature. For this will happen even if we do not wish it. But since we must die voluntarily together with Him who died of his own will, it is appropriate to think for us that death which takes place by free choice (ἐκ προαιρέσεως). For it is not possible to imitate (μίμησις) what is voluntary by means of what is necessarily imposed. Since, therefore, the death that is imposed on each one by nature happens in any case and necessarily, whether we want to or not, one cannot consider voluntary that which happens necessarily; therefore in another way we shall die together with Him who died voluntarily, that is, by being buried in mystical water through baptism. For it is said, "through baptism we have been buried together with Him in death" (Rom 6:4), so that the imitation of death may also be followed by the imitation of resurrection.[56]

---

[56] *Gregory of Nyssa*, Antirrheticus adversus Apollinarium: GNO III/1, p. 226,6–227,9: καὶ ὥσπερ (κωλύει γὰρ οὐδὲν σωματικῶς τὸ μυστήριον τῆς κατὰ τὴν ἀνάστασιν οἰκονομίας ἐνδείξασθαι) [καθάπερ] εἰ διχῇ κάλαμος διασχισθείη καί τις κατὰ τὸ ἓν πέρας τὰ ἄκρα τοῦ καλάμου τμημάτων ἑνώσειεν, ὅλον ἐξ ἀνάγκης τὸ τμῆμα τοῦ καλάμου πρὸς τὸ ὅλον συναρμοσθήσεται διὰ τῆς ἐν τῷ ἑνὶ πέρατι συμβολῆς τε καὶ σφίγξεως πρὸς τὸ ἕτερον πέρας συναρμοζόμενον, οὕτως ἡ ἐν ἐκείνῳ τῆς ψυχῆς πρὸς τὸ σῶμα γενομένη διὰ τῆς ἀναστάσεως ἕνωσις πᾶσαν κατὰ τὸ συνεχὲς τὴν ἀνθρωπίνην φύσιν διὰ τοῦ θανάτου ψυχῇ τε καὶ σώματι μεμερισμένην πρὸς συμφυΐαν ἄγει τῇ ἐλπίδι τῆς ἀναστάσεως, τὴν συνδρομὴν τῶν διεστηκότων ἁρμόσασα· καὶ τοῦτό ἐστι τὸ παρὰ τοῦ Παύλου λεγόμενον ὅτι Χριστὸς ἐγήγερται ἐκ νεκρῶν, ἀπαρχὴ τῶν κεκοιμημένων, καὶ Ὥσπερ ἐν τῷ Ἀδὰμ πάντες ἀποθνήσκομεν, οὕτως ἐν τῷ Χριστῷ πάντες ζωοποιηθησόμεθα. κατὰ γὰρ τὸ τοῦ καλάμου ὑπόδειγμα ἀπὸ μὲν τοῦ κατὰ τὸν Ἀδὰμ πέρατος ἡ φύσις ἡμῶν διὰ τῆς ἁμαρτίας ἐσχίσθη, τῷ θανάτῳ τῆς ψυχῆς ἀπὸ τοῦ σώματος διαιρεθείσης, ἀπὸ δὲ τοῦ κατὰ τὸν Χριστὸν μέρους πάλιν ἡ φύσις ἑαυτὴν ἀναλαμβάνει, πάντῃ τῆς διαιρέσεως πρὸς ἑαυτὴν ἐν τῇ ἀναστάσει τοῦ κατὰ τὸν Χριστὸν ἀνθρώπου συμφυομένης. διὰ τοῦτο τοίνυν συναποθνήσκομεν τῷ ὑπὲρ ἡμῶν ἀποθανόντι, οὐ τοῦτον λέγω τὸν ἀναγκαῖόν τε καὶ κοινὸν τῆς φύσεως ἡμῶν θάνατον· τοῦτο γὰρ καὶ μὴ βουλομένων γενήσεται· ἀλλ' ἐπειδὴ τῷ ἑκουσίως ἀποθανόντι συναποθνήσκειν χρὴ θέλοντας, προσήκει τὸν ἐκ προαιρέσεως αὐτοῖς ἐπινοῆσαι θάνατον· οὐ γάρ ἐστι διὰ τοῦ κατηναγκασμένου ἡ πρὸς τὸ ἑκούσιον μίμησις. ἐπειδὴ τοίνυν ὁ ἐκ φύσεως ἐπικείμενος ἑκάστῳ θάνατος πάντῃ καὶ πάντως γίνεται καὶ βουλομένων καὶ μή, οὐκ ἂν δέ τις τὸ πάντως γινόμενον τῷ ἑκουσίῳ λογίσαιτο,

In the text, it is clear how Gregory describes human nature as a reed, which has been cut in two horizontally by Adam's sin, which propagates syntactically. But Christ, at the other end of the reed, through the Mystery of His death and resurrection, has reunited the two divided parts at that concrete point in time and space, from where unity always rediffuses syntactically, reuniting the divided parts in one. It is extremely important to note that this reunification passes through freedom, because one cannot forcefully imitate what is essentially an act of love and, therefore, of supreme freedom. As we saw at the beginning, Christ does not die because he was born, like we who are on Adam's side of this divided reed, but Christ is born to die, that is, to restore unity and life to this reed.

The syntactic perspective allows us, then, to read the transmission of original sin in the negative, through the contemplation of the dynamic of the gift of salvation.

VI. Conclusion

The end point of the proposed route thus coincides with its beginning. For Gregory, the relationship between Adam and Christ is the fundamental axis through which life passes and death passes. What underlies universal salvation is exactly the same as what underlies universal guilt. The first in freedom, the second in necessity. The human being, in fact, was created in a state of continuous growth in goodness and life, which sin interrupted, transforming the dynamic condition of communion with God into a static condition of communion with evil, with nothingness. Baptism and the Eucharist restore the divine blessing that is at the origin of the existence of the human being, in such a way that the relational texture of human ontology is manifested both in evil, because of the syntactic transmission of sin, and in good, because the syntax of the two natures of Christ reunites nature in that unity that is now accessible to every human being who freely accepts it.

Gregory's perspective is very bold, as revealed by a change in his *chrêsis* of the Platonic myth of the cave after his trip to Jerusalem in 382. Before then he denied the original meaning of the myth, where darkness is identified with the material world, to reinterpret it precisely in terms of man's condition after original sin. We are born in the shadows facing the limit. But after his visit to Bethlehem he changed his perspective, because he saw that the sun had en-

---

διὰ τοῦτο ἕτερον τρόπον τῷ ἑκουσίως ἀποθανόντι συναποθνήσκομεν, τῷ μυστικῷ ὕδατι διὰ τοῦ βαπτίσματος ἐνθαπτόμενοι· Συνετάφημεν γὰρ αὐτῷ, φησί, διὰ τοῦ βαπτίσματος εἰς τὸν θάνατον, ἵνα τῇ μιμήσει τοῦ θανάτου ἀκολουθήσῃ καὶ ἡ τῆς ἀναστάσεως μίμησις.

tered the cave, the nativity grotto, in such a way as to bring light where before there was only darkness.[57] This means that the world and personal history are the place of encounter with life. The limit is where the infinite seeks us in Christ. Thus, "salvation (*Heil*) in history becomes healing (*Heilung*) of history (*reparatio, restauratio*)", as Max Seckler wrote in another context,[58] that is salvation history becomes salvation of history.

---

[57] *Gregory of Nyssa*, Antirrheticus adversus Apollinarium: GNO III/1, p. 171,11–17.
[58] M. Seckler, Das Heil in der Geschichte (München 1964) 91.

Svetoslav Riboloff, Sofia (Bulgaria)

Theodore of Mopsuestia on the Ancestral Sin

Abstract:
Theodore of Mopsuestia (352–428) is a highly original Antiochene author who tackled a wide range of exegetical issues in an innovative manner. His approach also informs his understanding of human sin and mortality, both before and after man's fall from grace. According to Theodore of Mopsuestia, death is not only punishment for men but also an important educational tool. It is precisely because men are mortal that they have been able to appreciate the value of immortality and to become aware of the wretchedness of their situation. At the same time, Adam's sin brought man's changeable nature to a state of confusion, which, in turn, provoked an outpour of passions. This event brought sin to man, yet it also taught man to search for a proper solution to this problem. In Theodore's logic, the sensibility of human nature is inevitably accompanied by changeability. Hence, man needs to be able to make a free choice because man is a reasonable being.

Traditional academic Church History has long considered Theodore of Mopsuestia (352–428) a key figure in Antiochian theology. During the second half of the 20th century, however, scholars have persuasively argued that he is also a highly original and inquisitive author who tackled a wide range of exegetical issues in an innovative manner. His innovative approach also informs his understanding of human sin and mortality, both before and after man's fall from grace.

Robert Devreesse, true to the method he employed for his entire work on Theodore's writings, adopts a consistent approach to editing Theodore's texts. Assuming that these texts have been subject to ill-intentioned interpolations, Devreesse ignores a number of fragments. His approach to Theodore's position on original sin follows the same logic. Devreesse also attributes to Theodore the assumption that sin may be hereditary, for after the fall, sin becomes inherent to human nature[1]. Refuting Devreesse's approach, Arthur Vööbus notes,

---

[1] See *R. Devreesse*, Essai sur Théodore de Mopsueste, StT 141 (Città del Vaticano 1948) 98–103. The Greek scholar, Chrysostomos Stamulis, shares the same view. According to Stamulis, Theodore of Mopsuestia's and Nestorios' writings present the sin that is engendered in

According to Theodore, sin has nothing to do with the realm of nature. The characteristic penchant cherished in the West that sin has to do with nature is simply abhorrent to him [...]. This possibility [i.e., that sin may be inherent to human nature], however, does not come into account, since Christ has taken on himself what is in the human nature, namely death[2].

Similarly, Frederick McLeod states:

> But Theodore is opposed to any notion of an "original sin" that has kept human nature sinful insofar as this would militate against his conviction that sin is a free act of the human will. Moreover, if Adam's "original sin" is a sin of nature, this would at least imply that Christ's humanity would also have been affected by sin and unable to serve as a sinless mediator[3].

If we accept Theodore's writings that have come to us as authentic[4], we cannot but agree with Vööbus, McLeod, and Norris' unbiased reading according to which Theodore does not view sin as inherent to human nature. In his *Commentaries on the Book of Psalms*, Theodore explicitly states that sin has nothing to do with nature[5]. Elucidating the words in Psalm 51:5, "Behold, I

---

the soul as immanent to human nature after the fall. Hence it becomes necessary that God's Word should accept human nature in its entirety so that the Word, during Its earthly life, can then gradually free human nature from sin. As I noted in my introduction, Stamulis concludes that even though Theodore and Apollinaris were theological opponents, they agree on the anthropological prerequisites for sin. (Apollinaris considers sin to be immanent to the human mind; hence the Word must replace sin in the human mind.) Yet Theodore and Appollinaris draw different conclusions about the effects of these prerequisites. See X. Σταμούλης, Ἀνθρώπινη φύση τοῦ Χριστοῦ καὶ ἡ ἁμαρτία στοὺς Ἀντιοχειανοὺς θεολόγους τοῦ 5^{ου} αἱ. Συμβολὴ στὴ μελέτη τοῦ Θεοδώρου Μοψουεστίας, τοῦ Νεστορίου καὶ τοῦ Βασιλείου Σελευκείας, Πρακτικὰ τοῦ ΙΑ' Θεολογικοῦ Συνεδρίου πρὸς τιμὴν τοῦ Παμβασιλέως Χριστοῦ (Θεσσαλονίκη 1991) 572-582.
[2] A. Vööbus, Regarding the Theological Anthropology of Theodore of Mopsuestia, Church History 33.2 (1964) 118.
[3] F. G. McLeod, The Roles of Christ's Humanity in Salvation: Insights from Theodore of Mopsuestia (Washington, D.C. 2005) 62. The same stance is elaborated on in R. Norris, Manhood and Christ: A Study in the Christology of Theodore of Mopsuestia (Oxford 1963) 173-178.
[4] Besides, the *Catechetical Homilies*, which Theodore's disciples preserved in their entirety, contain the same basic propositions as fragments of his work preserved in Byzantine catenae or in documents from the Church councils. See Frances Sullivan's detailed analysis of the origin of these fragments and their comparability with the *Catechetical Homilies*. F. Sullivan, The Christology of Theodore of Mopsuestia, AnGr 82 (Rome 1956) 35-158.
[5] Man was created innocent by nature, the Anthiochian writer says. If man had been created sinful, then the Creator himself would be accountable for man's sin. See *Theod. Mopsuest.*, Contra defensores peccati originalis III, 3: H. B. Swete, Theodori Mopsuesteni in epistolas B. Pauli Commentarii, vol. 2 (Cambridge 1880), p. 335.

was shapen in iniquity; and in sin did my mother conceive me" (ἰδοὺ γὰρ ἐν ἀνομίαις συνελήφθην, καὶ ἐν ἁμαρτίαις ἐκίσσησέ με ἡ μήτηρ μου), Theodore avoids the topic of sin's hereditary damage to nature and proposes,

> He [David] does not find any sin in the newborns' natures, he does not even hint to their natures; rather, he refers to their parents' wills. In other words, by referring to the mother in the expression, 'I was shapen in iniquity; and in sin did my mother conceive me,' he critiques the mother's sins, not the child's; he accuses the parents' will and not the children's natures as some madmen would have it[6].

Theodore may be rebuking the consistent trend in western theology of which he may have been informed.

The Bishop of Mopsuestia further suggests that the so-called hereditary aspect of sin is just the bad moral example set by the established practice of committing sins. In the same text he says:

> As their fathers had been committing sins for a long time, the next generations adopted their sins (indeed, they were often conceived in sin), and evil was never absent from their midst[7].

Consequently, the power of sin grew stronger with every successive generation[8]. Perhaps Theodore suggests that man must have been created both innocent and vulnerable to temptation. As a contingent creature prone to changeability, Adam was deceived by Satan, who misled Adam by presenting himself as Adam's helper. Satan assisted Adam in overcoming his fear of his Creator, as the prohibition against eating from the tree in the middle of Eden

---

[6] *Theod. Mopsuest.*, Expositio in psalm. L, 7: R. Devreesse, Le Commentaire sur les Psaumes (I–LXXX) de Théodore de Mopsueste, StT 93 (Città del Vaticano 1939), p. 337: Οὐ τὴν τῶν τεχθέντων φύσιν αἰτιᾶται, ἄπαγε, οὐδὲ γὰρ περὶ ἐκείνων φύσιν ὅλως εἴρηται, ἀλλὰ τὴν τῶν τεκόντων γνώμην ἐξαγγέλλει,—τὸ γὰρ ἐν ἀνομίαις συλληφθῆναι καὶ ἐν ἀνομίαις κισσηθῆναι ὑπὸ τῆς μητρός, δῆλον ὅτι τῶν γεννώντων ἀλλ' οὐ τῶν γεννωμένων μηνύει τὸ ἔγκλημα,— κἀκείνων γνώμην διαβάλλει, ἀλλ' οὐ φύσιν τῶν τικτομένων, ὡς οἱ ἀνόητοι βούλονται.

[7] Ibid.: ἐπειδὴ ἐκ πολλοῦ πταίοντες καὶ παρὰ τῶν πατέρων οἱ καθεξῆς τὰς ἁμαρτίας διαδεχόμενοι ἀπὸ τῶν τοιούτων καὶ τῆς γεννήσεως τὰς ἀφορμὰς πολλάκις ἐδέχοντο, οὐδέποτε ἐν μέσῳ τοῦ κακοῦ διαλείποντος ἐν αὐτοῖς. In fact, Theodore dedicated an entire essay to refuting the thesis of original sin's hereditory nature. Patriarch Photios entitled this essay: Θεοδώρου Ἀντιοχέως πρὸς τοὺς λέγοντας φύσει καὶ οὐ γνώμῃ πταίειν τοὺς ἀνθρώπους. See *Phot. Const.*, Bibliotheca cod. CLXXVII: PG 103, 513A–520A. Cf. *Barhadbesabba 'Arbaya*, Historia ecclesiastica XX: F. Nau, PO 9.5 (Paris 1913), p. 512.

[8] See *Theod. Mopsuest.*, Fragm. in ep. ad Rom. 7, 5: K. Staab, Pauluskommentare aus der griechischen Kirche: aus Katenenhandschriften gesammelt und herausgegeben (Münster 1933), p. 124–125.

encompassed both the promise of immortality, which obviously had to be fulfilled in the future, and the threat of punishment (Genesis 2:7; 3:3)[9]. Adam fell victim not only to his naivety, but also to his disregard for God's orders[10]. Thus, it turns out that in the act of the fall, Satan, rather than provoking bodily passions, provoked a volitional act of the human soul. Theodore states this explicitly in the *Catechetical Homilies*. He writes:

> It is obvious that the power of sin derives from the will of the soul. In Adam's case, it was also his soul, and not his body, who first heard sin's advice; for it was not his body whom Satan convinced to give in, to abandon God, and to believe that the deceiver was his helper. In his [Adam's] striving for superior things and following Satan's advice, Adam transgressed against God's order and chose for himself things that were at odds with it[11].

What Theodore finds particularly intriguing about the fall is Adam's irresistible ambition, which led him to disobey God's will and to rebel against God's law. Sin is an act of disobeying God's law and can only be committed as an act of free will[12]. As Adam was fully conscious of his actions, God justly punished his transgression. The punishment was death[13]. Paradoxically, however, for Theodore, human mortality both precedes sin historically and follows

---

[9] See pages 106–119 in the sources cited above, as well as Codex Barberinus graecus 569, f. 59ᵛ: Θεοδώρου. Δύο ταῦτα ποιεῖ, ἐξάγει τε ἡμᾶς τοῦ χείρονος καὶ προσάγει τοῖς κρείττοσιν, ἐπαγγελία καὶ φόβος, ὁ μὲν ἀφέλκων τοῦ κακοῦ, ἡ δὲ ἄγουσα τῷ καλῷ. Τούτου γὰρ ἕνεκεν καὶ ὁ Θεὸς τῇ τε ἀπειλῇ τῆς τιμωρίας ἠσφαλίσατο τῆς ἐντολῆς τὴν παράβασιν, καὶ τῇ ἐπαγγελίᾳ τοῦ ξύλου τῆς ζωῆς ἐπὶ τὴν φυλακὴν αὐτῆς προετρέψατο. Μοχθηρότητα τοίνυν ὁ διάβολος τόν τε φόβον ἀνεῖλεν τῷ εἰπεῖν Οὐκ ἀποθανεῖσθε, καὶ προτροπὴν εἰσήγαγεν τῷ εἰπεῖν Διανοιχθήσονται ὑμῶν οἱ ὀφθαλμοὶ φαγόντων, καὶ ἔσεσθε ὡς θεοί, γινώσκοντες καλὸν καὶ πονηρόν. Ἐνταῦθα δὲ τὴν οἰκείαν ἐξήμεσε κακίαν· οὐ γὰρ εἶπεν ἔσεσθε ὡς Θεός, ἀλλ᾽ ὡς θεοί, ἐντεῦθεν ἤδη προεθίζων αὐτοὺς τῷ μὴ μέγα τι νομίζειν τὸν Θεόν, μηδὲ μόνον οἴεσθαι τοιοῦτον εἶναι, πολλοὺς δὲ κατ᾽ αὐτὸν εἰληφέναι, ὡς καὶ ἑτέρους δυνατὸν εἶναι γενέσθαι τοιούτους. Since the manuscript has not been published, I am quoting here from R. Devreesse, Essai sur Théodore de Mopsueste. Devreesse quotes from the original. Cf. *Theod. Mopsuest.*, Contra defensores peccati originalis III, 3: H. B. Swete, Theodori Mopsuesteni, vol. 2, p. 335.
[10] See *Theod. Mopsuest.*, Hom. cat. XII, 8.19.25: A. Mingana, Commentary of Theodore of Mopsuestia on the Lord's Prayer and on the Sacraments of Baptism and the Eucharist, WoodSt 6 (Cambridge 1933), p. 148, 156, 162 (Syr.), p. 21, 28, 32 (Engl.).
[11] *Theod. Mopsuest.*, Hom. cat. V, 11: A. Mingana, Commentary of Theodore of Mopsuestia on the Nicene Creed, WoodSt 5 (Cambridge 1932), p. 190 (Syr.), p. 56 (Engl.).
[12] See R. Norris, Manhood and Christ, 179 et seq.
[13] See *Theod. Mopsuest.*, Fragm. in ep. ad Rom. 7, 9–11: K. Staab, Pauluskommentare, p. 128: ἐπειδὴ δέ, φησίν, ὁ θεὸς τὸν περὶ τοῦ φυτοῦ δέδωκε νόμον, καὶ διάκρισις ἐγένετο δύο πραγμάτων, ἡ μὲν ἁμαρτία παρείσδυσιν ἔσχεν, ἐγὼ δὲ τἀναντία ποιήσας τοῖς τῷ θεῷ δεδογμένοις, θανάτῳ κατεκρίθην, γέγονέ τε ἡμῖν λοιπὸν θανάτου παρεκτικὸς ὁ παρὰ τοῦ θεοῦ τεθεὶς νόμος ἐπὶ τῷ ζῆσαι πεισθέντας αὐτῷ. See also *Theod. Mopsuest.*, Fragm. in ep. ad Rom. 7, 12: K. Staab, Pauluskommentare, p. 128: Τῆς πρὸς τὸν Ἀδὰμ μέμνηται ἐντολῆς, ἐπειδὴ ἀρχὴ

naturally from sin, from an "objective" moral point of view. In fact, God had foreseen man's volitional act of renouncing his blessed state. It is in this sense that according to Theodore, death, in man's current state, amounts to separation between body and soul[14]. Theodore proposes that the incorruptibility of man following his resurrection will apply mostly to the body and to the relationship between body and soul, which is contingent upon rendering the soul unchangeable by cleansing it from sin:

> It could be possible—he says—to protect the body against death and decay if we first made the soul unchangeable and free from the passions of sin, so that by acquiring unchangeability, we could also acquire freedom from sin[15].

By sinning, man loses his power and his function as a link (σύνδεσμος) connecting contingent beings to one another, on the one hand, and all of them to God, on the other. Hence, by sinning, man has transgressed against God's

---

νόμου τοῖς ἀνθρώποις ἐκεῖνος ἐγένετο. καὶ συμπλέκων ἀμφότερα λέγει· ὥστε ὁ μὲν νόμος ἅγιος, καὶ ἡ ἐντολὴ ἁγία καὶ δικαία καὶ ἀγαθή, ἵνα εἴπῃ ὅτι ἀμφότερα τοίνυν ἄγαν ὠφέλιμα. καλῶς δὲ ἐπὶ τῆς ἐντολῆς πλείοσιν ἐχρήσατο τοῖς ἐπαίνοις, ἅτε δὴ καὶ τῆς δόσεως οὐκ ἐπ᾽ ἀναγκαίοις κατὰ τὸ πρόχειρον δοξάσης δεδόσθαι καὶ θανάτου παρεκτικῆς ἅπασι γενομένης. ἐκάλεσε δὲ αὐτὴν ἁγίαν μὲν ὡς τὰς ἀφορμὰς παρέχουσαν τῆς τε τοῦ καλοῦ καὶ τοῦ κακοῦ διακρίσεως καὶ τὸ κρεῖττον ἀπὸ τοῦ χείρονος ἀφορίζουσαν, δικαίαν δὲ ὡς ἀναγκαίως μετὰ τὸ δεῖξαι τὸ καλὸν ἐπάγουσαν τῷ παραβάτῃ τὴν τιμωρίαν, ἀλλὰ καὶ ἀγαθὴν ὡς καλῶν παρεκτικήν, τό τε παρέχειν τὴν διάγνωσιν καὶ τὸ μείζονα πειθομένοις ὑπισχνεῖσθαι καλά.

[14] In his *Commentary to the Psalm* singer's messianic words, "Into thine hand I commit my spirit" (Psalms 31:5), Theodore of Mospuestia explains why the separation between body and soul amounts to death. See *Theod. Mopsuest.*, Expositio in psalm. XXX, 6: R. Devreesse, Le Commentaire sur les Psaumes de Théodore de Mopsueste, p. 137–138: *Tuae tuitioni animam meam committo atque custodiae: tu eam saluam fac atque defende. Notandum uero quoniam hac uoce usus est Dominus in patibulo constitutus, non quod profetice de ipso dicta sit, sicut opinantur quidam, sed quod ei inter mortis ac passionis pericula posito haec uerba conuenerint. Usus <est> ergo hac uoce id temporis, cum anima eius separabatur a corpore, quam iuste commendabat Patri, ut eum corpori conpetenti resurrectionis tempore redderet.*

[15] *Theod. Mopsuest.*, Hom. cat. V, 12: A. Mingana, Commentary on the Nicene Creed, p. 191 (Syr.), p. 57 (Engl.). In his *Commentary on the Gospel according to Saint John*, Theodore explicitly declares that Christ's death is not like the death of ordinary people: his death is shorter "because [Christ] knew that His stay in the grave would be short and that death would be destroyed after His soul returned to His body" (*Theod. Mopsuest.*, Commentarius in Evangelium Joannis Apostoli X, 16: J.-M. Vosté, CSCO 116, SSyr 63 (Paris 1940), p. 146: *quia sciebat breve fore intervallum (in sepulcro) et mortem esse solvendam, reverente anima ad corpus.* See *Textus syriacus* in: J.-M. Vosté, CSCO 115, SSyr 62 (Paris 1940), p. 205–206. However, Theodore does not base this statement on his understanding of Christ as man's perfect prototype as he viewed this statement as a christological "inconvenience". In other words, this statement shows some inconsistency about his thinking. Cf. below, 157 et seq. The opposite is true: rather than base his understanding of man on Christology, in this case Theodore's understanding of man informs his Christology.

plan whereby man must represent all beings before God so that they may honor God through man. He points out in his commentary on Ephesians:

> But after death was introduced [in this order], because we commit sins, death caused separation between them [between the sensory and the spiritual]. The soul separated from the body, and the body—separated [from the soul]—was subject to complete decay. The link among the parts of creation started falling apart[16].

Adam sinned, even though he was given the opportunity to remain immortal and protected by God's grace (bestowed upon him when he was created) if he had obeyed God's orders. The effects of Adam's transgression are not just personal but expand upon the entire created world. All who partake in his "body" suffer the consequences: not only his offspring but also the entire visible created world that shares its constitutive elements with the human body. Not only did Adam transform the link between the created being and God into a subject who rebels against his Creator, rather than serve his function as a link; but he also brought about the soul's separation from the body as the harmonic unity of creation started falling apart[17].

In Theodore's thought, man's function as a universal link among the individual contingent creatures, on the one hand, and among all of them and God, on the other, is closely related to the notion of "God's image". Hence, we need to analyze the relationship between God's image and the fall in Theodore's works. Man can only fulfill his function of a unifying link and representative before God as long as man is in harmony with God, i.e., as long as man obeys God's orders. Following the fall, this unifying link stopped functioning, and, in Theodore's view, "God's image" within man transformed into "an image of Satan". Theodore writes in his *Catechetical Homilies*:

> if he [Adam] had been wise, he would have stayed with Him Who was the source of all blessings which Adam truly possessed. But Adam accepted and fulfilled the

---

[16] *Theod. Mopsuest.*, In ep. ad Eph. 1, 1: H. B. Swete, Theodori Mopsuesteni, vol. 1, p. 129–130: *Sed subintroducta est mors peccantibus nobis; fiebat autem hinc separatio quaedam utrorumque. Anima enim a corpore separabatur; et corpus separatum solutionem plenariam sustinebat. Dissoluebatur ergo secundum hoc creaturae copulatio.*

[17] In his *Commentary on the Epistle of Paul the Apostle to the Colossians*, Theodore of Mopsuestia even describes a rebellion of the angels who, aghast at Adam's transgression, refuse to serve mankind, but God promises them that he will restore the broken harmony of the world. The source to which Theodore refers in describing this story is unclear. See *Theod. Mopsuest.*, In ep. ad Col. I, 16: H. B. Swete, Theodori Mopsuesteni, vol. 1, p. 268 et seq.

image of Satan—the rebel who had risen against God and who had wanted to appropriate for himself the glory befitting God[18].

Thus, man ceased to be an image of fidelity to God—an image in harmony with creation—and instead accepted the image of God's opponent. Actually, Theodore interpreted the concept of "God's image" in an exclusively moral sense: for him, man's turning his will away from God equals man's adopting "Satan's image". Apparently, according to Theodore, when man fell, having turned his will away from God's will, man lost God's image within himself: "We lost the dignity of this image because we were not careful"[19], points out Theodore.

At the same time, Theodore proposes that the state of mortality threatening the first created humans reflects the weakness, vulnerability, and mutability of the human soul, or will, which eventually admitted sin into man's being after man has turned away from God by means of his disobedience: "There is nothing more terrible for men than death" (θανάτου γὰρ ἀνθρώποις οὐδὲν φοβερώτερον), the Antiochian thinker says in his *Commentary of the Gospel of Luke*[20]. The fear of death turned man into Satan's slave[21]. Theodore's statement follows, to an extent, the Apostle Paul's reflections upon man's wretched

---

[18] *Theod. Mopsuest.*, Hom. cat. XII, 8: A. Mingana, Commentary on the Lord's Prayer, p. 148 (Syr.), p. 21 (Engl.).
[19] *Theod. Mopsuest.*, Hom. cat. XII, 21: A. Mingana, Commentary on the Lord's Prayer, p. 160 (Syr.), p. 30 (Engl.). Frederick McLeod does not share this view: "Despite Adam's seeming acceptance of Satan's 'image' here, Adam has not lost 'God's image'. For Christ, in his humanity, is the true prototype who truly reveals God and unifies the Creation and God. Adam may have damaged his reflected image, but he cannot destroy it, because the role that was assigned to him has been fulfilled by Christ. 'God's image' is inherent to human nature." (F. McLeod, The Roles of Christ's Humanity, 132–133). McLeod's claims are based upon a logical reflection derived from Theodore's writings, yet McLeod fails to provide specific references to Theodore's texts in support of his proposition. Conversely, the two passages I cited above—the only extant fragments which discuss this issue—demonstrate that, according to Theodore, man lost God's image in himself in a moral sense.
[20] *Theod. Mopsuest.*, In Evangelium Luc. 22, 39: PG 66, 724C.
[21] See *Theod. Mopsuest.*, Fragm. in ep. ad Rom. 7, 8: K. Staab, Pauluskommentare, p. 127: Ὑποδείγματι κέχρηται τοῖς περὶ τὸν Ἀδάμ, ἐπεὶ κἀκεῖνος προκειμένων ἐπὶ τοῦ παραδείσου τῶν φυτῶν ἀδεῶς ἁπάντων μεταλαμβάνειν ἐδύνατο, εἰ μὴ νόμος αὐτῷ τις περὶ ἀποχῆς ἔτυχε δοθείς, καὶ οὐκ ἦν ἁμάρτημα τὸ μετὰ τῶν λοιπῶν βουληθέντα κἀκείνου φαγεῖν. ἐπειδὴ δὲ ἐντολὴν ἐδέξατο ἀποσχέσθαι τοῦ φυτοῦ τῆς βρώσεως, ἐπιθυμία μέν τις ἐνῆν αὐτῷ τῆς μεταλήψεως, ὡς εἰκός, τοῦ καρποῦ, ἐκωλύετο δὲ ὅμως ὑπὸ τῆς ἐντολῆς ἁμάρτημα εἶναι τὸ φαγεῖν τῶν ἀπαγορευθέντων ἡγούμενος. ἐντεῦθεν ἡ ἁμαρτία πάροδον ἔσχεν, τῆς μὲν ἐντολῆς ἐπεχούσης τὴν βρῶσιν, τοῦ δὲ Ἀδὰμ οὐ πρὸς τὴν ἀξιοπιστίαν τῆς ἐντολῆς βουληθέντος ἰδεῖν, ἀλλὰ πιστωθέντος μὲν τοῦ ἐπιβούλου τοῖς λόγοις, ὅλου δὲ τῆς ἐπιθυμίας τοῦ φαγεῖν γεγονότος. καὶ οὐ μόνον ἀφορμὴ τῆς ἁμαρτίας ἐντεῦθεν ἐγένετο, ἀλλὰ γὰρ ἔτι κἀκεῖνο ἐμάθομεν, ὡς οὐκ ἀπάτῃ ταῖς ἐπιθυμίαις προσήκεν ἕπεσθαι ἡμᾶς, δοκιμάζοντας δὲ ἃ χρὴ ποιεῖν, τῶν ἑτέρων ἀπέχεσθαι, οἷς οὐκ ἐμμένοντες

state. In his sermon, Paul adopts this state as a starting point for Christ's word (Romans 1:18-3:2; Ephesians 1:3-14, 3:4-12; and Colossians 1:24-29, 3:5-10; Ephesians 4:17-19; 1 Thessalonians 4:3-6; and Titus 3:3). Theodore of Mopsuestia examines Paul's reflections from a purely moral perspective. This leads Theodore's discussion in the direction of his specific hamartiology, which defines his perception of Christ's redeeming act and, in turn, his symmetric Christological model.

As in his examination of the soul's moral capabilities, here too Theodore is interested in the contingent human's abilities to obey God and freely to choose righteousness of his own, changeable free will. It is from this perspective that sin has nothing to do with nature but, instead, results completely from the work of will. This perspective also makes meaningful the proposition that God's creation of man as mortal was insightful and "pedagogical", since God had foreseen man's transgression. Failing to retain God's grace, man, being changeable by nature, is weak and vulnerable to the temptations of sin. In this state and in this world, man cannot avoid sin. Theodore writes in the *Catechetical Homilies*:

> As long as we live in this world, in our mortal and changeable nature, we will be unable not to transgress [God's will][22].

Theodore follows the same logic in the following passage from his *Commentary on the Epistle of Apostle Paul to the Ephesians* (2:10):

> Since we are mortal, in our present lives, certain susceptibility to sin accompanies mortality in some manner [...] for we cannot act [differently?], due to the weakness inherent in us through our mortality, and we are not capable of advancing on our own, straight toward perfect virtue[23].

δῆλοι πάντως ἐσμὲν ἁμαρτάνοντες. ὥστε οὐ κατ' ἐκεῖνο μόνον ἡ ἁμαρτία τὴν πάροδον ἔσχεν διὰ τῆς ἐντολῆς, καθὸ τοῦ φυτοῦ μετειλήφαμεν, ἀλλὰ γὰρ καὶ ὅτι μὴ πάσαις ἕπεσθαι ταῖς ἐπιθυμίαις ἁπλῶς ἐντεῦθεν μανθάνοντες ἡμαρτάνομεν, τὰ τῆς ἐπιθυμίας παρὰ τὸ δέον πληροῦν ἐπειγόμενοι· τοῦτο γὰρ λέγει τὸ κατειργάσατο ἐν ἐμοὶ πᾶσαν ἐπιθυμίαν ἀντὶ τοῦ παντὸς ἁμαρτήματος ἀπό τινος ἐπιθυμίας τικτομένου. ἐντεῦθεν ἡ ἀρχὴ γέγονεν ἡμῖν, ἅ τε δὴ τῆς διακρίσεως τὰς ἀφορμὰς δεξαμένοις ἐντεῦθεν.

[22] *Theod. Mopsuest.*, Hom. cat. XI, 12: R. Tonneau, R. Devreesse, Les Homélies catéchétiques de Théodore de Mopsueste: reproduction phototypique du ms. Mingana Syr. 561 (Selly Oak Colleges' Library, Birmingham), StT 145 (Città del Vaticano 1949), p. 304 (Syr.), p. 305 (French). I am quoting from the French edition of the *Catechetical Lectures* because Mingana's English translation for some reason omits this sentence, although the Syriac text contains it. See A. Mingana, Commentary on the Lord's Prayer, p. 9.

[23] *Theod. Mopsuest.*, In ep. ad Eph. II, 10: H. B. Swete, Theodori Mopsuesteni, vol. 1, p. 147: *Mortales cum simus secundum praesentem uitam, sequitur quodammodo mortalitatem*

In this manner, sinfulness deepens and gains strength from generation to generation[24].

This state, however, also applies to those who have been given the law[25] and threatens even those who have received the sacrament of baptism, after the Savior's coming, for they are still mortal[26]. Thus, the susceptibility to sin is inherent in all of Adam's offspring. Their free will—changeable and prone to straying—can move both toward virtue and toward sin:

> This is precisely why he [the prophet] says, 'I am a man' (cf. Isaiah 6:5), i.e., he is referring to our common nature, implying that the susceptibility to evil belongs to it[27].

In another commentary on Apostle Paul's words, "In Him we have redemption through His blood, the forgiveness of sins, according to the riches of His grace" (Ephesians 1:7), Theodore summarizes his thesis about man's susceptibility to sin. He writes: "It is impossible to see a mortal man, at any time, free from [committing] sin"[28]. Thus, Theodore considers Adam's offspring as inherently susceptible to sin, even though they do not carry in themselves their ancestor's guilt by nature.

Theodore adopts a position typical of his school (we certainly find it in John Chrysostom's works[29]) that views all humanity as one whole, one "body". The Bishop of Mopsuestia clearly conveys that in our present lives (man's first state), this unified body is headed by Adam, the rebellious and sinful father of all men. Not having been part of his nature, his transgression infiltrated

---

facilitas peccandi [...] *cum nos minime possemus propter infirmitatem illam quae nobis aderat per mortalitatem, et cum non sufficeremus ad perfectam uirtutem proficere directionem.*

[24] See *Theod. Mopsuest.*, Fragm. in ep. ad Rom. 7, 5: K. Staab, Pauluskommentare, p. 124–125; *Theod. Mopsuest.*, Hom. cat. I, 4 and VII, 6: A. Mingana, Commentary on the Nicene Creed, p. 119, 190 (Syr.), p. 20, 76 (Engl.).

[25] See *Theod. Mopsuest.*, In ep. ad Gal. II, 15,16: H. B. Swete, Theodori Mopsuesteni, vol. 1, p. 31.

[26] See *Theod. Mopsuest.*, Hom. cat. I, 6: A. Mingana, Commentary on the Nicene Creed, p. 122 (Syr.), p. 21 (Engl.).

[27] Also *Theod. Mopsuest.*, Hom. cat. XVI, 8: A. Mingana, Commentary on the Lord's Prayer, p. 241 (Syr.), p. 101 (Engl.).

[28] *Theod. Mopsuest.*, In ep. ad Eph. I, 7,8: H. B. Swete, Theodori Mopsuesteni, vol. 1, p. 126: [...] *nec fieri potest mortalem aliquando posse videri sine culpa*. See also: ibid., p. 103; *Theod. Mopsuest.*, Hom. cat. XI, 17: A. Mingana, Commentary on the Lord's Prayer, p. 140–141 (Syr.), p. 14–15 (Engl.).

[29] See the sources cited in I. Coman, L'unité du genre humain d'après saint Jean Chrysostome, in: P. Chrestou (ed.), Συμπόσιον. Studies on St. John Chrysostom (Thessaloniki 1973) 41–58.

all mankind, even the entire universe, because his transgression destroyed the "link" (σύνδεσμος), the harmonic unity within man (i.e., the unity between body and soul) as well as within the universe (the unity among its various constituting elements which Adam was called upon to keep connected): "Because of men's evil deed, the entire creation appeared destroyed" (*propter hominum etenim malitiam omnis* [...] *creatura disrumpi uidebatur*)[30]. All men together constitute a common being, a common existence, for all men partake in the same shared nature. Since Adam too partakes in this nature, all men constitute a composite "body", and Adam, the first man, is its head. The relationship between Adam and the rest of mankind is more complex than that of the representative to his species. Adam's mortality, changeability, and corruptibility affect the entire "body", allowing death to destroy all of its members. Theodore writes in his *Commentary on John*:

> After the first man was created by God, he became vulnerable to death because of his sin, together with all that were born from him. This is because they had received their existence from the first humans [i.e., Adam and Eve] who share with them their [common] nature. In this way humans may give birth too; consequently, they received a natural kinship with their parents. And since they share their parents' nature, humans also became susceptible to death, which was imposed on their nature[31].

In his *Commentary on the Epistle of Paul the Apostle to the Romans*, Theodore of Mopsuestia explains his view on why death spread among the rest of mankind even if they were not responsible for Adam's sin. His answer is in complete accord with his overall understanding of sin as a personal, volitional act of disobeying God's will:

> Death rules over all who sin, in any manner and at any time; the rest of mankind is not free from death because their sin is different from Adam's. Rather, all were sentenced to death because they sinned in all sort of ways and at all times. For

---

[30] *Theod. Mopsuest.*, In ep. ad Col. I, 16: H. B. Swete, Theodori Mopsuesteni, vol. 1, p. 267.
[31] *Theod. Mopsuest.*, Commentarius in Evangelium Joannis Apostoli XVII, 11: J.-M. Vosté, CSCO 116, SSyr 63 (Paris 1940), p. 224: *Postquam creatus est primus homo a Deo, reus factus est mortis propter peccatum cum omnibus qui ex eo nati sunt; quippe qui ex parte quadam naturali primorum hominum receperunt existentiam suam. Quia ita etiam gignere possunt homines, propterea merito participationem naturalem cum eis receperunt. Et quia communem habent naturam, ita etiam mortem naturae impositam, contraxerunt.* See *Textus syriacus* in: J.-M. Vosté, CSCO 115, SSyr 62 (Paris 1940), p. 313. Cf. K. McNamara, Theodore of Mopsuestia and the Nestorian Heresy, Irish Theological Quarterly 19 (1952) 262-263.

death has not been defined as a punishment for this or that kind of sin, but it is a punishment for all sins [in history][32].

Following the example of Paul, the Apostle's reflections upon the Old Testament law, Theodore too proposes that God's having given men the law—the Old Testament revelation—was not enough to help Adam's offspring overcome their susceptibility to sin[33].

An important distinction between the body and the soul is found in another of Theodore's text, his *Commentary on the Gospel according to Saint John*. While (as noted above) the soul's susceptibility to abusing its freedom derives from the soul's mutability, in this text the body's susceptibility to sin is explained in terms of the body's natural mortality:

> Likewise, talking about our souls and our bodies in his Epistle to the Romans and teaching us how our souls can reach toward virtue, the Apostle also said that the body, by the power of its movement, is susceptible to sin because of its mortality[34].

Conclusion

At this point, we can conclude that, according to Theodore of Mopsuestia, *death* is not only punishment for men but also *an important educational tool*. It is precisely because men are mortal that they have been able to appreciate

---

[32] *Theod. Mopsuest.*, Fragm. in ep. ad Rom. 5, 13-14: K. Staab, Pauluskommentare, p. 119: ὁ θάνατος ἐκράτησεν ἁπάντων τῶν ὁπωσδήποτε ἡμαρτηκότων· οὐ γάρ, ἐπειδὴ οὐχ ὅμοιον ἦν τὸ τῆς ἁμαρτίας εἶδος, τό τε τοῦ Ἀδὰμ καὶ τῶν λοιπῶν ἀνθρώπων, θανάτου γεγόνασιν ἐκτὸς οἱ λοιποί, ἀλλ' ὑπὲρ ὧν ἡμάρτανον ὁπωσδήποτε, τοῦ θανάτου τὴν ἀπόφασιν ἐδέξαντο πάντες· οὐ γὰρ τῆς τοιᾶσδε ἁμαρτίας τιμωρία ὁ θάνατος ὥρισται ἀλλὰ πάσης ἁμαρτίας. See also: ibid.: ἡμαρτηκότος γὰρ τοῦ Ἀδὰμ καὶ μὴν καὶ θνητοῦ διὰ τοῦτο γεγονότος, ἤ τε ἁμαρτία πάροδον ἔλαβεν εἰς τοὺς ἑξῆς καὶ ὁ θάνατος πάντων ἐκράτει τῶν ἀνθρώπων ὡς εἰκός. πάντων γὰρ ἡμαρτηκότων, εἰ καὶ μὴ παραπλησίαν τῷ Ἀδὰμ ἁμαρτίαν ἀλλ' οὖν γε ὁπωσδήποτε, τῶν μὲν οὕτω τῶν δὲ οὕτω, ἀνάγκη καὶ τὸν θάνατον ἦν κρατεῖν ἐφ' ἁπάντων ὁμοίως.

[33] Ibid.: ἀλλ' οὐδὲ ὁ νόμος ἐπεισελθὼν ἀνελεῖν αὐτὴν ἀπὸ τῶν ἀνθρώπων ἐδυνήθη· τοὐναντίον μὲν οὖν καὶ ἡ τοῦ ἁμαρτάνειν ἀφορμὴ ἐντεῦθεν ἡμῖν ἐπεγίνετο τῷ μηδὲ οἷόν τε εἶναι ἁμάρτημα κρίνεσθαι νόμων ἐκτός. ὄντων δὲ τῶν καθ' ἡμᾶς ἐν τούτοις ὡς μηδεμίαν τῆς ἐπὶ τὸ κρεῖττον μεταβολῆς ὑποφαίνεσθαι ἐλπίδα, λύσιν ἁπάντων ὁ Χριστὸς εἰργάσατο τῶν κακῶν. διὸ συντόμως ἐπήγαγε τὸ ὅς ἐστι τύπος τοῦ μέλλοντος, ἵνα εἴπῃ ὅτι ἐγένετο δὲ τὰ κατὰ τὸν Ἀδὰμ τύπος τῶν κατὰ Χριστόν, ἐπειδὴ ὥσπερ δι' ἐκείνου τῶν χειρόνων ἡ πάροδος ἐγένετο, οὕτω διὰ τούτου τῆς τῶν κρειττόνων ἀπολαύσεως τὴν ἀφορμὴν ἐδεξάμεθα.

[34] *Theod. Mopsuest.*, Commentarius in Evangelium Joannis Apostoli VIII, 16: J.-M. Vosté, CSCO 116, SSyr 63 (Paris 1940), p. 119: *Similiter et Apostolus, loquens de anima nostra et de corpore nostro in epistula ad Romanos, atque docens nos quomodo anima possit tendere ad virtutem, quomodo autem et corpus propter mortalitatem sibi naturalem faciliter motu naturae suae inclinetur ad peccatum.* See *Textus syriacus* in: J.-M. Vosté, CSCO 115, SSyr 62 (Paris 1940), p. 167.

the value of immortality and to become aware of the wretchedness of their situation. At the same time, *Adam's sin* brought man's changeable nature to a state of confusion, which, in turn, provoked an outpour of passions. This event brought sin to man, yet it also taught man to search for a proper solution to this problem[35]. The Antiochian thinker is convinced that God not only wanted to teach men how to live right but also to give them the opportunity to choose between dedicating their lives to God and dedicating them to evil[36]. The very possibility for sin (*peccato aditum*) has been given to men as an educational tool: sin represented a necessary choice, and not only the actual choice of sin but also the opportunity to choose God. Making good moral choices is man's highest pursuit. In Theodore's logic, the sensibility of human nature is inevitably accompanied by changeability. Hence, man needs to be able to make a free choice because man is a reasonable being. As part of his educational mission, God has also given men orders, laws that help man regulate his present life (κατὰ τὸν παρόντα βίον): life in man's first state, the first epoch of the *oikonomia* of salvation[37].

---

[35] See *Theod. Mopsuest.*, Hom. cat. XI: A. Mingana, Commentary on the Lord's Prayer, p. 124-142 (Syr.), p. 1-16 (Engl.). Cf. *Theod. Mopsuest.*, Hom. cat. XI, 1: A. Mingana, Commentary on the Lord's Prayer, p. 124 (Syr.), p. 1 (Engl.): "In this way he demonstrated to us that in addition to applying ourselves to correct worship of God and correct knowledge, we must also apply ourselves to bringing our lives in harmony with God's orders".
[36] According to Frederick McLeod, Theodore's thesis that for Adam, as well as for all men, mortality was educational emphasizes humanity's important, even central, place in Theodore's understanding of salvation (F. McLeod, The Roles of Christ's Humanity, 65-66; cf. R. Greer, Theodore of Mopsuestia: Exegete and Theologian [Westminster 1961] 16-17).
[37] *Theod. Mopsuest.*, Fragm. in ep. ad Rom. 7, 8: K. Staab, Pauluskommentare, p. 127: οὕτω καὶ ἐν τοῖς ἀνωτέροις τὸ τὴν ἐπιθυμίαν οὐκ ᾔδειν εἰ μὴ ὁ νόμος ἔλεγεν· οὐκ ἐπιθυμήσεις, ἀντὶ τοῦ οὐκ ἂν ᾔδειν ὡς οὐ δεῖ τι ποιεῖν τῶν ἐν ἐπιθυμίᾳ κειμένων, εἰ μὴ νόμος ἦν ὁ τοῦτο διορίζων ἡμῖν· καὶ γὰρ τὸ ἐν ἐμοὶ ὅτε λέγει, τὸ κοινὸν λέγει τῶν ἀνθρώπων καὶ τοῖς τοῦ Ἀδὰμ εἰς ἀπόδειξιν κέχρηται τῶν κοινῶν. ὅθεν ἐπὶ τοῦ οἰκείου κἀκεῖνο λέγει προσώπου, διὰ πάντων δεῖξαι βουλόμενος, ὅτι ἀναγκαίως μὲν κατὰ τὸν παρόντα βίον νόμοις πολιτευόμεθα, ὑφ' ὧν ἡ ἔμφυτος ἀνακινεῖται διάκρισις, παιδευομένων ὧν τε ἀπέχεσθαι καὶ ἃ ποιεῖν προσήκει, ὥστε καὶ τὸ λογικὸν ἐν ἡμῖν ἐνεργὸν εἶναι. χρεία δὲ τῆς μελλούσης ἡμῖν καταστάσεως ἐν ᾗ γεγονότες τὰ φαινόμενα ἡμῖν καλά, ταῦτα καὶ ποιῆσαι δυνησόμεθα ῥᾳδίως. ὅθεν τῆς οἰκείας ἐχόμενος ἀκολουθίας καὶ τοῦ δεικνύναι, ὡς οὐδ' ἂν τις ἦν ἐν ἡμῖν διάκρισις τοῦ τε καλοῦ καὶ τοῦ χείρονος, οὐδὲ ἁμαρτίας ἐπίγνωσις, εἰ μὴ νόμῳ ταῦτα διώριστο παρ' ἡμῖν, ἀλόγων δὲ δίκην τὸ προστυχὸν ποιεῖν ἅπαν ἐμέλλομεν, ἐπάγει· χωρὶς γὰρ νόμου ἁμαρτία νεκρά. οὐδ' ἂν ἐνεργηθείη, φησίν, ἁμάρτημα μὴ νόμῳ διωρισμένον. διὰ τί; ὅτι οὐχ ἡ πρᾶξις ἁμάρτημα ἁπλῶς, ἀλλὰ τὸ εἰδότα ὧν ἀπέχεσθαι προσήκει, ποιεῖν τι παρὰ τὰ ἐγνωσμένα καλῶς ἔχειν. Cf. *Theod. Mopsuest.*, In ep. ad Gal. II, 15-16: H. B. Swete, Theodori Mopsuesteni, vol. 1, p. 31.

Michel Stavrou, Paris (France)

« Héritiers de la malédiction survenue en Adam »
L'enseignement de saint Cyrille d'Alexandrie sur le péché des origines

Saint Cyrille d'Alexandrie est bien connu comme le grand docteur de l'Incarnation dans son combat contre le nestorianisme et les excès de l'École d'Antioche[1].

Dans son œuvre abondante, consacrée à l'exégèse et à la réfutation des hérésies arienne et nestorienne, il est notable que, de même que ses prédécesseurs Irénée de Lyon ou Athanase d'Alexandrie, il n'étudie pas vraiment le Premier Adam pour lui-même, mais il s'y intéresse surtout dans la perspective du salut que le Christ, Nouvel Adam, nous a apporté.

Dans ce court article, nous aimerions mettre en évidence l'originalité de la vision de saint Cyrille sur les causes et les effets du péché ancestral qui fait de tous les hommes les « héritiers de la malédiction survenue en Adam »[2]. Nous voudrions voir notamment dans quelle mesure sa vision se démarque de celle de saint Augustin d'Hippone sur la question d'une culpabilité des hommes héritée d'Adam. L'œuvre de ce Père étant considérable et souvent répétitive, nous nous appuierons sur l'examen de quelques passages emblématiques de ses écrits où sont présentées la signification et les conséquences de la chute d'Adam.

I. Les causes du péché d'Adam : la condition de créature et une liberté dévoyée

Pour Cyrille, l'homme a d'abord été créé « à l'image et à la ressemblance de Dieu ». En commentant Gn 2, 7 – « et sur sa face, [Dieu] souffla un souffle de vie » – Cyrille soutient que le « souffle de vie » (πνοὴν ζωῆς) auquel le texte biblique fait référence est, en fait, le Saint-Esprit qui a « marqué de son sceau »

---

[1] Parmi les ouvrages récents présentant une biographie renouvelée de saint Cyrille, on peut citer : *J. A. McGuckin*, St. Cyril of Alexandria : the christological controversy. Its history, theology, and texts (Crestwood ²2004) 1–125 ; *N. Russell*, Cyril of Alexandria (Londres – New York 2000) 3–58.

[2] *Cyrille d'Alexandrie*, De Dog. sol. 6 : L.-R. Wickham, Cyril of Alexandria. Select Letters (Oxford 1983), p. 202.

« *Héritiers de la malédiction survenue en Adam* »

(κατεσφραγίζετο) l'image de Dieu dans le premier homme. Pour lui l'homme a été créé en deux temps : Adam a d'abord été créé à l'image et à la ressemblance de Dieu ; puis il a reçu le Saint-Esprit dont l'effusion a donné la vie et les qualités divines au premier homme[3].

Cyrille reconnaît l'existence en l'homme d'une liberté originelle et fondamentale :

> L'homme a été créé au commencement en se voyant confier les rênes de ses propres volontés (θελημάτων) et en possédant l'inclination vers ce qu'il pouvait choisir. Libre en effet est la Divinité (τὸ Θεῖον) selon laquelle il a été formé (μεμόρφωτο)[4].

Au départ, l'homme, étranger aux passions et incorruptible, était tourné vers Dieu et « regardait vers ce bien sans se laisser distraire, comme s'il ne voyait que lui, inclinait vers lui avec tout le poids de sa volonté, et s'y appliquait avec tout son bon vouloir (ἐθελουργὸς εὖ μάλα) »[5]. Pour Cyrille, malgré la corruptibilité inhérente à sa condition de créature[6], l'homme, contre sa nature (παρὰ φύσιν), était rendu par Dieu supérieur à la corruption :

> Le Créateur de toutes choses faisait dès le commencement l'homme incorruptible et indestructible, affranchi sur ce point des lois de sa propre nature, et par suite établi hors des troubles. [...] Puis, en lui donnant le pouvoir de faire ce qu'il voulait, il le gratifiait de la gloire qui convient à des êtres libres. Car il fallait, oui, il fallait que la vertu [ἀρετὴν] apparaisse en nous comme le résultat d'un choix [προαιρετικήν][7].

Mais, en raison de l'instabilité foncière liée à son statut de créature muable (τρεπτός), l'orientation d'Adam vers le bien n'a pu se maintenir : cette orientation était une vocation et non une nécessité naturelle ; aussi restait-il libre de pencher vers le bien ou le mal, sachant que demeurer dans le bien résultait non de sa nature mais de son libre choix :

---

[3] *Cyrille d'Alexandrie*, In Joannem 1, 32-33 : P. E. Pusey, S.P.N. Cyrilli archiepiscopi Alexandrini in D. Ioannis euangelium, vol. I (Bruxelles ²1965), p. 182.
[4] *Cyrille d'Alexandrie*, Glaphyra in Genesim I, 4 : PG 69, 24C. Trad. française par nos soins.
[5] *Cyrille d'Alexandrie*, Contra Julianum III, 24 : J. Bouffartigue et al., SC 582 (Paris 2016), p. 212-213.
[6] Cyrille est ici directement tributaire de saint Athanase d'Alexandrie : « L'homme est par nature mortel car il est issu du néant », *Athanase d'Alexandrie*, De incarnatione Verbi IV, 6 : C. Kannengiesser, SC 199 (Paris 2016), p. 278.
[7] *Cyrille d'Alexandrie*, Epistulae paschales XV, 4 : W. H. Burns et al., SC 434 (Paris 1998), p. 197-199 (texte et trad.).

Il a été créé maître de lui-même [αὐτοκρατὴς], libre [ἐλεύθερος] et avec la faculté de s'élancer par les inclinations de ses propres volontés vers ce qu'il choisirait (ἕλοιτο), soit le bien, soit le mal[8].

Cyrille évoque constamment la « transgression » (παράβασις) par Adam et Ève, à l'instigation du diable, de l'ordre donné par Dieu de ne pas manger du fruit de l'arbre de la connaissance du bien et du mal (cf. Gn 2, 16–17). Du fait de leur fragilité, mais aussi surtout de leur choix de suivre la suggestion du tentateur, Adam et Ève ont transgressé les commandements du Créateur et se sont détournés vers le mal :

> Lorsque la femme fut portée vers la transgression [παράβασιν] par les ruses du diable et qu'elle fit consommation du fruit de celui des arbres qui était défendu, et que notre ancêtre Adam lui aussi glissa avec elle [συγκατώλισθε], aussitôt la nature était condamnée à mort [θανάτῳ κατεδικάζετο] [...][9].

C'est donc le fait de s'être détourné de Dieu et de ses commandements qui a provoqué la colère du Créateur et ramené l'homme à sa condition limitée de créature mortelle.

II. Les conséquences du péché d'Adam

Dans son *Commentaire sur l'Évangile de Jean*, Cyrille explique que la désobéissance d'Adam eut pour conséquence immédiate que sa « ressemblance avec Dieu fut défigurée » et que les « traits » divins (χαρακτῆρες) qui avaient été ceux d'Adam lors de sa création ne furent plus lumineux, mais devinrent plus pâles et plus sombres[10]. Mais c'est seulement lorsque le péché eut exercé sa domination sur l'humanité que l'Esprit cessa de demeurer dans les hommes :

> Du fait que le genre humain s'étendait jusqu'à devenir innombrable, et que le péché régnait sur tous, l'âme de chacun étant conquise de diverses manières, la nature était dépouillée de sa grâce primitive; et l'Esprit s'en va totalement [ἀπανίσταται παντελῶς] et l'être raisonnable (λογικὸς) tombe dans la pire déraison (ἀλογίαν), ignorant même le Créateur[11].

---

[8] *Cyrille d'Alexandrie*, Contra Julianum VIII, 24 : PG 76, 925B. Trad. française (légèrement remaniée) reprise de : M.-O. Boulnois, Liberté, origine du mal et prescience divine selon Cyrille d'Alexandrie, Revue des Études Augustiniennes 46 (2000) 61–82, ici 74.
[9] *Cyrille d'Alexandrie*, Glaphyra in Genesim I, 5 : PG 69, 20D–21A. Trad. française (légèrement remaniée) reprise de : B. Meunier, Le Christ de Cyrille d'Alexandrie (Paris 1997) 30.
[10] *Cyrille d'Alexandrie*, In Joannem 1, 32–33 : P. E. Pusey, vol. I (Bruxelles ²1965), p. 183.
[11] *Cyrille d'Alexandrie*, In Joannem 1, 32–33 : P. E. Pusey, vol. I (Bruxelles ²1965), p. 183. Trad. française par nos soins.

Ce thème du départ «total» de l'Esprit Saint, corrélé avec la prolifération du péché parmi les hommes, est essentiel. Il sera ensuite sous-jacent dans la compréhension cyrillienne lorsque le Christ ressuscité «soufflera» l'Esprit Saint sur les Apôtres (Jn 20, 22), comme signe d'une véritable recréation du genre humain.

La plupart des textes où saint Cyrille évoque la chute ancestrale sont construits sur une opposition globale entre la situation de perdition suscitée par Adam et la venue du salut par le Christ, Nouvel Adam. Le Père alexandrin est directement tributaire d'une péricope paulinienne qu'il cite fréquemment – 1 Co 15, 21-22 : «Puisque la mort est venue par un homme, la résurrection des morts est aussi venue par un homme. Car, de même que tous meurent en Adam, de même aussi tous revivront en Christ».

C'est dans le cadre de sa christologie que nous pouvons comprendre l'enseignement de Cyrille sur la chute des origines, exposé notamment dans son *Commentaire de l'Épître aux Romains*. Sinon, certaines de ses affirmations lues dans une perspective théologique postérieure pourraient facilement conduire à des conclusions éloignées de leur contexte et de la pensée de leur auteur.

Dans son *Commentaire sur l'Évangile de Jean*, Cyrille écrit de façon caractéristique : «Tu entends comment la transgression [commise] en Adam [ἡ παράβασις ἡ ἐν Ἀδάμ] et, pour ainsi dire, le fait de s'être détourné [ἀποστροφὴ] des commandements divins, nous ont arrangé la nature de l'homme, et comment cela l'a disposée à revenir à la terre qui lui est propre »[12].

On remarque ici que la transgression est présentée comme «[accomplie] en Adam». Ce mode d'expression typiquement biblique qui souligne la personnalité corporative du premier homme – à savoir le fait qu'il représente lui-même mais aussi tout le genre humain – ne manque pas de nous interroger. Nous verrons s'il peut signifier, pour le Père alexandrin, le fait que tous les hommes étaient présents mystiquement dans la transgression d'Adam.

Dans un premier temps, cette manière de parler entend souligner que la transgression initiale affecte, à travers Adam et Ève, «la nature de l'homme», donc tous les êtres humains. Cyrille emploie une expression très forte en ce sens : «Le péché s'est jeté [εἰσήλατο] sur la nature de l'homme »[13].

---

[12] *Cyrille d'Alexandrie*, In Joannem 14, 20 : P. E. Pusey, vol. II (Bruxelles ²1965), p. 488. Trad. française : B. Meunier, Le Christ de Cyrille d'Alexandrie, 30.
[13] *Cyrille d'Alexandrie*, In Ep. ad Romanos 5, 18 : P. E. Pusey, vol. III (Bruxelles ²1965), p. 186. Trad. française par nos soins.

Et de même, dans son *De adoratione*, il précise : « La nature de l'homme a glissé, cela est reconnu de tous, vers la mort et la corruption [κατώλισθεν ὁμολογουμένως εἰς θάνατον καὶ φθορὰν ἡ ἀνθρώπου φύσις] »[14].

Le passage permanent d'un sujet à l'autre – c'est-à-dire d'Adam à la « nature de l'homme », ou même aux « hommes » – pour décrire la chute veut sans doute exprimer la corrélation qui existe entre le péché d'Adam et la tendance universelle au mal qui sévit depuis cet événement primordial.

Processus mimétique d'accomplissement du péché

L'un des passages les plus délicats de l'œuvre sotériologique de saint Cyrille est constitué par ses remarques dans son commentaire de *Romains* 5, 12 :

> Comme je l'ai dit, par le péché la mort s'est introduite dans le premier homme et dans le principe de notre genre [γένους ἀρχῇ]. Ensuite, elle a été distribuée au reste, à tout le genre humain [ὅλον τὸ γένος]. [...] Ainsi, éloignés de la face du Dieu très saint, compte tenu de ce que la raison de l'homme se consacre avec soin aux choses néfastes dès sa jeunesse, nous vivions d'une manière très irrationnelle. Et la mort, s'étant répandue, dévorait, comme dit le prophète : « L'Hadès a élargi son âme et ouvert sa bouche sans mesure [μὴ διαλιπεῖν] » (Is 5, 14 LXX). Car puisque nous sommes devenus des imitateurs de la transgression accomplie en Adam [τῆς ἐν Ἀδὰμ παραβάσεως γεγόναμεν μιμηταί] dans la mesure où tous ont péché [καθ' ὃ πάντες ἥμαρτον], nous avons subi le même châtiment que lui [ταῖς ἴσαις ἐκείνῳ δίκαις ὑπενενήγμεθα][15].

Nous constatons qu'en lisant la fameuse finale de Rm 5, 12 : ἐφ' ᾧ πάντες ἥμαρτον, Cyrille interprète la locution ἐφ' ᾧ comme un adverbe et qu'il la transcrit par καθ' ὅ qui, compte tenu de l'absence de l'antécédent dans la proposition qui précède le pronom relatif ὅ, peut se traduire par « dans la mesure où ».

---

[14] Cyrille d'Alexandrie, De adoratione in spiritu et veritate III : PG 68, 289A. Trad. française : B. Meunier, Le Christ de Cyrille d'Alexandrie, 32-33.
[15] Cyrille d'Alexandrie, In Ep. ad Romanos 5, 12 : P. E. Pusey, vol. III (Bruxelles ²1965), p. 182. Trad. française par nos soins; cf. J. Townsend, Patristic Commentaries on Rom. 5:12-21: Translation and Analysis (New York 1967) 12; D. Weaver, The exegesis of Romans 5:12 among the Greek Fathers and its implications for the doctrine of original sin : the 5th-12th centuries, SVTQ 29/2 (1985) 133-159, ici 144-145.

L'archevêque d'Alexandrie met bien ici en évidence la forte référence symbolique et morale que constitue la transgression d'Adam. Pour lui, les hommes sont prisonniers d'un véritable syndrome mimétique par lequel ils reproduisent presque fatalement dans leurs péchés personnels le geste de leur ancêtre (τῆς ἐν Ἀδὰμ παραβάσεως μιμηταὶ), actualisant ainsi la déchéance ancestrale. Donc, si l'humanité a reçu un châtiment identique à celui d'Adam, c'est parce que tous pèchent *à la manière d'Adam*.

Transmission de la mortalité

Cyrille utilise une image biologique pour décrire le lien entre Adam et ses descendants : « La condamnation est passée à tous les hommes comme si le mal passait à partir de la racine vers ses rejetons [καθάπερ ἐκ ῥίζης ἐπὶ τὰ ἐξ αὐτῆς ἰόντος τοῦ πάθους] »[16].

Adam est présenté à plusieurs reprises, notamment dans le commentaire de Romains 5, comme la «racine» et même la «racine première» (ῥίζης πρώτης)[17] du genre humain. Ce titre non biblique est presque toujours associé au père de l'humanité dans le contexte de la mortalité héritée de la chute :

> Notre ancêtre Adam, en tant que racine du genre [humain] [ὡς ῥίζα τοῦ γένους], s'est entendu dire : «Tu es terre et à la terre tu retourneras» (Gn 3, 19)[18].

C'est à partir de cette racine que la mortalité s'est propagée à tout le genre humain. Mais, pareillement et inversement, la vie éternelle se répand du Christ ressuscité, et saint Cyrille – à la suite de saint Paul et de plusieurs Pères – dresse un parallèle entre Adam et le Christ :

> [...] Le Créateur, en se souciant de ceux qui péchaient selon la ressemblance de la désobéissance d'Adam, soutint par la Providence ses créatures et prépara une sorte de deuxième racine de la race humaine, qui nous ramène à l'incorruption du commencement [...][19].

---

[16] Cyrille d'Alexandrie, Glaphyra in Genesim I, 5 : PG 69, 28C. Trad. française par nos soins.
[17] Cyrille d'Alexandrie, In Ep. ad Romanos 5, 18 : P. E. Pusey, vol. III (Bruxelles ²1965), p. 186 ; Cyrille d'Alexandrie, Quod unus sit Christus 757c : G. M. de Durand, SC 97 (Paris 2008), p. 444–446.
[18] Cyrille d'Alexandrie, In Habac 3, 2 : P. E. Pusey, vol. II (Bruxelles ²1965), p. 125. Trad. française par nos soins.
[19] Cyrille d'Alexandrie, Glaphyra in Genesim I, 5: PG 69, 28D. Trad. française par nos soins.

Corrélation circulaire entre péché et mort

Si saint Cyrille affirme clairement que la mort et la corruption sont répandues dans tous les hommes à la suite du péché d'Adam, il souligne aussi que la peccabilité est entrée par le premier homme en se répandant à partir de lui à toute la race humaine. Cependant le terme de «péché» n'est pas bien défini chez Cyrille et la relation de causalité entre péché et mortalité n'est pas évidente. Comme l'écrit David Weaver,

> il est raisonnable de supposer que Cyrille utilise le mot «péché» dans un sens équivoque, tantôt voulant dire le premier péché d'Adam, et tantôt dans un sens collectif pour signifier les péchés personnels des descendants d'Adam[20].

Pour Bernard Meunier, l'un des meilleurs spécialistes de Cyrille d'Alexandrie, il existe chez celui-ci «une sorte de parallélisme entre la transmission de la mort et celle du péché, sans qu'il soit dit explicitement que la première est la cause du deuxième»[21].

Dans le commentaire de Romains 5, on trouve que le péché est nommé «le patron de la mort» (πρόξενος θανάτου), qui, par lui-même, produit la mort[22], mais dans la phrase suivante il appelle la mort la «mère» (μητρί) du péché. Il nous semble donc que, pour le docteur alexandrin, il existe une sorte de causalité circulaire entre le péché et la mort, chacun des deux renforçant le pouvoir de l'autre.

Culpabilité des hommes reçue du péché ancestral ?

La question d'un héritage éventuel, par tous les hommes, de la culpabilité d'Adam est abordée de manière indirecte par Cyrille dans son commentaire de Romains 5, 18, où il s'interroge sur la manière dont les hommes se sont éloignés de Dieu :

> Comment la multitude [οἱ πολλοί] est-elle devenue pécheresse par lui (Adam) ? Pourquoi sa transgression est-elle tombée sur nous ? Et comment ont été condamnés avec lui tous ceux qui n'étaient pas encore nés, alors que Dieu dit : «*Les pères ne mourront pas à cause de leurs enfants ni les enfants à cause de leurs pères, l'âme qui a péché mourra*» (Dt 24, 16) ? Quelle serait l'explication de cela ?[23]

---

[20] D. Weaver, The exegesis of Romans, 145. Trad. française par nos soins.
[21] B. Meunier, Le Christ de Cyrille d'Alexandrie, 56.
[22] *Cyrille d'Alexandrie*, In Ep. ad Romanos 5, 13 : P. E. Pusey, vol. III (Bruxelles ²1965), p. 183.
[23] *Cyrille d'Alexandrie*, In Ep. ad Romanos 5, 18 : P. E. Pusey, vol. III (Bruxelles ²1965), p. 186. Trad. française par nos soins ; voir D. Weaver, The exegesis of Romans, 147.

« *Héritiers de la malédiction survenue en Adam* » 423

Puis il donne une réponse synthétique qui récapitule les effets collectifs du péché ancestral :

> Eh bien, « *c'est l'âme qui a péché qui mourra* » (Dt 24, 16). Mais nous sommes devenus pécheurs par la désobéissance d'Adam de la manière suivante : [Adam] avait été créé pour l'incorruption et pour la vie ; au paradis des délices, sa vie était digne de sainteté [ἁγιοπρεπής] : son intellect [νοῦς] tout entier était constamment voué à la contemplation de Dieu, son corps était dans la sécurité et le calme, sans que se manifeste aucun plaisir mauvais, car le tumulte des mouvements inconvenants n'existait pas en lui. Mais lorsqu'il tomba par le fait du péché et glissa dans la corruption, alors les plaisirs et les impuretés pénétrèrent la nature de la chair, et la loi de la sauvagerie se développa dans nos membres. La nature tomba donc malade du péché *par la désobéissance d'un seul*, c'est-à-dire d'Adam. Ainsi « *la multitude fut constituée pécheresse* » (Rm 5, 19) ; non pas qu'elle ait partagé la faute [συμπαραβεβηκότες] d'Adam – puisqu'elle n'existait pas encore [οὐ γὰρ ἦσαν πώποτε] –, mais parce qu'elle était de sa nature qui était tombée sous la loi du péché. De même, donc, qu'en Adam la nature de l'homme est tombée malade de la corruption [ἐρρώστησεν τὴν φθορὰν] par la désobéissance, parce qu'ainsi les passions se sont insinuées en elle, de même, en Christ, elle en a été débarrassée ; car Il a été obéissant à Dieu le Père et n'a pas commis le péché[24].

On voit que Cyrille utilise volontiers le langage de la nature : « La nature tomba donc malade du péché ». Il explique qu'Adam, par sa chute, a affaibli sa nature, désormais « malade de corruption », en introduisant cette faiblesse : la propension à pécher et à s'éloigner de Dieu, héritée par tous les hommes[25]. En même temps Cyrille précise : « Non pas que [la multitude] ait partagé la faute d'Adam, puisqu'elle n'existait pas encore ». Il refuse clairement d'envisager, pour les héritiers d'Adam, une culpabilité personnelle qui résulterait mystiquement de la transgression originelle.

Un autre passage du *De dogmatum solutione* (chapitre 6), est encore plus explicite à cet égard :

> Il faut se demander comment notre ancêtre Adam nous a fait passer [παρέπεμψε] la sentence qui avait été portée contre lui à cause de la transgression. Car il lui avait été dit : « *Tu es terre et tu retourneras à la terre* » (Gn 3, 19), et il devint corruptible, d'incorruptible qu'il était, et fut soumis aux liens de la mort. Et puisque, après être tombé dans la mort, il a engendré des enfants, nous qui sommes nés de lui comme

---

[24] Cyrille d'Alexandrie, In Ep. ad Romanos 5, 18 : P. E. Pusey, vol. III (Bruxelles ²1965), p. 186-187. Trad. française par nos soins ; sur ce passage, voir aussi B. Bobrinskoy, L'héritage d'Adam selon le père Jean Meyendorff, La Pensée orthodoxe 6 (1998) 23.
[25] Cf. B. Meunier, Le Christ de Cyrille d'Alexandrie, 55-56.

d'un être corruptible, nous sommes nés corruptibles; ainsi sommes-nous aussi héritiers de la malédiction survenue en Adam [τῆς ἐν Ἀδὰμ κατάρας κληρονόμοι]. En effet, nous n'avons absolument pas été châtiés pour avoir désobéi avec lui au commandement qu'il avait reçu [ὡς σὺν ἐκείνῳ παρακούσαντες τῆς θείας ἐντολῆς ἧς ἐδέξατο], mais, comme je le disais, étant devenu mortel, il a fait passer la malédiction [παρέπεμψε τὴν ἀράν] à sa propre semence. Nous sommes en effet nés mortels, issus d'un mortel[26].

De nouveau, nous constatons que Cyrille limite à la personne d'Adam la culpabilité liée à la transgression initiale, tandis qu'il rappelle les effets transmis à tout le genre humain : la corruption et la mortalité. Il est donc bien clair qu'il ne partage pas la vision augustinienne d'une faute collective commise lors de la chute ancestrale. Certes la malédiction a ses effets sur tout le genre humain, mais il s'agit de celle d'Adam[27]. Comme le souligne Jean Meyendorff, à propos de la compréhension cyrillienne :

> La race humaine possède une nature corrompue dans la mesure où elle descend d'Adam, mais chaque hypostase humaine, celle d'Adam comme celle de chacun de ses descendants, demeure totalement responsable de ses actes; elle ne partage pas la faute d'Adam, elle l'imite[28].

Cyrille considère que les hommes sont « héritiers de la malédiction survenue en Adam » à travers sa « semence » : « Nous qui sommes nés de lui […] ». La tendance humaine au péché et à la mortalité est donc, selon lui, héritée d'Adam de manière biologique.

Condamnation paradoxale du genre humain « en Adam »

Un autre thème important du passage du commentaire de Romains 5, 12[29] que nous avons cité plus haut est celui du châtiment que subissent tous les hommes, puisque Cyrille cite Is 5, 14 (LXX) : « L'Hadès a élargi son âme et

---

[26] *Cyrille d'Alexandrie*, De dogmatum solutione 6 : L.-R. Wickham (Oxford 1983), p. 200-202. Trad. française (légèrement corrigée) : B. Meunier, Le Christ de Cyrille d'Alexandrie, 52.

[27] Voir par exemple : *Cyrille d'Alexandrie*, Glaphyra in Numeros III, 2 : PG 69, 620D : « Puisque Adam avait négligé le commandement donné et glissé vers la transgression, il fut immédiatement maudit [ἐπάρατος], et en lui le genre humain était condamné à la mort et à la corruption ». Trad. française : B. Meunier, Le Christ de Cyrille d'Alexandrie, 54.

[28] J. Meyendorff, Christ in Eastern Christian Thought (Crestwood 1975) 116. Trad. française par nos soins.

[29] *Cyrille d'Alexandrie*, In Ep. ad Romanos 5, 12 : P. E. Pusey, vol. III (Bruxelles ²1965), p. 182, cité plus haut.

« *Héritiers de la malédiction survenue en Adam* »

ouvert sa bouche sans mesure». André-Marie Dubarle considère qu'il serait contraire à la pensée de Cyrille de voir dans ce passage l'idée d'une condamnation éternelle de l'humanité :

> Cyrille connaît bien les suites néfastes du péché d'Adam : corruptibilité, mortalité, vie déréglée sous la tyrannie de la loi du péché. Mais, à la différence d'Augustin[30], il n'ajoute nulle part que le péché d'Adam entraîne en soi la damnation éternelle de tout le genre humain. Bien au contraire, il mentionne habituellement la restauration opérée par le Christ aussitôt après avoir décrit les conséquences ruineuses du péché d'Adam. Il rappelle le texte de la Loi : « Les pères ne mourront pas pour les fils, ni les fils pour les pères. L'âme qui pèche mourra », en contaminant les expressions de Dt 24, 16 par celles d'Ez 18, 4 et 20[31].

Ainsi, pour Dubarle, la citation d'Isaïe 5, 14 par Cyrille dans son explication de Romains 5, 12 ne signifie pas pour le docteur alexandrin une condamnation éternelle à l'enfer. Il s'agit d'une « simple illustration imagée » de la péricope paulinienne : « La mort a passé dans tous les hommes »[32].

Du fait du péché d'Adam la mort est entrée dans le monde et tous l'ont héritée. Cyrille affirme clairement la transmission à tous les hommes de la condamnation de l'ancêtre, ou plutôt des effets de celle-ci, c'est-à-dire la mort et la corruption. Mais la vision de la mort dont témoigne saint Cyrille est celle de ses prédécesseurs : plutôt que d'une malédiction, il s'agit pour lui d'un remède paradoxal. Dans les *Glaphyres sur la Genèse*, lorsqu'il rappelle que l'homme a été condamné à la mort et à la corruption, il ajoute :

> Dieu avait prévu ce qui serait le plus bénéfique dans l'événement [...]. Il a imaginé avantageusement la mort selon la chair ; elle n'envoyait pas à une destruction totale l'être vivant, qui était conservé plutôt en vue d'une nouvelle fabrication et pour être façonné de nouveau comme un vase brisé[33].

---

[30] *Augustin*, Enchiridion 26–27 : PL 40, 245 ; De civitate Dei XIV, 1 : PL 41, 403 ; De nuptiis et concupiscentia I, XXXII, 37 : PL 44, 434 ; Opus imperfectum contra Julianum I, 57 : PL 44, 1079.
[31] A.-M. *Dubarle*, Le péché originel : perspectives théologiques (Paris 1983) 30–31.
[32] Ibid., 31. En cela, il s'oppose à H. Rondet dans : H. *Rondet*, Le péché originel dans la tradition patristique et théologique (Paris 1967) 107.
[33] *Cyrille d'Alexandrie*, Glaphyra in Genesim 4 : PG 69, 24D. Trad. française par nos soins.

Dans le livre VIII du *De adoratione,* Cyrille réfléchit aux principes généraux de la justice divine dans le cas des crimes involontaires. Il explique que la convoitise mauvaise fait subir une sorte de violence à la volonté libre. L'acte, répréhensible en soi, qui en résulte n'est pas soumis par le juge divin à une peine définitive mais à un exil temporaire, tout comme le meurtrier involontaire qui dans la loi judaïque pouvait revenir dans son lieu d'origine après la mort du grand prêtre. Cyrille voit en ces dispositions des « ombres du mystère du Christ » et une annonce prophétique du salut apporté par la mort de l'unique Grand Prêtre qui est descendu dans l'Hadès et a dit à ceux qui y étaient enchaînés : « Sortez ! »[34].

Il en résulte, pour André-Marie Dubarle, et contre l'interprétation de Stanislas Lyonnet[35], qu'il est impossible de « mettre une égalité entre la pensée d'Augustin et celle de Cyrille, en attribuant à ce dernier la doctrine que l'humanité, à la suite du péché d'Adam, est ‹ privée du salut, de soi condamnée à l'enfer ›, même en ajoutant aussitôt qu'elle en est libérée par Jésus-Christ ». En effet, souligne Dubarle, « ce qui est affirmé expressément et à plusieurs reprises par Augustin est rejeté par Cyrille dans des textes explicites et ne s'accorde pas avec sa conception de la justice divine »[36].

Conclusion : une nature humaine « refaçonnée en Christ pour la sanctification »

C'est dans le cadre d'une doctrine originale sur le salut que saint Cyrille a réfléchi à la signification théologique du péché ancestral. Il s'est trouvé trop éloigné de la polémique entre Pélage et Augustin pour que celle-ci ait pu avoir eu une influence conséquente sur sa vision théologique. Son souci n'était jamais de brosser une hamartiologie mais de mettre en évidence les voies de la résurrection en Christ. Sa sotériologie est structurée selon une opposition marquée entre le Premier Adam, dont la chute a eu des conséquences universelles, et le Christ, Nouvel Adam, qui apporte le salut universel à la fois en tant qu'homme mais aussi en tant que Fils de Dieu rempli et donateur de l'Esprit Saint.

---

[34] Cf. *Cyrille d'Alexandrie,* De adoratione VIII : PG 68, 581, résumé dans *A.-M. Dubarle,* Le péché originel, 30.
[35] *S. Lyonnet,* Le péché originel et l'exégèse de Rom. 5, 12–14, in : J. Huby, Saint Paul. Épître aux Romains (Paris 1957) 528 ; *S. Lyonnet,* Le péché originel en Rom. 5, 12. L'exégèse des Pères grecs et les décrets du concile de Trente, Biblica 41 (Rome 1960) 325–355, ici 340–341, 344.
[36] *A.-M. Dubarle,* Le péché originel, 31.

Pour Cyrille, les hommes, plongés dans l'état de faiblesse et de corruption qu'ils ont hérité d'Adam se sont trouvés poussés à commettre leurs propres péchés, devenant ainsi à leur tour des pécheurs à l'image du Premier Adam. Quelle que soit la résistance qu'ils opposent au péché, celle-ci se révèle insuffisante au salut et elle nécessite la restauration de chacun par le baptême dans la mort-résurrection du Christ. En effet le baptême nous fait accéder, par l'Eucharistie, à la nature humaine sanctifiée en Christ.

Le Christ est le Second Adam, celui en qui « toute la nature humaine a été recréée pour une vie nouvelle et [...] a été refaçonnée pour la sanctification »[37]. Le but même de l'Incarnation était justement cette recréation et sanctification. Dans la préface du *Contre Nestorius*, Cyrille écrit très clairement :

> Si le Verbe n'était pas né parmi nous selon la chair et n'avait pas participé de manière si semblable [παραπλησίως] aux mêmes conditions de vie que nous, Il n'aurait pas délivré la nature de l'homme des fautes portées en Adam, Il n'aurait pas repoussé de nos corps la corruption [φθοράν] et la force de la malédiction n'aurait pas pris fin[38].

Désormais, conclut-il, en Christ, « nous voyons la nature humaine, comme dans les secondes prémices du genre humain, posséder la liberté d'accès (παρρησίαν) à Dieu »[39].

Se faisant l'écho de la vision de saint Paul (cf. Rm 5), Cyrille écrit :

> De même que, par la transgression et la désobéissance d'Adam, notre nature avait été condamnée à mort [...], de la même façon, je pense, par l'obéissance et la justice du Christ, [...] la bénédiction et la vivification [ζωοποίησις] par l'Esprit ont pu s'étendre à notre nature tout entière[40].

Désormais, par l'Esprit Saint, nous faisons l'expérience d'une « renaissance de l'intellect » (νοητὴν ἀναγέννησιν) et atteignons une « conformité spirituelle » (συμμορφίαν πνευματικήν) avec celui qui est le véritable Fils par nature. Grâce

---

[37] *Cyrille d'Alexandrie*, In Joannem 17, 18–19 : P. E. Pusey, vol. II (Bruxelles ²1965), p. 723. Trad. française par nos soins.
[38] *Cyrille d'Alexandrie*, Contra Nestorium I, 1 : E. Schwartz, ACO I.1.6 (Berlin – Leipzig 1928), p. 17,24–27. Trad. française par nos soins.
[39] *Cyrille d'Alexandrie*, Contra Nestorium I, 1 : E. Schwartz, ACO I.1.6 (Berlin – Leipzig 1928), p. 17,39–41. Trad. française par nos soins.
[40] *Cyrille d'Alexandrie*, In Joannem 17, 18–19 : P. E. Pusey, vol. II (Bruxelles ²1965), p. 724–725. Trad. française par nos soins.

à cette ressemblance avec le Fils, nous pouvons désormais appeler Dieu « notre Père » et être incorruptibles, affranchis de tout lien avec notre « premier père », Adam, en qui nous avions subi la corruption[41].

---

[41] *Cyrille d'Alexandrie*, Quod unus sit Christus 724d-e : G. M. de Durand, SC 97 (Paris 2008), p. 334.

Georgiana Huian, Bern (Switzerland)

The Sin of Adam and Eve and the Restoration of the Image of God through Baptism according to Diadochus of Photike

Abstract:
This study identifies four strategies to reframe theologically the story of the sin of Adam and Eve in Diadochus of Photike. The first links the drama of the Fall with a universal phenomenology of temptation, reenacted in every human sin, and offers a spiritual remedy. The second tells the fall from unity into duality suffered by all human faculties and pleads for a return to unity. The third looks at the consequences of Adam's transgression through the lens of the distinction between image and likeness, and rereads the story of the proto-parents through the theology of Incarnation and grace. The fourth strategy uses plastic imagery such as painting and sealing to account for the restoration of the human being affected by the consequences of the sin of Adam and Eve. Studying the vocabulary and the arguments of Diadochus in this framework, the essay shows that Diadochus integrates the notion of ancestral sin in an anthropology with strong incarnational, pneumatological and sacramental (especially baptismal) emphasis.

I. Introduction

Diadochus (ca. 400–486), Bishop of Photike in Epirus, is known for his teaching on discernment and spiritual perfection, included in the *Philokalia*, for his explicit mentioning of the Jesus Prayer[1], and for his debate against the presuppositions of the Messalian movement[2]. He was contemporary with the

---

[1] K. Ware, The Jesus Prayer in St. Diadocus of Photice, in: G. D. Dragas (ed.), Aksum-Thyateira. A Festschrift for Archbishop Methodios of Thyateira and Great Britain (London 1985) 557–568. *Idem*, The Origins of the Jesus Prayer: Diadochus, Gaza, Sinai, in: C. Jones, G. Wainwright, E. Yarnold (eds.), The Study of Spirituality (New York – Oxford 1986) 175–184.

[2] Fr. *Dörr*, Diadochus von Photiké und die Messalianer. Ein Kampf zwischen wahrer und falscher Mystik im fünften Jahrhundert (Freiburg im Breisgau 1937). Dörr considers that Diadochus had a strong polemic with the "Messalian" Macarius regarding the relation between grace and sin. In the meanwhile, several studies showed the "orthodox" content of the Macarian homilies, placing their author in the 4th–5th centuries, without considering him a proponent of the Messalian doctrine. See, for example, the introduction of P. Deseille to the French edition: *P. Deseille*, Les homélies spirituelles de saint Macaire. Le Saint-Esprit et le Chrétien,

Fathers of Chalcedon[3]: moreover, he defended the doctrine of the two natures of Christ in his writings[4]. Against the background of this spiritual and Christological setting, Diadochus is the author of a great synthesis regarding the understanding of the human being. Walking in the footsteps of both Evagrian and Macarian views[5], Diadochus articulates an anthropology uniting the mind and the heart. In his view, the height of the platonic *nous* meets with the depth of the biblical *kardia*, in an attempt to recover a holistic harmony of the human person.

In fact, all his spiritual recommendations can be read as a longing to recover the initial unity and beauty of the human being, a state of direct communication with God through prayer[6], in which God becomes manifest in a state of

---

SO 40 (Bégrolles-en-Mauges 1984), particularly 14-19. For a reconstruction of the Messalian controversy and its main topics and motives, see the monograph of C. Stewart, "Working the Earth of the Heart". The Messalian Controversy in History, Texts, and Language to AD 431 (Oxford 1991).

[3] *Photius*, Bibliotheca 231: R. Henry, vol. V (Paris 1967), p. 65. Diadochus was not yet bishop of Photike during the council, but became bishop "some time between 451 and 458", as notes N. Russell, The Doctrine of Deification in the Greek Patristic Tradition (Oxford 2004) 246. Photius mentions also hundred chapters as an ascetical writing of "Diadochus, Bishop of Photike in Old Epirus": *Photius*, Bibliotheca 201: R. Henry, vol. III (Paris 1962), p. 100.

[4] See *Diad. Phot.*, Sermo de ascensione 4-6: É. des Places, SC 5 bis (Paris 1955), p. 166-168. For the Christology of Diadochus, see J. E. Rutherford, Sealed with the Likeness of God: Christ as Logos in Diadochus of Photike, in: T. Finan, D. V. Twomey (eds.), Studies in Patristic Christology (Dublin 1998) 67-83.

[5] Being aware of the problem of authorship of the Macarian homilies, I will conventionally call "Macarius" the author of the Macarian corpus, resonating with most of the manuscript tradition; when "Pseudo-Macarius" occurs, it is to respect the choice of the cited scholars. For the heritage of Macarius, see M. Plested, The Macarian Legacy. The Place of Macarius-Symeon in the Eastern Christian Tradition (Oxford 2004) 142-143: "In teaching the organic and essential relationship between knowledge and experience, Diadochus reveals himself to be a disciple of the experiential epistemology pioneered by Macarius." *Idem*, Macarius and Diadochus: An Essay in Comparison, StPatr 30 (1997) 234-240. For the heritage of Evagrius, see M. Plested, The Macarian Legacy (Oxford 2004) 135. N. Russell, The Doctrine of Deification, 246 attests that Diadochus presents a synthesis of Evagrius and Macarius that leads to a description of the spiritual life culminating with deification. Elements taken from Macarius and Evagrius are also mentioned by C. Ermatinger, Introduction to the Life and Spirituality of Diadochus of Photike, in: Following the Footsteps of the Invisible. The Complete Works of Diadochus of Photike (Collegeville, Minnesota 2010) 6.

[6] For the importance of prayer in Diadochus, see J. E. Rutherford, Praying the Trinity in Diadochus of Photike, in: D. V. Twomey, L. Ayres (eds.), The mystery of the Holy Trinity in the Fathers of the Church (Dublin 2007) 65-78.

The Sin of Adam and Eve and the Restoration of the Image of God   431

plenitude and certitude[7] of the spiritual sensation[8]. It is a longing after the lost state of Paradise, one may say. But how did the human being loose this condition and what does it mean to restore it? It is therefore necessary to regard the question of sin, and more precisely the sin that parted the human being from its perfect (initial) condition, in order to understand the possibility of recovering this first[9] beauty and fullness of being, in uninterrupted communion with God.

II. Whose sin? The drama of Adam and Eve

Let us look closely at how Diadochus considers the sin that affected so much the human constitution that it now requires the struggles of spiritual combat, the ineffable touch of divine grace and finally the filling with grace for the human being to recover its perfection, its union with God. Whose fault is this sin, how is it to be named and understood, when and how can its consequences be "undone" or overcome? Assuredly, Diadochus does not have a doctrinal talk on the "original sin", nor does he regard it "as a juridical guilt imputed collectively to humanity"[10]. But does he assume an original sin in the sense of a "primordial root […] at the heart of every personal sin"[11], as a constitutive weakening of our will, or as the event of shadowing, tarnishing or hiding the image of God in the human?[12]

In chapter 56 of his *One Hundred Gnostic Chapters*[13], Diadochus introduces

---

[7] "La *plèrophoria* – la pleine certitude, la perception de l'origine lumineuse – est continuellement requise." *J. Touraille*, Introduction à Diadoque de Photicé, Cent chapitres spirituels, in: L. Regnault, J. Touraille (intr., tr. notes), Philocalie des Pères neptiques, Fascicule 8 (Bégrolles-en-Mauges 1987) 130.

[8] See *M. Plested*, The Macarian Legacy, 134–140 ("Diadochus of Potike", 6.2. The Language of Sense); *C. Stewart*, "Working the Earth of the Heart", 137–138 (for the language of spiritual sense and sensation in Diadochus); ibid., 123–131 (for its roots in Pseudo-Macarius).

[9] I use "first" in an ontological sense, meaning the state of being intended by God at the creation of the human being.

[10] Definition by *P. Rigby*, Original Sin in Augustine's Confessions (Ottawa 1987) 1.

[11] *P. Rigby*, Original Sin, 2.

[12] On the hypothesis of a weakened human nature because of the "original sin", see *C. Ermatinger*, Introduction to the Life and Spirituality of Diadochus of Photike, in: Following the Footsteps of the Invisible, 61.

[13] This is the title according to the edition of *É. des Places*, Diadoque de Photicé, Œuvres spirituelles, SC 5 bis (Paris 1955), p. 84: κεφάλαια γνωστικὰ ρ'. The work also circulated under the title: *One Hundred Chapters on Spiritual Perfection = Capita centum de perfectione spirituali* (abbreviated as Cap.). C. Ermatinger translates this title as: *Discourses on Judgement and Spiritual Discernment*. J. E. Rutherford proposes the translation: *J. E. Rutherford, One Hundred Practical Texts on Perception and Spiritual Discernment from Diadochus of*

the episode of the temptation and fall of Adam and Eve in the attempt to explain the dissipation of the memory of God under the influence of the immoderate use of the bodily senses. The trigger of temptation lies in looking at the tree with pleasure (ἡδέως), in touching the fruit with ardent desire (μετὰ πολλῆς ἐπιθυμίας), followed by tasting it with intense pleasure (μετὰ ἐνεργοῦς ἡδονῆς), which brings an all-embracing passion (πάθος). Once this passion makes Eve "slip" into a "bodily embrace" of the desired object, all her desire will be directed towards the rejoicing in present things (τὴν τῶν παρόντων ἀπόλαυσιν)[14]. This phenomenology of desire causes spiritual nudity—only in spiritual nakedness becomes possible the fault or the disobedience of Eve and Adam. In this state of nakedness, the human is left without the discernment assured by grace. Therefore, a passing and deceiving sweetness, "the sweet appearance of the fruit"[15], insinuates itself as true sweetness. The ephemeral joy and the deceiving appearance of the object of desire make the tempted human being attract the other one in the same deceit—this is why Eve attracts Adam in her fall[16]. Seduced through her senses, she pulls her companion and sharer in the same humanity in her own seduction. They both share in the fault, in the immoderation if the senses which brings passion and finally the dissipation of the "memory of the heart" (μνήμη τῆς καρδίας) which was previously continually oriented towards God[17].

This moment seems to be extracted from the history of humanity and transferred in the phenomenology of temptation. As such, it affects not only the heart, but also the intellect or the mind of all human beings: it *introduces* a weakness in the noetic/mental power of the human to remember God's commandments. One may legitimately ask if Diadochus points here to *an inherited weakness* from the first human exemplars to their followers, or rather to a *pattern of the expansion of forgetfulness of God* in the human mind. His mention of "the first Eve" (πρώτη ἡ Εὔα) may as well be typological (and not necessarily chronological), in the tradition of paralleling Eve with Mary, the second/new Eve, and Adam with Christ, the second/new Adam[18]. But the question of in-

---

Photike (Belfast 2000).

[14] *Diad. Phot.*, Cap. 56: É. des Places, SC 5 bis (Paris 1955), p. 117; transl. C. Ermatinger (Collegeville, Minnesota 2010), p. 93.

[15] Ibid.

[16] Ibid., transl. C. Ermatinger (Collegeville, Minnesota 2010), p. 93: "dragging Adam along in her own fall". The language is literally that of mixing or mingling Adam in her own fault: μίξασα [...] τῷ ἑαυτῆς καὶ τὸν Ἀδὰμ πταίσματι.

[17] Ibid.

[18] This tradition is exemplary represented by Irenaeus in *Adversus haereses*, as the contribution of Ysabel de Andia to this volume shows.

heritance due to a genealogical line is never posed as such. It seems that the story of Adam and Eve explains not so much the intergenerational inheritance of a weakened humanity, but the slippery path of forgetting God. More precisely, it illustrates that forgetting just one commandment leads to the *fall* in the difficulty to live in the continual remembrance of God and his commandments:

> Our sight, our taste, and all our senses (αἰσθήσεις) dissipate the memory of the heart (διαφοροῦσι τὴν μνήμην τῆς καρδίας), when we use them immoderately, as the first Eve demonstrated for us. Indeed, she carefully remembered the divine mandate as long as she did not regard the forbidden tree with pleasure. In a certain sense, she was sheltered beneath the wings of ardent love for God, thus unaware of her own nudity. But when she looked at the tree with pleasure, when she touched it with desire, and then tasted its fruit with intense pleasure, then, naked, she immediately slipped into a bodily embrace joining all her passion to it. She squandered all her desire on the joy of present things, dragging Adam along in her own fall, just for the sake of the sweet appearance of the fruit. Ever since then it has been difficult to subdue the human mind in order to remember God's commandments.[19]

Whose sin is the first sin? In other words: who falls? At first glance, the answer is narrative: the fault belongs to Eve and Adam, the parents of all humankind. At a second reflection, however, the sin belongs to human senses and their immoderation, causing the human, "the first Eve", to leave her shelter "beneath the wings of ardent love for God". The climax of passion, attracting the fall, goes through seeing, touching, tasting and embracing[20]. The fall is Eve's, the fall is Adam's, but in the end, this is the fall of "all our senses" every time we use them immoderately—the case of Eve and Adam is only a paradigm of being seduced through intense desire of appearances. In any case, Diadochus is not interested to explain how this propensity to immoderation, to dissipation of memory of the heart and mind is *transmitted to*, let alone *inherited by* other individuals. In turn, he explains the cure to this dissipation:

> Living our whole life long gazing into the depths of our hearts (εἰς τὸ βάθος τῆς καρδίας ἡμῶν) with undying memory of God, we ought to live as blind men throughout this deceptive life (ὡς πηροὶ τὰς ὄψεις τῷ φιλαπατεῶνι τούτῳ ἐνδιάγωμεν βίῳ).[21]

---

[19] *Diad. Phot.*, Cap. 56: É. des Places, SC 5 bis (Paris 1955), p. 117, transl. C. Ermatinger (Collegeville, Minnesota 2010), p. 93.
[20] Interestingly, the sense of hearing is not mentioned. Maybe because hearing is closer to listening to God.
[21] *Diad. Phot.*, Cap. 56: É. des Places, SC 5 bis (Paris 1955), p. 117, transl. C. Ermatinger (Collegeville, Minnesota 2010), p. 93.

To the immoderate use of the bodily senses, which caused the fall, we have to oppose "the highest self-mastery" (ἀκροτάτης ἐγκρατείας)[22].

III. Human faculties: the story of unity and duality

Another important question arises: did the proto-sin cause an ontological or a phenomenal change? Is this a change in the deep structure of the human constitution or a functional change? Diadochus speaks of a doubling or splitting in two energies or movements, which occurred in all human faculties following the disobedience of Adam and Eve. Even when touched by the grace (in the beginner's stage of spiritual life), the mind or intellect still experiences a duality in knowledge and thought:

> And so, from the moment in which our mind (νοῦς) has slid into this double knowledge (τὸ διπλοῦν τῆς γνώσεως), it then produces good and bad thoughts at the same time (καλὰ καὶ φαῦλα διανοήματα), even though it does not choose to do so.[23]

The memory is also subject to this duality: it is itself divided into the remembering of good/of God/of the Lord[24] and the remembering of evil[25]. The origin of this division is a change in humanity caused by Adam's disobedience:

> Even as the mind strives to think of good things, soon it remembers evil things, given that ever since Adam's disobedience (ἀπὸ τῆς Ἀδὰμ παρακοῆς) human memory (ἡ τοῦ ἀνθρώπου μνήμη) is divided in double thought (εἰς διπλῆν τινα ἔννοιαν).[26]

---

[22] Ibid., transl. C. Ermatinger (Collegeville, Minnesota 2010), p. 94.
[23] *Diad. Phot.*, Cap. 88: É. des Places, SC 5 bis (Paris 1955), p. 148, transl. C. Ermatinger (Collegeville, Minnesota 2010), p. 117.
[24] "Memory of the good" (μνήμη ἀγαθοῦ): Cap. 97. "Memory of God" (μνήμη τοῦ θεοῦ): Cap. 3, 11, 27, 32, 33, 56, 58, 59, 60, 81, 97. "Memory of the Lord Jesus" (μνήμη τοῦ κυρίου Ἰησοῦ): Cap. 61, 88, 96, 97. "Memory of the Lord of glory" (μνήμη τοῦ κυρίου τῆς δόξης): Cap. 96. "Memory of God our Father" (τοῦ θεοῦ καὶ πατρὸς ἡμῶν μνήμη): Cap. 61. Cf. É. des Places, Introduction, SC 5 bis (Paris 1955) 50. "Memory of spiritual love" (μνήμη τῆς πνευματικῆς ἀγάπης): Cap. 90.
[25] "Memory of evil" (μνήμη τοῦ κακοῦ): Cap. 5; Sermo de ascensione 1148A: É. des Places, SC 5 bis (Paris 1955), p. 86 and 168,20–21. Cf. Cap. 83: É. des Paces, SC 5 bis (Paris 1955), p. 143: "memory of non-good" (μνήμη τοῦ μὴ καλοῦ), whose cause is the first deceit. "Rather, it is through the original deceit that it [the heart] once and for all has as a habit the memory of evil." (transl. C. Ermatinger [Collegeville, Minnesota 2010], p. 113).
[26] *Diad. Phot.*, Cap. 88: É. des Places, SC 5 bis (Paris 1955), p. 148, transl. C. Ermatinger (Collegeville, Minnesota 2010), p. 117.

The Sin of Adam and Eve and the Restoration of the Image of God 435

Sensation is also double; its initial condition was that of a unified power of sensing God and his grace. However, because of Adam's fall, it lost its spiritual and undivided state (ch. 25, 29). Only when practising the holy knowledge, we find out about the natural—and primordial—modality of the sense (αἴσθησις):

> The exercise of divine knowledge itself teaches us that there is only one natural sense in the soul, henceforth divided into two operations on account of Adam's disobedience.[27]

Mind or intellect, memory, thought, spiritual sensibility—they all suffered a fall from unity into duality of operations since "Adam's disobedience" (παρακοὴ τοῦ Ἀδάμ)[28] or the "primordial deceit" (πρώτη ἀπάτη)[29]. This duality is not natural, as the natural state of the human person is that of unity: for example, Diadochus explains, the splitting of the mind in good and bad thoughts does not have its cause in the human interiority, in the heart. The evil thoughts are not produced naturally by the human being in his/her heart, but induced by external factors (the demons)[30]. Nevertheless, as long as the ascetic can remember and testify for the primordial unity, there is a sign that the deep levels of human constitution remained intact. These depths shelter the image of God—the imprint of the divine in the created humanity.

IV. Works of divine grace: the dynamic of the image and likeness

The puzzle concerning the original sin and its consequences cannot be completed without taking into account the distinction image—likeness. The difference between image and likeness (ch. 4, 88) is an important distinction to understand the anthropological view of Diadochus. Moreover, this distinction is essential to get a glimpse into the delicate dynamics of sin, spiritual combat and activity of the divine grace in the fallen human nature.

---

[27] *Diad. Phot.*, Cap. 25: É. des Places, SC 5 bis (Paris 1955), p. 96–97: Μίαν μὲν εἶναι αἴσθησιν φυσικὴν τῆς ψυχῆς αὐτὴ ἡ τῆς ἁγίας ἡμᾶς γνώσεως ἐκδιδάσκει ἐνέργεια, εἰς δύο λοιπὸν διὰ τὴν παρακοὴν τοῦ Ἀδάμ διαιρουμένην ἐνεργείας. Transl. C. Ermatinger (Collegeville, Minnesota 2010), p. 79.
[28] Ibid.
[29] *Diad. Phot.*, Cap. 83: É. des Places, SC 5 bis (Paris 1955), p. 143.
[30] Ibid.

In his introduction to Diadochus in the Romanian edition of the *Philocalia*, Fr. Dumitru Stăniloae[31] clarifies that the image of God, which was tarnished by the sin of the proto-parents, is purified by the grace of baptism. Baptismal grace works without the collaboration of the human; it does not need to be sensed in human consciousness. Reaching the likeness of God, nevertheless, requires human involvement, the movement of human will, personal efforts— it occurs only when the human being is filled with the love of God. This plenitude of love supposes the conscious experience of grace, and the spiritual sensing of grace indicates the progress in charity and in the likeness. In other words, the story of the image and likeness requires the distinction between two modes of manifestation of the works of grace: *not yet sensed* (or unconsciously present) and *sensed* (or consciously experienced). With this distinction, Diadochus offers a clear refutation of the Messalian confusion between the presence of the grace and the experience of the grace. Divine grace is present in the Christian person after baptism, even when it is not sensed or experienced. However, progress in the spiritual life means progress towards experiencing or sensing the presence and the work of the grace.

The drama of the image and likeness, so closely connected to the manifestations and works of the divine grace, has an unavoidable intrigue: "Adam's transgression" (παράβασις τοῦ Ἀδάμ)[32]. The image of God resides in "the intellectual movement of the soul", but it also reverberates in the body which is like the "house" (οἶκος) of this intellectual movement, therefore of the divine image[33]. Thus, Adam's transgression affects both soul and body: its consequences are the marred "lineaments of the soul's form" or imprint (αἱ γραμμαὶ τοῦ χαρακτῆρος τῆς ψυχῆς), as well as the corruptibility of the body[34]. To heal both soul and body of these consequences, the Logos of God was made flesh, and offered humanity the possibility of regeneration through "the water of salvation"[35]. The regeneration is explained in the logic of "eviction" of the sin (or of the Evil One) and indwelling of the Holy Spirit. It is a personal dynamic: the old resident of the soul is cast away, the new one—the life-giving Holy Spirit—"takes up residence in us"[36]. At no time can there be two

---

[31] D. Stăniloae, Viața și scrierile lui Diadoh al Foticeii [The life and writings of Diadochus of Photike], in: D. Stăniloae (tr.), Philocalia (Romanian edition) I (București 2008) 305–310.
[32] *Diad. Phot.*, Cap. 78: É. des Places, SC 5 bis (Paris 1955), p. 135, transl. C. Ermatinger (Collegeville, Minnesota 2010), p. 107.
[33] Ibid., my transl.
[34] Ibid., transl. C. Ermatinger (Collegeville, Minnesota 2010), p. 107.
[35] *Diad. Phot.*, Cap. 78: É. des Places, SC 5 bis (Paris 1955), p. 136, transl. C. Ermatinger (Collegeville, Minnesota 2010), p. 107.
[36] Ibid.: εἰς ἡμᾶς κατασκηνοῦντος. C. Ermatinger explains the literal meaning: "to pitch

persons (δύο πρόσωπα) in the soul, as "some" implied, because the soul's imprint (χαρακτήρ) is unique and simple[37]. Diadochus most probably addresses and corrects here the terminology of Macarius[38]. As Diadochus understands the term πρόσωπον not merely as an "aspect" of being, but as "person", as being (in the sense of ὑπόστασις)[39], he rejects the substantial presence of both Satan/Sin and the Holy Spirit in the soul after baptism[40]. Continuing the images of indwelling, Diadochus mentions "the treasure chamber of the intellect" as the place cleansed from the presence of the "multiform serpent" and filled with the light of the spirit[41]. In sum, the baptismal grace has the following works (effects): the adherence of divine grace to the lineaments of the image, the guarantee of the likeness[42], the eviction of the Evil One and of the sin from the soul/intellect, and the illumination of the inner chamber.

---

one's camp" (*C. Ermatinger*, Following the Footsteps of the Invisible, 107, n. 202). Compare with the vocabulary of indwelling in the Macarian writings and in Ephrem, surveyed by C. Stewart, "Working the Earth of the Heart", 294–300.

[37] K. Fitschen notes a rejection of a dualism inside the soul, considering that Diadochus is correcting Macarius (and not broadly the Messalians) on this point. See *K. Fitschen*, Messalianismus und Antimessalianismus. Ein Beispiel ostkirchlicher Ketzergeschichte (Göttingen 1998) 262.

[38] Cap. 76, 77, 78, and 80 bring further evidence to argue that Diadochus is criticizing Macarius' idea of the coexistence of sin and grace in the heart or intellect of the baptized. The Macarian theory of the two πρόσωπα is explicit in II 17.6: H. Dörries, E. Klostermann, M. Kroeger, PTS 4 (Berlin 1964), p. 169–170, transl. *M. Plested*, The Macarian Legacy, 152: "Nobody of any sense would have the temerity to say, 'Grace is in me, therefore I am wholly freed from sin', rather the two πρόσωπα [of sin and grace] are active in the intellect". See by M. Plested, The Macarian Legacy, 152: "The manipulation of the same scriptural texts (2 Cor 6:14; John 1:5), the description of sin and grace as πρόσωπα and the discussion of the sullying of the divine light (μολύνω in Diadochus; θολόω and μιαίνω in Macarius) make it palpably clear that Diadochus is directly criticizing Macarius on the specific issue of the coexistence of sin and grace." In my references to the Macarian homilies, the Roman numbers indicate the collection (I, II, or III) and the Arabic numbers indicate the homily and the paragraph.

[39] *M. Plested*, The Macarian Legacy, 153. Cf. *Macarius*, I 18.5.1: K. Fitschen, BGL 52 (Stuttgart 2000), p. 225. This passage illustrates the doctrine of coexistence using the image of the sun and the wind—both maintaining their own hypostasis while remaining in close contact to one another.

[40] See also the notion of "indwelling sin" in Macarius, which is different from the "ancestral sin", as clarified by *Mariya Horyacha* in her contribution to this volume. On the tendency of the Macarian homilies to "personify" the evil as "Satan" and the word of death (and subsequent evil deeds) as "the tempting serpent", see her doctoral thesis: *M. Horyacha*, The Journey Within the Heart. The Dynamic Anthropology of Pseudo-Macarius, Diss. (Lviv 2012) 110 and 190. I thank Mariya Horyacha for sharing with me her thesis and for our discussions on terminological differences between Macarius and Diadochus.

[41] *Diad. Phot.*, Cap. 78: É. des Places, SC 5 bis (Paris 1955), p. 136, transl. C. Ermatinger (Collegeville, Minnesota 2010), p. 107.

[42] Ibid.

However, if the bath of incorruptibility washes the marks of transgression completely, takes away the wrinkles of sin and restores the darkened image to its luminous state, it does not dissolve the duality of human will[43]. Nor does it turn the soul into a citadel unreached by the attacks of the demons, as they continue their assault, from outside the heart, "through the body's softness and the sweetness of irrational pleasures"[44]. The immediate regeneration of the image in Baptism needs therefore to be followed by the human response to God, by active participation in the divine love in order to reach the likeness[45]. Ascetic struggles against the double directedness of our desire and thoughts are necessary on the path to the likeness. But they are not sufficient. This path comprises the cooperation with the "power of God" to obtain the virtues (ch. 78). It finally brings the experience of the grace of God in terms of purifying and consuming fire (ch. 85), or in terms of light lifting the soul to perfect (and resplendent) transparency (ch. 40)[46].

V. Modes of restoration: the similes of the painting and the seal

Two extended similes retell the drama of the image and likeness, complicated by the human Fall, assumed in the Incarnation of the Word, and performed, at individual level, in the spiritual development starting with baptism and leading to perfection and deification[47].

---

[43] Ibid. Cf. *M. Plested*, The Macarian Legacy, 153. See also the remark of N. Russell that baptism "does not change the duality of our will" (*N. Russell*, The Doctrine of Deification, 246). Met. Kallistos Ware sees in this point a similitude between Diadochus and Mark the Monk, cf. *K. Ware*, Diadochus von Photice, in: G. Krause, G. Müller (eds.), Theologische Realenzyklopädie VIII (Berlin – New York 1981) 617-620.

[44] *Diad. Phot.*, Cap. 76: É. des Places, SC 5 bis (Paris 1955), p. 134, transl. C. Ermatinger (Collegeville, Minnesota 2010), p. 106: "So we find that just as deceit reigned in the soul before, so too after baptism truth reigns. Nonetheless, Satan continues to work on the soul as before and often even more strongly. This is not to say that he is present concurrently with grace—never!—rather, he clouds the intellect through the body's softness and the sweetness of irrational pleasures. And this occurs because God lets it happen, so that, passing through tempests and trials by fire, one might, if he so desires, come to enjoy the good."

[45] *Diad. Phot.*, Cap. 89: É. des Places, SC 5 bis (Paris 1955), p. 149, transl. C. Ermatinger (Collegeville, Minnesota 2010), p. 117: "Through the regeneration of baptism holy grace obtains two benefits for us, one of which infinitely surpasses the other. It grants us the first immediately, since we are renewed in the water itself which washes us of every stain of sin and it restores all the etchings of the soul—that is, making evident what is 'the image'—cleansing it of every stain of sin. The other part, which is 'the likeness', he [it] hopes to bring about with our cooperation."

[46] For the "imagery of light and fire", see *N. Russell*, The Doctrine of Deification, 247.

[47] Perfection is the goal of the human life in the *One Hundred Gnostic Chapters* (e.g. Cap. 89). Deification, as eschatological state, is mentioned once in the *Sermon on the Ascension* 6 (SC 5

The Sin of Adam and Eve and the Restoration of the Image of God 439

One simile is that of completing a painting: the image (εἰκών) is compared to a "sketch of a figure of a person in one color", while the resemblance is associated to the fully colored portrait, faithful in all details to its model. If at baptism grace restores the image as a simple monochromatic outline, it subsequently paints over the sketch the colors of the virtues, elevates the soul's beauty from glory to glory (2 Cor 3:18), and adorns it with the "distinguishing mark of the likeness" (τὸν χαρακτῆρα τῆς ὁμοιώσεως)[48]. The beginning of this process of painting is indicated by the spiritual taste[49]; finally, the "perfection of likeness" is known exclusively by illumination[50]. This artistic transformation occurs in the workshop of the grace, on the condition that the grace sees our whole-hearted desire for the beauty of likeness[51].

Another simile is that of the seal (σφραγίς) imprinted on the beeswax: the seal is God's virtue, and the wax is the human being. Just as the wax needs to be "warmed up and thoroughly softened", the human person should be "tested in efforts and weaknesses"[52]. This is the path of humility that enables the indwelling of Christ[53] in the human, as well as human receptivity to the divine seal. The "striving for perfection" is therefore inseparable from this dynamic of humbleness (ch. 94). Thus, the temptations that come (even after baptism) through the evil suggestions of the demons, because of the persisting duality of thoughts and will, or the moments of pedagogical retreat of the grace (ch. 85) belong equally to this dynamic. The spiritual combat prepares the heart to receive "the seal of the divine beauty" (τοῦ κάλλους τοῦ θείου τὴν σφραγῖδα), according to the words of the Ps 4:7: "the light of your face, Lord, is sealed

---

bis, 1145D) by the verb θεωθέω ("intensified form of the verb θεόω", according to N. Russell, The Doctrine of Deification, 246).

[48] Diad. Phot., Cap. 89: É. des Places, SC 5 bis (Paris 1955), p. 149, transl. C. Ermatinger (Collegeville, Minnesota 2010), p. 118.

[49] Diad. Phot., Cap. 89: É. des Places, SC 5 bis (Paris 1955), p. 149, transl. C. Ermatinger (Collegeville, Minnesota 2010), p. 117: "When the mind (intellect) begins to taste the goodness of the Holy Spirit with profound sentiments, then we ought to know that grace is beginning to paint the likeness over the image" (revised).

[50] Diad. Phot., Cap. 89: É. des Places, SC 5 bis, p. 150, transl. C. Ermatinger (Collegeville, Minnesota 2010), p. 118: "yet it is through illumination that we will know the perfection of likeness."

[51] This artistic imagery recalls Eph 2:9 ("we are God's work of art"). In other pictorial comparisons, Christ is the painter: Macarius, II 30.4: H. Dörries, E. Klostermann, M. Kroeger, PTS 4 (Berlin 1964), p. 242; Greg. Nyss., In Cant. Cant. 15: H. Langerbeck, Gregorii Nysseni Opera VI (Leiden 1960), p. 439, French transl. by Ch. Bouchet, Pères dans la foi 49–50 (Paris 1992), p. 294. Cf. C. Ermatinger, Following the Footsteps of the Invisible, 117, n. 258.

[52] Diad. Phot., Cap. 94: É. des Places, SC 5 bis (Paris 1955), p. 155, transl. C. Ermatinger (Collegeville, Minnesota 2010), p. 122.

[53] Ibid., citing 2 Cor 12:9.

upon us"[54]. Finally, the imagery of the wax that needs to be softened stays for the importance to "carry out the martyrdom of our conscience before God"[55].

Both similes invite a closer look at the question of the agency. They also allow for an analysis of the duality activity–passivity, essential for the theology of grace and for an anthropology taking seriously the consequences of sin on human will. On the one hand, the painting metaphor suggests that the divine grace is the author of the work of art, the colorful portrait, corresponding to the perfect likeness "painted over" the image restored in baptism. However, the human being needs to stay courageously in the workshop of the grace and show its profound desire to reach the likeness—without seeing this willingness and this desire, divine grace cannot proceed to complete its masterpiece[56]. Thus, the human person is not entirely passive; it is expected to cooperate with the work of the divine grace. On the other hand, the sealing metaphor seems to stress more the passivity of the human; the agency belongs to the divine, who imprints the seal. Nevertheless, the human should be actively involved (in the form of his engaging in a spiritual combat) in preparing the receptiveness of the soul for the seal. This interviewing of passivity and activity of the human in receiving and cooperating with the divine grace seems to counterbalance the phenomenological combination of activity and passivity in the "original sin". As we saw earlier, Diadochus spoke both of the "serpent" and of "deceit" (ch. 78), suggesting the agency of the Evil One, and of Adam's disobedience (ch. 25, 88) or transgression (ch. 78), underlining the free choice of the human in that act, his voluntary action. Also in the original sin, the human being was both passive and active: deceived by the Deceiver, the human being is the one who disobeyed and enacted the transgression.

VI. "Ancestral sin" and spiritual perfection

Diadochus has reframed the narrative of the Fall from Genesis 3 in four stories: the drama of Adam and Eve (and the phenomenology of temptation), the story of the one and the many in the human faculties; the conceptual story of the image and likeness (and the fine description of the works of grace to restore and elevate the human above the consequences of the Fall), and finally

---

[54] *Diad. Phot.*, Cap. 94: É. des Places, SC 5 bis (Paris 1955), p. 156, transl. C. Ermatinger (Collegeville, Minnesota 2010), p. 123.
[55] *Diad. Phot.*, Cap. 94: É. des Places, SC 5 bis (Paris 1955), p. 157, transl. C. Ermatinger (Collegeville, Minnesota 2010), p. 123.
[56] *Diad. Phot.*, Cap. 89: É. des Places, SC 5 bis (Paris 1955), p. 149; transl. C. Ermatinger (Collegeville, Minnesota 2010), p. 118.

the story of the divine painter and the divine seal (with its implications for the activity-passivity distinction). Speaking in terms of what seems to be chronological priority ("first Eve", "first deceit"), he is drawing the lines of a diagnosis which is crucial for anyone who embarks on the journey towards spiritual perfection. The term "first" refers to an underlying primordial fragility of the human being, healed only through the Incarnation of Christ and through the work(s) of divine grace. Phrases rendered as "ever since"—literally "for which reason" (ὅθεν) or "after/since/because of" (ἀπό)[57], referring to the event of the fall of Adam and Eve, show the universal presence of this fragility in all humanity. Although he speaks of "transgression", Diadochus is far from embracing a legalistic view on the sin of Adam and Eve. Neither does he imagine a hereditary explanation for the universal transmission of the consequences of the "ancestral sin", despite a clear view that the road to human perfection passes through the struggle against these consequences (the duality of operations in the human faculties, for example). The "ancestral sin" is entirely posited in an ascetical and mystical framework, with Christ as a key and the work of grace as healing horizon[58].

VII. Conclusion: from narrative of the fall to iconicity

The vocabulary of Eve's slipping or falling (ch. 56), Adam's disobedience (παρακοή, ch. 25, 88), Adam's transgression (παράβασις, ch. 78), first deceit (πρώτη ἀπάτη, ch. 83), or multiform serpent hidden initially in the human mind (ch. 78) fits into the narrative framework of the Fall. Anyway, this fall is depicted more as a paradigmatic fault than a historical guilt: any fall through intense desire and immoderation of bodily senses reenacts the story of Adam and Eve, sharing in the same phenomenology of temptation, deceit, disobedience and transgression. The consequences of the fall are powerful: the darkening of the image of God, the corruptibility of the body, the splitting of

---

[57] *Diad. Phot.*, Cap. 56, 88: É. des Places, SC 5 bis (Paris 1955), p. 117, 148.

[58] This approach is coherent with earlier correlations of the biblical narration of the Fall with considerations on moral perfection, such as those of Theophilus of Antioch († ca. 183). In *Ad Autolycum*, Theophilus considers Adam's fall as disobedience of God's commandment to follow a certain way of perfection. At the same time, it resonates with later spiritual understandings of the biblical testimony, such as that of Anastasius of Sinai (ca. 630 – † after 700). See J. S. Romanides, *The Ancestral Sin* (Ridgewood, NY 2008) 124–125. For reasons of systematization, I use sometimes in my analysis of Diadochus the term "ancestral sin" (corresponding to προπατορικὸν ἁμάρτημα), borrowed from Romanides' overview of patristic writings, but the concept does not occur as such in Diadochus. We encounter in the chapters the terms ἁμάρτημα (Cap. 87) and ἁμαρτία (for example, in Cap. 76, defined as "the spirit of error", μνεῦμα τῆς πλάνης, or in Cap. 80 and Cap. 83).

human faculties in two. Against these sharp formulations, Diadochus pleads, however, for an optimistic, Christological, pneumatological and sacramental anthropology[59], that revolves around baptism and the regeneration of the human in Christ, through the Holy Spirit. In the ascetical scenery, the drama of Adam and Eve turns into the story of the fall from unity into duality, affecting all human faculties. Retold conceptually, the story brings forward the dynamic of the image and likeness. Diadochus presents a differentiated description of how the image is affected through ancestral sin and may be restored in baptism to its clarity, opening the ascent to the perfection of the likeness. Therefore, the main concern of the regeneration of the human being is the restoration and the fulfilment of its iconic identity. The language of sealing and painting demonstrate the importance of lifting the image, through the work of divine grace, to its utmost clarity and beauty.

---

[59] Cf. *C. Ermatinger*, Introduction, in: Following the Footsteps of the Invisible, 6: "Diadochus's theology is a theology of baptism and its consequences."

Ioannis Kourempeles, Thessaloniki (Griechenland)

„Die Jungfrau, die die Erlösung vom Fluch gebar": Die Alte Eva und das neue Paradies in der Dichtung von Romanos dem Meloden

Präambel

Romanos widmet zwei *Kontakien der Geburt Christi* und zeigt somit die Koexistenz von Eva mit der Gottesmutter in diesem paradoxen Ereignis. Im ersten *Kontakion zur Geburt Christi*[1] erzählte er von der Anwesenheit der drei Weisen an der Krippe und verdeutlichte mit dramatischen Dialogen die folgenden theologischen Punkte:

1. Die Anerkennung der jungfräulichen Geburt Gottes durch die Weisen.
2. Die fühlbare Präsenz (Fleischwerdung) von Gott selbst in der Welt, welche die Weisen bestätigten.

Im zweiten *Kontakion*, das gleichfalls der *Geburt* Christi gewidmet ist, wird die Dramaturgie des Dichters in Dialogform verstärkt, um das orthodoxe Dogma anschaulich auszudrücken. Ich werde bei der Untersuchung dieser Verbindung von Dramaturgie und Ausdruck des Dogmas verweilen, mit detaillierter Bezugnahme auf das 2. *Kontakion über die Geburt Christi*, wo die Dialogpersonen in der Reihenfolge ihres Auftretens im Dialogdrama Eva, Adam, die Gottesmutter und schließlich Christus selbst sind.

---

[1] Über die kritische Herausgabe dieses Gedichts mit Analyse von Aufbau und Versmaß und mit seinen literarischen Parallelen siehe: *J. Grosdidier de Matons*, Romanos le Mélode. Hymnes. vol. 1, SC 99 (Paris 1964); vol. 2, SC 110 (Paris 1965); vol. 3, SC 114 (Paris 1965); vol. 4, SC 128 (Paris 1967); vol. 5, SC 283 (Paris 1981). In dieser Studie werden unsere Verweise auf die romanischen *Kontakia* der Oxford-Ausgabe (*P. Maas – C. A. Trypanis*, Sancti Romani Melodi Cantica. Cantica genuina [Oxford 1963]) entnommen werden. Die Nummer des Kontakions wird in arabischen Ziffern angegeben, der Verweis auf die Strophen des Kontakions wird im griechischen Alphabet und die Anzahl der Verse auch in der arabischen Nummerierung auf einem Exponenten angezeigt angegeben. Für die deutsche Übersetzung siehe auch *J. Koder*, Romanos Melodos: Die Hymnen, I–II, Bibliothek der griechischen Literatur 62 und 64 (Stuttgart 2005).

I. Das gottmenschliche Wunder und das gewonnene „Ich" der Eva

Wenn der Leser auch das zweite, sehr theologische Kontakion *über die Geburt Christi* liest, gewinnt er den Eindruck, dass es auf gewisse Weise die Handlung des ersten Kontakions über die Geburt Christi voraussetzt, wo die theologischen Punkte betont wurden, die ich bereits oben angeführt habe.
Was geschieht konkret im Fall des 2. *Kontakions*?
Während die Jungfrau den von ihr Geborenen Gott Logos lobpries und „den von ihr allein auf die Welt gebrachten Säugling verhätschelte" ($2γ^{1-2}$), hörte dies alles die „im Schmerzen Kinder Gebärende" ($2γ^{3-4}$), also die alte Eva. Romanos scheint darstellen zu wollen, wie Eva um die Rettung bangt: er zeigt sie in Erwartung des paradoxen Ereignisses der Inkarnation Gottes. Wir könnten sagen, dass sich Eva nach dem Sündenfall und dem Tod im Tiefschlaf befindet, sie unterliegt jedoch nicht dem vollkommenen *sensorischen Tod*. Daher fragt sich die *alte Frau* laut rufend:

> Wer ließ soeben meinem Ohr das erklingen, worauf ich meine Hoffnung baute,
> die Jungfrau, die die Erlösung vom Fluch gebar?
> Ihre Stimme allein beendete meine Leiden,
> und ihr Spross verwundete den, der mich verwundet hatte[2].

Im vorliegenden Fall bezieht sich Eva auf den entscheidenden Schlag, den Christus durch seine jungfräuliche Geburt dem Teufel versetzt, der das erste Menschenpaar getäuscht hatte. Als ob die Frau Adams zum Unterdrücker der Menschen, dem Teufel, sagen würde: *Wie du mir, so ich dir.*

Das dramatische Thema ist jedoch, erlaube ich mir zu sagen, dass Eva das Vertrauen Adams verloren hatte. Für seine Hörer, die eine einfache und bildliche Wiedergabe des Dogmas wollten, investiert Romanos stark in das dramatische Element. Der große Dichter nutzt daher dieses Element dramatisch aus, um den Charakter des Fluchs, der das Menschengeschlecht belastete, und seine Aufhebung zu erläutern. Die weibliche Präsenz spielt in diesem Fall die wichtigste Rolle. Die Frage, die Romanos freilich in der Erzählung stellt, ist, wie der durch seine alte Leichtgläubigkeit gepeinigte Vorvater Adam jetzt Eva glauben sollte.

Romanos drückt die Agonie und die Gewissheit Evas über das Heilsereignis wie folgt aus:

---

[2] $2γ^{3, 5-8}$: Τίς ἐν τοῖς ὠσί μου νῦν ἤχησεν ἐκεῖνο ὃ ἤλπιζον; / παρθένον τὴν τίκτουσαν τῆς κατάρας τὴν λύτρωσιν; / ἧς φωνὴ ἔλυσέ με τῶν δυσχερῶν, / καὶ ταύτης γονὴ ἔδησε τὸν τρώσαντά με.

Die Jungfrau, die die Erlösung vom Fluch gebar

Da du die Schwalbe hörtest, die mir am Morgen sang,
Adam, lass den todgleichen Schlaf fahren, erhebe dich! Höre auf mich, deine Frau!
Ich erhebe mich nun, die einst den Sterblichen den Fall brachte.
Erkenne das Wunder! Sieh, wie sie, die keinen Mann kennt,
durch ihr Gebären dich von der Verwundung heilt.
Einst erkor mich die Schlange und freute sich sehr;
jetzt aber sieht sie unsere Nachkommen und flüchtet, sich windend.
Gegen mich erhob sie das Haupt, jetzt aber winselt sie
Gedemütigt und spottet nicht mehr, voll Furcht vor dem, den gebar
Die Begnadete³.

Die Schwalbe zeigt offenbar den Frühling an, der mit der Geburt Christi verkündet wird. Diese Geburt muss das *Wiedererwachen* Adams aus dem ihm vom Teufel auferlegten Tiefschlaf auslösen. Eva übernimmt ihre Verantwortung, möchte aber gleichzeitig auch auf ihren jetzigen Beitrag hinweisen. Romanos hilft ihr offenkundig so gut wie nur möglich bei ihrem Bemühen, damit die alte Frau ihre ehrliche Position ausdrücken kann.

Tatsächlich beansprucht Eva nun eine aktive Rolle bei der Rettung der Menschheit, indem sie zu ihrem Mann sagt: „Ich, die ich den Sündenfall über die Menschen herrschen ließ, richte sie jetzt auf". Wir wollen nicht vergessen, dass die Gottesmutter ein Nachkomme der Eva ist, weswegen die Jungfrau sie weiter unten „Eltern" nennt (2ι⁵). Die Gottesmutter wird damit vom Meloden als „Evas Stolz" präsentiert. Im vorliegenden Fall ist das „Ich" der Eva ein soteriologisches „Ich".

Das theologisch Wunderbare ist hier freilich, dass die Rettung therapeutisch verstanden wird und mit der entsprechenden Terminologie wiedergegeben wird. Daher ist die Rede von „Wunde" und „Heilung", und nicht über Schuldgefühle und Recht bekommen⁴. Die Schlange, nun mit gesenk-

---

³ 2δ¹⁻¹¹: Τῆς χελιδόνος ἀκούσας κατ' ὄρθρον / κελαδούσης μοι / τὸν ἰσοθάνατον ὕπνον, Ἀδάμ, ἀφείς, ἀνάστηθι· / ἄκουσόν μου τῆς συζύγου· / ἐγὼ ἡ πάλαι πτῶμα προξενήσασα βροτοῖς νῦν ἀ-νιστῶ· / κατανόησον τὰ θαυμάσια· ἰδὲ τὴν ἀπείρανδρον / διὰ τοῦ γεννήματος ἰωμένην σε τοῦ τραύματος. / ἐμὲ γάρ ποτε εἶδεν ὁ ὄφις καὶ σκιρτᾷ, / ἀλλ' ἄρτι ὁρῶν τοὺς ἐξ ἡμῶν φεύγει συρτῶς· / κατ' ἐμοῦ μὲν ὕψωσε τὴν κεφαλήν, νυνὶ δὲ ταπεινωθεὶς / κολακεύει, οὐ χλευάζει, δειλιῶν ὂν ἐγέννησεν / ἡ κεχαριτωμένη.
⁴ Romanos, der in der Überlieferung bezüglich der Stellung der Gottesmutter im Heilsmysterium gut bewandert war, kannte auch sehr wichtige Reden über die Gottesgebärerin, wie die des Proklos von Konstantinopel *An die Allerheiligste Gottgebärerin* (siehe mehr I. Κουρεμπελές, Ἡ ὁμιλία τοῦ πατριάρχη Πρόκλου «εἰς τὴν Παναγίαν Θεοτόκον» καὶ ἡ ἀπάντηση τοῦ Νεστορίου [Θεσσαλονίκη 2004]). Tatsächlich beeindruckt in dieser Rede, dass beim Thema des Vergleichs von Eva mit der Gottesmutter nicht die Frage der Schuld gestellt wird, was L.-M. Peltomaa in einer neueren Studie sehr treffend bemerkt (*L.-M. Peltomaa, Die berühmteste Marien-Predigt der Spätantike, Jahrbuch der Österreichischen Byzantinistik 54 [2004]*

tem Kopf, verliert ihren Mut gedemütigt durch die Geburt Gottes. Theologie und Dichtung werden in den Versen von Romanos auf harmonische Weise zusammengefügt, sodass es völlig unnatürlich wäre zu versuchen, diese Dinge getrennt zu betrachten.

II. Das „Dogma" Adams

Was geschieht aber mit Adam? Die Worte Evas veranlassen ihn, die Schwere von seinen Lidern zu verscheuchen und „wie aus dem Schlaf aufzuwachen" ($2\varepsilon^{1-3}$). Adam öffnet also seine Ohren, die ihm „der Ungehorsam verschlossen hatte", und sagt zu seiner Frau

> Erfreulich ist das Gehörte, aber seine Melodie stellt ihn nicht zufrieden, da es von einer Frau ausgesprochen wird, deren Stimme er fürchtet[5].

Und er fürchtet sie natürlich, weil er die vorausgegangene Erfahrung des Sündenfalls gemacht hatte, den sein Vertrauen in Eva und der Ungehorsam gegenüber dem göttlichen Willen ausgelöst hatten. Obwohl daher der „Klang" der Worte bezaubernd ist, lässt ihn das „Instrument" (das heißt Eva) argwöhnen, ob sie ihn vielleicht wieder täuschen und Schande über ihn bringen wird.

Hier lässt Romanos die hohen Prinzipien seiner Dichtung erkennen, die offenkundig genaue Harmonie von Wort und Rhythmus gesucht haben sollte. Mit einem weiteren ausmalenden Oikos, den Romanos Eva widmet, wird Adam auch über das „Instrument" Eva überzeugt, die ihm beharrlich versichert, dass er gewiss sein und ihren jetzigen Worten glauben muss. „Du wirst nicht feststellen", sagt sie ihm, „dass ich dich bitter berate", und Eva ruft mit einem Zitat von Paulus (2 Kor 5, 17) aus: „Das Alte ist nämlich vergangen, und der Spross Mariams, Christus, zeigt alles neu auf" ($2\sigma\tau^{3-4}$).

Romanos unterstreicht die Rolle der Frau beim Menschengeschlecht, denn er kennt die heilsbringende Tiefe der Theologie gut und zielt auf diese Perspektive ab, welche die Frau mit der Rettung der Welt verbindet. Er spricht mit theologischer Perspektive über die gottempfangende Frau und die Rettung der Menschheit[6].

77–96, hier 84–85).
[5] $2\varepsilon^{5-6}$.
[6] Die Annäherung von N. Matsoukas (Ν. Ματσούκας, Ὁ Σατανάς: Δογματική καί Συμβολική Θεολογία, τ. Δ᾽ [Θεσσαλονίκη 1999] 107) an die biblische Darstellung der Schlange, die das erste Menschenpaar täuscht, ist nicht verfehlt, wenn er sagt: „Im vorliegenden Fall dominiert in der Parabel das patriarchalische Recht. Der Verfasser der Erzählung konnte in seiner Zeit keine andere Form verwenden. Zuerst wird Adam erschaffen, und Eva erliegt als erste der teuflischen Versuchung". Die Übersetzung ist von mir.

Die Jungfrau, die die Erlösung vom Fluch gebar　　　　　　　　　　　447

Daher dominiert im 7. Oikos die erste Person Plural. Die Übernahme der alten Verantwortung für den Sündenfall hat einen pluralen Charakter. Adam sagt:

> Frau, schon merke ich den Frühling, fühle die Erquickung,
> die wir einst verwirkten, und ich sehe ein Paradies,
> ein neues, ein anderes: die Jungfrau,
> die das Holz des Lebens am Busen trägt, das einst
> die Cherubim hüteten, das heilige, auf dass ich es nicht berühren konnte.
> Unversehrt sehe ich es sprießen[7].

Im Prinzip bestätigt also Adam sein *sensorisches Erwachen* und seine geschärften Sinnesorgane, was durch die Geburt Gottes aus dem weiblichen Schoß Wirklichkeit wird. Er nutzt Tastsinn und Sehen als die *Sinnesorgane*, welche den großen Unterschied zwischen früher (im Paradies) und jetzt (im neuen Paradies der Gottesmutter) bezeugen. Als ob er sagt: Jenen, den ich nicht im Paradies anfassen konnte, kann ich jetzt berühren, denn ich sehe ihn *sprießen*, nämlich als vollkommenen Menschen aus dem menschlichen Schoß wachsen.

III. Das neue Paradies

Am Schluss des von mir untersuchten Kontakions bestätigt Christus selbst, dass er nicht nur greifbar, sondern auch *viel leidtragend* für die Rettung des Geschlechts Adams ist. Aus all dem wird deutlich, dass die bittere Erfahrung der Sterblichkeit, die der Vorvater mit seinen Nachkommen erlebt hat, dynamisch und nicht statisch betrachtet wird. Das erste Menschenpaar hat nicht etwas verloren, was es nicht wiederfinden kann. Der Schöpfer des Menschengeschlechts befindet sich immer der Menschheit gegenüber und bleibt menschenfreundlich offen für Teilhabe. Das Paradies liegt nicht hinter den Menschen, sondern immer vor ihnen.

Hier reiht sich auch die Darstellung der Gottesmutter als „neues Paradies" ein, die auch aus der Rede des Erzbischofs Proklos „An die Allerheiligste Gott-

---

[7] 2ζ¹⁻⁶: Ἔγνων, ὦ γύναι, τὸ ἔαρ καὶ τῆς τρυφῆς αἰσθάνομαι, / ἧς ἐξεπέσαμεν πάλαι· καὶ γὰρ ὁρῶ παράδεισον / νέον, ἄλλον, τὴν παρθένον / φέρουσαν κόλποις αὐτὸ τὸ ξύλον τῆς ζωῆς, ὅπερ ποτὲ / Χερουβὶμ ἐτήρει τὸ ἅγιον πρὸς τὸ μὴ ψαῦσαί με· / Τοῦτο τοίνυν ἄψαυστον ἐγὼ βλέπω φυόμενον.

gebärerin" bekannt ist, die dem Meloden gut vertraut war[8]. Romanos verwertet solche Darstellungen und bearbeitet sie mit theologischen Farbnuancen, die auf die theologische Wahrheit hinauslaufen, dass Gott, der im verlorenen Paradies unsichtbar gewesen war, durch seine Geburt durch das sichtbare „neue Paradies", die Gottesgebärerin, sichtbar wird (als Fleischwerdung), die vor uns steht und eine aus unserem Geschlecht ist.

Deswegen setzen sich die oben angeführten Verse mit den folgenden Worten Adams fort:

> Und fühlte den lebensspendenden Hauch,
> der mich, der unbeseelter Erdenstaub war,
> beseelte. Von seinem Duft gestärkt
> will ich jetzt zu der eilen, die die Frucht unseres Lebens hervorbrachte,
> die Begnadete[9].

Adam erkennt in Christus seinen Schöpfer selbst und nicht irgendeinen einfachen Menschen[10]. Auf welchen anderen noch glaubwürdigeren Zeugen für diese Anerkennung (Identifizierung der Person) könnte sich Romanos berufen, dieser große „Kirchenregisseur"? So antwortet er allen, die in seiner Zeit Christus vom Göttlichen Wort selbst differenzierten. Mit dieser Überzeugung

---

[8] Siehe dazu mehr in meiner Studie: *I. Κουρεμπελές,* Ἡ ὁμιλία τοῦ πατριάρχη Πρόκλου, insbesondere 46f., 94f. Darüberhinaus siehe das Thema auch bei Basileios von Seleukeia in: *G. Martzelos,* Die Mariologie des Basileios von Seleukeia und Romanos der Melode, in: P. Hoffrichter (Hg.), Auf der Suche nach der Seele Europas: Marienfrömmigkeit in Ost und West: Studientagung der Pro-Oriente Sektion Salzburg aus Anlass ihres 20 jährigen Bestehens 7. und 8. Oktober 2005 (Insbruck 2007) 43–66, hier 51: „Basileios bezieht sich öfters festlich auf die Jungfräulichkeit der Gottesgebärerin, indem er sie als ‚unvermählte Braut', ‚jungfräuliches Brautgemach' und ‚unverdorrtes Paradies der Keuschheit', indem der Baum des Lebens eingepflanzt worden ist, damit die Frucht des Heils für die ganze Menschheit hervorsprießt, bezeichnet".

[9] 2ζ$^{7-10}$: ᾐσθόμην πνοῆς, σύζυγε, τῆς ζωοποιοῦ, / Τῆς κόνιν ἐμὲ ὄντα καὶ ἄψυχον πηλόν / ποιησάσης ἔμψυχον· ταύτης νυνὶ τῇ εὐοσμίᾳ ῥωσθεὶς / πορευθῶ πρὸς τὴν ἀνθοῦσαν τὸν καρπὸν τῆς ζωῆς ἡμῶν, τὴν κεχαριτωμένην.

[10] Es ist eine Tatsache, dass die Frage nach der Position Adams nach dem Sündenfall die Theologen noch sehr viel später beschäftigt hat. Beispielsweise schreibt Evgenios Voulgaris in seinem *Theologischen Buch* (siehe *E. Βούλγαρης,* Θεολογικόν ἢ Ἱερά Θεολογία [Θεσσαλονίκη ²1987] 380) das Folgende: „Wenn sie (die Vorväter) den Sündenerlass erhielten, dann nicht aus einem anderen Grund als wegen ihres Glaubens an den kommenden Messias. Es gibt nämlich keine Rettung durch jemand anderen (Handlungen/Akte, Kapitel d.) daher auch Augustinus (*Brief* 102 bzw. 49, Thema 2): und auch jene erfuhren die Rettung, sagt er, die vor seiner Fleischwerdung an seine künftige Inkarnation glaubten. Es ist nämlich unser eigener Glauben auch der ihrige, die (an den Kommenden) glaubten, dass er sein wird, wie auch wir glauben, nachdem es bereits geschehen ist". Die Übersetzung ist von mir.

eilt der Vorvater zur „Gnadenvollen"[11] um sie zu bitten, mit ihrem kummervollen Vater Adam „dem ganz Elenden, der im Hades alt wurde" (2η^5) Mitleid zu haben.

Eva fügt sich jedoch harmonisch in diese Bittszene. Ihr gehört der neunte Oikos. Auch sie kommt heran, um ihre menschliche Angst auszudrücken, ihre Agonie wegen der Leiden der Welt. Sie bittet daher die Gottgebärerin, die Schande zu tilgen, vor allem um ihres Ehemanns willen, dessen Wehklagen ihr in der Seele wehtun[12].

Sollten wir sagen, dass Romanos den Ausdruck „in der Seele wehtun" zufällig gewählt hat? Das wäre, meiner Meinung nach, verfehlt. Der Melode investiert in die Tatsache, dass die Vorväter den Tod erlitten haben. Adam erinnert sich somit an das paradiesische angenehme Leben und entgegnet Eva:

> Es wäre besser gewesen, wenn du nicht aus meiner Rippe gewachsen wärst und ich dich nicht zu meinem Helfer genommen hätte, denn dann wäre ich nicht in einen solchen Abgrund gestürzt[13].

Hier scheint es, dass der Sündenfall der ersten Menschen kein von ihrem kleinkindhaften Zustand (im Paradies) unabhängiges Ereignis war. Deswegen hört diese Szene nicht auf, an ein *kindisches Verhalten* von Seiten der ersten Menschen zu erinnern.

IV. Menschengestaltung

Romanos ist ein begabter Dramatiker, wie durch das oben Geschilderte bewiesen wird. Er stellt Szenen aus dem Alltagsleben einer Familie dar und hält dadurch bei seinen Zuhörern die Spannung aufrecht. Eva scheint über die Vorhaltungen («ἐλεγμούς») und Tadel («ὀνειδισμός») Adams verärgert zu sein, was wir heute *Nörgeln des Ehepartners* nennen, und „beugt daher den Hals" vor der Gottesmutter, damit die den Schöpfer Gebärende „sie aufrichtet" (2θ$^{1-10}$).

– Was macht Maria gegenüber der beharrlichen flehenden Aufforderung der Vorfahren, und vor allem der *alten Frau*?

---

[11] Dieses substantivierte Adjektiv bildet den Abschlusshymnus des konkreten *Kontakions*.
[12] 2θ^4: ἐγὼ ἡ τλήμων τοῖς ὀδυρμοῖς <τοῖς> τοῦ Ἀδάμ πάσχω ψυχήν.
[13] 2θ$^{7-9}$.

Bevor ich zur Antwort auf diese Frage komme, möchte ich betonen, dass alle von Romanos dargestellten Eheszenen einen guten Seelenbeschreiber, einen Psychographen, des Familienlebens zeigen. Sie gehören zu jenen ausdrucksvollen Stellen bei Romanos, durch die wir annehmen, wenn wir unsere Fantasie etwas spielen lassen, dass der Melode ein verheirateter Kleriker in Konstantinopel gewesen ist, da in der Forschung die Frage geäußert wurde, ob er ein unverheirateter Diakon geblieben war[14].

V. Das „Mitleid" der neuen Eva und die Therapie der Menschen

Aus den Augen Marias rinnen Tränen, als sie die Vorfahren erblickt, welche die Last der Leiden der Welt nach dem Sündenfall tragen und die Notwendigkeit der Fleischwerdung des Wortes für die Rettung der Menschheit hervorheben. Der Melode zeigt, wie die Gottesmutter mit ihren Eltern „mitleidet" und tatkräftig mit dem barmherzigen Christus *im Einklang steht* ($2\iota^{5-6}$). Sie sagt ihnen, dass sie das *Unheil* verscheuchen sollen, da sie selbst die *Freude* geboren hat, den ewigen Gott, den einzigen Barmherzigen und Menschenliebenden. Es ist das, was wir bereits oben erwähnt haben: *es dominiert die Heilsperspektive und nicht das Zuschreiben von einer gerichtlichen Verantwortung*[15].

Die Gottesmutter selbst verfügt über das greifbare Beispiel und beruft sich darauf. Der Dichter verwendet das typologisch weithin bekannte Beispiel des brennenden Dornbuschs, der doch nicht verbrennt, um die rettende Bedeutung des göttlichen Feuers in seiner Vereinigung mit der Menschheit zu betonen. Obwohl das göttliche Feuer in ihr gewohnt hat, also das göttliche Wort selbst sich im Schoß der Gottesgebärerin niedergelassen hatte, hat es sie, *die*

---

[14] Anlässlich der *Hymne an die Mönche* schreibt J. Koder (*J. Koder*, Romanos Melodos, 243) charakteristisch: „Auch wenn der Dichter selbst sich nicht für das Mönchsleben entschieden hat, ermahnt er die Mönche, in ihrem Bemühen um ein gottgefälliges Leben ohne Unterlass dem Leben der Engel nachzueifern [...]". Der große griechische Schriftsteller Odysseus Elytis (*Ο. Ελύτης*, Ἐν λευκῷ [Αθήνα 1993] 54), wiederum, mit dem Wort „Diakon" spielend, schreibt, dass „er war Diakon, und wie es scheint, blieb Romanos bis zum Ende seines Lebens Diakon". Ihm gefallen aber wirklich nicht die Mutmaßungen, die, meiner Meinung nach, das Salz in der Forschung und im Leben sind, deswegen schreibt er weiter unten: „In unserer Zeit sind wir verwöhnt und versuchen, die biographischen Lücken mit Vermutungen zu füllen [...]".

[15] Aus dieser Perspektive ist sehr treffend beschrieben von N. Matsoukas im vierten Band seiner *Dogmatik* das Thema des Ungehorsams (*N. Ματσούκας*, Ὁ Σατανάς, 111), indem er schreibt: „Anders gesagt, müssen wir an das Problem interpretierend mit medizinischer und nicht mit juristischer Terminologie herangehen. Die Erbsünde ist also eine Übertretung des Lebens, ein Herunterkommen, Verfehlen und Verlust Gottes, was jedoch den Lauf hin zur Vollendung betrifft und nicht die anderen Geschenke der göttlichen Präsenz. Der Verlust des Paradieses ist etwas anderes als der Verlust von Gott selbst". Die Übersetzung ist von mir.

Die Jungfrau, die die Erlösung vom Fluch gebar

Geringe, dennoch nicht verbrannt, sondern als Brücke für die Vorväter und die Menschheit hervorgehoben, welche die Welt mit ihrem göttlichen Spross verbindet (2ια').

VI. Theologische Topologie – Die Gottesmutter als dialogische Person

Wo spielt sich jedoch diese gesamte Szene ab? An der Krippe, wie auch im Fall der Weisen (im 1. *Kontakion über die Geburt Christi*). Die ärmliche Krippe ist der Auffindungsort der Freude, *obwohl die Vorfahren örtlich (szenisch) nicht an ihr zu sein scheinen*. Spielt es daher eine Rolle, dass die Vorfahren den Tod erlebt haben und in einem *Kontakion über die Geburt* das Szenarium aus dieser Sicht gebunden ist? Offenbar. Jedenfalls „neigt" dort an der Krippe die Mutter Gottes wieder flehend „den Hals" (2ιβ⁴), wie sie es auch bei den Weisen getan hatte, und bittet ihn, ihre Eltern von der Blöße zu bedecken, in die sie die Schlange gestoßen hatte. Nun ist es aber an der Zeit, Christus als Person zu sehen, die in diesem mystischen Zwiegespräch dialogisch handelt.

Tatsächlich lässt jetzt Romanos im 13. *Oikos* den Retter seiner Mutter antworten, wobei er offensichtlich miterlebt hat, was sich abgespielt hatte:

Mutter, um deinetwillen und durch dich rette ich sie.
Wollte ich sie nicht retten, so hätte ich nicht Wohnung in dir genommen,
wäre nicht aus dir erstrahlt, nicht hörtest du: Meine Mutter!
Die Krippe bewohne ich wegen deines Geschlechtes,
von deinen Brüsten trinke ich, wie ich es will.
In den Armen trägst du ihnen zuliebe mich, den die Cherubin zu sehen nicht ertragen,
du siehst und trägst und liebkost mich als deinen Sohn,
du Begnadete![16].

Mit diesen Worten scheint Christus zu seiner Mutter zu sagen, dass sie ihn um etwas gebeten hat, das auch Gott selbst wünscht. Er verstärkt mit seinen Worten daher noch mehr die heilsbringende Bedeutung seiner Fleischwerdung, seiner greifbaren Präsenz in der geplagten Welt durch die Gottesgebärerin.

---

[16] 2ιγ⁴⁻¹¹: Ὦ μῆτερ, καὶ διὰ σὲ καὶ διὰ σοῦ σῴζω αὐτούς· / Εἰ μὴ σῶσαι τούτους ἠθέλησα, οὐκ ἂν ἔν σοὶ ᾤκησα· / Οὐκ ἂν ἐκ σοῦ ἔλαμψα, οὐκ ἂν μήτηρ μου ἤκουσας· / Τὴν φάτνην ἐγὼ διὰ τὸ γένος σου οἰκῶ· / Μαζῶν δὲ τῶν σῶν βουλόμενος νῦν γαλουχῶ· / ἐν ἀγκάλαις φέρεις με χάριν αὐτῶν· ὃν οὐχ ὁρᾷ Χερουβίμ, / ἰδοὺ βλέπεις καὶ βαστάζεις καὶ ὡς υἱὸν κολακεύεις με, / ἡ κεχαριτωμένη.

Unser theologisches Thema ist bekannt, wie wir bereits anfangs betont haben. An dieser Stelle lohnt es sich jedoch, das Interesse von Romanos am christologischen Schema der Innewohnung (seinem Wohnen in der Gottesmutter) zu unterstreichen, das er in seinen *Kontakien* mit besonderem christologischen Interesse entfaltet. Er betont daher, dass Gott den Menschen *ersehnt*, dass er das menschliche Schicksal erleiden möchte, um zu zeigen, dass die leidgeprüfte menschliche Natur nicht der Existenzlosigkeit unterworfen ist.

Er spricht somit zu seiner Mutter:

> Erfährst du aber auch das andere, Ehrwürdige,
> das ich um ihretwillen tun will, dann wirst du mit allen Elementen
> erschüttert werden und wehklagen, du Begnadete [17].

Romanos legt dies nicht zufällig in den Mund Christi, noch möchte Christus die Gottesmutter erschrecken. Er will ihr seine unendliche Liebe für seine Geschöpfe zeigen, um derentwillen sie ihn bis jetzt gebeten hatte. Die Fleischwerdung des Wortes selbst als freudiges Ereignis verbindet sich soteriologisch mit dem Leid und der Trauer, die der äußerste Beweis für die Bejahung des menschlichen *Verfalles* sind[18]. Die Inkarnation des Wortes selbst als freudiges Ereignis wird hier soteriologisch mit Leiden und Trauer in Verbindung gebracht, was der wichtige Beweis dafür ist, dass er (Gott-Logos selbst) den menschlichen Verfall und die Qual vor dem Tod in sein Fleisch aufgenommen hat. Was nicht zur wahren Beziehung der Menschen zu Christus passt, ist die Korruption des freien Willens des Menschen und die Umwandlung der angemessenen menschlichen Trauer in unvernünftigen Pessimismus und Depression.

Welche Mutter würde jedoch solche Worte hören und nicht aus der Fassung geraten? Selbst wenn sie vom allmächtigen Göttlichen Wort selbst stammen, ist sie dennoch eine Mutter. Daher akzeptiert sie die Folge der Menschwerdung, also das Leiden ihres Sohns, verlangt aber trotzdem, ihr die Tiefe des Sinns der *Menschwerdung* zu erläutern. Im 15. *Oikos* möchte die Mutter sittsam die Zukunft erfahren („Was du zu vollenden strebst, was genau das ist, das will ich jetzt erfahren")[19]. Sie möchte, dass dieser ganze „ewige Wille" Gottes

---

[17] 2ιδ$^{10\text{-}11}$: ἂν δὲ καὶ σταυροῦσθαί με μάθῃς, σεμνή, νεκροῦσθαι δὲ δι' αὐτούς, / μετὰ πάντων τῶν στοιχείων δονηθήσῃ καὶ θρηνήσεις / ἡ κεχαριτωμένη.

[18] Leider haben westliche Theologen dieser Verbindung keine Bedeutung beigemessen, und auch die Forschung von Kirchenvätern, welche die *orthodoxe gottleidende Soteriologie* dynamisch bevorzugten, hat sich in eine andere Richtung gewandt, wie des großen Redners Proklos von Konstantinopel (siehe *I. Κουρεμπελές, Ἡ ὁμιλία τοῦ πατριάρχη Προκλού*, insbesondere 161f.).

[19] 2ιε^{7}: ὃ μέλλεις τελεῖν τί ἐστι θέλω νῦν μαθεῖν.

Die Jungfrau, die die Erlösung vom Fluch gebar

nicht vor ihr verborgen bleibt, wie auch sie als Mutter nicht einen Teil, sondern das *gesamte* Göttliche Wort selbst *im Fleisch* geboren hat. Nicht zufällig betont die Gottesmutter ihrem Sohn gegenüber, dass sie ihn im Ganzen und nicht nur teilweise geboren hat. Das hat eine besondere dogmatische Bedeutung[20]. Romanos möchte auch dem einfachen Gläubigen klarmachen, dass es nicht möglich ist, dass sie nur einen Teil der Wahrheit kennt, obwohl sie am Ereignis der Geburt vollständig teilnimmt. Sie fordert von Gott, der die personifizierte Wahrheit ist, Ehrlichkeit und nicht Verschlossenheit. „Sprich", sagt sie ihm daher, „was du über uns im Sinn hast", sag uns also, was du über uns denkst. Der nächste *Oikos* (16) mit den Worten Christi ist einer, der in seinen Gedichten durch die Weise herausragt, mit der er dem Hörer die Heilsbotschaft nahebringt. Wir zitieren ihn wortwörtlich:

> Von der Liebe werde ich besiegt[21], die ich für den Menschen empfinde,
> antwortete der Schöpfer: Meine Magd und Mutter,
> ich will dich nicht betrüben! Doch tue ich dir
> meine Ansicht kund, denn ich will deine Seele stärken, Maria!
> Den deine Hände tragen, dessen Hände wirst du in kurzer Zeit
> Von Nägeln durchbohrt sehen, weil ich dein Geschlecht liebe.
> Den du mit Milch stillst, werden andere mit Galle tränken.
> Den du zärtlich küsst, werden sie über bespeien.
> Den du das Leben nanntest, wirst du am Kreuz hängen sehen
> Und als tot beweinen. Doch sollst du mich auch als Auferstandenen umarmen,
> du Begnadedte[22].

VII. Göttliche Menschenliebe

Romanos lässt hier die *menschenliebende göttliche Kultur* dominieren, eine Theologie der Sehnsucht und der Leidenschaft Gottes für die gesamte

---

[20] Zur besonderen dogmatischen Bedeutung des Ausdrucks „im Ganzen habe ich dich geboren" und dieser holistischen christologischen Terminologie siehe: *I. Κουρεμπελές, Ἡ Χριστολογία τοῦ Ῥωμανοῦ τοῦ Μελωδοῦ καὶ ἡ σωτηριολογικὴ σημασία της* (Θεσσαλονίκη 1998) 126f. Romanos hat hier offenbar die aphthartodoketischen Tendenzen seiner Zeit im Sinn, denen er auf dichterische Weise gegenübertritt.
[21] Ich ziehe hier lieber das Verb „besiegen" statt des Verbs „bezwingen" der Übersetzung von J. Koder.
[22] 2ιστ$^{1-11}$: «Νικῶμαι διὰ τὸν πόθον, ὃν ἔχω πρὸς τὸν ἄνθρωπον» / ὁ ποιητὴς ἀπεκρίθη, ἐγὼ δούλη καὶ μῆτερ μου· / οὐ λυπῶ σε· γνωριῶ δὲ / ἃ θέλω πράττειν καὶ θεραπεύσω σου ψυχήν, ὦ Μαριάμ· / τὸν ἐν ταῖς χερσίν σου φερόμενον, τὰς χεῖρας ἡλούμενον / μετὰ μικρὸν ὄψει με, ὅτι στέργω τὸ γένος σου· / ὃν σὺ γαλουχεῖς, ἄλλοι ποτίσουσι χολήν· / ὃν καταφιλεῖς, μέλλει πληροῦσθαι ἐμπτυσμῶν· / ὃν ζωὴν ἐκάλεσας, ἔχεις ἰδεῖν κρεμάμενον ἐν σταυρῷ, / καὶ δακρύσεις ὡς θανόντα, ἀλλ' ἀσπάσῃ με ἀναστάντα, / ἡ κεχαριτωμένη».

Menschheit. All das, sagt der menschenliebende Gott weiter unten, „werde ich erleiden, weil ich es will", also nicht aus Zwang. Es handelt sich um einen alten und gleichzeitig neuen göttlichen Willen für die Menschheit, als Gott den Menschen zu retten, ohne den menschlichen Schmerz in seinem angenommenen Fleisch zu vermeiden (2ιζ^{14}). Das Seufzen Mariams, die nicht die Ermordung ihres unschuldigen Kindes sehen möchte, beugt nicht das sehnende Verlangen Gottes nach Rettung der geschundenen Menschheit. Diese Rettung erfolgt durch die Bedingungen der *homöopathischen Medizin* Christi, des einzigen wahren Arztes[23].

Christus sagt ihr sogar, mit dem Jammern aufzuhören, denn ohne das Leiden werden alle verlorengehen, für die sie selbst bittet (2ιζ$^{9\text{-}10}$). Das zeigt ausdrucksstark, dass die Gottesgebärerin als wahre fleischliche Mutter nicht den schmerzhaften Weg ihres Kindes erleben wollte, als sie für ihr Geschlecht bat, wie wir in den vorherigen Versen gesehen haben. Keine Mutter möchte sehen, dass ihr Sohn leidet und Schmerzen fühlt. Ihr Sohn sagt ihr aber, dass sie nicht ausschließlich bei der wundersamen jungfräulichen Geburt (Betonung der Göttlichkeit) bleiben dürfe, ohne um die schmerzvolle Zukunft zu wissen, die auf ihren Sohn wartet (Betonung der Menschlichkeit). In dieser Zukunft wartet der *menschenfressende Tod*, der jedoch in Christus nur das sichtbare Menschsein Christi sieht und seine verborgene Göttlichkeit übersieht.

Das Kontakion endet an dieser Stelle mit einem *Oikos* (18), der die theologische Bedeutung der Auferstehung zeigt. Voraussetzung für diesen Punkt sind jedenfalls der Abstieg in den Hades und das die Menschheit rettende Leiden, das die Tiefe der göttlichen Menschenliebe zeigt.

Christus spricht zu seiner Mutter, seinen Tod nicht zu fürchten, sondern ihn als Schlaf „anzusehen". In drei Tagen, sagt er ihr, wird er auferstehen und sie treffen (zuerst sie). Und er wird auf diese Weise die Erde und die Erdlinge erneuern. Ihre Pflicht ist es, Eva diese Freude zu verkünden, eine Freude, die freilich das abgeschlossene Werk Gottes für den Menschen voraussetzt (2ιη'). Zur gleichen göttlichen Person, die in die Erfahrung des Menschseins eintritt, gehören auch das fleischliche Leiden und der Tod, die Trauer der Mutter und die freudige Auferstehung[24].

---

[23] Christus ist nicht der vom zu behandelnden Menschen distanzierte Arzt, sondern jenes göttliche Subjekt (Hypostase), das in seinem Fleisch (*homöopathisch*) mit Schmerzen sein Geschöpf rettet.

[24] Im liturgischen Sinn des *Kontakions* postuliert Romanos hier freilich auch eine ekklesiologische Komponente, die sich auf das nicht scheinbare (doketische) Leiden Christi stützt. Die Größe der göttlichen Menschenliebe wird im Mysterium der Einheit des Leibes Christi gewebt, welches das Werk des Auferstandenen ist. Siehe mehr zu diesem dogmati-

Der anti-aphthartodoketische Charakter, den Romanos der theologischen Grundlage dieses Kontakions verleiht, ist deutlich erkennbar. Diese Erzählung ist also dogmatisch nicht losgelöst von den Auseinandersetzungen seiner Zeit, wo die tatsächliche Fleischwerdung Gottes von den aphthartodoketischen Kreisen angezweifelt wurde und die Bedeutung des Leidens des inkarnierten Gottes in seinem Fleisch herabgesetzt wurde[25].

Epilog

Wir haben gesehen, wie verständlich in der Dichtung das theologische Element werden kann, was auch das Anliegen von Romanos dem Meloden gewesen war. Und wir haben dies durch das theologische Thema der Geburt des Göttlichen Wortes selbst durch den (die) Menschen gesehen. Romanos war Unterstützer des Dogmas von Chalkedon, wo der *eine Christus* verkündet wurde, der „in zwei Naturen unvermischt, unveränderlich, ungetrennt und unteilbar erkannt wird". Er war der *neuchalkedonische Dichter* seiner Zeit[26]. Und wie wir aus seinen Worten entnehmen können, wusste er die dogmatische Wahrheit in poetische Sprache, dramatische Elemente und Melodie zu übersetzen, welche die Sinne des ganzen Menschen trainieren sollten. So wie der *ganze* Christus aus der Jungfrau Maria geboren wurde und mit ihm auch die *ganze* Wahrheit über sein Verlangen nach dem Menschen offenbart wurde, so wird den Menschen der *ganze* im Fleisch Leidende Christus angeboten.

Wir wissen nicht, warum das Kontakion aus der Liturgie verschwand (zum Glück gibt es in ihr als *in toto* zu singendes Lied den *Akathistos Hymnus*) und an seine Stelle der terminologisch eher dogmatischer und nicht mehr dramatische Kanon trat[27]. Sicher ist, dass in der Zeit Justinians diese freie dramatische

---

schen Thema der Auferstehung im Rahmen der Ekklesiologie *N. Ματσούκας,* Ἐκκλησιολογία ἐξ ἐπόψεως τριαδικοῦ δόγματος, Ἐπιστημονική Ἐπετηρίδα Θεολογικῆς Σχολῆς Πανεπιστημίου Θεσσαλονίκης 17 (1972) 115–214, hier 162.

[25] Über den Aphthartodoketismus im Zeitalter Justinians I. siehe *A. Grillmeier – Th. Hainthaler,* Jesus der Christus im Glauben der Kirche: Die Kirche von Konstantinopel im 6. Jahrhundert, Bd. II/2 (Freiburg – Basel – Wien 1989) 224ff.

[26] Zum theologischen Ausdruck des *Neuchalkedonismus* siehe *I. Κουρεμπελές,* Ὁ Νεοχαλκηδονισμός: Δογματικό σημεῖο διαίρεσης (Θεσσαλονίκη 2015). Zu den christologischen Ansichten nach Chalcedon im Westen siehe *Th. Hainthaler,* Lateinische Christologie nach Chalkedon: Eine Skizze, in: Th. Hainthaler – D. Ansorge – A. Wucherpfennig (Hgg.), Jesus der Christus im Glauben der Kirche (Freiburg – Basel – Wien 2019) 271ff.

[27] Das bedeutet jedoch nicht, dass das dramatische Interesse später verschwunden ist, da die Forschungen die Existenz eines religiösen byzantinischen Theaters nicht ausschliessen kann. Die Kunst von Romanos bot einfach nicht die Interessen, welche das byzantinische Theater besaß, denn der Schwerpunkt der Dichtung von Romanos lag auf der Musik, der

Dichtung ein Jahrhundert der theologischen Kultur und Grundlage der Bildung dieser Zeit anzeigt[28]. Vielleicht hat später die musikdramatische Dichtung jenen Tendenzen nicht gepaßt, die der Durchführung und dem Ausdruck des Gottesdienstes strengere Grenzen setzen wollten. Heute kennen wir jedenfalls den griechisch-syrischen Meloden der Dichtung und der Theologie, der Theologie und der Dichtung, hinreichend gut, der deutlich auf der klaren Beantwortung der Frage bestand: „Wer sagen die Leute, dass der Menschensohn sei?" (Mt 16, 13), indem er Theologie mit dem fleischgewordenen Gott und nicht ohne ihn und ohne seine Mutter auf Erden erlebte[29].

---

theologischen Qualität und der Teilnahme der Eucharistie-Gemeinde und nicht auf der Prominenz von „Schauspielern". Zum religiösen byzantinischen Theater siehe: Κ. Καλοκύρης, Τὸ ἀρχαιοελληνικὸ καὶ τὸ βυζαντινὸ θέατρο καὶ ἡ ἀρχαία λατρεία στὴ λειτουργικὴ παράδοση τῆς ὀρθόδοξης ἐκκλησίας, in: Χριστιανικὴ λατρεία καί εἰδωλολατρία. Πρακτικά ΣΤ' Πανελληνίου Λειτουργικοῦ Συμποσίου στελεχῶν Ἱερῶν Μητροπόλεων (Ἀθήνα 2005) 341–363, hier 350f.

[28] Mit erkennbaren seelischen Schmerzen sagt N. Tomadakis (N. Τωμαδάκης, Ἡ γέννησις τοῦ Χριστοῦ ὑμνουμένη ἀπὸ τὸν Ῥωμανὸ Μελωδόν, Λογοτεχνικὰ Χρονικὰ 2 [1970] 145–150, hier S. 147) als Abschluss seines Verweises auf das 1. *Kontakion* von Romanos über die Geburt Folgendes: „Seit der Zeit, als Konstantinopel in die Hände der Türken gefallen war, wurde dieser wundervolle Hymnus nicht mehr gehört, der fast tausend Jahre lang zu Weihnachten im Kaiserpalast von den Chören der Kirchensänger der Hagia Sophia rechts und von der Kirche der Heiligen Apostel links gesungen wurde. Heute findet er sich nur in den philologischen Ausgaben von Romanos gedruckt, und als Gegenstand von Universitätsvorlesungen, Sprachbearbeitungen, Seminarstudien und ästhetischen Analysen". Die Übersetzung ist von mir.

[29] Zur Verfälschung der Lehre von der ewigen Jungfräulichkeit der Theotokos durch moderne Theologen vgl. bei *Ι. Κουρεμπελές*, Ἡδονοδοξία: Κριτικὴ στὴ μεταπατερικὴ θεώρηση τῆς Παρθενίας τῆς Θεοτόκου (Θεσσαλονίκη 2019).

Georgi Kapriev, Sofia (Bulgaria)

Das Problem der Erbsünde in der Anthropologie des Maximus Confessor

Abstract:
The paper, without contrasting the positions of Eastern Orthodox and Roman Catholic theology in regard to the sin of Adam and Eve in general, attempts to establish the real points of difference. Further, the opinion of Maximus Confessor is explained, who is quoted by the two sides as a high authority. It is stated that the solution of this question is a core position of his anthropology, which plays a system-building role also in his Christology, as well as in his cosmology, ecclesiology and eschatology.

Die orthodoxe Theologie hat eine Stellungnahme zu der Frage nach der Sünde der Urahnen geprägt. Aus verständlichen Gründen erfolgte die strikte Formulierung dieser Position nach der Mitte des 20. Jahrhunderts. Ich fasse anfänglich nur drei repräsentative Konzepte zusammen: diese von Johannes Romanides (1957), John Meyendorff (1974) und Kalin Yanakiev (2020).

I. Drei maßgebende ost-orthodoxe Positionen

In seinem sonst insbesondere gegenüber dem Augustinismus zu leidenschaftlich polemischen[1] Buch formuliert Romanides schon durch den Titel die Hauptthese: Es geht nicht um eine Erbsünde, sondern um ein προπατορικὸν ἁμάρτημα, um eine Ahnensünde. Adam und Eva sind mit dem Potential erschaffen, die Gottebenbildlichkeit durch geistliche Arbeit und kraft ihres freien Willens zu bewahren. Dadurch würden sie die Unsterblichkeit und die Vergöttlichung erreichen. Nicht Gott hat den Tod geschaffen, sondern Adam und Eva durch ihre Trennung von Gott und der erstgeborene Kain, durch den der Tod in die Welt eingetreten ist. Auch wenn die Urahnen nicht gesündigt hätten, würden die Nachfahren gleichwohl weder unsterblich noch sterblich sein. Die Unsterblichkeit des einzelnen Menschen würde nicht von seiner Natur, sondern von seinem Bemühen, die Vollkommenheit zu erreichen (ἐκ τῆς

---

[1] Nach dem Spruch von Kalin Yanakiev: *К. Янакиев*, Метафизика на личността. Християнски перспективи (София 2020) 263.

πρὸς τὴν τελείωσιν ἀσκήσεως αὐτοῦ), von seinem Willen und von der Gnade Gottes abhängen. Die Ahnensünde hat die Menschennatur nicht sündig, sondern krank gemacht. Unter den durch die Geburt vererbten Krankheiten der Menschheit sind die Verwesung (φθορά) und der Tod die Grundlage aller anderen Krankheiten[2].

Meyendorff setzt diesen Gedankengang fort. Die Rebellion von Adam und Eva gegen Gott ist nur als ihre persönliche Sünde aufzufassen. Es kann nicht um eine ererbte Schuld oder um eine „Sünde der Natur" gehen, obwohl die menschliche Natur die Folgen von Adams Sünde trägt. Wegen des Ungehorsams Adams ist die Natur, die die von ihm geborenen Menschen aufnehmen, krank geworden und in diesem Sinn unter das „Gesetz der Sünde" gefallen. Die Krankheit der φθορά betrifft sowohl das Leibliche als auch das Sittliche. Die Menschen sind nicht wegen der Sünde der Ahnen schuldig. Sie sind von dem Zustand der Welt nach dem Akt des Ungehorsams abhängig, mit dem die erbliche Sterblichkeit verbunden ist. Tod und Sterblichkeit sind nicht so sehr als Vergeltung für die Sünde zu betrachten, sondern als ein Mittel, durch das die grundsätzlich ungerechte „Tyrannei" des Teufels nach Adams Sünde über die Menschheit ausgeübt wird[3].

Yanakiev betrachtet die Sünde Adams und Evas auch als eine persönliche und legt die Betonung auf die Entfremdung Adams von seinem gottgegebenen Sein. Der Mensch hat seinen existentiellen Umgang, sein Sein von Angesicht zu Angesicht mit Gott unterbrochen. Er hat sein Sein zu Eigen gemacht. Er hat sein Ich seinsmäßig von Gott entfremdet. Das entwendete Sein entblößt ihn. Daraus erfolgt das ontologische Drama des Menschen: seine Sterblichkeit und der Tod. Der Mensch ist seiner Erschaffung nach kein sterbliches Geschöpf. Der Grund der Sterblichkeit ist die Unterbrechung der Verbindung des menschlichen Werdens mit Gott. Der Tod war nie von Gott gewollt und es ist nicht widersprüchlich, dass Gott den Menschen mit ihrer Natur das Ewig-Sein spenden und sie von dem Tod befreien wird[4].

Mehr oder weniger scharf nehmen die Autoren Abstand von den Positionen der römischen Theologie. Keiner solidarisiert sich zwar mit Photius von Konstantinopel, der sich, innerhalb seines Kommentars über die Einwände von Theodor aus Antiochien, dem Bischof von Mopsuestia, gegen diese, die behaupten, dass die Menschen der Natur und nicht dem Willen (γνώμη) nach sündigen, äußert. Theodor habe gegen die entsprechende Lehre der Westler

---

[2] Ἰ. Σ. Ῥωμανίδης, Τὸ Προπατορικὸν Ἁμάρτημα (Θεσσαλονίκη ³2010) 156–161.
[3] J. Meyendorff, Byzantine Theology. Historical Trends & Doctrinal Themes (London – Oxford 1975) 143–146.
[4] К. Янакиев, Метафизика на личността, 248–260.

Das Problem der Erbsünde in der Anthropologie des Maximus Confessor 459

geschrieben, erklärt Photius, wobei er diese Lehre als Häresie und Absurdität bestimmt. Es ist die Lehre gemeint, dass nach der schlechten Handlung von Adam und Eva die Menschennatur eine andere geworden sei, so dass die Sünde schon in der Natur und nicht in der Willensentscheidung (προαίρεσις) Platz habe. Die geborenen Kinder sollen also in einer Natur sein, die durch die Sünde geprägt ist. Sie sollen die Sünde natürlicherweise innehaben. Photius lehnt diese Auffassung ab. Es geht im Fall der Menschwerdung Christi nicht um eine andere Natur, sondern nur um eine andere Figur (σχῆμα) der Natur. Die Taufe verleiht die Erneuerung, die nach der Auferstehung der Leiber bevorsteht[5].

II. Die Lehre der Katholischen Kirche

Einige Autoren berufen sich kritisch vor allem auf ausgewählte Thesen von Augustinus. Bei ihm sind Äußerungen zu finden, dass die Natur des Menschen sich mit der Sünde Adams gewandelt hat. Das Bild Gottes soll durch die ursprüngliche Schuld, die Ursünde (*peccatum originale*), wesenhaft deformiert sein[6]. Es wird eine „postlapsarische Natur des Menschen" angedeutet. Die offizielle aktuelle Lehre der Römischen Kirche ist jedoch viel subtiler und sie folgt diesen Thesen weitgehend nicht rigoros[7].

Dem *Katechismus der Katholischen Kirche* nach haben Adam und Eva eine persönliche Sünde begangen. Die Erbsünde hat bei keinem Nachkommen Adams den Charakter einer persönlichen Schuld. Der Mensch missbrauchte seine Freiheit und ließ in seinem Herzen das Vertrauen zu seinem Schöpfer sterben. In dieser Sünde zog der Mensch sich selbst Gott vor und missachtete damit Gott: Er entschied sich für sich selbst gegen Gott, gegen die Erfordernisse seines eigenen Geschöpfseins und damit gegen sein eigenes Wohl. Die menschliche Natur ist nicht durch und durch verdorben, wohl aber in ihren natürlichen Kräften verletzt[8]. Durch ihre erste Sünde geben Adam und Eva ihren Nachkommen die verwundete menschliche Natur weiter. Dieser Man-

---

[5] *Photius*, Bibliotheca 177: PG 103, 513A–516A.
[6] Cf. *Augustinus*, De trinitate 14, 4; De natura et gratia 3.
[7] Es wird dabei erklärt, dass die Lehre über die Weitergabe der Ursünde vor allem im 5. Jahrhundert geklärt worden ist, besonders unter dem Anstoß des antipelagianischen Denkens des hl. Augustinus, und im 16. Jahrhundert im Widerstand gegen die Reformation: die Kirche hat sich insbesondere 529 auf der zweiten Synode von Orange und 1546 auf dem Konzil von Trient über den Sinngehalt der Offenbarung von der Erbsünde ausgesprochen. – Catechismus catholicae ecclesiae 406, zit. nach: https://www.vatican.va/latin/latin_catechism.html.
[8] Catechismus 397, 398, 405.

gel wird „Erbsünde", *peccatum originale*, genannt und zu einer *essentialis veritas fidei* erklärt. Sie ist „Sünde" in einem übertragenen Sinn: Sie ist eine Sünde, die man „miterhalten", nicht aber begangen hat, ein Zustand, keine Tat.[9] Die Erbsünde wird zusammen mit der menschlichen Natur durch Fortpflanzung übertragen. Sie wohnt jedem Menschen als ihm eigen inne[10]. Infolge der Sünde werden die Menschen ganz allgemein verdorben – *universalis corruptio consequenter ad peccatum*[11]. In Rücksicht auf Röm 5, 12 und Röm 5, 19 wird geschlossen, dass alle Menschen in die Sünde Adams verwickelt sind[12]. Weil wir alle schon bei der Geburt von ihr betroffen sind, spendet die Kirche die Taufe zur Vergebung der Sünden selbst kleinen Kindern, die keine persönliche Sünde begangen haben[13]. Die Taufe spendet das Gnadenleben Christi. Sie tilgt die Erbsünde und richtet den Menschen wieder auf Gott aus. Aber die Folgen für die Natur, die geschwächt und zum Bösen geneigt (*debilitata et ad malum inclinata*) ist, verbleiben im Menschen und verpflichten ihn zum geistlichen Kampf[14]. Der Zustand des universellen Verderbens schließt allerdings die Möglichkeit einer Höherführung der Natur nicht aus[15]. Christus, der „neue Adam", hat den Ungehorsam Adams mehr als nur wiedergutgemacht. Der „neuen Eva", der Mutter Christi, ist als erster und auf einzigartige Weise der von Christus errungene Sieg über die Sünde zugutegekommen: sie wurde von jeglichem Makel der Erbsünde unversehrt bewahrt[16].

Die wesentlichen Unterschiede zwischen der römisch-katholischen und der orthodoxen Auffassung der Sünde von Adam und Eva als *peccatum originale* oder als *peccatum paternum* wurzeln vorwiegend in den Deutungen von Röm 5, 12, woraus der Sinngehalt der Taufe, wie auch das Konzept von der Menschheit der Gottesmutter abgeleitet wird.

III. Die orthodoxe Deutung von Röm 5, 12 und das Sakrament der Taufe

Der hermeneutische Kern des Verständnisses von Röm 5, 12[17] bildet die Deutung des Ausdrucks „ἐφ' ᾧ πάντες ἥμαρτον". Die philologische Analyse zeigt,

---

[9] Catechismus 404, 417, 388.
[10] Catechismus 419.
[11] Catechismus 401.
[12] Catechismus 402.
[13] Catechismus 403.
[14] Catechismus 405.
[15] Catechismus 412.
[16] Catechismus 411.
[17] Röm 5, 12: Διὰ τοῦτο ὥσπερ δι' ἑνὸς ἀνθρώπου ἡ ἁμαρτία εἰς τὸν κόσμον εἰσῆλθεν καὶ διὰ τῆς ἁμαρτίας ὁ θάνατος, καὶ οὕτως εἰς πάντας ἀνθρώπους ὁ θάνατος διῆλθεν, ἐφ' ᾧ πάντες ἥμαρτον.

Das Problem der Erbsünde in der Anthropologie des Maximus Confessor 461

dass es unmöglich ist, die Worte „ἐφ' ᾧ" auf Adam zu beziehen. Die Lektüre der Wendung im Sinne, dass alle Menschen in Adam gesündigt haben und also seine Sünde als eigene innehaben, erweist sich als grammatisch unhaltbar. Das Wort „ᾧ" ist ein Relativpronomen in Neutrum oder in Maskulinum. Im ersten Fall ist der Tod als das Los aller Menschen zu betrachten, weil jeder persönlich gesündigt hat. Der Mensch war weder als sterblich noch als unsterblich bestimmt[18]. Der Tod eines Menschen ist also als eine Strafe für seine persönlichen Sünden zu begreifen. Wenn es auf das Wort in Maskulinum, nämlich θάνατος, bezogen wird, dann ist der Satz so zu verstehen: Der Tod ist zu allen Menschen gelangt und wegen des Todes haben alle gesündigt. Der Ausdruck wird als „ἐφ' ᾧ θανάτῳ πάντες ἥμαρτον" gelesen. Wegen des Todes sündigen alle Menschen in dieser Existenzweise der menschlichen Natur. Die Sünde ist ein Ergebnis der Tätigkeit des einzelnen Individuums und keine ererbte Schuld. Beides schließt die Idee von einer Erbschuld aus. Die beiden Lesarten werden durch griechischsprachige christliche Autoritäten bekräftigt. Es werden vor allem Sätze von Theophilus von Antiochien, Gregor von Nyssa, Johannes Chrysostomus, Cyrill von Alexandrien, Theodoret von Cyrus, Maximus Confessor, Photius von Konstantinopel zitiert[19].

Die Taufe wird entsprechend nicht als Tilgung der Erbsünde gedeutet. Sie wird als Spende einer Lebenserneuerung, als Verleihen eines neuen Lebens und der Möglichkeit verstanden, mit Christus zusammen zu sterben und aufzuerstehen. Die Taufe ist keine Rechtfertigung und kein Erlass einer ererbten Schuld, sondern Kommunion im auferstandenen Leib Christi. Sie ist eine Teilhabe am göttlichen Leben und den göttlichen Lebensenergien, wodurch die Menschheit in ihren echten natürlichen Zustand versetzt wird[20]. Der Mensch, der unter der Herrschaft des Todes lebt, lebt widernatürlich. Die φθορά kommt nicht von Gott. Christus ist der echt natürliche Mensch, weil er gemäß der ursprünglichen Bestimmung des Menschen lebt[21]. Das Leben im gegenwärtigen Zustand ist als ein Leben παρὰ φύσιν zu verstehen. Vor diesem Hintergrund ist es nicht kompliziert zu vermuten, dass die Jungfrau Maria keine spezielle Gnade für ihre Natur braucht, um – durch ihre freie und demütige Annahme des Willens Gottes – Θεοτόκος zu werden.

---

[18] *Theophilus Antiochiensis*, Ad Autolycam 2, 24.
[19] *J. Meyendorff*, Byzantine Theology, 143–145; Ἰ. Σ. Ῥωμανίδης, Τὸ Προπατορικὸν Ἁμάρτημα, 167–168.
[20] *J. Meyendorff*, Byzantine Theology, 146.
[21] Ἰ. Σ. Ῥωμανίδης, Τὸ Προπατορικὸν Ἁμάρτημα, 133.

IV. Maximus Confessor und die Frage nach der Sünde der Stammeltern

Aussagen von Maximus Confessor werden nicht selten herangezogen, um das orthodoxe Konzept von der Ahnensünde zu bekräftigen. Es ist nach dem systematischen Charakter dieser Problematik in seinem Werk zu fragen.

1. Logos der Essenz und Existenzweise der Natur

Auf den entscheidenden Punkt in unserem Zusammenhang hat es Andrew Louth gebracht: Der Fall existiert nicht auf der Ebene des Logos, sondern des Tropos. Die Folge des Sündenfalls, erklärt Louth, ist nicht, dass die Natur an sich entstellt ist, sondern dass sie missbraucht wird. In einer gefallenen Welt bleiben die λόγοι von allem Natürlichen unangetastet, aber die Naturen können in einer Weise (τρόπος) handeln, die ihren grundlegenden λόγοι zuwiderläuft. Die λόγοι werden durch die τρόποι, die die Naturen annehmen, verdeckt. Die Tatsache, dass der Sündenfall die Ebene der Natur nicht berührt, bedeutet nicht, dass die Auswirkungen des Sündenfalls oberflächlich sind[22]. Weder die Sünde noch das Verwesen (der Tod) sind, bemerkt Basil Lourié, die Position des Maximus Confessor deutend, auch nach dem Sündenfall Teil der menschlichen Natur geworden. Die Sterblichkeit wird im Menschengeschlecht ererbt, aber nicht deshalb, weil sie ein Teil der Natur geworden ist[23].

Durch „Logos der Essenz (oder des Seins[24])" (λόγος τῆς οὐσίας oder τοῦ εἶναι) bezeichnet Maximus „das, was ist" (τὸ τί ἐστιν), die konstitutive Bestimmtheit der Essenz. Er ist konstant, variiert nicht und setzt in Kraft das göttliche Gesetz der Natur: der unveränderliche Logos ist das grundlegende Gesetz-νόμος jeder Natur, die kraft dieses Logos entsteht und existiert[25]. Die Existenzweise (τρόπος τῆς ὑπάρξεως oder τοῦ πῶς εἶναι τρόπος) ist die Ordnung der Naturwirkung. Sie ist das Areal des Variierens, der Modifikation oder der Innovation. Die Existenzweise ermöglicht Schwingungen mit unterschiedlicher Amplitude, wobei aber der Logos unverändert bleibt[26]. Die Existenzweise jeder geschaffenen Natur schließt die Äußerung von neuen, vorher geschichtlich nicht festgestellten Formen der Naturexistenz nicht aus. Der Logos bescheinigt das Sein und der Tropos bescheinigt das konkrete Vorhanden-

---

[22] A. *Louth*, Maximus the Confessor (London – New York 1996) 56.
[23] В. М. *Лурье*, История византийской философии. Формативный период (Санкт-Петербург 2006) 397.
[24] Cf. e.g. *Maximus Confessor*, Mystagogia 23: PG 91, 701A; Ambigua ad Thomam 5: PG 91, 1052B.
[25] *Maximus Confessor*, Ambigua ad Iohanem 31: PG 91, 1280A.
[26] *Maximus Confessor*, Amb. Ioh. 42: PG 91, 1341D.

sein dieses Seins. Der Begriff „Existenzweise" wird nicht direkt mit dem Begriffsbereich von „Hypostase" assoziiert. Der hypostatische Modus ist nicht mit dem Modus der Existenz (ὕπαρξις, ὑπάρχειν) identisch. Der in diesem Kontext gedeutete τρόπος τῆς ὑπάρξεως ist die Weise, auf die die Natur wirklich existiert[27].

In Rücksicht auf die Menschennatur unterscheidet Maximus zwischen zwei Sorten von Existenzweisen, die in einer spezifischen Korrespondenz untereinander stehen. Er spricht einerseits über Existenzweisen der Menschennatur in der Geschichte: vor dem Sündenfall, nach ihm, nach der Inkarnation des Logos und nach dem Gericht. Andererseits beschreibt er drei allgemeine Existenzweisen der Natur des Menschen: Sein – Gut-Sein/Böse-Sein – Ewig-Gut-Sein/Ewig-Böse-Sein. Der Übergang von Logos zu Tropos ist eine Übertragung von der essentiellen zu der existentiellen Ordnung. Der positiven Linie folgend, spricht sich Maximus eindeutig aus:

Unser Herr und Gott hat eine dreifache Geburt von uns gesegnet: die allgemeine Weise der Geburt im Sein, im Gut-Sein und im Ewig-Sein. Die erste ist die Geburt des Leibes und der Seele in ihrer gemeinsamen Existenz von einem anderen Leib. Dadurch bekommen wir Sein. Die zweite Geburt ist durch die Taufe. Dadurch bekommen wir reichlich das Gut-Sein. Die dritte Geburt ist in der Auferstehung, die Weise unserer Verwandlung durch Gnade in Ewig-Sein[28].

Maximus setzt die Existenzweisen der seienden Menschennatur mit der Geburt, mit der Inkarnation des Logos und mit der Taufe in einen Zusammenhang. Der Mensch war nach dem Bilde Gottes geschaffen, überlegt Maximus, so dass er nach seiner freien Willensentscheidung aufgrund der ihm inhärenten natürlichen selbstbewegenden und unabhängigen Kraft im Geist geboren werden konnte. Er werde dann Sohn Gottes und Gott der Gnade nach durch den Geist. Diese gottmachende und nichtmaterielle Geburt wurde von dem

---

[27] Um die Identifikation von „Existenzweise" und „Hypostase" zu vermeiden, spricht Maximus mit Rücksicht auf das hypostatische Sein, einen klaren Unterschied zwischen „Essenz" und „Hypostase" ziehend, über „Logos der Hypostase" und „Existenzweise der Hypostase", die er dem Logos und dem Tropos der Essenz gegenüberstellt – Cf. *Maximus Confessor*, Amb. Ioh. 36: PG 91, 1289C; Epistulae 12: PG 91, 493D. Λόγος τῆς ὑποστάσεως kennzeichnet hierin die eigene Verfassung der Hypostase: die Inhypostasierung der Natur, das Hineintun der Hypostase in die entsprechende Existenzweise der Natur, den Rahmen der Seinsbedingungen der Hypostase, die Struktur ihrer einmaligen Eigenschaften. Τρόπος τῆς ὑποστάσεως schildert seinerseits die Weise, auf die die Person ihre Naturvermögen oder Eigenschaften benutzt und ihren Willen richtet und gebraucht – Cf. *Maximus Confessor*, Disputatio cum Pyrrho: PG 91, 294A. Der τρόπος τῆς ὑποστάσεως ist jenes, das die Person von den anderen Personen ihrer Art innerhalb ihrer sonst gemeinsamen Weise der Naturexistenz unterscheidet.
[28] *Maximus Confessor*, Amb. Ioh. 42, 12: PG 91, 1325BC.

ersten Menschen frei abgestoßen. Er hat das überflüssige Vergnügen seiner Sinne bevorzugt. Infolge dessen war er auf eine materielle, tödliche und körperliche Geburt verworfen. Gott hat entschieden, dass der Mensch, wegen seiner Entscheidung für das Niedrigere, seine freie, nichtleidenschaftliche, willentliche Geburt durch eine Geburt ersetzen soll, die ihn mit den alogischen und anoetischen Tieren gleichstellt. Die Taufe ist die geistliche Geburt der Adoption[29]. Die geistliche Geburt der Taufe ist Rückkehr oder, präziser gesagt, Wiederschöpfung (ἀνάπλασις) des Menschen[30].

2. Erschaffung und Geburt

Der erste Mensch ist γενητός und sein Nachfolger ist γεννητός. Der Unterschied zwischen erschaffen und geboren, zwischen der Erschaffung des Menschen bei seinem Antreten ins Sein (γένεσις) und der Geburt (γέννησις), wodurch sich das Menschengeschlecht nach dem Fall Adams vermehrt, hat eine prinzipielle Bedeutung. Der Schöpfungsakt versieht den göttlichen Logos der menschlichen Natur mit dem entsprechenden Tropos der Existenz. Die Geburt ergibt die Existenzweise der Natur, durch die die Effekte der Sünde – und an erster Stelle das Verwesen und die Leidenschaftlichkeit – an die weiteren Menschengenerationen weitergegeben werden.

Die Differenz zwischen dem Logos des Erschaffens des Menschen (τῆς ἀνθρώπου γενέσεως λόγος) und der durch die Sünde hervorgerufene Tropos der Geburt des Menschen (τῆς γεννήσεως αὐτοῦ διὰ τὴν ἁμαρτίαν τρόπος) besteht darin, dass der Logos des Erschaffens im Grunde der Menschennatur steht und ewig beständig und unverändert bleibt. Demgegenüber ist der Tropos der Geburt nur eine Weise der Existenz der Natur, die dem Menschen wegen Erziehungsökonomie eigen geworden ist. Er findet sein Ende nach der Korrektur des Menschen und seiner vollständigen Rückkehr zum Prinzip seines Erschaffens. Dieser Tropos ist vergänglich und er ist nicht imstande, den Logos der Natur gemäß ihrem Erschaffen zu verletzen[31].

Unser προπάτωρ Ἀδάμ hat das göttliche Licht seines Seelenauges verloren und er ist in der Dunkelheit des Unwissens versunken. Wenn Adam Gott vertraut hätte, würde er von dem Baum des Lebens essen. Dann würde er die Gabe der Unsterblichkeit nicht verlieren. Der erste Mensch entfernte sich aber von dem göttlichen Leben und trat in einem anderen Leben an, wodurch er

---

[29] *Maximus Confessor*, Amb. Ioh. 42, 31: PG 91, 1345D–1348B.
[30] *Maximus Confessor*, Amb. Ioh. 42, 32: PG 91, 1348CD.
[31] Cf. *Maxiums Confessor*, Quaestiones ad Thalassium 21: PG 90, 312B–313; Amb. Ioh. 42: PG 91, 1316C–1320A, 1325C; Opuscula theologica et polemica: PG 91, 60C.

die ganze Schöpfung dem Tod überliefert hat. Der Tod verweilt bis heute, so dass wir nicht richtig leben, weil wir von dem Tode durch Verwesen (φθορά) unaufhörlich verschlungen werden[32]. Der Tod ist kein Ergebnis einer Transformation der Natur und ist demzufolge kein physisches, sondern ein metaphysisches Problem. Er ist ein Attentat gegen den göttlichen Schöpfungsakt. Die Unsterblichkeit ist kein Naturelement, sie war im Paradies eine gottgegebene Teilhabe am göttlichen Leben. Der Tod wird seinerseits auch nach dem Sündenfall kein Bestandteil der Natur, aber er ist eine Wirkung, die die Individuen dieser Natur zerbricht.

Die Samenvermehrung, die Geschlechtertrennung, die körperliche Geburt sind Elemente des neuen Gesetzes des Fleisches, d.h. der durch die Sünde eingerichteten Gesetze der Natur (διὰ τὴν ἁμαρτίαν νόμοι τῆς φύσεως)[33]. Sie widerstehen den durch den Ungehorsam des alten Adams verletzten geistlichen Gesetzen der Natur[34]. Diese neuen Gesetze variieren negativ das eigentliche Gesetz der Natur und sind gültig für die Weise, auf die die Natur in dieser Welt existiert. Die „Gesetze des Fleisches", auch „νόμοι τῆς ἀλογίας" genannt, stehen mit dem autonomisierten und favorisierten Leib in Korrespondenz. Sie entfremden den Menschen von seinem Logos; er ist übermäßig von Gott entfernt. Umgekehrt ist das Befolgen der richtigen inneranthropologischen Ordnung imstande, den Leib und das Leibliche zu transzendieren, ohne sie zu ignorieren oder zu unterschätzen. Auf diese Weise wird die Kluft zwischen Mensch und Gott vermindert. Die aktuelle ἀνωμαλία kann und soll beseitigt und überwunden werden, weil sie keinen Platz im Schöpfungsplan Gottes und keinen Grund in den Prinzipien-λόγοι der geschaffenen Dinge hat[35]. Christus hebt gerade die Gesetze der Natur des Fleisches auf und erneuert die Gesetze der göttlichen Schöpfung (δημιουργία) [36].

3. Leib und Seele, die psychophysische Einheit und ihre Ordnung

Die Seele und der Leib haben bei der γένεσις ihre eigenen λόγοι τὸ εἶναι und τοῦ γένεσθαι τρόποι erhalten[37]. Sie, Seele und Leib, sind zwei verschiedene Wesenheiten, sie können auch getrennt (nach dem physischen Tod) bestehen[38]. Im paradiesischen Zustand war aber der Leib Adams entschieden

---
[32] *Maximus Confessor*, Amb. Ioh. 10, 28: PG 91, 1156C–1157A.
[33] *Maximus Confessor*, Amb. Ioh. 31: PG 91, 1276B.
[34] *Maximus Confessor*, Amb. Ioh. 31: PG 91, 1276C.
[35] *Maximus Confessor*, Amb. Ioh. 8: PG 91, 1105B.
[36] *Maximus Confessor*, Amb. Ioh. 10: PG 91, 1172A, 1157D–1160A; 31: PG 91, 1276CD.
[37] *Maximus Confessor*, Amb. Ioh. 42, 10: PG 91, 1324D.
[38] *Maximus Confessor*, Amb. Ioh. 42: PG 91, 1321BD.

nicht ohne Anteil an der Unsterblichkeit der Gnade nach[39], weil er untrennbarer und vollwertiger Teil der zusammengesetzten Natur (φύσις σύνθετος) des Menschen ist. Der Mensch ist Bild Gottes und in dieses Bild ist der Logos, das natürliche und göttliche Gesetz des Menschen gelegt[40]. Das Bild Gottes ist der ganze Mensch: die Seele und der Leib. Der Mensch ist naturgemäß einer nicht erst in seiner Hypostase, die zwei Naturen enthält, sondern im Logos seiner Natur und in der einen Art „Mensch"[41].

Von diesem Standpunkt aus besteht Maximus darauf, dass das höchste in diesem Leben erreichbare Gut, nämlich das Leben des Lebens Gottes durch das Erfüllen des Menschen mit den göttlichen natürlichen Energien, dem ganzen seelisch-leiblichen Menschen geschenkt wird. Diese andere Lebensweise wird nicht nur „im Fleisch" gegeben, sondern sie wird auch durch das Fleisch geäußert, weil die Tugenden durch das Fleisch zur Erscheinung gebracht werden[42].

Im Kontext der Ahnensünde ist die Behauptung instruktiv, dass der Wechsel der Existenzwese der Natur zu Veränderungen in der Zusammensetzung des menschlichen Leibes führt. In der Körperlichkeit erweisen sich entgegenwirkende und sich gegenseitig vernichtende Eigenschaften, die die Unveränderlichkeit und die Unsterblichkeit des Leibes abschaffen. Der Effekt besteht in dem Verwesen und dem Tod des Leibes, in der chaotischen Bewegung, die zu den Leidenschaften neigt, in der Unbeständigkeit der äußeren und der eigenen Materialität[43].

Der Tod ist ein Zerfall des Körpers. Adam, der durch seine Willensentscheidung den Zerfall der materiellen Dinge in Materie und Geist zugelassen hat, ist selbst zum Opfer dieses Zerfalls geworden. Auf diese Weise hat er selbst den Tod für die ganze Zeit des gegenwärtigen Zeitraums (κατὰ πάντα τὸν χρόνον τοῦ παρόντος καιροῦ) geschaffen. Er ist während dieser ganzen Zeitspanne (χρονικὸν διάστημα) wirkend. Dieser Umstand wird im Weiteren durch das Wort „ständig" oder „immerwährend" (ἀεί) ausgedrückt. Damit ist nicht „ewig" im strengen Sinn des Wortes gemeint, sondern nur die allgemeine Gültigkeit des Todes im ganzen Zeitraum der irdischen Lebensweisen des Menschen[44].

---

[39] *Maximus Confessor*, Amb. Ioh. 45, 3: PG 91, 1353A.
[40] *Maximus Confessor*, Op. th. et pol. 1: PG 91, 37BC; Expositio orationis dominicae: PG 90, 901D.
[41] *Maximus Confessor*, Amb. Ioh. 42: PG 91, 1321D–1324B.
[42] *Maximus Confessor*, Amb. Ioh. 10: PG 91, 1124C.
[43] *Maximus Confessor*, Amb. Ioh. 8: PG 91, 1104B.
[44] *Maximus Confessor*, Amb. Ioh. 10, 28: PG 91, 1156C–1157A.

Die Zeit und die Bewegung, generell als Veränderung gemeint, stehen, behauptet Maximus, in keiner notwendigen Korrespondenz. Nicht jede Zeit wird durch Bewegung gemessen, so tritt er in eine offene Diskussion mit der Auffassung des Aristoteles[45]. Maximus hat an erster Stelle die geschichtliche Existenz vor Augen. Das erschaffene äonische Seiende (wie die Engel oder die Seelen) ist der Zeit untergeben: es hat seine Geschichte. Es hat einen Anfang und, unabhängig davon, dass seine Existenz nie aufhört, seine eigene Zukunft steht ihm bevor. Die geschichtliche Zeit der Existenz ist mit Notwendigkeit nicht Bewegung, sondern Entfaltung von Ereignissen. Das schließt nicht aus, dass im Rahmen des Geschichtskontextes selbst die Existenzweisen der Natur des geschichtlichen Seienden eine Veränderung erfahren können[46].

Die Veränderung, die die Prozesse des Verwesens und des Zerfalls impliziert, ist keine ursprüngliche Charakteristik der Schöpfung. Die sensitiven Wesen sind zwar als materielle geschaffen, aber sie sind Adam gegeben, damit er das Geistliche mit dem Auge seiner Seele durch die Materie schaut. Die Materialität ist ihm als Vermittler verliehen worden. Erst die von dem Geistlichen separierte Materie darf als verwesend bestimmt werden. Der Versuch Adams, das Sensitive ohne Gott und nicht Gott gemäß zu beherrschen, hat zur Folge die Herstellung des Todes für ihn und seine Nachfolger.

Das Fleisch des gefallenen Menschen bleibt Fleisch, wie Gott es geschaffen hat. Nun ist es aber viel „schwerer": es ist sterblich und innerlich widersprüchlich geworden. Man pflegt diesen Zustand als Strafe zu bestimmen. Es wird aber nicht der Leib für irgendeine Sündigkeit bestraft, sondern der ganze Mensch, der durch seine Seele und die alogische Bewegung seiner noetischen Kraft gesündigt hat. Gott erwählt als Strafe den Tod des Leibes, der von der Seele abstrahiert nichts ist, um offen zu machen, dass die Sünde eine Liebeswendung zum Nichts ist, das der Mensch anstelle Gottes bevorzugt hat. Kraft seines Geistes hat der Mensch seine Kraft zur Liebe verdorben. Der Mensch war und bleibt selbstständig, selbstbewegend, sich selbst bestimmend, αὐτεξούσιος. Er bestimmte sich für den Tod kraft seiner freien Willensentscheidung. Durch das Leiden (διὰ τοῦ πάσχειν) sollen wir einsehen, dass wir unsere Kraft wieder auf das Sein richten müssen. Der derart in dieser Existenzweise der Natur strukturierte Charakter des Fleisches (und nicht das Fleisch selbst oder der Leib) kann und muss durch die freie Rückkehr des Menschen zu Gott überwunden werden[47].

---

[45] Cf. *Aristoteles*, Phys. IV, 11, 219b3–7; 220a25–28.
[46] Cf. *Maximus Confessor*, Amb. Ioh. 67: PG 91, 1397AB.
[47] *Maximus Confessor*, Amb. Ioh. 7: PG 91, 1092D–1093A; 8: PG 91, 1104AB; 45: PG 91, 1352B–1353B.

4. Die Sünde und die Freiheit

Vielsagend ist die Tatsache, dass die römisch-katholische Deutung der Sünde Adams und Evas sich auf die Entscheidungen der Synode von Orange aus dem Jahre 529 stützt. Diese Synode verurteilte unter anderem die Willenslehre des Johannes Cassianus (um 360–435), der den sog. Semipelagianern zugeordnet wurde. Die östlichen Kirchen haben die Synodalbeschlüsse nicht akzeptiert. Ihre Position ist bis heute mit dem Standpunkt des Cassianus identisch.

Er betont, dass „Gott all das in uns wirkt, was gleichzeitig eine Sache der freien menschlichen Willensentscheidung (*liberum arbitrium*) ist"[48]. Die Totalität der Gnade auf dem Weg zur Erlösung wird in einem Vergleich mit Augustinus relativiert. Cassianus formuliert seine Position in drei Sätzen. Erstens: Es ist immer ein Gnadengeschenk Gottes, wenn ein Mensch dazu entflammt wird, das zu ersehen, was gut ist – so jedoch, dass dabei weder zur einen noch zur anderen Seite hin die Entscheidung des freien Willens (*liberae voluntatis arbitrium*) beeinträchtigt wird. Zweitens: Es ist gleicherweise göttliche Gnadengabe, wenn wir die Tugenden verwirklichen – ohne dass dadurch die eigene Entscheidungsfreiheit ausgelöscht wäre. Drittens: Es ist ebenfalls ein Geschenk Gottes, wenn einer in der Tugend verharrt, die er erworben hat – jedoch so, dass die uns geschenkte Freiheit keine Gefangenschaft (*captivitas*) fühle. Wenn der Gott des Weltalls wirkt, fasst er zusammen, alles in allen. Er schenkt das Anfangen. Er stärkt und schützt das Angefangene. Er entledigt uns dabei aber nicht der Entscheidungsfreiheit, die er selbst uns verliehen hat[49]. Gott hat uns als vernünftige Wesen geschaffen und uns mit der Macht der freien Entscheidung ausgestattet (*liberi arbitrii potestate donavit*)[50]. Der Grundsatz lautet, dass der freie Wille eine selbständige Kraft des vernünftigen Menschenwesens ist, die von ihm abhängig ist. Sie nämlich wirkt mit der göttlichen Gnade zusammen, wenn es um das Erreichen des Guten geht. Cassianus betont dementsprechend die lenkende Rolle der göttlichen *providentia*, wobei er die *praedestinatio* ablehnt und diese eigentlich nicht erwähnt[51].

---

[48] *Johannes Cassianus*, Collationes patrum XIII, 18: PL 49, 946BC. Deutsche Teil-Übersetzung der *Collatio* XIII in: *G. Sartory, T. Sartory*, Johannes Cassian. Ruhe der Seele (Freiburg im Breisgau 1984), p. 13–21.
[49] *Johannes Cassianus*, Collationes XIII, 18: PL 49, 946AB.
[50] *Johannes Cassianus*, De coenobiorum institutis XII, 18: PL 49, 455A–456A.
[51] *Johannes Cassianus*, Collationes XIII, 18: PL 49, 946 AB; 937B. Cf. *G. Kapriev*, Freier Wille und Vorherbestimmung in der Byzantinischen Tradition, Medioevo 42 (2017) 125–129 (=A. Beccarisi, F. Retucci (eds.), Moral Agency and its Constraints: Fate, Determinism and Free Will in the Middle Ages); *G. Kapriev*, Providenz, Vorherbestimmung, Schicksal und Freiheit im byzantinischen Geschichtsdenken, in: T. Hainthaler et alii (Hgg.), Pronoia. The Provi-

Das Problem der Erbsünde in der Anthropologie des Maximus Confessor 469

Maximus Confessor partizipiert an dieser Denkrichtung. Für ihn ist die Sünde Adams ein persönlicher Missbrauch der Freiheit, durch den er zu dem Niedrigeren gelangt, weil er sein Verlangen auf das Verbotene gerichtet hat[52]. Maximus folgt der Linie des Nemesius von Emesa, der eine Idee des Aristoteles aus christlicher Sicht entfaltet. Der Bereich der Willensfreiheit ist das von uns Abhängige (ἐν τοῖς ἐφ' ἡμῖν). Außerhalb des Kompetenzbereiches des Freiwilligen (ἑκούσιον) liegen die Gebiete des der Natur und des Zwanges nach Verrichteten, wie auch des Notwendigen, des Zufälligen und des Unbekannten[53]. Jedes Tun, das der Vernunfterwägung (λογισμός) und der freien Willensentscheidung (προαίρεσις), eigenem Trieb und eigener Neigung nach verrichtet wird, ist aus freiem Willen[54]. Maximus ordnet das von uns Abhängige (ἐφ' ἡμῖν), in welchem Feld die Willensakte entscheidend sind, dem Bereich des göttlichen Vorwissens (πρόγνωσις) zu, während er das nicht von uns Abhängige dem Bereich der Prädestination (προορισμός) zurechnet[55].

Maximus deutet die Sünde Adams nicht in einer essentiellen Perspektive, sondern als persönlicher Rückzug von den Normen, die Gott im Paradies aufgestellt hat. Die Quelle dieser Sünde ist die freie Willensentscheidung Adams, durch die die Anfänge des naturwidrigen Willensgebrauchs gesetzt worden sind. Auf diese Weise geschieht auch die Wendung zum Bösen, das immer Nichtsein, Nichtvorhandensein oder Abwesenheit von Sein (ἀνυπαρξία) im eigentlichen Sinne des Wortes ist. Die Sünde hat keinen Logos. Der Eintritt der Leidenschaft und des Leidens (πάθη) verbindet den Menschen mit den irdischen Dingen, lässt das Äußere im Innern des Menschen zu und bricht den Bezug des Menschen mit Gott[56].

Einem Verwesen unterliegen die Willensdisposition und die Willensentscheidung. Die Sünde hat ihren Grund in der Neuorientierung des Willens[57]. Die treibende Kraft der Bewegung nach dem Bösen wird nicht von der Natur, sondern von der autonomisierten γνώμη erzeugt. Im Grunde stehen Leiden-

---

dence of God (Innsbruck – Wien 2019) 380.
[52] *Maximus Confessor*, Amb. Ioh. 7, 32: PG 91, 1092D.
[53] *Nemesius Emesenus*, De natura hominis 32: PG 40, 728B; Cf. *Nemesius Emesenus*, De nat. hom. 34: PG 40, 757AC; 740B–741A.
[54] *Nemesius Emesenus*, De nat. hom. 32: PG 40, 729B.
[55] Cf. *A. Louth*, Pronoia in the Life and Thought of St Maximos the Confessor, in: T. Hainthaler et alii (Hgg.), Pronoia. The Providence of God (Innsbruck – Wien 2019) 341.
[56] Cf. *Maximus Confessor*, Amb. Ioh. 7: PG 91, 1092D; 31: PG 91, 1276B, 1277B; 42: PG 91, 1332A; Quaest. Thal. Prol.: PG 90, 257A; Capita de charitate 1, 5: PG 90, 969C; Cap. de char. 2, 3: PG 90, 984C; Op. th. et pol. 1: PG 91, 36B.
[57] *Maximus Confessor*, Quaest. Thal. 42: PG 90, 405D; 61: PG 90, 628AB, 629C; 62: PG 90, 635D–656A.

schaften, die zu einer Trennung von der göttlichen Selbstbewegung hinführen, wobei der θυμός und die ἐπιθυμία als die Gattungsleidenschaften gedeutet werden[58]. Der gnomische Wille ist die willentliche ἕξις, der feste innere Zustand des Willens, der aufgrund eingeborener und – vorwiegend – erworbener Einstellungen formiert wird. Die γνώμη ist der Faktor, der das Naturvermögen „Wille" personalisiert. Von der Perspektive des Gut- bzw. Schlecht-Seins ist einzusehen, dass Maximus den Antagonismus zwischen der sittlichen Wirkung und der Seinsverfassung des Menschen durch die Hexis-Lehre ablehnt. Die Selbstbestimmung für den betreffenden Seinslogos ist vorerst ein Ergebnis der menschlichen Willensaktivität und Praxis. In der Dimension des Gut-Seins erklärt diese Lehre die Art und Weise der Zusammenwirkung des heiligen Geistes und des einzelnen Menschen im Bereich des Persönlichen. Sowohl das Standhalten im Gut-Sein als auch die Vergöttlichung werden gemäß der menschlichen Hexis und durch die Gnade (κατὰ τὴν ἕξιν διὰ τῆς χάριτος) verwirklicht[59].

Als Bild Gottes ist der Mensch „selbstmächtig und der Natur nach wirkend" geschaffen[60]. Ihm ist eine „selbstmächtige Bewegung" (αὐτεξούσιος κίνησις) eigen, die ihm die Möglichkeit gewährt, sein höchstes existentielles Ziel, die Gottebenbildlichkeit, und also seine Authentizität zu erreichen. Diese von Natur aus aufgegebene „Selbstmächtigkeit" ist das „synergische Konstituens zwischen Gott und Mensch", das Privileg der Freiheit, das die dynamische Verwirklichung der Gottebenbildlichkeit ermöglicht[61]. Während das Bild mit der Essenz oder der Natur des Menschen assoziiert ist, ist das Erreichen des als Potenz gelegten Ebenbildes ein Werk der frei motivierten Person. Während der Mensch Bild Gottes der Natur nach ist, kann er Ebenbild Gottes nur persönlich und der Gnade nach werden[62].

Die Providenz stützt nicht nur den Logos der Natur, sondern sie gibt auch den Logos des Gut-Seins. Er kann jedoch nur denen eigen werden, die die entsprechende Bewegung von sich aus initiieren. Während das Prinzip des Seins

---

[58] Cf. *Maximus Confessor*, Disp. Pyr.: PG 91, 252AB; Amb. Ioh. 6: PG 91, 1068A; 10: PG 91, 1201AB. P. Sherwood, Maximus and Origenism, in: Berichte zum XI. Internationalen Byzantinischen Kongreß, III/1 (München 1958) 10–11.
[59] *Maximus Confessor*, Quaest. Thal 6: PG 90, 281AB.
[60] *Maximus Confessor*, Op. th. et pol. 1: PG 91, 157AC; Ep. 7: PG 91, 436AB.
[61] С. Тутеков, Добродетелта заради истината. Богословски и антропологични основи на аретологията (Велико Търново 2009) 167–170.
[62] Cf. В. В. Петров, Максим Исповедник: онтология и метод в византийской философии VII века (Москва 2007) 41–42.

Das Problem der Erbsünde in der Anthropologie des Maximus Confessor 471

und der Natur die Kraft-δύναμις verleiht, erklärt Maximus, verleiht das zweite Prinzip die ἐνέργεια[63].

Der Mensch kann seine Aufgabe erst nach der Überwindung der in der postlapsarischen Periode erschienenen Gegensätze zwischen der Seele und dem Leib erfüllen. Es wird möglich dank des Erlösungswerks Christi, der die naturwidrigen Gesetze der Natur außer Kraft setzt und die Geburt selbst heiligt, wodurch er den Seinshiatus zwischen dem Entstehen und der Geburt des Menschen kompensiert[64]. Der postlapsarische Zustand der menschlichen Existenz ist in Christus überwunden. Der Erlöser bahnt den Weg nach einem neuen Tropos der Natur. Der menschgewordene Gott hat nicht den Logos, sondern die Existenzweise der Natur erneuert[65]. Deshalb ist Christus der neue, sündenlose Adam. Der Gottmensch legt den Anfang des Wechsels der dem Logos der Natur widrigen Gesetze und der Rückkehr zur Harmonie mit dem Prinzip der Natur[66]. Er erlässt neue Gesetze der Existenz[67]. In den beiden Fällen geht es um Gesetze ein und derselben menschlichen Natur.

5. Christus und die Taufe

Christus, der inkarnierte Logos von Allem, richtet die Welt auf das Gerechte mit denen zusammen, die von ihm im Geiste geboren sind[68]. Das Ganze wird in die richtige Ordnung gebracht (ἀναρρυθμίζεται)[69]. Es geht jedoch nicht um irgendeine kreisförmige Wiederkehr nach dem anfänglichen Zustand des geschaffenen Menschen, keine Wiederherstellung des ursprünglichen adamischen Zustands. Das Reich Gottes ist höher als das Paradies. Es geht um keine origenische Rückkehr. Das neuplatonische Exitus-Reditus-Schema, das eine zyklische Bewegung und entsprechend eine Rückkehr zum Ausgangspunkt voraussetzt, ist wesentlich verstoßen. Nach Maximus und allen christlichen Denkern seit den Kappadokiern, abgesehen von dem Grad ihrer Beeinflussung von dem Neuplatonismus, fällt die Vollendung der Rückkehr mit dem Ausgangspunkt nicht zusammen, sondern sie übertrifft ihn, ihr Niveau ist ein höheres. Eine neue Wiederholung des Seinszyklus ist unmöglich. Es geht auch um kein Erhalten göttlicher Essenz. Die menschliche Natur erlangt einen Exis-

---

[63] *Maximus Confessor*, Amb. Ioh. 10: PG 91, 1116B, 1168B; 65: PG 91, 1392AC; Quaest. Thal. 2: PG 90, 272AB.
[64] *Maximus Confessor*, Amb. Ioh. 42: PG 91, 1325B.
[65] *Maximus Confessor*, Disp. Pyr.: PG 91, 320C.
[66] *Maximus Confessor*, Amb. Ioh. 31: PG 91, 1276CD.
[67] *Maximus Confessor*, Amb. Ioh. 31: PG 91, 1280AC.
[68] *Maximus Confessor*, Amb. Ioh. 31: PG 91, 1276C.
[69] *Maximus Confessor*, Amb. Ioh. 31: PG 91, 1276D.

tenzstatus, der höher als der ursprüngliche ist. Der Gottmensch verleiht der menschlichen Natur die Vergöttlichung durch die Energien seiner göttlichen Natur[70]. Die θέωσις ist eine existentielle Teilhabe an der essentiellen göttlichen Energie[71].

Der Gott Logos übernimmt von Maria die Menschennatur mit ihrem Prinzip, aber in einem ganz anderen Tropos, der sich von der jungfräulichen Zeugung auftut. Das der Schöpfung nach Vorhandene wird gänzlich erhalten, aber es besteht ein Unterschied in der Geburt: sie ist „ohne Same" oder vielmehr „aus eigenem Samen" verwirklicht. Christus bekommt von Maria alles, das der Menschennatur in ihrem postlapsarischen Tropos eigen ist, mit Ausnahme der Sünde. Die in der Hypostase Christi vollzogene περιχώρησις, die gegenseitige Durchdringung der Naturen durch ihre existentiellen Energien, verleiht der menschlichen Natur einen neuen Tropos, der dem in dem Logos dieser Natur eingepflanzten Ziel entspricht[72]. Die natürliche Bestimmtheit bleibt unverändert, die existentiellen Grenzen der Natur werden aber transzendiert. Im Unterschied zu der Einigung der Naturen in Christus, ist die Einigung der einzelnen Person mit Gott nicht hypostatisch, sondern nur der Energie nach[73]. Im Zustand der Vergöttlichung bleibt der Mensch völlig der Natur nach Mensch und wird mit Seele und Leib völlig Gott der Gnade nach[74].

Der neue Tropos des Menschlichen in Christus, betont Maximus, erfasst und umformt gründlich die menschliche Existenz im Ganzen, wobei die Empfängnis und die Geburt, die der Begriff „γέννησις" einschließt, eine entscheidende Bedeutung haben. Das heilige Fleisch Christi stellt die authentischen Kräfte der Natur wieder her und hebt die Macht des Todes auf. Die neue Geburt in Christus ist „πνευματικὴ ἀναγένεσις" – geistliche Neuentstehung. Der Mensch ist berufen persönlich das zu werden, was er gemäß der Natur nach dem Erlösungswerk Christi ist[75].

---

[70] Cf. *Maximus Confessor*, Quaest. Thal. 22: PG 90, 321A; 63: PG 90, 684A.
[71] Cf. *E. v. Ivanka*, Der philosophische Ertrag der Auseinandersetzung Maximos des Bekenners mit dem Origenismus, JÖBG 7 (1958) 28–29.
[72] Cf. *Maximus Confessor*, Amb. Ioh. 42: PG 91, 1317D–1321B.
[73] *V. Karayiannis*, Maxime le Confesseur: essence et énergies de Dieu (Paris 1993) 472.
[74] *Maximus Confessor*, Amb. Ioh. 7: PG 91, 1088BC. А. И. Бриллiантовъ, Влияние восточного богословия на западное в произведениях Іоанна Скота Эригены (С.-Петербург 1898) 363.
[75] *Maximus Confessor*, Quaest. Thal. 21: PG 90, 312B–316D; 42: PG 90, 405B–409A; Ep. 2: PG 91, 396C–401C; Amb. Ioh. 31: PG 91, 1281A; 42: PG 91, 1316C–1320B, 1325C, 1345C–1349A; Op. th. et pol. 4: PG 91, 60C–61A. Cf. *F. Heinzer*, Gottes Sohn als Mensch (Freiburg, Schw. 1980) 127–140; *I.-H. Dalmais*, Maxime le Confesseur, in: Dictionnaire de spiritualité, X (Paris 1980) 842; *J.-C. Larchet*, La divinisation de l'homme selon saint Maxime le Confesseur (Paris 1996) 232–238; *A. Riou*, Le Monde et l'Église selon Maxime le Confesseur

In diesem Kontext ist nicht zufällig der Akzent auf die Bedeutsamkeit der Taufe Christi. Die Taufe ist eine neue Geburt. Sie „kompensiert" die Geburt, die sich der Erschaffung gegenüberstellt. Christus verbindet die Geburt der Taufe mit der fleischlichen Geburt und überwindet die Effekte der letzteren[76]. In Einverständnis mit Gregorios dem Theologen verbindet Maximus die Geburt Jesu mit seiner Taufe. Der Gott Logos hat nicht nur die leibliche Geburt aufgenommen, sondern er hat sich auch einer anderen Geburt unterworfen, die auf die geistliche Adoption lenkt. Durch die Taufe verwirklicht Christus die wahrhafte Neuschöpfung des Menschen. Die Taufe, der Anfang des christlichen Lebens, gründet sowohl auf der Geburt des inkarnierten Wortes als auch auf seinem Leiden und Tod. Sie hat den τύπος des Todes und der Auferstehung inne. Die von Christus erteilte neue Existenzweise der Natur äußert ein göttliches „Wie" des menschlichen „Was"[77].

Lourié betont, dass in dieser Existenzgestalt die Natur als „der Auferstehung entsprechend", d.h. von dem Verwesen frei, besteht. In der Teilhabe an Christus nehmen die Christen an der Unverwesenheit der Menschennatur teil, die sie gemeinsam mit ihm haben. Die Sakramente, die Taufe und insbesondere die Eucharistie, befreien den Menschen – durch die Einbeziehung zum verwesungsfreien Fleisch Christi – von der Wirkung des Verwesens auf seinen Willensgebrauch und seine Willensentscheidungen. Die Erlösung wird dadurch seitens des Menschen ein Werk des persönlichen Willenswirkens[78].

Die Taufe lässt am Tropos der Geburt Christi partizipieren. Sie „regeneriert" die menschliche Natur. Durch die Taufe werden Charismen gewährt, die die Potenz für ein neues Leben verleihen, deren Aktualisierung die Anstrengung des einzelnen Menschen, der menschlichen Hypostase fordert. Der Mensch erhält die Gnade der Tadellosigkeit, der Kraft des Nichtsündigens (ἀναμαρτησία), aber es wird ihm auch die Pflicht auferlegt, wirklich nicht zu sündigen, weil seine Fähigkeit zu sündigen erhalten bleibt. Die Gnade wird in der Taufe gänzlich gegeben, aber ihre Entfaltung in Wirklichkeit ist ein Werk der persönlichen Praxis und Schau[79].

(Paris 1973) 83-84; *А. И. Брилліантов*, Влияние восточного богословия, 113-114; *В. В. Петров*, Максим Исповедник, 46-47.

[76] Cf. *Maximus Confessor*, Amb. Ioh. 42: PG 91, 1348AD. *F. Heinzer*, Gottes Sohn als Mensch, 169-170.

[77] Cf. *Maximus Confessor*, Quaest. Thal. 21: PG 90, 312B-316D; 42: PG 90, 405B-409A; Ep. 2: PG 91, 396C-401C; Amb. Ioh. 31: PG 91, 1281A; 42: PG 91, 1316C-1320B, 1325C, 1345C-1349A; Op. th. et pol. 4: PG 91, 60C-61A.

[78] *В. М. Лурье*, История византийской философии, 399.

[79] Cf. *Maximus Confessor*, Capita theologica et oeconomica 1, 87: PG 90, 1120B; Quaest. Thal.: PG 90, 280C-281B; 61: PG 90, 636C; *J.-C. Larchet*, La divinisation de l'homme, 413-

Nach dem Sühnopfer Christi erhalten die verkirchlichten Christen die erlösende Gnade nicht mehr zwecks einer besonderen Aufgabe oder Mission, wie es für die alttestamentlichen Heiligen galt[80]. Sie ist prinzipiell allen zugänglich. Gott hat uns mit dem Tropos der Erlösung vereinigt, betont Maximus, und hat uns die Kraft gegeben, ewig Söhne Gottes zu sein: von nun an steht unsere Erlösung in unserer Kraft[81]. Der Geist wendet sich aber auf verschiedene Weise an jede Person in Rücksicht auf ihren Glauben, ihre Lebensweise, Tugend und Liebe. Hiermit wird die Synergie zwischen den Charismen des Geistes und dem freien Willen der Person verwirklicht[82]. Die Natur selbst leistet keinen Widerstand gegen die Gnade, weil die Natur von Beginn an charismatisch und mit der Gnade komplementär ist. Wenn die menschliche Natur in aller Wirklichkeit entfaltet ist, ist sie für die göttliche Gnade vollständig offen. Es wird die Verbindung der menschlichen Natur mit Gott ausgeführt, für die sie überhaupt geschaffen ist[83].

6. Kosmologie und Eschatologie

Die Vergöttlichung der leiblich-seelischen Einheit des Menschen ist – laut der kosmologischen Lehre des Maximus – der Motor und der Garant für die Vergöttlichung der ganzen Schöpfung, d.h. für die Rückkehr der ganzen Schöpfung zu Gott und die Teilhabe aller geschaffenen Naturen an Gott. Der Mensch wird als allumfassende Werkstatt (συνεκτικώτατον ἐργαστήριον) bestimmt, in der alle geschaffenen Naturen aktiv vertreten sind, die an Gott gerade durch den Menschen und in ihm teilhaben werden. Die Natur des Menschen umschließt die Natur des ganzen Kosmos. Die eschatologische Aufgabe des Menschen ist, für die Vergöttlichung aller geschaffenen Naturen mitzuwirken, insofern ihre λόγοι in ihrem Anfang und Ziel, also im einen Λόγος, vorhanden sind. Ihre Vergöttlichung wird als ihr optimales Zusammenfallen mit ihren Seinsnormen, d.h. mit ihren λόγοι, gedeutet. Die Rolle des Men-

---

423; *Г. В. Флоровский*, Отцы V–VIII веков (Париж 1933; репр. Москва 1992) 220.
[80] Cf. *G. Kapriev*, Die Begegnung Moses' mit Christus (Gregorios Palamas, Triaden, II, 3, 55), in: T. Hainthaler et alii (Hgg.), Sophia. The Wisdom of God – Die Weisheit Gottes (Innsbruck – Wien 2017) 387–394.
[81] *Maximus Confessor*, Liber asceticus 42: PG 90, 953B.
[82] *Maximus Confessor*, Quaest. Thal. 59: PG 90, 604B–609C; 63: PG 90, 672B–673C; cf. *J.-C. Larchet*, La divinisation de l'homme, 217–219, 394–397.
[83] Cf. *P. Evdokimov*, De la nature et de la grâce dans la théologie de l'Orient, in: 1054–1954. L'Église et les Églises: neuf siècles de douloureuses séparation entre l'Orient et l'Occident. Études et travaux de l'Unité chrétienne offerts à dom Lambert Beauduin, vol. II (Paris 1955) 177–178, 184; *L. Thunberg*, Microcosm and Mediator. The Theological Anthropology of Maximus the Confessor (Lund 1965) 461.

schen ist eine vermittelnde und er ist imstande sie erst nach der Erneuerung seiner Naturexistenz zu realisieren. Er soll wieder die „Extreme" der ganzen Schöpfung „sammeln", sie in sich wie in einer Mitte und allgemeiner Bindung (σύνδεσμος) verbinden und mit Gott durch seine Einigung mit ihm einigen[84]. Maximus erklärt, dass in ihrem gegenwärtigen Zustand die Hypostase der ganzen Natur in fünf Teilungen zergliedert ist. Es geht um die Teilung in nichtgeschaffene und geschaffene Natur; die Teilung der geschaffenen Natur in noetische und sensitive; die Teilung der sensitiven Natur in Himmel und Erde; die Teilung der Erde in Paradies und bewohnten Erdteil (οἰκουμένη); die Teilung in Mann und Frau[85]. Der ewige göttliche Wille ist, dass die ersten drei Teilungen überwunden werden sollen. Statt dessen hat der Mensch durch seine verderbliche Tätigkeit zwei weitere geschaffen. Der Mensch ist verantwortlich sowohl für die Zerstörung des ursprünglichen Zustandes, als auch für die Rückkehr der Schöpfung zu Gott und ist das einzige Wesen, das es leisten kann.

Seine Fähigkeit, diese universelle περιχώρησις hervorzurufen, ist nur wegen seiner Teilhabe an Christus möglich. Entscheidend ist, dass Jesus Christus diese Überwindung verwirklicht und das Paradigma für ihre Ausrichtung gegeben hat. Er erfüllt die kosmische Aufgabe des gescheiterten Adam. Christus fügt die Abbrüche der kosmischen Natur zusammen. Durch seine Geburt von der Jungfrau beseitigt er die Polarität zwischen Männlichem und Weiblichem. Durch sein menschliches Verhalten heiligt er die οἰκουμένη. Sein Eintreten ins Paradies mit dem guten Schächer verbindet den bewohnten Erdteil und das Paradies. Himmel und Erde werden bei seiner Himmelfahrt geeinigt. Die Vergöttlichung und das Integrieren seiner geschöpflichen Kräfte nach der Himmelfahrt überwinden die vierte Teilung. Mit dem Sitzen zur Rechten des Vaters hebt er auch die letzte Teilung auf[86]. Auf diese Weise erfüllt er den ewigen Willen und den immerwährenden Plan (βουλή) des Vaters und erlöst zugleich den Menschen. Aus dieser Perspektive wird der ganze Umfang des natürlichen und persönlichen Horizonts des Menschen, wie auch der Forderung nach der Nachahmung Christi in seinem vollen Sinn, sichtbar.

---

[84] Cf. *Maximus Confessor*, Amb. Ioh. 41: PG 91, 1304D–1305B; Amb. Th. Praef.: PG 91, 1032B.
[85] *Maximus Confessor*, Amb. Ioh. 41: PG 91, 1304D–1305A; Quaest. Thal. 48: PG 90, 436AB.
[86] *Maximus Confessor*, Amb. Ioh. 41: PG 91, 1308D–1309D. Cf. *Maximus Confessor*, Quaest. Thal, 48: PG 90, 436AB; Pater: PG 90, 877BC.

Die Lösung der Frage nach der Ahnensünde, die Maximus Confessor darbietet, erweist sich als eine Kernposition seiner Anthropologie, die eine systembildende Rolle auch in seiner Christologie, wie auch in seiner Kosmologie, Ekklesiologie und Eschatologie spielt.

Karolina Kochańczyk-Bonińska, Warsaw (Poland)

Human Sexuality—One of the Ontic Consequences of Adam's Fall—Maximus the Confessor's Interpretation

Abstract:
This paper focuses on the status of the division into the sexes in the prelapsarian state and the consequences of Adam's sin for the distinction between the sexes in Maximus the Confessor's writings. Before the Fall, Adam had a different kind of subtle body and experienced harmony in his corporality. He was naked because he was not burdened with mortality, patience or any passions (πάθη) but if, according to the Confessor, the Fall was supposed to be somehow nearly simultaneous with the creation, then the original state should be treated as the ultimate aim rather than the important starting point. While teaching about Adam's sin, Maximus points out the wrong human use of freedom and the choice of passions over God's love. By Adam's Fall, man was condemned to be born through pleasure and sin, however, it is not about making sexual intercourse sinful. Sexuality, therefore, is being understood as a certain function within human nature, which appeared only after Adam's sin, and it is necessary for human nature to be transmitted in its postlapsarian condition. Hans Urs von Balthasar referring to Maximus' views, wrote that human sexuality is a "sacrament of sin", because although it is not sinful itself, it is a visible sign of the condition in which man found himself after the Fall.

Maximus the Confessor is a figure particularly popular in recent years among researchers of Christian antiquity and, the topic of Maximus' understanding of the distinction between woman and man has been analysed in several current studies[1]. Most researchers concentrate on the problem of the existence

---

[1] E. Brown Dewhurst, The Absence of Sexual Difference in the Theology of Maximus the Confessor, Philosophy and Society 32/2 (2021) 204–225; D. Costache, Living above Gender: Insights from Saint Maximus the Confessor, JECS 21/2 (2013) 261–290; S. Mitralexis, Rethinking the Problem of Sexual Difference in Maximus the Confessor's Ambiguum 41, Analogia 2 (2017) 107–112; S. Mitralexis, An Attempt at Clarifying Maximus the Confessor's Remarks on (the Fate of) Sexual Difference in Ambiguum 41, Philosophy and Society 32/2 (2021) 194–203; D. Skliris, The Ontology of Mode in the Thought of Maximus the Confessor and its Consequences for a Theory of Gender, in: S. Mitralexis (ed.), Mustard Seeds in the Public Square: Between and Beyond Theology, Philosophy, and Society (Wilmington 2017) 39–60; C. E. Partridge, Transfiguring Sexual Difference in Maximus the Confessor,

(or not) of the division into man and woman in eschatological times as the original approach proposed by the Confessor seems interesting to contemporaries for various reasons (e.g. in gender studies). In this paper I will not omit these issues altogether, but focus on a thread that is much less elaborated, namely, the status of the division into the sexes in the prelapsarian state and the consequences of Adam's sin for the distinction between sexes.

As my topic concerns ontic consequences of Adam's Fall as far as human sexuality was concerned I will divide my paper into three parts: I will present what was, according to Maximus, the status of human sexuality before the fall, the nature of Adam's Fall and what changes in human nature were the consequences of sin and the reasons for these.

The first general remark that should be made is the fact that for Maximus the Confessor the anthropology, cosmology and the history of salvation are combined into one system, the keystone of which is the person of Jesus Christ. Sexual differentiation is connected to various crucial elements of Maximus' thought: on the one hand, it is strongly connected to such theological problems as the original sin and eschatological vision, as I have already mentioned, and, on the other, with Maximus' understanding of human nature and the idea of man as a microcosm, which are philosophical ideas and a part of his world vision[2].

I. Human condition before the Fall

Maximus does not pay much attention to the original human condition, and his reflection on the state before the fall are rather curt. First of all, the Confessor points out that the prelapsarian state was different from the present one:

> The creation of our forefather Adam took place in a hidden, secret manner, and his soul had both a different principle of being (εἶναι λόγον) and a different mode of generation (γενέσθαι τρόπον), while his body obviously was formed on the basis of a different principle and mode, just as the Divine Scripture has so sublimely taught us, allowing us no room to lump together according to nature the creation of the soul and the body according to one and the same mode of origin, losing sight of each

---

PhD diss. (Harvard Divinity School 2008); K. Kochańczyk-Bonińska, The Philosophical Basis of Maximus' Concept of Sexes: The Reasons and Purposes of the Distinction Between Man and Woman, in: S. Mitralexis, G. Steiris, M. Podbielski, S. Lalla (eds.), Maximus the Confessor as a European Philosopher (Oregon 2017) 229-239.

[2] K. Kochańczyk-Bonińska, The Philosophical Basis of Maximus' Concept of Sexes, 229-230.

one's distinctive principle of being (οὐσίας λόγον) and mode of origin (γενέσεως τρόπον)³.

In *Ambiguum* 45, which is the explanation of Gregory the Theologian's *Oratio*⁴, Maximus develops his theory of different kinds of bodies which human beings were supposed to have before the Fall⁵ and underlines that Adam experienced harmony in his corporality. According to one of the researchers, and I agree completely with this interpretation, Maximus rejects the connection between the punishment of sin and corporeal creation of a human being⁶: the first Adam was innocent, although he was corporeal⁷.

I therefore hazard the conjecture that the teacher said these things wishing to point out the difference between the temperament of the human body in our forefather Adam before the fall, and that which is now observed within us and predominates, because then the temperament of man's body was obviously not torn apart by mutually opposed and corrupting qualities, but was in a state of equilibrium devoid of flux and reflux, being free of continuous alternation between each of these two, depending on the predominance of one quality or another, for surely man was not without a share in immortality by grace, nor was he suffering, as he is now, from the blows rained down on him by the scourge of corruption, since his body had a different temperament, obviously suited to him, and held together⁸.

Before the Fall, Adam was sinless by virtue of creation (γένεσις). For Maximus, the first human being is an example of a perfect man who enjoys direct vision of God and has a different, subtle kind of corporeality. Living in communion with God, Adam had the opportunity to experience spiritual pleasure and true freedom⁹.

Moreover, this harmony was not destroyed even after the original sin. Adam's nakedness was not, as the Origenists wanted, disembodied: he was naked because he was not burdened with mortality and patience; he did not have to cover himself because he experienced neither lust nor coldness. The

---

[3] Maxim. *Confess.*, Amb. 42, 10: PG 91, 1324D. English transl. *N. Constas*, On Difficulties in the Church Fathers The Ambigua, vol. II (Harvard 2014), p. 141.
[4] Gregor. *Naz.*, Or. 45, 8: PG 36, 633A.
[5] Maxim. *Confess.*, Amb. 45, 3: PG 91, 1353AB (English transl. *N. Constas*, vol. II, p. 80).
[6] A. *Cooper*, The Body in St Maximus the Confessor: Holy Flesh, Wholly Deified (Oxford 2005) 80.
[7] Maxim. *Confess.*, Amb. 45, 3: PG 91, 1353AB (English transl. *N. Constas*, vol. II, p. 195); Amb. 42, 10: PG 91, 1324D (English transl. *N. Constas*, vol. II, p. 141).
[8] Maxim. *Confess.*, Amb. 45, 3: PG 91, 1353AB (English transl. *N. Constas*, vol. II, p. 195).
[9] Maxim. *Confess.*, Amb. 42, 4: PG 91, 1317A (English transl. *N. Constas*, vol. II, p. 127).

first man remained in love with God and needed nothing but God; he was naked in his simplicity. In the Paradise state, Adam experienced only the movements and spiritual pleasures of communion with God, any sensory experience (πάθος) was alien to him: not only pleasure, but also feeling pain or chill.

Another important remark, and it should be strongly stressed is, that if, according to the Confessor, the Fall was supposed to be somehow nearly simultaneous with the creation (ἅμα τῷ γενέσθαι)[10], then the original state should be treated as the idealistic vision or model, as the ultimate aim rather than the important starting point[11]. Maximus seems to draw the prelapsarian state parallel to the state of heavenly happiness foreseen for man at the end of time. Researchers discuss whether there are any differences in the understanding of the human condition in both states in his writings[12].

This strong link between protology and eschatology is especially important in the context of the existence of sex distinction in the beginning; sexual difference can be connected only to the lapsarian state, as a consequence of the Fall. The first Adam seems to be a creature without sex and, although it runs counter to the biblical accounts of creation, it is strongly connected with the Confessors' eschatological vision[13]. The most important proof of such ideas can be found in *Ambiguum* 41 which is devoted to the end of the times that may be identified with universal harmony and lack of divisions in the entire created world. As it is the crucial argument of our paper, the extensive quotation is warranted.

> He (Christ) became a perfect man, having assumed from us, and for us, and consistent with us, everything that is ours, lacking nothing, *but without sin*, for to become man He had no need of the natural process of connubial intercourse. In this way, He showed, I think, that there was perhaps another mode, foreknown by God, for the multiplication of human beings, had the first human being kept the commandment and not *cast* himself down to the level of irrational animals by misusing the mode of his proper powers—and so He drove out from nature the difference and division into male and female, a difference, as I have said, which He in no way needed in order to become man, and without which, existence would perhaps have been pos-

---

[10] *Maxim. Confess.*, Qu. Thal. 61: C. Laga, C. Steel, CCG 22 (Turnhout 1990), p. 85.
[11] K. Kochańczyk-Bonińska, The Philosophical Basis of Maximus' Concept of Sexes, 229–230.
[12] L. Thunberg, Microcosm and Mediator: The Theological Anthropology of Maximus the Confessor (Chicago 1995) 154; P. Sherwood, The Earlier Ambigua (Rome 1955) 91.
[13] S. Mitralexis, An Attempt at Clarifying Maximus the Confessor's Remarks, 196.

> sible. There is no need for this division to last perpetually, for in Christ Jesus, says the divine apostle, there is neither male nor female[14].
>
> Thus He united, first of all, ourselves in Himself through removal of the difference between male and female, and instead of man and woman, in whom this mode of division is especially evident, He showed us as properly and truly to be simply human beings, thoroughly formed according to Him, bearing His image intact and completely unadulterated, touched in no way by any marks of corruption [...][15].

As we can see there is a strong connection between the prelapsarian and eschatological state and one of their features presented by Maximus is cosmic harmony and lack of divisions—also the division into man and woman[16]. This background allows us to better understand what in our human condition is "unnatural", that is, introduced after the Fall. We can also see that the distinction between male and female has inner meaning in Maximian thought, which will be elaborated on later.

II. What was Adam's sin?

Since Adam was in perfect fellowship with God, what caused his fall? What was his sin? In his teaching, which is not original, Maximus points out on the one hand to the wrong human use of freedom and, choosing passions instead of God's love.

> Since man was created for and to this end—but because our forefather Adam misused his freedom and turned instead to what was inferior, redirecting his desire from what was permissible to what had been forbidden (for it was in his power of self-determination *to be united to the Lord and become one spirit with Him, or to join himself to a prostitute and become one body with her*; but being deceived he chose to estrange himself from the divine and blessed goal, preferring by his own choice to be *a pile of dust* rather than God by grace) [...][17].

Some scholars[18] suggest that Maximus, using the quotation from *The Letter to Corinthians*, claims that Adam followed Eve, who was the direct impulse for the Fall and is being called *a prostitute*. In fact, the Confessor explains in another place as to who he understands as "the prostitute".

---

[14] Maxim. Confess., Amb. 41, 7: PG 91, 1309AB (English transl. N. Constas, vol. II, p. 111).
[15] Maxim. Confess., Amb. 41, 9: PG 91, 1312AB. English transl. N. Constas, vol. II, p. 115.
[16] Maxim. Confess., Amb. 41: PG 91, 1305A–1316A (English transl. N. Constas, vol. II, p. 103–121); K. Kochańczyk-Bonińska, The Philosophical Basis of Maximus' Concept of Sexes, 233–237.
[17] Maxim. Confess., Amb. 7, 32: PG 91, 1092D (English transl. N. Constas, vol. I, p. 121).
[18] Cf. e.g. D. Costache, Living above Gender, 265.

For what reason does the law forbid "a fee from a dog" and "wages of a prostitute" (Deut 23:18)? It signifies through these that one must offer to God the virtues unmixed with the anger and desire, calling anger a "dog" and "prostitute" the desire (ἐπιθυμίαν)[19].

The key problem in Maximus' teaching about Adam's sin is the theme of sensual pleasures and desires. This view should be associated with the Stoic tradition[20], not only because of the terminological similarity, but above all, because the Stoics recognize passion as the source of evil, and Maximus as the cause of turning away from God[21]. In the Paradise state, Adam experienced the perfect dispassion, which he had lost after his Fall: from then on, human nature is subjected to the πάθη. This fact in itself is not bad or sinful as such. Maximus underlines that Christ accepted the πάθη that flowed from birth[22].

Lars Thunberg points out how, in *Quaestiones ad Thalassium*, the Confessor carries out a detailed analysis of whether πάθη are bad or sinful. The affects that are analysed are the desire, fear, suffering and pleasure which are used, above all, by the Stoics[23]. They were not created in the beginning, but only after the Fall when they were introduced into the irrational part of the soul[24]. However, in themselves, they are not evil, as they can be used in obedience to Christ, but they can also be the weak point where we are tempted and, ultimately, lead to death. The nature of the affects, prone to sin rather than virtue, are transmitted to every human being by virtue of the bodily birth[25].

As the Fall is strongly connected with πάθη, it seems clear why one of the consequences of sin is linked with sex engendering

> When (the first man) had sinned while transgressing the commandment, he was condemned to an engendering through passion and sin. Because of this, natural genesis became a law in the passible element of sin (ἐν τῷ παθητῷ τῆς ἁμαρτίας)[26].

---

[19] Maxim. Confess., Quaest. et Dub. 156: J. H. Declerck, CCG 10 (Turnhout 1982), p. 109: Τίνος χάριν ἄλλαγμα κυνὸς καὶ μίσθωμα πόρνης ἀπαγορεύει ὁ νόμος; Σημαίνει διὰ τούτων ὅτι δεῖ τῷ θεῷ τὰς ἀρετὰς προσάγειν θυμοῦ καὶ ἐπιθυμίας ἀνεπιμίκτους, θυμὸν λέγων τὸν κύνα, πόρνην δὲ τὴν ἐπιθυμίαν. English transl. D. D. Prassas, Maximus the Confessor. Questions and Doubts (Washington 2003), p. 220.
[20] M. Grahn-Wilder, Gender and Sexuality in Stoic Philosophy (London 2018).
[21] C. Moreschini, Introduzione, in: C. Moreschini (tr.), Massimo il Confessore. Ambigua. Problemi metafisici e teologici su testi di Gregorio di Nazianzo e Dionigi Areopagita (Milano 2003) 51–52.
[22] Maxim. Confess., Amb. 42, 4: PG 91, 1317A (English transl. N. Constas, vol. II, p. 127).
[23] Maxim. Confess., Qu. Thal. 1: C. Laga, C. Steel, CCG 7 (Turnhout 1980), p. 47–49.
[24] L. Thunberg, Microcosm and Mediator: The Theological Anthropology of Maximus the Confessor (Chicago 1995) 161.
[25] Maxim. Confess., Qu. Thal. 21: C. Laga, C. Steel, CCG 7, p. 135.
[26] Maxim. Confess., Qu. Thal. 21: C. Laga, C. Steel, CCG 7, p. 127–129; J.-C. Larchet, An-

The sexual differentiation itself, which is a consequence of the Fall and sexual procreation, which becomes an instrument of the transmission of the consequences, are being used as an instrument of the transmission of the consequences of the sin, which are part of the human mode of existence after the sin[27].

III. The consequences of Adam's Fall

The Confessor points out that, after Adam's sin, the human way of being changed and this is described by Maximus with different terminology for the creation of the first man and, the beginning of the existence of other people. By creation (γένεσις), Maximus understands the first formation of man through which Adam received, directly from God, perfect human nature[28]. For him, as for Gregory of Nyssa, in the original plan of the Creator, spiritual nature was to be transmitted asexually for reproduction was not related to sexuality. The term γένεσις is referred by Maximus only to the creation of the sinless Adam and the incarnation of Christ. All people born after the fall of Adam receive the corrupted nature through the way of procreation related to sensual pleasure that was introduced after the Fall. Maximus however, decides to introduce another term, namely, birth or bodily birth (γέννησις), which refers to the way in which man comes into the world after original sin, which has become similar to the animal reproduction. The Confessor emphasizes that Christ, as the New Adam, was born differently to other people. Maximus writes extensively about the salvatory mission of Christ in the face of the split between γένεσις and γέννησις in *Ambigua* 42. It seems that in this distinction, γένεσις and γέννησις, or rather in the bodily manner of birth, Maximus contains all the consequences of sin. Moreover, the very way of giving birth is tantamount to passing on to the next generations a sin-tainted nature. Sexuality, therefore, is being understood as a certain function within human nature, which appeared only after Adam's sin, and it is necessary for human nature to be transmitted in its postlapsarian condition. Hans Urs von Balthasar referring to Maximus' views, wrote[29] that human sexuality is a "sacrament of sin",

---

cestral guilt according to St Maximus the Confessor: A bridge between Eastern and Western conceptions, Sobornost 20/1 (1998) 30.

[27] K. Kochańczyk-Bonińska, The Philosophical Basis of Maximus' Concept of Sexes, 230.
[28] A. Cooper, The Body in St Maximus the Confessor, 216.
[29] H. U. von Balthasar, Cosmic Liturgy: The Universe According to Maximus the Confessor (San Francisco 2003) 199.

because although it is not sinful itself, it is a visible sign of the condition in which man found himself after the Fall.

By Adam's Fall, man was condemned to be born through pleasure and sin, however, it is not about making sexual intercourse itself sinful. The Confessor does not condemn either the body that Adam had from the beginning, or the sexual mode of reproduction that was only later inscribed in the law of nature. In *Ambigua* 42 he writes emphatically:

> And if these refutations raise doubts in your minds, and cause you to take refuge in this final argument, saying that it is not right that the image of God and "divine element" (for this is what you call the rational soul) should coexist with sordid pleasure and bodily secretions, so that you think it more seemly to introduce the soul into the body forty days after conception, you will clearly be seen to be indicting the Creator, and rightly be subject to the frightful danger provoked by such blasphemy. For if marriage is evil, then it is obvious that the natural law of creation is also evil. And if the natural law of creation is evil, it is equally obvious that the One who created nature, and who gave it this law, should justly fall under your indictment[30].

As we have discovered, Maximus not only presents his own, highly controversial theory of the origin and final annihilation of sex distinction, which is part of his vision of the deified and united world. The Confessor understands our sexual existence (as men and women) as a sign of our postlapsarian condition, which is deeply rooted in the whole understanding of the history of salvation.

---

[30] *Maxim. Confess.*, Amb. 42, 24: PG 91, 1340B. English transl. *N. Constas*, vol. II, p. 167–169.

Ivan Christov, Sofia (Bulgaria)

St Cyril the Philosopher on the Meaning of Theology for Restoring the Image of God in Man and Overcoming Original Sin

Abstract:
The paper aims to reassess the testimony of medieval sources about the life of St Cyril, the great Apostle to the Slavs, in terms of synergy with God leading man away from sin in a spiritual ascent. For many generations it has exemplified Christian life dedicated to spirituality, which at the same time includes intellectual activities. The epithet "Philosopher" he was commemorated with in medieval times, actually denoted St Cyril's pursuit for true wisdom as his main motive prevailing over his interest in secular wisdom, of which he had renowned expertise. There was no contradiction between the two insofar as both will and knowledge are internal activities of man and knowledge is in a subordinated position in the spiritual ascent to God. Theology may use elements of Philosophy, first, to turn the human mind back to God, which makes it a genuine search for wisdom, a true "philosophy" and, second, what is more important, to exhaust its resources in the mystery of God thus leading it to repentance in the apophatism of Mystical theology. Mystical Theology is a kind of repentance of the intellect where it denies all that gave rise to its pride and intellectual deception. This fundamentally changes the attitude of man, which initially led him to the misuse of his free will and it is through this activity that he restores the image of God in himself and exterminates the roots of original sin and its consequences.

***

Among the variety of approaches to the problem of *inherited sin*, there is one of particular importance to Eastern-Orthodox Theology. It offers an alternative interpretation to the undeniable fact that sin exists in each and every man, not relating it to a corruption of human nature caused by the original sin and passed down the generations. According to this approach, sin is caused not by the corrupted nature of man but rather by his inner (natural) activity forming an voluntary attitude determining his deeds. The difference between nature and activity is the key point. Sin is related to an undue exercise of free will leading to the aversion of man from God. Therefore, it does not penetrate human nature and is not inherited by posterity but rests in an attitude of will, which is not substantial. Will itself is an *inner activity* (inner ἐνέργεια) expanding *ad extra* in human deeds—in the *external activity* of man. Two consequences follow from this point. First, the original sin is void of natural causality. It is first in the series and its crucial meaning to the history of mankind is that it unlocked the mechanism of decline that in a latent state ever existed before. The same mechanism—the free will, however is first of all the basis of spiritual progress. It is a gift from God to all rational beings. It functions with no natural necessity and could generate both sinful and virtuous life. Historically, this led to a particular reading of the Scriptural evidence in the Eastern-Orthodox tradition treating the original sin in an allegorical way not in terms of nature and therefore not as a historical fact that happened once and is all the time passed down the generations but as an allegory of the particular reality of will inherent in the activities of each and every man. Second (and closely related to the first point), this approach to the nature of sin in terms of activity is both optimistic and demanding. It opens a dual prospective to human being distinguishing between his very essence and his mode of existence. While human nature has a spiritual background (the inherent λόγος), being a creature its activities are divided between the spiritual and physical life. It is up to man to find a proper balance between them and to coordinate his activity with the Divine activity—with the Divine grace. This synergy of man and God leads away from sin in a spiritual ascent and is demanding for Christian life. Such approach is at the same time strongly optimistic—sin and virtue according to him have a common source. That is why man could always change his attitude and choose the right way. There is nothing predetermined, it is all a matter of his free choice.

Turning back to the origins of Christianity in the Slavonic world we could see elements of this doctrine in the medieval sources for the life of the great Apostle to the Slavs St Cyril. For many generations it exemplifies the Christian life dedicated to spirituality, which at the same time combines spiritual and secular activities. The main point in the medieval *vitae* of the saint is his search for true Wisdom that is not neglecting the high culture of the time but puts it in a spiritual context. Void of theological depth because of their broad audience, the medieval sources nevertheless contain the most important points of the teaching of synergy and especially the meaning of the internal activities of man such as will and knowledge in the spiritual ascent to God. Not quite unexpectedly Theology is of especial importance. It is knowledge of particular spiritual nature and is regarded as a remedy of spiritual deception to clear the image of God in man and to eradicate the roots of sin. It is in Theology that man changes the attitude of his mind from creature to the Creator. It is part of the way to true wisdom. Following the etymology of the word *philosophy* the medieval *vitae* use it both for the Christian pursuit of wisdom by St Cyrill and for his interest in secular Philosophy not opposing but rather coordinating them. The right balance between his secular and spiritual activities is an important message to the Slavonic reader. Now let us consider it closer.

It is striking from a modern point of view that the epithet *Philosopher* is regularly applied to St Cyril. This occurs not only in his *vitae* but also in the texts of medieval Slavonic Church usage such as the *Service of St Cyril and Methodius* (April 6)[1], in the *Synaxarion* for February 14[2] and August 25[3], in the *King Boril's Synodicon*[4], and in the *Encomium of St Cyril*[5]. Unlike the Old Slavonic tradition, modern times prove to be sensitive and conscious to such an epithet. For many Orthodox Christians, there is, as it were, a contradiction between the general assessment of St. Cyril as a holy man equal to the apostles and at the same time, the recognition of his philosophical interests. Whatever the epithet philosopher could mean in the 9th c., it is difficult to imagine that a newly shined saint in the 20th and 21st centuries will be commemorated by the Church with such a name.

That is why there are many ways today of naming the great Apostle to the Slavs and brother of St Methodius: 1) St Cyril[6], 2) St Cyril the Philosopher[7], 3) Constantine the Philosopher–St Cyril[8], 4) St Constantine-Cyril[9] 27–34.,

---

[1] Служба на Кирила и Методия: А. Теодоровъ-Баланъ, Кирил и Методий, т. 2 (София 1934), p. 74.
[2] See Житие Кирилово: А. Теодоровъ-Баланъ, Кирил и Методий, т. 2 (София 1934), p. 34 (from: http://www.scripta-bulgarica.eu/bg/sources/zhitie-na-sv-kiril-ot-prostiya-prolog [accessed 07.03.2021]).
[3] See Житие на Константина и Методия: А. Теодоровъ-Баланъ, Кирил и Методий, т. 2 (София 1934), p. 42.
[4] Борилов синодик 202a5: И. Божилов, А.-М. Тотоманова, И. Билярски, Борилов синодик (София 2012), p. 150.
[5] Похвала Кирилу: А. Теодоровъ-Баланъ, Кирил и Методий, т. 1 (София 1920), p. 109.
[6] E.g. *М. В. Безобразова*, Изречения св. Кирилла и Послания митрополита Никифора (Санкт-Петербургъ 1898).
[7] It occurs mostly in medieval texts like the *Encomium of St Cyril*, *Synaxarion*, some *Services of St Cyril and Methodius*, etc. See notes 1–5.
[8] It occurs in the *Church service of St Cyril* (February 14): Служба свети Кирилу: А. Теодоровъ-Баланъ, Кирил и Методий, т. 2 (София 1934), p. 53. See also *С. Алексиев, Ю. Трифонов*, Църковно-мисионерското дело на Константин Философ – Св. Кирил (София 1996); Съчинението на Константина Философа (Св. Кирила) Написание за правата вяра, Списание на БАН т. LII (София 1935) 1–87.
[9] E.g. *А. Стаматов*, Към корените на християнската ни култура. Св. Константин-

5) (St) Constantine-Cyril the Philosopher[10], 6) which is absolutely not correct but is accepted in a broad Church usage and by the media—St Cyril the Slavonic and Bulgarian. One would hardly find such a variety of names applied anywhere else to a holy man. St Cyril the Philosopher is the one that causes the most confusion today. All the other names either omit the epithet *Philosopher* or make it less confusing by adding the secular name Constantine. Therefore it is essential to realize the true meaning of this epithet and appreciate the significance of Philosophy proper in Theology for turning man back to God to restore His image in himself and for completing a repentance of the intellect in the Mystical Theology to cut the roots of sin and dignify him for divine grace of and finally for *theōsis*.

Let us first consider the information from the primary sources concerning St Cyril's interest in philosophy. Theophylact of Ohrid in the *Vita Clementi* qualifies him as "great [...] in the exterior (i.e. Gentile) philosophy"[11]. The *Italian Legend* says that "due to the astonishing gift, by which he was remarkably distinguished from early childhood, he was deservedly called a Philosopher"[12]. According to the *Vita Constantini* by St Clement of Ohrid, he was a student of Leo the Philosopher and Photius the Great in dialectic and all philosophical teaching[13]. Two important remarks should be made for the range and nature of the competence of St Cyril's teachers, Leo the Philosopher and Mathematician and Patriarch Photius. First, they were highly educated bibliophiles, well informed about the history and traditions of philosophical knowledge. Patriarch Photius was mostly attracted by the Alexandrians and his approach to their texts was analytical and not just historical or motivated by a wish just to broaden the outlook of his disciples. Second, philosophy for

---

Кирил за философията, Християнство и култура VII/10 (33) (2008)

[10] E.g. *И. Панчовски*, Философски и богословски концепции на св. Константин-Кирил Философ, Годишник на Софийския университет, Богословски факултет 2 (1995) 227–298; *К. Станчев*, О философско-эстетических взглядах Константина-Кирила Философа, Palaeobulgarica 2 (1979) 7–11; *Е. Георгиев, Г. Данчев* et al. (eds.), Константин-Кирил Философ. Материали от научните конференции по случай 1150 годишнината от рождението му (София 1981).

[11] *Theophylactus Achridensis*, Vita Clementis Achridensis II, 4: А. Милев, Гръцките жития на Климент Охридски (София 1966), p. 78: πολὺς [...] τὴν ἔξω φιλοσοφίαν.

[12] Vita cum Translatione S. Clementis (Италианска легенда) 1: А. Теодоровъ-Баланъ, Кирил и Методий, т. 2 (София 1934), p. 196: *qui ob mirabile ingenium, quo ab ineute infantia mirabiliter claruit, veraci agnomine Philosophus est appellatus*. The English translation is mine.

[13] *Clemens Achridensis*, Vita Constantini (=VCon) IV: Б. Ангелов, Х. Кодов, Климент Охридски. Събрани съчинения, т. III (София 1973), p. 91: наоучи же се ѹ дька, и оу Фотїа патриарха въсеи философꙗ҆ ѹчѥнїѥмъ.

St Cyril the Philosopher on the Meaning of Theology

Photius was not an end in itself. It was integrated in the Christian education he was keen to spread as well as in his theological thinking[14]. Now I will try to connect these points to the evidence we have about St Cyril's philosophical interests.

Two moments in the Slavonic *Vita of St Cyril* could be taken as a testimony that he belonged to the most advanced category of their students. First, when the Logothete realised that St Cyril was ready to take the monastic vow, he looked for a way not to lose him from the community[15] and after the Logothete's solicitation to the empress, St Cyril had his hair tonsured, and was given a spiritual title and the position of patriarchal secretary. Secondly, soon after having escaped from the capital and having tried to hide in a monastery, St Cyril was offered a position as a philosophy teacher[16], which he accepted. These two episodes testify to the respect St Cyril received in Constantinople as a man of letters whose accomplishment was highly appreciated by the Logothete who did his best to retain him within the Byzantine academic community.

The definition of philosophy St Cyril gave to the Logothete is the only explicit statement of a philosophical nature we can attribute to him although it occurs in an indirect source his Slavonic vita written by St Clement of Ohrid. The evidence concerning St Cyril's philosophical interests is less than scarce. To say that it is not representative to the level of Byzantine intellectual life and even to education in the 9th century Byzantium means to say nothing. It was not representative as well to the depth of philosophical interests St Cyril testified by the Logothete's concern to keep him in his circle and by an explicit statement of Theophylact of Ohrid in his *Vita of St Clement of Ohrid*: he qualifies St Cyril as "great in the exterior (i.e. Gentile) philosophy"[17]. Therefore the scare evidence of St Cyril's philosophical occupations stays against an extremely rich background. It is tempting to look for the hidden motives he could have. Any attempt in this direction is praiseworthy but will never be

---

[14] See *I. Christov*, Neoplatonic Elements in the Writings of Patriarch Photius, in: M. Knežević (ed.), S. Press The Ways of Byzantine Philosophy (California 2015) 289–309 (an English version of paper published in Bulgarian in 2004).

[15] *Clemens Achridensis*, VCon IV: Б. Ангелов, Х. Кодов, Климент Охридски. Събрани съчинения, т. III (София 1973), p. 91: да ие ѿкѹстимъ єго ѿ цръкѵ.

[16] *Clemens Achridensis*, VCon IV: Б. Ангелов, Х. Кодов, Климент Охридски. Събрани съчинения, т. III (София 1973), p. 92: оучити философїи.

[17] *Theophylactus Achridensis*, Vita Clementis Achridensis II, 4: А. Милев, Гръцките жития на Климент Охридски (София 1966), p. 78: πολὺς […] τὴν ἔξω φιλοσοφίαν. The English translation is mine.

proved and would remain no more than a hypothesis, which does not exclude a variety of other options.

Now let us look at the definition. Asked by the Logothete to explain what philosophy was, St Cyril defined it this way:

> Knowledge of divine and human things, to the extent that man can get close to God, a knowledge that teaches him to become, through his activity (дѣтѣлїю), an image and likeness of the One who created him[18].

There is a variety of approaches to St Cyril's definition, but this falls out from the topic of this paper. I would rather examine the Christian element in it. It is contained in the final part, which has both Hellenic and Christian aspects: *Philosophy* is "a knowledge [...] that teaches him to become **through his activity** an image and likeness of the One who created him". Insofar as it defines philosophy as "becoming a [...] likeness of God", the definition goes back to Plato. In the *Theaetetus,* Plato describes philosophical concern as an escape from this world striving to "assimilation to God as far as it is possible"[19]. This part of St Cyril's definition however takes the assimilation of man to God in a Christian sense as becoming, through man's activity, an image and likeness of the One who created him. This does not mean that "becoming an image of God" is acquiring a state man does not already have. Man is an image of God by nature. The definition means restoring it, cleansing it from the pollution of original sin. We see this aspect of philosophy in other parts of the *Vita Constantini* where it states that Christian philosophy is the knowledge of how to restore our ancestors' image of God to what it was in the Garden of Eden: "to acquire the ancestral dignity". With the following words, St Cyril declines the Logothete's offer to marry a noble lady:

> for me there is nothing greater than knowledge, through which I will acquire wisdom and seek for the ancestral dignity and spiritual wealth[20].

---

[18] *Clemens Achridensis*, VCon IV: Б. Ангелов, Х. Кодов, Климент Охридски. Събрани съчинения, т. III (София 1973), p. 91: Бжїимъ и чл҃вѣскыимъ' вѣщемъ разоумъ, елико можеть чл҃къ приближити се ест, такожь дѣтѣлїю оучить чл҃ка, по ѡбразѹ и по подобїю быти сътворшоумоу и. The English translation is mine.

[19] *Plato*, Tht. 176b, 1: I. Burnet, Platonis opera omnia, I (Oxford 1995), p. 182: ὁμοίωσις θεῷ κατὰ τὸ δυνατόν.

[20] *Clemens Achridensis*, VCon IV: Б. Ангелов, Х. Кодов, Климент Охридски. Събрани съчинения, т. III (София 1973), p. 91: мнѣ болшее оученїа ничтоже ѥ [мнѣ] им' же разоумъ сьбравъ, прадѣдьнее чьсти и богатьства хощѹ искати. The English translation is mine.

This raises a principle question: is such a spiritual knowledge philosophy or theology?

Before answering to this question, I need to make an important remark. It seems that there is an essential difference between acquiring wisdom and seeking ancestral dignity in this passage and becoming an image and likeness of the God in the definition of Philosophy insofar it is through activity. Normally we are apt to take it in its external meaning as designating the human deeds. Activity (дѣтѣль, syn. дѣтѣльство, дѣиство), however, which in this context is traditionally translated as *deed* or *virtue*[21] corresponds to the greek ἐνέργεια and has a broader meaning, also including the activity of the human soul, led by intellect (John the Exarch)[22]. Theology in the Eastern-Orthodox tradition plays an important role in restoring the image of God in man. Summarising the main points of this teaching, Gregory Palamas described theology as a contemplation and knowledge of God.

> a knowledge of Christian doctrines (δογμάτων γνῶσις), and a corresponding to nature application and movement of the capacities of soul [...] that restores in man his rational image (τῆς λογικῆς εἰκόνος)[23].

Gregory follows the teaching of the great Cappadocians and Maximus, according to which the human mind is the image of God in man. The mind was given to man by the Creator so he could know God and to be a mirror in human nature reflecting Him. Mental activities, according to Maximus, play an important role in the history of salvation. The fall was a result of pride and intellectual deception, when the mind realised its ability to penetrate into the nature of things and to create knowledge that had power over nature and served the needs of the body. This led to man's turning away from God toward the creation and to the darkening of the divine image in him. Now, it is the mind that should correct its mistake and act in a way that corresponds to its nature, since it was created to know God. Theology is the activity of the mind needed to restore the image of God in man. At its highest stage—Mystical theology—all mental activities cease in repentance when the apophatic modes of thought have also been exhausted. It is this repentance that clears the mind of its sinful pride and intellectual deception that led to the fall. Now, the mind restores

---

[21] See the survey in: С. Николова, Проблемът за философските възгледи на Константин-Кирил, Кирило-Методиевски студии кн. 5 (1988) 27–28.

[22] Cf. И. Христов, Art. дѣтѣльство, дѣиство, in: А. М. Тотоманова, И. Христов (eds.), Терминологичен речник на Йоан Екзарх (София 2019) 101–102.

[23] *Greg. Pal.*, Triad. I, 3, 15, 12–16: Π. Κ. Χρήστου, ΓΠΣ, τόμ. Α' (Θεσσαλονίκη 1988), p. 425. On θεολογία and its distinction from θεοπτία in Gregory see: И. Христов, Византийското богословие през XIV в. (Дискурсът за Божествените енергии) (София 2016) 89–90.

its dignity as the image of God in man[24]. Another important note should be added here. Theology, as intellectual activity, should not be opposed to ascetical activity. The Greek ἐνέργεια and the Old Slavonic дѣтѣль embrace them both. So, in Maximus the Confessor's teaching, ascetical activity (πρᾶξις or πρακτικὴ φιλοσοφία) is a part of theology because it is based on free choice which, in its turn, is not possible without deliberation and presupposes mental activity. Deeds, virtuous acts, ascetical practices and theological discourse are all part of man's activity that cooperates with God's activity, with his grace, to restore man to the lost paradise and dignify him to deification[25].

Therefore, spiritual knowledge that, according to St Cyril's words, leads to becoming an image and likeness of God is actually theology, and St Cyril's being called a "philosopher" has a particular meaning here. Even his only explicitly "philosophical" statement, the definition of philosophy, conforms to such spiritual knowledge. Let us examine this closer. When Theophylact of Ohrid qualified St Cyril as great in the exterior philosophy, he went further and praised him for his real greatness, which was in Christian philosophy:

> Cyril who is great in exterior [pagan] philosophy is even greater in inner [Christian] philosophy, and having true knowledge of the nature of beings, he has rather such knowledge of the One Being by whom everything received existence from non-being[26].

This distinction between interior and exterior philosophy illustrates an important point about the partial integration of philosophy within theology. For apologetic purposes, Christians often used very prestigious, Greek words to demonstrate that these terms finally acquired their true meaning when used in a Christian context. The same happened with the term *philosophy*. Its nominal definition is "love of wisdom". Christians used this word to demonstrate that they, not pagans, were the genuine *philosophers* because, unlike the pagans,

---

[24] И. Христов, Тема смерти в богословии св. Максима Исповедника, in: Proceedings of the V International Theological Conference Dedicated to St Maximus the Confessor (Tbilisi 2017) 79–91. See also И. Христов, Божественное руководство над умом в синергии Бога и человека согласно св. Максиму Исповеднику, in: Proceedings of the V International Theological Conference Dedicated to St Maximus the Confessor (Tbilisi 2017) 92–105.

[25] This is a common place in the Cappadocians and later Eastern-Orthodox tradition. Cf. I. Christov, Synergetic Aspects in St Gregory of Nyssa's Teaching on the Salvation of Man, in: T. Hainthaler, F. Mali (eds.), For Us and for Our Salvation. Soteriology East and West (Innsbruck – Wien 2014) 103–111.

[26] *Theophylactus Achridensis*, Vita Clementis Achridensis II, 4: А. Милев, Гръцките жития на Климент Охридски (София 1966), p. 78: Κύριλλος, ὁ πολὺς μὲν τὴν ἔξω φιλοσοφίαν, πλείων δὲ τὴν ἔσω, καὶ τῆς τῶν ὄντως ὄντων φύσεως ἐπιγνώμων, μᾶλλον τοῦ ἑνὸς ὄντος, ᾧ τὰ πάντα ἐκ μὴ φαινομένων τὸ εἶναι ἔλαβον. The English translation is mine.

Christians knew true Wisdom. Philosophy is not knowing existing things *qua* existing but knowing God who created them out of nothing. Initially, Christians called monks philosophers because they lived in Christ, and Christ is the true Wisdom[27]. Later, the term acquired a new meaning, not just a consecrated Christian life, but also knowledge of God as a pursuit of true wisdom. That is how the term *philosophy* was also used for theology. The last development resulted from the need to better formulate Christian doctrines and identify heresies. Such formulating could benefit from the thoughts and methods developed in philosophy. Thanks to the Cappadocian Church fathers from the 4th century, some of the basic concepts of ancient philosophy were integrated into the dogmas. The integration of philosophical language into theology and the establishment of such language in the practice of Eastern theology were two of the most significant contributions of the Cappadocian fathers. In the text under examination, Theophylact of Ohrid praises St Cyril the "the inner philosopher" i.e. the Christian theologian who knows God and is, therefore, directed to true Wisdom.

The two great theologians of immense influence on St Cyril—Dionysius the Areopagite and Gregory the Theologian—used the term *philosophy* in its transformed Christian meaning. Gregory's works had a special importance for St Cyril who learned them by heart[28]. According to Anastasius Bibliothecarius' testimony, when St Cyril brought St Clement's relics to Rome, the great teacher of the Slavic people, St Cyril, used to say that Dionysius the Areopagite would have been of great use to the holy fathers against heresies, had his works been known earlier[29]. In the *Ecclesiastical Hierarchy*, the Areopagite explicitly talks about "the philosophy of monks"[30]. The Greek scholia that are an inseparable part of the *Corpus areopagiticum* make important comments on the synergy of man and God, explaining the nature of the most important human activity (ἐνέργεια) that unites them with the immortal, rational beings,

---

[27] *Dionysius Ps.-Areopagita*, EH VI c 2: G. Heil, PTS 36 (Berlin 1991), p. 117,24; *Eusebius Caesariensis*, HE II, 17, 5: G. Bardy, SC 31 (Paris 1952), p. 73; *Sozomenus*, HE I, 12–13: J. Bidez, G. C. Hansen, GCS 50 (Berlin 1960) p. 24–30; F. Dölger, Zur Bedeutung von φιλόσοφος und φιλοσοφία in byzantinischer Zeit, in: F. Dölger, Byzanz und die europaeische Staatenwelt (Ettal 1953) 197–208.
[28] *Clemens Achridensis*, VCon III: Б. Ангелов, Х. Кодов, Климент Охридски. Събрани съчинения, т. III (София 1973), p. 90: ογчє се нєоγчтъ кънігамъ сто Григоріа Богословца.
[29] *Anastasius Bibliothecarius*, Ep. ad Carolum Calvum de scriptis Dionysii Areopagitae: И. Дуйчев, М. Войнов et al. (eds.), Латински извори за българската история II (София 1960), p. 207–208.
[30] *Dionysius Ps.-Areopagita*, EH VI c 2: G. Heil, PTS 36 (Berlin 1991), p. 117,24: τῶν μοναχῶν φιλοσοφία.

the angels. Humans and angels are "intelligent beings" because they both have the privilege of participating in divine providence through intellectual activity. Thus, they are able to participate in the Wisdom of God[31]. The *Dionysian corpus* is one of the best examples of what we call *Christian philosophy* that is a theological discourse using philosophical language which has been integrated into theology itself[32].

Longing for true Wisdom marked St Cyril's life right from his childhood. He was seven when he had a dream: he was given the choice of any girl in the city, and he chose the most beautiful and with a shining face. Her name was Sofia (Wisdom)[33]. This was his lifelong choice. It is quite indicative that the *Vita Constantini* starts with this story and continues to demonstrate St Cyril's progress in learning and his special interests in philosophy.

No doubt, St Cyril was keenly interested in both secular and Christian philosophy. The sources we have, however, testify rather to the second. His definition of philosophy subordinates knowledge to becoming like God and means participation in Divine Wisdom. All other passages of a philosophical nature found in medieval sources are either related to expounding the Christian doctrine or are reduced to his capacity to build sound arguments and to persuade the Gentiles. This is what characterised his theological discourse.

***

There is an issue of great importance. The fact that theology could partially integrate philosophical elements into its discourse did not mean that in Byzantium philosophy was abolished or made a servant of theology. They coexisted until some philosophical doctrine gave rise to heresy. This coexistence was beneficial to theology insofar it could enrich its instrumentation allowing it to borrow expressions, mental structures and methods from philosophy, but theology only used these elements as tools and adapted them to its spiritual needs.

---

[31] I. *Christov*, Pronoia and Sophia in the Greek Scholia to the Corpus Areopagiticum, in: T. Hainthaler, F. Mali et al. (eds.), Pronoia. The Providence of God (Innsbruck – Wien 2014) 303–313. See *Iohannes Scythopolitanus*, Schol. in DN V.1, 309,27–31 (in νοερὰ): B. Suchla, TS 62 (Berlin – Boston 2011), p. 315,1–4.

[32] A. *Christova*, I. *Christov*, Lexical Morphology and Syntactic Formation of Philosophical Terms in the Translation of the Corpus Areopagiticum by the Starets Isaija, in: H. Goltz, G. Prochorov (eds.), Das Corpus des Dionysios Areiopagites in der slavischen Übersetzung von Starec Isaija (14. Jahrhundert), Monumenta linguae Slavicae dialecti veteris LV/5 (Freiburg i. Br. 2013) 536.

[33] *Clemens Achridensis*, VCon III: Б. Ангелов, Х. Кодов, Климент Охридски. Събрани съчинения, т. III (София 1973), p. 90: Σοφία, сиръчъ прѣмѫдрость.

This is a result of the dual prospective Byzantines had on human being, distinguishing between the spiritual essence of man and his natural mode of existence. He has both a spiritual background (λόγος) and a natural reality. It is up to man to find a proper balance for them and to coordinate his activity with the Divine activity—with the Divine grace. This synergy of man and God leads away from the sin in a spiritual ascent. The intellectual activity of Theology may use elements of Philosophy, first, to turn the human mind back to God, which makes it a genuine search for wisdom, a true "philosophy" and, second, what is more important, to exhaust its resources in the mystery of God thus leading it to repentance in the apophatism of mystical theology. The mystical theology is a kind of repentance of the intellect where he denies all that what gave rise to its pride and intellectual deception[34]. This fundamentally changes the attitude of man which initially led him to the misuse of his free will and it is through this activity that he restores the image of God in himself and exterminates the roots of sin.

Here is the main challenge for modern studies of St Cyril: to keep the right balance between the secular and the spiritual aspects of his life and neither to exaggerate his interest in secular philosophy nor totally deny it. The great Apostle to the Slavs embodied in his life the patristic ideal of the unity of faith and reason and remains a "philosopher" in the Church's memory, that is a theologian who managed to integrate the achievements of high culture into the preaching of Christian doctrine. The spiritual ascent to God may integrate elements of them in itself. But this is not only and not so much for the purpose of positive theology as to exhaust the resources of intellect thus leading it to repentance in the apophatism of mystical theology. In this way its pride and self-conceit—the roots of original sin are cut, restoring the purity of image of God in man and dignifying him for divine grace.

---

[34] On the "repentance of intellect" in Mystical Theology see: *И. Христов*, Божественное руководство над умом в синергии Бога и человека согласно св. Максиму Исповеднику, in: Proceedings of the V International Theological Conference dedicated to St. Maximus the Confessor (Tbilisi 2017) 92–105.

Georgios Martzelos, Thessaloniki (Greece)

The Concept of inherited sin in the Orthodox Tradition

Abstract:
The Orthodox tradition, due to the ontological premises of the Greek Fathers, unanimously accepts that after the fall of Adam his descendants do not inherit his personal sin and guilt, but the morbid state of sin, decay and death, in which he fell and from which sin is born on a personal level. For this reason the deliverance of Adam's descendants from this morbid state is only done by abolishing of decay and death through the death and resurrection of Jesus Christ, and His victory over decay and death can be appropriated by sinful man through his participation in the sacraments of Baptism and Eucharist.

Introduction

The notion of inherited sin, as formulated by the Greek Fathers, significantly differs from that of the Latin Fathers and especially of Augustine. This is understandable, because the premises that existed in the two traditions for the theological reflection on this issue, as well as the challenges that contributed to the development and formation of this notion, were different in East and West. Apart from the fact that the Latin Fathers had legal rather than ontological premises facing this issue, there was never such a challenge in the East as the one posed by the heresy of Pelagianism, which the Latin Fathers, and mainly Augustine, had to deal with. Although this heresy was condemned in the East and even on ecumenical level at the Council of Ephesus (431), it did not occupy on a wide scale the theological thought of the Greek Fathers, which had been absorbed for several centuries mainly by the Christological problem.

However, the Greek Fathers were not indifferent to the essence and the consequences of inherited sin. Only they dealt with these issues not independently and systematically, but in the context of their effort to address the various heresies, such as Gnosticism, Manichaeism, Arianism, Apollinarism, Nestorianism, Monophysitism and Monothelitism, that essentially forged the salvific teaching and experience of the Church regarding the reality of salvation and deification of man.

From this point of view, the patristic teaching on inherited sin does not constitute, in orthodox tradition, an autonomous and systematic dogmatic teaching that faces an isolated and independent soteriological challenge. It is a teaching that is inextricably and functionally linked to the core of orthodox dogma, and especially to Cosmology, Anthropology, Christology and Soteriology.

Of course, due to the variety of heretical challenges, which occur even during different periods of time, as well as the lack of systematic development of this teaching, there are often differences between the Greek Fathers in certain aspects of it. However, it should be emphasized that in the basic points of this teaching there is a *consensus patrum* in the Orthodox tradition, which is mainly due to the common theological premises of the Greek patristic theology.

For this reason, before we go into the actual examination of our subject, let us first look as briefly as possible at these common theological premises, which have played a decisive role in the development and formation of the teaching of the individual aspects of inherited sin in the Orthodox tradition.

I. Theological premises

The first basic premise is the concept in which the Greek Fathers understand the relationship between God and the world[1]. For them only God is by nature uncreated, unchangeable and immortal, while the world is created and changeable, coming into being "out of nothing" (ἐξ οὐκ ὄντων) by God's energies[2]. Already its origin from non-being into being constitutes a change and alteration[3], which makes it constantly lean to zero, from which it came. For this reason, in order to remain in being, it is necessary to depend on the cohesive power of God. Otherwise, it will return to zero and non-existence.

---

[1] *J. S. Romanides*, Τὸ προπατορικὸν ἁμάρτημα (Athens ²1992) 39–57; *N. A. Matsoukas*, Δογματικὴ καὶ Συμβολικὴ Θεολογία Β' ('Έκθεση τῆς ὀρθόδοξης πίστης) (Thessaloniki 1985) 202–203.

[2] *Joh. Dam.*, Exp. fid. 2–3: P. Ledrux, SC 535 (Paris 2010), p. 138–148. See also *G. D. Martzelos*, Οὐσία καὶ ἐνέργειαι τοῦ Θεοῦ κατὰ τὸν Μέγαν Βασίλειον. Συμβολὴ εἰς τὴν ἱστορικοδογματικὴν διερεύνησιν τῆς περὶ οὐσίας καὶ ἐνεργειῶν τοῦ Θεοῦ διδασκαλίας τῆς Ὀρθοδόξου Ἐκκλησίας, (Thessaloniki ²1993) 15–16, 91–100.

[3] *Gregor. Nys.*, De hom. opif. 16: J. Laplace – J. Daniélou, SC 6 (Paris 1944), p. 157–158; Or. catech. magna 6: E. Mühlenberg – R. Winling, SC 453 (Paris 2000), p. 176; *Joh. Dam.*, Exp. fid. 3: SC 535, p. 11.

In other words, the created world cannot live on its own regardless of its relationship with God. The interruption of its relationship and communion with God will necessarily lead to zero and death. In this sense, man as created, is in himself changeable and mortal. In order to achieve immortality, which is a natural attribute only of uncreated God, he must be in constant communion and relationship with him. Both death and immortality are two possibilities that open before him, dependent solely on his relationship with God. It is this relationship with God or its interruption that determines whether he will be led to immortality or fall to death[4]. In this context we must clarify that when the Greek Fathers speak of death and immortality, they do not perceive these situations only in biological, but also in spiritual sense. Death means for them not only the separation of the body from the soul, but also the separation of the soul from the God who is the source of life. So is immortality: it is not only understood as the survival of man as a psychosomatic entity, but also as the vitalization of the soul by the life-giving energy of the Holy Spirit[5].

The second basic premise, connected to the previous one, is that sin in the Orthodox tradition is not understood simply as a violation of a commandment of God or much more as an insult to divine justice, but as an unhealthy psychosomatic situation that originated from the interruption of communion and relationship with God, the source of life, and therefore leads inevitably to death[6]. For this reason, sin and death are inextricably linked and often identified in the Orthodox tradition[7]. As Gregory Nyssa characteristically points out, expressing in this case the unanimous conception of the other two Cappadocian Fathers, "Sin is nothing else than alienation from God, Who is the true and only life"[8]. In other words, sin, according to the Orthodox tradition,

---

[4] Concerning this matter see *N. A. Matsoukas*, Τὸ πρόβλημα τοῦ κακοῦ. Δοκίμιο πατερικῆς θεολογίας (Thessaloniki ²1986) 36-39, 113-115.

[5] See *Iren. Lugd.*, Adv. haer. 5, 2, 3: A. Rousseau – L. Doutreleau – Ch. Mercier, SC 153 (Paris 1969), p. 37-41; *Gregor. Nys.*, Or. catech. magna 8: SC 453, p. 192; Contr. Eunom. 8: PG 45, 797C-800A; *Marc. Erem.*, De baptismo: G. M. de Durand, SC 445 (Paris 1999), p. 372; *Isid. Pelus.*, Epist. 252: PG 78, 932B; *Joh. Dam.*, Exp. fid. 100: P. Ledrux, SC 540 (Paris 2011), p. 300-312; *Gregor. Palam.*, Homilia 16: PG 151, 196A-C.

[6] See *J. Karawidopoulos*, Das paulinische Sündenverständnis bei den griechischen Kirchenvätern, Κληρονομία 2/1 (1970) 45, 49.

[7] See *Clem. Alexandr.*, Cohort. ad gentes 11, 115: C. Mondésert, SC 2 (Paris 1949), p. 184; Paedagog. 1, 2, 5: H. Ir. Marrou – M. Harl, SC 70 (Paris 1960), p. 116; *Basil. Caesar.*, In martyr. Julit. 9: PG 31, 260A; *Gregor. Naz.*, Or. 18, 42: PG 35, 1041A; *Joh. Chrysost.* (spur.), In parabol. ejus qui incidit in latrones: PG 62, 755; *Marc. Erem.*, De baptismo: SC 445, p. 372. See also *J. Karawidopoulos*, Das paulinische Sündenverständnis, 48.

[8] See *Gregor. Nys.*, Contr. Eunom. 2: PG 45, 545B. Cf. *Basil. Caesar.*, Quod deus non est auctor malorum 7: PG 31, 345A; 8: PG 31, 348A; De spiritu sancto XVI, 40: B. Pruche, SC

is not simply a legal fact that disturbs the divine judicial order and therefore implies the punishment of God to the transgressive man, but above all and *par excellence* an existential event that disturbs the ontological relationship between God and man, resulting in the interruption of this relationship with God, which inevitably leads man to sickness, decay and death.

In this sense, death is not understood as a punishment imposed by God Himself, but as a natural consequence of sin which constitutes, as we have said, a breakdown of communion with God. God as the source of all good things cannot be considered the cause of death[9]. As Irenaeus characteristically emphasizes,

> To as many as continue in their love towards God, does He grant communion with Him. But communion with God is life and light, and the enjoyment of all the benefits which He has in store. But on as many as, according to their own choice, depart from God, He inflicts that separation from Himself which they have chosen of their own accord. But separation from God is death, and separation from light is darkness; and separation from God consists in the loss of all the benefits which He has in store[10].

For this very reason, salvation is not understood in the Orthodox tradition as the restoration of a legal relationship between God and man, but as a healing and deliverance from the sovereignty of decay and death.

II. Man's original state and fall

Despite the different way in which the Greek Fathers sometimes describe the original state of man, there are in this case many common points among them that constitute the starting point and the basis for the Orthodox understanding and interpretation of the event of the fall.

Before his fall, man, created in the image and likeness of God, was, as they point out, in communion with the persons of the Holy Trinity. Adorned with the grace of the Holy Spirit was a sharer of divine glory and a knower of divine truths. His life was free from anxiety, calm and impassible, and he was in complete harmony with the whole creation, without running the risk of disturbing his relation to it or much more of being endangered by it. There was no fear of death and no carnal desire in him. However, being created and changeable

---

17 (Paris ²1968), p. 388–389; *Gregor. Naz.*, Carmina moral. 8, 184: PG 37, 662A.
[9] See *Basil. Caesar.*, Quod deus 7: PG 31, 345A. See also J. S. Romanides, Τὸ προπατορικόν, 19–20, 160; J. Karawidopoulos, Das paulinische Sündenverständnis, 49.
[10] *Iren. Lugd.*, Adv. haer. 5, 27, 2: SC 153, p. 343. English translation from: https://www.new advent.org/fathers/.

in his nature, it was not possible for him to be immortal and utterly perfect by nature[11]. Besides, if he had been created perfect from the beginning, he would have been deprived of the most essential feature of his existence that is the freedom of his will. But such a thing would be highly contradictory to the concept of the creation of man, because according to the Greek Fathers the freedom of will or in other words the free and sovereign will (αὐτεξούσιον), which they consider as inextricably linked to reason (λογικὸν), is what constitutes the essence of man[12].

The purpose of man's creation according to them was therefore to enable man, as a rational being with free will in communion with the Triune God, to achieve immortality and deification through his moral and spiritual perfection[13]. This is, after all, the deeper meaning of man's creation "in the image" (κατ᾽ εἰκόνα) and "in the likeness" (καθ᾽ ὁμοίωσιν) of God in the patristic tradition. The creation of man "in the image" of God refers according to the majority of the Greek Fathers to the rational and to the free and sovereign will, which man was endowed with[14], while man's creation "in the likeness" of God

---

[11] See *Joh. Dam.*, Exp. fid. 26, 44: SC 535, p. 300, 366-372, where the previous patristic tradition on this matter is summarized, and *Gregor. Palam.*, Hom. 16: PG 151, 204A, 220A. See also the studies cited below, where there is abundance of related patristic references: A. Gaudel, Péché originel, in: DThC 12.1 (Paris 1933) 318-340, 343-344, 347-353, 429-430; M. Jugie, Péché originel dans l'Église Grecque après Saint Jean Damascène, in: DThC 12.1 (Paris 1933) 610; *J. S. Romanides*, Τὸ προπατορικόν, 121-123, 156; J. Gross, Entstehungsgeschichte des Erbsündendogmas (Von der Bibel bis Augustinus) (München - Basel 1960) 76-110, 125-140, 143-144, 148-163, 168-172, 182, 209-214; A. V. Vletsis, Τὸ προπατορικὸ ἁμάρτημα στὴ θεολογία Μαξίμου τοῦ Ὁμολογητοῦ. Ἔρευνα στὶς ἀπαρχὲς μιᾶς ὀντολογίας τῶν κτιστῶν (Katerini 1998) 227-237; Ch. Filiotis-Vlachavas, La création et la chute de l'homme dans la pensée de Cyrille d'Alexandrie selon ses œuvres d'avant la querelle nestorienne (Strasburg 2003) 122-140, 163-184; Y. Spiteris, Il peccato originale nella traditione orientale, PATH 3 (2004) 338-362.

[12] See *N. A. Matsoukas*, Κόσμος, ἄνθρωπος, κοινωνία κατὰ τὸν Μάξιμο Ὁμολογητή (Athens 1980) 123-127; A. V. Vletsis, Τὸ προπατορικό, 191-200; *G. D. Martzelos*, Ὀρθόδοξο δόγμα καὶ θεολογικὸς προβληματισμός. Μελετήματα δογματικῆς θεολογίας Β' (Thessaloniki 2000) 107-126.

[13] See *Theoph. Antioch.*, Ad Autolycum 2, 24: G. Bardy - J. Sender, SC 20 (Paris 1948), p. 158; *Iren. Lugd.*, Adv. haer. 4, 38, 3: A. Rousseau, SC 100 (Paris 1965), p. 955-956; *Athanas. Alexandr.*, Contra gentes 2: P.-T. Camelot, SC 18bis (Paris 1977), p. 52-53.

[14] See *Athanas. Alexandr.*, De incarnat. Verbi 3, 6: Ch. Kannengiesser, SC 199 (Paris 1973), p. 270-271, 282; *Basil. Caesar.*, In psalm. 48, 8: PG 29, 449BC; In illud: Attende tibi ipsi 6: PG 31, 212BC; De gratiarum actione 2: PG 31, 221C; Hom. dicta tempore famis et siccitatis 5: PG 31, 317A; Quod deus 6: PG 31, 344BC; Regul. fusius tractatae 2, 3: PG 31, 913B; Epist. 233, 1: Y. Courtonne, Saint Basil: Lettres, tome III (Paris 1966), p. 39; *Gregor. Nys.*, De hom. opif. 11, 12, 16: SC 6, p. 122, 131-132, 157-159; Or. catech. magna 5, 21: SC 453, p. 168, 240; De virginit. 12: M. Aubineau, SC 119 (Paris 1966), p. 402; *Constantin. diacon.*, Laudatio omnium martyrum 14: PG 88, 496C; *Maxim. Confess.*, Disputat. cum Pyrrho: PG 91, 304C;

refers to the possibility of his likeness with God, that is of his deification, after a free course of spiritual maturity and moral progress, with the contribution of the Holy Spirit[15]. Therefore, man's fall occurred according to the orthodox tradition, during this moral and spiritual progress from the "in the image" to the "in the likeness" situation. Although it overturned God's initial plan and definitely constitutes a tragic event for man, it is seen as nothing more than an episode in the whole history of Divine Economy[16].

Let us see now how orthodox tradition understands the original sin as an episodic event and, above all, what its tragic consequences are for the fallen man. Besides, as Roman Catholic theologians aptly observed, the Greek Fathers insist on these ontological consequences and are more interested in them in order to develop their teaching on Christ's salvific work[17].

While God set, as we have said, as the purpose of man's existence from the very beginning of his creation his moral-spiritual perfection and deification, which would be achieved only through his communion with God and obedience to his commandments, man, carried away by the devil who moved out of envy towards him, wanted to reach equality with God (ἰσοθεΐα) and deification in his own way, bypassing the divine plan and violating the commandment of his creator[18]. This is how the biblical narrative about Adam and Eve's transgression of God's commandment not to eat from the fruit of the tree of the knowledge of good and evil is basically interpreted in the Orthodox tradition[19]. The only exception seems to be the view of Clement of Alexandria

---

Joh. Dam., Exp. fid., 26: SC 535, p. 300; See also G. D. *Martzelos*, Ὀρθόδοξο δόγμα, 109, 121–122; *idem*, Vernunft und Wille als das "Ebenbild Gottes" im Menschen in der griechischen und lateinischen Tradition, in: Th. Hainthaler, F. Mali, G. Emmenegger, A. Morozov (Hgg.), Imago Dei. Forscher aus dem Osten und Westen Europas an den Quellen des gemeinsamen Glaubens Studientagung L'viv, 12. – 14. September 2019 "Imago Dei", Pro Oriente Bd. XLIII (Innsbruck – Wien 2021) 431–435.

[15] See *Clem. Alexandr.*, Strom. 2, 22: P.-Th. Camelot – Cl. Mondésert, SC 38 (Paris 1954), p. 133; *Method. Olymp.*, Sympos. 1, 4: H. Musurillo – V.-H. Debidour, SC 95 (Paris 1963), p. 62–63; *Basil. Caesar.*, In 'Faciamus hominem' 1, 16–17: A. Smets – M. van Esbroeck, SC 160 (Paris 1970), p. 206–208; *Joh. Chrysost.*, In Genesim 9, 3: PG 53, 78; *Joh. Dam.*, Exp. fid., 26: SC 535, p. 300.

[16] See also *N. A. Matsoukas*, Δογματική καὶ Συμβολικὴ Θεολογία Β΄, 203–204.

[17] See *M. Jugie*, Le dogme du péché originel, 166; *A. Gaudel*, Péché originel, 360–361, 381.

[18] See *Athanas. Alexandr.*, Adv. Apollinar. 2, 9: PG 26, 1148B; *Basil. Caesar.*, Quod deus 8: PG 31, 348B; *Gregor. Naz.*, Or. 38, 12: C. Moreschini – P. Gallay, SC 358 (Paris 1990), p. 126–130; Or. 39, 13: SC 358, p. 176–178; *Joh. Chrysost.*, Contra Judaeos, gentiles et haereticos (spur.): PG 48, 1078; De statuis 11, 2: PG 49, 121, 269; De fato et providentia 2: PG 50, 754; In venerabilem crucem (spur.): PG 50, 820; In Genes. 16, 3–4: PG 53, 129–130; 18, 2: PG 53, 150–151; Comment. in Joann. 9, 2: PG 59, 72; *Joh. Dam.*, Exp. fid. 25: SC 535, p. 286–298.

[19] Gen 2:16–17; 3:1–7.

in this case, who, using the allegorical method of interpretation of the Holy Scripture identifies original sin with the conclusion of premature and therefore illegal carnal relationships between Adam and Eve[20].

However, the Greek Fathers and ecclesiastical writers, obviously facing abstinential views of Platonic, Gnostic and Manichaean origin[21], based exclusively on the biblical narrative of Genesis, clearly and categorically reject the identification of original sin with Adam and Eve's connection by carnal relations[22]. Identifying the cause of the fall not only in man's voluptuousness but also in his vanity[23], they emphasize *par excellence* the spiritual dimension of original sin, considering it essentially as an act of disobedience and rebellion of man against the will of God. With this disobedience, the man, as they point out, broke his relationship and communion with God, and as a result of that he was deprived of the life-giving energy of the Holy Spirit and thus fall into the dominion of the devil, sin, decay and death. He lost his holiness and childlike innocence, his mind was darkened, his reason and his free and sovereign will, that is his situation "in the image" of God, was blackened, and his previous knowledge of God was driven away[24]. Creation became hostile to him, so he felt strongly from it the threat of death. Man and creation are now in a competitive and hostile relationship with each other, with the aim of neutralizing and overcoming the threat of death that came from it[25]. This is how orthodox tradition understands the fact that after the fall, not only man but also the whole of creation "laments and suffers pain together" with him

---

[20] See *Clem. Alexandr.*, Strom. 3, 14: PG 8, 1193C-1196A; 17, PG 8, 1208AB.
[21] See for example *Clem. Alexandr.*, Strom. 3, 13: PG 8, 1192C-1193B; 17: PG 8, 1205A-1208A.
[22] See *Athanas. Alexandr.*, In psalmos 50, 7: PG 27, 240CD; *Joh. Chrysost.*, In Genes. 15, 4: PG 53, 123: Μετὰ [...] τὴν παράβασιν τὰ τῆς συνουσίας γέγονεν; 18, 4: PG 53, 153; *Theod. Cyr.*, Eranistes 3: PG 83, 245D-248A; *Joh. Dam.*, Exp. fid. 97, SC 540, p. 286.
[23] See *Marc. Erem.*, De baptismo: SC 445, p. 372; Consult. intellect. cum sua ipsius animae 5: SC 445, p. 410.
[24] See *Athanas. Alexandr.*, Contra gentes 3-4: SC 18bis, p. 56-62; *Joh. Dam.*, Exp. fid., 44: SC 535, p. 370; 45: SC 540, p. 8-12. See also the following cited bibliography where there is abundance of more related patristic references: A. Gaudel, Péché originel, 318-344, 348-349, 351, 429-430; J. S. Romanides, Τὸ προπατορικόν, 156-158; J. Gross, Entstehungsgeschichte, 79-80, 82-86, 89-90, 110-111, 127-128, 140-141, 144-148, 151-155, 168-169, 171-172, 182-190, 212-213; A. V. Vletsis, Τὸ προπατορικό, 256-275; M. Filiotis-Vlachavas, La création, 262-277; Y. Spiteris, Il peccato, 339-362.
[25] See *Theoph. Antioch.*, Ad Autolycum, 2, 17: SC 20, p. 142; *Symeon Nov. Theol., Or. ethic.* 1, 2: J. Darrouzès, SC 122 (Paris 1966), p. 190. See also A. Kesselopoulos, Ἄνθρωπος καὶ φυσικὸ περιβάλλον. Σπουδὴ στὸν ἅγιο Συμεὼν τὸ Νέο Θεολόγο (Athens 1992) 93ff.

(Rom 8:22) and "creation was subjected to vanity, not willingly, but because of the one who subjected it" (Rom 8:20)[26].

At this point we must emphasize that the fall of man into decay and death for the Greek Fathers, who rely in this case on the Holy Scripture[27], is not a punishment imposed by God, but a natural consequence of original sin by which his existential communion and relation with the source of life was cut off[28]. Moreover, the biblical passage "on the day you eat of it you shall most surely die" (Gen 2:17) is not understood in the Orthodox tradition as a threat of God for the punishment He would impose on Adam and Eve if they violated His will, but as a loving warning, in order to protect them from the danger of violating the divine commandment[29]. In fact, even death itself was allowed by God for reasons of charity towards man, "so that evil does not become immortal"[30]. Thus, the rational and possessing free will creature of God, which was created for immortality and deification, was suddenly found because of his disobedience and the misuse of his freedom under the rule of the devil, decay and death.

Although original sin, according to the Greek Fathers, was not an act of necessity on the part of Adam's changeable nature, but an act of his free choice[31]

---

[26] See *Joh. Chrysost.*, De statuis 10, 5: PG 49, 117; In diem natalem Domini nostri Jesu Christi 6: PG 49, 360; Comment. in epist. ad Romanos 14, 4–5: PG 60, 529–530. See also J. Galanis, Ἡ σχέση ἀνθρώπου καὶ κτίσεως κατὰ τὴν Καινὴ Διαθήκη (Thessaloniki 1984) 89–96; idem, Τὸ καινοδιαθηκικὸ ὑπόβαθρο τῶν σχέσεων ἀνθρώπου καὶ κτίσης κατὰ τὴ λατρευτικὴ πράξη τῆς Ἐκκλησίας, in: Ἐπιστημονικὴ Ἐπετηρίδα Θεολογικῆς Σχολῆς Ἀριστοτελείου Πανεπιστημίου Θεσσαλονίκης (Thessaloniki 1985) 385–400.

[27] Wis 1:13; 2:23–24.

[28] See *Theoph. Antioch.*, Ad Autolycum 2, 27: SC 20, p. 164; *Basil. Caesar.*, Quod deus: PG 31, 345A; *Nemes. Em.*, De nat. hom. 1: PG 40, 513B–516A; *Joh. Dam.*, Exp. fid. 42: SC 535, p. 356.

[29] See *Athanas. Alexandr.*, De incarnat. Verbi 3: SC 199, p. 268–274; *Joh. Chrysost.*, Adver. Judaeos 8, 2: PG 48, 929; In Genes. 14, 2: PG 53, 114; 18, 1: PG 53, 147; *Gregor. Palam.*, Cap. phys. 51: PG 150, 1157D–1160A.

[30] See *Maxim. Confess.*, Quest. ad Thalasium 44: J.-C. Larchet – F. Vinel, SC 554 (Paris 2012), p. 40. See also *Gregor. Naz.*, Or. 38, 12: SC 358, p. 130. Cf. *Basil. Caesar.*, Quod deus: PG 31, 345A. See also J. S. Romanides, Τὸ προπατορικόν, 157.

[31] See *Athanas. Alexandr.*, Contra gentes 4, 7: SC 18[bis], p. 60, 68–69; *Basil. Caesar.*, In Hexaemeron 2, 5: S. Giet, SC 26 (Paris 1949), p. 160; Quod deus. 3: PG 31, 332C–333A; 5: PG 31, 337D–340A; 6: PG 31, 344BC; *Gregor. Naz.*, Or. 14: PG 35, 892AB; Or. 38, 12: SC 358, p. 126–130; Or. 45, 28: PG 36, 661BC; *Epiphan. Cypr.*, Adv. haereses 1, 3, 42: PG 41, 776D–777A; *Gregor. Nys.*, De mortuis: PG 46, 521D–524B; In Ecclesiasten 2, 3: F. Vinel, SC 416 (Paris 1996), p. 156–160; *Joh. Chrysost.*, In Genes. 16, 5: PG 53, 132; *Joh. Dam.*, Exp. fid. 26, 44: SC 535, p. 302, 366–372; 86: SC 540, 202. Generally sin, according to the Fathers, has its cause not in nature but in man's free will. (See for example *Nemes. Em.*, De nat. hom. 40: PG 40, 769B; *Theod. Cyr.*, Eranist. 1: PG 83, 40D).

it did not remain limited to the level of will. It also extended to the ontological carrier of the will, which is nature. Because of original sin, human nature became ill in Adam's person, was ontologically eroded and, cut off from the source of life, unavoidably ended in decay and death[32]. It is precisely this morbid state of decay and death, into which Adam fell, that the Greek Fathers consider as a sinful state, not only because decay and death are the fruit of sin, but mainly because they constitute the source and cause for the birth of sin in Adam's life after the fall. By his fall into decay and death, they claim, passions, carnal pleasures and sin in general have dynamically invaded his life[33]. That is why sin, decay and death are for them, as we have seen, inextricably linked to each other. Although the causal relationship between sin and the sick and mortal human nature will be discussed in more detail below, we must clearly emphasize here that the Greek Fathers consider the mortality of human nature not only as the result but also as the cause and root of sin. And this very patristic position is the key to understanding not only the concept of inherited sin in the Orthodox tradition, but also orthodox anthropology and soteriology in general.

III. The inheritance of original sin

Based on these facts, the answer of the Greek Fathers to the question of inherited sin, that is how sin was passed on to the whole of human race by Adam's fall, so that all people became and are considered sinners, according to what Paul writes in his Epistle to the Romans, differs significantly from the Western and especially the Augustinian view.

The Greek patristic tradition, in contrast to Augustine, unanimously emphasizes that what the descendants of Adam inherit is not his personal sin and his guilt for it, but his sick and mortal nature[34]. Adam's personal sin and guilt is only his own, not of his descendants. The fact that Adam, because of his personal sin, remarks John Chrysostom, became mortal and therefore also his descendants became mortal is understandable and reasonable. But to make someone else sinful because of Adam's disobedience would be unjust

---

[32] See *Cyril. Alexandr.*, In epist. ad Romanos: PG 74, 789B: [...] ἠρρώστησεν ἡ ἀνθρώπου φύσις ἐν Ἀδὰμ διὰ τῆς παρακοῆς τὴν φθοράν.
[33] See *Joh. Chrysost.*, Comment. in epist. ad Romanos 13, 1: PG 60, 507; *Cyril. Alexandr.*, In epist. ad Romanos: PG 74, 789AB; *Theod. Cyr.*, Interpret. in Psalmos 50, 7: PG 80, 1245A.
[34] See characteristically *Joh. Chrysost.*, Comment. in epist. ad Romanos 10, 1: PG 60, 474; 10, 2-3: PG 60, 477; *Marc. Erem.*, De baptismo: SC 445, p. 372; *Cyril. Alexandr.*, In epist. ad Romanos: PG 74, 789AB.

and unreasonable[35]. That is why the holy Father, unanimously expressing the Greek patristic tradition, considers that submission to the sin of Adam's descendants and their characterization as sinners is understood exclusively as their submission to death[36]. This is because death, as we have seen above, is generally for the Orthodox tradition not only the result, but also the source and cause of sin. Therefore, according to Greek patristic tradition, Adam's descendants are characterized as sinners by the apostle Paul, not because they are considered to participate in Adam's personal sin and guilt, but because they inherit from him their sick and mortal nature, from which inevitably sin is born[37].

It is very characteristic, as J. Meyendorff already points out, that two Greek Fathers of the 5th century, and in fact contemporaries of Augustine, Cyril of Alexandria and Theodoret of Cyrus, although they belonged to different schools of interpretation and in opposite camps during the Christological controversies of their time, present at this point an impressive *consensus* on Adam's sin and its consequences for the entire human race[38].

In fact, regardless of their different interpretation of the much-discussed Pauline phrase "for that all have sinned" (Rom 5:12), they fully agree that sin for the descendants of Adam is born from the perishable and mortal nature they inherited from their ancestor[39]. This is the theological basis, on which mainly Cyril of Alexandria explains in a thorough and detailed way how it happened so that "by one man's disobedience many were made sinners" according to Paul (Rom 5:19). As he points out, they became sinners not as co-transgressors of Adam and heirs of his guilt, but as heirs of his sick and mortal nature, from which their personal sins are necessarily being produced. What he writes on this matter in his *Explanation of the Epistle to the Romans* is very interesting and representative of orthodox tradition:

---

[35] See *Joh. Chrysost.*, Comment. in epist. ad Romanos 10, 2: PG 60, 477.
[36] See *Joh. Chrysost.*, Comment in epist. ad Romanos 10, 3: PG 60, 477.
[37] See also *J. S. Romanides*, Τὸ προπατορικόν, 162–168; *J. Karawidopoulos*, Das paulinische Sündenverständnis, 46–48.
[38] *J. Meyendorff*, Ἐφ' ᾧ (Rom. 5, 12) chez Cyrille d'Alexandrie et Théodoret, SP 4 (1961) 158: "Leur unité dans l'exégèse de Rom. 5, 12 indique que nous nous trouvons devant un consensus de la pensée du Ve siècle sur le péché d'Adam et de ses conséquences. En gros, on peut dire que ces Pères considèrent que ce qui est hérité d'Adam, ce n'est pas le péché lui-même, mais la mort ; le péché d'Ancêtre a eu pour conséquence de rendre mortelle la race adamique tout entière". See also *idem*, Byzantine Theology. Historical trends and doctrinal themes (New York 1974) 145.
[39] See *J. Meyendorff*, Ἐφ' ᾧ (Rom. 5, 12), 158–159.

But one would say: yes, Adam slid away and by disregarding the divine commandment he was condemned to decay and death; and then how were the many made sinners because of him? What do his faults have to do with us? And how have the ones not yet born been wholly condemned together with him [...]? So what would be the way for us to be excused? [...] But we have become sinners through Adam's disobedience in such a way: he was created for incorruption and life, and his life was holy in the paradise of delight, the whole mind was always in vision of God, the body was in a state of calmness and tranquility, and all disgraceful pleasure was at rest; for in him there did not exist any disturbance of inordinate movement. But because he fell under sin and slid away into decay, henceforth pleasures and impurities ran into the nature of flesh, and the angry law in our members sprang up. So nature became ill with sin through the disobedience of one person, that is Adam; in this way the many were made sinners, not as having transgressed together with Adam, because they had not yet come into being, but as having his nature which is fallen under the law of sin[40].

Therefore, original sin in the Orthodox tradition, although it was the fruit of Adam's free will, had painful and inevitable consequences for human nature. Sin, now because of Adam's disobedience, passed from the will, which is considered a "syndrome" of nature[41], into human nature itself, not as guilt but as a morbid condition of decay and death that has infected like an epidemic the entire human race. It is precisely this morbid state of decay and death transmitted by Adam to all his descendants that constitutes the essence of the inherited sin for the Orthodox tradition.

The connection of sin with nature and not only with the will of the fallen man, not only emphasizes the ontological conditions, by which the Greek Fathers understand the meaning and significance of original sin, but also reveals the philosophical and psychoanalytic depth of their thought and their whole reflection concerning the origin of sin.

John Chrysostom, specifically connecting the origin of sin to the mortality of human nature, notes suitably that together with death, which followed Adam's fall, human nature was invaded by:

> the throng of passions [...]. For when the body had become mortal, it was henceforth a necessary thing for it to receive concupiscence, and anger, and pain, and all the other passions[42].

---

[40] Cyril. Alexandr., In epist. ad Romanos: PG 74, 788D–789B. It's my own translation.

[41] See Gregor. Nys., Contr. Eunom. 1, 440: R. Winling, SC 524 (Paris 2010), p. 198; Contra Apollinar. 31: PG 45, 1192B; Cyril. Alexandr., De sancta et consubst. Trinitate 2: PG 75, 780B.

[42] Joh. Chrysost., Comment. in epist. ad Romanos 13, 1: PG 60, 507–508. En-

As the holy Father points out, these things certainly do not constitute *per se* the essence of sin, but they turn into sin because of man's excessive and unbridled behavior[43], which is obviously due to the fact that man, as he stresses, "submits to all things rather than die"[44].

Theodoret, moving a step further from John Chrysostom's thought, emphasizes that human nature after the fall is governed by the instinct of self-preservation and therefore has various needs, the selfish satisfaction of which gives birth to sin on a personal level[45]. This is indeed the way in which he understands how "sin reigned in death" according to the words of the apostle Paul in Romans 5:21[46]. Theodoret's thought in this case, as J. Meyendorff remarks, is strikingly connected with certain contemporary conceptions, such as those of M. Heidegger, regarding the relationship between death and the instinct of self-preservation[47].

Besides, it is not at all by chance that in orthodox tradition the three sinful inclinations of the soul, that is love of pleasure, love of glory and love of money, which constitute the component of human sinfulness[48], are considered as the greedy and selfish reaction of the fallen man against the threat of death[49]. The selfishness and greed that are displayed in these three sinful inclinations, are in the context of the fall the only possibility for psychological balance opposite the threat of death.

This orthodox patristic conception is, as we understand, of enormous psychoanalytic importance, because it fully enlightens and fully interprets the psychic processes of the fallen (that is the empirical) man based not only on one, but on all three basic sinful tendencies that essentially converge on his

---

glish translation from: https://www.documentacatholicaomnia.eu/03d/0345-0407,_Iohannes_Chrysostomus,_Homilies_on_The_Epistle_To_The_Romans,_EN.pdf (p. 167).
[43] Ibid.
[44] *Joh. Chrysost.*, In epist. ad Hebraeos 4, 4: PG 63, 41.
[45] See *Theod. Cyr.*, Interpret. epist. ad Romanos 5, 12: PG 82, 100AB.
[46] See *Theod. Cyr.*, Interpret. epist. ad Romanos 5, 21: PG 82, 104C.
[47] See *J. Meyendorff*, Ἐφ' ᾧ (Rom. 5, 12), 160.
[48] See *Athanas. Alexandr.*, In sanctum Pascha 7: PG 28, 1089BC (Actually it is probably a work of Basil of Seleucea. See *B. Marx*, Der homiletische Nachlass des Basileios von Seleukeia, OCP 7 [1941] 365); *Joh. Chrysost.* (spur.), In Pascha 5, 2: PG 59, 736; *Marc. Erem.*, De lege spirituali 107: SC 445, p. 100; Consult. intellect. cum sua ipsius animae 2: SC 445, p. 400–402; *Joh. Climac.*, Scala Paradisi 8: PG 88, 836A; 26: PG 88, 1024A; *Doroth. Gaz.*, Doctrina 13, 145: L. Regnault – J. de Préville, SC 92 (Paris 1963), p. 416: […] φιληδονία, φιλοδοξία καὶ φιλαργυρία, ἐξ ὧν συνίσταται πᾶσα ἁμαρτία. See also *J. Kornarakis*, Μαθήματα Ποιμαντικῆς μετὰ στοιχείων ποιμαντικῆς Ψυχολογίας (Thessaloniki 1969) 51, 54–59.
[49] See *Joh. Chrysost.*, Comment. in epist. ad Romanos 13, 1: PG 60, 507–508; In epist. ad Hebraeos 4, 4: PG 63, 41; *Theod. Cyr.*, Interpret. in Psalmos 50, 7: PG 80, 1245A; Interpret. epist. ad Romanos 5, 12: PG 82, 100AB.

selfish satisfaction and self-determination[50]. In this respect it provides, we believe, a more complete picture of the basic psychic trends and processes and is therefore far superior to the psychoanalytic theories of S. Freud, A. Adler and C. G. Jung which are based only on one of the above psychic trends and constitute only one-sided attempts to explain the behavior of the human soul[51].

However, we must emphasize that considering the fallen human nature as the cause of sin does not mean for the Orthodox tradition the irresponsibility of Adam's descendants for the sins they commit. This is because sin certainly springs from the perishable and mortal human nature, but it manifests itself with the free consent of the human will. Without it, there is neither sin nor responsibility for committing it on a personal level. That is why both Cyril of Alexandria and Theodoret of Cyrus, in their own way, unanimously emphasize that the personal death of Adam's descendants is not directly due to the sin of their ancestor, but to their own personal sin born out of their perishable and mortal nature[52].

IV. Liberation of man from inherited sin

Adam's fall into sin, decay and death, according to the Greek Fathers, led the whole human race in a vicious circle from which it could not be released: Original sin brought to mankind as a direct consequence the morbid state of decay and death, and this situation in turn gave birth to sin again, that resulted in decay and death, and so on. It is this vicious circle that constitutes for the Orthodox tradition the essence of the tragedy of the post-fall man.

The post-fall man could not achieve by his own might his freedom from sin, his moral-spiritual perfection, and the restoration of his relationship with God while he was under the rule of decay and death. Death had to be abolished so that man could be released from the cause of sin and his diseased nature could be healed. As the Greek Fathers unanimously emphasize, this is exactly what the incarnated Word of God took upon Himself with His salvific work. With His death on the cross and His resurrection He defeated and abolished death that is the source and cause of sin and of the devil's power over mankind. The fear of death, which kept people enslaved to sin and devil, loses now its power

---

[50] See also J. Kornarakis, Μαθήματα Ποιμαντικῆς, 59–60.
[51] See also J. Kornarakis, Μαθήματα Ποιμαντικῆς, 52–53.
[52] See Cyril. Alexandr., In epist. ad Romanos: PG 74, 784BC; Theod. Cyr., Interpret. epist. ad Romanos 5, 12: PG 82, 100B.

The Concept of inherited sin in the Orthodox Tradition

with Christ's resurrection[53]. In this way, man is truly liberated and saved, because, as John Chrysostom aptly remarks "he that fears not death is out of reach of the devil's tyranny"[54].

In this respect, the resurrection of Christ is considered in the Orthodox tradition as the most salvific event in the history of Divine Economy. That is why it is celebrated in the Orthodox Church with great pomp, as an event that achieves the liberation of man from the monocracy of death, and the provision of a new life free from the authority of sin and the devil.

> Christ has risen from the dead, trampling upon death by death, and giving life to those who were in the graves[55],
>
> We celebrate the death of death, the destroying of Hades, the beginning of another life, the eternal one[56],

the faithful chant on Easter day. In other words, it is an event, with which the passage (Hebrew: *Pascha*) of man from death to life takes place in Christ.

At this point, however, we must emphasize that the salvific significance of Christ's resurrection is not limited only to man. It is extended through man to the whole of creation, thus restoring the relationship between them. Man and creation are now related to each other and function harmoniously, free from the destructive power of death in the light of Christ's resurrection. This fact is precisely underlined in a very brilliant way by John Damascene, when he proclaims in a *Troparion* of his *Easter Canon*:

> Now everything is full of light, both the heavens and the earth and also the underground. Therefore, let all creation celebrate Christ's resurrection, in which it has been established[57].

---

[53] See *Joh. Chrysost.*, Katecheticus in sanctum Pascha: PG 59, 723–724; In epist. ad Hebraeos 4, 4: PG 63, 41–42; *Gregor. Palam.*, Homilia 16: PG 151, 209AB, 212A–213A.
[54] *Joh. Chrysost.*, In epist. ad Hebraeos 4, 4: PG 63, 41–42. English translation from: http://www.documenta-catholica.eu/d_0345-0407-%20Iohannes%20Chrysostomus%20-%20Homilies%20on%20the%20Epistle%20to%20the%20Hebrews%20-%20EN.pdf (p. 49).
[55] Apolytikion of Easter.
[56] Easter Canon, Troparion of the 7th Ode.
[57] Ibid., Troparion of the 3rd Ode.

Based on these facts it is now easy to understand why, despite the tragedy of the event of the fall, from the very beginning we talked about the episodic character of original sin in the Orthodox tradition. Christ as a new Adam opens with his resurrection new ontological perspectives not only for mankind, but for the whole creation. Free from the power of decay and death, man can now achieve the purpose for which he was created, i.e. to win incorruptibility, immortality and deification. All that is needed in contrast to the old Adam is to show faith and obedience to Christ, keeping his commandments and participating existentially in his death and resurrection. And this is where the special significance of the sacrament of Baptism in the Orthodox tradition is highlighted.

By Baptism, the believer is being buried with Christ, stripping off the old man of sin, decay, and death, and is being resurrected with him, dressing the new man, "who is renewed unto knowledge, according to the image of his creator"[58]. Thus participating existentially and sacramentally in the death and resurrection of Christ, he is spiritually reborn in a new life free from the fear of death and the authority of sin. Baptism is for the Christian the beginning of the new life in Christ, which is increased and maintained by the other two important sacraments of the Church, the Chrism and the Eucharist[59].

Within the framework of these data it becomes obvious that Baptism in the Orthodox tradition is not aimed solely at the remission of sins, which is certainly one of the basic gifts of Baptism, but does not exhaust the wealth of its saving gifts. Apart from the provision of the remission of sins, the Greek Fathers unanimously emphasize that the nature of man, which is worn out by sin, is through Baptism ontologically renewed, and the Christian, becoming a shareholder of the death and resurrection of Christ, receives his new substance, becomes a participant of the gifts of the Holy Spirit, and God's son and heir by grace[60]. This is the only way to remove the consequences of original sin. In other words, the question of removing them according to the Orthodox tradition is not the remission of sins but the liberation of man from the rule of the devil and death and the healing and renewal of his sick fallen nature.

More generally, the salvific work of Christ is not understood in the Orthodox tradition on the basis of the judicial scheme "sin–remission", but on the basis of the ontological scheme "death–life" or "disease–healing". And it is precisely this passage from death to life or from disease to healing that takes

---

[58] Col 3:10.
[59] See *Nicol. Cavas.*, De vita in Christo 1, 19: M.-H. Congourdeau, SC 355 (Paris 1989), p. 94.
[60] See *Theod. Cyr.*, Haereticar. fabular. compendium 5, 18: PG 83, 512AB.

place with Baptism. This is the reason why the Church, as Theodoret of Cyrus points out, accepts infant baptism, even though toddlers have not committed personal sins[61]. If the purpose of Baptism was simply the remission of sins, infant baptism should have no place in the Church. Moreover, as Nikolaos Kavasilas (14th century) points out on this matter, Baptism as a birth in the new life in Christ is a gift from God, and therefore does not presuppose the voluntary participation of man. Just as God creates us without our will, so He recreates us in Christ without our own voluntary collaboration[62]. Perhaps there is no more comprehensive and clearer patristic position in the Orthodox tradition than that which constitutes the theological background of infant baptism.

Conclusion

After what we have said, it becomes understandable that the Orthodox tradition, due to the ontological premises of the Greek Fathers that characterize their theology in general, unanimously accepts that after the fall of Adam his descendants do not inherit his personal sin and guilt, but the morbid state of sin, decay and death, in which he fell and from which sin is born on a personal level. This is precisely why the release of Adam's descendants from this morbid state occurs by the abolition of decay and death that takes place with the death and resurrection of Jesus Christ, something that is particularly emphasized in the Hymnography of the Orthodox Church.

Therefore, what is needed to enable sinful man to personally appropriate the salvific gifts of Christ's victory over sin, decay, and death is to participate existentially and sacramentally in the death and resurrection of Christ through the sacraments of Baptism and Eucharist. Only in this way is the human race restored to its ancient beauty and becomes capable of fulfilling the primary purpose for which it was created, i.e. its deification.

---

[61] Ibid.
[62] See *Nicol. Cavas.*, De vita in Christo 2: PG 150, 541C.

Presse

Pressemitteilung (Wien, Pro Oriente-Informationsdienst, 13.09.21)

Patristische Tagungen feiern in Wien ihr 20-Jahr-Jubiläum

Internationale Tagung von 16. bis 19. September mit hochrangigen Expertinnen und Experten aus ganz Europa – Festakt am 16. September mit Kardinal Schönborn und Metropolit Hilarion

Vom 16. bis 19. September findet in Wien die zehnte Patristische Tagung statt, zu der orthodoxe und katholische Wissenschaftlerinnen und Wissenschaftler aus ganz Europa erwartet werden. Höhepunkt der Tagung ist ein Festakt am Donnerstagabend, 16. September, im Wiener Kardinal-König-Haus, bei dem u.a. Kardinal Christoph Schönborn und der Leiter des Moskauer Außenamts, Metropolit Hilarion (Alfejew), das Wort ergreifen werden. Die Patristischen Tagungen feiern heuer ihr 20-Jahr-Jubiläum. Sie finden alle zwei bis drei Jahre in unterschiedlichen Städten Europas statt.

Bei diesen Tagungen kommen führende Expertinnen und Experten für die christliche Literatur der sogenannten „Kirchenväter" des ersten Jahrtausends aus dem Osten und dem Westen Europas, aus unterschiedlichen Kirchen, Ländern und Kulturen zusammen. Die Tagungen dienen so dem wissenschaftlichen Austausch und der Vertiefung der Beziehungen und des Dialogs zwischen Ost- und Westkirche.

Neben Kardinal Schönborn und Metropolit Hilarion (er wird sein Grußwort online von Moskau aus sprechen) kommen beim Festakt auch Bischof Atanáz Orosz, Bischof von Miskolc der Ungarisch-Katholischen Kirche, und Prof. Andrew Louth zu Wort. Eine Video-Grußbotschaft wird außerdem Bischof José Rico Pavés (Diözese Asidonia-Jerez) beisteuern. Auch PRO ORIENTE-Präsident Alfons Kloss und die frühere Leiterin der Tagungen, Prof. Ysabel de Andia, werden das Wort ergreifen. Moderiert wird der Abend von der nunmehrigen langjährigen Leiterin der Tagungen, Prof. Theresia Hainthaler. Im Rahmen des Festakts soll die kirchliche und gesamtgesellschaftliche Relevanz des Forums gewürdigt werden.

Von 2001 bis 2009 veranstaltete die Stiftung PRO ORIENTE die Tagungen. Ab 2010 wurden die Tagungen unter der Leitung von Prof. Hainthaler auf eigene Initiative weitergeführt.

Pressemitteilung (Wien, Pro Oriente-Informationsdienst, 13.09.21)

Die erste Tagung in Wien im Jahr 2001 fand zu einer Zeit statt, als der offizielle katholisch-orthodoxe Dialog ausgesetzt war. Die Anregung dazu kam von Christoph Kardinal Schönborn und Prof. Ysabel de Andia. Zahlreiche orthodoxe und katholische Wissenschaftlerinnen und Wissenschaftler, von denen heute mehrere auch in der Leitung orthodoxer oder katholischer Kirchen wichtige Positionen innehaben, waren und sind beteiligt.

Die diesjährige zehnte Tagung behandelt das Thema: „Inherited sin?". Die „Erbsünde" wird dabei aus verschiedensten Perspektiven und in fast 40 Vorträgen und Impulsen von katholischer und orthodoxer Seite behandelt. Die breite Reichweite der Tagung zeigt sich an den Herkunftsländern der Teilnehmenden bzw. den Ländern, in denen diese ihre Lehrtätigkeit ausüben: Deutschland, Ukraine, Großbritannien, Serbien, Frankreich, Polen, Tschechien, Russland, Schweiz, Italien, Rumänien, Spanien, Griechenland, Niederlande, Bulgarien, Irland und Österreich. Die Tagung wird von PRO ORIENTE, Renovabis und der Fritz-Thyssen-Stiftung für Wissenschaftsförderung unterstützt.

Veröffentlicht: Pro Oriente-Informationsdienst (13. September 2021).

Pressemitteilung (Wien, Pro Oriente-Informationsdienst, 16.09.21)

Wien: Ökumene braucht Einsatz auf allen Ebenen

Leiterin der Patristischen Tagungen, Prof. Hainthaler, zieht zum 20-Jahr-Jubiläum der ökumenischen Initiative positive Zwischenbilanz

Dialog-Foren wie die Patristischen Tagungen sind zur Vorbereitung und Begleitung offizieller Dialoge zwischen den Kirchen von unerlässlicher Bedeutung. Das hat die Ökumene-Expertin Prof. Theresia Hainthaler gegenüber dem PRO ORIENTE-Informationsdienst betont. Die zehnte Patristische Tagung, die coronabedingt in hybridem Format stattfindet, hat unter der Leitung Hainthalers am Donnerstag, 16. September, in Wien begonnen.

Übereinkünfte des offiziellen Dialogs, und wären sie noch so gut, „sind für die Archive, wenn sie nicht lebendig in den Kirchen vor Ort rezipiert werden". Dazu brauche es den Einsatz auf allen Ebenen, betonte Hainthaler. Die Patristischen Tagungen gehörten wesentlich zu diesen Dialog-Formen.

Wissenschaftlerinnen und Wissenschaftler aus ganz Europa sind zur zehnten Tagung ins Kardinal-König-Haus gekommen. Im Blick zurück auf die bisherigen Tagungen resümierte Hainthaler: „Der Horizont weitet sich deutlich, sowohl für den Westen zum Osten hin wie umgekehrt." Die Begegnung mit den Kolleginnen und Kollegen aus dem Osten „inspiriert und bereichert uns, auch im Denken und Forschen". Für viele orthodoxe Wissenschaftlerinnen und Wissenschaftler aus Osteuropa seien die Patristischen Tagungen zudem eine sehr willkommene Gelegenheit, sich international zu profilieren und in Austausch mit westlicher Theologie zu treten. Man sehe das auch an wissenschaftlichen „Karrieren", so Hainthaler.

Sie hob zudem die zwischenmenschliche Ebene hervor: „Ein herzliches Miteinander hat sich entwickelt", in das auch neue Kolleginnen und Kollegen integriert würden: „Ich würde sagen, es ist ein Netzwerk, in das immer wieder Neue integriert werden können."

Auch ökumenisch brisante Themen würden bei den Tagungen immer wieder angesprochen, „aber eingebettet in einen breiteren Kontext". Man wolle ja auch dem offiziellen katholisch-orthodoxen Dialog zuarbeiten. Orthodoxe Vertreter hätten immer gerne an den Tagungen teilgenommen, auch in den

Zeiten, wenn es im offiziellen orthodox-katholischen Dialog Schwierigkeiten gab, so Hainthaler, die seit 2005 Mitglied des offiziellen Dialogs ist.

Prof. Hainthaler wies zudem darauf hin, dass eine Reihe von Teilnehmern aus verschiedensten Kirchen inzwischen Bischöfe wurden: Metropolit Hilarion (Alfejew) von Wolokolamsk (Russland), Metropolit Elpidophoros (Lambriniadis) von Amerika (Ökumenisches Patriarchat), Bischof Atanáz Orosz, ungarisch griechisch-katholischer Exarch von Miskolc (Ungarn), Bischof José Rico Pavés von Jerez de la Frontera (Spanien), Erzbischof Alexander Golitzin von Dallas (USA) oder Bischof Johan Bonny von Antwerpen (Belgien). Auch das sei für die Ökumene sicher förderlich.

Die Patristischen Tagungen feiern heuer ihr 20-Jahr-Jubiläum. Sie finden alle zwei bis drei Jahre in unterschiedlichen Städten Europas statt. Von 2001 bis 2009 veranstaltete die Stiftung PRO ORIENTE die Tagungen. Ab 2010 wurden die Tagungen unter der Leitung von Prof. Hainthaler auf eigene Initiative weitergeführt. PRO ORIENTE war aber auch in der Zwischenzeit unterstützend tätig, und ist für die Durchführung der aktuellen Tagung gemeinsam mit Prof. Hainthaler verantwortlich.

Die Tagung (16. bis 19. September) steht heuer unter dem Generalthema „Inherited sin?". Die „Erbsünde" wird dabei aus verschiedensten Perspektiven und in fast 40 Vorträgen von katholischer und orthodoxer Seite behandelt. Höhepunkt der Tagung ist ein Festakt mit Kardinal Christoph Schönborn und dem Moskauer Außenamtsleiter Metropolit Hilarion.

Veröffentlicht: Pro Oriente-Informationsdienst (16. September 2021).

Pressemitteilung (Wien, Pro Oriente-Informationsdienst, 17.09.21)

Schönborn: Freundschaften wichtige Voraussetzung für Ökumene

Festakt im Wiener Kardinal-König-Haus zum 20-Jahr-Jubiläum der Patristischen Tagungen – Moskauer Außenamtsleiter Metropolit Hilarion würdigt ökumenische Initiative – PRO ORIENTE-Präsident Kloss: Patristische Tagungen sind Beispiel für fruchtbare Ökumene

Freundschaften über Konfessionsgrenzen hinweg sind eine wesentliche Voraussetzung für gelingende Ökumene. Das hat Kardinal Christoph Schönborn beim Festakt zum 20-Jahr-Jubiläum der Patristischen Tagungen Donnerstagabend in Wien betont. Bei diesen Tagungen kommen führende Fachleute für die christliche Literatur der sogenannten „Kirchenväter" des ersten Jahrtausends aus ganz Europas zusammen. Schönborn bezeichnete die Initiative als ein „Netzwerk der Wissenschaft und der Freundschaft". Und er fügte im Blick auf den offiziellen Dialog zwischen der Katholischen und Orthodoxen Kirche hinzu: „Auch wenn der offizielle Dialog bisweilen mühsam ist – der Dialog bei den Patristischen Tagungen funktioniert sehr gut."

Der Wiener Erzbischof berichtete davon, wie ihm in jungen Jahren ein orthodoxer Geistlicher aus einer Glaubenskrise geholfen hatte. Andrei Scrima, ein rumänisch-orthodoxer Mönch und bedeutende Theologe, der u.a. auch als orthodoxer Vertreter am Zweiten Vatikanischen Konzil (1962–65) teilgenommen hatte, habe ihm und anderen jungen Dominikanermönchen die Kirchenväter auf so lebendige und existenzielle Weise näher gebracht, dass er bis heute davon zehre, betonte der Kardinal. Das sei auch eine wesentliche Motivation dafür gewesen, dass er sich für die Patristischen Tagungen stark gemacht habe.

Die erste Patristische Tagung in Wien im Jahr 2001 fand zu einer Zeit statt, als der offizielle katholisch-orthodoxe Dialog ausgesetzt war. Die Anregung dazu kam von Schönborn und der Pariser Kirchenväter-Spezialistin Ysabel de Andia. De Andia war auch in Wien beim Festakt mit dabei und erinnerte an die Anfänge des Projekts und unterstrich dessen drei wesentliche Dimensionen: ökumenisch, akademisch und europäisch.

Ziel sei gewesen, „Orthodoxe und Katholiken zusammenzubringen, die Patristik oder Theologie an den Philosophischen oder Theologischen Fakultäten lehren" und „denen die Liebe zu den Kirchenvätern des ersten Jahrtausends gemeinsam ist", so die Patrologin. Die Begrenzung auf das erste Jahrtausend weise auf den Wunsch hin, „sich in eine Zeit vor der großen Spaltung der griechischen und lateinischen Kirche zu versetzen, eine Zeit, in der die Kirchen die Vielfalt ihrer Traditionen entfalteten und ihre Einheit in den Ökumenischen Konzilien fanden".

Die Teilnehmenden der Tagungen würden zudem „als Europäer eingeladen", betonte de Andia weiter. Dabei habe man ein Europa im Blick, „das sich nicht an den Grenzen der Europäischen Union orientiert, sondern an der Nachwelt der byzantinischen und lateinischen Kirche".

Aus Moskau war Metropolit Hilarion (Alfejew), Leiter des Außenamts der Russisch-orthodoxen Kirche live zugeschaltet. Er hatte an den ersten vier Patristischen Tagungen teilgenommen und würdigte in seiner Rede die Initiative, die unbedingt weitergeführt werden soll, um auch weiterhin Beiträge zur gegenseitigen Bereicherung zu leisten. Bei den Kirchenvätern handle es sich nicht nur um ein Thema der Wissenschaft. Vielmehr gehe es – auch heute – ganz praktisch um Leitlinien und Orientierungshilfen für ein geglücktes christliches Leben.

PRO ORIENTE-Präsident Alfons Kloss nannte die Patristischen Tagungen als Beispiel einer gelungenen fruchtbaren Ökumene. Die Kirchenväter seien starke Zeugen der Einheit der Kirche „und sie helfen uns dabei, den Weg zurück zur Einheit zu finden", zeigte sich auch Kloss überzeugt.

Von 2001 bis 2009 veranstaltete die Stiftung PRO ORIENTE die Tagungen. Ab 2010 wurden die Tagungen unter der Leitung von Prof. Theresia Hainthaler auf eigene Initiative weitergeführt. PRO ORIENTE war aber auch in der Zwischenzeit unterstützend tätig und ist für die Durchführung der aktuellen Tagung gemeinsam mit Prof. Hainthaler verantwortlich, die lebendige Zeugnisse aus den vergangenen 20 Jahren in die Moderation des Festakts einfließen ließ.

Atanáz Orosz, Bischof von Miskolc der ungarischen Griechisch-katholischen Kirche, der die Patristische Tagung 2012 in Esztergom organisiert hatte, zitierte in seinem Grußwort den Präsidenten des Päpstlichen Einheitsrats, Kardinal Kurt Koch, mit den Worten: „Je näher wir Christus kommen, desto näher kommen wir auch einander." Als ein künftig bedeutsames ökumenisches Thema ortete er die Bemühungen um ein gemeinsames Osterdatum.

Weitere Grußworte kamen von José Rico Pavés, Bischof der südspanischen Diözese Jerez de la Frontera, vom griechisch-orthodoxen Erzbischof von Amerika, Elpidophoros (Lambriniadis) sowie dem britischen orthodoxen

Priester und Patrologen Prof. Andrew Louth. Seit dem ersten Treffen 2001 habe die Teilnehmenden der Tagungen der Appell von Papst Johannes Paul II. bewegt, dass die Kirche in Europa wieder mit beiden Lungenflügeln atmen solle, so Louth, der sich davon überzeugt zeigte, „dass die Kirche weniger durch die Hierarchie zusammengehalten wird als durch das, was man als geistliche Sehnen bezeichnen könnte, die uns alle miteinander verbinden".

Der Festakt im Wiener Kardinal-König-Haus war eingebettet in die zehnte Patristische Tagung, die das Thema „Inherited sin?" behandelt. Die „Erbsünde" wird dabei aus verschiedensten Perspektiven und in fast 40 Vorträgen und Impulsen von katholischer und orthodoxer Seite behandelt. Die breite Reichweite der Tagung zeigt sich an den Herkunftsländern der Teilnehmenden bzw. den Ländern, in denen diese ihre Lehrtätigkeit ausüben: Deutschland, Ukraine, Großbritannien, Serbien, Frankreich, Polen, Tschechien, Russland, Schweiz, Italien, Rumänien, Spanien, Griechenland, Niederlande, Bulgarien, Irland und Österreich. Die Tagung dauert noch bis Samstag.

Am Festakt nahmen u.a. auch der Wiener armenisch-apostolische Bischof Tiran Petrosyan, der Vorsitzende der Österreichischen Ordenskonferenz, Erzabt Korbinian Birnbacher, der Generalvikar des Ordinariats für die Gläubigen der katholischen Ostkirchen in Österreich, Yuriy Kolasa, sowie der Vorsitzende des Ökumenischen Rates der Kirchen in Österreich und PRO ORIENTE-Vizepräsident Prof. Rudolf Prokschi teil.

Veröffentlicht: Pro Oriente-Informationsdienst (17. September 2021).

Пресс-релиз (Вена, Служба коммуникации ОВЦС, 18.09.2021)

Митрополит Волоколамский Иларион в дистанционном режиме принял участие в конференции патрологов в Вене

16–18 сентября 2021 года в Вене (Австрия) состоялась международная конференция патрологов, посвященная раскрытию темы наследственной греховности в творениях восточных и западных Отцов Церкви. В конференции приняли участие ведущие патрологи из разных стран мира.

Вечером 16 сентября митрополит Волоколамский Иларион посредством дистанционной связи обратился с приветственным словом к участникам конференции, особо отметив присутствие в зале архиепископа Венского кардинала Кристофа Шёнборна, с которым председателя ОВЦС связывают долгие годы сотрудничества, начавшиеся еще в то время, когда он был епископом Венским и Австрийским. Митрополит Иларион также тепло приветствовал профессора Высшей школы философии и теологии Санкт-Георгена (Франкфурт-на-Майне) Терезию Хайнталер, одного из главных организаторов конференции.

В своем выступлении митрополит Иларион подчеркнул, что изучение наследия Святых Отцов не может сводиться только к исследованию написанных ими текстов. Очень важно изучать контекст, в котором они жили и творили. А это невозможно без практического освоения основ христианской веры и духовности.

Святые Отцы, как отметил иерарх, не были академическими богословами, которые сидели за столом, обложив себя книгами других авторов. Их богословие рождалось, прежде всего, из молитвенного опыта, а также из опыта участия в сакраментальной жизни Церкви. Именно поэтому их труды сохраняют актуальность для всех, кто стремится найти путь ко спасению.

В качестве примера современного исследования, посвященного святоотеческому богословию, митрополит Иларион привел вышедшую только что в переводе на русский язык книгу бывшего архиепископа Кентерберийского Роуэна Уильямса «Безмолвие и медовые лепешки.

Мудрость пустыни», посвященную египетскому монашеству IV–V веков. В простой и доступной форме автор книги излагает основы монашеской духовности, пытаясь актуализировать мудрость египетской пустыни и обозначить ее ценность для современного читателя.

В заключение своего выступления митрополит Иларион пожелал успехов участникам конференции и выразил надежду на то, что сможет принять личное участие в одной из будущих конференций.

Московский патриархат
Отдел внешних церковных связей
Служба коммуникации (18.09.2021)

Press Release (Vienna, DECR, 18.09.2021)

Metropolitan Hilarion of Volokolamsk takes part remotely in a conference of patristic scholars in Vienna

On September 16–18, an international conference of patristic scholars took place in Vienna, Austria, devoted to exploring the topic of inherited sinfulness in the works of eastern and western Church Fathers. The conference was attended by leading patrologists from various countries.

In the evening of September 16, Metropolitan Hilarion of Volokolamsk addressed the participants remotely, making a special mention of the presence in the hall of Archbishop of Vienna Cardinal Christoph Schoenborn, with whom the DECR chairman is bonded by long years of cooperation, which began as far back as the time when he was Bishop of Vienna and Austria. Metropolitan Hilarion also warmly greeted Prof. Theresia Hainthaler of the Sankt Georgen Graduate School of Philosophy and Theology (Frankfurt am Main), one of the chief organizers of the conference.

In his speech, Metropolitan Hilarion stressed that the study of the heritage of Holy Fathers cannot be reduced only to the study of their already written texts. It is very important to study the context in which they did their creative work. And this is impossible without the practical mastering of the foundations of Christian faith and spirituality.

Holy Fathers, as the hierarch noted, were not academic theologians who would sit at a table surrounded by books written by other authors. Their theology was generated primarily from the experience of prayer, as well as the experience of participation in the sacramental life of the Church. Precisely for this reason, their works remain topical for all who seek to find the way to salvation.

As an example of modern study on patristic theology, Metropolitan Hilarion cited the Russian version of the book, which has just come out, by the former Archbishop of Canterbury Rowan Williams entitled Silence and Honey Cakes. The wisdom of the desert devoted to the Egyptian monasticism of the 4th–5th centuries. In the simple and intelligible form the author sets forth the foundations of monastic spirituality seeking to actualize the wisdom of the Egyptian desert, to accentuate its value for the modern reader.

In conclusion of this speech, Metropolitan Hilarion wished success to the attendees and expressed a hope that he will take part in person in one of the future conferences.

The Russian Orthodox Church
Department for External Church Relations
Communication Service (18.09.2021)

Fotos

Bilder der Tagung

Gruppenfoto beim Kardinal-König-Haus

1. Reihe v.l.: Franz Mali (Fribourg), Gordian Gudenus (Wien), Theresia Hainthaler (Frankfurt), Bischof Atanáz Orosz (Miskolc), Christoph Kardinal Schönborn (Wien), Ysabel de Andia (Paris), Präsident Dr. Alfons Kloss (Wien), Andrea Riedl (Regensburg), Georgiana Huian (Bern/Bukarest), Ilaria Vigorelli (Rom).

2. Reihe v.l.: Tomasz Stępień (Warschau), Hilary Mooney (Stuttgart), Marta Przyszychowska (Pego), Dominique Gonnet SJ (Lyon), Giuseppe Caruso OSA (Rom), Viola Raheb (Wien), Pablo Argárate (Graz), Georgios Martzelos (Thessaloniki), Vittorino Grossi OSA (Rom), NN (St. Pölten), Sebastian Mateiescu (Bukarest/Leiden).

3. Reihe v.l.: Bernd Mussinghoff, Mariya Horyacha (Lviv), Gregor Emmenegger (Fribourg), Jana Plátová (Olomouc), Hans-Jürgen Feulner (Wien), Zdravko Jovanović (Belgrad), Ivan Christov (Sofia), Alexey Morozov (Fribourg), Svet Ribolov (Sofia), Hubert Philipp Weber (Wien), Johannes Arnold (Frankfurt), Vít Hušek (Olomouc).

Das Auditorium im Kardinal-König-Haus

Christoph Kardinal Schönborn, Bischof Atanáz Orosz und Dominique Gonnet SJ im Gespräch

Bilder der Tagung

Metropolit Hilarion online, Podium (Theresia Hainthaler, Bischof Atanáz Orosz, Kardinal Schönborn, Ysabel de Andia)

Theresia Hainthaler, Bernd Mussinghoff und Viola Raheb

Register

Biblische Schriften

Altes Testament
Gen
Gen 1, 2 120
Gen 1, 5 385
Gen 1, 26 .... 68, 120, 253
Gen 1, 28 .... 222, 288
Gen 2, 7 .... 71, 197, 407, 416
Gen 2, 16–17 ... 290, 397, 418, 501, 503
Gen 2, 21–22 329
Gen 3, 1–7 .... 273, 501
Gen 3, 3 407
Gen 3, 5 147
Gen 3, 6 120
Gen 3, 16 188
Gen 3, 19 .... 421, 423
Gen 3, 20 94
Gen 3, 21 .... 169, 230, 257, 281, 395
Gen 3, 22 110
Gen 5, 5 121
Gen 8 21 229
Gen 16, 5 503
Gen 19, 25 312

Ex
Ex 12, 1–42 38
Ex 13, 2 233
Ex 20, 5 312
Ex 20, 6 313
Ex 32, 26 398
Ex 34, 1 233

Num
Num 21, 8 122

Dtn
Dtn 13, 4 263
Dtn 23, 18 482
Dtn 24, 16 .... 422, 423, 425

2 Kön
2Kön 2, 19 327

Ijob
Ijob 4, 18 221
Ijob 14, 4–5 ...... 94, 226, 231, 256, 290
Ijob 15, 15 .... 221, 227
Ijob 25, 5 227

Ps
Ps 1, 1 .... 90, 311
Ps 4, 7 439
Ps 5, 8–9 89
Ps 7 15 116
Ps 31, 5 408
Ps 32, 1–2 90
Ps 49, 17 89
Ps 50, 5 .... 118, 311
Ps 50, 7 .... 94, 97, 229
Ps 51, 7 36
Ps 57, 4 .... 62, 233
Ps 59, 10 230
Ps 103, 13 89
Ps 126, 1 263
Ps 126, 5 89
Ps 128, 1 89
Ps 133, 2 221

Spr
Spr 1, 7 87
Spr 11, 5 89
Spr 20, 9 226

Hld
Hld 1, 1 259
Hld 1, 5 330
Hld 1, 15 389
Hld 1, 17 389
Hld 4, 9 393

Biblische Schriften

Weish
Weish 1, 13 . . . . 116, 503
Weish 2, 23–24 . . . . 116, 121, 503

Sir
Sir 10, 14 289

Jes
Jes 5, 14 . . . . 420, 424, 425
Jes 6, 5 412
Jes 14, 11–12 173
Jes 14, 19 173
Jes 44, 22 90

Jer
Jer 20, 14 94
Jer 27, 20 90
Jer 27, 44 90

Ez
Ez 18, 2 312
Ez 18, 4 . . . . 312, 425
Ez 18, 20 . . . . 313, 397, 425
Ez 47, 1–5 229

Hos
Hos 6, 6–7 228
Hos 13, 14–15 229

Jona
Jona 3, 5 227

Mi
Mi 1, 16 224
Mi 2, 1–5 224

Hab
Hab 1, 15 223

Mal
Mal 1, 2 162

Neues Testament
Mt
Mt 3, 13 244
Mt 3, 15–16 248
Mt 4, 1 244
Mt 5, 23 247
Mt 5, 28 90
Mt 10, 16 68
Mt 11, 29 331
Mt 12, 29 61
Mt 13, 25 128
Mt 16, 13 456
Mt 19, 13–15 245
Mt 19, 16–30 249
Mt 20, 20–28 . . . . 243, 265
Mt 24, 23 243

Mk
Mk 1, 40 93
Mk 3, 27 61

Lk
Lk 1, 26–38 273
Lk 1, 35 . . . . 70, 197
Lk 1, 78 . . . . 61, 66
Lk 6, 30 191
Lk 10, 38 129
Lk 13, 7–9 261
Lk 15, 1–7 374
Lk 15, 8–10 221
Lk 15, 22 328
Lk 18, 6 120
Lk 18, 10–14 258
Lk 19, 10 . . . . 321, 397
Lk 20, 37 281
Lk 22, 39 410

Joh
Joh 1, 5 437
Joh 1, 9 259
Joh 1, 13 . . . . 203, 215
Joh 1, 17 267
Joh 1, 29 348

Joh 3, 5-6 242
Joh 3, 14 122
Joh 3, 36 274
Joh 5, 6 93
Joh 6, 63 71
Joh 8, 16 414
Joh 9, 3 329
Joh 9, 7 61
Joh 17, 11 413
Joh 20, 17 399
Joh 20, 22 419

Röm

Röm 1, 18-3, 2 411
Röm 5, 6 331
Röm 5, 12 .... 32, 119, 122, 124, 125, 270, 271, 278, 281, 286, 287, 290-295, 298, 300, 304, 321, 336, 342, 345, 361, 385, 420, 424, 425, 460, 505
Röm 5, 12-21 . 31, 38, 220, 303, 316, 319
Röm 5, 13 .... 119, 314, 414
Röm 5, 14 . 168, 226, 227, 229, 233, 280, 281, 292, 314, 414
Röm 5, 18 .... 173, 291, 318, 422
Röm 5, 19 .... 32, 224, 291, 423, 460
Röm 5, 20 333
Röm 5, 21 507
Röm 6, 4 401
Röm 6, 6 .... 275, 277
Röm 6, 7 244
Röm 7, 5 .... 126, 412
Röm 7, 8 .... 410, 415
Röm 7, 9-10 120
Röm 7, 9-11 .... 113, 407
Röm 7, 11-25 91-93
Röm 7, 12 407
Röm 7, 13 121
Röm 7, 14 309
Röm 7, 14-25 97
Röm 7, 17 119
Röm 7, 18 306
Röm 7, 19-20 .... 85, 307
Röm 7, 22-25 290
Röm 7, 23 .... 185, 308
Röm 7, 24 .... 275, 308
Röm 7, 25 .... 253, 264, 308, 343
Röm 8, 2 185
Röm 8, 3 .... 275, 277
Röm 8, 6-7 .... 121, 130
Röm 8, 20 503
Röm 8, 22 502
Röm 8, 28-30 .... 253, 265
Röm 9, 9-21 279
Röm 9, 10-13 162
Röm 9, 11 .... 161, 276, 279
Röm 11, 29 400

1 Kor

1Kor 1, 30 327
1Kor 2, 12 130
1Kor 3, 16 96
1Kor 4, 7 .... 253, 264
1Kor 5, 6 127
1Kor 5, 7 .... 70, 127
1Kor 6, 16 128
1Kor 9, 24 333
1Kor 15, 20 401
1Kor 15, 21-23 ... 62, 70, 168, 182, 220, 223, 224, 229, 271, 280, 293, 328, 350, 401, 419
1Kor 15, 31 364
1Kor 15, 42-50 188
1Kor 15, 42-50 71
1Kor 15, 50 242
1Kor 15, 55 241
1Kor 15, 56 132

2 Kor

2Kor 3, 6-17 71
2Kor 3, 15 128
2Kor 3, 18 439
2Kor 4, 7 240
2Kor 5, 17 446
2Kor 6, 14 437

Biblische Schriften

2Kor 11, 28 328
2Kor 12, 2–4 160
2Kor 12, 9 439

Gal
Gal 2, 15–16 .... 412, 415
Gal 4, 1–2 223

Eph
Eph 1, 3–14 411
Eph 1, 5 253
Eph 1, 7 412
Eph 1, 10 57
Eph 2, 9 439
Eph 2, 10 411
Eph 3, 4–12 411
Eph 4, 17–19 411
Eph 4, 25 331
Eph 5, 1 265
Eph 5, 2 331

Phil
Phil 2, 8 65
Phil 3, 21 160

Kol
Kol 1, 13 129
Kol 1, 16 .... 409, 413
Kol 1, 18 63
Kol 1, 24–29 411
Kol 2, 14 124
Kol 3, 3–11 54
Kol 3, 5–10 411
Kol 3, 10 510
Kol 4, 6 327

1 Thess
1Thess 4, 3–6 411

2 Thess
2Thess 2, 4 120

1 Tim
1Tim 2, 5 65
1Tim 4, 4–5 246
1Tim 6, 9 133

Tit
Tit 3, 3 411

Hebr
Hebr 2, 14–15 32
Hebr 5, 8–9 48
Hebr 7, 19 327
Hebr 10, 26–27 .... 85, 88–90, 97

Jak
Jak 3, 2 226

1 Petr
1Petr 4, 8 90
1Petr 5, 8 357

2 Petr
2Petr 2, 19 321

1 Joh
1Joh 1, 8 311
1Joh 2, 1 311
1Joh 5, 16–17 90
1Joh 5, 19 .... 245, 246

Frühchristliche und anonyme Schriften

4 Esra 5, 35 94

Barnabasbrief 123

Diatessaron 137, 141
Didache 141

Liber Graduum 137–155

Opus imperf. in Matthaeum . . 237–251
Oracula Chaldaica 164

Pastor Hermae 88, 123, 141
Petrus-Evangelium 36

Synoden

Karthago (418) 299
Ephesos (431) 496
Chalcedon (451) 455
Orange (529) 300, 318–333, 459, 468
Konstantinopel (543) 157
Nicaea II. (787) 381
Trient 276, 297, 299, 300, 459
Syrische Schatzhöhle 149

Thekla-Akten 141
Thomasakten 140
Thomas-Evangelium 141, 142

Vita Adae 149

Antike und mittelalterliche Autoren und Personennamen

Adelphios v. Edessa 138
Alexander v. Aphrodisias 368, 376
Alkinoos 163, 164
Ambrosiaster 281, 303–317
Ambrosius v. Mailand 32, 190,
   252–268, 287, 296, 304
Anapsychia 210
Anastasius Bibliothecarius 493
Anastasius II., Papst 219
Anastasius v. Sinai 441
Anaximander v. Milet 74
Antonius d. Einsiedler 355–367
Aphrahat 141
Apollinaris 210
Apollinaris v. Laodicea 369, 405
Apuleius 163
Areios Didymos 204
Aristoteles . . . 82, 85, 87, 89, 90, 92, 97,
   167, 197–216, 467, 469
Athanasius v. Alexandrien 157,
   355–367, 370, 385, 416, 417, 500–
   503, 507
Attikos 163
Augustinus v. Hippo 32–34, 43,
   44, 52, 119, 122, 123, 126, 156, 178,
   190, 196–220, 230, 231, 252, 266–
   302, 317–322, 330, 331, 333, 342,
   343, 345–347, 349, 416, 425, 426,
   431, 448, 459, 496, 504, 505

Barhadbšabba 406
Basilides, Gnostiker 85, 92, 95
Basilius v. Caesarea . . 32, 157, 299, 370,
   377, 498–501, 503
Basilius v. Seleukia 448, 507
Bonifatius II. 320

Caesarius v. Arles 318–333
Celsus 280–283
Cicero 88
Clemens v. Alexandrien 32, 85–97, 195,
   395, 498, 501, 502
Clemens v. Rom, Ps. 140

Antike und mittelalterliche Autoren und Personennamen 537

Constantinus Diaconus 500
Cyprian v. Karthago . 195, 267, 274, 287
Cyrill v. Alexandrien 157, 162, 416–428, 461, 504–506, 508
Cyrus v. Edessa 40

Damasus I. v. Rom 221
Diadochus v. Photice 136, 429–442
Didymus der Blinde 32, 370
Diogenes Laertios 73
Dion Chrysostomos 376
Dionysius Ps.-Areopagita 493
Dorotheus v. Gaza 507

Ephraem d. Syrer 39, 40, 437
Epiphanius v. Salamis 503
Eunapius v. Sardes 377
Eunomius v. Cyzicus 377, 381
Euripides 165
Eusebius v. Cäsarea . 196, 204, 376, 493
Eustathius v. Sebaste 377
Evagrius Ponticus 139, 430

Faustus v. Riez 266, 319

Galen v. Pergamon . 202–204, 207, 215, 218, 376
Gottschalk v. Orbais 343
Gregor Palamas 491, 498, 500, 503, 509
Gregor v. Nazianz . . . 32, 157, 267, 479, 493, 498, 499, 501, 503
Gregor v. Nyssa . 32, 157, 280, 304, 340, 368–403, 439, 461, 483, 497, 498, 500, 503, 506

Harpokration v. Alexandrien 163
Hermogenes 197, 200
Hesiod 75
Hieronymus 98, 172, 210, 220–236, 267, 274, 278, 280, 287, 294, 299, 304, 310, 326
Hilarius v. Poitiers 212, 215, 292
Hinkmar v. Reims 343

Homer 74, 75
Iamblichos v. Chalkis . . . 73, 82, 83, 377
Ignatius v. Antiochien 123
Irenaeus v. Lyon 32, 43–72, 123, 156, 172, 254, 304, 328, 330, 368, 375, 376, 385, 386, 395, 416, 432, 498–500
Ishodad v. Merv 40
Isidor v. Pelusium 498
Isidor, Gnostiker 92

Jakob v. Sarug 33, 39, 40
Johannes Cassian 266, 468, 469
Johannes Chrysostomus . 123, 126, 157, 237, 412, 461, 498, 501–507, 509
Johannes Exarch 491
Johannes Klimakos 138, 507
Johannes Scottus Eriugena . . . 334–352
Johannes v. Damaskus 497, 498, 500–503, 509
Julian v. Eclanum . . 213–219, 252, 267, 271, 286, 295–297
Julius Cassianus 93
Justinian I., Kaiser 157

Kelsos 163, 173
Kliment v. Ohrid . . . 488–490, 492–494
Kyrill v. Saloniki 485–495

Leon d. Mathematiker 488

Macarius, Ps. . . . 118–136, 429–431, 437, 439
Macrina 392
Marcellinus 210
Markion v. Sinope 65, 197, 200
Markus Eremita 438, 498, 502, 504, 507
Maximos v. Tyros 163, 164
Maximus Confessor 349, 350, 383, 457–484, 491, 492, 495, 500, 503
Melito v. Sardes 31, 33, 36–38
Methodius v. Olympus . . . 98–117, 368, 375, 376, 501

Narsai v. Nisibis 33, 39, 40
Nemesius v. Emesa 469, 503
Nestorius 404, 445
Nikolaos Kabasilas 510, 511
Novatian 254, 268
Numenios v. Apameia 163, 164

Optatus, episcopus Hispanus . 215, 218
Origenes 32, 123, 156–174, 195, 223, 224, 235, 256, 269–285, 302, 326, 369, 395

Pelagius 32, 126, 178, 229, 232–234, 252, 266, 270, 276, 281, 303–317, 426
Petrus v. Alexandrien 157
Philo v. Alexandrien .. 39, 94, 162, 172, 395
Philoxenos v. Mabbug 140, 142
Photios v. Konstantinopel 406, 430, 458, 459, 461, 488, 489
Platon ... 73–84, 92, 157, 159, 163, 170, 281, 282, 284, 359, 490
Plotin ... 73, 78–84, 284, 368, 377–380
Plutarch 163–166
Porphyrios 81, 232, 301
Proklos v. Konstantinopel 445, 447, 448, 452
Prosper v. Aquitanien 320, 333

Prudentius 345
Pythagoras v. Samos 74

Romanos Melodos 443–456
Rufin v. Aquileia 158, 229, 277, 280, 281

Severus v. Antiochien 138
Sokrates 258
Soran v. Ephesus 199–210
Sozomenos 493
Symeon d. Neue Theologe 502

Tatian d. Syrer 162
Tertullian 32, 177–219
Themistios 376
Theodor v. Mopsuestia ... 39, 404–415, 458
Theodoret v. Cyrus . 461, 502–505, 507, 508, 510, 511
Theophilus v. Alexandrien 157
Theophilus v. Antiochien ... 39, 43–59, 254, 441, 461, 500, 502, 503
Theophylakt v. Ohrid 488, 489, 492, 493
Thomas v. Aquin 66

Valentin, Gnostiker 92

Zenon v. Kition 162, 196, 204

Moderne Autoren

Abramowski, L. 40
Adorno, T. W. 34
Alder, A. 508
Aleksiev, S. 487
Alexandre, M. 384
Alexopoulos, T. 392
Andia, Y. de 44, 54, 60, 66, 376, 432
Apostolopoulos, C. 392
Argárate, P. 137, 142, 155
Armstrong, A. H. 379
Arnaldez, R. 39

Badurina, T. 98
Baker, A. 141
Balás, D. L. 373, 377, 378
Balthasar, H. U. v. 477, 483
Bammel, C. P. 167, 172
Banning, J. van 238, 245
Baumann, U. 33, 36
Baumert, N. 32
Baumstark, A. 138
Beatrice, P. F. ... 32, 178, 180, 188, 190, 194, 197, 218, 274, 304, 394

Moderne Autoren

Bengsch, A. 53
Berthold, H. 120
Bezobrazova, M. V. 487
Bigg, Ch. 279
Blank, J. 36
Bobrinskoy, B. 423
Bochet, I. 213, 219, 302
Böhlig, A. 140
Boersma, H. 56
Böttigheimer, Ch. 41
Bonner, G. 274
Bostock, G. 162
Boulnois, M.-O. 162, 418
Braun, R. 179
Bray, G. L. 178
Brennan, B. 356
Breuning, W. 34
Brilliantov, A. I. 472, 473
Brown Dewhurst, E. 477
Brown, P. 315
Brown, R. F. 57
Brox, N. 51
Bucchi, F. 223
Buckert, W. 76
Bürke, G. 167, 280

Cadiou, R. 279
Caluori, D. 377
Canellis, A. 233
Caner, D. 140
Capone, A. 235
Cappuyns, M. 340
Caruso, G. 233
Castagno Monaci, A. 279
Castellanos, M. A. B. 55
Cavallera, F. 223, 231
Chelius Stark, J. 270
Christov, I. 489, 491, 492, 494, 495
Christova, A. 494
Clark, E. 90
Colless, B. 138
Coman, I. 412

Cooper, A. 479, 483
Coppa, G. 235
Cornford, F. M. 74
Costache, D. 477, 481
Crehan, J. H. 238
Crouzel, H. 160
Cullmann, O. 53

Dalmais, I.-H. 473
Daniélou, J. 164, 369, 370, 377, 392–394
Dausner, R. 41
Davids, A. J. M. 134
Davids, E. A. 128, 129
De Clerck, P. 333
Debidour, V.-H. 99
Debreucq, E. 301
Dehandschutter, B. 133
Delaroche, B. 270, 271
Delmulle, J. 266
Deseille, P. 429
Desprez, V. 134, 140
Devreesse, R. 404, 407
Di Palma, G. 271, 293
Dietze-Mager, G. 167
Dölger, F. 493
Dörr, Fr. 429
Dörries, H. 130, 134
Drecoll, V. H. 211
Dubarle, A.-M. 425, 426
Dunaev, A. 120, 127
Durkheim, E. 74
Duval, Y.-M. 234
D'Alès, A. 181, 188, 190, 191, 194

Edwards, M. . . . 157, 158, 161, 167–170,
  172, 174
Elytis, O. 450
Emmenegger, G. 202, 203, 219
Englezakis, B. 142
Ermatinger, C. . 430, 431, 436, 439, 442
Ernest, J. 356
Esser, G. 200
Evdokimov, P. 474

Fairbairn, D. 355, 359
Falque, E. 56
Farge, J. 98
Fatti, F. 377
Fédou, M. 300
Ferguson, E. 392
Ferwerda, R. 215
Filiotis-Vlachavas, Ch. 500, 502
Fitschen, K. 437
Florovskij, G. V. 474
Franchi, R. 98
Fredouille, J.-C. 200
Freud, S. 508
Fritz, G. 319
Fuchs, G. 143, 144, 149, 154
Fürst, A. 231

Gaith, J. 373
Galanis, J. 503
Gaudel, A.   178, 188, 190, 191, 304, 307,
  309, 500–502
Gerson, L. P. 377, 379
Gignoux, Ph. 39
Gilson, É. 44
Girard, R. 33, 36
Görgemanns, H. 165
Gorday, P. 123
Grahn-Wilder, M. 482
Grant, R. M. 47
Green, M. H. 196
Greer, R. 415
Gregg, R. 357
Grillmeier, A. 37, 38, 455
Groh, D. 357
Gross, J. 34, 210, 302, 305, 500, 502
Grossi, V. 268, 271, 299, 301
Guillaumont, A. 155
Guthrie, W. K. C. 75

Haag, H. 33, 35
Hadot, P. 256
Hainthaler, Th. 40, 455
Hall, S. G. 36

Hammond Bammel, C. P.   277, 279–281
Hanson, A. E. 196
Harl, M. . . . 157, 158, 162, 167, 172, 280
Harmless, W. 365
Harnack, A. von 277
Hauke, M. 33, 123, 156, 381, 382
Hausherr, I. 138
Havrda, M. 93
Heidegger, M. 507
Heinzer, F. 473
Herren, M. W. 348
Hesse, O. 134
Hick, J. 57
Hoek, A. van den 94
Horyacha, M. 118, 134, 437
Hunter, D. G. 309, 310
Hušek, V. 281, 304–306, 313, 316

Ivanka, E. v. 472

Jacobsen, A.-C. 160
Jäntsch, J. 307
Janakiev, K. 457, 458
Jay, P. 235
Jeanjean, B. 233
Jeauneau, É. 337, 348–350
Jedin, H. 300
Jonas, H. 47
Jugie, M. 500, 501
Juhl, D. 140, 155
Jung, C. G. 508

Kalokyris, K. 456
Kapriev, G. 469, 474
Karavites, P. 89
Karawidopoulos, J. 498, 499, 505
Karayiannis, V. 472
Karfík, F. 92
Karfíková, L. .. 156, 161, 270, 276, 279,
  283, 284, 317
Karmann, TH. R. 36
Karpp, H. 199, 200
Keech, D. 277

Moderne Autoren

Kelly, J. N. D. 178, 229, 231
Kenny, A. 92
Kerschensteiner, J. 141
Kesselopoulos, A. 502
Kiraz, G. A. 40
Kitchen, R. A. 138–140, 142, 155
Kmosko, M. 137–139, 141
Knauer, P. 32
Kniewasser, M. 134
Kochańczyk-Bonińska, K. 478, 480, 481, 483
Koder, J. 450, 453
Komosko, M. 138
Kornarakis, J. 507, 508
Kourempeles, I. 445, 448, 452, 453, 455, 456
Kowalski, A. 146, 149
Kraus, Th. J. 36
Kremer, Th. 39

La Bonnardière, A.-M. 278
Lagouanère, J. 302
Lamberigts, M. 197, 211, 215
Lane, A. N. S. 48, 51
Larchet, J.-C. 473, 474, 482
Lawson, J. 44
Le Guillou, M.-J. 134
Leal, J. 178, 180, 181, 188, 190, 191, 194
Lesky, E. 214
Lies, L. 158
Löhr, W. A. 91, 95
Lössl, J. 271
Lohfink, N. 31, 33–36
Lona, H. 163
Lourié, B. 462
Louth, A. 462, 469
Lunn-Rockliffe, S. 311
Lure, V. M. 462, 473
Luther, M. 300
Lyonnet, S. 271, 292, 426
Lytvynenko, V. 366

Macé, C. 356

Madec, G. 258, 343
Maloney, G. A. 127
Markschies, Ch. 92
Martens, P. W. ... 158, 162, 167–169, 174
Martzelos, G. D. 368, 448, 497, 500, 501
Marx, B. 507
Maspero, G. 383
Mateo-Seco, L. F. 381, 385, 392
Matsoukas, N. A. ... 446, 450, 455, 497, 498, 500, 501
Mattei, P. 253, 254, 266–268
Matteoli, S. 314–317
May, G. 369
McClear, E. V. 370, 373, 381
McCoy, A. M. 44, 51, 53
McGuckin, J. A. 416
McLeod, F. G. 405, 410, 415
McNamara, K. 413
Méhat, A. 88
Meister, Ch. 100
Mejzner, M. 99
Ménard, J.-É. 141
Meunier, B. 418–420, 422–424
Meyendorff, J. . 122, 424, 457, 458, 461, 505, 507
Mitralexis, S. 477, 480
Molin Pradel, M. 235
Moreschini, C. 482
Morin, G. 234, 235, 322
Morozov, A. 98, 99
Moser, P. K. 100
Moutsoulas, E. 394
Munier, C. 194
Musurillo, H. 99, 393

Nicklas, T. 36
Nikolova, S. 491
Norris, R. 405, 407

Old, H. O. 142
Orbe, A. 375
Osborn, E. 178
Outrata, F. 271

O'Connell, R. J. 284
O'Daly, G. 215, 284

Panchovski, I. 488
Parmentier, M. F. G. 142
Patridge, C. E. 477
Paul VI., Papst 35, 301
Pazzini, D. 162
Pellegrino, M. 392
Peltomaa, L.-M. 445
Pennacchio, M. C. 228
Peri, V. 235
Perler, O. 36
Petrov, V. 471, 473
Pisi, P. 167, 279
Places, É. des 431, 434
Plested, M. 124, 131, 430, 431, 437, 438
Poirier, A. 141
Polito, R. 199
Pollastri, A. 305–307, 309, 310, 317
Prinzivalli, E. 98
Przyszychowska, M. 280, 305, 378

Quispel, G. 141

Raduca, V. 381
Rassinier, J.-P. 214
Ricœur, P. 269, 270
Rigby, P. 431
Riou, A. 473
Rist, J. 44
Roberts, R. E. 178, 188, 194
Rogers, R. 47
Romanides, J. S. 441, 457, 458, 461, 497, 499, 500, 502, 503, 505
Rondet, H. . 44, 178, 185, 189, 190, 425
Roukema, R. 162
Rücker, A. 141
Russell, N. 416, 430, 438, 439
Rutherford, J. E. 430, 431

Sand, A. 34
Sanlon, P. 44

Scheffczyk, L. 31, 33, 34, 38, 373
Scherer, G. 34
Schmöle, K. 88
Schönborn, Ch. 34, 35
Schwager, R. 36
Scribona, C. G. 211
Seckler, M. 403
Sfameni Gasparro, G. ... 167, 170, 222, 226, 277, 279
Sferlea, O. 392
Shakespeare, W. 334
Shaw, G. 82
Sherwood, P. 470, 480
Sieber, J. 99
Simonetti, M. 237, 238
Skliris, D. 477
Smith, A. J. 281
Smith, J. Z. 44
Spanneut, M. 188
Spiteris, Y. 500, 502
Srawley, J. H. 395
Stählin, O. 92
Stamatov, A. 487
Stamulis, Ch. 404, 405
Steenberg, M. C. 44, 47, 50, 51, 55, 189, 190, 210
Stewart, C. 127, 430, 431, 437
Stewart-Sykes, A. 36
Stickelbroeck, M. 33
Stăniloae, D. 436
Stępień, T. 368, 377, 380
Strothmann, W. 141
Sullivan, F. 405

TeSelle, E. 123
Testa, E. 188
Theobald, M. 336
Thunberg, L. 474, 480, 482
Tomadakis, N. 456
Touraille, J. 431
Townsend, J. 420
Trifonov, Ju. 487

Abkürzungen 543

Tutekov, S. 470

Vaillant, A. 99, 100
Valero, J. B. 303–305, 309, 317
Van Rompay, L. 40
Vannier, M.-A. 253
Veder, W. 355
Vigorelli, I. 383
Visonà, G. 253
Vives, J. 55, 374, 375, 381
Vletsis, A. V. 500, 502
Völker, W. 381
Vööbus, A. 140, 141, 404, 405
Vorst, N. Z.-V. 47
Voulgaris, E. 448

Ware, K. 134, 429, 438

Waszink, J. H. 199, 214, 215
Weaver, D. 420, 422
Wermelinger, O. 276
Westerhoff, M. 141, 142
Wickham, L. 138–140, 142
Widmann, M. 47
Williams, N. P. 178, 187, 188, 279
Wingren, G. 48
Wirth, K. H. 194
Wohlmann, A. 347

Yanakiev, K. 457, 458

Zachhuber, J. 369, 373, 378, 379
Zañartu, S. 56
Zorzi, M. B. 99
Zumkeller, A. 215

Abkürzungen

Die Abkürzungen für Zeitschriften und Reihen richten sich nach:
S. M. Schwertner, IATG². Internationales Abkürzungsverzeichnis für Theologie und Grenzgebiete (Berlin, New York ²1992).

Abweichend bzw. ergänzend dazu wird verwendet:
CCG   Corpus Christianorum, series graeca, Turnholti 1, 1977 ff.
CCL   Corpus Christianorum, series latina, Turnholti 1, 1953 ff.
LACL   Lexikon der antiken christlichen Literatur,
       hg. S. Döpp und W. Geerlings, Freiburg i.B.²1999.